Myra Waldo's
Travel and Motoring
Guide to Europe
1973

Myra Waldo's Travel and Motoring Guide to Europe

1973

Collier Books, *New York, New York*
Collier-Macmillan Ltd., *London*

CONTENTS

THE COUNTRIES OF EUROPE

INTRODUCTION

Travel, at all times, is an intensely personal experience. We all see the same sights, but we react differently to them, depending upon our own background, nature and personality. Therefore, what is absorbed, remembered or treasured varies from one individual to another.

Based upon interviews of many hundreds of travelers and careful reading of letters from readers, it seems clear that the vast majority of Americans are willing to try almost anything during the day, but at night they want a good dinner, a hot bath and a comfortable bed. With that general premise, I suppose there can be little or no argument.

In this book, I have tried to avoid travel-folder writing, in which there is nothing but good and everything is wonderful. I have said precisely what I thought, even where the results are somewhat unflattering and less than ideal. But then, not everything in life is wonderful and ideal. On the other hand, where warranted, I have tried not to be repressed and unenthusiastic. Although I regularly visit Europe almost every other month during the year and have spent long periods in different countries over the years, I am almost never bored and still derive enormous pleasure from traveling throughout the many and varied countries.

In our country, sightseeing attractions are separated, very frequently, by hundreds of miles, occasionally by overnight trips. One of the great wonders of Europe is the fact that everything is so close. One worthwhile destination is usually only a matter of an hour from still another not-to-be-missed spot. Furthermore, creature comforts are often at their absolute best in Europe, where fine hotels and restaurants abound. Even the most chauvinistic American would have to admit that a good meal is not easy to find in certain parts of our country, but this is surely not true on the Continent.

European travel, once reserved for the wealthy, the retired, and the overprivileged, has now become an American way of life. Everyone goes to Europe nowadays, as indicated by the vast number of passports which show the Continent as a destination. One note of caution: first-time visitors want to see everything and often schedule too many countries. Even for the most enthusiastic sight-seer, a degree of moderation is in order. In my opinion, three countries are enough on any visit, or else all the impressions will become jumbled and blurred. When I read advertisements scheduling nine countries in 17 days, I wonder whether any of these travelers will have time to do anything more than merely look out of a train or bus window.

The most important single thing that any American visitor to Europe can take with him is an open mind. Please don't arrive with preconceived ideas or impressions supplied by others. Make up your own mind about what you like and what you want to see or do. This book, hope-fully, can assist you in that most important regard.

Have a wonderful trip!

MYRA WALDO

Myra Waldo's
Travel and Motoring
Guide to Europe
1973

How to Get to Europe

Back in the spring of 1927, when a young American (who had been delivering mail in the Middle West) decided to go to Europe, he flew his own plane from New York to Le Bourget airport in Paris. He traveled light, except for a spare gas tank, which he stored in the front cockpit of the plane. With the romantic flair of a genuine traveler, he called his plane the *Spirit of St. Louis*. The young man was Charles A. Lindbergh, and he was making the first nonstop flight from New York to Paris.

The chances are when you head for the continent this season you will fly—although not necessarily in your own monoplane, sitting alongside a tank of high-octane fuel. But you might just possibly decide to go by ship. In the years just after Lindy's sensational flight, those embarking on the Grand Tour of Europe started out with a voyage aboard ship. There was not much choice. Even when commercial airlines began making regular flights to Europe, ships continued to be the most popular way of getting across the Atlantic. But then, in the mid-50s, things started changing dramatically. When jets replaced piston engines, there was no holding back the airplanes in their competition with ships for the patronage of the continent-bound traveler. A crossing that had taken eleven to sixteen hours by piston-engine plane was made by jets in six hours—even less!

In 1956 the contest between ships and planes was over. Until then, ships had been carrying more passengers between the United States and Europe than the airlines. Since that year, the planes have been out in front. It is not even close any more. A few years ago, for instance, of the million persons who crossed the Atlantic, five-sixths of them went by plane—and the percentage of air travelers keeps growing.

But no matter what these figures prove, they have not settled the argument of which is the best way to travel. The ship group and the plane group are no closer to agreement than they ever were. Each presents irrefutable

1

arguments showing the obvious advantages of one method of travel over the other. In the near future the introduction of subsonic jets will cut the travel time even more. Then, when the supersonic jets go into service, it will take about as long to get from America to Europe as it now does to travel from a downtown terminal to the airport. That is not likely to convince the ship enthusiasts, however. They will still be patiently explaining why a sea voyage is half the fun of going to Europe.

This is one of those personal decisions that you—or whoever makes the decisions in your family—are going to have to make. You should make it on your own, after sizing up the pros and cons within the context of your travel aims. If you went by air the last time, perhaps you want to try an ocean voyage this season and see what all the ship talk is about. Maybe, it is the other way around.

Here's what you will have to weigh:

Ship enthusiasts claim that ocean travel involves a vacation en route, with luxurious accommodations, fine meals, a relaxed atmosphere and never a dull moment. They point out that the traveler rests up both going and returning and that one sees Europe completely refreshed after the sea voyage. The plane people, meanwhile, argue that travel by air is superior because you get to Europe in a matter of hours; that the swiftness of the trip leaves you refreshed and ready for anything; that no time is lost and, besides, there's no other possible way to travel in the twentieth century. One point can be made objectively from the sidelines: ship travel takes time. If you are budgeting your time—as well as your money— then the speed of travel will be a major element in your decision. The loss of days involved in travel aboard ship, plus time consumed with connecting trains after you arrive in Europe, will drain away too many vacation hours that could be better applied to seeing the sights and enjoying life on the continent. Let's consider both methods of travel, starting first with the ships (after all they were first to cross the ocean) and then go on to the high-level newcomers, the planes.

All About Ships

SELECTING YOUR SHIP ¶ Even though the United States has virtually abdicated from the trans-Atlantic passenger business, and other nations are making cutbacks, there is still a relatively large number of passenger liners and combination passenger-cargo ships on the high seas. They come in all sizes and shapes. Do you want the biggest and the longest? That's the French Line's *France*. The two big decisions you will have to make after deciding to go by ship is what flag you will sail under and what class of accommodations you reserve—First, Cabin or (at the bottom of the list) Tourist.

The *British*, in the corporate person of the Cunard Steam-Ship Company, have the world's greatest seagoing tradition, with high marks in seamanship, navigation and the general care and comfort of the passengers. Their stewards (meaning actually all of the service personnel other than the ships' officers and crews) have been doing the same work for generations, with positions frequently handed down from father to son. To put it flatly, you'll probably never get better service anywhere than you do from the experienced, skilled stewards aboard a British Cunard liner. The food varies greatly. In First Class, the dishes are often superb, just about as good as anyone might have reason to expect. In the less expensive, popular Tourist Class, the British tendency toward fatty vegetable soup, boiled mutton (with caper sauce) and floury white puddings seems to take over. It is really not very complicated: the British aren't any great shakes as cooks (an understatement if ever there was one!) and, to remedy the situation, have hired French *cordon bleu* chefs for First Class. The rub is that they use English food murderers (laughingly called cooks) for Tourist Class.

French ships are special in their own ways. Let's get the complaints over with right away—*tout de suite*. The housekeeping could be a little better, particularly if you're the kind of person who looks in dark nooks or lifts up carpet corners. But the French shipowners, like all Frenchmen, think that one of the nicest pastimes in the world is eating and drinking, as undoubtedly it is. On any French ship in *any* class, the cooking will be delightful, the meals inviting and the wine flowing freely. Then, too, the French have natural gaiety and *joie de vivre* that permit them to convey a sense of pleasure and enjoyment, more so than any other nation in the world.

The *Italians* run a ship with some of the joy of living that the French seem to have. The atmosphere frequently is quite gay and everyone does his best to make the crossing pleasant. Some of the décor is weird—let's admit it—but the service, almost without exception, is just about superb. The food is variable—sometimes absolutely magnificent, sometimes very mediocre. It's like that little girl with the curl: when it's good, it's very good, and when it's not so good—it's covered with tomato sauce.

The *Dutch* have a wonderful record afloat. You'll find most Dutch ships scrubbed down to a state of hygienic cleanliness that would satisfy even the most persnickety American. The service is excellent. Sometimes it is so good it seems as if the steward has been reading your mind. How could he possibly have known you wanted a cheese sandwich and a glass of milk before you went to bed? In general, the food is generously served, in king-size portions. Unfortunately, the Atlantic crossings have been greatly curtailed, generally only in the spring and fall.

Scandinavian ships are so clean you'll feel guilty if you drop a match stick. (And on ships, by the way, please remember to be very careful about matches, cigarette stubs and smoldering ashes.) A friend of mine once said she always straightened up her stateroom *before* allowing the steward in to make it up, because she didn't want him to think she wasn't neat. The personnel aboard Scandinavian ships are polite and willing, although not nearly so skilled as their French and British counterparts. The food is good, particularly if you have a yen for smorgasbord. Don't look for creations by Escoffier, however. Like the Dutch ships, the Scandinavian ones sometimes lack the sparkle and light-heartedness that seem to be a French trademark.

Canadian ships apparently combine the best and the worst of American and British qualities. The ships are clean, and the cabins and general shipboard décor are moderately attractive, if uninspired. The food, although palatable and appetizing, is hardly thrilling. But service and seamanship get a top vote. The trips to Europe take longer because of the run through the St. Lawrence River and Seaway. This trip can be a source of great pleasure for those with lots of extra time, but it's somewhat frustrating if you are in a hurry to get there. *There* meaning Europe.

WHICH CLASS ¶ Some ships have eliminated the class problem entirely by sailing as one-class passenger liners which makes things much easier. There is no need to weigh another set of pros and cons, and that annoying matter of class distinction never crops up. The innovation of one-class ships, furthermore, does not make an ocean voyage one bit less pleasant. But most steamship lines stick to the old custom of classes—three of them. Back in the days when the big migrations to America took place, there were *four* classes. They were called First, Second, Third and Steerage (which was down in the bottom of the ship). In the contemporary fashion of resorting to euphemisms to brighten up words that don't sound too nice, the terms for the different types of accommodations aboard ship have been changed. Steerage, for one thing, has been dropped from the vocabulary. Now there are just three classes: First, Cabin (the old Second Class) and Tourist. No matter how these carefully burnished words sound—and no matter how the various types of accommodations look in the travel folders —First Class is definitely more luxurious than Second (pardon, *Cabin*), and Cabin is far superior to Tourist. And why should it not be that way when the prices are scaled accordingly?

First Class is the best there is. It means the largest staterooms, the best and the most food and the finest service—and, in general, it is the deluxe way to travel if you don't mind paying for it. You'll pay, because the big problem with First Class travel is not only the substantial initial fare but also the question of living up to your accommodations. That means tips for just about everyone in sight of course, and most important of all, the additional clothes required. There never was a woman born—well, practically never—who had enough clothes for a trip to Europe. So a gown or two must be bought (these will be completely unnecessary in Europe), and this type of expenditure has to be logically considered as an addition to the cost of the ticket. And what does a ticket cost, you ask? Prices vary with the ship, but traveling First Class on a topnotch liner costs an average of $100 a day.

Cabin Class is usually selected by the discriminating voyager who enjoys the better things of life, but hesitates to spend the whopping outlay for First Class. Cabin Class accommodations and the public rooms (salon, dining room, bar, etc.) are usually quite attractive, the food is quite good (although, naturally, not so good as in First

Class) and the passengers are *generally* younger. At the risk of breaking with tradition, let us consider the popular myth that all of the fun aboard ship is to be had in Cabin Class, where everyone is swinging around the clock while up in First Class—where all the passengers are rich—the biggest excitement of the day is the stock market report from the ship's radio room. This just isn't so. The proof lies in the fact that once at sea the biggest headache for the ship's officers is keeping the Cabin Class passengers out of the First Class area. In fact, the first thing many Cabin Class passengers try to learn when they get settled aboard is how to sneak into First Class for dancing and the after-dinner shows—or even just a look to see how different things are. The fact remains, nevertheless, that very good times may be had in Cabin Class, although not necessarily better than in First. And in that same the-grass-is-always-greener spirit (maybe the adjective is not precise), there are always First Class passengers who insist on barging into Cabin Class parties and then reporting to fellow First Class travelers the next day— usually a trifle smugly or patronizingly—that they had "gone down to Cabin last night for a little while, and it was quite a bit of fun."

Tourist Class may or may not be a pleasant experience. Accommodations are located in the least desirable parts of the ship—fore (up front), aft (back where the propeller whirs away) and down below decks near the engine room. These locations, besides taking a long time to reach, are extremely sensitive to all the twists and turns that ships get involved in en route. The pitching (when the vessel dips and rises, fore and aft, in a steady but not steadying rhythm) and the rolling (the wallowing in the water from side to side) are particularly noticeable in the Tourist Class area. Tourist Class food is limited in variety and is usually plain—very plain. (Exception: French ships.)

How to Get Started ¶ Maybe I should have first said *when*, rather than *how*, to get started. The sooner the better is the answer. Shipping space is getting tighter all the time because many of the lines use their luxury vessels on quickie as well as longie (round-the-world) cruises, and passenger liners are not parked at the piers in New York, like sightseeing buses, waiting for customers. They fill up fast, especially in Cabin and Tourist

Class, where the lower rates attract the largest number of travelers. Usually you can get First Class accommodations—although not the minimum-priced ones—right up to sailing time on many ships. But Cabin and Tourist Class accommodations go fast—often a year ahead, and frequently even earlier (particularly on a few favorite ships) during the eastbound (toward Europe) rush, from May through July, and the westbound peak period, from August through late September. So, if you want to go to Europe by ship—particularly in Cabin or Tourist Class—run, do not walk, to your travel agent and get your request in immediately.

This might be a good place to mention that your travel agent can be extremely helpful to you in many, many ways—and does not charge you for his services. Ship tickets (as well as airline ones) are the same price whether he gets them for you or you buy them yourself from the company. He receives an agent's commission from the company. You gain nothing from dealing directly with the company because, aside from the rates being exactly the same, you cannot save the agent's commission and you do not get the helpful free service and advice that an experienced travel agent will give you.

CHOICE OF ACCOMMODATIONS ¶ The amount of money you have budgeted for the ocean trip will largely determine the type of stateroom. But you can get the most for your money by carefully studying a deck plan of the ship before you pick your cabin. An outside cabin (with a porthole) is obviously more pleasant than an inside one, no matter how nicely decorated and air-conditioned it is. Cabins at the center of the ship—amidships, as you'll be saying once you get your sea legs—are not as subject to rolling and pitching as those toward the stern or bow. By studying the deck plan and matching prices with such factors as location, you will have the best chance of choosing accommodations that meet your budget and taste. If the sizes of the cabins are not clearly indicated, you can usually find some dimension measured out on the plan that will serve as the basis for determining the approximate lengths and widths of the accommodations. If you are not picking a cabin with private bath, look on the plan to see where the nearest lavatory and bath are. This will be quite important once you are aboard. But you can also be too close to these facilities. If your cabin turns out to be adjacent to them, you might be annoyed by the continuous running of water and the closing (never gently!) of doors. It is also best to stay your distance from pantry, linen closet and other service doors (which, traditionally, make a good deal of noise), elevators and entrances to public rooms.

Pointer: During Low Season, ask your travel agent to get you a First Class cabin on the "borderline" that switches to Cabin Class rates—or to get you a Cabin Class cabin at the border when it switches to Tourist Class rates. This can't be accomplished on every ship, but where done, you'll save a substantial amount of money.

Then, there is the question of decks. If you bought tickets to a New York legitimate show and the tickets were marked row B, you'd automatically assume that you were in the second row. But if you did so, you'd probably be mistaken, because most theater owners usually mark the first row AA, the second row BB, the third CC and then comes row A—actually the fourth row. This same peculiar logic is applied by steamship owners, who know that most people would rather be on A or B deck than C or D deck. What do they do? They call the upper decks by all sorts of fancy names: Veranda, Sun Deck, Boat Deck, Promenade Deck, Main Deck and the like. Then, when they've used up all the upper decks, the last two decks may be called A Deck (actually about the fifth deck down) and B Deck (say, the sixth deck). These designations sound nice and are reassuring. But you're liable to get tired of the sound of the ocean water slapping against the bulkheads (walls).

GOING ABOARD SHIP ¶ From the travel agent or the steamship company, you will get a supply of baggage tags and stickers. It is wise to use them. (The stickers, because they stick, are the best.) Fill in your name and cabin number in a clear, easy-to-read way, and you'll have no baggage worries. If you wish, you can bring your baggage to the pier the day before sailing or early on the morning of embarkation. Checking baggage early can simplify things amid all the hustle and bustle of sailing time and permit you to stroll up the gangplank in that carefree, joyous way the people do in the magazine ads. In any event, travel light and keep in mind that no matter how much space you have in your cabin you will not have such roomy quarters when you begin traveling around the continent by train, car or bus. And, definitely! the days of the old-fashioned steamer trunk are over.

In checking in at the pier, keep one hand free for displaying your ticket and embarkation card at the drop of a hat. Make a last-minute check to be sure that you have your passport. No one is likely to ask for it until you reach port on the other side. But by then it won't be very helpful to remember that you left it in the top drawer in the bedroom.

The inspection of your cabin and any sailing festivities going on there will occupy you during the first moments aboard. But as quickly as possible, you should drop into the dining room and reserve a table, at which you will have all your meals (except breakfast, which you can have in your room, if you wish). This table matter is important and will have a lot to do with your general enjoyment of the voyage. If there are specific people with whom you would like to sit, the dining room steward will do his best to arrange this. If you have no preference other than a desire to be seated with some congenial people, the best thing is to leave the whole thing up to the chief steward and hope for the best. Chief stewards are seasoned, wise men and are pretty good at working out table patterns and partners. If you're traveling alone, it's best to have yourself placed at a large table. There are few things more frustrating to the average unmarried woman than to be seated at a small table with a couple of unmarried women or with an older couple, while some nearby table seems to be filled up with a covey of eligible bachelors talking to themselves (or worse, to only one woman). But don't ask to be seated at the Captain's Table. The seating there is decided by the captain himself, with an assist from the chief dining room steward. On some ships, the guest list for the Captain's Table remains the same for the entire voyage—a movie star, a diplomat, a bearded writer, a pop music artist and other recognizable, or notable, personalities. Sometimes, on a small ship, just about everyone gets a chance to sit at the Captain's Table at one meal during the crossing. The Captain's Table, of course, is only in the First Class dining room, but other officers of the ship usually eat in the Cabin Class dining room.

Pointer: There are usually two sittings for lunch and dinner. The first is invariably too early (noon for lunch; six for dinner). Sign up for the second sitting. The ship's social activity revolves around that one.

DECK CHAIRS ¶ For some quaint, if not stubborn, reason, the ships ask you to pay for the use of a deck chair, as well as for a rug and cushion. If you want a chair, you'll have to do this even though you have already paid out perhaps $500 or more for your passage. The chair will cost a dollar a day (more or less) and the blanket (rug, they call it) will also have a slight fee attached—a kind of cover charge. Imagine paying a dollar for a blanket aboard an airplane! The deck steward, in return for all this, will place your chair in a sheltered or sunny spot or on whatever part of the deck you want it and furthermore will print your name on a little card and slip in into an identification slot to prove that it is yours for the entire voyage. After the first day or so most passengers leave their chairs and start floating around the ship, rarely settling down in one spot any more. The tip-off is that on eastbound voyages to Europe almost all of the chairs are sold out, while on the homeward journeys a smaller number of the passengers bother to reserve one.

PROTOCOL ¶ Aboard ship, the captain is the king of his domain. Each captain decides for himself how much socializing he does with the passengers. Some attend all meals. Others are only on hand for the gala Captain's Dinner at the end of the voyage. Some ships have two "captains"—one who remains on the bridge in charge of navigation matters and another who handles the social routine. If you have any complaints, tell them to the ship's purser (he is addressed as *Purser*). The purser usually has an office on the Main Deck and is available to passengers at practically every hour of the day or night. If there is something about the food or wines at meals that does not please you, tell the chief steward about it. In addressing the various service personnel—the room attendant, barman, waiter—the term "steward" is used. If you have a stewardess for your cabin, she is called stewardess.

Pointer: If there is a special dish you would like and you don't see it on the menu, let the chief dining room steward know what it is. Regardless of what it is, he will do his best to produce it for you.

DRESSING ABOARD SHIP ¶ During the day, most passengers wear *conservative* sports clothes. For men, this means slacks and a sport shirt. (A jacket must be worn in the First Class dining room, however.) Women usually wear blouses and skirts, sweaters and what is generally known in the garment trade as cruise wear. Practically no one except a British diplomat wears a hat (too much danger of its being blown overboard, you know). On the way to the swimming pool, wear a robe, jacket or some kind of beach coat over your bathing suit. And, by the way, never go into the dining room in a bathing suit, or you'll get thrown out (asked to leave, that is).

In First Class only, evening clothes are theoretically worn each evening for dinner except on sailing day, the last night at sea (when you're supposed to do your packing) and Sunday. The general wave of informality has caught up with First Class, even on the high seas, and so dressing formally for dinner has become more or less optional. This state of affairs means that a short cocktail dress for women and summer formal clothes for men are adequate during the main tourist season. No formal dress is required in Cabin or Tourist Class; however, especially on gala nights, many people do get dressed up.

TIPPING ABOARD SHIP ¶ About two or three days before your ship is due into port one of your shipboard companions, in a very confidential way, is going to ask you what your plans are about tipping. Regardless of how many times a passenger has sailed to Europe he will seek advice, counsel or just plain information from traveling companions about the tipping question. This is an eternal question, and there is almost an infinity of answers. Once upon a time when steamship rates were a lot lower than they are now, a general rule of thumb was to set aside for tips an amount equal more or less to 10 percent of the cost of passage. But passenger fares have increased so steadily in recent years that a somewhat lower scale is presently used. There are certain fixed ground rules, but except for them everyone is on his own. For instance, tips are expected by any of the service personnel who do something for you that can be interpreted as being above and beyond their normal duty. This might be even nothing more than a cheerful Good Morning from the elevator operator—and if he addresses you by name, then by all means a tip is in order. You do not tip any of the ship's officers—not even the purser—but otherwise everyone else on the horizon is a potential receiver of your largesse. How large the largesse is depends on you and how you assess the services given you. The cabin steward and the waiters will be the main recipients. I say *waiters*—plural —because the chances are that a second dining room steward (waiter) will join your table somewhere along the line, and he will have to be remembered, too. His tip, however, will be somewhat smaller than the one you give the waiter who started out with you on the first day. Also, depending on how crowded a social life you lead aboard ship, tips might be in order for the stewards at the swimming pool, the gym and, of course, the lounge (the steward who serves you afternoon tea and after-dinner coffee and who so good-humoredly helps you place bets on the ship's pool). The deck steward gets tipped automatically, and if you have had a stateroom without private bath, you will have to tip the bath steward. At the end of the voyage—or after you have had your last drink— the bar bill will be presented to you as discreetly as if it was an invitation to Buckingham Palace. This is the one point where you do not have any leeway in your tipping. The barman gets 15 percent of the bill. Tips for the other personnel are given on the last day or, as in the case of the dining room stewards, after the last meal aboard. I have worked out a little tipping guide that can give you an idea of what to give the key people on your list. But you can give more or less depending on the service you received. The guide is based on *two* passengers in one stateroom:

	First Class	Cabin Class	Tourist Class
Cabin steward	$15	$10	$ 5
Cabin stewardess	15	10	5
Dining room steward	20	15	10
Wine steward (no need to tip if not used)	7	5	3
Deck steward	2	2	1
Bath steward (no need to tip if not used)	2	2	1

Pointer: One of the greatest pleasures of air travel is the absence of tipping of any kind. The Holland-American Line, which has been trying for some time to solve the tipping problem, eliminated tipping on all its ships in the spring of 1968. Tips are included in the fares, and additional tipping is not required or encouraged.

FREIGHTERS ¶ More and more cargo vessels are being converted into container ships, and that means less and less passenger-carrying freighters are available to trans-Atlantic travelers. Still, some freighter lines continue to carry passengers. So a word about this method of ship travel is in order. The word is this: freighters take even longer than the usual passenger liner but have their good points. For about half of what you would pay in First Class on a passenger liner, for instance, you can sail by freighter. Don't think they are going to stow you among the crates and bales of cotton, either. You will have a fine outside room—a large one, too. It will probably be larger, as a matter of fact, than the one you would have aboard a liner. The food will be very good, but unless you are on a French freighter, it won't be cooked by a French chef—and that makes a tremendous difference. You will be at the Captain's Table for meals. That's certain. There will be no more than a dozen passengers (that is the limit allowed), and the captain, accompanied by one or two other officers, dines with them. If the other passengers are the convivial type, all will be smooth sailing on the voyage. If you find them antipathetic, the trip will seem even longer than it actually is. Most freighters take anywhere from a week to eight or nine days to a North Atlantic port (such as Antwerp, Rotterdam, Le Havre) and ten days or more to a Mediterranean one (such as Genoa). Life is very informal aboard a freighter, and the captain usually gives you the run of the ship. Freighters are booked up heavily during the summer months, and reservations have to be made at least six months ahead of time. There are American, Norwegian and other countries' freighters serving European ports. In some cities there are travel agents who specialize in booking reservations on freighters, but most of them do not handle this type of seagoing transportation. Not all freighters carry passengers, by the way. In fact, the majority of them do not. But any freighter line will give you the names of companies that do, and you can start from there in making arrangements for your slow boat to Europe. That is a lot of fun, too.

Pointer: With the development of container ships, a large number of the old-style passenger-carrying cargo ships are being retired. This makes it harder than usual to book passage on a trans-Atlantic freighter.

All About Air Travel

Going by air means that almost your entire vacation time will be spent abroad. In recent years the cost of flights has been getting lower and lower, and that is undoubtedly one of the big reasons people have been switching to planes. The airlines keep working out new arrangements and possibilities (including package hotel and sightseeing tours on arrival). The result is that air rates are a big bargain for the Europe-bound traveler. Under one plan, for instance, it is possible to make a round-trip flight between Europe and the United States for about what it would cost in Cabin Class on a ship for only *one way*. Your travel agent or an airline office will give you complete details on the latest flight plans available. Before you make up your mind on which method of travel you are going to use, take a look at the latest air fares being offered.

SELECTING YOUR AIRLINE ¶ There are over a dozen airlines flying regularly scheduled flights from the United States to Europe. The largest proportion of business is in the hands of three airlines—Pan American, TWA, and BOAC. Americans, as a group, tend to fly the American carriers, the statistics indicate, and I suppose that's the way it should be, all things considered, because most foreign nationals tend to travel by *their* own national airline. With only rare exceptions (the Czech airline, and Aeroflot, the Russian carrier), airlines tend to use American equipment. And, of course, with respect to airline fares, they're all the same by agreement. The one major exception is Icelandic, which is not a member of IATA, the international organization of airlines which sets the fares each year. The theory behind fixing fares is that no airline should compete by lowering its fares, thus inviting the disregard of passenger safety, which might be induced by an airline trying to cut corners due to lowered income. The theory has been criticized, but nevertheless it's a definite fact of life that almost all airlines flying to Europe belong to IATA, and the fares are the same on all airlines (except Icelandic, as mentioned before).

Until recently, the biggest and best plane flying was the Boeing 707, the standard for overseas flights. Now, the newest and biggest is the Boeing 747, a veritable monster plane, carrying some 350 (or even more) passengers.

Although there have been some critical words about the enormous size of the aircraft, and that it's often difficult to visit the rest rooms, somehow or another the public has taken to the 747 and it's surely here to stay. Certainly the major airlines have invested so many hundreds of millions of dollars in the 747, that if for no other reason, it's almost certain to be the airplane of the 1970s.

Now a word about charter flights: The scheduled airlines have been fighting a war of words with the non-scheduled airlines. The latter differ from the scheduled airlines in that they only fly when they have a full load of passengers, whereas the scheduled airlines leave according to their time-table, regardless of how many passengers show up. As a result, the non-scheduled airlines are in a position to offer lower fares, providing the plane is chartered by an organization. There are a whole series of complicated rules about what constitutes a valid charter, and what doesn't. However, at various times and places, people have found themselves stranded at the airport, unable to board their long-anticipated charter flight to Europe, because the government has decided the flight was illegally or improperly chartered. It is very important —and this cannot be overemphasized—that you verify, well in advance, whether or not the charter is a *bona fide* one, and you should look into the reputation of the travel agent involved. If not, it's within the bounds of possibility that you may find yourself sitting on your baggage, pondering what to do next, upon learning that the charter flight has been canceled.

To us the principal goal of an airline is to get us there safely. All of the nonessentials—including the luxurious lounges, the red carpet leading to the plane, the pretty stewardesses, the elaborate meals served aboard with vintage champagne, the free toothbrushes and the handy flight bags—are merely trimmings. Call us old-fashioned, but we can never forget the basic premise that the airline's principal job is to arrive at the destination safely and quickly.

Now let's tackle the secondary part of this question of getting there safely. Sometimes an airline will announce a delay in beginning a flight. Or, while en route, an airliner will make an unscheduled stop at some point such as Gander or Shannon for a look-see at something mechanical or for additional fuel. Occasionally passengers in a hurry will groan and complain about the delay.

But you will never hear a word from us. We're delighted to think that the airline has enough regard for the safety of its passengers to delay a flight in order to check on the equipment. This unscheduled stopping costs the airline a large sum of money. But they gladly take on this cost in order to be certain, rather than continuing the flight and hoping for the best. Frankly, we'd rather arrive in Paris an hour later than take *any* chance of winding up in the water without our bathing suit on. We can swim pretty well, but do not like unscheduled swims.

Since we like that safety factor, we prefer to travel on an American airline. American aviation ability and skill cannot be surpassed. Even the Europeans have begun to admit this on occasion. When that plane stops at Goose Bay, it's comforting to know that the airline is spending money on extra safety for its passengers. A smaller airline, because of fewer planes and a more restricted operation, cannot afford the number of mechanics and the maintenance of million-dollar stockpiles of spare parts around the world the way a large airline can. Furthermore, when a canceled flight is necessary, the giant airline because of its big inventory of equipment can put another plane into service at once. It may come as a surprise to you, but several of the European lines operate with as few as four (yes, f-o-u-r) overseas aircraft. Naturally, when one of these planes is incapacitated, it might take a day or more to get a replacement and put it into service.

SELECTING YOUR CLASS ABOARD THE PLANE ¶ Trans-Atlantic passengers in recent years have had a choice of about five different classes. All have varied in one degree or another on such factors as space available to the passenger, fancy groceries, free liquor and length of time in which the return portion of the ticket could be used. It now appears that the airlines have settled down to two types of service—First Class (Deluxe) and Economy. There is a big price difference between the two, let me point out right away. This differential can range—depending on when and where you are going—from $150 to $180 or more *per person one way*. Thus, a couple making a round trip by air in Economy Class can save as much as $600—and maybe more. To put it another way, it costs about $20 extra per hour of flying for First Class compared with Economy.

You pay for this bargain in other ways. That is obviously logical. For one thing, the baggage allowance in Economy Class is limited to 44 pounds. In First Class you can take a whopping 66 pounds. Actually, 44 pounds is enough for the average European vacationer if he packs sensibly and uses judgment in what he takes. (If not, the overweight charge is pretty stiff. So think twice before taking along that 2-pound French dictionary.) Another reason why Economy is less expensive than First Class is the food. In First Class, they feed you cocktails, a rich meal and all the elegant trimmings—course by course and accompanied by the appropriate wines and liquors. Everything is designed to give you a very luxurious vacationy feeling. In Economy Class, on the other hand, the food consists of a blue plate-type meal; coffee and other non-alcoholic beverages are served. (You can buy drinks, however.) Possibly the major distinction between First and Economy Class is the amount of leg room. In First Class there are two seats together on each side of the plane. There is a fair amount of room in front of you, also, to stretch out and be really comfortable. Not so in Economy Class. In this lower-priced section there are more seats abreast and less leg room. Say what you like —it's a close fit, although roomier, on the 747s.

Despite the lower baggage allowance, the more simple food and the limited leg room, three out of four travelers use Economy. Why? It is a wonderful feeling to step off a plane in Europe with the realization that during the seven-hour flight you have actually saved at least $150!

First Class, of course, is ideal for those who are working for big corporations, who are on an expense account or whose grandfather thoughtfully remembered them in his will with a gift of 2,000 shares of U.S. Steel. Also, First Class should be considered by those people who dislike the idea of being crowded or of having a third party sitting alongside them while they're cooing away on a second (or first!) honeymoon. Whatever the reason, the decision must be yours.

How About Baggage ¶ First, you will need lightweight baggage. The canvas or nylon types are the most desirable. The perfect suitcase has yet to be devised for the air traveler, however. As far as we are concerned, the lighter-weight bags aren't strong enough, and the stronger ones are too heavy. In any event, don't spend too much money for a suitcase. No matter how fine a one you purchase, it will get scratched and bruised somewhere along the line. Size is important, too. Don't take a bag over 30 inches in length, about 10 inches deep and 20 inches wide. A bag not meeting these general measurements (you don't have to be exact about it) gets unwieldy. You have to keep in mind that at times you'll have to handle the baggage yourself or push it through train windows for reluctant porters if you journey through Europe by rail. Try to limit yourself to two bags (three pieces for a husband and wife). You will probably be carrying a flight bag or two, so there will be more than enough for you to handle.

Obligingly, the airlines do not weigh certain extra items you take along with you, and that helps expand your weight allowance. Coats, an umbrella, a camera, a lady's handbag, binoculars, a reasonable amount of reading material and an infant's carrying basket and food are not weighed. But the airlines *do* weigh briefcases, typewriters, overnight bags, heavy professional-type cameras, radios, hat boxes and lady's vanity or cosmetic cases. But there is one further consoling point when you are working with your weight allowance. Two or more people traveling together—or headed for the same destination and "weighing in" at the same time—can pool their allowances.

What You Should Take

The main rule—for both men and women—is to take *less* than you think you will need. Let's look at the problem carefully—first for women, then for men

WOMEN ¶ Most women, especially first-time travelers to Europe, take too many changes of clothing. Those who have been in Europe previously know that unless you plan to stay at one resort for several weeks (where repetition might prove tiresome or embarrassing), extensive changes are not necessary. You'll be on the move every few days and meeting new people all the time. Thus, you can wear the same few dresses time and time again, merely by changing your accessories (belts, blouses, shoes) and adding a sweater or scarf. European cleaning service is expensive, slow and not usually equal to American standards. So it will be helpful, and a lot easier, if you pack synthetic fabrics. We have traveled around the world on several occasions, taking only one 29-inch suitcase and staying well within the baggage allowance. Yet—and this is 100 percent true!—we still had all the necessary clothing for seasonal changes.

To simplify your wardrobe, select colors that can be worn with one particular color accessory. In this way, your clothing problem will be lessened and you'll be able to wear all your shoes with all your dresses, all your blouses with all your suits and so forth.

Where are you going in Europe? It's a big place and has about the same weather changes as the different regions of the United States. If you are going to tour only the Scandinavian countries (where the weather is cool) or if you are going to stick to the warm shores of the Mediterranean, planning should not be too difficult. If you're ranging from warm to cool—and in-between or moderate—climates, a little more thought will have to be given to the matter. We've found it a good rule, in any case, to be prepared for cool days on occasion even though the area we were touring was, basically, a warm one.

Here are the basic items you'll need on a month's vacation (and, wherever possible, they should be the wash-and-wear variety):

2 nightgowns or pajamas
3 petticoats or slips ⎫
3 bras   ⎬ These can include the ones you're
3 girdles or panties ⎭ wearing
6–12 pair nylon hose
1 pair sturdy, *comfortable* walking shoes
1 pair dressy shoes
1 dressy handbag (in case you're carrying one of those overlarge carry-all traveling bags)
2 dressy dresses
3 daytime dresses
1 suit (you'll probably be traveling in another one)
2–3 blouses
1 sweater
1 scarf
1 coat (tweed or all-weather type, which you'll carry)
12 handkerchiefs
1 robe
1 pair bedroom slippers (preferably the lightweight traveling type)
Shower or bathing cap
Bathing suit (if you plan on swimming)
Jewelry
Cosmetics, medicine and *accessory* toilet articles (don't take too much; they're available everywhere)

Fur stole (depending on your travel plans)
Sunglasses
Sewing kit

MEN ¶ Like a woman's wardrobe, yours depends on where and when you plan to travel—the fjords of Norway or the Riviera sun spots, the Alps in the winter, or the Mediterranean islands in the summer. As a general rule, you can't go wrong if you emphasize conservative clothes when you pack. On the other hand, you can go wrong if you figure on wearing nothing but sport clothes on your European travels. European men are extremely conservative in their clothes. If you're driving through southern France, for instance, you can enter a luxury, four-star restaurant along the road in sport clothes for lunch. But if you go to a simple city restaurant to eat in the evening, all eyes in the place will be on you if you're not wearing a tie and suit. Some eating establishments, as well as all casinos and night clubs, will not admit a man not wearing a tie—tourist or not.

As in the case of women, it is a good idea to build your wardrobe around a single color scheme. European men prefer a dark color. Blue is a good one, because it harmonizes with just about everything except brown. In the evening, a blue, dark gray (charcoal) or black suit will look dressy, whereas a brown one would be definitely out of order. If your sport jacket and slacks match or harmonize with each other, you are bound to get full usage out of everything you take along.

Even though you might want to make some variations to satisfy your own taste, the following packing list is basic and can be a useful guide:

1 dark suit (blue, charcoal gray or black)
2 pairs slacks (blue, gray or charcoal)
1 sport jacket (to match slacks; it should be a lightweight one for southern areas; a heavy tweed for Scandinavia)
5 shirts (three will do, if they are dacron or another synthetic)
1 sport shirt (preferably a no-iron type)
4 ties
4 sets underwear
8 handkerchiefs
6 pair socks
1 pair shoes
1 sweater
2 pair pajamas (drip dry)
1 lightweight robe
1 pair slippers (preferably the lightweight traveling type)

1 pair swimming trunks (if you're planning to swim)
Shaving kit
Miscellany: Sunglasses, medicine, and so forth.

THE WEIGH-IN ¶ You will have enough clothes with you if you follow the above basic guides for men's and women's packing, because you will also be wearing a complete outfit. When you have assembled everything, weigh it all (including the suitcases, but excluding a raincoat or topcoat, which you'll *carry* separately) and find out whether you are under the weight allowance. If you are overweight (that is, if your baggage is above the allowance), remove a heavy item, such as the extra pair of men's shoes—which can tip the scales at 3 pounds or more. (You won't have to go barefoot. You've got one pair on, remember?) Or if you are set against removing any items, then get prepared to pay some stiff excess-baggage charges. The rate is 1 percent of the one-way fare for each 2.2 pounds over the allowance. In dire emergency, you can always put a few heavy items in your topcoat (or raincoat) pocket. This is not exactly the correct thing to do, but it is only slightly improper. After all, you *are* permitted to carry a coat, and no one says the pockets have to be empty.

HOW TO PACK ¶ Lay clothes flat in the suitcase and separate them with successive layers of tissue paper. Stuff the sleeves of suits and jackets with crumpled tissue paper to reduce wrinkling. Place the heavier items (like suits) on the bottom and the shirts, blouses, underwear and lighter articles at the top. Before starting your packing, visit a dime store and buy several large plastic bags (the transparent ones, such as cellophane). You can put shoes in these bags and keep them from soiling your other clothing. A zippered container for shaving gear, toothbrush, toothpaste and so forth, will keep these things from rattling around in the suitcase and will keep everything handy for use when needed. If by some chance your suitcase is not completely filled up, add some crumbled tissue paper. Otherwise, everything will be jumbled up when you open the lid in Europe.

EXTRAS ¶ Those of you who have been going back and forth to Europe during the past two decades know how, progressively, American items have been showing up on shelves and counters all over the continent. American cigarettes are more expensive (in most countries) than at home, but you can get most brands. It's a good idea to buy cigarettes at tax-free airport shops. The same goes for liquor. For a while, the term "whisky" to the European meant Scotch exclusively, but Europeans have since discovered bourbon. Liquor prices, by the way, are frequently cheaper than in America. Europe is also well stocked with film—color, as well as black and white. Your favorite brands of vitamin pills, toothpaste, drugs and cosmetics are all available—and often are cheaper. If you have a special medicine, bring the prescription with you so that you can have it made up in a European pharmacy if your own supply runs out.

Be sure to bring along a large cake of soap in a plastic container. European hotels frequently do not supply soap, and even when they do, it is too small for bath use (or, at least, most Americans think so). Liquid soaps or soap flakes in individual paper envelopes are marvelous for doing your dacron shirts or blouses and underwear and are not generally available in Europe. Whether you plan to drive around Europe or travel by train, you'll be happy to have a towel handy on many occasions. Not even paper towels are available in many continental washrooms. If your weight allowance discourages you from packing a towel, at least remember to get one among your first European purchases.

Take along, too, a portable transistor radio; it will weigh only a few ounces but will be worth having as a traveling companion. By tuning in on the BBC or the American Armed Forces Radio in Germany, for instance, you will be able to hear the latest news in English. A portable travel clock is often worth its weight in gold, because telephone operators have been known to forget early morning calls. Also, a European model travel iron, with dial settings for 220 as well as 110 current, will help you freshen up articles that get creased in your travelings. Unfortunately irons are fairly heavy—about 2 or 3 pounds—and not worth the excess-baggage charge if you have to go over the weight limit. (However, you could slip one in your coat pocket.) And if you wear eyeglasses, by all means bring an extra pair with you.

First Aid ¶ About the only typical ailment that troubles most travelers is diarrhea caused by the change in water.

Paregoric or kaopectate are also helpful. One of the myacins, in capsule or tablet form, is an excellent precautionary item, but your doctor will have to write a prescription for it. A few Band-Aids will also come in handy for nicked fingers. Don't forget to bring along a thermometer—European ones (except in England) are in Centigrade. When you're sick, the last thing you'll want to be bothered with is a table that converts Centigrade readings to Fahrenheit.

Making Travel Arrangements

If you cannot make up your mind on which method to use to cross the ocean—plane or ship—consider compromising by going one way by ship and the other by plane. If you do that, it's wisest to make the eastbound (toward Europe) crossing by plane and the homeward voyage by ship. Inevitably, you'll buy things in Europe, and returning by ship avoids the problem of charges for excess baggage. Also, most returning vacationers could use a few days of rest on board ship. Going to Europe, you'll be anxious to get there, and the plane is the obvious choice.

Once you have decided how you're going to travel to Europe, you will have to give some thought to the matter of how you will travel when you get there. Fundamentally, there are three ways of doing this: (1) the conducted group tour, with many variations; (2) the independent but planned trip; (3) traveling completely on your own.

The *conducted tour* comes in just about every version possible. You can have everything and every minute arranged for your entire trip—from hotels and meals to local sightseeing excursions and shopping trips. Or, you can take a conducted tour in which you will be free to go on your own from one main meal a day. Or, you can choose between traveling by train or by bus. Or—well, as we said, the variety seems to be without limit. The principal thing is that you will be doing your touring in a group —the same group for every single day, morning and night, day after day, right down to the rainbow at the end of the tour. Many of you who have taken the "group" tour in the past have sworn, "Never again!" Others are all for it. Some people object to the regimentation, the feeling of being "herded about like cattle." Or, they don't like the idea of being in such close proximity to the same group of fellow tourists all the time and being, in effect, cut off from the human contacts they would naturally have with local Europeans if they were not on a conducted tour. But there are the enthusiasts who say that it takes all the headaches out of traveling. The organizers of the tour do all the worrying about hotel arrangements, tipping, schedules and the like, leaving the tourist completely free to enjoy himself. Also, it should be remembered that such tours are set up for the common denominator of interest—that is, what the travel agent thinks the group will want to see and do. This may or may not jibe with your own desires. The conducted tour might call for journeying from one monument to another in a city, such as Pisa. You, after taking a quick look at the tower to see if it is still leaning, might want to spend most of your time wandering around the flower market. A fifteen-minute bus stop in Assisi might be enough for some people. But, while the driver is saying, "Folks, remember we've got to reach Florence tonight," you might climb back into the bus and huddle up in your seat with a feeling of deep disappointment that such a short interval was allotted to the Umbrian hill town. One thing is sure: A conducted tour is the least expensive way of traveling —that is, if you consider the prices you yourself would have to pay for the same hotels, restaurants and sightseeing excursions.

The *independent planned trip* is like a conducted tour in a way—but without the group. You will be on your own, except that everything will have been worked out for you and you will be met by uniformed representatives along the line, such as at railroad stations and piers. Travel agents call this type of travel FIT (*Foreign Independent Trip*). You can set up a FIT for yourself by telling your travel agent which countries you'd like to visit, how many days you have for the whole trip and how much money you are prepared to spend. You also have to tell him—and this is a point of fundamental importance to the success of a FIT—the types, or maybe just *the* type, of things you want to see. Is your interest Roman ruins in France and other countries, bikinis anywhere or vineyards? Or, do you want only a general once-over look? It is obviously cheaper to arrange transportation and accommodations for people traveling in a group, rather than by themselves, so the FIT is more expensive than a conducted tour. The big advantage—if everything works out all right—is that you see exactly what you want to see. But you must be specific in your talks with the travel agent, and he must know how to translate your wishes into a precise, custom-made itinerary.

Traveling on your own, those of you who have been to Europe time and again will agree, is the ideal way to do it. For those who have taken conducted tours or FITs in the past—or who are heading for the continent for the first time—a few warning signals have to be hoisted. First, it is suitable for two people at the least. The individual traveler who can explore, and *enjoy*, Europe on his own is rare. Second, this type of trip can be extremely difficult during the height of the tourist season, when all available accommodations are being spoken for by Europeans themselves, as well as by those people who arrange conducted tours or FITs. Third, you must have that wonderful sort of nature that can bear up gracefully under all sorts of petty annoyances (such as being told at one hotel after another that there is not a room in town on a hot July night when you're dying to get undressed and take a bath).

If you're going to make the trip on your own, a few preparations should be made. Before leaving the United States, line up a return reservation. If the mood strikes you to change plans once you arrive in Europe, your reservation home can be used for a trade in getting later (or earlier) or different accommodations. Otherwise, with lots of other Americans wanting to go home at the same time, you might run into trouble getting the space you ask for. A day spent in a ticket office waiting hopefully for a last-minute cancellation to turn up not only will be a nuisance but—prorating the cost of your entire trip— can be an expensive one.

Another predeparture preparation is to make a hotel reservation in the first city at which you're landing. (Have it confirmed, too.) Nothing is more frustrating than to arrive in a strange city and have to go from hotel to hotel, looking for a room, while the taxi driver frets at each succeeding stop and the meter simultaneously shows its uneasiness by clicking away in the local currency. Most European capitals are short of hotel space all year around, and the hotels that offer good rooms at the right price are always in scant supply. At mountain and sea resorts during the summer, it is the same story. The lone traveler is often told, for instance, that only double rooms are available. If he wants a room he has to take the "double" and pay the higher rate. Often, especially during the summer vacation period (High Season), the only available rooms are in the luxury—and most expensive— hotels. The most critical time in the year for hotel space is around August 15, the high point of summer vacation time for Europeans. But Easter and Pentecost are also busy times. So, the lone traveler should be guided accordingly. Furthermore, if he plans to set off somewhere by train as soon as he gets to the continent, advance train reservations are in order. There are just so many berths on European trains. If the traveler does not have one reserved by the time he gets to the station, he might have to stand up in an aisle all night; or, he might not even be allowed standing room on the train. In Spain, for instance, even if you are traveling in Second Class, you have to have a reserved seat on main line trains. If you don't have a reservation, you have the choice of trying to get aboard a milk train that makes every stop or waiting until you arrange space for yourself on the next express—or the one after that. So even if you prefer to travel on the spur of the moment and as free as the wind, you will still have to pay some obeisance to that venerable BE PREPARED motto.

Passports and Visas

Visas have become a thing of the past for the American tourist in Western Europe, and the day might be coming when the nations of Eastern Europe follow suit. A visa is formal permission by a country for a person to enter it and is indicated by an appropriate rubber stamp put in the individual's passport by a consular or other representative of the government doing the authorizing. The nations of Western Europe dropped visa requirements for American citizens years ago and have gradually been giving this same visa-free privilege to neighbors and some other countries. Yugoslavia abolished visas in 1967 but re-established them in 1969 for citizens of those countries which require visas from Yugoslav citizens. So now you need a visa again, but you can get it at the border (if you do not have time to go to a Yugoslav Consulate) and it is issued with a minimum of formality. Actually it is more like a tourist card than a real visa. The only country covered in this book that requires an old-fashioned visa is the Soviet Union.

Even though you do not need a visa to travel in Western Europe, you definitely have to have a passport—that now-familiar blue (some people think it's gray) booklet issued by the Department of State in Washington, D.C. A passport, in effect, is a representation to foreign countries that you are an American citizen. Most Europeans will think you're very lucky to own that precious blue booklet. The old passport you used on earlier trips abroad might still be good. Under the new procedure, passports are now valid for five years. However, if you have an old passport, check the issuance date. It may still be good, or possibly renewable for an additional two years, in some cases.

To get a passport, you have to apply in person at the main Passport Office in Washington, D.C., or at a branch office of the U.S. Passport Agency. In the case of new applications, you have to bring along a birth or baptismal certificate or some other proof of the place and date of your coming into this world, plus a driver's license or other suitable identification. You also have to have two duplicate photographs that were taken no later than six months ago and are about 2½ by 2½ inches. They can be black and white or color. Oh, yes. Bring some money with you. The application fee for a passport is $10 plus a $2 service charge. You can make a "package" deal, if you wish—that is, a husband and wife (and their children) can travel on one passport for one fee.

Here are the addresses of the offices of the U.S. Passport Agency:

Boston: Salada Building, 330 Stuart St.
Chicago: Federal Office Building, 219 S. Dearborn St.
Los Angeles: Federal Office Building, 300 North Los Angeles
   St.
Miami: Federal Office Building, 51 S.W. First Ave.
New Orleans: New Federal Building, 701 Loyola Ave.
New York: 630 Fifth Ave.
San Francisco: Federal Office Building, 450 Golden Gate
   Ave.
Seattle: 1410 Fifth Ave.
Honolulu: Room 304, Federal Building

Note: If you don't live in or near one of the above
cities, inquire at the nearest federal (U.S. District) court
or at your city or county clerk's office about the closest
facility where passports are issued. Certain courts have
this authority.

Timing the Tour

The tourist with limited vacation time—say, two or
three weeks—has to make every day (yea! *minute*) count.
It follows, therefore, that he (or she) has to be extremely
selective.

This calls for two things: adequate preparation beforehand; and once you get there, really moving on your
holiday. It is considerably more entertaining to spend
two or three energetic weeks loaded with charm and
pleasure than two or three months of boredom endured
in strange and expensive surroundings.

Since every hour, minute and second count, flying to
Europe is your inescapable choice. If a vacation begins
—as it so often does—after work on Friday, take right
off that evening. In that way you gain a day. The flight
to Europe will allow plenty of time for rest. (Because
the eastward course of the plane reduces nighttime darkness to only four or five hours, it is a good idea to take
along some black eyeshades. Some airlines have them
aboard.)

If a tourist has cared little for art galleries and museums at home, it is not necessary to spend too much
time in them in Europe merely because this seems to
be the thing to do. By eliminating many things that other
people have told you to do when you go abroad, it is

surprising how much time will be left for doing what you really want to.

Get a breather now and then from your busy schedule by stopping for a coffee or whatnot at a sidewalk cafe. You can watch the city go by while you are having your well-earned sustenance. (Can't afford to waste time even when you are resting!)

Don't forget to be choosy. To get the best from a short trip, as we want to mention once more, the tourist in a hurry must be selective. If the schedule, for instance, allows only five days in France, spend them all in Paris. In attempting to see the whole country in so short a time, you would end up seeing nothing. Selectivity also avoids duplication. It certainly is not necessary, or advisable, to see every monument, museum, ruin and church in any particular place. Sightseeing (for those with limited time) should be concentrated on representative places—the high spots.

Equally important is to do a little sightseeing of human beings and not exclusively of objects. The kindness of a shopkeeper who leaves his store to give you street directions will remain much longer in your memory than the statue or whatever other object it was that you had been looking for.

Most Americans look forward eagerly to foreign food —especially French and Italian—and, as a result, consume stupendous lunches and multicourse dinners accompanied by numerous wines. What happens? In a few days, gorged with huge meals and unaccustomed sauces, they are languid and not at all hungry. The traveler in a hurry has no time to spend on a sluggish liver. To minimize the chance of this happening, the wise traveler eats sensibly and does not have more than one rich or unusual dish at each meal.

Weather

Europeans have "weather" just as we do, and they talk about it in the same way. But you will not see and hear references to it in newspapers, on radio and TV and on billboards or outdoor displays to the extent that we do here at home. A newspaper, for instance, will *usually* (no guarantee) inform you and other readers what the temperature high and low were *yesterday*. But in a European country, if you want to know the correct temperature at any moment, you'll probably have to call up the official weather bureau, although the weather forecasts are regularly included in radio and TV news reports. In most of the capitals and large cities in Central Europe, you can dial the weather number on the phone to get a recorded forecast. The problem: you have to know the language of the country. Something else you will have to get used to in European weather reporting is that temperatures are given in Centigrade, rather than Fahrenheit.

To help give you an idea of what the temperature is likely to be in the places on your itinerary, we have included weather strips throughout this book. The weather strips give the low, high and average temperatures for many of the places you'll be visiting. The temperatures, too, are in Fahrenheit. Even so, they might be confusing. To make things easier for you, here are some average temperatures and the average number of days of rain in representative American cities. By comparing the weather record of one of these cities in your general area with one in Europe, you will find it easier to understand and "forecast" the temperatures on your journey ahead.

	JAN.	FEB.	MAR.	APR.	MAY	JUNE	JULY	AUG.	SEPT.	OCT.	NOV.	DEC.
EAST												
Boston	29°	29°	37°	47°	58°	67°	72°	70°	64°	54°	43°	32°
	12	10	12	11	11	10	10	10	9	9	10	11
New York	31°	31°	39°	49°	60°	69°	74°	73°	67°	56°	45°	35°
	12	10	11	11	11	11	11	10	9	9	9	11
Washington, D.C.	35°	36°	44°	54°	65°	73°	77°	75°	69°	57°	46°	37°
	11	10	12	11	12	11	11	11	8	8	9	10
SOUTH												
Atlanta	43°	46°	53°	61°	70°	77°	79°	78°	73°	63°	52°	45°
	12	11	11	10	9	11	12	12	8	7	8	11
Charleston	51°	52°	58°	65°	73°	79°	82°	81°	77°	68°	58°	54°
	10	9	9	8	8	11	13	13	10	6	7	9
Houston	53°	56°	63°	69°	75°	81°	83°	83°	79°	71°	62°	55°
	10	9	8	7	7	8	10	9	9	6	8	10
Miami	68°	68°	71°	74°	77°	80°	82°	82°	81°	78°	72°	69°
	8	6	7	7	11	13	16	15	18	15	10	8
New Orleans	55°	57°	63°	69°	76°	81°	83°	83°	80°	72°	62°	56°
	10	9	9	7	8	13	15	14	11	7	8	10

	JAN.	FEB.	MAR.	APR.	MAY	JUNE	JULY	AUG.	SEPT.	OCT.	NOV.	DEC.
CENTRAL												
Chicago	25°	27°	36°	47°	58°	68°	73°	72°	65°	54°	40°	30°
	11	10	12	11	12	11	9	9	9	9	10	11
Cleveland	25°	26°	35°	46°	58°	68°	72°	70°	64°	53°	39°	29°
	17	15	15	13	13	11	10	9	10	11	14	16
Dallas	45°	50°	57°	65°	73°	81°	84°	84°	78°	68°	56°	48°
	8	8	8	8	9	7	5	7	5	6	6	7
Detroit	25°	25°	34°	46°	58°	68°	73°	71°	64°	53°	40°	29°
	13	12	13	11	13	11	9	9	10	10	12	13
Minneapolis	14°	17°	30°	46°	58°	68°	73°	71°	62°	50°	33°	20°
	8	7	8	9	12	12	9	9	9	9	8	8
Omaha	22°	26°	38°	52°	62°	72°	78°	75°	67°	55°	39°	28°
	6	6	8	10	12	11	9	9	8	7	5	6
Pittsburgh	31°	31°	40°	51°	62°	70°	74°	72°	67°	55°	43°	34°
	16	14	15	13	13	12	12	10	9	10	12	14
St. Louis	32°	35°	45°	56°	66°	75°	80°	78°	71°	59°	46°	36°
	9	9	11	11	12	11	8	8	8	8	8	9
WEST												
Denver	31°	33°	39°	48°	57°	67°	73°	71°	63°	52°	40°	33°
	5	6	8	9	10	8	9	9	6	6	5	5
Los Angeles	56°	56°	58°	60°	63°	67°	71°	72°	70°	66°	62°	57°
	6	6	6	4	2	1	0	0	1	2	3	6
Phoenix	52°	56°	61°	68°	76°	85°	91°	89°	86°	71°	60°	53°
	4	4	4	2	1	1	5	6	3	2	2	4
Salt Lake City	29°	34°	42°	50°	59°	68°	77°	75°	65°	53°	41°	32°
	10	10	10	9	8	5	4	6	5	7	7	13
San Francisco	50°	53°	54°	56°	57°	59°	59°	60°	62°	61°	57°	52°
	11	11	10	6	4	2	0	0	2	4	7	10
Seattle	40°	42°	46°	50°	56°	60°	64°	64°	60°	53°	46°	42°
	18	16	19	16	12	9	5	5	8	13	17	16

Pointer: To convert Centigrade into Fahrenheit, multiply by 2, deduct 10%, and add 32. For example: 20° C. multiplied by 2 equals 40; deduct 10%, or 4, and you get 36. Plus 32 equals 68° F.

To convert Fahrenheit into Centigrade, reverse the above process. For example: 68° F. minus 32 equals 36. Plus 10% equals 40. Divided by 2 equals 20° C.

United States Customs

CLEARING THE U.S. CUSTOMS WITHOUT DIFFICULTY ¶ For many tourists the number-one mental hazard when they return from Europe is going through customs. Clearing American customs does not have to be a problem at all if you follow a few simple rules. For one thing, don't pay any attention to advice that supposedly helpful fellow passengers try to give you. If you violate customs regulations, you can lose the property itself and be fined. Flagrant violations are sometimes prosecuted. Another thing to remember is that just because you use a foreign item abroad before getting home does not eliminate the need for you to declare it. Everything purchased abroad, whether already used or not, has to be declared when you arrive in the United States from your trip abroad. Now this is not something that a traveler who has never been in Europe before has to worry about when he is packing his bags for the journey. But travelers making a repeat voyage definitely must think about the matter of customs before they set off. That is why we mention "going through customs" at this point. Why? Every article of foreign origin—whether it is a watch, a camera, a piece of jewelry or whatever—is subject to duty every time it is imported into the United States. That means you might still have to pay duty on a watch you bought on a previous trip but took back to Europe with you this time. You can avoid this, however, by proving to the customs officer that you possessed the article in the United States before embarking on your latest trip. Bills of sale, purchase receipts and cleaning or repair bills are acceptable ways of proving prior possession. But you must have these papers with you. So, when packing for your European trip, make a careful check to see whether you are taking, or wearing, articles acquired the last time you were abroad. Either leave such articles home or bring along with you papers that prove you possessed them before leaving the United States.

If you are taking cameras, jewelry, or the like with you, ask the airline (at the time of checking in) to register these articles on an appropriate custom's form. They will constitute proof of your ownership *prior* to leaving the country.

WHO ARE YOU? ¶ Before you reach the United States on your return voyage, the ship or plane steward will give you a customs form. If you are a "returning resident," you will fill in the answers on one section of the form. The "returning nonresident" uses another. Are you resident or nonresident? The customs people have a pretty easy way of helping you decide. Generally speaking—they say—a returning resident is one who has not abandoned his permanent residence in the United States and taken up a permanent residence abroad.

CUSTOMS EXEMPTIONS ¶ Back in the early part of the postwar period, when the United States was helping Europe get back on its feet, the customs exemption was $500. Nowadays, a returning resident of the United States is granted a $100 exemption on the articles acquired abroad. The exemption is given to those persons who have been abroad at least forty-eight hours and who have not used a similar exemption—or any part of one— during the previous thirty days. This $100 exemption is figured on the fair retail value of the items. Be as exact as humanly possible on this. If you have sales receipts with you, all the better. Make sure the receipts are for exactly what you paid. The customs people are well aware that some European merchants, in a misguided effort to satisfy a client, will use a lower figure than the actual cost when filling out a receipt for an overseas-bound article. Comparison-shopping reports, coupled with long experience, enable the customs inspectors to know exactly what things are selling for in Europe at any particular moment. This $100 exemption, by the way, applies only to the articles accompanying you at the time of your return and does not cover anything being shipped or arriving separately.

One other "significant" change in the customs routine in recent years is the liquor allowance. The multiquart allowance has evaporated. The allowance now is one quart, which must be included as part of your $100 exemption. This alcohol exemption, incidentally, is available only to a returning resident who is at least twenty-one years old. There is no problem, however, about cigarettes. You can bring in as many as you want for your personal use. Not so with cigars, however. One hundred cigars may be imported free if they are declared part of your $100 exemption. More than one hundred cigars are subject to duty.

MAKING THE DECLARATION ¶ The U.S. Customs inspectors do their very best to make things simple and easy for the returning traveler. The customs form is now so abbreviated that unless you have more than the usual number and type of articles, it can be filled out in a matter of seconds. The actual declaration of the foreign articles in your possession can be made orally in most cases. You must make a written declaration, however, when the total fair retail value of the articles tops $100, or if you have more than a quart of liquor or more than a hundred cigars with you. A written declaration is also necessary if some of the articles are not for your own personal use.

Making out the customs declaration can be a family affair. The head of the family can file a joint declaration for all members of his household who are returning with him. They can pool their exemptions. If one member has purchased $150 worth of things and another $50, everything averages out nicely. Children, even babes in arms, are granted the same $100 exemption as adults. But the youngsters do not get the alcohol exemption. There is one further subtle exception. Children who have been born overseas and who have not yet set foot in the United States do not get the $100 exemption.

Note: Antiques can be brought in without paying duty if they are at least one hundred years old.

PROHIBITED AND RESTRICTED ARTICLES ¶ Certain articles are banned altogether. Among them are lottery tickets, obscene articles and publications, narcotics and wild birds. Other things—such as fruits, vegetables, plants, meats, poultry—are either prohibited or subject to specific restrictions concerning their import. Animals being brought back with you are subject to health, agriculture and customs requirements. If you need help or information about possible restrictions on articles you're thinking of bringing home, the American consulates overseas will gladly be of service. The consulates are in each capital city as well as in certain other cities, such as major ports and tourist or commercial centers.

SHIPPING PURCHASES HOME ¶ You yourself, or the shop where you have bought an article, can ship a purchase home. This saves you the trouble of carrying it. But the item cannot be included in your $100 customs exemption.

You can use the mails, a ship or a plane to send your articles to the United States, but regardless of how they travel they must be cleared through U.S. Customs. The easiest shipping method for the average traveler, the experts say, is the mails. The mailman does the delivering for you—right to your home. If there is no duty to pay on the article, fine! If a duty has to be paid, the postman will collect it when he delivers the article. For this service the post office asks a very reasonable fee For each dutiable package the fee ranges up to a maximum of 50 cents in the case of parcel post and 20 cents for letter mail.

What about shipping by air or sea express, you ask? The initial freight charges look attractive, to be sure. But there is a good likelihood that you will have to pay some forwarding and handling charges you were not counting on. If you happen to be living in the area of the first port of arrival for the package and are able to go down and handle the entry formalities yourself, that is fine. Otherwise, the package will have to be consigned for handling to a custom-house broker. The brokers are private businessmen, not employees of the U.S. Customs service, so they charge a fee (usually quite substantial) for their service. Before the package finally reaches you, the handling, forwarding and miscellaneous charges can be more than what the article cost in the first place.

SHIPPING GIFTS ¶ A very nice wrinkle in the general customs situation is that you are allowed to send home by mail certain low-priced gifts without paying duty on them and without affecting your basic $100 exemption. This is the ideal way of making sure your friends and family get a little souvenir from Europe, and at the same time the tranquillity of your baggage allowance is not disturbed. This welcome gesture on the part of U.S. Customs and postal officials can be rescinded at any time. No one—except tourists—seems to be too happy about it. But as things now stand, you are permitted to send duty-free a gift not valued at more than $10. The limit is one gift to the same person a day. Thus, you can send a dozen gifts of less than $10 each in value to a dozen different people in the same day. Looking at it another way, you also could send a new under-$10 gift to the same person every day for a week or more. Just write on the outside of the package: "Unsolicited Gift— Value under $10." Almost any shop will ship little gifts for you in this way if you ask them to; postage extra, of course.

THE ACTUAL CUSTOMS EXAMINATION ¶ Before the customs inspector comes to where you and your luggage are, have the bags open and waiting. It is a good idea to keep your purchases together in one place for easy examination.

Don't *ever*, under any circumstances, offer a tip to the customs inspector. That would be a very serious offense.

There are two attitudes, both equally wrong, that definitely will slow up the customs examination for you. The first wrong approach is to give the impression that the entire proceeding is an undue invasion of your privacy. The second incorrect attitude is to act as if a fortune in drugs is hidden in your luggage. The best, and easiest, way to clear customs is to be responsive to the inspector's questions, look him right in the eye and answer him with frankness. Under normal circumstances, the entire proceeding should not take more than five or ten minutes.

Getting Around in Europe

As at home, the American tourist in Europe has a choice of traveling by bus, train, air or car. Let's take a look at each and see its advantages and drawbacks—if any.

Bus ¶ Europe has lots of buses, but they are usually not like those on the United States roads. They are primarily local operations—moving people from one town to another in areas where no railroad line exists or where train service is infrequent. In other words, don't expect to find a Greyhound or Trailways depot in every town you come upon. Greyhound, as a matter of fact, has bought an interest in a bus company in Holland, called VAVO-Greyhound. The name's the same, but the multischedule service available in the United States is not. There is also—as many of you who have already been abroad know—a Europabus system, which crisscrosses Europe, covering just about all the high spots. But service is limited, there is practically no choice of schedules (you either go *that* day, at *that* time, or wait for the next time around) and you cannot interrupt and resume your journey with the freedom possible at home.

It is unlikely, for that matter, that buses will become a means of rapid transportation in Europe to the dramatic extent they are in the United States. The principal reason, it seems to us, is that European railroads are generally owned and operated by national governments. The government people have enough budgetary problems as it is and are not in any mood to encourage a competing transport system that will put railroads in the red by taking customers from them. Nevertheless, there are some very nice trips you can make by bus. The day-long bus ride from Lisbon to Seville is almost twice as fast as the train service between the two points and is many times more interesting. The Riviera—both French and Italian—unwinds splendidly as you view it from one of the interurban buses operating on very frequent schedules (several times an hour). Trains connect Rome with Florence in a few hours, but it is much more enjoyable to go by bus and spend a full day sightseeing along the way. The same applies to the Paris-Riviera run. It is an overnight trip by train and two days by bus, but they are two magnificent days. Unlike in the United States, bus travel is not automatically cheaper than train travel. It *can* be dramatically cheaper, but not always is. Accommodations are not necessarily very comfortable or roomy.

TRAINS ¶ The railroad service in Europe is remarkably good. Switzerland, Germany, Italy, France and just about every country have excellent trains. Schedules are frequent, service is magnificent and the trains really move along. Most capitals are no more than an overnight journey away, and the extra-fast Trans-Europe Express trains (TEE) connect major cities with swift, pleasing smoothness. (You pay an extra fare—a supplement—on the TEE trains, but the service is well worth it.)

Europe, since World War II, has dropped Third Class on its railroads, except that this category of service still exists on some local trains in Spain.

All international and express trains traveling at night have sleeping cars (*wagons-lits* or, in Germany where sleeping cars are operated by a different company, *Schlafwagen*). There are also *wagons-lits* nowadays for Second Class ticket holders. Until recently you had to have a First Class ticket to ride—that is, *sleep*—in a *wagon-lit*, but the railroads have been making things easier and simpler for the traveler all the time. Don't, by the way, confuse a *wagon-lit* with a *couchettes* car (*Liegewagen* in the German-speaking areas). The *wagon-lit* is as much like a bed in a bedroom as is possible, and only one, two or—in the case of the Second Class ticket holders—three persons share one compartment, which is fairly expensive. The *couchette* has six bunks—three on each side of the compartment aisle. Users are given a blanket, a pillow and—well, that's about it. *Couchettes* are better than sitting up in a crowded train all night or standing in the aisle! At least you can stretch out. But they do not compare with *wagons-lits*. Some people like *couchettes* because they are cheap. It depends on the journey, of course, but the price is $3 on the average. One quaint factor about *couchette* travel is that men and women occupy the same compartment. Complete strangers, that is!

The railroads, in their imaginative and energetic efforts to improve service, have added a facility that will interest the car user. They have introduced "sleeping cars for automobiles" (*auto-couchettes*) on many major routes, especially on lines leading from Paris, and even more from Germany (*Autoreisezüge*, "trains for automobiles"), to southern Europe and Mediterranean points. The *auto-couchette* makes it possible for the car user to get a good night's sleep on the train and still cover hundreds of miles overnight. His car is placed aboard the same train he is traveling on and is quickly returned to him on arrival the next morning at his destination.

If you think you'll be doing lots of train traveling on your European journey, then before you go—let us repeat, *before you go*—buy a Eurailpass through your travel agent. Once you arrive in Europe, it will be too late to get one. The Eurailpass can be sold only in the United States. What good is it? Well, it is a tremendous money saver on rail fares. For a fixed sum of money you can travel by train throughout Europe, in First Class, as often as you like and as far as you like. But, remember, the real benefits will pile up *only* if you plan to do a lot of traveling. If you are going to spend a week or two in one place and then the rest of your vacation in some other city not too far away, then the Eurailpass will probably not be a saving for you.

AIR ¶ Airlines are not used for travel in Europe to anywhere near the spectacular degree to which we use them at home—and which we take for granted. In some cases, a TEE train connects two European cities faster than a plane can, when you count the time going to and from airports. But for the long flights, the European air service is wonderful. Traveling from Paris to the French Riviera, for instance, takes less than an hour. Scandinavia—a journey that seems to take forever by train and ferry— is a couple of hours away. In general, if you are in a hurry and want to cover widely scattered points in Europe, take to the air.

CAR ¶ There cannot be the slightest question or the vaguest hint of a doubt that driving a car is the best way for two people (or more) to tour Europe. Buses and trains are all right for the individual traveler who would feel lost by himself and for the more timorous souls who cannot cope with language problems. But for the vast majority of self-reliant Americans, a motor trip through Europe is far and away the most satisfactory way to travel. Incidentally, motoring is often less expensive than public transportation.

Europe by Car

WHOSE CAR ¶ This calls for some analysis on your part. Should you take your own—as, perhaps, you'd like to do —buy one over there and ship it home, lease one in Europe or sell it back to the manufacturer by prearrangement or just rent one?

If you're traveling by ship, your automobile can go along with you as excess baggage (if you arrange everything beforehand). But the baggage charges run high. The round-trip charge for a typical 4,000-pound car is about $475. If you go by plane (or a ship different from the one the car is on), freight charges will be even higher. A medium-size car, for instance, costs something like $800 to ship purely as freight, round trip. And that is as deck cargo—unboxed. If you want it crated (or placed inside a container) you have to figure on spending $200 more each way. Once you get in Europe with your car, you quickly realize that the roads are not like turnpikes. Europe's roads, let's face it, were not built for American cars. Nor are gasoline prices at the high-octane and low-cost levels we know here at home. Gasoline prices on the continent can be as low as 40 cents a gallon but go on from there up to 80 cents or so (although for the large gallon). Filling an American gas tank with such high-priced fuel and trying to navigate mountain passes with low-octane gasoline that your car is not accustomed to will have your automobile and you yourself pinging.

What about *buying* a car? This is now quite a popular approach. You can order the car before you leave home and have it waiting for you in Europe. By considering what you save by owning your own car rather than renting one, your transportation outlay can be quite small. A six-week driving trip in Europe, for instance, can cost as little as $100 after you subtract the savings in car rental fees from the cost of shipping your automobile home. If you order the car before you leave the United States, your $100 customs exemption cannot be applied to it. You can only use the customs exemption on the car if you actually order and buy it abroad. The customs inspectors will put a "used car" appraisal on the vehicle that will probably be one-fourth less than what you paid for it. The customs duty on an automobile (right now) is only 3 percent.

Pointer: Foreign cars being imported into the United States must meet new (and rigid) emission standards in accordance with the Clean Air Act. All 1971 and subsequently produced vehicles must carry a compliance sticker.

There are several other possibilities. If you want to buy a car but do not have any interest in bringing it back home, you can *lease* an automobile or arrange for its repurchase. In either case, you get a brand new automobile.

The lease arrangement is made for a definite period— say, as little as a month and up to six months. You figure out how long you plan to use the car in Europe and pay a fixed depreciation fee for this period. The payment is made in advance before you leave the United States. A leased car can cost as little as $320 for somewhat less than a month. You drive it as if it were your own automobile (it is yours, in effect), putting on it as many miles as you like without a worry about mileage charges.

Buying the car and arranging at the time of purchasing it for its *guaranteed* repurchase are variations on the lease arrangement. Here again, you must decide in advance how long you will be using the car. The manufacturer agrees to buy back the car from you at the price you paid for it—less the fixed depreciation charge for the period the car is to be in use. This works like the lease arrangement in the sense that you pay the depreciation charge in advance in the United States. But since you are also purchasing the car, you have to do some paperwork, certainly more than if it was only a lease arrangement. You sign a promissory note for the remainder of the car's purchase price. When the trip is over and you return the car to the manufacturer, he cancels the promissory note. This guaranteed car-repurchase plan can give you your own automobile in Europe for as little as $260 a month.

Renting a car abroad is undoubtedly the simplest way of obtaining auto transportation in Europe and has the merit of involving practically no paperwork. It is ideal for those who wish to begin their holiday with a minimum delay. If your trip is scheduled for the peak season (the summer), it would be advisable to order your car as far ahead as possible. At your request, it will usually be possible to have the car waiting for you at a pier or airport. This delivery service is often made without any additional charge to you.

A rental car costs various prices in different countries. In Denmark, for instance, a Volkswagen might rent for $4.50 a day and the mileage charge might be 5 cents for each kilometer; next door in Western Germany the same car might cost $5 a day and 4½ cents for each kilometer. For short periods, such as a month or less, it will be easier and cheaper all the way around to rent a car. Don't forget, too, when doing comparative price shopping, to find out whether the leasing and repurchase prices quoted include complete insurance and miscellaneous fees for "papers."

Pointer: You can usually arrange to rent a car in one city and leave it in another city, even in another country. Often, there is no extra charge for this service. If there is a charge, it is fairly nominal.

MOTORING MISCELLANY ¶ That famous piece of documentation fondly called the *Carnet de Passage en Douanes*, which you probably had to tote along on your last driving trip through Europe, is no longer needed. Nowadays, the *carnet*—which in effect is a passport for the automobile—is only necessary if you venture off into the Middle East. The only documents needed are proof of ownership (the registration), the *Carte Verte* ("Green Card" for insurance which affirms that you are covered for third-party liability) and a valid driver's license. Your home state driver's license will be good in most countries. To be on the safe side and to avoid unnecessary complications in out-of-the-way places, it is best to have an International Driving Permit, which costs only $3 and requires no test. Your local automobile club at home can arrange for it before you leave, or when you are in New York City you can obtain it from the American Automobile Association, 750 Third Avenue. Or, you can get it at one of the AAA offices in Europe. Their addresses are: 15 Pall Mall, London; 9 Rue de la Paix, Paris; and 84 Via Veneto, Rome.

A FEW USEFUL MOTORING TERMS

ENGLISH	FRENCH	ITALIAN	GERMAN
axle	essieu	asse	Achse
battery	batterie	batteria	Batterie
bearing	coussinet	cuscinetto a sfere	Lager
bolt	boulon	bullone	Bolzen
brake	frein	freno	Bremse
bulb	ampoule	lampadina	Birne
bumper	pare-choc	paraurti	Stosstange
carburetor	carburateur	carburatore	Vergaser
clutch	embrayage	innesto	Kupplung
cylinder	cylindre	cilindro	Zylinder
distributor	distributeur	distributore	Verteiler
engine	moteur	motore	Motor
fan belt	courroie de ventilateur	cinghia del ventilatore	Ventilatorriemen
gasoline	essence	benzina	Benzin
gears	engrenage	ingranaggio	Getriebe
hood	capot	cofano	Motorhaube
horn	klaxon	tromba	Signalhorn
hub	moyeu	mozzo	Nabe
ignition	allumage	accensione	Zündung
muffler	silencieux	silenziatore	Auspufftopf
oil	huile	olio	Ol
piston ring	segment de piston	fascia elastica	Kolbenring
pump	pompe	pompa	Pumpe
puncture	crevaison	bucatura	Reifendefekt
radiator	radiateur	radiatore	Kühler
spark plug	bougie	candela	Zündkerze
spring	ressort	molla	Feder
switch	contact	contatto	Kontakt
tank	réservoir d'essence	serbatoio	Tank
tire	pneu	copertone	Reifen
transmission	transmission	transmissione	Getriebe
valve	soupape	valvola	Ventil
wheel	roue	ruota	Rad
windshield	pare-brise	parabrezza	Windschutzscheibe

(Courtesy European Travel Commission)

**Pointer: Sweden in 1967 switched from its old practice
of driving on the left-hand side of the road. So,
everywhere except in Great Britain and Ireland, keep
to the right.**

Parking conditions in European capitals are becoming
as chaotic as those in the United States. A number of
cities have adopted the blue zone no-parking or limited-
parking system of Paris. Special disks have to be exhibited
in the windshield when you park in a blue zone. The
disks can be regulated to show the hour at which you
parked your car and the maximum parking time you are
allowed. Parking meters have now found their way onto
the streets and boulevards of France and some other
countries. Be sure to have small coins of the country
with you if you intend to use a meter. Two basic parking
rules should be remembered. One is that parking restrictions on some European streets are not clearly
indicated at all times (Rome is a good example of
this). The other parking rule to keep in mind is that
European police are very tolerant of tourists' cars. (Rome
is a good example of this, too. The *vigili* there stick a
little note in the windshield of an overparked tourist car.)

France has ended the coupon system, which made it
possible for tourists to get lower-priced gasoline. So
gasoline is on the high side there. It is also on the high
side in Italy, but the Italians, helpfully, still issue gasoline
coupons at the border.

About Being a Good American

During our country's first years, the troubles and problems of European nations seemed very far away indeed.
An early edition of the *Encyclopedia Britannica* refers to
the United States standing army as a token force needed
only for symbolic purposes.

That delightful state of affairs no longer exists.

World War I brought a change in our thinking. World
War II involved a complete revolution. Now, more than a
quarter of a century after the end of World War II,
there is not an American who does not realize that we are
not alone in the world. The many days of travel once
needed for spanning the distance between our isolated
shores and foreign lands have dwindled remarkably. A

jet plane crosses the oceans in hours; an armed missile could do it in minutes. We can no longer live alone in the world. Now we have to recognize that our next-door neighbors are the French, the Italians, the Brazilians and, equally, the Zulus, who once seemed so far away. No man is an island, and no one can retire to a mental island and let the world go by.

In the struggle to win the minds of men, the United States needs friends all over the world. We send out a pitifully small handful of professional ambassadors in the person of diplomats and members of economic and social missions. But our truest ambassadors to the world at large are American tourists. You, by force of circumstances, are an American ambassador of good will—or, if not, then of bad will.

Repeater travelers among you have undoubtedly noticed this more and more with each passing season. Wherever Americans travel in Europe, the local people watch their actions closely and discuss them in detail. American customs, ideas and concepts are followed avidly and, more often than not, adopted. We are watched especially by the younger people, who, even if they don't say anything or if they pretend not to be looking, have us under close surveillance. Drugstores, public relations, management techniques, anything-on-the-rocks, Hollywood westerns (with Justice always triumphant) on Saturday night TV programs, pop music, press conferences—the American influence is everywhere noticeable. There is no question but that the United States is the most powerful nation on earth. We, Americans, also believe we are the greatest. It is understandable, therefore, that Europeans are interested in knowing everything possible about us—how we got that way and what makes us the kind of nation we are.

One day, seated in a small restaurant in Venice, we listened to an American sounding off to his long-suffering wife about a subject that was hardly of earth-shattering import—except to him at that moment. The object of his ranting was a cup of coffee. He talked so loudly that the poor waiter could not fail to hear him. To hear him tell it, Italians were this and Italians were that (everything derogatory), the cup was too small and the coffee was so bad that it must have been made in a dirty coffee pot. This American went on in that vein endlessly and boringly. Meanwhile, the waiter continued his work silently, although you could see by his face that he did not like this kind of talk one bit. The fact remains that the coffee was superb and delicious—if you like strong, black coffee. (It's the Italian way of doing things and *they* like strong, black coffee.) If the waiter said anything, there was a very good chance he might be fired. So he listened in silence. He was, without doubt, thinking of his wife and three children. (We couldn't know for sure, but all Italian waiters have a wife and three children.) The United States certainly did not make an Italian friend that day. Later, we saw the complaining American leave the restaurant. On his way out he came face to face with the establishment's huge coffee-making machine. Standing motionless in his tracks, he watched the *espresso* machine being carefully taken apart and washed. If he had stayed longer, he would have found out that it is cleaned after each usage. With a bemused expression on his face, the American walked out of the restaurant slowly. But he didn't go back and apologize to the waiter.

As a matter of fact, Americans are very well treated in Europe. An American in France, for instance, even if he does not know a word of French, will always be catered to and given courteous attention. But American demands must be within the bounds of reason. It would be definitely unreasonable to demand buckwheat cakes for breakfast in a village in France's Midi. It would be just as unreasonable for a French visitor to the United States to insist on being served brioches or croissants for his *petit déjeuner* at a lunch counter crowded with office workers on the way to work, say, in Altoona, Pennsylvania. It's just not part of the early-morning lunch counter scene in Altoona, just as buckwheat cakes are not usually served for breakfast in villages in southern France.

If an American, not knowing a word of Finnish, walks into a restaurant in Helsinki, the waiter will make every possible effort to understand him and to bring him what he wants. Imagine, for contrast's sake, the reception awaiting a Finn who, without a word of English in his vocabulary, drops into a busy New York restaurant. See what we mean?

Because it is so vitally important today that the United States and its citizens are understood by the peoples of the world, we must all make an effort to be real ambassadors of good will. It is hard to believe that many Europeans have never actually met an American face to face, but you might be the first one! That is quite a responsibility. The Europeans are sophisticated enough to know that not all of us are millionaires, nor are we all Chicago gangsters, despite what they have heard. They know that there are rich and poor Americans, and many in between. They know, too, that there are some who are not so good. The point is, though, that they think there is something special about Americans. They'll be sizing you up closely to see for themselves and draw their own conclusions.

This wasn't meant to be a sermon. We merely wanted to point out an important problem of understanding that now exists. When you go to Europe, have a wonderful time. Be a good American.

A Different World

Philosophically, we can agree that people everywhere are pretty much the same. There is no argument about that. But just because people are the same does not mean that they do everything in an identical way or have similar customs and habits. *Pas du tout!* The way of life in Europe—despite the borrowing of American ideas—is noticeably different from how we live and do things in the United States. This difference is a big reason why a visit in Europe is so exciting and absorbing. It can be an adventure to see new things from breakfast to nightcap. All we have to do is keep our eyes—and our minds— open as we travel about. Europeans, when they do something in a way different from ours, have a reason. Perhaps it is a poor one. It could be a brilliant one. Studying the different habits and customs we come across can be lots of fun. It also gives travelers something to talk about—and think about—when they get back home.

Even within any one European country you will find that customs change abruptly from one section to another. These changes cannot be dismissed as "regional differences," either. There is much history, tradition and trial-and-error experience behind them.

Let's look at some of the general differences that crop up in every tourist's path on the continent.

ALL ABOUT NUMBERS ¶ Europeans write numerals in a manner different from ours. The best example is the number 7. They put a short line across it at the center, as 7̶. In writing out a date, Europeans reverse the order of the month and day from the way we're used to seeing it. For December 25, 1972, we would write 12/25/72. Not the Europeans. They make it 25/12/72. You can usually figure this out without too much trouble. The difficulty comes, however, when the day of the month is the twelfth or earlier. If a European or an American writes 9/8/72 for the other person, neither will know what day it is unless they are operating on the same ground rules.

In street address the number and the name of the street are often written in reverse order, as in Via Roma 6, rather than 6 Via Roma.

THE EUROPEAN CLOCK ¶ The twenty-four-hour clock is standard all through Europe. Hours from 1 P.M. to midnight are generally designated as 13:00 (for 1 P.M.), 14:00 (2 P.M.) and so on *until* 24:00 (midnight). European timetables are set out in the twenty-four-hour system. It is therefore quite important to familiarize yourself with the way it works as quickly as possible.

HOTELS ¶ Not all European hotels have the trimmings top American ones do. We mean the TV sets, recorded music, cracked ice and other amenities. They do, however, carry the fine art of personal service to its highest peak. If you want a maid, valet or waiter, you don't ordinarily use the telephone. A panel of buzzers is on the wall or alongside the bed. Symbols identify which buzzer to push. It still is the custom in European hotels, too, to leave your shoes outside the door at night so that they can be shined by the time you need them in the morning.

The *concierge* is, if possible, a bigger institution than ever on the European hotel scene. Concierges have their own association and hold conventions now just like other tycoons. Make no mistake about it. The concierge is a powerful, resourceful personage. He'll handle the mailing of letters, the getting of theater tickets and train or plane reservations and questions about where you can park your car overnight. But he specializes in the difficult.

That's where he shines, and that's how he earns handsome tips. A couturier showing, a ticket for an opera performance that is sold out, a lower berth on the Paris-Nice express in mid-August? Try him out. If he is so good, you might ask, why is he standing behind a desk in the lobby, wearing a dark uniform with a pair of crossed keys on the lapel? If he is so smart, why doesn't he own the hotel? He's behind the desk because being a concierge in a top hotel is a wonderful way to make a fortune. Instead of owning the hotel, he's probably investing his money in new apartment houses on the French Riviera.

LES HOMMES ET LES FEMMES ¶ Subtitle: What's all this about men's and ladies' rooms in France? Well, what you've heard is true—and not only in France but most everywhere in Europe. Europeans have an entirely different concept about wash room privacy, if you know what we mean. Most of the time the "rest room" has one common anteroom, with a basin or two for handwashing. Presiding over this activity, usually, is a woman of mature years. This is a comfort to women handwashers and very disconcerting to men handwashers. Sometimes there will be only one toilet. When there are two or more, these will be separated from each other by partitions. When the partitions reach from floor to ceiling, there isn't too much of a problem. But when the separating partition starts about two feet off the ground and rises only a brief distance, the situation is calculated to startle most circumspect Americans. To say the least, it is extremely disconcerting to see an adjacent pair of man's (or woman's) feet. But it is even more staggering to view the top of a man's (or woman's) head, unexpectedly, in the next-door cubicle. The Europeans say we are prissy about rest rooms. True or false as that may be, it seems that most tourists become reconciled to the European custom after a few days.

With the increasing affluence of the continent in the past few years, Europeans have done wonders with their rest rooms. Some are now quite good. You will find, however, that as you proceed southward the rest rooms become progressively less attractive. To put it another way, they become increasingly primitive. In Scandinavia and all through the Low Countries, Germany, Switzerland and Austria, the rest rooms generally are fine. They are good in most of Paris as well as northern Italy, also. But as you continue southward you will find them less and less satisfactory. This north-south progressive deterioration in rest room facilities must have some significance but, as yet, we have not been able to determine the rationale of the whole thing.

WOMEN ON THEIR OWN IN EUROPE ¶ During the day, there can be no question about the propriety of women wandering about a European city with the same degree of freedom as they might feel in Kansas City, Kansas. Nighttime is something else. European women do not go window shopping or take walks by themselves, in general, late in the evening. A great place to observe this "prohibition" is Rome. At 8:15 P.M. any evening the streets will be thronged with men, women and children talking, walking and making themselves seen. Fifteen minutes later, as if by an electronic signal, the streets of Rome except the Via Veneto and a few other tourist thoroughfares are absolutely deserted. This no-women-on-the-streets-alone-after-dark tradition varies somewhat from city to city and country to country. Venice in the summer, Viareggio at carnival time and such places as the promenade at Ostend on a balmy, happy evening are among the many exceptions to the general tradition. Any woman, as a matter of fact, can size up the situation for herself in the city being visited. It really is not much different than here in the United States. The difficulty really arises only when a tourist thinks it is different or wishes to act differently than she would at home.

Except for a few chi-chi restaurants most European *brasseries, trattorie* and other eating places do not object to parties composed exclusively of women. They would *prefer*, however, that at least one man is included in a party. Incidentally, several proprietors of European establishments have told us that they would be even more pleased with parties of women if they would keep their voices low and maintain the conversation at a moderate level. With this, we must heartily agree. It appears that groups of women dining alone seem duty-bound to make considerable noise, as if driven by a psychological impulse to show the world that they're having a good time despite the lack of escorts.

Now we come to a big However. Women, alone or in groups, are definitely unwelcome in European night clubs without at least one male escort. Unescorted women should embarrass neither themselves nor the night clubs (nor foster the impression among Europeans that all American women are excessively aggressive) by seeking admission without at least *one* man. Peculiarly enough, one male escort is regarded as sufficient for numbers up to a sewing circle of nine. Why a European night club proprietor should assume that one mere male could possibly cope with nine women is far too much for our comprehension. The fact remains that unescorted women, even though of unquestioned virtue and financial resources, are *absolutely* unwelcome in European nighttime places. The same general rule holds true for most bars after 9 P.M. The occasional one that admits unescorted women generally assumes that they are in search of male companionship, which may or may not be true.

Before You Go

Vaccination certificates are no longer required when you reenter the United States unless you've come from a country where there's been a smallpox scare. So, if you have one take it with you, otherwise, forget it.

Don't forget to take some money with you. We mean *foreign* money. A few dollars worth of the currency (in small change) of the first country you reach will be helpful for tips, taxis and unexpected expenditures. All airports, air terminals and railroad stations have money-exchange facilities. But not all of these places operate on a twenty-four-hour basis—like Saturday afternoon or Sunday evening. It is an awful nuisance to try to figure out with a grumpy taxi driver, in a sidewalk conversation, what the fare from the air terminal to the hotel comes to in the one-dollar bills you're clutching. Such spur-of-the-moment money transactions as well as the use of dollar bills for tips can be expensive, too. You'll invariably spend more than you would if you were using the currency of the country.

Information Points

Seldom in life do we receive something for nothing. A rare opportunity is offered by the amiable and obliging official tourist bureaus set up in the United States by the

European governments. These offices exist for the sole purpose of disseminating free information, folders, maps and booklets about their respective countries. By all means, don't fail to obtain all the available tourist information material from the office (here in the United States) of the countries you're planning to visit. Write to these government offices while your trip is still in the planning stage and specify subjects you are particularly interested in (beach resorts, gastronomy, archaeology, Flemish paintings and so on). They will send you, without any cost, an assortment of maps and reading material that will assist you in planning your trip and enjoying to the fullest your European vacation.

All European cities (even small towns) operate official tourist offices, where you can get very specific details about everything of interest to the tourist locally. This information includes such things as the time and price of sightseeing trips, hours of museums, restaurants—in a word, everything. The offices also have available a free map of the city or town and local bus or trolley routes and schedules. Try to find out in advance the address of the official tourist office in the next place on your itinerary. You can usually get this address from the official tourist office where you are at the time. All the European nations also maintain official tourist offices in Paris, and many of them have such bureaus in other continental capitals and large cities as well. When you are writing to the official tourist offices in the United States, ask them for the addresses of the local offices at points you will be visiting in their country.

Here, as a starter, are some helpful addresses:

AUSTRIA
Austrian National Tourist Office
545 Fifth Avenue, New York, N.Y. 10017
BELGIUM
Official Belgian Tourist Bureau
589 Fifth Ave., New York, N.Y. 10036
FINLAND
Finnish National Travel Office
505 Fifth Ave., New York. N.Y. 10017
FRANCE
French Government Tourist Office
610 Fifth Ave., New York, N.Y. 10020
GERMANY
German National Tourist Office
500 Fifth Ave., New York, N.Y. 10036

GREAT BRITAIN
British Travel Association
680 Fifth Ave., New York, N.Y. 10017

GREECE
Greek National Tourist Office
601 Fifth Ave., New York, N.Y. 10017

IRELAND
Irish Tourist Board
590 Fifth Ave., New York, N.Y. 10036

ITALY
Italian State Tourist Office
626 Fifth Ave., New York, N.Y. 10022

NETHERLANDS
Netherlands National Tourist Office
605 Fifth Ave., New York, N.Y. 10022

PORTUGAL
Casa de Portugal
570 Fifth Ave., New York, N.Y. 10036

SCANDINAVIA (Denmark, Finland, Norway, Sweden)
Scandinavia House
505 Fifth Ave., New York, N.Y. 10017

SPAIN
Spanish National Tourist Office
589 Fifth Ave., New York, N.Y. 10036

SWITZERLAND
Swiss Center
608 Fifth Ave., New York, N.Y. 10020

YUGOSLAVIA
Yugoslav State Tourist Office
509 Madison Ave., New York, N.Y. 10022

Pointer: France, Western Germany, Ireland, Italy, Holland, Spain and Switzerland also have national tourist offices in San Francisco; Austria, Great Britain, Greece and the Scandinavian countries are represented in Los Angeles.

AUSTRIA

National Characteristics

Austrians first danced to Johann Strauss' "Blue Danube" over a century ago, when his famous waltz was introduced during the height of the society ball season in Vienna. The Danube is not exactly blue—frankly- - and maybe it would not win a beauty contest on its own. But this is certain: The lands stretching back from the shores of the Danube as it wriggles through Austria—and the people living within the borders of the country—will make you wish you had some of Johann Strauss' skill and could compose a song of your own as a joy-filled salute to a truly wonderful part of this world.

This is a country of song and music. Perhaps the people will not be dancing in the street, as you might expect. But the sound of music is never far away. It might come from the stage of the Vienna Opera or from a village square on a Sunday afternoon as a brass band plays. Or, perhaps you will hear the Vienna Boys Choir singing in the Hofburg Chapel, just as it did when Emperor Franz Josef kneeled in a pew. Or, if it is a spring day and you are in Vienna, you might hear an old woman singing as she walks down the street, to announce that she has lavender blossoms for sale. You will see and hear much music. Perhaps, too, as you travel around the country, meeting the people, enjoying the sights and the food and getting to know the Austrian mentality, you might even begin to feel the *presence* of music regardless of whether it is audible.

Austria is a land, too, of burly alpine peaks and breath-takingly landscaped valleys, of women elegantly dressed both in Paris *haute couture* clothes and in native dirndls and of the Old World as we like to think it was or of the New World with many subtle differences.

There are cosy and very smart bars with red damask on the walls and Biedermeier candlesticks on the grand piano. There are also wine cellars where the massive wooden tables are not even covered by a piece of paper.

It is not a place of contrasts. It is just *Austrian*.

At adjoining tables in Grinzing might be a high official from the federal chancellery and a Vienna streetcar conductor, drinking new wine and encouraging the zither player to play something old. When the musician responds with an old-time favorite, such as "My Mother was a Viennese," the groups at both tables will sing it with the same Vienna accent—an accent that is as nostalgia-filled as a family album. The merrymakers at the government official's table would not have the slightest feeling of condescension at being in the same place as the trolley conductor's family and friends. The streetcar man and his party, on the other hand, would not give a second thought to who the people at the next table are. They are all Viennese together, and as such they like to enjoy themselves. No one is trying to prove anything about democracy, one way or the other. All they seek is the reassurance that the old songs are still the best songs.

This is Austria. Austria *is* different.

The husky man in the well-worn lederhosen getting out of a car in Innsbruck might be the publisher of a Vienna daily newspaper or he might be the baker from a tiny Tyrolean village somewhere along the Inn valley. That beautiful woman you see in a dirndl walking across the bridge at Salzburg on a July afternoon might well be a shopkeeper's wife, proudly wearing the regional costume. Or, she could be a Viennese opera star just returned from a Metropolitan Opera engagement and recording sessions in New York.

Austrians are warm-hearted, friendly, extra polite. We don't have quite the word for it in English. The French say *sympathique*; in Italian, it is *simpatico*. It will not be long after your arrival in Austria that you learn to describe an Austrian as *sympatisch*.

Under the streets of Vienna are bits and pieces left over from the Roman settlement of twenty centuries ago. Throughout the country are signs of many of the peoples who at one time or another have crossed and crisscrossed Austria. Some of these signs are scars that have healed as much as they ever will. Others are happy memories. Every major power of the past—*and* of the present—has come through Austria, or has tried to. The Turks made their last attempt in 1683 and were stopped at the walls of Vienna. From the scattered supplies of the vanquished Turks were salvaged coffee beans, unknown at the time in this part of the Western world. The Viennese quickly refined the Arabic method of coffee brewing and developed it as a pleasant pillar of Vienna's social life.

Europe literally danced in Vienna a century and a half ago when crowned heads and rulers gathered in the city to map out the continent's fate—and to celebrate their fateful decision. A century later, in the defeat of World War I, the Austro-Hungarian empire collapsed. An empire that reached out from Vienna in all directions for hundreds of miles—and back into history for centuries—shrank into a small, impoverished, helpless nation. Hitler, with his *Anschluss* of 1938, "annexed" the little country to Germany. The four Allied Powers—the United States, Great Britain, France and Russia—occupied Austria for ten years after World War II. The State Treaty of 1955 ended the occupation, and Austrians thought happy times were here again. Now, a decade and a half after, they are not quite as sure as they were. Things have improved spectacularly, but the economic future would be a lot more certain if Austria could join the Common Market. Russia, describing the Common Market as a "Western instrument," waves the State Treaty, which fixed a neutral status for Austria. But Austrians are not discouraged. They are hoping for the best. They always do.

When to Go

Spring reaches Vienna very early in April, and visitors begin to flock to the city not long afterward. May and June are particularly crowded (making hotel reservations *very* necessary), and even September (the time of the Vienna fall fair) and early October are busy. Summer in Vienna is less crowded, because activity swings to the provinces. In the summer, therefore, hotel space in Salzburg, Innsbruck and resort areas—particularly, the Salzammergut—is something that should definitely be arranged for in advance. Vienna can get dark and rainy in the fall, but a busy round of activities—opera, concerts, traditional cafés—screens out the weather. Skiing is possible from December until late spring and even later if one wishes to move higher up on the alpine slopes.

WEATHER STRIP: VIENNA

Temp.	JAN.	FEB.	MAR.	APR.	MAY	JUNE	JULY	AUG.	SEPT.	OCT.	NOV.	DEC.
Low	28°	29°	35°	41°	50°	55°	58°	57°	51°	43°	35°	31°
High	36°	38°	48°	56°	65°	70°	73°	72°	65°	55°	42°	38°
Average	32°	34°	42°	49°	58°	63°	66°	65°	58°	49°	39°	35°
Days of rain	7	5	7	8	9	10	10	8	7	8	7	7

TIME EVALUATION ¶ On a month's trip to Europe, allow a week or slightly more for Austria, unless you're planning to tour the country. In that case, two weeks would be required. Out of a seven- to ten-day visit, allow three days for Vienna and the balance for Salzburg and Innsbruck, at the very least. If you have only three or four days for Austria, spend all of them in Vienna and the suburbs, including possibly a steamer ride on the Danube. On a brief stopover, there wouldn't be time to see the countryside so just have a marvelous time in Vienna.

PASSPORT AND VISA ¶ Passport, but no visa, required.

CUSTOMS AND IMMIGRATION ¶ There is no limit on how much foreign or Austrian money the foreign visitor is allowed to bring with him on entering the country. On leaving, you can take with you as much foreign currency as you like (or *have*), but there is a limit on the amount of Austrian money that may be exported. It is 15,000 schillings, just in case you're interested; nobody will really ask you. As far as the articles you're carrying with you, there will be no problem under normal circumstances. The Austrian customs are among the world's friendliest and easiest to pass—as a rule. You can have with you two cameras (with ten rolls of film for each) and one of such things as record player, transistor radio, portable typewriter, binoculars (pair, that is) and even portable TV. On tobacco, you are limited to 400 cigarettes, *or* 100 cigars, *or* 500 grams (a little over a pound) of tobacco—or some combination of these three smoking classics. What about liquors? Two liters (about two quarts) of wine and a quart of liquor (whisky, gin, brandy, etc.) are permitted duty-free entry. All frontier stations, by the way, are open around the clock daily.

HEALTH ¶ Public health standards in Austria are very high. Naturally, however, stay away from unpasteurized milk. Water in Vienna is excellent—right from mountain springs. In the rest of Austria, the tap water is also tops. If you are uneasy, anyway, there is a big choice of bottled waters. Preblauer is a popular one. In some Alpine areas the water traditionally has been deficient in iodine. But this is of no possible significance unless you're planning to stay there and drink water for twenty years or so. Perhaps not even then.

TIME ¶ Six hours later than Eastern Standard Time. When it's 6 P.M. in Vienna, it's noon in New York. When Daylight Saving Time is in effect, the time difference is only 5 hours.

CURRENCY ¶ The Austrian *schilling* (abbreviated in Austria as S.) is somewhat similar in value to our 5-cent piece. The actual rate fluctuates daily, according to supply and demand, and also changes of course when there is an official currency revaluation. The schilling is composed of 100 *groschen* (abbreviated Gr.). Small-denomination groschen coins are aluminumlike; half-schilling and schilling pieces are brass; and large coins (5 S. and 10 S.) are silver.

PRICE LEVEL ¶ *Leider, leider*—prices are not what they used to be. They keep inching up. Transportation tariffs —railroads and Vienna trams—went up a couple of years ago after staying at pleasantly low levels for a long time. Hotel rates are relatively high, although not so high as a number of other European countries. A single room in Vienna—with taxes, service charges and heating costs included—can be about $25 in a luxury hotel, and a double room is $30 or more. But there are comfortable hotels in town and nonresort areas where a room will be only a few dollars. Food prices are still low. You can have a good meal in a *Gasthaus* anywhere for $2 to $3. For a few more dollars, you can dine in a top eating place. Coffee is expensive, but very good. Austrian wines are relatively inexpensive.

TIPPING ¶ Austrians love traditions, and an old one is the custom of giving a few extra coins to the waiter, doorman or whoever has been particularly helpful (and all of them, almost always, are). These few extra coins, called *Trinkgeld* (what we would call the money to "buy yourself a drink"), are in addition to the 10 to 15 percent service charge that will be automatically added to hotel and restaurant bills. As a tip to a hotel porter for carrying your bag, don't give less than 5 schillings, and increase it by a couple of schillings for each additional bag. One wonderful thing about tipping in Austria is that no matter what you give you will always receive warm and friendly thanks. There is never any muttering about the size of a tip, nor are there any disdainful looks.

TRANSPORTATION ¶ A *rail* network of 4,000 miles extends through the country, and all the main lines (more than half of the system) are electrified. Service, generally, is rapid and good. There used to be a train that struggled through the valleys and over the hills and dales between Salzburg and Bad Ischl. You were not allowed to lean out the windows and pick flowers as the train huffed and puffed lazily along. The famous Salzburg-Bad Ischl train has been scratched (although still remembered in song), but some local trains in high places move at low speeds even today. You can see the scenery better! Fares are proportionately lower as the distance traveled increases. Rates are among the lowest in Europe, and there are reductions of 25 percent for round-trip journeys and 20 percent on circular tours of more than 600 kilometers (370 miles). A supplement of 15 S. is charged for travel on express trains which are identified in timetables by EX, D and TS. There is also a surcharge for the Trans-Europe Express (TEE) trains.

Taxis in most parts of the country are relatively high priced—especially in Salzburg. In that festival city the cab drivers operate on the old supply-and-demand economic theory, which is coupled with a new one holding that all visitors are wealthy and like to spend lots of money on cabs. Alas! high cab fares seem to be a part of resort life just about everywhere on the continent. Cab fares in Vienna are lower than in other Austrian cities. Here are some approximate Vienna cab rates (starting from St. Stephen's Square and excluding tips): Sudbahnhof, 25 S.; Westbahnhof, 22 S.; Schwechat airport, 150 S.; Opera, 12 S.; Burg Theater, 12 S.; Volksoper, 20 S.; Grinzing, 35 S.; Kahlenberg, 65 S.; Kobenzl, 60 S.;

the Prater, 30 S. (Remember, in all large cities taxis have officially sealed meters.) Vienna taxi drivers have taxi tours of the city that range from about $4.50 to $15 in accordance with the number of hours involved.

Bus service is handled by the Post Office and private operators on certain routes. Bus service is primarily available from Vienna to towns in Burgenland and Lower Austria. In the summer a private line runs a service to Salzburg. Excursion buses are everywhere. Even in small villages you will find a bus for sightseeing in the area—though it might be nothing more than a seven-passenger Volkswagen bus. But you will see the sights! Bus rates are low—about the same as Second Class rail travel. The advantage of buses is that you get a better look at the scenery (if you're seated by a window). Often, another advantage is that it's better than walking. Some places are served only by buses.

Steamer service on the Danube is churning along like the old days after being pretty much anchored throughout the war years and even much of the postwar era. You can sail from Passau, at the German-Austrian border, right to Vienna, singing, humming and/or dancing the "Blue Danube" all the way. Or, you can stop off at one of a score of points en route. The trip can be made in a westerly, or Vienna-Passau, direction as well. Keep in mind, though, that the Danube travels downhill, from west to east. This means that a trip eastward from Passau does not take as long as one from Vienna toward some place up the river.

Fares on the Danube are not high. Passau to Vienna, for instance, costs a little over $10 on an express boat (the one to travel on). Cabins can be reserved (as far in advance as possible is our advice), and they cost something like the price of a good hotel room. If you have a cabin you can board the ship in Vienna or Passau on the evening before departure. The ships do not carry automobiles but arrangements can be made with Auto Leasing Lermer, Nikolastrasse 4, Passau, Germany, to have your car driven to any destination. For faster travel on the Danube there are hydrofoils which journey from Vienna to Linz and also to Budapest.

Air travel within the country is provided by Austrian Airlines, which has had a very fine operating and service record.

By car Austria's valleys and mountain tops are easily

available. There are autobahns connecting Vienna and Salzburg; Vienna and Wiener Neustadt; and Innsbruck and the Brenner Pass. The Grossglockner high-in-the-Alps road is open only in summer.

COMMUNICATIONS ¶ One of those everyday expenditures that has a habit of going up is postal rates. An *airmail letter* to the United States will be about a quarter for five grams (a thin sheet of paper, an envelope and an unlimited number of kind words). *Cables* to the New York area cost about a half dollar a word, and slightly higher if they are headed beyond the Big City. A *night letter* is half the rate, but you must use twenty-two words. *Telegrams* within Austria are close to a nickel a word, with a minimum length of ten words. A *telephone call* remains a bargain—1 schilling! (Remember when a telephone call in the U.S.A. cost a nickel?) Incidentally, the main and railroad terminal post offices in large cities are open around the clock. Post offices are also points for sending telegrams and cables. Oh, yes—mail boxes are painted yellow.

BASIC WORDS AND PHRASES ¶ See the section on Germany.

ELECTRICITY ¶ If outlets are not marked, the chances are that everything is 220 A.C. But always check to be sure. Otherwise, your electric razor might begin to smell like burning toast.

SPAS ¶ Austria has a number of spas, along with so many other wonderful things. In general, it is always wise to follow medical advice before "taking the cure" at a spa. A mineral spring water that is good for one thing might be not so good—or even bad—for another ailment. Spas always announce the ailments and physical conditions for which their waters are "indicated," as well as for those for which they are "counterindicated." By all means try to visit Bad Gastein, a lovely spa in a superb setting. The sight and sound of the foamy spring waters gurgling down the hill under your hotel window are unforgettably wonderful.

SPORTS ¶ They say you could put on a pair of *skis* at the western border of Austria and, on any day during the winter, ski all the way to Vienna—almost 500 miles. We don't know if anyone has done this recently. We certainly haven't, and have no immediate plans. The point, though, is to emphasize the mountainous nature of the country —this is the eastern half of the Alps, you know—and the popularity of skiing as a winter sport. Skiing is really something for everyone here in Austria. There are very smart winter resorts—St. Anton, Lech and Kitzbühel, for example—where the international set gathers. There are hundreds of other resorts where you are not likely to meet anyone you have seen or heard of before. There are also plenty of informal "weekend slopes," such as those in the Vienna Woods, where the local people gather, when they can, for some free fun in the snow. This is real ski country.

With more than two-thirds of Austria's area covered by mountains and foothills of the eastern Alps, it should be no surprise that *mountain hikes* and *Alpine tours* are quite popular. Many mountain routes are relatively easy going. Others are like trying to climb up the side of the United Nations building in New York. But, whether you are going for "just a short walk" or a real cliff-hanging expedition, there are certain basic rules to follow. Have the proper equipment and clothes with you, and pay particular attention to having clothing that will protect you in case of a sudden cold snap or snowstorm. Also, listen to what the local people say. If they shake their heads and advise you not to do any mountaineering —even if it is only to inspect the area around the upper station of a cable car—please follow their advice.

Austria is bracketed by lakes (Lake Constance, on the west; the Neusiedlersee, in the east) and spotted across the country are 100 or more lakes—all ideal for *sailing* to a greater or lesser degree. The really perfect yachting lakes are in three federal states: Upper Austria, Salzburg and Carinthia. In the northern part of the country are the Attersee, the Traunsee, the Mondsee and the Wolf-gangsee. Three other ideal lakes for sailing are in the southern part of the country: the Wörthersee, the Mill-stätter See and the Ossiachersee. (Say, don't forget that *see* means "lake" and is pronounced "say.") Boats can be hired if the boatowner is satisfied of your ability to handle his craft. Otherwise, you will have to take a local yachts-man aboard. The boat rental ranges between 60 cents and $2 an hour. Information is available at the Austrian Yachting Association, 12 Prinz Eugen Strasse, Vienna IV.

There must be at least a hundred communities throughout the country that make possible *horseback* excursions for visitors. The number keeps growing. The equestrian sports can vary from horseback riding in an indoor riding hall during the winter (or in bad weather) to cross-country rides on a fine summer day. One hour's riding usually costs $2 or so. The Austrian Riding Club, the Hofburg, Vienna I, can be helpful in providing details about possibilities for horseback holidays.

Golfing is nowhere near the popular sport it is here. But you won't have to drive (by car, that is) too far to find a course. They are evenly situated, more or less, across the country. There are a dozen golf courses in all, ranging from Innsbruck on the west to Vienna in the east, and from Linz in the north to Dellach (near Klagenfurt) on the south. Fees, which are quite reasonable, are about the same at every course. At Bad Gastein, for instance, the green fee is $2.40 a day and $12 a week; caddies, 80 cents for 18 holes and 40 cents for 9 holes; and the pro, $2.40 an hour. The Austrian Golf Association, 11 Rüdengasse, Vienna III, will provide details.

CASINOS ¶ Gambling may or may not be a sport. So just to play safe—what a gambler we are!—let's put the subject of games of chance under this category rather than Sports. There are casinos in Vienna and six other localities in the country: Baden, Kitzbühel, Bad Gastein, Velden, Salzburg and Seefeld. Roulette and baccara are played in accordance with international rules. Guest's cards are issued for a day, or a week, or a month. Bring your passport with you (not to mention your billfold!) when you drop into a casino; you will be asked for identification. The casino at Vienna (called Cercle Wien) is open daily, the year round, from 7 P.M. The others have a mixed schedule that ranges from year around to only the summer and winter season, as in Kitzbühel.

FOOD SPECIALTIES AND LIQUOR ¶ Forget about counting calories in this land of delicious things to eat. The average Austrian eats possibly as many as six times a day. There are even those who seem to be eating all the time. The word *Calorie* is in their dictionary, but not on their minds. Their breakfast can be coffee, tea or cocoa, with rolls liberally toned up with butter, jam and/or honey. A word about those rolls is in order. Vienna produces a roll called the *Semmel*, which dates from imperial days, and it is as wonderful as any that was ever baked for an emperor or empress. Sometimes at breakfast there are soft boiled eggs. They are fresh and delicious in Austria! After that breakfast comes a second one—about midmorning—which can consist of a sandwich or two brought from home, a pair of frankfurters or a small bowl of beef or veal stew (goulash). This second breakfast is called *Gabelfrühstück* ("fork breakfast") because it is the kind of breakfast that is eaten with a fork. Logical? Right! The midday meal is eaten between noon and 2 P.M. Before going into a restaurant an Austrian will look at the day's bill of fare, which is posted outside. Usually there is a specialty for the day that is a big attraction. In the evening, Austrians start dinner around 6 P.M. But in the afternoon—somewhere between 3 and 5 P.M.—there is another mouth-watering institution, called the *Jause* (pronounced like *Yowsah*—and you'll be saying *Yowsah* after confronting this calorie-filled custom). The *Jause* is a pause to have coffee or tea with cake—and the cake is absolutely fantastic. Then, in the evening—especially in Vienna—the Austrian returning home from the movies or some social engagement will have a late snack. In Vienna this is easy because there is a mobile sausage stand—called a *Würstelstand*—set up at several strategic places after the dinner hour. Two of these stands operate near St. Stephen's, and a third, whose genial operator describes it as "The Little Sacher," is set up across the street from the Opera (and the Sacher Hotel). The stands sell frankfurters, several varieties of thick sausages and roll mops (herring). By the time the Austrian goes to bed he has had a busy day. He probably dreams of what wonderful things will be on tomorrow's menu.

Austrian food generally follows the "Vienna cuisine," which in turn is filled with many pleasant, if spicy, overtones of dishes popular in the long-ago Habsburg Empire. Aside from being occasionally piquant, Austrian food is almost invariably heavy. But it is good! *Leberknödel* (liver dumpling) and *Nudelsuppe* (noodle soup) are items you will be coming across on menus all the time. Try a goulash soup—at least get a half portion of it. The paprika will pep it up so much you might not even notice how filling it is. If you're lucky enough to find it on the menu, do try *Krebsuppe*, a crawfish bisque. There will also be several different kinds of thin slices of veal,

Schnitzels—from *natur* (plain) to *Holstein* (with a fried egg and anchovies). But in Wien, naturally, you must have at least one *Wienerschnitzel* (that is, breaded). The old favorite in Austria is boiled beef, customarily served with horseradish, pickles and maybe as many as a half dozen or more vegetables (including such items as lentils). Look on the menu for the entry *Tafelspitz*. When the word *garniert* is added, that means it is served with vegetables.

Only freshwater fish is available, as a rule, because Austria has no seacoast. The mountain trout are pretty special, but most Americans aren't too fond of muddy pike and carp from the somewhat muddy Danube. *Fogasch*, on the other hand, is an interestingly flavored whitemeat lake fish that is unlike anything we know.

The Austrians are wild about all sorts of desserts— and all of them are wonderful and, needless to say, laden with ingredients that add weight. You'll be eating delicious *Palatschinken*, thin rolled pancakes filled with either jam or chocolate sauce or chocolate sauce with nuts and/or with some other good things. Or, would you rather have *Kaiserschmarrn*, which begins life as an omelet, but is later shredded, often mixed with raisins, sprinkled with powdered sugar and frequently served with cranberry sauce. *Kastanienreis*, "the chestnut rice," looks like rice but actually is a sort of chestnut pudding made with rum or maraschino and surrounded by whipped cream (*Schlag*). Outside of Vienna there are certain special desserts. Salzburg, for instance, has its famous *Salzburger Nockerl*, which is a sort of egg soufflé. Linz is known for its *Linzertorte*—a luscious almond cake with a layer of jam. In Vienna, naturally, you won't neglect trying a *Sachertorte*, a remarkable chocolate cake. Generations of Viennese have been seriously discussing whether a real *Sachertorte* should, or should not, be served with the classic apricot jam layer that often enriches it. Oh, well, we've gone this far, so we might as well mention the *Gugelhupf*, a puffy sponge cake powdered with sugar, and of course *Apfelstrudel*. Another delightful pastry is an *Indianer*, a round chocolate-covered puff that is about 50 percent whipped cream. Even if a piece of pastry or cake does not have whipped cream as part of its natural ingredients, feel perfectly free to ask the waiter to serve it *mit Schlag* (with cream). He will nod knowingly and to himself classify you as a wise person.

Austrians are fond of both beer and wine. The beers are very good and quite inexpensive. Beer is sold either right out of the keg or in bottles. If you would like a draft beer, ask for a *Krügel*, which is a half-liter, or a *Seidel*, three-tenths of a liter (a liter is slightly more than a quart, so when ordering beer, be guided accordingly). The Romans used to cultivate the vine, as they say, in the hills around Vienna twenty centuries ago and wine production is still faithfully, and expertly, carried on to this day. Austrian wines, since the end of the occupation in 1955, have been constantly increasing in quality. One of the best known white wines is *Gumpoldskirchner*, but you may find it too heavy to drink with meals. *Kremser* and *Dürnsteiner*, we think, are better. The Austrian reds are not great, but the best of them come from the Baden and Bad Vöslau area in Lower Austria and from Burgenland. Don't drink the local "champagne" (called *Sekt*) and expect to be pleasantly surprised. You won't be. It's more likely to produce an unpleasing surprise, because it's so bad. The same goes for Austrian brandy. *Slivovitz,* an heirloom from empire days, is a plum brandy that is plumb powerful. It is raw and invigorating and has a sneaking-up-on-you quality. Martinis and bourbon are available at hotel bars, the *international* and *American* bars that keep cropping up, and in general wherever there are tourists.

To enjoy wine drinking in the Viennese way, make a short trip (twenty minutes by cab) to Grinzing, a pleasant suburb in the Vienna Woods, and visit a *Wiener Heurige,* as it is called. This is a warm, friendly and informal establishment where the vine grower sells the wine he has produced from his own vines. The word *heurige* is an adjective meaning "of this year." Thus, it refers to this year's wine as well as to the place where the wine is served. Wine of this year in any event is called *heuriger* and it is drunk in a *heurigen*. Remember it that way. Technically, the new wine is theoretically introduced on St. Martin's Day, November 11, but actually it probably does not start flowing until December. On St. Martin's Day, the wine that had been the "new" until then suddenly becomes the "old," or *alter*. Either because of Viennese wine-drinking habits or a limited supply, there is rarely much wine left by St. Martin's Day to be called *alter*. The *heurigen* places at Grinzing are open all year around, but some are not open every day. A green branch is hung outside the door to show whether it is open. If you don't have a table reserved for a particular *heurigen*—and that's not necessary—just walk along the main street of Grinzing, drop into a place that has the green branch outside and see if you like the looks of things. If not, go next door. Everything is very informal; there is music and much singing. Some places sell food—simple dishes, such as a *Wienerschnitzel*, fried chicken and a pair of frankfurters. It is more fun—and more practical—to stop at one of the food shops you see in the center of Vienna and have them make up some sandwiches. Just tell the man behind the counter you want a *Heurigen-paket* for as many people as will be in your party. He'll do the rest. Almost all the *heurigens* are pleasant and not very costly, and they give you the opportunity of seeing just how nice the Viennese really are. And they are nice!

The principal tourist areas are Vienna, Salzburg and its surroundings, Innsbruck and the Tyrol and the southern part of the country. A classic trip is the one across the glaciers of the Grossglockner.

Capital City

Vienna has been described as "the largest village in Austria"—which gives you an idea of how friendly a place it is. The population of Vienna is 1.7 million out of a total of 7 million inhabitants in all of Austria. Vienna itself is one of the nine Austrian federal states. (Right around it are the federal states of Lower Austria and Burgenland. To the south are Styria and Carinthia. In about the middle of the country are Upper Austria and Salzburg. The two federal states in the western end are Tyrol and Voralberg.) Vienna, the capital city, is an impressive place.

Viennese architecture is of the type generally described as *baroque*—or, occasionally, as *Austrian baroque*, which means even more so. Baroque is a style of architecture based upon unevenness, exuberance and considerable flamboyance, all executed in a florid style. In other words, too much of everything. It's eye-catching and intriguing, but you probably wouldn't want to live with it. (Unless you're Austrian.) When baroque really goes wild, loses control and casts caution to the four winds, the style becomes known as *rococo*—a condition that first occurred about 1775. Much of everything you'll see will be either baroque or rococo.

The city is divided into twenty-three districts—called *Bezirke.* You won't have to remember the numbers of these Bezirke. The main one, called (quite naturally) the First Bezirk, is the very heart of Vienna and is the one that is most rewarding for tourists. This complete inner district is surrounded by a wide, circular (more or less) boulevard, called the Ringstrasse. The *Ring* changes its name frequently before completing the circle, but don't worry too much about this. Usually everyone calls it the Ring, regardless of what section of it is being referred to. Because of the heavy traffic along the Ring, a series of underpassages have been built. They are quite attractive and have shops, or display windows, that are worth looking at or into.

SIGHTSEEING ¶ More or less in the center of the inner town—the First Bezirk, remember?—lies a large square. Stephansplatz, flauntingly located alongside of Vienna's beloved St. Stephen's Cathedral, familiarly known as *der alte Steffl*—"the dear little old Stephen," is the way we make it. Coming into the square from the south and west, at a right angle, are the Kärntnerstrasse and the Graben. These two thoroughfares are the heart of Vienna's shopping district. At the end of the Kärntnerstrasse, at a junction with the Ring, is the Opera, one of the most beautiful opera houses in the world and the musical heart of Austria. It was heavily damaged in World War II but the Austrian people—even though flat broke—contributed the equivalent of $10 million for its rebuilding. The job took ten years—which gives you an idea of how magnificent it is. Tickets for good seats are about the same as in New York, although balcony and standing-room tickets are less. But you can take a guided tour for a half dollar or so that takes you backstage, out front and everywhere. In July and August (when there are no performances) the tours are at 9, 10 and 11 A.M. and at 1, 2 and 3 P.M. From September to June the tours are not at any fixed hours, so you have to check.

Not far from the Opera is the Hofburg, the former imperial palace of the Habsburgs. The Hofburg has merely 2,000 rooms, and most of it is rather old except for a new part (new!—built about a century ago). You'll want to see the state apartments (conducted tours from

9 A.M. to 4 P.M. weekdays; and Sunday and holidays, except May 1, from 9 A.M. to 12:30 P.M. If you like crown jewels, look in on the Treasury (Monday, Wednesday, Saturday from 9:30 A.M. to 3 P.M.; Tuesday and Thursday 2 to 7 P.M.; Sunday and holidays 9 A.M. to 1 P.M.; Friday closed). By circling about the Hofburg you'll come upon Michaelerplatz and St. Michael's Church. The route that follows along the edge of the Hofburg leads to the Albertina Museum, with a very important collection of prints, engravings and etchings, including many by Dürer. The Albertina's hours are Monday, Tuesday, Thursday and Friday 10 A.M. to 4 P.M.; Wednesday, 10 A.M. to 6 P.M.; and Saturday and Sunday 10 A.M. to 1 P.M. But, between July 1 and September 15, the museum is closed on Sundays and holidays.

There are loads of other sights to see in Vienna, such as the Kapuziner Church, which contains the imperial vaults, the resting places for 140 Habsburgs (including more than two dozen emperors and empresses).

Although the name is unnecessarily awe-inspiring, the Kunsthistorisches Museum (Museum of Fine Arts) has a wonderful collection of paintings. The schedule at the Museum of Fine Arts goes like this: Tuesday through Saturday 10-3; Sunday 9-1; Tuesday and Friday 8 to 10 P.M. with special illumination; from May through September it is also open on Wednesdays from 3 to 6 P.M.

Another place worth seeing is the Belvedere Palace, where the State Treaty was signed in 1955. The palace, set out in a lovely and immense garden, is used for official receptions nowadays. It has a picture gallery that is open to the public, and at times there are special exhibitions. Many of the palace's rooms are available for viewing.

Almost everyone who comes to Vienna wants to see the famous Spanish Riding School of Lippizaner horses. Most of the horses, born dark gray, turn white. The riders, in fancy uniforms and without stirrups, execute the most complicated maneuvers with this remarkable group of animals. Performances are given in the Hofburg on Sunday mornings and Wednesday evenings. Be sure to ask your concierge for tickets as far in advance as possible. If you can't make the Sunday morning performance, you can attend a training session during the week for a half dollar or so, and that might be even more interesting. For an extra 5 schillings, you can look around the mahogany stalls of the horses. For a free look, stand on the Stallburggassee about noon and see the horses parade across the street on their way back to the stables. Those training sessions, by the way, are held from early March to the end of June and from early September to mid-December from 10 A.M. to noon daily, except Sundays and Mondays.

Also, you should drive out to Schönbrunn Palace, once the summer residence of Austrian royalty. Leave from the intersection of the Ring and Babenbergerstrasse which continues into Mariahilferstrasse (those are *really* street names!) and less than a couple of miles later, you will come upon this grandiose palace, set back amid landscaped gardens and lines of trees. The Imperial Apartments are open (guided visits only) daily 9 A.M. to noon and 1 to 5 P.M. There are guided night tours, with all the lights burning in a festive fashion from June 1 to August 31 on Wednesdays, Thursdays and Saturdays, 7:30 to 9:15 P.M. Many other sights in the Schönbrunn area will charm you, including the zoo and botanical gardens, the miniature theater and the coach house. You had better allow a good part of the day for the Schönbrunn excursion. There is an adequate restaurant in the palace courtyard, by the way.

Throughout Vienna are places that have become shrines for great composers—Schubert, Beethoven, Mozart and Strauss, for example—because of their direct association with the city. Sightseeing in Vienna is made easy by plaques on walls of many of the buildings and monuments of historical and artistic renown. These plaques are easily recognized white wooden scrolls with gold lettering. In the summer they are adorned with small Austrian red-white-red flags. Just look for these wall plaques. They call attention to a couple of hundred points of interest—ranging from the site of Vienna's first coffee house to the seventeenth-century Obizzi Palace, which now houses the city's Clock and Watch Museum.

Besides the Danube, another area that inspired Strauss' enthusiasm was the Vienna Woods, a range of forested hills reaching out west and southwest. On the way to them, you'll pass delightful villages and have the opportunity (on pleasant days) to view the Viennese enjoying their natural woodlands. They love to hike through the woods and pick suitable spots for a pleasant (and filling!) picnic. For another worthwhile trip, take the drive south from Vienna in the direction of Baden, a noted spa.

PUBLIC HOLIDAYS ¶ New Year's Day, Epiphany (Jan. 6), Easter Monday, Labor Day (May 1), Ascension Day, Whit Monday, Corpus Christi Day, Assumption (Aug. 15), National Holiday (Oct. 26), All Saints Day (Nov. 1), Immaculate Conception (Dec. 8), Christmas and St. Stephen's Day (Dec. 26).

ACCOMMODATIONS ¶ There are just a shade under 14,000 hotels of various types in Austria, plus some 450 others at spas. Thus, you will not have too much difficulty finding some place to stay. In August, during the festival season, it used to be impossible to find a room anywhere near Salzburg. The festival draws more enchanted visitors than ever, but the growing use of automobiles makes it possible for them to stay in colorful out-of-town inns and drive into Salzburg at concert time. The result is that hotels in Salzburg during the music festival have rooms available *sometimes*. So, when you have no advance reservation and things look the blackest, don't give up the ship. Well, you know what we mean.

One of the finest ways to get into the right mood for a visit in Austria, we think, is to use one of its castles as your hotel. Dozens of these timeworn, timeless structures, hanging on the side of a cliff or perched on a plateau speckled with alpine flowers, have been made into small, luxury inns. They are removed from the main currents of activity—no discothèques are around the corner, for instance—but perhaps that is just what you want. Some of the wonderful ones are Schloss Fuschl, near Salzburg; Schloss (that's the word for "castle") Sighartstein, which is at Neumarkt-am-Wallersee, also near Salzburg; the 12th century Burg Kapfenberg ("Burg" means fortress) in Styria; Schloss Rabenstein, also in the federal state of Styria, not far from Graz. Schloss Grubhof, a luxurious old manor in great mountain landscape at St. Martin near Lofer, and Jagdschloss Graf Recke, the hunting lodge of the Counts of Recke at Wald, are both in Land Salzburg; Schloss Haunsperg with antique interiors and luxurious facilities is at Oberalm near Salzburg. Some of these castles are quite roomy. Fuschl, for instance, has 130 beds; Rabenstein, on the other hand, has 12. All the castles have rich histories and are in splendid locations. Let's look at it this way. When these places were "homesteaded" centuries ago, their royal owners could take their pick of the neighborhood sites—and they chose the best because they figured that was none too good for them, at that.

VIENNA HOTELS

Imperial: An extremely fine hotel, renowned for its attractive good-size rooms and pleasant accommodations. It is the kind of hotel where you, after checking in on the main floor, are greeted by name by a hotel employee when the elevator whisks you to the floor where your room is located.

Intercontinental: A new hotel in a fine location just a block or so from the Ring. Excellent accommodations are offered in good-size rooms; several different restaurant facilities.

Ambassador: A famous Viennese hotel, carefully maintained in capable fashion. Rooms are quite pleasant and the atmosphere is gracious. Don't be misled by the hotel's somewhat depressing exterior.

Bristol: One of Vienna's famous traditional hotels. It has been remodeled in recent years and has a beautifully decorated restaurant. The location is marvelous albeit noisy because of street traffic: on the Ring and just across the street from the Opera. Rooms are large and gracious.

Sacher: A truly famous hotel, in the great Viennese tradition and spirit. Crystal chandeliers, red damask—everything to make life enjoyable. For those who enjoy turn-of-the-century atmosphere, it is charming. Others might think it old-fashioned.

Palais Schwarzenberg: Located in a wing of the palace of the same name which still belongs to one of the oldest Austrian aristocratic families. Although almost in the center of the city, it nevertheless is quiet because, naturally, the palace has a park. Small but exclusive (and sometimes booked months in advance), it is furnished with authentic antiques. No restaurant.

Schloss Laudon: Modern comfort in an Old World setting; a large secluded park with swimming, tennis, riding, boating. It is on the outskirts of Vienna, near the junction of federal highway number 1 (as it comes in from the west) and Mauerbachstrasse.

Clima-Villenhotel: In a wonderful location away from the downtown part of the city at the foot of the vineyards in the suburban wine-growing village of Nussdorf (near Grinzing)—very quiet but difficult to get to without a car—this hotel consists of several small and modern buildings with pleasant garden grounds. Accommodations include kitchenettes and refrigerators.

Among the conveniently located First Class hotels are:

Am Stephansplatz: Well located, but the rooms are somewhat small.

Kahlenberg: In a beautiful, unique location atop the Kahlenberg hill, overlooking the city; however, you need a car.

Europa: A modern-style hotel with a fine main-floor coffee house, and a good upper-floor restaurant with Viennese music in the evening.

Kaiserin Elisabeth: In a romantic old street and, literally, just a few steps from Stephansplatz.

VIENNA RESTAURANTS

The city's restaurants run the full scale—from gourmet to economy. Some of the luxury hotels mentioned above have excellent restaurants. The Sacher is especially popular in the evening—*late-ish*—and also for lunch during the summer (its sidewalk terrace faces the Opera). The Hotel Europa has a First Class restaurant, also.

Zu den 3 Husaren: Some consider this Vienna's leading restaurant. It is sophisticated, elegant dining. The menu is interesting. Prices are fairly high, but worth it. Closed for part of the summer period, unfortunately.

Am Franziskanerplatz: An excellent place, staid and dignified. Attractive surroundings and very good Austrian and international food. High prices, but offering luxurious dining.

Altes Kerzenstüberl: Old-world atmosphere, charming ambiance, and high prices. Several rooms; dining is best in downstairs room, by candlelight.

Wegenstein-Weisser Schwan: Ten minutes from center of town, but worth the trip. Austrian cuisine, but noted for game, cooked by the owner and his family, and probably the best restaurant for game in Austria. Despite fashionable clientele, prices are moderate.

Weisser Rauchfangkehrer ("The White Chimneysweep"): Nobody is cleaning up chimneys here, only plates of very fine Viennese food in a setting of hunting-style wood-panelled rooms. Medium prices.

Eckel: A bit out of the way, perhaps, in the direction of the wine suburb of Sievering, but you will not regret a trip there. Viennese food prepared by the owner himself, very reasonable prices and a pleasant garden in summer.

Balkan Grill: Offers both summer and winter gardens, gypsy music and the best Balkan-type food in Vienna—most likely also better than you get in the Balkans these days. High prices if you take the full swing, i.e. from Slivovitz to special gypsy music requests.

SHOPPING ¶ *Knitwear* is the stand-out item, with smart designs in sweaters, skirts and complete ensembles. *Cashmere* sweaters for men and women are good buys, although not precisely cheap even here. *Leather goods* are good values—particularly handbags, wallets, belts, cigarette boxes and the like. *Glassware and porcelain* are specialties of Austria (*Alt Wien* porcelains from the old times are works of art). Old Vienna silver was another masterpiece, and the silver work still remains good. *Petit point* is a unique finely executed embroidery that is used on many articles of clothing (ladies' handbags, principally). The price depends (natch!) on the quality of workmanship. The more stitches per square inch there are, the higher the price. There is also *gros point*, in which the stitches are large, and which is used for tapestry. Naturally, exceptional handwork must be well paid for. But you'll never wear out a petit point bag. So consider that fact, even though the price seems high (a Fifth Avenue shop would charge double or triple what you'll pay for a good bag in Vienna).

Lodencloth overcoats for men are one-third the price at home. This makes sense. Austria is where lodencloth comes from.

Pointer: Except for food stores, most downtown shops are open from 8 A.M. to 6 P.M. Monday to Friday and until noon on Saturday. Food shops keep a 7 A.M. to 1 P.M. and 4 P.M. to 6:30 P.M. schedule daily except Saturday when they are open only in the morning.

Costume jewelry is always listed as an Austrian specialty, but many of the old-fashioned designs could stand updating. *Antiques*, needless to say, are good values. An excellent place for antique shopping is the Dorotheum, a national government-run auction house. There are several branches in outlying sections of the city, but the main place—and the one where you should go—is in the First Bezirk in the Dorotheergasse. You'll need some time for this—at least a couple of days. Sales are held toward the end of the week, and goods are on display early in the week. Furniture, china and all manner of household items —from clocks to bird cages—are put up for auction regularly. You do not have to do the bidding yourself. If you see anything you like, leave a bid with one of the licensed bidders at the Dorotheum. The bidder will try to land the article for you at the price limit you authorized. Sometimes you'll get it for less than you figured on bidding for it. You pay the bidder a very small fee. It is all very honest and aboveboard, so have (absolutely!) no doubts. There is a sale every week, and from time to time special groupings of articles—like cameras or clocks, maybe—are put up for sale. Your hotel concierge can tell you about what is up for bid this week.

If you're planning to go native with *dirndls* and *peasant blouses and skirts*, you may wait until Salzburg, Innsbruck or Graz although Vienna now also has several shops in this field. Even then, choose with care and look for becoming clothes. *Men's clothing* buys are pretty much confined to haberdashery items: shirts, ties and accessories. *Alpine hats* look pretty good on everyone, but the leather pants, *lederhosen*, only become the young and slim (even though Austrians themselves pay no attention to that). The hats now run about $10, and the pants are from $20 up, depending on the type of leather used.

ENTERTAINMENT ¶ *Music* is what makes Austria tick (to the tempo of a metronome), and you'll find plenty of it in Vienna—from chamber concerts to full-dress grand opera. The classical operas are presented at the Staatsoper, as the Opera in Vienna is called. There are no performances in the summer, but many of the opera singers perform at the festival in Salzburg. The Vienna Volksoper features light opera and operetta, and sometimes musicals, nightly except in summer. In mid-May to mid-June Vienna has a big music festival.

One of Vienna's oldest institutions is the *coffee house*. It has been part of Vienna social life for almost three centuries. With the swift surge of the espresso bars a decade ago, it looked to some as if the coffee house might be a victim of modern times. But it is still holding its own, although a number of the real old-timers have closed their doors. In a coffee house you can read newspapers and magazines (free), write letters or reports, meet friends, hold business (or other) conferences or just sit before your empty coffee cup contemplating (anything). You can do that all day, and no one will ever ask you to leave—nor will anyone ever hint that you should order something else. Every half-hour or so the waiter in the black tie (black jacket and trousers, white shirt) will bring a fresh glass of water for you. The waiter with the water is a tradition, too. Even if you never touch a drop of water, you get a fresh glass every thirty minutes.

A cup of coffee, in this cosmopolitan city where the West first practiced the art of coffee drinking, is not merely a "cup of coffee, please, Herr Ober." Almost everyone has a favorite way of having his coffee served. Here are some of the popular ones:

Mélange: Coffee with milk
Schale Braun: Just a touch of cream
Schale Gold: Enough cream to give the coffee a golden color
Kapuziner: More coffee than milk, making it dark brown

Einspänner: Coffee served in a glass with whipped cream
Obers: Cream
Schlagobers: Whipped cream

Some of these coffee houses also serve meals, but, in any case, you'll never go hungry in one. If nothing else, there will always be a pair of frankfurters handy.

By all means, you must visit Demel's, an Old World establishment that serves out-of-this-world pastry and ice cream. Drop by at lunchtime and sample the imaginative and exquisite variety of their specialties—all superb and fattening. Sunday afternoon is a favorite drop-in time for ice cream and cake.

With Vienna's sweet tooth the number of pastry shops and places where you can get a *Mehlspeis* (dessert) to go with your coffee keeps climbing. The Aida chain has four handy *Konditorei* in the First Bezirk and a couple of others not far away, where you can entertain yourself with a delicious piece of pastry in between sightseeing and shopping tours. Gerstner's and Lehmann's are ranked by some as almost on a par with Demel's.

Late in the afternoon many Viennese, as a source of entertainment, drop into a huge (usually), below-street-level *Keller* for a relaxing *Viertel* (a fourth of a liter) of wine and conversation at big wooden tables. They also usually have a little sandwich of cheese or ham along with their wine. Some kellers, like Urbanikeller, operate till about midnight and have some informal music. Others shut up earlier and stick pretty much to the wine drinking. Other popular kellers are the Twelve Apostles and Augustiner.

The Moulin Rouge has been Vienna's best-known international-type night club for a long time now. It has floor shows and high prices. Maxim, Eve and a couple of other places in the First Bezirk also provide entertainment. But remember, you're on your own. Please note, too, that these are not typically Austrian, but merely exist to cater to foreign visitors. If you have never seen a floor show in Las Vegas, New York, or Paris, you might want to drop in on one of these Vienna night clubs; otherwise, skip it.

The "Old Vienna" style of music these days is now confined, generally, either to restaurants (where there is frequently a piano or zither player) or to the *heurigens* at Grinzing.

Vienna's young people are a step ahead of everyone

else when it comes to waltzing. But they are not listening to Strauss music all the time. There are several nicely decorated, lively discothèques you will enjoy—just to look and listen, anyway. The Atrium, just off the Schwarzenbergplatz, is the best, in our opinion. It calls itself "Austria's First Beer Bar," but don't let that confuse you. It is quite elegant and is jammed with handsome young Viennese couples. The Scotch, a two-level affair on the Ring, is also a place to visit. A modern espresso bar is on the street-floor level. Downstairs is the dancing bar. The Chattanooga, on the Graben, is a kind of night club for young people and is not expensive. The music is modern and somewhat noisy. Maybe "cacophonous" would express our point better. On second thought, it *is* noisy. But it is a nice place to drop into—there's a coffee bar on the street level—to see how the new sounds are reverberating in Old Vienna against the background of the Danube and the old masters. More "conservative" dancing places include Eden Bar, not far from St. Stephen's, and Cobenzl Bar on Cobenzl hill in the Vienna Woods. At the latter, you can dance outdoors in summer, with a beautiful night view of Vienna as a backdrop.

Vienna's Prater (amusement park) has been a major attraction for more than two centuries. The shooting galleries, make-believe autos and other amusement park fixtures are not unlike those that one used to see in Coney Island. But this setup is only a very small part of the Prater's great lure. Of course, there is the unique Big Wheel—the highest or biggest or tallest ferris wheel in the world. It all depends how you say it. It *is* pretty big and provides an impressive view of the city from one of its swinging gondolas. But the Prater is also an immense park, with lovely lanes and promenades. It is particularly pleasant to ride through it in one of Vienna's famous horsedrawn carriages, the *Fiaker*.

ဧ A Tour of Austria

Vienna to Krems—51 miles

Leave Vienna from the intersection of Liechtensteinstrasse and the Ring; head northward on Liechtensteinstrasse until it joins with Heiligenstädterstrasse. Soon you'll find the Danube River on your right as you head in the direction of Klosterneuburg, whose most important attraction is an old abbey.

Then continue on toward Tulln via an unnumbered road; Tulln has an old church, ruined walls, ancient doorways. Onward to Traismauer, in the direction of Mautern. Just before reaching Mautern you'll find the junction of the Krems–St. Pölten road. (If you are so inclined, turn left here for three miles to see the 900-year-old Benedictine abbey—guides conduct visits during both morning and afternoon hours. This side trip we heartily recommend, although there are more abbeys along the way, a fact that probably may discourage all but abbey lovers.)

At Mautern, cross to the other (north) side of the Danube because the south ride offers a much less impressive view of the beautiful valley ahead. Here, after a turn to the right, is the old market town of Krems, with its suburb, or rather twin-town, of Stein. There is a little local joke here wherein everyone tells you that "Krems Und Stein (i.e., Krems *and* Stein) are three towns." Apparently it doesn't take much to amuse the inhabitants of this area, for that is indeed a little joke.

Krems to Linz—84 miles

Leaving Krems via route 29 toward Dürnstein, you'll soon encounter a land of fairy-story castles, cliffs with houses perched on the rocks and a general air of romantic music and medieval madrigals, for this is the beginning of the region known as the Wachau. The next twenty miles (tourist folders notwithstanding) is a truly enchanted vista, with the Danube at the bottom of a narrow valley and picturesque old towns lining its banks.

Dürnstein is a small, colorful, walled-in town with extremely narrow streets; if you're driving a large car, perhaps you'll do better to take the special tunnel that bypasses the center, and then return to the town on foot for sightseeing. History was made here; in the year 1193, England's King Richard the Lion-Hearted was returning in disguise from the Holy Land after a Crusade. He was recognized and imprisoned by Duke Leopold. (Hisses from the audience!) Because Richard had offended the Duke during the Crusade, Leopold was concerned about his own honor. He imprisoned Richard despite excommunication from the Church; at the time anybody who harmed a Crusader, whatever the circumstances, was excommunicated. Legend says that Richard's minstrel, Blondel, traveled across Europe, singing outside of each castle to learn whether it was the prison of his king. At Dürnstein, Richard the Lion-Hearted answered his minstrel's plaintive song and today you'll find the two hotels named in their honor—the Gasthof Zum Richard Lowenherz and the Gasthof Zum Sänger Blondel. Hardy walkers might choose to ascend past the early medieval cemetery toward the ruined castle, the Feste Dürnstein, where Richard was imprisoned, which Swedish marauders destroyed about 500 years later. In 1805, the French fought the Russians here in a fiercely contested battle and defeated them.

No, Dürnstein has not had a peaceful existence, but today, all is mellow and quiet. To enjoy the town's unique setting, take the little ferry across the river to Rossatz, a village boasting a charming old chateau.

Next comes Weissenkirchen, quaint as are all the towns of the Wachau and with a small beach; then after miles of vineyards, you'll find Spitz, best known for its parish church and the nearby ruins of Hinterhaus, an old castle. Spitz is dominated by the imposing Tausendeimerberg, or Hill of a Thousand Buckets of Wine. Here, also, is a passenger ferry across the Danube, to Arnsdorf, a tiny village with an interesting church.

On to Aggsbach; across the river is Aggsbach-Dorf, known for the Aggstein fortress, which, unfortunately, is some distance from the ferry landing. Your route follows along to Rollfähre Melk, and here you might do well to consider crossing to Melk, site of a truly impressive abbey, an outstanding example of baroque architecture (open 10 A.M. to noon, 2 to 5 P.M.); the extremely interesting interior contains a museum, lovely rooms and the famous gold cross of Melk. (If you wish, take your car across on the ferry and drive to the Melk abbey, returning to the north shore at either of the two next towns, Pöchlarn or Marbach.)

Klein-Pöchlarn is the twin town of Pöchlarn, across the Danube. Marbach is situated at the foot of a hill crowned by the twin-spired Maria Taferl pilgrimage church, the landmark seen from far away. This section of the Danube valley is called the *Nibelungengau* because, according to legend, the Nibelungs came here. The road soon cuts inland, losing sight of the river, toward Persenbeug and then Sarmingstein and its ruins. Grein is colorful, followed by Perg, with a castle and a moat in the medieval tradition; and then Linz.

Because it lies on the road toward Salzburg and Innsbruck, Linz doesn't receive its proper share of attention from tourists; you'll find a large city (population 200,-000) spread along both banks of the Danube, with a few good places for a stopover, notably the Parkhotel, where most of the rooms feature balconies, and the new, modern Esso Motor Hotel, located half way between the autobahn and the downtown center, pleasant for an overnight stop. Klosterhof is an interesting and inexpensive eating establishment, with series of rustic rooms downstairs and upstairs, good local food and excellent beer. The building long ago used to be the library of—you guessed it—an abbey. Anyone who leaves the city without having a *Linzertorte* (a special almond cake), the culinary landmark of Linz, is a traitor to organized tourism.

During the summer, from June 15 to September 15, there are regular excursions to St. Florian, another famous baroque abbey, as well as sightseeing tours of the city. You can get help with accommodations and details on things to see and do from the Tourist Office at Hauptplatz 8 or the one in the railroad station.

Linz to Salzburg—90 miles

From Linz, take route 1 toward Wels and Lambach, where you may visit another Benedictine abbey, dating back to the eleventh century (unless you've seen all the Benedictine abbeys you intend to). At Lambach, make a left turn onto route 145, toward Gmunden on the Traunsee (which means Gmunden is on the lake). This is a resort town with beaches, theaters, fishing and all the rest of it; be sure to see the famous twin castles of Schloss Orth. Herein lies a story for some motion picture producer: Archduke Salvator (Johann Orth) renounced his title and disappeared, according to the rumors of the time, with a safe containing the true story of Prince Rudolph (son of Emperor Franz Josef), who died under very mysterious circumstances—remember the film *Mayerling*? It is said (in low whispers) that the world couldn't stand the secret of the cause of his death. (Sorry, we can't say another word. Not in print, in any event.) Johann Orth headed for South America where he went down with his sailing ship in 1890. His twin castles span both land and water (one is on a tiny island connected by a footbridge).

The road continues alongside the west bank of the Traunsee, eight miles long, sky-lined on its east shore by three magnificent mountains. After the town of Ebensee comes Bad Ischl, which sounds like the name for a local juvenile delinquent but is actually a water place, or spa. Of all things, this town is famous for an outstanding *Konditorei*, a pastry shop with cakes and tarts and little doodads that are absolutely delicious. Zauner's is the name of this fabulous establishment, and even Emperor Franz Josef (himself) frequented the remarkable shop during his summer visits. For an overnight stay try the Hotel Austria facing the river, or the traditional Post, both moderately priced.

It's route 158 from Bad Ischl to Strobl, where you should make a right turn toward the fascinating little town of St. Wolfgang on the shores of the Wolfgangsee. If you remember the operetta *White Horse Inn*, here is situated its inspiration, the Weisses Rössl. A miniature railway to the top of Schafberg Mountain takes about an hour (operates May through September) and offers a remarkable view of the region. On summer holidays and Sundays, the entire side trip to St. Wolfgang may be slowed to the proverbial snail's pace because of heavy traffic, narrow streets and scant parking space.

From Strobl drive to St. Gilgen, a summer resort, where one can rest at the Hotel Excelsior. On to Fuschl (with castle converted to elegant hotel) and Salzburg.

Salzburg! We don't want to be monotonous about it, but the hotel situation in and around Salzburg during the summer is difficult. We therefore want to mention it once more. The classic favorite inn, both as hotel and restaurant, is the Goldener Hirsch; but it's small. The Oesterreichischerhof is charming and elegant. Gastschloss Mönchstein is a small exclusive castle hotel on the Mönchsberg hill, rising above the center of the city. Grand Hotel Winkler and the 15-story Europa are very modern, all rooms having baths. All rooms in Europa also have very fine views of the city and the mountains, but the building itself, called locally "the matchbox," badly spoils Salzburg's baroque skyline. A nice place to stay, on the edge of the city, is on the grounds of a former castle, the Schlosshotel Klessheim (Kavalierhaus). Dine at the Goldener Hirsch. It is a wonderful (and expensive) experience to have a meal in this four-centuries-old place. The venison, the boiled beef—everything is splendid. Don't leave Salzburg, of course, without trying a *Salzburger Nockerl*.

Beautiful Salzburg stretches along both banks of the peaceful Salzach River, with the older town on the south shore. Behind the old town looms the fortress of Hohensalzburg, which may be reached by funicular railway (frequent service) and offers tours between 8 and 6:30. Inside, you'll hear the famous musical (?) instrument called the Bull of Salzburg, because it bellows before and after each selection. Residenzplatz, in the heart of town, contains the Archbishop's Residence, a marvelous baroque fountain, the cathedral, and Residenz-Neugebäude, "the New Residence Building," constructed in 1592–1602 (which will give you an idea of what "new" means in Salzburg). Incidentally, don't fail to see the renowned Salzburg marionettes, a fascinating theatrical experience. Four miles outside of town, easily reached by exorbitantly priced taxis or more reasonably by bus, is the crazy Hellbrunn Castle, built for a bishop with (very!) eccentric ideas. The gardens are filled with mechanical figures operated by water, and it's all very amusing until a hidden fountain suddenly sprays you with an unnecessarily large flow of water, which sort of takes an edge off the fun; we advise wearing a raincoat.

Salzburg is one of the best shopping regions of the country; walk along the narrow Getreidegasse and try to resist the bargains. It's almost impossible. Marvelous handmade sweaters for men and women, table mats, ceramics and coats made of lodencloth at a fraction of their American prices are typical of the bargains to be had. Antiques, too, are a great specialty of the town; don't worry about shipping them home, for they always arrive.

But we neglected explaining that Salzburg, wonderful as it is, has come to the fore primarily because it was the home of one of the world's most gifted composers, Wolfgang Amadeus Mozart, who, though he died at the age of thirty-five, wrote some of the outstanding musical creations we have today. During his lifetime, Mozart sought in vain financial and musical recognition of the type now extended to Rodgers and Hammerstein or Duke Ellington. Ah well, to be appreciated, one must die. From the last week in July through all of August, the music festival changes the nature of this charming city. In short, the town is a complete madhouse of people seeking hotel rooms, waiting in line at restaurants, lacking tickets for the musical events, even though as many as a half dozen are presented each day. If you can put up with all this frenzy, go. But be sure you have a *written* confirmation from the hotel; the fact that *you* merely write or wire is no assurance that the room will be waiting. If you have no advance reservation, avoid Salzburg during the two summer months and see it at its very best in the spring or fall.

An interesting excursion from Salzburg, if you like the mountains, is the trip to the top of Untersberg via the recently constructed aerial cableway; the valley station of the cable railway can be reached by bus from Salzburg.

Salzburg to Innsbruck—99 miles

Leave Salzburg, heading toward Bad Reichenhall; then cross the border (now route 21) into Germany (later to reenter Austria—we're not getting lost). Here is an opportunity to drive southward for a side trip to Berchtesgaden, now a resort community but principally known because it was the retreat of one Adolf Hitler of unbeloved memory. You'll reach his Eagle's Nest by elevator and find an outdoor restaurant and a magnificent view. You'll also want to visit the local salt mines, dressed up as you would for a walk under Niagara Falls. If great heights don't bother you, try the *Jennerbahn*—a cableway in which you are lifted in a chair and everything is great, provided you don't look straight down.

Back on German route 21, you return to the Austrian

border, pass through customs readily (we hope) and head for Lofer, via route 1.

Now you come to a crossroad; if time does not permit a visit to Innsbruck, the tour may be shortened by turning south on route 168, to Zell am See and Bruck, rejoining this tour on page 84.

After Lofer, the route winds through the narrow Pass Strub, St. Johann, Wörgl and then into Innsbruck, the capital of the federal state of Tyrol. This really lovely university town has the standard attractions, but in point of fact its own natural setting makes Innsbruck outstanding. Facing north from the main street, Maria-Theresien Strasse, you'll surely get a thrill just gazing at the towering Alps, which almost seem to encroach upon the city. Incidentally, the town is so named because originally it formed a bridge over the river, which is called Inn. Oh, of course Innsbruck has its points of interest, notably the Goldenes Dachl, the so-called Golden Roof of an old mansion; but all that glitters is not gold—in this case it's heavily gilded copper—however, on a sunny day, it does look like gold. Then, too, there's the Hofkirche, the Court Church which actually is the mausoleum of Emperor Maximilian (called "the Last Knight") and contains 28 larger-than-life bronze statues portraying his ancestors and legendary kings, among them King Arthur. There is the Triumphal Arch built by Maria Theresa, St. Anne's Column and an interesting Tyrolean museum, the Ferdinandeum. If you're a restless soul, Innsbruck probably won't make too much impression on you, for it takes a little time to absorb the slow-paced, mountain charm of the region.

Innsbruck's leading hotels are the very modern Hotel Tyrol, which overlooks the railroad station, and Holiday Inn, the latest addition, scheduled to open during 1971. A few steps from the Tyrol is another new and fine hotel, the Europa. On the Maria-Theresien Strasse is the traditional, comfortable Maria Theresia Hotel. (Notice how the endings of German words can change? It's very confusing.) Among the best and most interesting restaurants are Ottoburg, Goldene Rose and Das Alte Haus, all located in centuries-old buildings. Goldener Adler is a fine, historic inn (founded in 1390!), with good food and Tyrolean music in its cellar restaurant. In Innsbruck try Tyroler *Knödelsuppe* (beef broth with Tyrolean-style dumplings). If you are really famished and would like a typical Tyrolean farmer's meal, then have a *Tiroler Bauernschmaus* (it has everything—frankfurters, sausages, boiled pork chop, sauerkraut, dumplings, etc.). The *Kalterersee* wine—red—is excellent. There's a variety of cable cars to the three levels of the alpine summit at the edge of town, and the view of the slender green Inn valley—"the land amid the mountains," as the antique phrase goes—is one you'll long remember.

West of Innsbruck the Inn Valley rises slowly among the great Tyrolean mountain ranges up to the Arlberg Pass area, which is known especially for some of the most famous skiing centers in the world: St. Anton, Zürs and Lech. The latter two are located already within the borders of the most western Austrian federal state—Vorarlberg, with its main city Bregenz resting on the shores of Bodensee (Lake Constance).

Innsbruck to Zell am See—90 miles

After leaving Innsbruck, you'll duplicate a stretch of some 25 miles (39 kilometers) by returning on route 1 in the direction of Salzburg. After about 18 miles, you'll come to Schwaz; 6 miles farther along, there's a right turn (route 169) that passes through Schlitters, Fügen, Kaltenbach, Aschau and Zell am Ziller. This general area, the Zillertal, a pastoral region popular as a resort, is probably the most beautiful valley of the Tyrol. If you're on a slow, unhurried schedule, make a short side trip south on an unnumbered road to Mayrhofen, for some reason a British favorite, perhaps because it is a center for walking tours. Unlike Americans, the British still retain the use of their legs and even seem to enjoy exercising them. From Mayrhofen you could continue on to isolated villages like Ginzling, Tux or even Hintertux.

From Zell, route 169 continues toward Gerlos; from here the road begins a moderately steep ascent through the Gerlos Pass and then descends to reach Wald; at Wald, turn right to the village of Krimml, which hasn't much to offer (although handsomely situated) except its celebrated three-stage waterfalls, a scene you shouldn't miss as long as you're in the neighborhood. After all, how often *do* you get to Krimml? And so, on through Bramberg to Mittersill; here you could turn right (that is, south) and drive over the new Felber Tauern Road (toll charge is about $5 for cars having up to six seats—

even if they are not filled or if you are alone), which cuts
the Hohe Tauern range here through a 3½-mile tunnel
at an elevation of 5,250 feet. The road represents the
latest in Alpine road engineering, has only a few easy
curves and a grade that is never steeper than 7 percent.
On the other side of the tunnel you come to East Tyrol
with its quiet valleys tucked away from the traffic and
the town of Lienz at the foot of the spectacular Lienzer
Dolomites.

From Mittersill, continue on to Uttendorf (route 159)
to Zell am See, where you might stay at the Grand Hotel
or at Latini, which is the newest and largest addition to
the numerous hotels in this "hotel town"; if you come
here during July or August, be sure to have a reservation.
North of the town a cable railway leads to the top of
Schmittenhöhe and another superb view of the Alps (but
we're beginning to wonder if the Austrians haven't overdone this cable railway bit, just a trifle).

Zell am See to Spittal—85 miles

Next we go toward Bruck, the beginning of the most
fascinating ride in all of Austria. We're referring, of
course, to the wonderfully engineered Grossglockner road,
which extends from Bruck to Heiligenblut, a truly amazing feat of engineering, principally because the roadbed
is so good and presents so few dangers (when the weather
is clement). The road opens in June, the date depending
upon the weather, and closes down (as a rule) in October
or November, but a sudden freak storm can cause the
closing of the road briefly, even during the middle of the
summer. Don't forget, there is a toll charge on the
Grossglockner road of about $5 for a six-seat car or
smaller, which is the minimum charge. The round-trip
ticket is about $8.50 and can be used on the Felber
Tauern Road nearby as well. Drive carefully, please,
especially when you encounter buses, and get up and out
early in the morning, at dawn (if possible) for fullest
enjoyment of the wonderful vistas.

This is route 107, but you can hardly lose your way.
Head toward Fusch and then on to the toll house, where
you should be sure to fill up with gas, just in case. Then
comes Ferleiten, where the scenery becomes unbearably
magnificent and the road begins its serious ascent. As
you climb, there are various parking places for further
enjoyment of the view, and if only one person in your

car is a driver, play fair and stop occasionally for the driver's benefit. Parking on the road is, of course, forbidden. Soon you'll note that all trees and grass have disappeared, replaced by moss. In a short while you'll see a sign for the Edelweiss road, which leads to the Edelweissspitze, where the view is so sensational you won't believe it, and the favorite (outdoor) sport is counting the dozens and dozens of mountain peaks.

Onward, ever onward. Through the Hochtor Tunnel with a parking lot and refreshments at its exit. Three miles farther on, there's a right turn onto the Glacier road, a definite must. This road extends about five miles and begins on a fairly level grade but gradually climbs higher until it reaches the heights of Franz-Josefs-Höhe, where you can leave your car in a large garage and admire the view. There is a mountain inn on the heights, the Alpenhotel Franz-Josefs-Haus, but to reach it you must go by foot, for there is no road for cars.

Back on Grossglockner road, you continue to Heiligenblut and Winklern, where there is a right turn which takes you over the Iselsberg Pass, with a magnificent view of the jagged Lienzer Dolomites, to East Tyrol and Lienz, the main town in this area; you can proceed further west from here to South Tyrol (now located within the borders of Italy) and return via South Tyrol to Innsbruck over the Brenner Pass. The left turn from Winklern takes you onto route 106 toward Obervellach, through the Moll valley. Soon you'll be driving in an attractive valley, passing Rangerdorf and Stall and coming to Ausserfragant, where a pleasant diversionary road may be followed toward Innerfragant (no, we don't make up the names!). The main route leads to Flattach and Obervellach; the Groppenstein waterfall is not too far (about fifteen miles), if you're in the mood for a waterfall.

From Obervellach, continue on route 106 through Perk and into Spittal, a busy little town. (Interesting side trips may be made northward from Spittal, a town that still wears a medieval face, to Gmünd [via route 99] or to the shores of a lake, the Millstättersee [via route 98].

Spittal to Klagenfurt—53 miles

Follow the main road, route 100 from Spittal to Villach, an important town of about 35,000 people. From Villach, take the road (route 70) to Velden, a resort situated on the lovely Wörthersee, a ten-mile lake renowned for its extremely warm water. Here are the usual complement of resort hotels, beaches and sightseeing boats. The top hotel at Velden is the Schloss Velden, a converted castle with a lakeside restaurant where you get the best food thereabouts.

The road follows the north shore of the lake, passing through Pörtschach, another leading resort, and Krumpendorf and into Klagenfurt, a town with many remnants of its historic past and the capital of Carinthia. You should visit the Old Square (the Alterplatz), the sixteenth-century Landhaus (open 8–12, 2–5), with its twin towers, and if you're hungry there's a fair enough restaurant in this magnificent building. For an overnight stay, give thought to the Hotel Sandwirt which is reputed to have the best food in town. Just outside of Klagenfurt, on the city's western edge, is Freyenthurm Castle. It's an interesting and completely renovated castle, beautifully furnished—a delightful place to stay if you're looking for atmosphere. If you've an urge to explore Yugoslavia by heading south from Klagenfurt, visas may be obtained at the border or at the Yugoslav Consulate in Klagenfurt.

Klagenfurt to Graz—95 miles

From Klagenfurt, take route 70 to Völkermarkt, a small fortified town, where an optional right-hand turnoff on route 82 brings you to the bathing resorts on the Klopeiner Lake. On route 70, continue toward Griffen, after which careful driving is in order—hairpin turns, steep grades, narrow winding roads. You'll pass through St. Andrä, Wolfsberg and Twimberg (sounds like baby talk!).

Next comes Waldenstein, a small town guarded by an ancient castle. At Pack Höhe (the top of the pass), there is an open area in the forest (with a gas station where you can fill up your tank); then Pack, where the road begins to descend, twisting and turning sharply in the process. Continue through Köflach and Voitsberg and then into Graz, the second largest city in Austria and the capital of the federal state of Styria.

In Graz, you will be pleased with a stay at the traditional Steirerhof Hotel in the center of town, at the modern Daniel at the main station or at the Wiesler on the river bank (ask for rooms on the new top floor, which have fine views). Graz, a very old university town, is on the Mur River and has retained its charm of past centuries. The old town, the Altstadt, has the Hauptplatz as its focal point; on the southeast end of the square is the Rathaus. Nearby is that wonderful old building the Landhaus, dating back to the sixteenth century; during warm weather it doubles as a theater, so make inquiries locally as to performances if you're staying overnight. In the northern part of the old town is the Schlossberg, or Castle Hill, on which still stands the Bell Tower (with the famous Liesel bell) and the Clock Tower, the traditional emblem of Graz. Shopping, incidentally, is a great pleasure on the main drag, the Herrengasse. You'll find Graz worth a little investigation because it receives fewer tourists than more widely publicized centers like Salzburg, Innsbruck and Vienna.

Incidentally, the best food in Graz is probably at the Steirerhof Hotel; next best, we think, is the Herzlweinstube, which features Styrian dishes plus a little pleasant music. A large restaurant with fine view and garden is on the Castle Hill. Krebsenkeller, in the courtyard of an old Renaissance house, has a long bill of fare of good, local, inexpensive food and wines.

If you want to visit an exceptional museum, drive to Stübing in the environs of Graz where *Österreichisches Freilichtmuseum* (Austrian Open Air Museum) was recently opened. Thirty old original farm houses from various sections of Austria have been transplanted here and stand in an area of about 40 hectares; it will take you about three hours to visit all of them.

Graz to Vienna—127 miles

From Graz, take route 67 north toward Bruck, passing Gratkorn and Peggau, with a castle in ruins; a famous cave, the Lurgotte, is open daily 8–6. In Bruck, the Town Hall square, Hauptplatz, has a fine old building in Gothic style, called the Kornmesserhaus, and a weird-looking wrought-iron fountain dating back some 350 years.

A side trip from Bruck will take you to the old mining town of Leoben (the seat of the mining engineering university) and further west through the magnificent mountains of Upper Styria to the Enns Valley which is topped by Dachstein, the highest mountain in Styria. From the medieval town of Schladming you can drive to the foot of the Dachstein's "south wall" and glide over the vertical rock in a new aerial cable car; at the top of the mountain you can take a glacier tour in a taxi-snowmobile. Here you are actually much nearer Salzburg than Vienna and you can continue on to Salzburg if you wish, proceeding west from Schladming.

Back in Bruck and continuing in the direction of Vienna, you head for Kapfenberg (dominated by a castle housing a hotel). Then take route 17 to Kindberg, Mitterdorf and Mürzzuschlag, a particularly busy place during the skiing season, and don't forget the sport is said to have originated in this Austrian town (although Norway claims the honor)—then to Semmering, a luxury health resort; you might spend a pleasant day or so at the hotel Südbahnhotel (where the swimming pool is enclosed, just in case). If you still can digest more scenery, make a side trip to the nearby Hirschenkogel Mountain, the summit of which can be reached by a chair lift; or drive your car to the top of Sonnwendstein Mountain—40 cents toll.

On to Gloggnitz, a summer resort overpowered by Gloggnitz Castle, a mere 900 years old; if you want an exciting ride, try the aerial ropeway to the Raxalpe, 6,500 feet high. Then Neunkirchen and Wiener Neustadt, which were heavily bombed during the war. A little further is the famous spa of Baden, which after the war had the misfortune of being the headquarters of the Soviet occupation troops in Austria; when the Soviets departed in 1955, they left Baden in such poor shape that the rebuilding and cleaning has only recently been completed. The best hotels here are the new Park, overlooking the beautiful spa park (Kurpark), and Herzoghof with its own thermal spring. The next and final stop on this Austrian tour is Vienna, where you started.

For a last look around, you can take the elevator up to the observation platform on Vienna's new Danube Tower, which rises more than 750 feet above the city. Near the top is a good restaurant. There is also a nice coffee bar.

❧ Motoring in Austria

Austria uses the principle of "confidence" as the basis for driving practices. This means that in general the driver can be confident that all other drivers are proceeding in a proper manner. But don't get overconfident. Be careful all the time, because anything from a farm tractor to a tourist bus can unexpectedly turn upon the road just ahead. The driver approaching from the right, as a general rule, has the right of way. There are some exceptions. Here again, before exercising your priority as you come to an intersection, look both ways.

There is no speed limit as a general rule, but in towns and built-up areas the maximum permitted is 50 kilometers an hour (about 30 miles).

When overtaking a streetcar, you pass on the *right* and stop when the streetcar stops to discharge and load passengers; you are allowed to proceed only after the streetcar starts moving again and after all the passengers have safely reached the sidewalk. The streetcars always have right of way and you are not permitted to drive on the streetcar tracks.

In the central sections of cities there are the so-called blue zones (marked by shields and blue lines) where you are allowed to park only up to 1½ hours; you have to use special cardboard parking shields (obtainable from the automobile club, the police, and tobacco shops at no charge) indicating the time of your arrival.

Gasoline is about 50 cents a gallon for "regular" and 60 cents for "super."

There are almost 20,000 miles of roads in Austria, and they are of all types—from autobahns (superhighways) to mountain passages. Roads are very good, although frequently narrow. Close to cities, road surfaces are cement, but farther out they usually are asphalt. It is part of Austria's charm that one can wander about, completely at random, on the side roads that seem to lead nowhere. You'll see rural countryside, sometimes delightful national costumes and loads of local color.

Austria has a number of toll roads, and they usually lead up some mountain. The special maintenance required to keep roads open in the high altitudes is the explanation for the tolls. The Alpine highway stretching across the Grossglockner is a toll road, but, most important, it is one of the most spectacular mountain roads you can encounter anywhere. Nearby is another extremely scenic high Alpine road, the Felber Tauern Road, which carries the same toll as the Grossglockner Road (minimum about $5; a round-trip ticket, about $8.50, is valid on either of these two roads).

An autobahn—*free!*—has been built between Vienna and Salzburg, one is under construction to connect Vienna with the south and has been finished as far as Wiener Neustadt. Happily, the Tyrol Autobahn from Kufstein to Brenner has now been completed and the section between Innsbruck and Brenner is operated as a toll road (about $2.50 a car; close to $4 for a round trip). But why ride on an autobahn? It's dull, uninteresting and not recommended unless you are pressed for time. Why come to Austria if you're looking for a superhighway where you won't see a thing?

Be particularly careful on mountain highways. During July and August, the experienced bus drivers tear up and down the narrowest roads, often passing the timid tourist with an inch to spare (or less, it seems sometimes). Remember that a vehicle climbing a hill *always* has the right of way over one going downhill. Don't plan on going through any Alpine pass without checking locally as to the road's navigability and such happenstances of nature as snow and rock slides. A good source of information is (are you ready?) the Oesterreichischer Automobil, Motorrad and Touring Club—the Austrian Automobile Club—at 7 Schubertring, Vienna I. The club's abbreviated name is ÖAMTC, thank goodness!

Most of the customs formalities have been removed for tourists' automobiles. Merely show your passport and the green insurance card and, usually, you will be waved on your way at the border crossing. Occasionally you'll be asked to produce the car ownership registration and your driver's license. Your home-state license is good *if* it is accompanied by a translation in German that has been made by an Austrian consular or tourist official or by an Austrian or foreign automobile club. It's easier to have an international license with you. Oh, yes. Foreign-registered cars coming into the country should have a nationality identification plate at the rear of the vehicle— USA for an American-registered car, F for French, I for Italian, etc.

In very small towns, the ancient streets are extremely narrow, and American cars frequently find the going difficult. Use care and exercise patience because, when all is said and done, you're an unofficial American ambassador. Avoid small incidents, even if you have to give up the right of way once in a while. Any accident or collision may cost you a precious afternoon or so in clearing up a lot of paper work.

Pointer: You can "piggyback" your car through the Tauern Tunnel, between the train stations of Boeckstein and Mallnitz, and through the Arlberg Tunnel, between the stations of St. Anton am Arlberg and Langen. The average tarriff is a little over $5.

BELGIUM

National Characteristics

Remember those nice words Julius Caesar said about the Belgians? On his conquering journey through Gaul he had encountered many different armies. "Of all these," he said, "the bravest are the Belgians." They are brave indeed. The small section of land that is present-day Belgium has been traversed, fought over and occupied by many of the major powers of history. But the Belgians, each time the shooting is over, gather up the pieces and with great energy confidently rebuild. They did that at the time of the Norman invasion, and, a thousand years after the Normans, they rebuilt when World War I ended. The Nazis invaded and occupied their country during World War II. When *that* war was over, the Belgians set out once again to rebuild their homeland.

The Belgians are an amazing people. They like the creature comforts and the good things of life—whether it is food, a big American car or the latest in filter cigarettes. But they work for these things.

The Belgians work hard, too. In big cities as well as villages you will find many shops open early in the morning and late in the evening—and on Sundays, too. Two decades ago, when just about all of postwar Western Europe was still buying food and clothing with ration cards, the Belgian economy was already moving into high gear. Their economic philosophy is much like America's. They prefer to rely on initiative and hard work, rather than on economy-controlling rules and doctrines.

Belgium is one of the world's few remaining monarchies. But don't look for too much pageantry or ceremonial show. The immense palace in Brussels usually looks as if it were uninhabited. King Baudouin and his queen, Fabiola, generally reside at the smaller palace at Laeken, on the northern edge of Brussels. Belgium's monarch, by the way, is not called "the Belgian king." His title is King of the Belgians.

The Belgian people have a colorful, important ancestry —from painters to men of political affairs. The counts of Flanders and the dukes of Brabant helped shape European history.

At the big international exposition in Brussels a decade ago, science and technology were basic themes. Interest in things technical is nothing new for Belgians. The first European railroad was inaugurated at Brussels in 1835. The first international telephone link was the one between Paris and Brussels, set up in 1886. Brussels is now the home of the headquarters of the Common Market. NATO, meanwhile, has established its headquarters near Mons in southern Belgium.

The country is densely populated. There are about 9.3 million people in Belgium—750 to each square mile. Most live in the urban centers. There are more than 1 million in Brussels.

Belgium is divided into two linguistic zones, which are roughly the same size. In the northern zone Flemish dialects of Dutch are spoken. In the southern zone, French (and Walloon dialects) are spoken. The Dutch-speaking Belgians are called Flemings and the French-speaking ones are Walloons. Brussels, as the capital, is an island mixed linguistically. Both languages are spoken in the city proper, but on the outskirts the people speak just one language—Flemish. In the eastern corner of Belgium, in the Eupen and St.-Vith regions, some 80,000 Belgians speak German.

Except for language there are no main differences between Flemings and Walloons. The Flemish people probably look a bit more Nordic, while the Walloons are more easily identifiable with southern neighbors.

When to Go

The best weather months are April through September, but even if the outside temperature is on the down side, the insides of homes, buildings and hotels are heated in the American manner. Fog often moves into the Ardennes in the fall. Summer throughout the country is generally warm but not really hot. A day of cloudy skies in the summer can bring the temperature down. Rain, especially in the autumn and winter, is not at all unusual. So bring that lightweight raincoat.

WEATHER STRIP: BRUSSELS

Temp.	JAN.	FEB.	MAR.	APR.	MAY	JUNE	JULY	AUG.	SEPT.	OCT.	NOV.	DEC.
Low	30°	33°	35°	40°	46°	52°	55°	55°	52°	44°	38°	33°
High	39°	43°	49°	57°	64°	70°	73°	72°	67°	56°	48°	42°
Average	35°	38°	42°	49°	55°	61°	64°	64°	60°	50°	43°	38°
Days of rain	15	15	15	16	16	17	16	16	16	17	18	18

TIME EVALUATION ¶ On a month's trip to Europe, about four days would be ideal for seeing Belgium. Two days are sufficient for Brussels, and the balance could be used in visiting Bruges and Ghent and/or the Ardennes area. If you're planning to tour the Benelux countries by car, it would be best to allow at least a week (ten days, possibly, if you want to do it leisurely). Even on a very short visit to Belgium, it would be possible to drive out to Bruges and Ghent and return the same day, if necessary. Of course, it would be more enjoyable if you could take more time.

PASSPORT AND VISA ¶ Passport required; no visa for a stay of three months or less.

CUSTOMS AND IMMIGRATION ¶ If you are entering Belgium from one of its Common Market neighbors (France, Luxembourg, Germany or the Netherlands) you might not even meet a customs inspector. Even if there is a customs inspection, it will be quick and easy as a rule. Two cartons of cigarettes or 100 cigars or 200 cigarillos or 500 grams (17½ ounces) of tobacco—or a combination of these tobacco products—are permitted into the country without duty. You can also have with you two bottles of wine or a bottle of liquor. Perfume (maximum of 50 grams), toilet water (one liter), one portable musical instrument, one portable radio, one pair of binoculars, one camera (12 rolls of film), one movie camera (reasonable amount of film), one record player (20 records) and such sports gear as fishing and hunting equipment (including one gun and 50 cartridges) may be brought into Belgium by a visitor without duty.

HEALTH ¶ The water is safe, but it is best in rural areas to follow the European practice of drinking bottled waters. Make sure the milk you drink is pasteurized. There is also a sterilized type of milk (*lait sterilisé*), which keeps indefinitely. But this is not like the milk you drink at home.

TIME ¶ Six hours later than Eastern Standard Time. When it's 6 P.M. in Brussels, it's noon in New York. When Daylight Saving Time is in effect, the time difference is only 5 hours.

CURRENCY ¶ The Belgium *franc* is the unit of currency in Belgium. Its value in relation to the dollar fluctuates with changes in the international money market but for quick calculation you can figure a franc is worth about 2 cents. The franc is composed of 100 *centimes*.

PRICE LEVEL ¶ This country has a high standard of living, and prices generally are on the high side. But quality is high, too. Luxury hotels in Brussels run from $25, or thereabouts, for a single room and $35 for a double. Restaurant charges in Brussels can be low in good cafeteria-style places, but they will be on the high side (from about $10 up per person) in the luxury restaurants. In the provinces, a gastronomic meal in the best restaurant in town will usually be $6 and up. In the free enterprise system of Belgium, hotel rates are the kind of thing that can change without too much notice.

TIPPING ¶ A 15 percent service charge is added to hotel and restaurant bills, and that's enough. Do not confuse it with a 6 percent government tax that is added as well. However, in cafes, pastry shops and cafeterias the bill is usually presented without *service*. So, as a tip give 15 to 25 percent, depending on the size of the bill. If a coffee, for instance, costs 12 francs, give a 3-franc tip. At all railroad stations the official rate for porters is 10 francs for one or two bags; 15 francs for three or four; and 20 francs for five or six. If you are part of a group, a flat charge of 7½ francs a person is made, regardless of the number of pieces of luggage. Between 10 P.M. and 5 A.M. there is a 25 percent boost in tariffs.

TRANSPORTATION ¶ *Taxicab* drivers require a lot of watchfulness. They dearly love to extract their own tip, in advance, out of your money (and they have very big ideas on the subject of tipping!). So keep an eye on the meter when it comes to cab-paying time. Don't agree to any extra charges except those for a big suitcase or several pieces of luggage. They will also usually try to charge you "for the distance back to the cab stand." Rates are pretty much like New York's. Give a tip of 20 percent (yes, that's right) on the meter, but at least 5 francs.

Rail service in Belgium is excellent. The Belgian National Railways goes everywhere in the country, and very often. To travel the main line points, such as Liège, Bruges, Mons, Antwerp, Namur, Ostend and Malines (among others), a timetable is not necessary for the traveler who happens to be in Brussels. Trains leave at ten-, twenty-, or thirty-minute intervals for most places you'll be headed. In Brussels—and also in Antwerp—check on the particular railroad station you'll be arriving at or departing from. Brussels has three main stations; Antwerp, two. First Class rail travel costs about 8 cents a mile; Second Class, about 6 cents; although as the mileage goes up the charge per mile goes down. But you don't need to go First Class. The trains are good in Second Class and distances are not great, anyway. There are special reduced-rate tickets for unlimited rail travel, and commutation tickets good for five, ten and fifteen days. If you're going to be a big train rider while in Belgium, check into them.

Helicopters connect Brussels with many other Belgian cities. The new Brussels airport at Zaventem is about ten miles from the city. Trains operate every half-hour between the airport and the Gare Centrale in Brussels (the air terminal is nearby and there is direct access to it from the station).

Trams or trolley cars are a principal means of getting around many cities, especially big ones like Brussels. The average Brussels fare is about 20 cents, and varies with the zone. Trolly cars also operate through the countryside and along the entire coastline of Belgium, from the Netherlands to France. Gradually, the sturdy trams are being replaced by buses.

COMMUNICATIONS ¶ *Airmail letters* to the United States cost a minimum of about a quarter. The Main Post Office, which used to be at the Place de la Monnaie in

Brussels, has been moved a few blocks away to the Rue des Halles. So if you don't see it where it was the last time you were in Brussels, don't blame your memory. It is only open until 8 P.M. (weekdays), but the post office at Gare du Midi (Avenue Fonsny) is open night and day, including Sunday (between 8 P.M. and 8 A.M., however, only for special delivery and air mail). Long-distance *phone calls* can be made either from your hotel or from a post office. You can place a local call from a sidewalk cabin or from a cafe. Direct dialing is old stuff in Belgium for calls around the country. Local calls are 5 francs, the first long distance zone within Belgium 10 francs for six minutes, the second zone 20 francs for the same time. *Telegrams* are definitely not suggested here, for one simple reason—they probably never will reach their destination. I'm sorry, but that's the way it is, despite what the hotel concierge may say to the contrary.

BASIC FRENCH AND FLEMISH ¶ See the sections on France and the Netherlands. Written Flemish is the same as Dutch, although the spoken language has its own characteristics.

ELECTRICITY ¶ Both 110 A.C. and 220 A.C. are used, so be sure to inquire before plugging in an American appliance. Because of the different type of sockets you will need an international plug.

FOOD SPECIALTIES AND LIQUOR ¶ The food of Belgium, particularly in Brussels, is just about as good as the best in Europe, *including* France. Naturally, the fare varies between the elegant, expensive restaurants in cities such as Brussels and Antwerp, which serve international French-style cuisine, and the menu you are served in a small, unpretentious spot in the countryside. But both meals can be memorable.

Generally, dining is a treat throughout the country. You'll eat well almost anywhere you go. Among the appetizers, *jambon d'Ardennes*, thin slices of smoked ham, is a memorable choice. Shrimp are excellent, although the Belgians have an absolute mania for serving them stuffed in a tomato, *tomate aux crevettes*. Crayfish are a must when they appear on the menu (mostly along the seacoast). That goes for trout, too. The favorite preparation is *à la meunière*, with melted butter. Sausages are popular. *Boudin noir* is a black sausage that could not, in all honesty, be recommended to everyone. On the other hand, *boudin blanc aux raisins*, the white type of sausage served with grapes, is a delicacy anyone can eat —and, what's more, is sure to enjoy.

A popular meat dish is *carbonade flamande*, small cuts of beef prepared in a rich beer sauce, and when it is good, it's very good indeed. The *waterzooï* is another specialty, a sort of thick soup-stew usually made with chicken and beloved by the Belgians. A *hochepot* is nothing more or less than a stew with vegetables, but properly appetizing on a cold day.

The most popular single meat is a steak, served, naturally, with fried potatoes (called *frites*). Another big favorite is goose. Look for it prepared *à l'instar de Visé*, with cream sauce. *Poularde Bruxelloise* is excellent, and game dishes in the fall are a treat—particularly in the Ardennes region.

Along the seacoast, the fishermen bring in loads of mussels (*moules*). They are not particularly popular with Americans but are beloved by the local folk when served, boiled, in a big bowl. If you are so inclined, try them with fried potatoes, *moules et frites*—not a bad combination. Pickled or fried fish and eels are also specialties here. In traveling along the western coast, try the sole —fresh from the sea. Many of the Belgian soups are good but, we think, too rich and fatty as a rule. Brussels sprouts and endives (called *chicorées* in French, so don't get confused) are the favorite vegetables, and you owe it to yourself to try them. And don't overlook another vegetable specialty: *asperges de Malines*. A novel vegetable is hop shoots. These tender young greens of the hop plant, otherwise best known for flavoring beer, are called *jets d'houblon* and are a springtime specialty, served with shirred eggs.

Cheese fanciers will be pleased with Belgian varieties, although they are not often classed with the French greats. If you chance to be here during the autumn fruit season (especially the grapes), you are fortunate indeed. Belgium has also specialized in growing hot-house grapes that are magnificent. Every area in the country offers its own local tart, candy, cake, cookie, sweet bread, macaroon, shortcake, pastry, wafer or biscuit—all very good and properly fattening. Even the smallest towns have topflight *patisseries* that produce a wonderful array of homemade, cream-filled pastries and cakes. Usually, pastry shops have tables and you can have a coffee or a pot of tea with your calorie-filled cake.

Theoretically, the sale of strong liquors is restricted in Belgium. The semiprohibition law goes back to the old days when dockers in the port of Antwerp were paid by the day and spent a good part of their wages in a bar before heading home. But don't give the prohibition on strong liquors a second thought. Few Belgians seem to. Generally, the visitor will have no difficulty in being served French wines, cognac, whiskies and liqueurs. The same goes for a Martini or mixed drink. The beer drinker will be in seventh heaven in Belgium. Because of restrictions on alcoholic purchases, the Belgians lean toward beer—and have the highest per capita beer consumption in Europe. Beer ranges from the mild *bière de table* to the really potent kind. There is a lot of leeway in the liquor laws for the brewers to come up with quite a beer. As a result, some beers are quite powerful. The best and the strongest are the so-called Trappist beers (not all of which are produced by Trappists), such as Orval or Westmalle.

CASINOS ¶ Gambling is forbidden by law in Belgium. But don't bet on it! What we mean is that gambling, although forbidden, is "tolerated" in eight watering places conveniently located around the country. The casinos at these places are private clubs, but you can become a member for a couple of dollars or so. The only people banned from these clubs (among Belgians) are notaries public, civil servants and military officers—in other words, people who have positions of public responsibility and who have to be protected from the temptation to gamble with other people's money. Four of the casinos are on the coast (Middelkerke, Blankenberg, Knokke and Ostend) and the other four are in the Ardennes (Spa, Chaudfontaine, Namur and Dinant). The Ostend Casino, along with about 70 percent of the city, was destroyed in World War II, but it has been beautifully rebuilt and is once again gleaming and alluring at the seaside.

SPAS ¶ Don't think we have made a mistake if we say a famous Belgian spa is Spa in the Ardennes area. That is exactly the name: its waters were attracting the equivalent of the jet set in the eighteenth century and the word "spa" was applied eventually to all delightful places on the continent where springs bubbled and social life was lively as well. For a while the resort lost its old-time popularity. But a great deal of money and attention have been devoted in recent years to improving everything, and it is again a fine place to visit. The other most famous Belgian spa is Chaudfontaine, whose name can be translated as "warm fountain." Its mineral springs are very warm, too!

SPORTS ¶ The most popular sport in Belgium is *bicycle racing*. It is to the Belgians what bullfighting is to the Spaniards. There is a big Paris-Brussels bike race in April, but whenever you're driving around the country—from spring to autumn—you are likely to encounter a platoon of bike racers on the highways. So be warned! Usually the races are on a Sunday afternoon, and at strategic crossings in the countryside *gendarmes* take up posts to control automobile traffic. The bike riders, quite naturally, have the right of way. There are two topnotch *golf courses* in Brussels (at Tervueren and Ohain) and other first-rate courses throughout the country at Antwerp, Ghent, Houyet, Knokke, Liège, Mons, Ostend and Spa. Brussels has four hippodromes that feature *horse racing* at different times of the year. At Boitsfort hippodrome, there is flat racing on Sunday afternoons from September to April; Sterrebeek, trotting, flat racing and hurdles, the year around; Zellick, flat racing from September to April; and Groenendael, flat racing and hurdles, Sunday afternoons from September to April. Ostend has a splendid race track, too, Hippodrome Wellington, which provides plenty of *divertissement* for horse fanciers in the summer. On Saturday, Sunday, Monday and Thursday afternoons in July and August, the horses are running at Ostend. The first two weeks of September are for the trotters. Along the sandy beach stretching from La Panne, near the French border, to Middelkerke (just below Ostend) Belgians like to practice a favorite and spectacular sport, *land yachting*. It is a form of sailboating on sand with sail-driven platforms on wheels.

PLACE-NAMES ¶ The use of two languages in Belgium results in some spectacular differences in the names of many towns and cities you'll be looking for on your drive through Belgium. Usually, the name is given both in French and Flemish on the road signs, not always. In the troubles over language in recent years, bilingual road signs are often illegally altered at night to show only the language that is the official (or popular) one for the particular linguistic zone in which the sign is located. So it is good to know the names of main places in both languages. "Brussels" (in English) is no real problem. The Flemish word is "Brussel," and in French it is "Bruxelles." But "Mons" (French and English) becomes "Bergen" in Flemish. Did you know that? "Liège," spelled the same in English and French, is "Luik" in Flemish. Here are some other names of places you'll be visiting that undergo a change from one language to another:

French	Flemish
Alost	Aalst
Anvers	Antwerpen
Audenarde	Oudenaarde
Bruges	Brugge
Courtrai	Kortrijk
Furnes	Veurne
Gand	Gent
Grammont	Geraardsbergen
La Panne	De Panne
Laethem-St. Martin	Sint-Martens-Latem
Leau	Zoutleeuw
Louvain	Leuven
Malines	Mechelen
Renaix	Ronse
Roulers	Roeselare
Saint-Nicolas	Sint-Niklaas
Saint-Trond	Sint-Truiden
Tamise	Temse
Termonde	Dendermonde
Tirlemont	Tienen
Tongres	Tongeren
Ypres	Ieper

MOTORING IN BELGIUM ¶ Two peculiarly Belgian characteristics are gradually disappearing from the roads of Belgium. One is the cobblestones. The other is the absence of driver's licenses. Licenses are being introduced (slowly), but a number of drivers still do not have them. The cobblestones, which used to make postwar driving bumpy, are being replaced by fine highways and *autoroutes*. There are, as a result of these road improvements, no real distances in Belgium. The *autoroute* to the west—to Ostend—makes it possible to cover the sixty miles in an hour. There is another new *autoroute* that goes to Liège, on the east, and on to the German border at Aachen (Aix-la-Chapelle). The drive to Antwerp, on the north, and the one to Mons, to the south, are on a fine highway. You'll find good roads in all directions.

There are no particular customs formalities for bringing a car into Belgium. You need your home-state driver's license and an international certificate of insurance (the Green Card, *Carte Verte*). If you don't have this Green Card you can buy, at the border, an insurance policy for about $5 that will be good for ten days. Gasoline is about 65 cents a gallon for regular and near 70 cents for super. Oil is 70 cents a quart. A *Touring-Secours* (help to drivers) service will help you in breakdowns on the highway or in the city. Inspectors, in cars or on motorcycles, cover the highways and if your car gets balky, it won't be long before one of the Touring-Secours people shows up on the horizon. Parking space in this prosperous country is hard to find—that is, if you want to park your car in the center of a big city rather than on a village side street. But many parking stations have been built in the major cities. Brussels has one on the Boulevard Pachèco for 1,500 cars. It is called, appropriately, Parking City.

Oh, yes, it's been said that the Belgians are the worst drivers in Europe. I find no reason to argue with that very moderate statement, which seems true on every possible count.

SIGHTSEEING ¶ From sand dunes set out like giant works of sculpture along the west coast to prehistoric grottoes in the Ardennes and from medieval monasteries to the mining area of the Borinage that Van Gogh painted, Belgium has lots of things for the sightseer to see. The great port of Antwerp, as cosmopolitan and as interesting a port city as any you'll come across in your continental travels, is only thirty miles from Brussels. Beyond the forests south of Brussels you can continue on through the celebrated Ardennes forestland, a wonderplace of nature brightened at fitting intervals by wondrous inns with comfortable fireplaces, perfect table settings and food of excellent quality. In the fields of Flanders, in western Belgium, are graves of Americans who died in World War I or II. On the eastern frontier of Belgium, not far from the Grand Duchy of Luxembourg, is Bastogne, where American General McAuliffe, when asked by the Nazis to give up, gave a one-word reply: "Nuts!" Or so they say. The tranquil life in towns and villages is a pleasant, fascinating contrast to the busy routine of the big cities. Formally laid-out bicycle paths line the highways, along which high-powered cars speed. Belgium has much for the sightseer to see, and to note, and to ponder. There are traditional celebrations of a spiritual nature, such as the Procession of the Holy Blood at Bruges early in May. There are also a large number of happy events and festivals that are traditional but have no religious association. The pre-Lenten carnivals at Malmédy, Fosse, Eupen, Aalst and Stavelot are spirited and lots of fun. Tens of thousands of people gather in the little town of Binche at carnival time each year for the big parade and the unique street battle that is fought with oranges. Yes, oranges! For ten centuries a classic saga from Germanic folklore has been presented each May 1 at Russon. In other words, there's lots doing everywhere. The marionette shows at Brussels, Antwerp and Liège are renowned (that means they are really wonderful!). On the boulevards of Brussels and in villages around the country a weekend *kermesse* (fair) is usually under way. The town of Bokrijk has an open air folklore museum, which in a genial, intriguing fashion gives an easy bird's-eye view of Belgium and Belgians.

There is lots to *hear*, also. All the main cities have opera companies, theaters, music halls and concert halls. What is particularly unique in Belgium is the number of carillons, which are still played from belfries, cathedral towers and town halls. Malines (Mechelen, in Flemish) is the home of a world-famous school for carillon players, and the bells are always sounding through the streets. In other cities, especially in Flanders, the carillons generally play on the hour and the half-hour.

Capital City

One of these days Brussels is going to be recognized, all of a sudden, as the most modern Old World capital on the continent. Ever since the end of World War II it has been tearing down old ramshackle buildings in the general area of where the Gare Centrale is now situated and erecting massive modern palaces that are used for government and private offices. It is quite a complex and, as we said, is growing and being added to all the time.

Brussels is today a twentieth-century metropolis, a

patina overlaid upon a base of history, offering the tourist the best of two worlds—an opportunity to examine various phases of the past in modern comfort. The city is completely enclosed by a series of wide boulevards that were laid out by Napoleon. (He was the one who met his you-know-what in 1815 at, er, Waterloo, just south of Brussels.) Technically, the city of Brussels is only the general downtown area and it is small suburban communities such as St.-Gilles, Schaerbeek and Ixelles that give it its great size. You don't have to concern yourselves with such technicalities. We mention it, however, because it can be a bit confusing to be walking along a Brussels street and suddenly see two foot patrolmen wearing uniforms that have on their shoulder patches an identifying name you never heard of before.

Because of a hill that slopes upward from the Grand' Place toward Porte Louise and Porte Namur, Brussels gives the appearance of being divided into an upper and lower town. But the people of Brussels do not refer to their city that way. They'll use some geographical landmark, like Porte Louise, the Bourse (which is near the Grand' Place) or Place Rogier (which is not far from the North Station, the *Gare du Nord*).

The Grand' Place is the heart of Brussels, impressive in scope and charming at all hours of day or night, although everyone you meet has his favorite time there —dawn, early morning, late afternoon, sunset or evening (with or without moonlight). The Grand' Place is particularly interesting at dawn, when the fruits and vegetables arrive, much as they did in the old days at the now-departed Les Halles in Paris (but on a much smaller scale). Later in the morning it becomes a riot of color once more, like a flower market. On Sundays it metamorphoses into a twittering bird market. At night, the square is floodlit, an oasis of romance and memories of past eras.

The 500-year-old Hôtel de Ville (Town Hall), which is in the Grand' Place, is unquestionably the architectural gem of Brussels. The exterior, with its statue of St. Michael (the patron of the city) and the Dragon, and a 295-foot tower; and the interior with the Lion Staircase, the elaborately adorned Council Chamber and Salle des Marriages, will not disappoint any viewer. (Visiting hours are weekdays 9 A.M. to noon and 1:30–5 P.M.; Saturdays, Sundays and holidays, 9 A.M. to noon.) The Maison du

Roi, opposite the Hôtel de Ville, is a 16th century building and not, we find, terribly fascinating.

In 1695, the lower part of Brussels was set afire and razed during one of the innumerable wars that plagued the city, and therefore most of the buildings date after that historic event. Flanking the Hôtel de Ville are a series of opulent, overornamented but nonetheless remarkable-looking buildings, which were headquarters of medieval trade guilds. These guild houses for bakers, tailors, painters and many others are worth examining. Only a block west of the Grand' Place is the Eglise St. Nicolas (St. Nicholas' Church), which dates back to the origins of the city. It once collapsed during a bombardment (in 1695), but was later rebuilt. The latest restoration work was done on the façade a dozen years ago.

A few steps from the Grand' Place is the mascot of Brussels—the world-renowned statue of Manneken-Pis— a small bronze figure of a young boy making water, you should excuse the expression. Some few people find the statue slightly distasteful, but to the vast majority, it is Brussels' most amusing landmark. The figure was sculptured by Duquesnoy in 1619 but was broken into pieces by mischievous boys about 150 years ago. The pieces were found, however, and a new figure cast from them. As a matter of fact, the Manneken is called the oldest resident of Brussels.

At another time, when you are in the Grand' Place, head past St. Nicholas' Church and you'll find yourself on the Rue du Marché aux Herbes. Near the intersection of this street with Rue de la Montagne are interesting glass-covered arcades: Galerie de la Reine, Galerie du Roi, and Galerie des Princes (Queen's Arcade, King's Arcade and Arcade of Princes). This hundred-year-old structure contains fine shops, restaurants and theaters. You can pass several pleasant hours in the arcade, particularly if the weather happens to be bad.

Other sights worth viewing include the cathedral, dating back almost 800 years; the Church of Notre Dame de la Chapelle, where artist Pieter Breughel the Elder is buried; the Law Courts (Palais de Justice) absolutely immense— one of the largest buildings in the world; and the Place Royale, on the hill overlooking the downtown area. The Place Royale is an impressive French-designed setting of majestic proportions built in the eighteenth century.

Just north of Brussels at Laeken, and not far from the royal chateau, are the Japanese Tower and the Oriental Pavilion. Here are the famous greenhouses, open during the last week of April and the first week of May.

Waterloo battlefield, where Wellington once and for all time took the measure of Napoleon, is only a short ride from Brussels. The Butte de Lion, or Lion's Mound, approximately 150 feet high, is a hill raised in 1825. On the top there stands a statue of a lion. Nearby you'll find a museum that has on display an oil painting depicting a panorama of the great battle. Unless you are very much interested in the Napoleonic Wars, all of this is not apt to be terribly exciting, nor an exceptional day's outing.

(Note: A tour of the Belgian countryside is included in the section on the Netherlands.)

BRUSSELS HOTELS

Hilton: This is a typical Hilton Hotel—large, good-size rooms, pleasant public area and rather good service. The food is wholesome and very American. Room prices are fairly high. Like other Brussels hotels, there is a service charge of 15 percent, plus 6% government tax.

Westbury: A new 252-room, very modern hotel in the downtown Grand' Place area; very elaborate; several restaurants; on the expensive side.

Amigo: Rather modern, and conveniently located downtown. Prices of some smaller rooms are relatively low—*relatively,* we said; others are high—yes, *high*!

Palace: An outstanding, old-style hotel. Very attractive rooms, all with private bath; rooms with a view of the park are quieter than those facing the Place Rogier. A fine hotel; from $15 to twice that for a double room.

Metropole: A big, well-run establishment right on the Place de Brouckère. Rooms are larger than average, although the décor is routine. Often a bit more expensive than the Palace.

Plaza: Very spacious rooms in this moderate-size establishment. An excellent hotel, located on the main Brussels downtown boulevard. Rates are remarkably reasonable for a hotel of this caliber.

Albert I: Convenient location on the Place Rogier. An older hotel, but one that has maintained its traditional excellence; moderately priced.

Atlanta: A medium-size hotel on the edge of Place de Brouckère. Average-size rooms and routine furnishings; but the rates are quite reasonable.

Mayfair: A new and very modern place on Avenue Louise with 100 luxurious rooms, among them 40 with private bars and 20 with kitchenettes; the hotel also has a 50-car garage.

MacDonald: A new luxury establishment on the Avenue Louise. Has a delightful Continental ambiance. Among its amenities are several splendid bars and a topnotch restaurant.

Pointer: About two dozen former castlelike mansions in Belgium now have accommodations for guests.

BRUSSELS RESTAURANTS

Villa Lorraine: If you're a gourmet and don't mind a high check, you might want to see if you agree with the general opinion that this is about the best restaurant around. Very expensive.

Aux Armes de Bruxelles: A cheerful, attractive and appealing restaurant serving good food in very pleasant surroundings. Medium to expensive.

Le Cygne: Extremely fine food served in attractive, dignified surroundings. Well located near the Grand' Place.

Epaule de Mouton: An excessively publicized restaurant, small and inviting, serving very good food. Very few tables; reservations absolutely essential. Dishes are quite rich by American tastes; fairly expensive.

La Couronne: Please try to reserve a table for yourself at the window looking out into the Grand' Place. The view through the window will complement the superb setting of the restaurant. Very fine French and Belgian food in this sophisticated, soigné establishment. Fairly expensive, but the food and service warrant the prices.

Filet de Boeuf: Small, intimate and excellent. Because there are only a few tables in the whole place, it is wise to make reservations very early.

Canterbury: A pleasant restaurant serving about average food at moderately high prices; classic French dishes are the specialty. There is a long menu and everything is wonderful.

Rôtisserie d'Alsace: An Alsatian-style, featuring the light Alsatian wines that go so well with *choucroute garnie* (a hot sauerkraut dish with frankfurters, sausages and other pork items). Alsatian dishes are always on the menu.

Le Carlton: An excellent and outstanding restaurant serving first-quality food; not inexpensive but worthwhile. A favorite of Belgians who want to show visitors how excellent Belgian cuisine is.

Provençaux: Very good seafood, some of it in southern French style. The suggested fixed-price menus are usually very acceptable. Prices are moderate unless you order the most expensive a la carte dishes.

PUBLIC HOLIDAYS: ¶ New Year's, Easter Monday, Labor Day (May 1), Ascension Day, Whit Monday, Independence Day (July 21), Assumption (Aug. 15), All Saints Day (Nov. 1), Armistice Day (Nov. 11), Dynasty Day (Nov. 15) and Christmas.

SHOPPING ¶ Sad to relate, Belgium is not a bargain treasure trove for shoppers, although attractive articles and good values are to be found. Because the country has high living and labor standards, mostly everything you can think of is readily available—at realistic, no-bargain prices. There are, however, a few exceptions that warrant discussion.

Lace, of course, is the favorite Belgian shopping specialty and as a rule represents good value. Belgian lace is usually white, although occasionally beige or honey color, and there is even black lace from Beaumont. You'll see lace being made, and sold, in Brussels, Bruges, Malines and some smaller towns. If the weather is nice and you're lucky, you'll see old women in white bonnets making lace in their doorways along the canals in Bruges. Lace ranges in price from a few dollars for a simply doily or place mat to several hundred dollars for a tablecloth and napkins—and higher for some wedding dresses. Some good shops are clustered around the cathedral in Brussels.

Glassware design and quality are superb. Val St. Lambert is in a unique class; its prices match the standards, and both are high. Don't worry about shipments home, because delivery is guaranteed. If you want an unsolicited piece of information, don't buy just a dozen of a type of glassware. Take three or four extras so that if a piece breaks later, your set will be intact—and so will your nerves.

Copper pots, stoneware and earthenware cooking utensils are marvelous for the gourmet or hobbyist cook. Prices are low and these make unusual gifts. The *dinanderie* (copperware) of Dinant is well known. If you're driving along the Meuse, look at the Dinant copperware and also taste the city's famous cakes.

Leather goods are excellent although not so cheap as in Italy. Purses, wallets, belts and gloves are very well made and the prices represent good value, if not startling bargains.

Shoes, particularly the higher-priced ones, are made in Brussels and Bruges and are smart, up to date and well styled. By far the leading woman's shoemaker is the firm of De Busschere of Bruges; superb quality may be found in their outstanding styles. Make sure you are fitted properly, because European lasts vary slightly from American ones.

Rifles and shotguns are high priced but are still bargains because the same articles cost substantially more in the United States. Belgian guns have been bought by the American army and many a general shopping for a hunting rifle. If you are in the vicinity of Liège, do your shopping for firearms there.

Chocolates are a big local specialty because Belgians have a sweet tooth and are fond of luscious confections. These may be eaten as you walk, or in your hotel room; given to anyone who is kind enough to ask you to lunch or dinner; or shipped home.

Lingerie and blouses in the higher-priced category are beautifully executed, but appear sleazy and unimpressive when mass-produced and low in cost.

Doodads and geegaws make up the sort of junk inexperienced tourists tend to bring home, admire momentarily when they unpack and then push into some dark closet. Please don't buy them. But, if in spite of our urging you insist, there are such things as carvings made in "Spa" wood, slate figurines, miniature stained-glass windows, miniature anchors, miniature baskets of fish and—for heaven's sake—even seashells glued on top of a Kleenex box!

Antiques and all sorts of odds and ends may be bargained for at the Brussels Flea Market (Marché aux Puces) in the Place du Jeu de Balle, or on Sunday mornings in the Rue des Radis. Go just for amusement, even if you don't want anything.

The Rue Neuve (right behind Place de Brouckère) is the favorite shopping street of the Brussels residents, because of both the shops and the handy *patisseries*. It is a very narrow and crowded street, but this only adds to its charm. Around the Porte Louise, in the chic residential area, are some fine specialty shops.

WHAT NOT TO BUY ¶ Anything imported into Belgium, because the custom duty makes prices extra-high. Exception: goods from Common Market countries. Men's clothing is mediocre and that goes double for women's dresses, although a few shops carry passable merchandise at very high prices. An exception might be made in the case of high-fashion hats—which aren't bad.

SHOPPING HOURS ¶ In Belgium there is, technically, no closing time for shops. (As we said, the people like to rely on themselves and not on a long list of rules and regulations.) In recent years, this situation has been modified somewhat. The law now provides for a shop to close one day a week. Family-operated shops (but not department stores) can choose the day—and it does not have to be Sunday, necessarily. As a matter of fact, some satisfy the law, as well as their own strong sense of individualism, by closing from Sunday noon to Monday noon (that's one day, see?). During the summer, especially in holiday places, the one-day closing is not generally required.

Pointer: Brussels department stores are open without interruption from 9:30 A.M. to 6 P.M. daily except Sunday. Department stores and shops in the lower part of the city are open Wednesdays till 8 P.M.

ENTERTAINMENT ¶ Night clubs in Brussels, or Antwerp for that matter, are commercial and brassy, with little of the light and gay. The shows are lively, well organized and right off the assembly line, all with particular customers in mind—the tourist and the tired international businessman with lots of francs to spend. Night club impressarios closely follow an established pattern—the success of Paris night life (and its prices!). Drinks average $2 or $3 each, champagne (and none too good!) is as much as $20 a bottle—maybe more—and a new bottle is brought as soon as the last drop leaves the first. In most such places, you'll never see so much as a brassiere. The local bar girls hang about to swoop down on any unsuspecting male laden with that precious commodity—money.

But night clubs aren't the whole Brussels (or Belgian) story of an evening's entertainment. Your hotel concierge or the Official Tourist Office in the Place de Brouckère in Brussels can help you pick out an opera, music hall or theater performance that can interest you or can suggest one of the concerts at the Palais des Beaux Arts. Incidentally, the Brussels opera house, the Theatre de la Monnaie, has been completely remodeled and looks wonderful (and the performances are better than ever, too—or so it seems).

Movies sometimes are "dubbed." So if you go to a movie, be prepared to hear French voices dubbed in for American or English ones that you had been expecting. However, some American and English films are shown in their original version (*O.V.* is the way such films are advertised), and French or Dutch—usually both—subtitles are added.

MISCELLANEOUS ¶ If any courtesies have been extended to you, send your hostess flowers or chocolates. This is customary.

Even though the country will remind you of the United States in many ways, don't call anyone by his first name on the first meeting, or even the second one for that matter. Belgians are friendly, but are inclined to formality, like other Europeans. So let the first overture in that direction come from them.

Be very careful when driving. The Belgians have lovely manners—but not when they're behind a wheel.

The average person is wild about a sport that seldom occurs to the average American—pigeon racing—and it reaches its peak of intensity on Sunday mornings. As a matter of fact, Belgian immigrants—years and years ago—introduced the pigeon-racing sport in America.

DENMARK

National Characteristics

Once upon a time, as they say in the fairy tales, in the long-ago days of piston planes, Scandinavia seemed far away from the rest of Europe. It is still about 660 miles from Paris to Copenhagen. But, by jet, the distance is covered nowadays in an hour and a half—give or take a few minutes either way. The European road network, which has been improved tremendously in the past quarter of a century, leads swiftly and smoothly to Denmark's door.

The Danes have a big welcome mat at their door, too. Mr. William Shakespeare talked about the Melancholy Dane. If such a Dane exists outside of a Shakespearean play, he either keeps out of sight of tourists or has long since migrated to some other land. There are 4.7 million people in Denmark, and after a visit in this happy country you'll be wishing there were many more of them. They are friendly, warm, hospitable—well, they're wonderful people. They enjoy fun, and they like to make things as pleasant and as good spirited for the visitor as is possible.

Don't expect to find a nation of Hamlets here; more than likely, the people you meet will resemble that other Danish ham, Victor Borge, with much of his offbeat elfin humor. The national sense of humor, incidentally, was a main line of defense for the Danes in enduring the dreary, sad years of the German occupation, from 1940 to 1945.

Denmark is a land of a big peninsula named Jutland (what else would *you* call a peninsula?) and 500 islands. Windmills, castles such as Hamlet's at Elsinore, red-coated postmen with brass bugles, policemen halting traffic to let a gaggle of geese cross a road—these are some of the everyday sights encountered on a drive across the 16,500 square miles that, as far as the map makers go, is Denmark. You'll come across the initials "H.C.A." frequently. They are as well known in Denmark today as the letters "J.F.K." have been to Americans in recent years. Hans Christian Andersen was a storyteller, and his famous tales are still being told almost a century after his death. So be prepared. If a Danish friend refers to "H. C. Andersen," please don't look blank and say, "*Who?*"

Out in the countryside, particularly at farms, you might be told about a special house guest—and even be shown him. He is the Nisse Man, a tiny gnomelike figure who, dressed impishly and colorfully, often occupies some favored spot on a farm, such as a hay loft perch that is close to the barn door. The Nisse Man is more of a "house spirit" than a house guest. But although inanimate, the Nisse Man is someone to be reckoned with. If a crop is bad, Danish farmers frequently blame their Nisse Man. They know, too, that if you are good to the Nisse Man, he will reciprocate the kindness.

This is Denmark—a land of high spirits and a Nisse Man here and there making sure he receives his due. It is the land of H.C.A. and the Little Mermaid, of bicycles and ballet, of shipyards and bright farms.

Denmark is a keystone of democracy—with a difference, for this small land has a monarch, the lovely Queen Margarethe. In extremely unkinglike fashion, her father and grandfather often were seen strolling through the downtown streets of Copenhagen or bicycling along country roads. The Danish people traditionally hesitate to stare at members of the royal family when they encounter them along the way out of fear of invading their privacy. There are titles here, too—counts and barons—although the holders are shorn of all power, except possibly the ability to get a good table in a restaurant.

Also, the Danes deserve credit for smiling in the face of a completely unpronounceable language. When read in print, Danish doesn't seem terribly difficult. But apparently this is only a trap for the unwary. The spoken language is another story, with one syllable emphasized, another held back, still another gargled and trilled until the whole effect is calculated to make the prospective student of Danish throw in the sponge. But don't despair of communicating with these vigorous folk. They speak English, and what is even more incomprehensible, speak it well—frequently without an accent. Not all Danes speak English, of course. But all Danes are so obliging that even those who do not speak English will try to.

When to Go

A frequent target of the Danish sense of humor is the weather. On a March morning, for instance, a hotel doorman in Copenhagen might give you a cheery Good Morning and then, putting on a straight face, remark, "Well—in another few months spring will be here." Copenhagen people will also good-humoredly tell a visitor, "We have a fifth season here. It's a green winter or a white summer."

As we said, the Danes like to joke. The Danish weather is not that bad at all. Winters, it is true, are on the cool side and days are short. But in the middle of the summer the sun might be shining from very early in the morning until very late in the evening. Although June through August are the busiest and most popular times of the year, Denmark is pleasant for a visit beginning in April (even though the nights are frequently chilly). May and June are ideal, with much sunshine and low rainfall. It never gets terribly warm in Denmark even during the summer months. If the temperature hits 80 degrees, the Danes consider it a heat wave. September is usually delightful, although rain begins at the end of the month.

WEATHER STRIP: COPENHAGEN

Temp.	JAN.	FEB.	MAR.	APR.	MAY	JUNE	JULY	AUG.	SEPT.	OCT.	NOV.	DEC.
Low	29°	29°	31°	37°	45°	53°	56°	56°	51°	44°	37°	34°
High	35°	35°	39°	47°	57°	65°	68°	66°	60°	51°	43°	38°
Average	32°	32°	35°	42°	51°	59°	62°	61°	56°	48°	40°	36°
Days of rain	15	14	15	12	13	12	15	16	14	17	16	17

TIME EVALUATION ¶ On any European vacation, whether a brief two-week trip or one for as long as six weeks, allow two to three days for Copenhagen. If you're going to drive around this small country, allow an extra two to three days, or even longer if you wish.

PASSPORT AND VISA ¶ A passport is required but no visa is necessary if you are not staying more than three months. This three months, keep in mind, includes your stay not only in Denmark but in the other Scandinavian countries (Finland, Iceland, Norway and Sweden). So if you are going to travel in all of the Scandinavian countries for a *continuous* period of more than three months, you will have to apply to the police for an extension-beyond-ninety-days visa.

CUSTOMS AND IMMIGRATION ¶ You're allowed 400 cigarettes or 500 grams (a little over a pound) of other tobacco, and in case you roll your own you may bring in 200 pieces of cigarette paper. You also are permitted two bottles (liters) of wine or spirits and two liters of beer, but who would bring beer to Denmark? The duty-free tobacco allowance can be claimed only by persons over fifteen years of age. In the case of the alcoholic spirits, the minimum age is seventeen. No restrictions are made on articles for your own use in the country, such as a radio, a camera, jewelry and so forth. There is no limit whatsoever on the amount of money you bring into the country—whether it is Danish currency, foreign money or travelers' checks. (Just be sure to bring money.) For practical purposes, there is only one limit on what money you take with you on leaving: The restriction is on Danish currency. There is an export limit of 2,000 crowns (*kroner*) unless such an amount of local currency was brought into the country by you—and declared at the time of entry—or if it was acquired by you in cashing checks or other foreign currencies within Denmark (and you have the receipts with you). The quarantine on dogs and cats is no longer required but there are special rules on vaccination and border exams. Check on them before you arrive with your pet.

HEALTH ¶ Denmark is a spotless, sanitary country, with a typical scrubbed-clean look. It's a matter of opinion, but this little country is probably the cleanest in all of Europe. The water and milk may be drunk without a worry in the world. As a matter of fact, the milk is about the best you'll ever drink *anywhere*.

TIME ¶ The country is six hours ahead of (later than) Eastern Standard Time. If it's noon in New York, it's 6 P.M. in Copenhagen. No Daylight Saving Time is used here because the midnight sun makes the summer days long enough to suit anyone. However, when Daylight Saving Time is in effect in the United States, the time difference is only 5 hours.

CURRENCY ¶ The unit of currency is the Danish *krone* (*kroner,* in the plural). The word in English is *crown,* but you'll be getting into the habit quickly of saying *krone* and *kroner.* The krone is composed of 100 øre. Thus, 10 øre are one tenth of a crown. (So much for higher mathematics.) The Danish money comes in 10, 50, 100 and 500 kroner notes. The coins are 1, 2, 5, 10 and 25 øre, and 1 and 5 kr. (the typical abbreviation).

PRICE LEVEL ¶ In the rather high-price range—not the highest among continental countries, but nonetheless not very cheap. International currency changes cause shifts in local prices depending on which way they have been made—up or down. But in general you can expect to be meeting high prices for many creature comforts. A single room at the Royal Hotel in Copenhagen can cost anywhere from $17 to $25, and doubles start near the $25 plateau. In restaurants a pot of coffee, or tea, will run from 3.50 to 6 kr.; a bottle of beer, 3 to 7 kr.; a bottle of red wine, 28 to 50 kr.; a glass of snaps (akvavit), 3.75 to 4.70 kr.; a continental breakfast, 9 to 15 kr. Dinner in a fine restaurant will run $6, or more. In general imported items will be high (such as film for your camera). There are some taxes on tobacco and liquor that boost such products sky high. Cigarettes, for instance, are more than a dollar a pack. A glass of Scotch, at less than a dollar, will be a bargain. Of sorts. It usually is anything from 6.25 to 11.50 kr. a glass. Anyway, you get the idea.

TIPPING ¶ The standard tipping rate of 15 percent is added on restaurant and hotel bills (along with a 15 percent tax). If the service has been exceptional and you're very pleased, you might leave the waiter some extra change. That is the general custom throughout Europe. But this change should not be more than a third or a half of what the service charge came to. The local residents get annoyed with Americans who are over-generous because it throws the whole tipping system out of kilter. Porters in hotels, railroad stations and on ferryboats expect 1.75 to 2.40 kr. for each bag carried.

The customary tip to taxi drivers is 10 to 15 percent of the meter. If the night valet has been doing a good cleaning job on the shoes that you left outside your door each evening, he should be remembered with a tip of one and a half kroner for each night's work. The concierge will also expect some kind of remembrance (a few kroner). If he has done something special for you, then this tip should be increased accordingly. The chambermaid and the valet, if they have done their best to keep your room pleasant, should each get a tip of a krone and a half for each day you've been in the hotel. Wardrobe attendants at the opera, in restaurants and in other public places will expect a tip of 1 krone. Washroom attendants receive about the same. You do not have to tip ushers in movie houses and theaters.

TRANSPORTATION ¶ *Taxis* are reasonably priced and distances are short, but (wouldn't you know it?) you'll never be able to find one when it rains. The Taxa taxi company in Copenhagen has a staff of capable, pleasant drivers who know their way around town; their cabs can be spotted easily. Drivers wear a green-triangle badge on their uniforms and the cabs themselves are fitted with the same identifying insignia. The telephone number for taxis in Copenhagen is easy to remember. It is 35-35-35.

Buses cover just about every place you can think of—or think of going to—in Denmark. Prices are relatively low, and reservations are rarely necessary. Just get on the bus and get your ticket then. The bus information office in the Town Hall Square will provide all you want to know about times and places.

Ferries link Denmark's islands, many of the ports and foreign countries. It is a very pleasant way of travel. A night boat from Copenhagen to Aalborg or Aarhus in Jutland during the summer can be a memorable excursion. In general, there are so many ferries it will not be necessary to make reservations for your car, although they are necessary over weekends and during the summer. But if you are traveling by car to Norway or Sweden, it will be a good idea to check in advance to see whether you will need a reservation on the ferry, or whether you will be able to just drive on. On certain days during the summer the Scandinavians themselves do a lot of traveling, and ferry space gets limited.

Hydrofoils connect Copenhagen and Malmö in Sweden

every hour in both directions all year round; the crossing takes a little over half an hour.

Trains operate with First and Second Class service. The longest time involved is nine hours. That's on one train ride that takes you from one end of the country to the other (or another, depending on how you look at it), including about one and a half hours on a ferry. The best train is the *Lyntog*, or Lightning Train, an all-seats-reserved, extra-fare type of thing, and very pleasant. Your concierge at the hotel can get these reservations for you more easily than you can yourself. You can save money on the relatively stiff train fares by checking into the range of reductions available for round trips, children between four and twelve, families with at least one member under twenty-one, persons over sixty-five and groups of four adults or more. There are also reduced prices on ten-day, one-month and one-year tickets which give you freedom to travel wherever you want and as often as you want.

Airlines serve all the tourist spots in Denmark as well as such offbeat places as Greenland and the Faroe Islands. There are frequent flights throughout the day to and from Copenhagen and the major cities of Denmark, and service is fast. From Copenhagen to Aalborg, flight time is sixty-five minutes; to Odense (the birthplace of H.C.A.—remember what we said?), it is forty minutes; to Esbjerg, seventy; Arhus, forty. At most airports in the country you can hire a private plane.

Cars can be rented easily. Major international firms have agencies in the center of Copenhagen. Cars can be rented only to drivers over twenty-one, however. Sorry, collegians.

Bicycles, as we mentioned, are a favorite means of transportation of the Danes. You'll see that for yourself as you drive along the highway on a summer day. Bikes can be rented almost anywhere. In Copenhagen you can rent bikes at Kbh.Cyklebørs, which is at Gothersgade 157; telephone 14-07-17. *Motorscooters* are also available, often at the same places as bikes. They cost a bit more and the minimum age for the scooter rider is twenty-one.

COMMUNICATIONS ¶ The airmail rate to the United States is approximately a quarter. However, if you use only one sheet of airmail paper and an airmail envelope, and if you write "Five Grams" on the envelope (and do not write "Airmail"), the charge will be about half the usual rate and the letter will be flown to New York and from there will be put aboard a train to its destination. If the destination happens to be somewhere along the eastern seaboard of the United States, this is a very good value. The telephone and telegraph service within Denmark, as well as overseas, is excellent.

Pointer: Telegrams can be sent from your hotel or from a post office.

BASIC DANISH

English-Danish

Waiter: *Tjener*
Bill of fare, menu: *Spisekort*
Napkin: *Serviet*
Bread and butter: *Brod og Smor*
A glass of orange juice: *Et Glas Appelsinaft*
Boiled egg: *Kogt Aeg*
1. soft   1. *blodkogt*
2. medium   2. *smilende*
3. hard-boiled   3. *haardkogt*
4. egg cup   4. *Aeggebaeger*
Fried eggs: *Spejlaeg*
Bacon and eggs: *Bacon og Aeg*
Coffee, black: *Sort Kaffe*
Coffee with cream and sugar: *Kaffe med Sukker og Flode*
Coffee with hot milk: *Café au lait*
Tea: *Te*
Water: *Vand*
Ice water: *Isvand*
Mineral water: *Mineralvand*
Breakfast: *Morgenkaffe*
Lunch: *Frokost*
Dinner: *Middag*
Shampoo: *Haarvask*
Haircut: *Haarklipning*
Manicure: *Manicure*
I want . . . liters of petrol: *Jeg vil gerne have . . . Liter Olie*
Change the oil: *Olien skal skiftes*
Grease the car: *Vognen skal smøres*
How are you?: *Hvordan har De det?*
Fine, thank you: *Tak, jeg har det godt*
Please: *Vaer saa god*
Thank you very much: *Mange Tak*
Good morning: *God Morgen*
Good afternoon: *God Dag*
Good night: *God Nat*
Yes: *Ja, Jo*
No: *Nej*
Morning: *Morgen*
Noon: *Middag*

Afternoon: *Eftermiddag*
Evening: *Aften*
Night: *Nat*
Sunday: *Søndag*
Monday: *Mandag*
Tuesday: *Tirsdag*
Wednesday: *Onsdag*
Thursday: *Torsdag*
Friday: *Fredag*
Saturday: *Lørdag*
One: *Een*
Two: *To*
Three: *Tre*
Four: *Fire*
Five: *Fem*
Six: *Seks*
Seven: *Syv*
Eight: *Otte*
Nine: *Ni*
Ten: *Ti*
Twenty: *Tyve*
Thirty: *Tredive*
Forty: *Fyrre*
Fifty: *Halvtreds*
One hundred: *Hundrede*
One thousand: *Tusind*

ELECTRICITY ¶ Denmark uses an assorted, miscellaneous variety or range of electric current. Sometimes it is 110 volts; other times it is 220. Sometimes, it is A.C.; other times, D.C. Nowadays, the usual voltage is 220 A.C. Also, the cycle frequency is usually 50 rather than our own customary 60 cycles, so the timing on phonographs and electric clocks will be off and electric razors will not be as perky as they are back home. A few hotels have transformers (available to guests), which enable one to use travel irons and electric shavers.

PUBLIC HOLIDAYS ¶ New Year's and Christmas are each as big a holiday in Denmark as they are at home. But the Danes also have a number of other days of celebration, and in doing your planning (especially if you're figuring on shopping on a certain day) it is best to make sure that a Danish holiday does not creep up on you unsuspectingly. These other holidays are Maundy Thursday and Good Friday of Easter Week, Easter Monday, the fourth Friday after Easter (Store Bededag), Ascension Day, Whit Monday and June 5 (Constitution Day). Boxing Day, the day after Christmas, is also a holiday, as in England.

MEET THE DANES ¶ You will have no difficulty meeting the Danes; they're all over the place. But if you would like to visit a family in their home, it will be arranged by the National Travel Association. There is no cost involved. As soon as you arrive in Denmark, visit the nearest official government tourist office. They will set up an appointment with an English-speaking family that has interests similar to yours, and you will be invited to spend an evening (after dinner) at their home. After operating very successfully in Copenhagen for many years, the program was eliminated there in 1971. It has continued, however, in Esbjerg, Fredericia, Herning, Horsens, Kolding, Nyborg, Odense, Silkeborg, Skive, Aalborg and Arhus.

FOOD SPECIALTIES AND LIQUOR ¶ Whenever you awake, ring for your breakfast, *morgen complet*, which consists of coffee with hot milk and several sweet rolls. They will not be the "Danish" pastry served at breakfasttime in New York, but will be wonderful. A very popular, mouth-watering item at breakfast is *Wienerbroed*. It means "Vienna bread," but peculiarly enough, it is Danish pastry and not something you'll find in Austria's capital. That's logical, no? No. Anyway, ask the waiter to serve you *Wienerbroed* at breakfast. It is very fluffy, marvelous and light as a feather. Danish housewives usually buy it direct from their bakery shop because it is difficult to make at home. Eggs—and wonderful eggs!—are available for breakfast, as well as bacon—plus butter (that magnificent *Danish butter* you've heard about).

Most of the local folks bring a sandwich or two with them to work. They're so anxious to finish work and leave early that they hate to lose time with long lunches. Tourists, however, will enjoy the midday specialty of *smørrebrød*, which means "buttered bread." What the Danes put on top of the butter and bread is worth watching, knowing and eating. First, you select the bread—rye, whole wheat, etc. It is never just plain white bread. This is spread evenly and smoothly with creamery-fresh Danish butter (sweet and unctuous) and carefully topped in eye-appealing fashion with anything or everything that appeals to you. The classic *smørrebrød* item is a pyramid (Danes call it a "crowd of") Danish miniature shrimp. Another possibility is roast beef with onions and a fried egg. And so on, far into the afternoon. Three of these open-faced sandwiches are considered the polite limit. (You might start with fish, go on to meat and finish with cheese—then coffee and dessert.)

Fish in Denmark is particularly good and it is plentiful. You can be sure that the fish offered to you in a restaurant has been caught within the last twenty-four hours. Those small shrimp we mentioned for the open-faced sandwiches are a Danish specialty. In the winter-time they are a little bit larger, but just as excellent. The shrimp are hand peeled and it takes about twenty minutes to peel enough shrimp for one of those open-faced sandwiches. It is traditional to go to Tivoli Gardens in Copenhagen for shrimp on May 1, when "summer" starts.

There is plenty of fine food in Denmark. Food is a major industry, and the products are excellent. They are served at every possible opportunity, because the Danes love to eat well. Copenhagen has more than 1,000 restaurants, and in addition there are over 100 mobile sausage stands at which snacks are available at all hours of the day (a hot sausage and roll costs around 1 krone).

In a Danish restaurant it is usually enough to order only a main dish, as portions are always more than ample. Anything you order for dinner, for instance, will have a number of vegetables with it, plus two or three kinds of potatoes. So, unless you are really hungry, there is no need to order a three-course dinner. The dinner hour in Copenhagen is 7 or 8 P.M., and even a bit later. The hot kitchens in restaurants close about 11 P.M. In the countryside, dining is usually earlier, especially when summer rolls around. Some dishes you might enjoy include roast pork with apples and prunes, rice fritters, Danish-style red cabbage, the famous jellied raspberry dessert with the unpronounceable name—*rodgrød med flode*. Also look for *frikadeller*, miniature meat or fish balls; *biksemad*, a sort of hamburger made with fried onions and potatoes, with an egg on top; and *røget laks*, the wonderful salmon. In fact, and this is a bold statement, no matter what you order, you'll get delicious, appetizing food anywhere you go.

Don't look for domestic wine in Denmark; this is beer-making country. The two leading brands are Tuborg and Carlsberg, and which is the better is an argument we prefer to avoid. They're both excellent. French wines are obtainable in top restaurants—and such places usually have a surprisingly fine wine cellar. Anjou, Bordeaux,

Champagne—you name the wine! The Danes have it on hand. Any type of alcoholic drink you can name—from Fernet Branca to cognac, from Scotch to *pastis*—is available in leading restaurants. So have no fear about finding your favorite *apéritif, digestif* or what-have-you, including sour-mash bourbon.

Scandinavia's typical hard drink—and we say *hard* advisedly—is the light-colored spirit called *aquavit,* or *akvavit*—or just plain *snaps.* It varies from one Scandinavian country to the other, depending on how it is made (potatoes, etc.). In any event, drink it straight, ice-cold (because it tastes horrible when warm). Don't sip, don't taste, but just toss it down manfully and hope for the best. And you'll need that hope because even though it is light-colored, *snaps* is heavy and powerful. Danes, even at lunchtime, like to have a beer chaser with their slug of *snaps.* If you don't wish to be considered crude and of low character, never (repeat) never order *snaps* without food.

What about the custom of the *skål?* Although the young people are inclined to minimize its importance, the *skål* (pronounced *skawl*) is still a live custom at the more formal dinner parties. In any case, it amounts to nothing more or less than not drinking your drink (snaps, whisky or whatever it is) by yourself. Your host will usually say a word (or lots more) of welcome and then say, "Skål!" You skål to him in return, and then drink. If you wish a drink on your own, look someone in the eye (preferably a member of the opposite sex), say the magic word "Skål," and then drink—or, vice versa, if someone catches your eye and says the word. One must never skål the hostess. The reason: if everyone did, she'd soon be loaded to the gunwales.

Denmark's food is meant for the home-produced alcoholic beverages, such as the beer and snaps. The favorite after-dinner drink, furthermore, is another Danish product, Cherry Heering. It is probably the best cherry cordial in the world and comes in several flavors. In the past the Danes used to drink snaps when eating cheese. But the trend now is to have a Cherry Heering. Cherry Heering, served ice-cold on the rocks, as a liqueur, is also very popular. By the way, this is a very good item to bring home as a gift because it sells in the United States for about three times the Danish price.

The principal tourist areas of Denmark are Copenhagen, Zealand, the islands of Funen and Jutland.

Capital City

Copenhagen, which must—under penalty of not being allowed to eat a Danish pastry—be pronounced Copen-HAY-gen (never Co-pen-HAG-en) is a fine, trim, immaculate city of almost 1.5 million inhabitants. On a Danish map or on roadside markers, it'll appear as Köbenhavn, which means "Merchant's Port," an appropriate name for this important seaport. Prepare to find a modern city, bustling and lively, with loads of charm and waterfront color, even though it may not have much in the way of medieval structures.

Across the street from the Palace Hotel is one of the city's natural landmarks, the Raadhus (Town Hall), which fronts on a big square that is the heart of Copenhagen. The square is called the Raadhuspladsen. The Town Hall is no old-timer. It was built as recently as 1905.

The ground floor of the Town Hall has busts of notable citizens, none of whom will ring a bell with you except H. C. Andersen (remember him?) and perhaps Bertel Thorvaldsen, the sculptor. The second floor (which Europeans always refer to as the *first*) has the reception room and the council chamber. On the third floor is a wonderful selection of relics and clothes from the early history of Copenhagen. If you wish, it's possible to get to the top of the Town Hall tower for a view of the city—provided you bought your tickets on the ground floor.

Leaving the Town Hall, walk into H. C. Andersen Boulevard, with the Tivoli Gardens on your right. Walking ahead, you soon come to the end of the Tivoli Gardens. The next large building on the right is the Glyptoteket, a museum with a renowned collection of sculpture and French paintings. From here, cross H. C. Andersen Boulevard and walk up Stormgade—*gade* means "street" —for two blocks until you arrive at the National Museum, the most modern in all of Scandinavia; it has a very complete and varied collection. The sections that are sure to interest any visitor are the ones devoted to Denmark's earliest history.

When you come out of the National Museum, you'll be facing Frederiksholm Canal, which you should cross. Here is Christianborg, where the Danish Parliament (*Rigsdag*) meets. Excavations have indicated that Christianborg is on the site of a fortress erected by Bishop Absalom in the twelfth century. (The State Rooms are open daily except Monday for guided visits from 10 A.M. to 4 P.M., during April-October; the rest of the year, Thursday through Sunday. The excavations under the castle may be seen daily from 10 A.M. to 4 P.M.; the Parliament, during the same hours when not in session.) You'll surely want to see the Royal Gate, which separates Parliament (northern portion) from the Supreme Court and the Ministry of Foreign Affairs (to the south). Castle Church is connected to the castle itself. From the church there is a narrow path leading to the Thorvaldsen Museum, where Denmark's famous sculptor is buried. (The museum is open daily from 10 A.M. to 4 P.M., the entrance is free on Wednesdays, Fridays and Sundays.) Many of the exhibits of his works are originals, but quite a few others are copies. (If you're in the mood to explore this section of the city further, behind Christianborg are the Royal Library and the arms museum. You will be intrigued by the unusual architecture of the Børsen, the Stock Exchange, whose twisted spire is used as an identifying symbol for Copenhagen.)

From Castle Church, cross the canal toward the statue of Bishop Absalom. There is usually a small market in progress around the statue. From the bishop's monument continue into Hojbro Plads and then to the Ostergade, one of the main shopping streets. At the Ostergade, turn right. This street forms part of the main shopping area collectively designated as the Strøget, consisting of a series of one-way streets that frequently change their names from one sector to another. After turning right at the Ostergade, continue until you reach the big square at Kongens Nytorv; a baker's dozen of streets radiate from this busy hub. On the right-hand side is the imposing Royal Theater and alongside it is the Charlottenborg, home of the State School of Arts (where you might inquire if there is any special exhibit being presented). Now you're in the famous—or it is *infamous*—Nyhavn area of ships and sailors. The Nyhavn Canal is lined by old buildings (with someone usually sitting on the steps), shops, sailors' hangouts and cafes with jukeboxes blaring, some fine one-flight-up restaurants—in other words, plenty of color and sights to see. On the other side of the canal, take Toldbodgade to Amaliegade by way of Sankt Annae Plads (St. Ann's Square). This is the route to Amalienborg, the royal residence of the king of Denmark. The *borg* consists of four great palaces that are approximately two centuries old. The style is rococo, which in those days was so very popular. During the winter when the king is in residence, there is a colorful ceremony of the changing of the guard, and it is quite wonderful to see the guard parading solemnly through the small, old streets of the city. It is also possible to witness an occasional flurry of excitement when the royal coach is used.

On another day, visit Rosenborg Castle (open daily from 11 to 3, June through October) in King's Park. This one-time castle, elegantly decorated inside, is now the showcase for the crown jewels. All tourists feel dutybound to see the small figure of Copenhagen's Little Mermaid, the Langelinie, who gazes so wistfully out to sea. The statue was inspired by a story of Hans . . . well, you know who. A few years ago when the statue's head was destroyed, all Denmark—and friends of the Little Mermaid around the world—mourned. But she is once again as lovely and wistful as ever. The trip to the Little Mermaid's lookout point could be combined with a visit to the nearby Kastellet, the Citadel, which was built three centuries ago to protect the entrance to Copenhagen's harbor. Other sights you won't want to miss in Copenhagen include the Round Tower, which may be climbed by the young or ambitious; the student district; the Marble Church; the Botanical Gardens. Also, you must visit one of the beer factories and enjoy a sample or two of the national brews. Alas! the Cherry Heering folks do not have any guided tours of their premises but why not drop down to their place anyway, along the really idyllic Christians-Havns Canal (not far from the Town Hall). It is a picturesque area, and if you knock at the door of the Heering house we don't think you'll be turned away. Don't fail to take at least one sightseeing trip by boat through the city's canals. Boats with English-speaking guides leave from the Stock Exchange (Børsen) behind Christianborg Castle.

ಌ Short Trips from Copenhagen

There are two interesting trips that can be made from the city. Each involves only a morning or an afternoon.

Frilandsmusseet

The first trip is to Frilandsmusseet, an open-air museum near Kongens Lynby, which can be reached by No. 23 or No. 24 bus from Norrepark, or by taxi, of course. Here, in a vast area, you'll find old houses, windmills, farms (completely furnished) representative of all the provincial districts of Denmark. If you want to spend the day there, lunch can be had in a good restaurant on the site. Another interesting trip is by No. 30 bus from Town Hall Square to the island of Amager, which has a fascinating history. King Christian II once brought a few hundred Dutch families to the island to farm the land near the center, at Store Magleby, and the place retains to this day a Dutch personality and atmosphere. The people have Dutch names and even Dutch holidays are celebrated. Further along on the island is the village of Dragor, with winding streets and old houses. Dragor is more than worth the trip in itself. It is a rustic, charming corner of Denmark with geese strutting in the streets and those light-haired Danish youngsters looking like animated figurines from a porcelain factory.

Elsinore

The classic one-day trip from Copenhagen to Hamlet's castle at Elsinore is one that should not be missed—unless you really want a guilt complex. (Incidentally, this is the same road you'll take in case you plan to drive to Sweden by way of the Elsinore—Danish: Helsingør—ferry, which crosses over to the Swedish mainland at Hälsingborg.)

Leave Copenhagen for Elsinore by way of the Bredgade, which in turn leads into the wide Osterbrogade that heads north along the sea. The name of the seaside road changes to Strandvejen, which, as you might have guessed, means "beach road." There are beautiful sandy beaches along here and it is a favorite of the Copenhagen people on *any* sunny day. Just inland from the seaside resort of Klampenborg is the celebrated Deer Park

(Dryehaven), a real woodsy area of tall trees and pleasant walkways and roads. Continue along the coast road through Rungsted and into Humlebaek, a tiny fishing village. From there it is just a short drive into Elsinore. The distance between Copenhagen and Elsinore is only twenty-five miles, and the trip takes about an hour or so.

At Elsinore is the renowned Kronborg Castle, the home of Hamlet. Shakespeare used the castle as the setting for his great dramatic play and Shakespeare enthusiasts will be able to recognize the place from the way he described it. Castle or not, it is a splendid setting. Sweden is just a few miles across the sound, and during the summer, ferries, yachts, cargo ships and small boats provide a holiday ambiance. During June—in case you're at Elsinore then—there is a week of gala performances of *Hamlet*. There are other attractions here: the Svea Column, the two Gothic churches, the supposed tomb of Hamlet (but does anyone really know?) and, most interesting of all, the old chemist's shop in the Faergestraeded.

For the return ride to Copenhagen, take the inland route, proceeding by way of Fredensborg Castle (at Fredensborg), which is the king's summer residence. When the royal family is not at the castle, it is open for inspection. The thing to do after sightseeing is to have lunch or tea at the Store Kro, the well-known inn at Fredensborg, one of the outstanding small hotels in Europe.

At Hillerød, stop for a while and visit the Frederiksborg Castle, an imposing Renaissance residence, which is famous for its banquet hall. Another great inn on the way back to Copenhagen is the Søllerød Kro at Søllerød, a country village of white-painted shops and houses and a fountain in the middle of the little square, that is just outside of Copenhagen. The Søllerød Kro was founded in 1677 and is one of the most pleasant places you'll find, *anywhere*, to lunch or dine in an elegant setting.

Pointer: There are various excursions which originate, by bus, at the Palace Hotel in the Town Hall Square.

ACCOMMODATIONS ¶ If it's possible to single out one country as outstanding for cleanliness and the generally inviting atmosphere of its hotels, Denmark deserves that accolade. Wherever you go throughout this tiny land, you'll be greeted by perfectly kept attractive rooms, with immaculate beds. But now comes a note of protest: Why, in heaven's name, are these beds covered with a feather, or down, comforter that is guaranteed to induce fever-level temperatures in the unsuspecting American who must cover himself with something? The Danes say that this is all a state of mind. Perhaps you'll agree; perhaps not, as you bathe in perspiration on a mild summer evening when it's too cool to sleep without a covering and much too warm for the bulky comforter. By dint of persistence, a blanket may be substituted by the hotel housekeeper. But it takes patience to convince her that you won't catch a cold under a mere blanket.

Other than the above mild snarl, we have nothing but praise for the fine hotels of the nation.

COPENHAGEN HOTELS ¶ To repeat the obvious, hotel space in Copenhagen is in very short supply during the middle of the tourist season. So, be sure to make advance reservations. In case you don't have any reservation, and you're arriving at a time when hotel space is hard to get, check with the Hotel Bureau in the Central Station. From May 1 to the middle of September it is open every day from 9 A.M. to midnight. The rest of the year the hours are shorter. There is also a Hotel Bureau on the main road, the A-2 just outside of Copenhagen in the area of Køge. It's open from July 1 to the last week or so in August.

D'Angleterre: One of Europe's leading hotels, with a distinct, gracious personality. Rooms are large, service and food are good, rates are only moderately high and what more can one expect from a hotel? Be sure to have *Danish* pastry for breakfast. It's so delicious, it's almost unbelievable.

Sheraton-Copenhagen: A large twenty-story establishment with over 500 rooms and suites, four restaurants and three bars; all rooms are air-conditioned, have TV and all other ultramodern facilities. Brand new, and very good.

Royal: A streamlined skyscraper near the Tivoli Gardens. It is operated in a most modern, efficient manner. Top staff members, for instance, have a radio paging system, with which they can be called instantly regardless of where they are. It was the first hotel in Copenhagen to install a *sauna,* which is available for outside users as well as hotel guests.

Palace: A compact, modern hotel, which is more conveniently located than the d'Angleterre because it is near the Town Hall; rooms are average size, but pleasantly decorated. Very good dining facilities.

Europe: A very good, modern hotel near Tivoli (it's on H. C. Andersen Boulevard). Rooms are moderately large, pleasantly furnished. This hotel offers a very good value in its price range.

Terminus: Near the railroad station, this older hotel may be recommended. Fairly large rooms, furnished in modern décor. Some of the old remodeled rooms are extremely attractive.

Imperial: A Royal Danish Automobile Club-affiliated hotel, very up to date in midtown Copenhagen. Efficiently operated and pleasant, appealing to the popular-priced trade; features a cafeteria among its restaurants.

Dan Hotel: A very large, modern hotel at Kastrup, the suburban area that houses the greatly enlarged international airport; frequent taxis to town.

Codan: Right at the harbor's edge; the masts of moored ships at the quayside will almost touch the picture windows; a small hotel but situated picturesquely and conveniently; has a fine rooftop restaurant. Rooms are modern and pleasing.

Bel Air: Opened in 1969 as a hospice for economy-class, jumbo-jet travellers, this is a very functional hotel, with 215 rooms, all with bath or shower, very reasonably priced.

Note: This is only a partial list. Other top hotels include Alexandra, Astoria, Belle France, Grand, Hafnia, King Frederick V, Mercur, 71 Nyhavn and 3 Falke.

COPENHAGEN RESTAURANTS

Coq d'Or: Strictly speaking, not a Danish restaurant, for it features French food, but serving the finest cuisine in the city. Small, intimate. Not very expensive, all things considered.

Frascati: Excellent for lunch, when you can try several of the smørrebrød specialties; very attractive surroundings.

Langeliniepavillonen: Although it's part of the Royal Yacht Club, the restaurant is open to the public. The food is rather good, the service and atmosphere fine.

Oskar Davidsen's: This is the place with that superlong sandwich list. Old-time patrons who have not been in Copenhagen recently will be happy about the establishment's location right on a lake in the middle of town—a much more splendid setting than in the old days. The open sandwiches are as fine as ever.

Krogs Fiskerestaurant: A popular spot for seafood, near the docks. If fresh sole is available, be sure to order it.

7 Smaa Hjem: An attractive restaurant with seven different small rooms. The food is good, but not extraordinarily so.

7 Nations: A newish restaurant featuring food from seven different nations. Interesting and amusing, although not authentic.

Café de Paris: Small, cheery spot serving local specialties; also has good French food.

A Porta: Tiny spot featuring excellent Danish food.

In Tivoli Gardens, you'll find several worthwhile restaurants where evening dining outdoors on a terrace can be very pleasant:

Belle Terrasse: One of Copenhagen's best restaurants. Beautiful, attractive surroundings; varied, interesting menu; fairly high prices. Certainly the best in Tivoli.

Divan II: Very good, although not in the same category with Belle Terrasse; prices somewhat more moderate. Features French and Danish food, with some emphasis on seafood.

Note: The Nimb restaurant, another fine eating place, has dancing.

SHOPPING ¶ Denmark is a marvelous place for bargains, especially in the field of home furnishings. This is probably the result of great Danish emphasis upon the home and family. You'll find your best buys among such articles.

Things are made easy for the shopper by the Permanent Exhibit for Danish Arts and Crafts (*Den Permamente*), which shows the products made by the skilled people of Denmark. The Permanent Exhibit is handily located, just a couple of blocks from the Tivoli Gardens and from the air terminal. It is open daily from 9 A.M. to 5:30 P.M. and remains open on Fridays till 7 P.M. The closing hour on Saturdays is 2 P.M. The Permanent Exhibit was started in 1931 as an undertaking of Danish craftsmen (mostly small ones). Today, the association sponsoring the Permanent Exhibit has 260 members, and between 70 and 80 percent of them are still small craftsmen.

For *sterling silver*, of course, everyone knows the works of Georg Jensen. The showroom has a tremendous selection of flatware, bowls, serving pieces, dishes, candelabra, vases and jewelry. Jensen, regardless of those who have vied with him, is still the pacesetter in design for the industry, although his work is not necessarily better (although more expensive) than that of his competitors. There are a series of annoying regulations about importing certain quantities and pieces of Jensen silver to the United States. To avoid this, request a release certificate from the Georg Jensen shop in Copenhagen at the time of making the purchase. As a rule, however, if the silver is merely listed on the customs declaration as "Danish silver," the inspecting officer will seldom inquire further. Other silversmiths of renown include Just Andersen, Dragsted, A. Michelsen, Kay Bogesen and Hans Hansen, who offer similar quality and workmanship, and lower prices, than Georg Jensen.

Porcelain is another great specialty here. The craftsmanship of much of the porcelain pieces by Bing and Groendahl, Royal Copenhagen and Dahl-Jensen can scarcely be surpassed. If you wish to send articles home, have no hesitation, for shipments invariably arrive in good order. Have the shop insure your purchase.

Furniture executed in the modern style by outstanding designers and craftsmen is offered at bargain rates—and doubly so when compared with United States prices for the identical articles. Remember, however, that shipping charges and insurance are also involved (and possible customs duties, too). However, shipments made during recent years seem to arrive without undue delay or damage. You may want to make sure that the furniture is not shipped in "knocked down" condition—that is, requiring assembly on arrival. This could be a difficult and tedious job.

Gift items are marvelous here: cigarette boxes, lighters, ashtrays, modern ceramics, small bronze pieces, copper and brass figurines—these are merely a few items that can give you an idea of the wide scope of the possibilities. *Table linens* and *place mats* are usually quite smart and represent good values. Modern *crystal glassware* is extremely attractive, and there need be no doubt about having this shipped home safely. Hand-woven *textiles* sold by the yard are another Danish specialty. *Kitchen equipment*, such as copper pans, cheese knives, stainless steel cutlery and kitchen gadgets, should not be overlooked.

Visitors to Denmark frequently mention mink and other precious *furs* as outstanding values. To our way of thinking, unfortunately, this is just not true, because the skins aren't worked properly (to American taste and standards, anyway) and the furs do not have the appearance their cost warrants.

The main shopping street in Copenhagen is the Strøget, a shopper and pedestrian paradise, because it has some 200 stores and there is not a car in the street. It is banned to traffic, permitting the shopper to wander from one side of the street to the other if a display window looks very inviting. The Strøget—you can pronounce it something like "Stroy-it"—is a succession of old streets, extending from Kongens Nytorv (where the Royal Theater is located) to the Town Hall Square.

Denmark's *food products* are exhibited in a fine display center with the easily pronounceable name *Ekko Denmark*, which is near the Town Hall Square. The exhibit has existed for more than a half dozen years now, but two years ago a restaurant, a delicatessen with Danish food and the Grill Shop were added. Grilled chickens and a variety of those Danish open sandwiches can be bought in the Grill Shop. Besides the restaurant, which has table service, there is a counter snack bar (a very smart-looking affair, too). During the day—at 11 A.M., noon, 1, 2, 3 and 4 P.M.—there are food demonstrations (the last demonstration on Saturdays is at noon) consisting of both a film and a practical use of Danish food products. There are always samples, *afterward*. There is no problem about the language. In the winter, it is Danish. But if Americans happen to be in the audience the demonstrator switches into English. In the summer, of course, there are always English-language demonstrations. The restaurant, by the way, is open until midnight but is closed Sundays.

Pointer: Danish store hours—Open from either 8:30 or 9 A.M. to 5:30 P.M., Monday through Thursday; to 7 or 8 P.M., Friday; to 1 or 2 P.M., Saturday. Bakers, florists and candy shops are open on Sunday to noon.

ENTERTAINMENT ¶ Of all the Scandinavian countries, the only one with night life, as Americans define it, is Denmark, and this area might be even further limited to Copenhagen. The Danish capital, for that matter, has been described as "the Paris of the north." This description is not very imaginative, nor is it particularly accurate. But the point is that there is lots of fun to be had in Copenhagen, and if you don't find this out, then it's no one's fault but you-know-who. No, not Hans Christian Andersen.

Once upon a time, as H.C.A. might say, the most famous and sought-after undraped female figure in Copenhagen was the statue of the Little Mermaid on the waterfront. Now Copenhagen features in "sex shops," kiosks and other handy places a variety of undraped figures, the likes of which are unknown on many of the world's waterfronts. They are depicted in film, photographs and in person. In other words this aspect of Copenhagen contemporary life-style is—depending on one's point of view—as good or as bad as reports indicate.

That venerable institution the pub has reached Copenhagen, and there are a couple of good examples of the English-style drinking establishments right in the neighborhood of Town Hall Square. They are popular with pop-in guests who arrive just before or after dinner.

The main hotels entertain guests, as well as drop-in visitors, in smart style. The Palace Hotel has two night spots. The sidewalk terrace of the Hotel d'Angleterre is a comfortable, agreeable place to watch the bicycle traffic on a balmy evening. Up higher, on the twentieth floor of the Royal Hotel, is the Panorama Lounge, which is open from 7 A.M. to midnight—for a cup of coffee, a drink or just a look-around. During the winter the Royal Hotel serves a Candlelight Dinner every Wednesday evening. It is a gourmet-type meal that starts around 7:30 P.M. and ends at midnight. Early in the evening a string orchestra provides appropriate music, and then a combo takes the stand for dancing. It is very pleasant and costs little, relatively speaking ($6.50, plus beverages).

All around the Town Hall Square area are numerous bars of various types. Some are quite good, and there is usually at least a pianist. A lot of visitors like to stroll through the Nyhavn area of the ships and seamen in the evening. It is quite colorful, naturally. But don't do it alone. The more in the party, the better.

The favorite entertainment spot of the Danish people, bar none, is Tivoli, a twenty-acre amusement park set in the heart of Copenhagen, right alongside of the Town Hall. It has been compared to Coney Island, but it is much more refined than that and a great deal more comprehensive. As a matter of fact, Coney Island has now been virtually eclipsed as an amusement park by modern-day events, but Tivoli, which was founded in 1843, is still going strong. At Tivoli you'll find all of the standard entertainment of a fun fair—scenic railway, games of chance, fireworks, etc. But it also has some pretty good free (or almost free) entertainment of a better class, including excellent concerts, a pantomime theater, and even a very good restaurant, the Belle Terrasse. Tivoli opens on May 1 and usually closes on September 1. But if the weather stays nice, they now keep it open till the end of September. It is a place that shouldn't be missed by anyone who really wants to see Copenhagen people enjoying themselves.

An even older amusement park than Tivoli is Bakken, which goes back a couple of hundred years. It is near Klampenborg, a thirty-minute ride on the S-train subway from the center of town. The taxi fare will come to around $5, including the tip. There is also plenty of parking space, if you've rented a drive-yourself car.

SPORTS ¶ *Golf* courses and *tennis* courts are everywhere, and there are even hotels with their own tennis facilities. The two main golf courses in the Copenhagen area are at Rungsted and Eremitagen. There are *trotting* races at Copenhagen, Aalborg, Aarhus, the island of Bornholm, Odense and Skive, and racetracks for *flat racing* at Copenhagen, Aalborg, Aarhus and Odense. If you want to ride the horses, instead, you will find riding academies in most cities. The rate is about $2 an hour. If you enjoy *surf bathing*, you'll be in your element in Denmark, particularly in the west coast beaches of Jutland. In fact, anything connected with the water is worthwhile here—boating, sailing and particularly fishing. There are any number of lakes and streams, and the landowner at the fishing site can give you the necessary license. To do any fishing in the sea, however, you'll need a license from the Fishery Control people, who can be reached in Copenhagen at 22 Kalvebod Pladsvej. There is marvelous *deep-sea fishing* for tuna from about the middle of August through October 1, notably near Elsinore and the neighboring village of Snekkersten. To hire a *sailboat*, check with the Continental Boat Charter, 6 Vester Farimagsgade, in Copenhagen.

Pointer: If you come across the term MOMS on a bill, don't jump to any wrong conclusions. MOMS refers to Denmark's 13 percent purchase tax.

৯ *A Tour of Denmark*

Motorists planning to tour this country and then head south into Germany should certainly drive north to Elsinore (Hamlet's place) before undertaking the main portion of the trip.

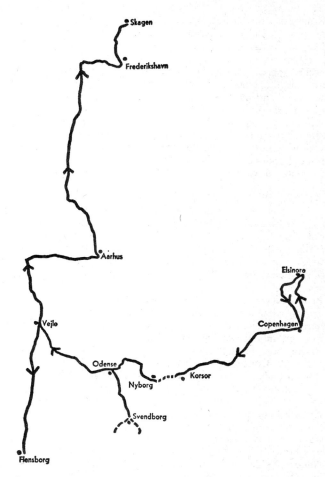

Copenhagen to Korsor—66 miles

Leave Copenhagen from Town Hall Square, following the Vesterbrogade westward (route 1), which changes into the Roskildevej (street). The road goes through Hedehusene and into Roskilde, a beautifully located town alongside a fjord. The B.P. Motel (yes, motel!) is the place for an overnight stay if you have made a late start. Continue on route 1 through Osted and Ny and into Ringsted, once an important medieval town, but now a quiet village; see St. Bendt Kirke and its many tombs of Danish royalty.

From Ringsted, continue on the road through Fjenneslev and Slaglille (after which there is an optional left turn to the beautiful town of Sorø, with many quaint scenes). The main road continues to Slagelse and down to Korsør, the ferry station. (There is frequent ferry service every day, but advance reservations are strongly advised during the summer season. In Copenhagen, reservations should be made at the Copenhagen Central Station, telephone Central 8880; elsewhere at any station of the state railways.)

Nyborg to Vejle—75 miles

The ferry trip terminates at Nyborg, formerly an important fortress, of which the principal reminder is Dänehof Castle, constructed in 1170 to prevent pirate ships from sneaking through the waters separating Nyborg from Korsør; interestingly, these waters are called the Store Baelt, or the "Great Belt." Proceed from Nyborg via route 1 to Avnsley, turning right at that village to Bovense (via an unnumbered road) and into Kerteminde, a little seaside village located on both shores of a fjord; here you'll be able to take a scenic motorboat trip through inland waterways to Ladby, where an original Viking boat found in 1935 may now be seen in a small museum. Continue on from Kerteminde to Munkebo, Aasum and then Odense. Here you'll find two American-style places to stay, the Odense and Ansgarhus motels, or, for a more conventional overnight stop, the Grand Hotel is very modern and pleasant.

Odense, of course, is the town where that favorite storyteller of children's tales, Hans Christian Andersen, was born. It has been said, by modern psychologists, that Andersen's desire for a world of make-believe was caused by his own desperately unhappy childhood. His family was not highly regarded, for Andersen had a half-wit grandfather and an alcoholic mother; poor Hans was himself homely and awkward, the butt of ridicule of the children of his neighborhood. You'll probably want to visit his home and the museum (open daily 10–5). The town also has Odense Castle (1720), now occupied by the town's mayor. A pleasant short trip from Odense is to Fynsk Landsby, the open-air museum with buildings typical of the island of Funen.

SIDE TRIP ¶ From Odense, a short journey of about twenty-seven miles is recommended via route 9 through Ringe to Svendborg, magnificently located on the waterfront. Svendborg is particularly known for its half-timbered houses, but its chief merit lies in the opportunity offered for boat trips to the neighboring islands to the south; we have no hesitation in approving the Hotel Svendborg as a delightful base of operations.

The nearest island is Taasinge, easily reached in a matter of minutes from Svendborg; on the island, the leading sights are Valdemar's Castle, built in 1678, and the neighboring small villages, notably Troense. The large island of Langeland is reached by ferry from Svendborg to the port of Rudkobing, with service every few hours; this is a slumbering, quaint village, and there are two famous old castles located in the northern portion of the island. But the best shall be last, for the most interesting island of all is Aerø, reached from Svendborg by ferry service; the trip takes about an hour and a quarter, and before starting, check the return schedules or you'll have to remain overnight at the charming little village of Aerøskøbing, and that would be terrible, wouldn't it? Should you wish to remain overnight in Aerøskøbing, there is the pleasing Old Worldish Hotel Aerøhus, which hasn't any private bathrooms and the bedrooms are small—but it *is* charming.

So much for the side trip to Svendborg. Continuing the tour from Odense, leave via route 1 toward Skallebølle, Gribsvad and Middelfart, the last town on Funen Island, where the principal place of interest is a folk museum. Follow route 1, subsequently picking up route 18; you are now on Jutland Island. (Should you wish to call it a day and stay overnight at a local hotel, take any of the several right turns indicated toward Fredericia, where you'll find the pleasant Hotel Landsoldaten. Formerly an important fortress town, Fredericia is best known today for its old fortifications and ramparts, which are in surprisingly good condition.) Then on to the tourist center of Vejle, located on a fjord; close to the road is the pleasing Hotel Australia, and there is the Grand Hotel, which is pleasant, and centrally located. If you enjoy good food, especially pastry, why not make an eighteen-mile

excursion to Kolding and pay a visit to the Saxildhus,
which has excellent smørrebrød, but also fabulous pastry.
Abandon all calorie counts before entering the Saxildhus!
Vejle is the base for trips to nearby Jelling (which is,
of course, pronounced YELL-ing); here are the burial
mounds of King Gorm and Queen Thyra, the first rulers
of Denmark. An outing to Jelling is lovely, the scenery
is lovely and you should have a lovely, lovely time; then
back to Vejle.

From this point, motorists heading for Sweden will
go north via route 10 to Frederikshavn, where there is
ferry service to Göteborg; incidentally, this is a good
time to remind you that reservations are important, particularly during the summer months. (A description of
the route south to the German border follows at the conclusion of the description of the northern route.)

FROM VEJLE NORTHWARD TO FREDERIKSHAVN

Vejle to Frederikshavn—179 miles

Take route 13 north through Tørring and Høllund and
toward Paarup, up to intersection with route 15; take a
right turn toward Silkeborg, where the Dania Hotel is
old but comfortable. Silkeborg is the starting point for a
waterborne trip to interesting old Himmelbjerget. Via
motorboat, steamer or even the old paddleboat, the entire outing requires just under an hour and a half.

From Silkeborg, continue on route 15 through Linaa
eastward to Aarhus, Denmark's second city. Here you'll
find the Hotel Royal, fascinatingly decorated in the
medieval style; or if you prefer American-style accommodations, there is the Motel la Tour. You should see
the cathedral (the largest in Denmark) and the open-air
museum in the middle of "Old Town," which includes
forty-eight decorated and completely furnished homes
representing the various Danish provinces. If you feel
like dinner with music, head for the Varna Restaurant;
for quiet (perhaps better) food, you might prefer to dine
at Frederik VI's Kro, which is situated in the nearby
town of Risskov.

From Aarhus follow route 10 north through Lisbjerg
to Randers, a town with colorful streets and medieval
homes; the Hotel Randers is very pleasant should you
wish to stay overnight. The best all-around dining room

in Randers is at the Centralen, which features Danish cooking. Continue on route 10 to Hobro, at the end of a long fjord, then through Rold and Støvring and into Aalborg, which has the very nice Phønix Hotel. This town manufactures a variety of products, but the most famous single item is the *snaps*, or *akvavit*, often considered the best of its type. The streets offer many pleasant sights, with old houses and narrow lanes, but just a scant distance away are broad boulevards and modern shops lit by neon. Close by is Rebild Park, where July 4 is celebrated with great vigor, at the request of Danes now living in the United States.

Then across to Nørresundby and route 14 north to Hjørring and then route 11 to Frederikshavn, all of which are in that upper portion of Jutland called Vendyssel. Frederikshavn is the ferry embarkation point for Göteborg, Sweden, and travel time is approximately three and a half hours. (Reservations are essential during the summer months.) If time permits, an interesting side trip may be made from Frederikshavn via route 10 to Skagen, the northernmost part of Denmark. "The Skaw," as it is called, is an artists' colony; the chief sights include the Buried Church (the roof is all that shows of the structure buried in the drifting sands) and the long, curving sand dune called Grenen. For a stay at Skagen, try the Brøndums or Foldens Hotel. Another daytime excursion is the boat trip from Frederikshavn to the island of Laesø; the trip takes an hour and a half and the island is exceedingly primitive and barren, but very interesting.

FROM VEJLE SOUTHWARD TO THE GERMAN BORDER

Vejle to Flensburg—63 miles

Leave Vejle via route 10 heading toward Viuf and into Kolding, a town situated on a fjord; the Saxildhus Hotel is pleasant and famous for its food.

SIDE TRIP ¶ For trips from Denmark to England by steamer, follow route 1 westward to Esbjerg, where the new Hotel Esbjerg is extremely pleasant. (From Esbjerg, there is steamer service, taking nineteen hours, to Harwich, England; also to Newcastle, England, taking twenty-four hours. Reservations may be made in advance at DFDS Rejesebureau, Axelborg, Copenhagen.) It's a short ride south from Esbjerg to Ribe, one of the most fascinating towns in all of Denmark, having retained its distinctive medieval quality over the years. Here you'll find storks' nests on the housetops, fine old buildings right out of the Middle Ages and a series of narrow, charming lanes. The Hotel Dagmar is extremely attractive and would be pleasant for a stop of several days.

From Kolding, continue on route 10 to Haderslev, a busy little city on a fjord; you could hardly do better than to stay at the Hotel Norden, facing the water. Continue on to Aabenraa, whose best hotel is the Søgaardhus. Then on to Krusaa and the German border at Flensburg. (For a continuation of the trip through Germany, via route 76, please refer to the tour section for that country.)

࢝ Motoring in Denmark

The entire country is mostly flat, with some slightly hilly areas in the countryside to break the monotony. You won't find the superhighways that exist in other parts of Europe, but the roads will be well paved and in excellent condition in the vast majority of cases. Travel distances are short and there is seldom any need for the tourist to hurry. The islands making up Denmark—there are 500 of them, remember?—are connected by busy ferries that generally offer frequent service, except in really outlying parts of the country. Some ferries you can drive on, as we said, without any reservations, but others are so busy during the summer touring season that it is best to check beforehand on the situation. The Royal Danish Automobile Club at Nyropsgade 47, in Copenhagen, will help you. Please don't trust to luck in the summertime.

As for the documents you need when you drive *into* the country from abroad, there are only a few. Your home-state driver's license, for one thing, is good. You'll also have to have registration papers for the car. That's natural. Then there is that Green Card, the third-party insurance coverage. Your coverage—and this is important

—must extend to travel in Norway, Sweden and Finland, as well as Denmark. If your insurance does not meet this specification, or the minimum coverage required, you'll have to get a White Card at the border. This costs 10 kr. a day for up to thirty days; 4 kr. a day, thereafter, with a maximum charge of 600 kr. for a year. One other thing you'll have to have is a nationality plate identifying the country in which the car is registered (USA for an American-registered car, F for France, etc.). Rental cars have them as a rule, but check.

There is no automatic priority given to cars on main highways. But anyone entering a main road from an approach or side road has to halt. It is best to be careful in all cases.

Gasoline prices are high—regular, 1.37 kr. a liter; premium, 1.43. Oil ranges from 5.10 to 7.20 kr. a liter.

The one and only big problem for the motorist here is the tremendous number of bicycles everywhere. A good deal of practice is required before you become accustomed to driving surrounded by dozens (sometimes hundreds!) of erratic cyclists. There is even danger of an accident when a traffic light changes suddenly and all the bicyclists stop equally suddenly. Exercise extreme care under such circumstances. Fortunate indeed is the motorist who finds himself driving on a highway where there is a separate lane for bicycles.

Scandinavia is extremely tough on drivers who have been drinking. Notice, we did not say "drunk driving." Even a small amount of alcohol can cause you problems should you become involved in an accident. The accompanying annoyance will often interfere with your trip and at the very least you'll almost surely lose your right to drive in Denmark.

The speed limit in built-up areas is usually posted in kilometers. Otherwise, there is no speed limit; but distances are never very great. So why hurry?

In some places, you'll have to park on the even-numbered side of the street on even days of the month; odd on the odd. Get it? Other times, there are signs telling about the parking arrangement. In the middle of Copenhagen, parking is generally limited to one hour—and the police are expert in that tow-away procedure in balky cases!

Traffic keeps to the right, just as in the United States.

If a vast generalization will be forgiven, it's our considered opinion that Danish drivers, as a group, are among the most law-abiding and best in Europe.

Pointer: Copenhagen's parking meters come in colors. At the yellow-painted ones you pay 1 kr. an hour; at the green, 50 øre; blue, 25 øre. But you cannot use any meter longer than three hours.

ENGLAND AND SCOTLAND

National Characteristics

People started coming to England 2,000 years ago—at least the arrival time of the Romans is the first date written down in the country's guest book. Other names, like the Saxons and Danes, the Vikings and Normans, have been added to the guest book as the centuries have flown by. The result is that England's guest book reads like a family album of the civilized world.

You'll feel at home here—like one of the family. And why not?

All those people coming here over the past 2,000 years, with the abbeys and castles the British built, their laws and customs, their tenaciousness and sense of tradition, created one of history's great nations and at the same time affected the lives of other men and women across the face of the earth—sometimes for the good, sometimes for the not so good. Some of the oldering folks among us—here as well as in England—would probably wish to mute the current impact from swinging London, as represented in the merciless Mersey beat of the Beatles, the Stones (the Rolling ones, we mean) and other merrie (?) men. The din from London town causes some to turn a thought nostalgically to the days—were they really in the pre-Norman times?—when the music that brought Manchester renown was played by the distinguished Hallé Orchestra.

But England is alive, and the world knows it!

For almost a thousand years—since the Normans made their celebrated arrival in 1066—England had been at the center of the world's attention in one way or another. Britannia no longer rules the waves—or the air, land or space, for that matter. The British have been buffeted by one economic storm after the other since World War II. Although they won the war, conditions have been tough for the English people in the postwar decades. Currently they're banking a rosy future on their entry into the Common Market. But the Englishman himself will be the last to tell you that life is difficult. That stiff-upper-lip attitude is part and parcel of the English spirit. They have been tightening their belts and pulling up their socks so much that one would think they had reached their limit and could not make another effort. But only someone who does not know the British would think that. Please do not underestimate them or sell them short. It would be neither a nice thing to do nor a wise one.

The British come as a pleasant surprise to Americans, in many ways. There is the matter of little courtesies, for everyday contact between people has been smoothed to a greater degree than in our own country by small civilities. "Thank you" and "Beg pardon" are not only everyday, but every-minute expressions here.

Critics proclaim, with some justification, that the English are insular. For example, they feel sorry for anyone so unfortunate as not to have been born an Englishman. They are patient and magnificently civilized. Nothing seems to fluster them. Whether they were waiting in a ration line in the days after the war or for a bus on a snappy morning on Regent Street this past winter, they took their turn calmly. They are stubborn, too; so stubborn that they didn't know they were licked in the last war. And now, unfortunately, the English seem to have become infected with an inferiority complex on a national scale. No longer the leaders in world affairs after generations of rule, some English people criticize American foreign policy and political strategy, conveniently forgetting their magnificent flubs when *they* had a chance at leadership. Of course, there are some disgruntled Englishmen who are annoyed that the world's power is now in the hands of their cousins over here, just as there are some Americans who feel a bit smug that life is sweeter for them than it is in the Mother Country. But, happily, such people are a minority.

Lots of people are still pouring into England as visitors each year. The number of visitors each year is well into the millions, and the American representation is close to the million mark. Americans are very welcome all over the nation. The language will make you feel at home right away. But that won't be the reason you feel that way. Language, as it is supposed to, will be only a vehicle for transporting you right into the world and the lives of the English people without any intermediaries of translators or interpreters. Language will simplify, facilitate and sharpen your awareness and understanding of those special characteristics that make English peoples so very *English*.

When to Go

The phrase "Spring comes early to England" is more than just a light-hearted bit of poesy. It does get there early, and it is splendid. The English take their weather calmly, except that they do get enthusiastic about the balmy, soft days of spring. The tourist season runs from April all the way through October, with the greatest emphasis upon June, July and August. The very best season in England may well be April (when spring begins delightfully in the countryside) and May. The fall months are more variable. In fact, the word for weather in England is "variable," because most days the poor weatherman is likely to change his forecast without too much forewarning. It is wonderful to listen to the BBC announcer pass on to listeners the weatherman's warnings. The accent is always on the affirmative. "There will be bright intervals in some places," he will say hopefully. "Today will be fair with some showers in the afternoon" is another twist. A light rain, as a matter of fact, may be expected almost any day you're here, but successive days of rain are comparatively rare during the tourist season. Incidentally, it never gets terribly hot during the summer, but some years it can be really cold in the winter. One recent winter, however, Londoners were practically sunbathing at lunch hours in Hyde Park. But you cannot bank on a mild winter. Not a bit. We would be less than honest if we didn't mention the fact that the winter months can be rainy and foggy, although the old-time "pea-soup fogs" seem to be practically gone if not forgotten. On the other hand, if your visit is confined to London, come even during the winter, because the city is particularly fascinating then. Let's phrase that again: Don't come to England and expect two weeks of perfect weather, even though that might have happened sometime between 1066 and today. Nonetheless, several days of superb weather in a row are commonplace. What's been said previously goes double for Scotland, where the climate is even cooler, damper and rainier. (Is that possible?)

WEATHER STRIP: LONDON

Temp.	JAN.	FEB.	MAR.	APR.	MAY	JUNE	JULY	AUG.	SEPT.	OCT.	NOV.	DEC.
Low	35°	35°	36°	40°	45°	51°	54°	54°	49°	44°	39°	36°
High	43°	45°	49°	55°	62°	68°	71°	70°	65°	56°	49°	45°
Average	39°	40°	43°	48°	54°	60°	63°	62°	57°	50°	44°	41°
Days of rain	17	13	11	14	13	11	13	13	13	14	16	16

TIME EVALUATION ¶ If you have a month for your entire European trip, allow not less than a week for England, unless you are just planning to visit London, in which case three to four days would be sufficient. For a little sightseeing, allow no less than a week, or as much more time as you can spare—England is worth it.

PASSPORT AND VISA ¶ For a ninety-day stay, all you need is a passport. No visa is required. For longer stays, you'll have to make an application, and permission is customarily granted.

CUSTOMS AND IMMIGRATION ¶ Just as, geographically, Great Britain is between the United States and Europe, the British customs are between American and continental ones if you were to classify them on a scale from Easy to Efficient. Well, you get the idea. So many things are taxed in the British Isles that the gentlemen of Her Majesty's Customs Service have to be on their toes to make sure that visitors are not lugging with them articles that will find their way onto the local market without benefit of the appropriate tax. The customs men have a chart that, before the examination begins, they hold up in front of you. This is not an eye test for a driver's license. The chart, in big, easy-to-read lettering, lists a dozen or some items that are especially dutiable and therefore of prime interest to the customs people. This chart comes in all languages, too. But the chances are the customs men will not say anything more to you than wish you a pleasant stay. As a practical matter, they are extremely lenient toward Americans and only bear down if they have a reason for doing so. If you're courteous, you'll find them courteous. But they can really give you the business when they're annoyed. You're allowed (if you are 17 years of age or over) 400 cigarettes, a fifth of liquor and about the same-size bottle of wine, one quarter pint of perfume, a reasonable amount of film, a camera, a transistor and personal articles.

Antiques and miscellaneous works of art may be taken out of the country, providing they are not worth more than £500. There are restrictions, also, on exporting stamp collections. Applications for licenses to export items on the restricted list should be made to the Board of Trade, Export License Branch, at Gavrelle House, 14 Bunhill Row, London. Better check there, too, if you have bought any furs or valuable gold articles while you were in the country.

HEALTH ¶ The water, vegetables and milk are completely safe all over England, and there is no reason to give any more consideration to the health problem than you would at home. As a resident—even though a temporary one —you will be covered by the famous British socialized medicine program. That means doctor bills will (or should) be small, unless you go to the "rooms" of one of those celebrated Harley Street specialists. The hotel manager either will send you to a doctor or will have one call on you if that is required.

Bring some fairly warm clothes, particularly during the spring and fall season. The stoic British don't believe that central heating (from radiators) is healthy, and they frequently hesitate to light a fire unless it really gets chilly —you know? snow on the ground, ice on the lake and all that sort of thing. We've had dinner in several country inns where the temperature in the dining room hovered in the low sixties. While we shivered, our hearty British neighbors were comfortable in their long woolies (we couldn't see them, but guessed), sweaters and heavy tweeds. Be forewarned!

TIME ¶ England is now on Central European Time, which is six hours ahead of Eastern Standard Time. When Daylight Saving Time is in effect in the United States, the time difference is only five hours.

CURRENCY ¶ Well, they've done it. Done what? Gotten rid of the fantastically complex system of money and coins which drove everyone a little crazy, especially the British. Gone, gone, is the whimsical British system of counting and computing money. That currency system had the pound (£) divided into 20 shillings, each shilling divided into 12 pence.

Now, Britain has gone "decimal." As a result, there are 100 new pence in each pound. They are written as 100p. In order to cope with expected fractions which are likely to arise, they've issued a new halfpenny piece, a tiny coin that looks like something that might be included in a children's game. There's also a new penny, much like an American penny, plus a new bronze 2-penny piece, slightly larger than an American quarter. But that's not all. Those are the three bronze coins that have been added. There are also three new cupronickel silver coins—5 pence (5p), 10p and 50p. The 50p coin, by the way, has seven sides. Oh, yes—the old 2-shilling, 1-shilling and 6-pence coins will continue in circulation. Under the new system they will be the equivalent of 10p, 5p and 2½p, respectively.

You might breathe a trifle easier knowing the bank notes will be unchanged in denomination. There will be one, five, ten, and twenty pound notes.

Here's how the old and new look. Under the old system, four pounds ten shillings was written as £4 10s; under the new, it is £4·50.

The new currency is written on checks, or price tags, in either of two ways. To indicate 29 pounds, you would write (or read) either £29–00 or £29·00, the dash being used for handwritten figures, and the decimal point for those that are typed or printed.

Sorry, there's one additional complication. For centuries, the professional fees of doctors and lawyers have been quoted in guineas, each equal to 1 pound and 1 shilling. Quite a few of the more expensive shops had developed the snobbish habit of quoting prices in guineas as well, and although they're not supposed to do so any longer, it's a difficult habit to break, and no one knows precisely what will happen in the future.

If you really are confused when paying a bill, perhaps the best advice I can offer is to pay with a note and take your change. After all, the British do have a good reputation for honesty.

PRICE LEVEL ¶ The various revaluations of recent years have at times made it difficult for the visitor to keep track of. In any case, the price level is generally high. Prices, perhaps, are something like American ones to a certain extent. At least in regard to food. In cafeteria-like places and snack bars the food is inexpensive. But then there are the smart restaurants where you can spend $15 per person. Hotels in London can run to $40 and more for a double room, but out in the countryside you will be able to find a pleasant inn where you'll spend $4 (per person) for a comfortable room that includes a hearty breakfast. It's all very confusing. Theater tickets remain a great bargain, especially compared with the fabulous New York tariffs. For two or three pounds, you can get a good seat. Hair-cuts, shampoos and sets run about one-third the prices in the United States. So keep having your hair cut and set as often as possible.

TIPPING ¶ With the confusing British currency, you'll have to be especially careful on the tipping procedure. If you can, try to work out a system for yourself, giving at least 5p (a shilling) for small services and twice that as the usual tip. In other words, the porter should get a 10p coin for each bag he carries for you. The usual taxi tip, if it is a short ride, is 5p. But at night, or on a ride across town, give at least 10p.

In restaurants, tip 10 to 15 percent of the bill if the service charge has not been added. If it has, nothing more is in order unless you're feeling extra generous. Hat check girls should be given at least 10p and, in a top restaurant, at least 15p.

Some hotels add a 10 percent surcharge, which takes the place of tips all around. But if this is not on your hotel bill, you are expected to distribute tips yourself in about the same amount (the 10 percent of the bill, we mean). With regard to the hall porter (the equivalent of the continental concierge), don't bother tipping him if you're only at the hotel for a day or so. For longer stays, or if he has done some service for you (tickets, reservations, etc.), a 50p tip is proper in a small hotel and double that in a larger, more expensive establishment.

TRANSPORTATION ¶ Getting around England is easy. All cities have fine public transportation systems (usually, those wonderful double-decker buses), and there is excellent service between cities by train, bus, air and highway.

Taxi rates in London are close to what they are in New York. Fairly high, we think. Between midnight and 6 A.M. an extra charge of about a quarter is added to the meter fare. If you arrange with a taxi driver to take you on an extended tour or beyond the city limits, make sure the arrangement includes a flat price definitely agreed upon in advance. You can hire a "Minicab," too.

Pointer: The taxi fare from Heathrow Airport to Piccadilly Circus is about $8. The fare on the bus that operates around the clock between the airport and the air terminal at Cromwell Road is a little over a dollar.

Buses in London are worth a ride or two just for the fun of peering around from the upper deck of a red double-decker. The fares vary according to the distance you travel—so much for each zone. So you have to let the conductor know in advance how far you plan to travel. If you wish to go to the end of the line, just let him know. He can be helpful, too, with sightseeing suggestions.

Bus trips (which the British refer to as coach trips) into the countryside are not nearly as enjoyable as driving your own car, but you can see more than on a train. Long-distance bus travel is about two-thirds the price of a Second Class rail ticket, ranging from 3 to 5 cents a mile. The London-Edinburgh express bus fare, for example, is about $8. If you are going to do a lot of bus traveling in England, get a copy—before leaving New York—of the A.B.C. Coach and Bus Guide. Thomas Skinner & Co., Trinity Building, 111 Broadway, in New York City has it. There is a summer section and a winter one, and the guide has timetables for most British bus lines.

The *underground* (what we would call the subway) is something that should be tried in London, because it's an experience.

The London *transportation system* is the biggest in the world, with something like 8 million passengers carried every weekday. For about $10 you can buy a master ticket allowing you seven days' unlimited travel on buses and trains of the London Transport system. There is also a Go-as-You-Please ticket, costing around $7, that provides the same service except for travel on the Green Line coaches. You can buy these tickets at any office of the British Railways or in London at the Fares Office of London Transport, 55 Broadway, Westminster, S.W. 1. Get a free map of the transport system from the Travel Enquiry offices at Piccadilly Circus and St. James's Park Station, at Eccleston Bridge (Victoria), and the City Information Center, St. Paul's Churchyard. There's around-the-clock transport information by calling 01-222-1234.

Pointer: London Transport buses make an inexpensive two-hour twenty-mile tour of local landmarks morning, afternoon and evening throughout the year (except Christmas). Starting point is in Buckingham Palace Road between Victoria Station and Eccleston Bridge. There are no reserved-in-advance seats, so come early.

Train service has improved greatly in Britain in recent times, thanks to an extensive modernization program of British Railways. Just about every nook and cranny in the country is within reach. Second Class travel costs about 5½ cents a mile, and First Class is 50 percent higher. There are various reduced-price tickets for day and half-day excursions, as well as for unlimited travel over a week or a two-week period. Rail-Rover and such other reduced-fare tickets as Freedom of Scotland and Freedom of Wales are bargains for those traveling in the March to October period. Trains have such wonderful names as *The Flying Scotsman* (serving Edinburgh from London), *The Royal Scot* (Glasgow), *The Cornish Riviera Express* (Penzance) and *The Irish Mail*, a venerable, colorful train that meets the Irish mail boats (which also carry passengers) at Holyhead, not far from Liverpool. All the train service to the continent can be recommended, particularly the *Golden Arrow*, a luxury train in which meals are served directly at your well-upholstered seat. In the event that you want to combine car and train travel to some holiday point, British Railways now operates both car-sleeper service (like the continental *auto-couchette*) for overnight trips and daytime car-carrier service. There also are, of course, sleeping accommodations on leading trains for travelers who do not have a car with them. A top overnight sleeper is the *Night Ferry*, connecting London with the continent. It leaves Victoria Station after dinner and arrives in Paris at breakfast time. The train makes the trip by ferry just as smooth as can be.

To speed up service even more, British Rail has introduced a fleet of one thousand Inter-City expresses which link two hundred cities of Britain day and night. Here are some typical Inter-City schedules from London: to Birmingham, 110 miles, 90 minutes; Edinburgh, 393 miles, 347 minutes; Manchester, 183 miles, 151 minutes; Oxford, 63 miles, 60 minutes; Southampton, 79 miles, 70 minutes; York, 188 miles, 158 minutes.

Pointer: A reserved seat on main trains costs about 60 cents extra.

Air transportation is good, but most tourists won't make much use of internal service except to Ireland or to some comparatively distant points from London such as Scotland, Wales, the Isle of Man and the Channel Islands.

Water travel is possible on excursion boats traveling along the inland waterways of England and Wales or by the regular passenger service to England's islands and to the islands around Scotland's Clyde coast. Remember, this is a seafaring nation, so travel by boat is an ever-present, and often extremely delightful, possibility.

COMMUNICATIONS ¶ You'll have no difficulty recognizing public *telephone* booths because they're painted red (a distinctive red, at that) and are scattered all over the place. But England and Scotland are doing some switching on their phones that will be going on for a couple of years yet. Previously, as well as currently in a good majority of cases, telephone numbers were a combination of letters and numerals. But now London, Birmingham, Manchester, Liverpool, Glasgow and Edinburgh are changing to all-numeral telephone numbers. So it is possible that you will encounter a combination of both types of numbers—and that will make things all the more interesting. No? To make everything even more fascinating (I doubt it) in the field of communications, "pay on answer" telephones are being installed to replace the old-type prepayment ones. Calls are 2 pence. The old-style telephones have A and B buttons. Deposit 2 pence and dial your number. When the person at the other end speaks, press button A and complete the call; if there is no answer, press button B and your money will be refunded. The new phones simplify this procedure. You pay only when the other party answers.

Long distance calls within England range up to a dollar or so, but there is a reduction on the tariffs in the evening. Calls to the United States for three minutes are about $6 during the day and about 20 percent less than that at night.

Pointer: It is now possible to dial many U. S. cities direct from the United Kingdom.

There are something like 25,000 *post offices* in England, Scotland and Northern Ireland. A book of stamps— sold at various, convenient rates—is handy and saves the trouble (and often the hidden cost) of having the hotel concierge mail letters for you. Furthermore, these stamp books have current postal rates in them. Mail rates are something that change relatively frequently, as they are a direct means of revenue. Airmail to the United States costs close to a quarter for letters; postcards are about a third less. Service is excellent, with airmail delivered within two or three days after mailing.

Telegrams come close to a dollar for regular messages of a dozen words within England; night telegrams, with a minimum of 20 words, are cheaper and are worthwhile for hotel reservations and the like.

USEFUL TELEPHONE NUMBERS ¶ By dialing 01-246-8041 you can hear a recorded announcement of main events taking place in London during the day. The same type of service operates in Scotland's beautiful city of Edinburgh from May to September. The number there is 031-246-8041.

Weather, as could be expected, is also something to inquire about in England, and forecasts are available (but not guaranteed) by telephone. In London, dial 01-246-8091; in Edinburgh, dial 031-246-8091.

In case of a real emergency—when you need police, fire or ambulance—dial 999.

INFORMATION SERVICE ¶ Since hotel space is often so difficult, it is extremely advisable to keep in mind that there are a number of hotel information services in London. Their names and numbers are usually indicated in public telephone areas at airports and rail terminals. There is no charge for the service.

In addition, there are several official tourist offices in London and at main railroad stations. The British Travel

Association, 64 St. James's Street, London, S.W. 1, will help you with your sightseeing plans. The City of London has an information center at St. Paul's. There are also official information offices at the West London Air Terminal in Cromwell Road, the Airways Terminal in Buckingham Palace Road, Victoria Railway Station and Waterloo Railway Station.

BASIC ENGLISH ¶ We do speak the same language, but there are certain differences in terms, pronunciations and accents. Most of us, after watching all those English films, know that a *bonnet* is the hood of an automobile, a *brolly* is an umbrella—and other little niceties of the language. You'll have little trouble until you encounter a Cockney (unless it is Michael Caine) or Lancashire-man, both of whom speak British English in the same way a hillybilly speaks American English.

ELECTRICITY ¶ Most of Britain has 200–250 volts, A.C., although once in a while you'll run into D.C. Since most American appliances—except international types—are 120 A.C., you'll need a transformer for an electric razor, for example. Before running out and buying one in an English store, check with your hotel. Many of them have them on hand for such emergencies. Also, you'll always need an adaptor plug with round prongs.

FOOD SPECIALTIES AND LIQUOR ¶ Mrs. Beeton, the acknowledged authority on food in Britain, has stated that the chief purpose of cooking food is to assist in mastication. Not a word about making it delicious or tempting! That attitude, in capsule form, summarizes what is wrong with typical British food.

But the canny traveler can lick most of the problem, chiefly by knowing what to order and what to avoid. About meals, first: breakfast is a good meal, often the best of the day. If you're not a member of the coffee and toast set, you can have porridge and thick cream followed by kippers or eggs and bacon. If you don't specify coffee, you'll get tea. Many Britishers are cutting down on large breakfasts and having "elevenses," a snack in the mid-morning. Tea about 4:30 or 5 in the afternoon is the classic British meal and may consist of a cup of strong tea with a scone or a bun or even a crumpet (attention, all P. G. Wodehouse fans!). But tea might also mean a meal of several courses, in addition to tea and cake. Both breakfast and tea are excellent and you need give no concern to eating heartily at those meals.

But lunch, at about 12:30 or 1 P.M., and dinner, beginning at about 7 P.M., are meals requiring a little thought (and planning). The British do know how to make some fine dishes, but in general the food is unimaginative. Among the appetizers, there's nothing to equal Scotch smoked salmon, a truly great delicacy. The local oysters are absolutely superb and with these, order a glass of Chablis or whatever type beer or ale suits your fancy. Potted shrimp are worth a try, too. Soup is never a thrilling item in typical English restaurants. Fresh fish is, and if you've never had the real, the genuine, the one and only Dover sole, you've missed a great treat. No matter how it's prepared, it's delicious—particularly grilled. The same goes for almost all fresh fish, especially salmon. Fish and chips (fried fish sticks and French fried potatoes) are to the British what hot dogs are to Americans. Some places serve them in newspaper shaped into a cone.

Now comes a kind word for the British way of handdling roast beef: excellent, although not necessarily better than the same dish at home; the British prefer to slice it thin and serve several slices, rather than one thick slice in the American fashion. Roast lamb is good, but there seems to be some sort of law requiring it to be served with caper or mint sauce. Beware of roast mutton! It's too strong for American tastes. Don't look for or anticipate American style steaks—unless you're very lucky, they'll be disappointingly bad. Meat pies are rarely good (ye gods, what an understatement!) and should be avoided except in the better places. The British have a word for vegetables, but that word invariably is Brussels sprouts— oh well, stretch it a point and add boiled cabbage. With rare exceptions, the British dearly love to overcook vegetables, and that goes for potatoes, too, which they boil to excess. Salads are just about nonexistent, if you're looking for crisp, crunchy ones. Most puddings and sweets are fairly insipid to American tastes, but fruit tarts and "fools" (notably raspberry and gooseberry) can be superb. If you are a cheese enthusiast, look for Stilton, or anything in the way of a local cheese.

But all of the above applies to typical British food; good restaurants abound, mostly of the foreign type— the best French restaurants in London serve almost as good a meal as you can get in Paris. But don't expect spectacular fare at very low cost, because first-rate food here, as elsewhere, is expensive. Around the Soho district, close to the theatrical area, are clusters of small foreign restaurants (particularly suitable for dining if you're going to see a show); these are all interesting. A good suggestion for theater nights is to have a large tea, and then dinner after the performance, which ends at about 9:30 or so.

When you want Scotch, ask for whisky, because *whisky* means Scotch to Britishers. If you've never had Irish *whiskey*, try it—many people like it. Don't be surprised if your whisky portion is pretty small and seemingly weak; both are probable because the average drink is only one ounce and its alcoholic strength is less than the export version we're used to. Gin is another favorite in England but seldom taken neat; it's usually served with tonic, with Italian vermouth (gin and It), bitters, lime, etc. There have been so many American soldiers and tourists in England that bartenders rarely will fall over in a dead faint when you ask for ice in your drink, but they *do* get very pale.

Now what about beer? Most Americans are accustomed to light beer, dark beer and ale; that's it. In England, land of beer, they brew up a whole world of varieties including mild, bitter, ale, stout, old, pale brown and so far into the night. Beer drinkers like to order combinations of two beers—mild and bitter, for example. Many drinks have special nicknames; a stout and bitter is called a "mother-in-law." The beers are all good, without exception, but the national custom is to serve them warm.

WHAT TO EAT IN ENGLAND

British specialties are rarely served in large tourist restaurants.

Cornish pastries: Individual miniature pies with various fillings
Lancashire hotpot: A famous stew with lamb and vegetables
Exeter stew: A beef stew with onions and dumplings
Stargazy pie: A rich fish pie
Kedgeree: A rice and fish dish
Plaice: A local fish similar to, but not quite so good as, sole
Brawn: Pickled meats, served cold
Rarebit or rabbit: A melted cheese dish, usually served with toast
Yorkshire pudding: The favorite accompaniment to roast beef

—a flour, milk, eggs and fat preparation with a taste similar to that of a popover

Marmalade: Refers to lemon or orange preserves; any other fruit flavor is called jam

Marlborough pudding: An apple-flavored sweet dessert

Fruit fool: Puréed fruits combined with milk and cream

Fruit trifle: A classic dessert of sponge cake with various fruits

Clotted or Devonshire cream: Extra-rich and thick cream, usually cannot be poured

Savoury: A piquant, small preparation of anchovies, bacon, cheese, etc., served at the conclusion of a meal, after dessert

WHAT TO EAT IN SCOTLAND

Scottish specialties are rarely served in large tourist restaurants.

Bannock: A flat cake of dough, made with white or barley flour

Baps: The standard breakfast roll served in Scotland

Scots broth or barley broth: A vegetable and mutton soup

Haggis: The classic Scottish dish of a sheep's pluck (liver, lights and heart) cooked in the sheep's stomach; only recommended to the fearless

Cock-a-leekie: A chicken and leek soup

Finnan-Haddie: Smoked haddock

Partans: Local crabs

Stovies: A type of peeled, baked potatoes

Skirlie: Cooked onions and oatmeal, served instead of potatoes

Scones: Raised tea cakes, customarily split and spread with butter or jam

Shortbread: Delicious, rich cookies made with plenty of butter

Parlies: A sort of ginger cooky

Capital City

London's newest sight is the tall tower atop the Post Office Building on New Oxford Street, and on a fine day it is a very fine place to visit for an espresso and a lofty look around. It's the highest point in the city. But no matter how you look at London—whether it is from the Post Office Tower or from street level—you will find that it is one of the most civilized and sophisticated cities in the world, even if its climate isn't. Another point: No one knows whether New York, Tokyo or London is the largest city in the world because this depends on how much miscellaneous suburban territory and population are included in the computations by overzealous politicos. But London is *big.* Make no mistake about that!

Let's get oriented first. The Thames River cuts across the city, and very little south of the river (the left bank)

offers much of interest to the vast majority of tourists. A central focal point north of the river is Piccadilly Circus, which you've probably seen pictured in many English movies or on a TV screen. Piccadilly Circus is not a circus, of course, but an open area surrounding a group of statuary and bears the same relationship to London as does Times Square to New York. Leading away from the circus westward is Piccadilly, an important, heavily trafficked street. For a little sightseeing on foot, walk down Coventry Street (which leads to the east away from Piccadilly Circus) to Leicester Square. Here is the heart of the theatrical district. All around the square are legitimate theaters, cinemas and restaurants. In the center is an attractive green park, with a statue of Shakespeare. At the square's western edge is Leicester Street, which you now follow southward (it becomes St. Martin's Street) to 250-year-old St. Martin's-in-the-Fields, a pleasing old church. Across the way is the National Portrait Gallery, which calls for a visit on the first rainy day—or now, if you have the time (open Monday to Friday, 10 to 5; Saturday, 10 to 6; Sunday, 2 to 6; admission free).

This region is busy Trafalgar Square, whose central figure is the famous statue of Lord Nelson. On one side is Canada House; on the other, South Africa House. Cut around this square directly into Whitehall, a double-size street lined with government offices. On your right you'll see the Admiralty, then the War Office on your left, followed by the Horse Guards on your right again. At the first turn on your right is Downing Street, and is there any other number but No. 10? This is the home of the prime minister, but the other houses are interesting, too; these are set aside for other government officeholders. "No. 10" has been thoroughly renovated in recent times —inside, that is.

Now walk toward the Thames (being sure to call it "Tems," even when merely thinking about it), where you'll find New Scotland Yard—yes, where all those tight-lipped, tweed-wearing, pipe-smoking detectives do their detecting. Early in 1967 they moved most of their operations to a modern skyscraper that probably in time will be called the New New Scotland Yard. Walking alongside the Thames in the direction of Westminster Bridge, you'll see Big Ben, the clock that held a special significance to the British during the last war. The Germans finally did manage to blast it out of operation for a short time, but the BBC was ready with a recording and the Germans never did find out the truth of the matter (good show!).

Here are the Houses of Parliament—the House of Commons nearest the bridge, the House of Lords extending southward. It's easy to tell if the Commons are sitting, for there is always a flag flying during the daytime and a light burning over the Clock Tower at night whenever this ancient body is in session. In front, facing onto Parliament Square, is Westminister Hall, one of the outstanding buildings in London, dating back to 1099. In this historic spot were held the trials of Charles I, Sir Thomas More and Guy Fawkes—losers all. If you would like to attend a session of the Commons, apply through the American Embassy in Grosvenor Square. Otherwise, there are guided tours on Saturdays, Easter Monday, Easter Tuesday, Easter Wednesday, Whit Monday, Whit Tuesday, Whit Wednesday, the bank holiday in August and those Mondays and Tuesdays during August when neither House of Parliament is sitting. On these same days, you can visit the House of Lords from 10 to 4:30.

Across the street is Westminister Abbey, probably one of the most interesting buildings in all of England. No one knows for sure the earliest origins of this venerable structure, but it seems probable that a Benedictine abbey first stood on the site during the eighth century. Many rulers of Old England lie in its vaults, and coronation ceremonies for present-day kings and queens of England are conducted here. The interior, unfortunately, is a hodgepodge of miscellaneous alcoves and crannies. Great and not-so-great men (but of political influence) are buried within its walls. The abbey is suitable for a visit of almost any duration. Two years ago Westminster Abbey celebrated the 900th anniversary of its consecration. It is generally open to visitors all day, except when there are special services. A quarter hour may be pleasantly spent in the abbey, or half a day. At any time the abbey holds something for the viewer. But we've had enough for one walk, haven't we?

Another day, you'll have to visit the museums. Even if you don't care for tripping through the ordinary ones, the British Museum is something quite special, although to be ultracritical we might say that it is coldly arranged (open weekdays, including bank holidays, 10 to 5; Sundays, 2:30 to 6; admission free). No matter how hasty the visit, everyone should see the famed Rosetta Stone, noted for its hieroglyphics. Jean François Champollion, the famous archaeologist, was the first person able to read the inscriptions, thus permitting translations of many of the previously incomprehensible writings of ancient Egypt. In the Elgin Rooms are the renowned marbles, the Parthenon sculptures, often considered the British Museum's prize possession. Among art exhibits, the Tate Gallery (open daily, 10–6; Sundays, 2–6; admission free) is best known for its collection of French Impressionists and the work of the English painter and water colorist, J. M. W. Turner. The National Gallery, which we already mentioned, has a tremendous collection covering all nations, but with greatest emphasis upon the English masters (now in comparative artistic obscurity).

One day make a trip to St. Paul's Cathedral, the third to be built on the identical spot, both of those previous having been destroyed by fire. You may reach the cathedral from Piccadilly by taking an eastbound No. 13 bus, which runs through Trafalgar Square into the Strand and then into Fleet Street, the newspaper district. When the bus begins to climb Ludgate Hill, get ready to alight at the cathedral. Or just ask the conductor to let you know when to get off. During the war, St. Paul's (No. 3, the one dating back to the Great Fire of 1666) was hit twice by bombs. But it has since been restored according to the original specifications of its great designer, Sir Christopher Wren. Americans will be especially interested in the American Memorial Chapel, where the number of its visitors indicates that not everyone forgets. There are small fees (5p or 10p) charged for admission to the crypt, the Whispering and Stone galleries and the Golden Gallery. The cathedral is open, April to September, from 8 to 7. The crypt, galleries and upper dome are open from 10:45 to 3:30 the year around, as well as from 4:45 to 6:30 P.M. during the summer. Inasmuch as St. Paul's is a tall structure located on a high point of ground, the view from the dome is unexcelled on a clear day.

Leave the cathedral and walk east on Watling Street, passing Friday and Bread (those names!) Streets and turning left on Bow Lane. Bow Church is on the left. (By definition, a Cockney is anyone born within the sound of the bells of Bow Church.) Continue ahead to Cheapside and turn right. You'll come to King Street, where you turn left and walk to the Guildhall, one of the most historic buildings of the city (open weekdays, 10–5; Sundays, from May to September, 2–5; closed on certain holidays and also on days preceding special events, such as a ceremonial banquet).

Now walk back on King Street until you come to Gresham Street. Turn left and go straight ahead for about four blocks to the Bank of England. This is the heart of "The City," London's financial district. If you enjoy just watching people, here is your opportunity to see the epitome of an English clerk (pardon us, "clark"), with his striped trousers, dark jacket and bowler and carrying the slim, furled umbrella. (In the City, it's not an umbrella if it isn't slim and furled.) King William Street cuts in front of the Bank of England. Follow this to Cornhill Street and pass the Royal Exchange. Continue on Cornhill, passing Gracechurch Street to Lloyd's, the insurance syndicate's building—that is, Lloyd's of London. Go back to Gracechurch Street and head south toward the Thames, where you will see the monument designed by Sir Christopher Wren to commemorate the Great Fire of 1666. The fire is said to have started close to where the monument now stands. The bridge over the river is London Bridge—you know, the one in the song that's supposed to be falling down. An ancestor of the present London Bridge has been reassembled in western Arizona, and is now a big tourist attraction there.

Now walk eastward along Monument Street, passing (at the waterfront) Billingsgate Market, the world-famous fish market, which might be worth a visit if you can manage to be there shortly after 6 A.M. (the opening time), when it is going full blast. It is open on Sunday, too (also starting at 6 A.M.), but only shellfish are on sale. The neighborhood around here isn't too choice, but shows you a side of London you may have missed. Monument Street joins lower Thames Street, and you'll pass the Custom House and finally come to the Tower of London. (Incidentally, this all calls for a spot of walking, as the British say.)

The tower dates back to 1078, when William the Conqueror built it to hold a few die-hard recalcitrant English who didn't know when to stop fighting—which proves they were stubborn, even then. Admission to the tower is 10 pence (10p). It is open from 10 A.M. to 5 P.M.

(4 P.M., in winter) on weekdays, and during British Summer Time from 2 to 5 P.M. on Sundays. Many a famous person has been executed here, including the noted princes, smothered (they say) by order of their uncle, the Duke of Gloucester, who later became Richard III. He was a nasty one, that uncle. Many ladies also came to a sudden and definite end here: Anne Boleyn, Catherine Howard and Lady Jane Grey—not to mention numerous others. If you have a spare shilling in your pocket, take a look at the Crown Jewels in the Jewel House. You'll see Victoria's Crown (containing a mere 2,927 diamonds), the royal scepter with the largest cut stone in the world (530 carats) that is known as the First Star of Africa and other dazzling items.

(Near the tower is Tower Bridge, the most famous span in the city. If you wish, it's possible to take one of the small boats that leave from Tower Pier, right at the entrance to the tower, and disembark at Westminster Pier, at the foot of Westminster Bridge, close to Big Ben.)

If you're in the mood for further interesting exploration via a bus ride, take a No. 78 bus at Tower Bridge *northward* to Liverpool Station, and there change for a No. 11. The No. 11 bus is famous as one of the cheap sightseeing trips across London. The route is through the center of London, the fare is less than a quarter and the run takes about an hour (depending on traffic). The bus travels toward the west through Fleet Street, the Strand and Trafalgar Square (duplicating the trip out to the tower), then swings southward through Whitehall, passing the Houses of Parliament and Westminster Abbey. It then proceeds around Victoria Station and down Buckingham Palace Road (which becomes Pimlico Road). The next point is Sloane Square, a sort of artists' area in the Chelsea district. A turn brings you into King's Road, once filled with antique shops; some remain. Here we will probably lose some of our sightseers, tempted by the chance of a bargain.

King's Road on Saturday afternoon should not be missed. The street is lined with "mod" boutiques, long-haired boys (I think), mini-skirted and unwashed girls and lots of excitement. Be sure to visit one of the coffee bars. Repeat—this is a "must."

Others will continue on, for this is one of those rare occasions when it's possible to see suburban London, with its neat, narrow houses and tidy shops, and the mode of life of the average Briton who commutes daily to the City. No. 11 plies its way bravely on to Hammersmith, the end of the line. Those who feel in need of liquid refreshment should walk just a little farther along to Shepherd's Bush and ask for a colorful pub called the World's End, definitely worth visiting. A No. 12 bus will bring you back to the center of town, near Piccadilly Circus.

Let's think about what else the conscientious sightseer should visit: Buckingham Palace is not open to the public, but it is possible to gain admittance to see not all, but some, of the Queen's horses and carriages in the Royal Mews. They are open on Wednesday and Thursday afternoons throughout the year (except during Ascot Week in June) from 2 to 4. The entrance fee is 15 pence (15p). The Queen's Gallery is open from Tuesday to Saturday from 11 A.M. to 5 P.M. and on Sunday afternoons from 2 to 5. The entrance fee here is also 15p.

Hyde Park has seen some turbulent events, but is all quite peaceful and placid now. While the park is pretty and has some pleasant walking paths, the most fascinating portion is in the northeast corner, at Marble Arch. On any pleasant evening, but especially on Sunday (all day), this is the place to hear the lunatic fringe of soapbox oratory, and everything you could possibly care to learn about: the Carnaby Street fashions, the general scene, the benefits of sunbathing, sending a man to the moon, juvenile delinquency, astrology, bad manners, the art of finger painting, support of a law to protect Arctic swallows during their migration and several other assorted burning issues of the day. Occasionally, very occasionally, mixed in all of this free-wheeling public speaking, is a person who seems to know what he's talking about and who has something to say. Definitely recommended on a pleasant Sunday.

The Temple and Lincoln's Inn (plus Grey's Inn) are two of the Inns of Court that have exclusive control of the legal profession in England. The name "Temple" is derived from the Knights Templar (of the Crusades), and its connection with the law goes back to the fourteenth century. The grounds of the Temple have loads of tradition and local color and extend from Fleet Street to the Thames. Alongside the river you'll see two famous ships: H.M.S. *President* and the *Wellington*. Farther along the Embankment (just below Waterloo Bridge) is

LONDON BOAT SERVICES

Destination	When Available	Leaves from	Elapsed Time
Tower	10:20 A.M. till dusk Daily April–September	Westminster or Charing Cross Pier	20 minutes

This is a pleasant way to get from central London to the Tower.

Greenwich	10:00 A.M. till dusk Daily April–September	Westminster or Charing Cross Pier	45 minutes

Greenwich is a good-size city of 100,000 and the site of the Royal Naval College; see the observatory in Greenwich Park. The reconstructed three-master *Cutty Sark* is a beautiful sailing ship; open 11–6 weekdays, 2:30–6 Sundays.

Kingston	Half-hourly 10:30 A.M.–4 P.M. Daily April–September	Richmond Pier	1 hour

Kingston was the scene of the coronation of several Saxon kings from 902 to 978; there is a coronation stone near the Guildhall.

Hampton Court	Half-hourly 10:30 A.M.–4 P.M. Daily April–September	Richmond Pier	1 hour 30 mins.

Hampton Court was given by Cardinal Wolsey to Henry VIII; it is especially attractive for a visit during springtime and the gardens are world famous. Be sure to see the State Apartments (all of Henry's wives lived here), the Great Hall and the Tudor Gate.

Putney Hammersmith Kew Richmond Kingston Hampton Court	At half-hour intervals to various destinations between the hours of 10 A.M. and 5 P.M. approximately. Time- tables are available at embarkation points. Daily April–September	Westminster or Charing Cross Pier	30 minutes 45 minutes 1 hour 45 mins. 2 hours 15 mins. 3 hours 30 mins. 4 hours

This is a local service that takes quite a long time to reach Kingston and Hampton Court. Anyone who is at all interested in gardening will enjoy a visit to Kew to see the Botanical Gardens. The greenhouses include a fabulous orchid collection, and there is a Chinese pagoda.

Southend Margate	9 A.M. daily except Fridays Whitsun to mid- September	Tower Pier	3 hours 5 hours

Southend resembles Coney Island; very lively and colorful on weekends. Margate is a busy seaside resort with good bathing.

London Docks	Summer months 2:30 P.M. Wednesday, Thursday and Saturday.	Tower Pier	4 hours

A wonderful way to see all the ships in London's great harbor; be sure to go on a pleasant day.

Canal trips leave daily (May through September) from Bloomfield Road, W. 9. (Take buses No. 1, 6, 8, 16 or 60; or take the tube to Warwick Avenue.) The small, narrow boats make several round trips every afternoon through Regent's Canal. The fare is about a half dollar. Reservations are admissible.

Canal cruises are made during summer months for one or two weeks; fares average about $30 per person per week. There are cabins with running water, pleasant companionship and a chance to see the country-side. Get in touch with any of the following:

    Sloan's New-Way Holidays, Oxford Mews, London, W.2.
    Inland Navigators, Banbury, Oxford.
    Inland Waterway Cruising Co., Braunston, Rugby.
    Waterborne Tours, Penkridge, Staffordshire.

Hostelboating, by horse-drawn canal boat, covers 100 miles in seven days for just under $20 per person. Low-pressure relaxation. Write to Waterway Projects Ltd., Autherley, Tettenhall, Wolverhampton (yes, that's all one address).

Captain Scott's ship *Discovery*. The *Discovery* is the vessel on which the explorer left for the Antarctic in 1890 and returned four years later. It is open to the public daily (including Sundays) from 1 to 4:45 P.M., and there is no admission charge. The *Wellington* is the headquarters for the Master Mariners; the *President* is used by the Royal Naval Volunteers Reserve. On the other side of Fleet Street, where it joins the Strand, are the Law Courts. The public galleries are open during sessions from 10 to 4, Monday through Friday. If the court is in session, you'll surely be rewarded by viewing the bewigged judges and lawyers in their court attire.

The Port of London is not easy to reach. The distance is great and much of the area is closed to the public. But there is a boat service touring the docks and the port area, leaving from Tower Pier. Check schedules with one of the official tourist offices which we have mentioned.

On Your Guard

A classic spectacle that will brighten up any day in London—regardless of the weather—is the Changing of the Guard. This custom is such a part of the London tradition that one almost gets the feeling that it has been going on since the days when the first monarch was enthroned. Actually, the protection of the British sovereign by a personal guard goes back only (!) three centuries and it was merely two centuries ago, when George III's acquisition of a piece of property called Buckingham House, introduced the custom of mounting the guard at what is now Buckingham Palace. It is a splendid ceremony.

The Queen's Guard is mounted each day at 11:30 A.M. at Buckingham Palace during the summer and also in the winter if she is in residence there. Otherwise, it is mounted from St. James's Palace. If the Queen is at Buckingham Palace during the winter, the Guard is mounted on weekends at St. James's. Then, there is the Queen's Life Guard, which is mounted from Horse Guards Parade, Whitehall, at eleven o'clock each weekday morning and at ten o'clock on Sundays throughout the year. These places are relatively close to each other, and since the time of the mounting of the guards is slightly different, it is possible—with some advance planning—to be present at both operations on the same morning. Sometimes special regiments mount the Guard, while the regular units of Guards are off on summer maneuvers. The individual regiments of Guards can be easily identified by the plume worn in their headdress: the Foot Guards, Grenadiers (white), Coldstream (red), Irish (blue) and Welsh (green and white); Cavalry, Life Guards (white) and Royal Horse Guards (scarlet). The Scots Guards do not wear plumes, poor fellows!

There is also the celebrated Trooping the Colour ceremony, a fascinating demonstration of pageantry and precision, which takes place once a year—on the Queen's official birthday, in June. A certain number of tickets are made available for this event by means of a drawing. If you want to have your name in the pot, write to Headquarters, Household Brigade, Horse Guards, London, S.W. 1. But you must have your letter there before March 1 for the following June's ceremony. If you don't get a ticket, the Mall offers plenty of viewing space. But better get there early—say, around daybreak!

LONDON'S MARKETS

Caledonian Market: This is now at Bermondsey Market, S.E. 1. It is open Fridays from 10 to 4. Specializes in silverware, pewter and plate—plus antiques. No longer a bargainer's paradise, but well worth a visit.

Petticoat Lane: Middlesex Street, E. 1. Open Sundays. This is a street market. The best time to go is on Sunday morning, from 9 to noon, before things get picked over too much and/or sold. Specializes in everything and anything, providing it's not new.

Whitechapel: Outdoors market, pushcarts, open stalls on Saturday and Sunday in the Jewish district; bustling, fascinating and alive.

Berwick Street Market: Weekdays only, preferably in the mornings. A general market with a wide assortment of articles.

Portobello Road: Although not exactly a London market, this should not be missed if you're here on a Saturday afternoon. Originally a flea market of sorts featuring miscellaneous junk, authentic or nonauthentic antiques and a food market, its personality has begun to change in recent years. Portobello Road involves a taxi ride costing about $2.50 or so, but that shouldn't deter you. You'll probably do better and enjoy it more on a sunny day, but it's always amusing unless the rain is just too much. There are characters galore—bearded and long-haired (no, not the girls) and feminine get-ups that will invite triple-takes; take along a camera with color film. Go hungry—there are lots of appetizing snacks to be had as you walk along Portobello Road. Don't buy antiques for substantial amounts without knowing what you're doing. As the dealers say, "We buy junk and sell valuable antiques."

𝕖❧ Short Trips from London

Windsor Castle and Eton

By automobile, depart from Hyde Park Corner through Knightsbridge, Kensington Road, Kensington High Street, Hammersmith Road, King Street and Chiswick High Road onto the Great West Road. The 22-mile ride takes about forty minutes via route M-4. There is frequent train service from Waterloo and Paddington stations, and the train ride is about an hour. Green Line buses No. 704 and 705 have an express service from Hyde Park Corner frequently, and No. 178 passes through Hampton Court.

Eton, founded in 1440 by Henry IV, is one of England's outstanding public schools (meaning *private*, in the British scheme of understatement); the buildings and facilities are Spartan, with perhaps an overemphasis upon games. The young boys undergo considerable physical punishment (although now lessened when compared to prewar years)—the exact antithesis of the American idea of progressive education. For visits, apply to the school office. A half-mile away is Windsor Castle, the largest lived-in castle in the world and the principal residence of British royalty since Norman days. The castle area is open daily from 10 A.M. to sunset. There is no admission fee.

The State Apartments may be visited when the royal family is not in residence. Usually visits are not possible in April and during certain parts of March, May and June. The general timetable is 11 to 5 on weekdays from

June 1 to September 30. Other times in the year the weekday closing is at 4 P.M., and from November 1 to March 31 it is 3 P.M. Sundays; from May to September, visiting hours are 1:30 to 5; in October, 1 to 4. Sundays are crowded, however.

It's possible to come here by boat from Hampton Court in about five hours. If you do, you'll want to stay overnight at the Old Court, a hotel designed by Sir Christopher Wren in 1676. It is in a wonderful location at the edge of the Thames. The Old House is also the best place to eat—but it's not great, at that. If possible, try to arrive in Windsor before the 10:30 A.M. changing of the guard. You might like it better than the ceremony at Buckingham Palace because you'll be closer to what's going on and can follow the guardsmen into the courtyard. Be sure to keep an eye out, on your tour, for the Queen's Doll House and for St. George's Chapel, where Henry VIII and wife Jane Seymour, one of many, are buried.

If you've really got stamina, on the way back from Windsor to London, continue through Runnymede. (Does that strike a familiar note? If it does, you've got a good memory. It's where evil King John was forced to sign the Magna Charta, a document intended to curb the evil king. It is also the site of a monument to our late President Kennedy). Then on to Hampton Court, where you'll find the great Tudor mansion built by Cardinal Wolsey. The State Rooms are open weekdays 9:30 to 6, from May through September; Sundays, 11 to 6. The rest of the year closing time is an hour or two earlier. A general admission will cost somewhere around a half dollar from April through September. There is a slight reduction in the admission charge from October through March. The place to eat at Hampton Court is undoubtedly the Mitre, which is pretty good.

Trips to Oxford and Cambridge and their famous colleges are certainly high on the list for any visitor. Which one to see? Well, both have their points. The solution: if possible, see both.

Oxford

Drive out route A-40, leaving from Hyde Park Corner, via Bayswater Road, Holland Park Avenue and Uxbridge Road and into Wood Lane. The run is fifty-seven (fast) miles, passing through Beaconsfield en route. Train service from Paddington Station takes 75 minutes. There is frequent bus service from Victoria Coach Station, with the running time taking between 2¼ and 2¾ hours.

At Oxford, see High Street (called the High), very impressive and attractive. The most interesting colleges are Corpus Christi, Magdalen (pronounced Maud-lin), University and New College. The Bodleian Library is definitely worth visiting. It is open daily from 10 to 5. There are tours of the colleges conducted by various student organizations. If you want to stay overnight, and you should, the Mitre Hotel is quite pleasant. The Randolph Hotel is the largest in town, and many think it is just about the best. Other fine places are Eastgate, in the High; the Excelsior Motor Lodge and Cotswold Lodge.

If you're in the mood to combine sightseeing and a resort vacation, consider the Weston Manor, located about nine miles north of Oxford in the village of Weston-on-the-Green. The rooms are pleasant, and there is a swimming pool, along with tennis courts. The food is fairly good. If you're only having lunch in Oxford, the Roebuck features meat and the Mitre's dining-room is fair enough. If you're looking for real atmosphere, drive two miles south of Oxford to Tudor Cottage on Churchway, in the miniature community of Iffley (fairly good food, but bring your own wine).

Although a one-day round trip from London to Oxford is perfectly possible, it makes an arduous day. If possible, try to remain overnight.

Cambridge

Getting to Cambridge involves some complicated driving northward from Marble Arch until you get onto route A-10. You'll surely have to make inquiries to find this road. The trip involves only fifty-six miles, but requires about two hours of moderately slow driving. Train service to Cambridge from King's Cross and Liverpool Street stations takes 75 minutes. Buses from Victoria Coach Station make the run in 2¾ hours.

At Cambridge, the outstanding single sight is the famous Backs, extensive stretches of lawn from behind the colleges toward the River Cam. Be sure to visit King's College and the beautiful College Chapel. While Cambridge, too, may be seen in a one-day excursion from London, this would be a mistake. Stay overnight at the very nice University Arms. Or, if you like a garden-surrounded hotel, choose the Garden House, a pleasant place, especially the new wings. This is somewhat more expensive than the University Arms. Other nice places are the West House, the Blue Boar and the Royal Cambridge. I would prefer to eat my meals at the Bath Hotel's restaurant. Miller's serves good, but plain, food with good wines. However, if you enjoy English country-side and local color, drive over to nearby Grantchester at tea time —worthwhile, we assure you.

The architecture of Cambridge is almost unbelievably harmonious in style, although built over a period of seven centuries (from 1277 to 1934). See if there will be an even-song service by candlelight in the chapel. If there is, go!

Pointer: For a real bargain price of less than $5, you can buy a comprehensive ticket to see some four-hundred major cultural attractions. For details, write to British Rail International, 270 Madison Ave., New York, N. Y. 10016.

ACCOMMODATIONS ¶ The hotel situation throughout England is a complicated one that permits only a few generalties—but with enough exceptions to make the rule. In London, hotels are extremely good. In fact, it would not be overdoing it to say that several of the world's best are located there. Unfortunately for the budget-minded traveler, almost all of these are extremely expensive. When one bears in mind the lower wages and generally moderate scale of prices for many other commodities and services, London hotel prices seem strangely out of line. But for those Americans who demand American comforts, the best hotels in London are fully prepared to supply this demand—at a price. Better figure about $30 (or more!) for a double room at a top hotel and $20 at a typical one. Of course, all hotels have some rooms at lower rates. But these are difficult to obtain unless reserved well in advance.

Once out of the luxury First Class category, London hotels revert quickly to type, which unfortunately means rather depressing, slightly seedy establishments, with bare patches of carpeting and antique plumbing. Rates in the countryside are much lower, but facilities and food are extremely variable. The typical British countryside small hotel has rather moderate prices, say approximately $10 for two people, including a hearty, appealing English breakfast. But the rooms, sad to relate, will frequently be depressingly old-fashioned, lack adequate bath facilities and seem completely out of date. However, to offset all of this, the service is invariably friendly and willing. If there is no central heating, a maid will make a fire in your rooms; if there is no hot water (which is not infrequently the case), she'll bring it up on request.

The atmospheric British inns are something else again; these are the historic spots with loads of history and squeaking stairs and locks that don't work and names like "Bramble," "Thistle" and "Hedge." Staying at a place like this, it's obvious that creature comforts must be sacrificed for local color and you wouldn't expect to find central heating, indirect lighting and air conditioning, but it would be worthwhile as an experience.

LONDON HOTELS

Claridge's: Generally regarded as London's outstanding hotel; specializes in a dignified, retiring clientele able to pay its very high tariff. Very luxurious, well-decorated large front rooms with oversize bathrooms. Rooms in the rear are smaller.

Berkeley: An extremely luxurious, individualistic hotel, which resembles a private home; personalized service. Many studios and suites. A very good, but costly restaurant. Recommended if you enjoy elegance and don't mind the prices, which are quite high.

London Hilton: A thirty-story skyscraper, with lovely view of Hyde Park. Rooms are moderate size, with marble bathrooms. Very attractive interior; fairly expensive.

Dorchester: A once elegant hotel, now in need of redecoration. Excellent location opposite Hyde Park, and with good service.

Savoy: A very popular hotel with Americans, particularly the theatrical crowd. Lively, bustling atmosphere; busy bar. Rather large rooms, pleasantly furnished. Well located near the theatrical district and opposite the Thames River.

Grosvenor House: One of the leading hotels, with a marvelous location facing Hyde Park (if you get a front room). Very large, well run, pleasant, elegant atmosphere. Rooms are extremely attractive.

Ritz: An elegant, distinguished small hotel with a definite London personality. Opposite Green Park; large bedrooms furnished in old world style. Excellent service, fine surroundings.

Portman: A new 300-room first-class hotel managed by Inter-Continental, not too far from Hyde Park Corner and shopping areas. Well-run, popular, and less expensive than hotels listed above. Completely air-conditioned; wide selection of restaurants in the hotel.

Churchill: Another new hotel with 500 rooms, close to the Inter-Continental (above) at Portman Square. A Loew's hotel, with rather good rooms, completely air-conditioned. Choice of restaurants within the hotel.

Royal Garden: A very large new hotel; has 550 bedrooms; on a superb site overlooking Kensington Gardens.

New Cavendish: A newly opened 250-room luxury hotel on Jermyn Street, with penthouse suite, private baths and deluxe facilities.

Royal Lancaster: Twenty stories tall, a Rank Organization operation. Often used for large conventions, inasmuch as it can accommodate meetings of 1,500 people. Fair rooms, somewhat commercial.

Lancaster: A Rank Organization hotel; 400 topnotch rooms; nicely situated on Bayswater Road.

Londonderry House: Right in Park Lane; 130 rooms that are superbly styled and furnished; opened in mid-1967; on the very expensive side.

St. George: A Trust House hotel that is a favorite with Americans seeking comfort in the fine British tradition and style.

Connaught: A quiet, dignified hotel with old-fashioned furniture and décor. An ideal spot for anyone wishing to live in the classic English atmosphere. Rooms are fairly large; furnishings are comfortably pleasant.

May Fair: A First Class hotel well located on Berkeley Street. Although an older building, the renovated public and guest rooms are now attractively decorated.

Westbury: London's first American-style hotel, built by the Knott Corporation. Good location on Bond Street; all the newest conveniences. Rooms are quite small, furnished in modern décor.

Carlton Tower: A new luxury hotel of the Hotel Corporation, American-style, with television in each room, good restaurant facilities.

Park Lane: A very dignified, almost staid, older hotel; excellent situation on Piccadilly Street opposite Hyde Park, convenient for theater, shopping.

Hyde Park: Fine location opposite Hyde Park. Very good rooms; attractive décor. Draws a fairly conservative clientele.

Quaglino's: A very small hotel in the West End, near Piccadilly. Two restaurants; good food. Rooms are pleasantly large and attractive.

Piccadilly: Moderate-size busy hotel, just off lively Piccadilly Circus. Popular for years, English atmosphere and surroundings in public rooms and guest chambers.

Waldorf: Friendly, homey hotel near the theatrical district. Average-size rooms, traditional décor. Not too many rooms with private baths.

Brown's: A very famous, quiet old British hotel steeped in tradition. Old World furnishings in the dining room, public halls and guest rooms.

White's: A small hotel located opposite Hyde Park. Average-size, pleasant rooms, nicely furnished.

Cumberland: An enormous, modern hotel in the Marble Arch district. Rooms are smallish, comfortably decorated. Good for hurried businessmen.

Athenaeum Court: A pleasant, medium-size hotel opposite Green Park. Moderate rooms, fair furnishings.

Royal Trafalgar: On Trafalgar square, with over 100 good rooms. Among the newest in London.

AIRPORT HOTELS ¶ Should you arrive by air late at night or have a very early departure, or if you have a rented car meeting you at the airport and don't intend to drive into London, there are two satisfactory hotels at the London airport. The Ariel Hotel has a unique circular design, and the Skyway Hotel looks like a modern American motel; both are quite new.

LONDON RESTAURANTS

The leading, fashionable dining spots:

Mirabelle: One of London's (and England's) outstanding restaurants; marvelous French food, frequently equal to Paris. Delightful, luxurious surroundings; high prices. Reservations essential.

Caprice: Superb French dishes served in this first-rank restaurant. Very smart fashionable clientele; prices quite high. Reservations are necessary.

Dorchester and Savoy Hotel grills: Excellent places for lunch; very good food, fairly high prices.

Manetta's: Very pleasant restaurant, featuring good continental food.

L'Ecu de France: An extremely well-known French restaurant, serving quite good meals. More moderate-priced than the previous restaurants.

Le Chateaubriand: A very good place for French food; known also for its grilled meats.

Le Coq d'Or: An outstanding restaurant, with French atmosphere and cuisine.

Colony: A fashionable restaurant in an excellent location. Very good for lunch; dancing at dinner.

Boulestin: A renowned French restaurant in the classic tradition of excellence. Dignified dining; fairly high.

Wilton's: An excellent, although quite expensive place featuring oysters and salmon.

Angus Steak House: A series of establishments in well-located parts of the city specializing in steaks and chops.

Aperitif: The French cuisine is nicely accented here.

Barque and Bite: This is a floating restaurant—London's first —that is near the Zoo; it floats on the Regent Canal.

Beachcomber: A wondrous South Sea setting for wonderful Chinese and Polynesian food.

Belle Meunière: French food in a beautiful manner.

Celebrity: Dancing and a cabaret is also on the fashionable menu here.

De Hems: Right in the heart of the theater district, with fine English fare.
Pavillon: Very pleasant surroundings for a superb meal.

SEAFOOD RESTAURANTS

Bentley's: Popular dining room, with emphasis upon oysters; moderately high, but worthwhile.
Cunningham's: An attractive, fairly small place. Emphasis upon Dover sole, many other seafood specialties.
Maison Prunier: Exceptional cuisine, principally based upon French seafood creations. Draws a fashionable, well-dressed clientele.
Wheeler's: There are several branches of this established seafood chain, serving very good fish preparations. Medium to expensive.
Overton's: Several medium-size dining rooms, each with an oyster bar; popular, moderate prices.
Scott's: Traditional English surrounding; three floors, but the cellar is most interesting. Lobster is the specialty here.
Vendôme: More elaborate than most seafood restaurants, this smart place features excellent seafood preparations.

BRITISH ATMOSPHERE AND FOOD

Simpson's in the Strand: A famous old restaurant, featuring roast beef, sliced in front of the diner (very thin slices to most Americans); quite reasonable.
Gore's: The Elizabethan Room features the food and atmosphere of Queen Elizabeth's (1) times; amusing, pleasant (often gay) evening's entertainment, passable food. Reservations essential.
Brown's: A dignified dining room in this ultradignified hotel; classic English food, English surroundings, English waiters. Quiet, high priced.
Guinea: Pleasant, clublike atmosphere in this cozy, old pub; fairly good steaks—for England, that is.
Rules: Old British tavern atmosphere and surroundings, with emphasis upon solid British food; medium prices.
Verrey's: A rather small, pleasant dining spot to try British dishes; sedate but friendly service.

SHOPPING ¶ As you've probably heard, London is a man's town, which means most of the good values involve men's apparel. But women will have a wonderful time here, too, because there are many specialties to attract them. Still, let's consider the men's purchases first.

There's nothing to equal the cut and appearance of an English *raincoat.* Cotton or mixtures, the starting price is somewhere under $50. They hold their shape almost indefinitely; Burberry and Aquascutum are the two most famous names.

Ready-made men's *suits* are not advisable, because British mass-production methods do not equal ours; however, ready-made topcoats or *overcoats*, where fit is not quite so important, are usually good values. If you're going to be in England for ten days or two weeks, a tailor-made suit or coat might be a good investment; figure anywhere up to $200, or so, depending upon the fabric, cut and reputation of the tailor you select. Almost any firm in Sackville Street or Savile Row will produce a beautifully tailored suit that you'll treasure for years.

Most men who use *smoking articles* will want to buy a pipe or lighter, or both; British cigarettes and pipe tobacco are worthwhile purchases. Incidentally, smoking items make perfect gifts for the men on your gift list.

For *men's accessories*, ready-made shirts are fairly good, but if you've the time or patience to order some custom-made shirts, you'll be delighted with their fit and wearing qualities. Ties are marvelous here; if you like foulards, there's a wonderful selection. Sweaters, both regular and sleeveless, should not be overlooked; N. Peal (in the Burlington Arcade) has an outstanding selection. Doeskin gloves are superb and only half of the United States price. Woolen and Argyle socks are worthwhile, as are leather belts and suspenders (don't forget that the British call them braces). Of course you'll want to bring back an English hat, particularly one from Lock or Herbert Johnson. As a general rule, ordinary run-of-the-mill British footwear isn't too good, but Peal and Co., Ltd. (on Oxford Street), does an excellent job; their custom-made shoes cost $50 or more and are reputed to last a lifetime. Hairbrushes, toothbrushes and every other kind of a brush are worth buying here; look for Kent products, although there are several other good manufacturers.

The Britisher is a sportsman, first and foremost, and British *sporting goods* are just about the best in the world. Ogden Smiths specializes in fishing tackle and has a wide and impressive selection; Lillywhites has a six-story building filled with all sorts of sporting gear; from a perfect set of matched golf clubs all the way to equipment required for a six-month safari into the African bush.

English *leather goods*—wallets, billfolds, passport cases, desk sets and attaché cases—are of unequaled excellence; luggage is well made but quite heavy; Finnigans on New Bond Street has a fine selection.

Pointer: Most West End shops close at 5:30 or 6 P.M. Monday through Friday, but on Wednesdays or Thursdays many shops stay open to 7 P.M. London's main shopping districts close on Saturday at 1 P.M., except for the Bayswater area, which stays open on Saturday afternoons and closes early on Thursdays.

Now how about letting the women in the party have some fun?

Ballantyne, Braemar and Pringle *cashmere sweaters* are about the finest; in addition to the classic styles, sweater manufacturers have been making dressmaker styles with soft necklines. Many of the newer models are suited for dressy or evening wear. In department stores, go to the export section for dressmaker sweaters.

Excellent *yard goods* including tweeds, cashmere, silks and wrinkle-proof cottons and linens (especially Tootal) are available at good prices. Liberty silks are world-famous; the scarves make excellent gifts.

For *women's coats and suits*, London couture has a thousand light years to go before it can even hope to catch up with Paris or Rome, although there are a few exceptions. Ready-made suits and coats of Shetland, Irish, Harris or Angora tweed are exceptionally low in price, but be sure that they fit at least reasonably well; the British tailors are notoriously fond of *extremely* loose-fitting tweeds, which is why most Englishwomen have the unenvied sartorial reputation that they (usually deservedly) bear. Women's raincoats are, we think, an outstanding purchase on two counts—styling and price. Cashmere coats and especially vicuña aren't cheap, but they feel so nice you'd better not touch one or you'll end up buying it.

For *accessories*, most English shoes are unsuited to the American foot and, while on the subject of feet, British nylons don't wear too well. Leather handbags are quite smart; although the prices aren't very low, the workmanship is superb. Umbrellas are obtainable in a wide selection and should be considered as possible gifts (after you've bought one for yourself). Kent hairbrushes, English soaps and other small bath items are good values. Linen blouses are worthwhile, but be sure the linen is Irish. Viyella robes have a softness that makes them irresistible.

Pointer: Have items costing over $20 shipped directly to your plane or ship to avoid the purchase tax, which is extremely high and minimizes a good portion of your savings. Inquire at time of purchase.

London is the place for *books* of all sorts—old and new. The district around Foyle's on Charing Cross Road is a center for new and secondhand books. Foyle's is a series of small shops, something like the inside of a rabbit warren, haphazardly joined together, and the sort of place a book collector can get lost in for hours . . . or days.

For *food and liquor*, Fortnum and Mason's is undoubtedly one of the most interesting food shops in the world, with gourmet delicacies from every country; probably you'll be tempted to ship yourself all sorts of cocktail snacks, cheese and exotic soups. (We always buy some of their clotted or Devonshire cream to eat for breakfast with porridge in our hotel room; absolutely delicious!) If you've a liking for port or sherry, visit Justerini & Brooks for a tasting under ideal circumstances; and even if you just want to send home Scotch whisky, the same holds true.

New silver isn't recommended; *antique silver* is, but remember that collectors of fine pieces have pushed the prices up into the stratosphere for the very choicest items. Small articles are often good values, however, although superb Georgian pieces can run into the thousands. Percy's (London Silver Vaults) in Chancery Lane has an enormous selection in all price ranges.

Old and rare pieces of *china* in perfect condition have become very expensive. Modern china, including Spode, Wedgwood, Crown Derby and the like are about half (or less) of American prices and the shipment is guaranteed. You'll have choice of dinner service for six, eight or twelve, tea services, individual cups and bowls, or almost anything you desire.

ENTERTAINMENT ¶ London's best bet for an evening's entertainment is a *legitimate show*, available at very reasonable prices. How reasonable? Well, stalls (orchestra seats) can be cheaper than a New York movie ticket; and as you go upward to the dress circle, the upper circle and the gallery (balcony) prices go downward. Ticket box offices are usually open from 10 A.M. to 8 P.M. daily. Unless you're near the theater, obtain your tickets through the ticket agency in your hotel lobby or from a broker such as Keith Prowse & Co. in New Bond Street. It's simpler. The broker's charges are extremely moderate, averaging less than a half dollar or so. With rare exceptions, seats for any of London's forty or more shows may be obtained the same day; or, at worst, on two or three days' notice. Have a late tea or early dinner, or postpone your evening meal until after the performance. Theater performances begin at varying times, but a lot earlier than in New York in any case. Some start at 7:30 or 8 P.M. Others have "twice nightly" shows, with one at 6:15 P.M. and the second at 8:45 P.M. You can also find matinee performances for some shows. Dine in nearby Soho, where many restaurants feature after-theater suppers. Most of the theaters are in the same district, except for the Old Vic (which specializes in Shakespeare). The Old Vic is south of the Thames.

Vaudeville, which died out in the United States a generation ago, still flourishes here. The leading theater is the Palladium, where you'll hear and see outstanding stars on the same bill with magicians, strong men, ventriloquists —some good, some poor. An interesting experience—at least once. If you liked the Ed Sullivan Show on TV, you'll love the Palladium; they're quite similar.

Night clubs come in several categories: first, the swank type, in which membership is required; second, the popular, large-scale operation; and last, the Greenwich Village–type arty spot. "Membership clubs" are generally in existence solely to get around the local liquor laws. Membership, if you can call it that, is granted without question by merely exhibiting your American passport. Don't feel the slightest hesitation about "membership clubs." Just go.

Gambling spices up night life on the London scene. The 21 Club is in a beautiful mansion and attracts a smart crowd in the winter season. The Embassy Club, in Old Bond Street, has many theatrical celebrities among its clientele. The Stork Room is for men only who are looking for feminine (female?) companionship. Quaglino's is extremely fashionable and attracts a well-dressed group; there is a floor show late in the evening. The Astor, Casanova, Churchill's, Edmondo Ros's, Eve, Gargoyle and Murray's provide dance music and floor shows of varying degrees of elaborateness. Les Ambassadeurs and the River Club have dance music but no floor show or cabaret program. There's dancing in leading hotels, such as the Dorchester, Hilton, May Fair, Berkeley and Grosvenor House and also in a number of restaurants, including Hatchett's and Sir Harry's Bar.

If you consider *dining out* a complete evening's entertainment (as many sophisticated people do), you'll find that London has nothing like Paris' range of superb restaurants. Head and shoulders above the rest in the city are Mirabelle and Caprice, both with French cuisine about as good as to be found in Paris. Neither of these is inexpensive—in fact, they're very expensive—they are very fashionable, attracting the best people in London and serving the finest food.

Pubs and bars in England are often loads of fun. A "pub" is the popular term for a public house, meaning in plain language a bar. Just so you'll know, public houses are almost always divided in two sections—the public bar (with the "high bar") and the saloon bar. Women do not usually go in the public bar, but rather go into the saloon bar even though the two sections might not be separated by anything more than the service area. In Scotland, women usually do not frequent pubs, except those in large tourist hotels.

Those of you who have visited a British pub know they are much more than a bar. In small villages the local pub is the social center. Even in large cities, there is a lively social atmosphere. You might not know anyone in the place when you come in, but the chances are you'll have a large acquaintanceship by the time you leave. There is always a game of darts in a British pub, and some pubs have dominoes, shove a penny and other simple *divertissements*, including a handy piano for the guest anxious to play a song. In a number of pubs, there is a cold buffet, with cold meats and salads, which are paid for in addition to the drinks. Hot dogs, as a recognition of American culinary habits, have been added in a number of establishments. Each region of Britain has some kind of a food specialty, and in the area's pubs you'll usually find such items available. The popular pub tidbits are Cornish pastry (in Cornwall), a closed pie of meat and potatoes, and pork pies. Some pubs do their own cooking and serve simple but good food at reasonable prices. There is really no typical pub. There are old ones, new ones. Each has its own clientele, and personality. In London, the open (licensing) hours are from 11 A.M. to 3 P.M. and then again from 5:30 to 11 P.M. At closing time, you will hear the host call out, "Time, gentlemen," and the bar shuts down on the minute.

You can order whisky if you like, but most pubs specialize in beer. Remember, as mentioned previously (in Food Specialties and Liquor), you never order merely "beer." An Englishman asks for "mild," or "bitter," or "old" or "stout" or, best of all, combinations of any two of these. Then, one never asks for a glass of anything, but rather "a pint" or "a half," and unless you have a remarkable capacity, better stick to "a half." Thus, you shouldn't ask for a glass of beer, but rather "a half of mild and bitter," possibly the favorite drink in most pubs.

Wherever you happen to be, the pub nearest you is worth trying. But certain places have a very special air and if you're in the Piccadilly area, look for the Captain's Cabin and Ward's Irish House. In the Fleet Street area, there's El Vino's and the Cock; around Soho, there's the Crown and Two Chairmen, and the Swiss House. Not precisely a pub is the atmospheric Cheshire Cheese (which was a favorite with Garrick, Goldsmith, Johnson and Boswell); here you can have a light lunch. Another very quaint spot is the Prospect of Whitby at 57 Wapping Wall, facing the Thames, possibly the most famous and colorful of all, although a bit far into East London.

Most tourists are anxious to see the Royal Ballet (formerly the Sadler's Wells); inquire locally as to which dancers are appearing. Frequently the ballets will feature lesser known performers while the principals of the company are off on tour. Opera lovers who arrive during the season surely will want to see a performance or two at Covent Garden; during the winter months there is almost always a touring opera company from the continent to permit an unequaled opportunity for comparisons. But of course, the leading attraction for opera fans is the Glyndebourne Opera, which specializes in works by the one and only Mozart. Performances are given at Glyndebourne in Sussex (near Lewes); the grounds are extraordinarily attractive, the attractions inevitably polished and near perfect and the whole proceeding quite delightful. But: dinner clothes are required, which means either reserving rooms in the vicinity of Lewes or taking a train (or driving out by car) in dinner clothes; meals are served on the grounds. A must for all opera lovers, no matter how much advance preparation is required.

London has three first-rate symphonic orchestras: the London Philharmonic, London Symphony and BBC Symphony, to list them in their accustomed order of excellence; there are seldom any performances during the summer months except at the Royal Albert Hall, where the Promenade Concerts are given at very low prices.

On a pleasant evening, a visit to Battersea Park (London's answer to Coney Island) is amusing and you'll get a chance to see the so-called man in the street having a good time. Also worthy of mention is Mme. Tussaud's Waxworks Museum, where you can see a unique display of life-size wax images, including members of the Royal Family, noted personalities and famous figures of the day. If you can face it, for a small extra fee, there's the basement Chamber of Horrors, but don't take children or squeamish people (or even yourself, if you are similarly susceptible).

SPORTS ¶ How about a horseback ride in Rotten Row? Or would you like to go rowing in the Serpentine? Maybe you would like to sail in Regent's Park. These are just some of the sports possibilities available in London, and throughout the British Isles there will be similar opportunities for amusement, in case you wish to become actively engaged in an athletic activity.

As anyone who was anywhere near England in 1966 knows, its football team won the World Cup, and that was a major and happy event for everyone. *Football* is the most popular game in England, but the game is different from our own. It is most like our game of soccer; rugby is actually closer to our version of football. You might enjoy a game, particularly if it's one of the important matches, which have all the excitement of a Rose Bowl and World Series wrapped in one. A lot of money is bet on the outcome of games, but it is all legal.

Cricket is a complicated game, at first glance resembling baseball in a very, very vague way, but there all similarity stops; difficult to follow at first, but pleasant in a low-key fashion, to watch for an hour or so. Unless you're a devoted enthusiast, you probably won't want to see a complete match, which might last fifteen hours (usually spread over a three-day stretch). If possible, try to see a game at Lord's Cricket Ground (near London) or just any pickup match in one of the city parks or in the countryside; please remember never to shout "kill the umpire" or any other crude Americanisms—merely mumble (it's not good form to speak distinctly) in a low voice, "Well played, old chap, well played, indeed." That's about as far as a chap can go, after all.

Golf can be played on more than 1,500 courses; they're every place and any place and rates are pleasantly low, with a very few exceptions. London alone has some 300 links within a fifty-mile radius; Wentworth and Sunningdale are probably the best-known local courses. The most famous course, as you probably know, is St. Andrews, in Scotland; anyone can play, but the clubhouse is not open to nonmembers. At Inverness, summer tournament play is usually at night, because the light holds good until 11 P.M.

Tennis is played everywhere: in parks, public courts, private clubs and resort hotels—you'll never lack a court. *Horseracing*, flat or steeplechase, is marvelous throughout England; check the sports sections of local newspapers for details and be sure to go to one of the special racing events like the Derby (held during the first week in June and not to be missed, if humanly possible), the Eclipse Stakes or the Grand National Steeplechase. *Hunting* in England doesn't mean hunting as we understand it—for the British think of that sport as stylized, with huntin' dogs, tally-ho, yoicks and all that sort of thing. *Shooting* for birds or game is complicated, most of the land being privately owned; game licenses cost $2.80 to $8.50, depending upon the number of guns and length of time involved.

Here's the place for trout and salmon fishing: no charge for a license in Scotland, but in England they're issued by local river boards and range from just a few cents for ordinary fishing permits all the way up to $15 for salmon. In every town near fishing waters, you can join the local fishing club for about $6. Inquire locally for a hotel that has its own fishing preserves (private); that will solve your problem. For information and details, inquire of the British Travel and Holidays Association or the British Field Sports Society, both in London.

There is good *deep sea fishing* at Cornwall, chiefly for blue shark.

GETTING YOUR BEARINGS ¶ This little list of place-names might be helpful to you in understanding the geography of England, and matching up vaguely familiar places with main regions of the country:

Home counties and southeast England: Essex, Hertfordshire, Kent, Middlesex, Surrey and Sussex.
South and southwest England: Berkshire, Cornwall, Devonshire, Dorset, Hampshire, Isle of Wight, Somerset and Wiltshire.
East Anglia: Cambridgeshire, Norfolk and Suffolk.
East Midlands: Bedfordshire, Buckinghamshire, Derbyshire, Huntingdonshire, Lincolnshire, Northamptonshire, Nottinghamshire and Rutland.
West Midlands: Gloucestershire, Herefordshire, Oxfordshire, Shropshire, Staffordshire, Warwickshire, and Worcestershire.
Northeast England: County Durham, Northumberland and Yorkshire.
Northwest England: Cheshire, Cumberland, Lancashire and Westmorland.

DISTANCES ¶ London is not really very far from anywhere you might be planning to go on your itinerary in the British Isles. The following highway distances in *miles* will help prove this point: Aberdeen, 532; Aintree, 199; Ascot, 25; Bath, 105; Birmingham, 108; Blackpool, 226; Bradford, 193; Brighton, 52; Bristol, 114; Cambridge. 51; Canterbury, 55; Cardiff, 154; Coventry, 90; Dover, 70; Durham, 258; Edinburgh, 375; Epsom, 15; Exeter, 167; Folkestone, 69; Glasgow, 401; Gloucester, 103; Grimsby, 162; Hastings, 63; Harwich, 70; Holyhead, 257; Hull, 197; Inverness, 565; Leeds, 188; Lincoln, 133; Liverpool, 196; Manchester, 182; Newcastle-on-Thyne, 272; Norwich, 109; Nottingham, 121; Oxford, 58; Penzance, 280; Perth, 450; Plymouth, 210; Portsmouth, 70; Salisbury, 83; Scarborough, 208; Sheffield, 158; Shrewsbury, 151; Southampton, 76; Southend, 36; Stoke-on-Trent, 145; Stratford-on-Avon, 90; Swansea, 190; Torquay, 189; Weymouth 131; Whitehaven, 309; Winchester, 64; Windermere, 261; Windsor, 20; Worcester, 110; and York, 195.

The principal tourist areas are London, the university towns of Cambridge and Oxford, the Shakespeare country, Wales, the West Country and Scotland.

৯ A Tour of Great Britain

ENGLAND

London to Lincoln—133 miles

Note: A section on Motoring in Great Britain starts on page 204.

Leave London heading northward from Hyde Park Corner via route A-10; you'll probably have to ask directions to pick up the route markers, but the tour is easily followed from that point on. The road is heavily traveled at first, passing through Waltham Cross, Hoddesdon, Ware, Buntingford and Royston and into lovely old Cambridge.

Here, the outstanding single sight is "The Backs," the charming lawns running from the college building down to the River Cam; be sure to see King's, Jesus, St. John's and Queen's the most interesting of the member colleges that go to make up Cambridge University. To do the colleges justice in the way of sightseeing, an overnight stay is recommended at the University Arms Hotel, or possibly at the charming Garden House, but be sure to ask for one of the new wings. Neither of these hotels serves good food, so better head for the restaurant of the Bath Hotel, or if you want to dine with the students, go to Miller's Wine Parlour, which has rather good meals, plus plenty of wine. (If you wish, take a diversionary trip via route 45 from Cambridge to Newmarket, the famous racing town where you might care to see English race horses being trained at one of the stables.) If not, continue on to Ely, believed to have received its name from the great number of eels in the surrounding marshes. Ely is a tiny town with no suitable accommodations, but you'll want to see the magnificent cathedral, the Bishop's Palace and St. Mary's Church, in whose vicarage none other than Oliver Cromwell once resided for almost ten years.

Continue on A-10 through Littleport to King's Lynn, an old seaport with many fine old houses; be sure to see the Old Custom House and the Tuesday and Saturday marketplaces and visit the Duke's Head Hotel, with fascinating carvings in its lounge. Proceed to Sutton Bridge, Long Sutton, Holbeach and Sutterton, being careful to turn on route 17 to Sleaford; here, take a right turn

onto route A-15, the road for Lincoln. (At Sutterton, if
you're curious, there's a short run of six miles to Boston,
an old market town, from which our own Boston gets its
name.)

Lincoln is worth a little time, chiefly to explore the castle built in 1068 by William the Conqueror and the cathedral, a superb Gothic structure. The White Hart
Hotel, adjacent to the cathedral, is extremely pleasant.

This hotel, incidentally, has the best food in town, so you needn't wander about looking for anything better. Another very nice place to stay is the Eastgate. It is twice the size of the White Hart and is a bit more expensive.

Lincoln to York—76 miles

From Lincoln, take routes 158 and A-57 to East Markham, just past which there is a right turn onto route 1 northward to East Retford and Bawtry. At Bawtry, be careful to turn onto route 614 to Thorne. After Thorne, watch for a left turn to Snaith (route 19), which leads into Selby, birthplace of Henry I; make certain to see famous old Selby Abbey. From Selby it is a fast run to York, one of the most interesting medieval towns in England, filled with narrow, tortuously twisting streets. Don't hurry through York; walk through the old streets, visit the York Minster Cathedral (the largest medieval cathedral in England), the ancient fortifications, the Treasurer's Houses (open daily except Wednesday mornings), the Museum (open weekdays and Sunday afternoons). The Chase Hotel is conveniently located nearby and makes a pleasing overnight stop. The Royal Station Hotel is larger, more imposing and more expensive; a room with private bath is hard to come by, however. I suppose, all in all, that the Royal Station has the best food in York, but that's not saying too much. For lunch-time only, you might try Terry's Restaurant; for dinner, you might squeeze into Betty's Restaurant, which isn't bad.

York to Newcastle—75 miles

From York take route A-59 to Harrogate, a resort town that has all the usual attractions of any well-known spa (plus over eighty sulfur and saline springs). The Granby Hotel is pleasant and modest; the busy season here, when advance reservations are desirable, is July through late September. Leave Harrogate via route A-61 to Ripley and Ripon, an early center of Christianity, boasting of a fine old cathedral. It might be interesting to stay here for the rare pleasure of hearing the traditional curfew horn at 9 each evening; the Spa Hotel is the logical place to stay. If time permits, make an interesting trip of just a few miles (via route B-6265) to Fountain's Abbey, a ruined Cistercian monastery founded in 1132 and destroyed during the Reformation. Would you believe it? There's a really good restaurant on Minister Road, Ripon, called the Old Deanery. If it's anywhere near mealtime, be sure to eat there or you'll be sorry later on.

From Ripon, continue on route A-61 until it joins route 1, where you make a left turn, heading north to Leeming, Scotch Corner and Darlington; continue on to Durham, a well-situated town encircled almost completely by the River Wear. Durham has loads of quiet charm and dignity, with many fine old buildings. See the 800-year-old cathedral, a superb example of Roman architecture; open daily except Sunday for guided tours. There is also a Norman castle, originally built by William the Conqueror. From Durham on to Chester-le-Street and then Gateshead, a busy port town, and Newcastle-upon-Tyne, an important shipping port and industrial city. The leading hotel here is the venerable Royal Station Hotel, with rather good Old World accommodations.

Newcastle is not a tourist city as such, but nearby is one of the most outstanding architectural wonders of England, built by the aggressive Romans during their occupation of England. Take route A-695 eastward from Newcastle to Wallsend, where you'll see the end of Hadrian's Wall, constructed under the Roman Emperor's direction during a four-year period, A.D. 122–126, to protect the Roman occupation forces from attacks by the northern barbarians. Should you wish to see Tynemouth, a seaside resort, continue on from Wallsend for some five miles. (If you care to see more of Hadrian's Wall while you're here, take route 69 from Newcastle westward to Heddon.)

Newcastle to Edinburgh—112 miles

Leave Newcastle by route 1 north through Gosforth and Morpeth and into Alnwick (which the inhabitants pronounce An-nick) and see its feudal castle (open for visits Wednesday through Saturday from 1 to 4:30). The next village is Belford, where there is Joyaus Garde Castle (open for visits during the afternoons).

SIDE TRIP ¶ Here is an opportunity for a side trip recommended only to the heartier and more ambitious tourist: Six miles above Belford is West Mains, where a narrow road runs eastward toward the North Sea and remote Lindisfarne, the Holy Island. When the tide is out, it's easy to cross the sands on foot, but refuges have been provided for those who are caught by incoming tides; it is also possible to drive across, but inquire locally as to tidal conditions. The reddish stone ruins of the Abbey of Lindisfarne date back to the seventh century; there are also ruins of a church and the castle of Beblowe, the latter open only on Thursday afternoons.

Now, on to the town that England and Scotland fought over for many years, Berwick-upon-Tweed. Behind Berwick, running inland, are the Cheviot Hills—a name to conjure with, for this is the heart of the fabric industry. From Berwick, route 1 passes through Burnmouth and Cockburnspath, and later there is a right turn to Dunbar, a beach resort; a little farther on there is another right turn to North Berwick, with a lovely, colorful harbor, and then on into Edinburgh.

This city is well-located on top of a high cliff and is an extremely interesting metropolis of almost a half million. Magnificent Princes Street, lined with fine shops, divides the town into two halves—the old and the new. The best hotels in town (all quite good) are the Caledonian, George, North British and Royal, but they are moderately expensive. The most interesting restaurant in the vicinity is the Cramond Inn, at Cramond, a few miles outside of Edinburgh. In town, the best bets are the Albyn, Apéritif, Beehive Inn, Cafe Royal, Epicure and the White Cockade. The restaurant at the Turnhouse airport is quite good, too. Don't leave Edinburgh without seeing the famous castle, high above the city, and Holyrood House, the official residence of the monarch in Scotland.

(At this point, the traveler must decide whether or not he has the time to continue on through Scotland to Inverness; if not, drive from Edinburgh via route 8 to Glasgow, approximately forty-four miles. Pick up your trip on page 199 and continue southward from Glasgow.)

SCOTLAND

Edinburgh to Perth—69 miles

The tour of Scotland begins on route A-8, leaving Edinburgh; this soon joins route A-9 to Linlithgow, famous for Linlithgow Palace, the birthplace of Mary, Queen of Scots (open every day from 9 to 4 or even later during summer months). Then through Folkirk (industrial and not too interesting) and on to Stirling, which bears a strong resemblance to Edinburgh, for it, too, has a historic old castle looking condescendingly down from the heights. Stirling Castle is open weekdays 9–4, Sundays 2–4 or later during summer months. From Stirling the road goes through Bridge of Allan; the nearby Allan Water is definitely worth seeing for its beautiful setting. On to Blackford and then on to the famous Gleneagles Hotel, an extremely luxurious resort (the largest in Great Britain) with two superb golf courses; marvelous for a break in your trip with or without its famed golf facilities, just to enjoy deep-down luxury.

Next comes the lovely town of Perth on the banks of the River Tay, delightful for a short stop. The best hotel here is the Station, with its attractive gardens; almost as good is the Royal George (much less expensive), which has the best food in town, but that isn't saying too much either.

SIDE TRIP ¶ If you're interested in viewing royalty's home in Scotland, make a side trip of fifty-seven miles north from Perth via route A-93 passing through Blairgowrie; soon afterward the road begins to enter Glen Shee, climbing steadily until it reaches the renowned and treacherous Devil's Elbow (a curve that should be executed with great care), and finally goes into Braemar, a very popular resort town. Here you'll find the lovely, country-style Invercauld Arms Hotel, many rooms being filled with fine antique pieces. If you come during September, you'll see the Braemar Gathering for the Highland Games, usually attended by the Royal Family. From Braemar, drive over to Balmoral Castle, the Scottish residence of the Queen; if the court is not in attendance, it is possible to visit the grounds, so make local inquiry. Continue to Ballater, another pretty resort town, where one can stay at the Loirston Hotel. Then, to Aberdeen; the descriptive portion of the tour is resumed on a subsequent page.

Perth to Aberdeen—87 miles

At Perth, if you choose not to take the drive north to Braemar and Balmoral Castle, follow route 85 to Dundee, where everyone feels duty-bound to buy some marmalade, the well-known local product.

Important Note: All motorists heading north from Dundee toward Aberdeen, Inverness and the north-western Highlands are cautioned about Sunday driving. In the large cities, it's difficult to obtain food and gasoline on Sundays; in the villages and along country roads, just about everything is closed down, including ferry services. This condition is particularly acute after leaving Inverness, so arrange your schedule accordingly; it is advisable to spend a pleasant lazy Sunday at a resort rather than experience a frustrating day on the road searching for food and gas.

While driving about Scotland, you might be interested to keep a lookout for the famous Scottish tenant farmers, called crofters. Ever since those early days when the Highland clans were fighting the English, the crofters have clung tenaciously to their small holdings. If you look high on the ridges of the moorland, you can often see the crofters' stone houses, small, sober and stiff. About 300 years ago, the clans governed the Highlands; after 1746, the date of the last unsuccessful clan uprising, British lords (lairds, in the local dialect) received vast land grants and pushed most of the crofters from their small lands. Only a small percentage remained, holding their acreage at the whim of the landowners and paying small rentals for the use of the land. At long last, however, things are looking up for the crofters, and their future now seems brighter, for the government is attempting to improve their general situation.

Twelve miles northward from Dundee is the world-renowned Glamis Castle (which is carefully pronounced Glahms), now the property of the Earl of Strathmore, brother of the Queen Mother (Elizabeth), and the birthplace, in 1930, of Princess Margaret Rose. If you recall your Shakespeare, it was in this very castle (although others compete for this dubious distinction) that one Macbeth, the Thane of Glamis, reportedly murdered Duncan. Incidentally, another king, Malcolm II, died (or was killed) here in 1033. The castle is open to visitors during summer months on Wednesdays, Thursdays and Sundays from 2 to 6. (Just five miles north from Glamis, on route A-928, is tiny Kirriemuir, the birthplace of the author James Barrie, but there is little left to remind us of this fact.)

From Glamis to Forfar and Arbroath, a seaside town, route A-92 continues to Montrose and then makes a fast run to Stonehaven, with its charming scenery and coastline. Then on into Aberdeen.

This large, dignified metropolis is known as "Granite City" or "Silvertown" because most of its structures are built of the "silvery-whitish-grayish granite quarried right inside the city limits. The standard sightseeing attraction in the vicinity is a bridge called the Auld Brigg o' Balgownie (a name quaint enough for the most whimsical); it's a venerable Gothic arch affair, dating back to 1320, spanning a salmon pool. Equally (if not more) interesting, to our way of thinking, is the excitement and early morning (7:30–8:30) activity centering about the fish auctions at the waterfront. The Caledonian Hotel in central Aberdeen is modest but pleasing. The Station Hotel has been remodeled and the rooms are now quite attractive, but it's difficult to get a room with a private bath, if that's important to you. The best meals in Aberdeen are at the Northern Hotel, however, providing you order the local food—especially Scottish salmon.

Aberdeen to Inverness—154 miles (via shore road)

From Aberdeen the motorist has a choice of two roads to Fochabers: Route 96 is a moderately interesting run of fifty-six miles; route 92 is recommended, for it offers more sightseeing although there are forty-one additional miles of driving. On the longer trip, route 92 toward Ellon, the road scans close by the North Sea and then finally turns inland. Then come Boddam and Peterhead, ports specializing in herring fishery, as does the next village, Fraserburgh. Here you leave the main highway and follow the coast road through Rosehearty to Macduff; be sure to take the short detour directing you to Gardenstown, set in a semicircular bay and quite delightful. From Macduff to Banff (again on route 92); here is a pleasant place for a day at the beach, stopping at the Fife Arms, a very quaint inn. Then on to Cullen, where again you leave the highway for the little coast road that goes through Portknockie and Findochty. Don't miss Portknockie—it's absolutely the prettiest coastal village in Scotland; if you don't agree, we'll be terribly disappointed.

Next into Fochabers, which is the juncture with route 96, the road proceeds into Elgin (with its ruined cathedral, razed in 1390); then comes Forres and the road begins its run through a heavily forested region. Along the road, there's an optional left turn to Cawdor, a medieval castle set in a lovely valley, and another place where

Macbeth is reputed to have murdered King Duncan (No. 2 on the murder parade). The castle is almost too perfect: moats, drawbridge, ramparts, battlements—almost as if taken from a Walt Disney picture. Then back to the main road and into Inverness, the capital of the Scottish Highlands.

This town is so named because it is on the lovely banks of the River Ness; there are attractive walks, cool and green, along the riverbanks, landscaped in imaginative fashion. The best place for an overnight stop is the Station Hotel, adjacent to the railway station. The food situation is not exciting in Inverness; better have your meals at the Station Hotel, which is fairly good.

SIDE TRIP ¶ A pleasant sightseeing tour of Loch Ness may be undertaken, by heading southwest from Inverness on route 82 to the far end of the lake, then returning by the road on the east shore, although it travels inland part of the way.

Reminder: The motorist is cautioned once again about traveling on Sunday through this region, where the Sabbath is scrupulously observed.

Inverness to Bonarbridge—61 miles (via main road)

Leaving Inverness, it's possible to take the Kessock Ferry (service every half-hour), join route A-9 and save eight miles, or drive around the Beauly Firth to Beauly, a town with fine fishing for sea trout at the mouth of the river. Then on to Dingwall and Evanton; shortly after Evanton, look for a fork in the road offering a choice of routes: a left turn through the mountains or the main road via route 9 through Invesgordon, Fearn, Tain and Edderton. (The mountain road climbs briefly, then comes out onto an elevated ridge overlooking almost deserted moorlands, brooding forlorn and extremely romantic.) It doesn't matter which road is selected, for both connect at Easter Fearn, which leads into Bonarbridge, an attractive little village surrounded by magnificent scenery.

Bonarbridge to Kyle of Lochalsh—172 miles

Here, take a left turn toward Invercassley and through Glen Oykell, a most delightful ride; the road also passes Oykell Bridge, Ledmore and Elphin, coming into Ullapool, a lovely summer resort in picturesque surroundings. From Ullapool, the ride is absolutely spectacular (via route A-835) toward Braemore. There is a right turn onto route A-832 toward Dundonnell; the road then cuts overland until it reaches Gruinard Bay, then across another neck of land to Loch Ewe. Next comes Poolewe, where you should stop and view the truly remarkable gardens (featuring unusual and subtropical plants) at Inverewe; shortly thereafter is the village of Gairloch, with fine bathing beaches and a perfect setting. The Gairloch Hotel is quite good, should you wish to remain overnight. From here, the scenery becomes even more breathtaking all the way through Herrysdale, Loch Maree, Kinlochewe and Achnasheen. (A final and last warning: if it's Sunday, the Strome Ferry won't be running, so if you can pull yourself away from this magnificent scenery and insist on continuing on Sunday, be sure you have plenty of gasoline, and drive from Achnasheen to Achnalt all the way back to Inverness, then take route 82 southward to Fort William.)

If it's not Sunday, take route A-890 out of Achnasheen toward Achnashellach (we can't pronounce them) to Stromemore, crossing on the ferry to Stromeferry. From here, the road climbs steeply, then descends to Loch Alsh; then make a right turn to the Kyle of Lochalsh, where ferries leave for Skye, the largest island of the Inner Hebrides group—also to other islands in the vicinity.

FERRY SERVICES FROM KYLE OF LOCHALSH
(MID-MAY THROUGH MID-SEPTEMBER)

Crossings to Skye: Frequent daily service.
Short morning cruises: Frequent service by motor vessel.
Loch Scavaig Excursion: Leave Kyle of Lochalsh Thursday at 10 A.M., returning 7:30 P.M.; time allowed ashore, weather and circumstances permitting, to visit Loch Coruisk. Be sure to bring sturdy footwear; the terrain is rough.
To Mallaig: Several trips daily except Sunday, allowing time ashore.
Sound of Sleat and Armadale (Isle of Skye): Daily except Sunday by ferry to Kyleakin, bus to Armadale and steamer back to Kyle of Lochalsh.
Stornoway mail service: Daily except Sunday service from Kyle, leaving 2:30 P.M., arriving at Stornoway at 7 P.M.; returning the following morning; passengers may obtain berths.
Note: Schedules frequently change; be sure to make local inquiry.

SIDE TRIP ON SKYE ¶ The crossing takes but a few minutes from Kyle of Lochalsh to Kyleakin, at the other end of the ferry run. Skye's roads are fair enough, although scarcely superhighways, and the only caution involves narrowness of the routes at certain points. From Kyleakin to Broadford the road is not especially interesting, but thereafter it becomes progressively more so. From the highway you can see three lovely, remote islands to the north—Raasay, Crowlin and Scalpay. At Portree, a pleasing hotel is the Royal; at Sligachan, there's the Sligachan Hotel.

Kyle of Lochalsh to Fort William—71 miles

From the Kyle of Lochalsh (incidentally, the word "kyle" means a narrow channel or strait), follow route 87 through Dornie, Shiel Bridge and Cluanie Inn into Invergarry. This run is considered one of the prettiest roads in all of Great Britain. At Invergarry, you make a right turn onto route 82; the road goes through Laggan, Invergloy, Spean Bridge, alongside Ben Nevis (only 4,406 feet high, but the tallest mountain in Britain) and then into Fort William.

Fort William, sad to relate, isn't much of a place: crowded, often damp and drizzly, unless luck (meaning clear weather) is with you; it's not the fault of poor Fort William—the cause lies in its physical setting close to the sea, backed by mountains. The moisture hits the mountains, condenses and bingo! rain. The hotels here include the Alexandra and Palace. The Alexandra Hotel is the better of the two and has quite good food, all things considered, so wherever you stay, better eat there. Incidentally, if the weather is nice, we take back everything we said about Fort William.

EXCURSIONS FROM FORT WILLIAM
(MID-MAY THROUGH MID-SEPTEMBER)

Oban: Excursions on Monday, Wednesday and Friday afternoons, allowing time ashore (Wednesday afternoon service begins in June).

Staffa and Iona islands tour: Trips to these fascinating outlying islands on Monday and Wednesday beginning in June, departing 7 A.M., returning 8 P.M.

Mallaig, Sound of Sleat, Kyle of Lochalsh, Isle of Skye: By train to Mallaig steamer to Kyle of Lochalsh, ferry to Kyleakin, bus to Armadale, back by train to Fort William.

SIDE TRIP ¶ If you enjoy ocean bathing under practically ideal conditions on almost empty, snow-white sands, take route 830 out of Fort William for a thirty-three-mile side trip toward Arisaig, Morar and Mallaig. The road winds and twists, climbs and drops, but the drive is an extremely beautiful one, passing lovely lakes en route. Morar, the outlet for Lake Morar, is particularly noted for its beach; in its own way, Morar is among the great beauty spots of Scotland. The road ends at Mallaig, an active colorful port filled with fishing boats; a cozy hotel here is the West Highland. If you wish, there is ferry service from Mallaig to Armadale (Isle of Skye) but autos are not carried; the trip is lovely . . . on a lovely day.

Mallaig specializes in kippers; don't fail to have kippers and eggs; the smoky taste is delightful when they're fresh. If you wander about the town, using your nose as a guide, you'll surely encounter a kipper processing yard; here you can see the fish split, boned, washed and pickled, then smoked.

EXCURSIONS FROM MALLAIG
(MID-MAY THROUGH MID-SEPTEMBER)

Loch Scavaig: Thursday only, leaving at noon, returning about 5:30, with time allowed ashore (weather and circumstances permitting) to visit Loch Coruisk. Bring sturdy shoes.

Small Isles Tour: Saturday morning at 7 A.M., returning 1:30 P.M., to see the little islands of Eigg, Rum and Canna; no landings.

Fort William to Oban—60 miles

Leave Fort William by route 82 to North Ballachulish; there is a choice of driving about thirteen miles or taking the ferry to South Ballachulish, a well-chosen name indeed, because it *is* south of North Ballachulish. From here the road heads south to Portnacroish and into Oban, which means "Little Bay." This town is a favorite resort spot, filled with hotels, but getting a room during August is often an insurmountable problem. Among the good hotels are the Marine, Station, Park and Alexandra. If you're here during the season, feast on one of the delicious ocean-fresh lobsters caught off the Hebrides.

EXCURSIONS FROM OBAN
(MID-MAY THROUGH MID-SEPTEMBER)

Six Lochs cruise: Through Loch Innhe and the Firth of Lorne, usually on Tuesday.

Staffa and Iona: Tuesday, Thursday and Saturday (daily except Sunday during July and August), leaving Oban 9 A.M., returning 6 P.M.

Tobermory: Daily service departing in the morning, returning late afternoon.

Oban to Glasgow—81 miles

From Oban, take route 85 to Connel, driving through the Pass of Brander, a divide between two ranges of hills. The road goes through Dalmally, Tyndrum, Crianlarich and Lochearnhead; here a left turn will bring you to the lovely shores of Loch Earn. Then on to Callander, a beautiful town located on the banks of the River Teith; here you'll find the castlelike Hotel Dreadnought and the smaller Roman Camp Hotel, which is somewhat more expensive.

The road from Callander south (via 821) is one of Scotland's most beautiful trips—but haven't we said that before? This region is known as the Trossachs, which actually means "bristling countryside"; the "pass" is merely a mile in length, but the cliffs, rocks, heather, woodland exuberance and splashing ravines make this a famous beauty spot. The Trossachs Hotel is located here, should you wish to spend a day or so. Then comes pretty Loch Katrine, Aberfoyle (with the Bailie Nicol Jarvie Hotel) and then Glasgow.

WEATHER STRIP: GLASGOW

Temp.	JAN.	FEB.	MAR.	APR.	MAY	JUNE	JULY	AUG.	SEPT.	OCT.	NOV.	DEC.
Low	35°	35°	36°	39°	43°	48°	51°	51°	48°	42°	38°	35°
High	42°	43°	45°	51°	57°	63°	65°	63°	59°	52°	46°	43°
Average	39°	39°	41°	45°	50°	56°	58°	57°	54°	47°	42°	39°
Days of rain	18	15	15	16	15	15	17	17	16	18	18	17

Be sure never to say Glas-gow, but rather Glass-go; many local people refuse to admit that a town pronounced Glas-gow exists. To make things worse, they call themselves not Glasgoers, Glasgoans or Glasgoites but Glaswegians! This is a smoky industrial city (the largest in Scotland) with over 1.5 million people and much too much traffic. The Central Hotel would be an excellent hotel any place and has fine food. More's Hotel is much smaller, but very good. Other top hotels are Lorne, North British, Royal Stuart, St. Enoch and Tinto Firs. The newest and most modern is the ten-story Excelsior Glasgow Airport Hotel with over 300 rooms and suites; it is linked with the airport terminal building. The Gay Gordon, speaking of eating, specializes in steaks and has dancing. The Grosvenor has a fine wine cellar and food to match. One-O-One is a splendid eating place, and there's music, too. To try local Scottish specialties, go to the Royal. For seafood, Rogano is the place. For some unknown reason, Glasgow coffee houses are exceptional and worth visiting. In spite of all the so-called tourist attractions, Glasgow is one place where conventional sightseeing may be completely omitted. Instead, take an informative, entertaining boat trip on the Clyde, one of the greatest shipping rivers of the world and a vast beehive of industry.

EXCURSIONS FROM GLASGOW
(MID-MAY THROUGH MID-SEPTEMBER)

There are complete day trips from Glasgow combining trains or motor coaches with steamer services through the various lochs and isles of the western Highlands. For particulars, write to the steamship company of David MacGrayne Limited at 44 Robertson Street, Glasgow, or phone CENtral 9231.

Glasgow to Carlisle—181 miles (via route 77)

Leaving Glasgow, you have two choices of roads: Route 8 travels around the coast through Gourock and Ardrossan into Ayr; the shorter way is via route 77 through Kilmarnock and into Preswick and Ayr. An interesting resort island, Arran, lies to the west; ferries leave frequently from Ardrossan. Arran, a lovely island much like the mainland but even less crowded, has two good hotels, the Kildonan and the Douglas (at Brodick, where the ferries arrive).

Ayr is another resort town with a famous racetrack, very lively and spirited during the September meet. The entire Ayrshire region is famous for two specialties, which it offers in profusion: (1) Robert Burns, the bard, who was born in Alloway (two miles south), and (2) golf, golf, golf (pronounced gowf, gowf, gowf). From Ayr, take the coastal road, A-719, which later turns slightly inland to pass Culzean Castle, open for visits from 10 A.M. until dark; the local residents call this Eisenhower Castle because an apartment has been presented to him, in recognition of wartime services, as his Scottish home. Near Milton, the road joins route A-77 running into Girvan, a seaside resort. From here, interesting trips may be made into the Firth of Clyde, which Girvan faces; don't miss visiting Ailsa Craig Island, a bird sanctuary, if you like bird sanctuaries. The road continues, closely following the sea, into an untamed, fierce region of rocks, crags and cliffs; you'll pass Ballantrae and come into Stanraer, where there is boat service across the North Channel to Larne, in Northern Ireland, should you wish to make the trip. The Hotel George is the place to stay in Stanraer.

Route A-75 travels through Glenluce (with its 700-year-old abbey), Newton Steward, passing several interesting old castles en route, all the way to Dunfries, a center of Scottish history. Beloved Robert Burns lies buried here and both the house in which he died and his grave may be visited.

Next comes Gretna Green, the very first spot across the Scottish border, once famous for the marriages performed at the local blacksmith shop; runaway couples from England no longer come here, but the famous blacksmith shop (now a very commercial enterprise) may still be visited, although the town itself is a disappointment. Then into Carlisle, formerly a bitterly contested border town with medieval castles and a twelfth-century cathedral, where none other than Sir Walter Scott was married.

SIDE TRIP ¶ Carlisle is a good starting point for exploring further the Roman Wall built by Hadrian; take route A-69 to Greenhead, then route B-6318 toward Housesteads, Chesters, Chollerford, Halton and Rudchester, then route A-69 to Heddon-on-the-Wall; the great wall may be viewed frequently along this drive.

ENGLAND

Carlisle to Blackpool—85 miles

From Carlisle, take route 595 to Cockermouth; in this old village was the home of Wordsworth (which may be visited daily except Thursday). Take route B-5292 to Keswick, a vacation spot where you'll find the pleasant

Keswick Hotel; be sure to see Lake Ullswater. Nearby is Penrith; the Edenhall Hotel has very nice accommodations. Take A-591 to Grasmere and B-5286 to Ambleside, the latter near the head of Lake Windermere. Leave Ambleside by route B-5286 going through charming Old Hawkshead and into Coniston. See the home where John Ruskin spent the latter part of his life; his grave is in the peaceful old churchyard. Now take A-593 to Torver, then follow the signs carefully to Newby Bridge, mostly on A-590; then A-592 into beautifully situated Windermere and then Kendal, a market town with loads of local color.

From Kendal, it's route A-6 down to Carnforth and Lancaster, whose checkered history goes back to Roman times. Leave Lancaster, soon picking up a right turn onto A-586 for Blackpool. This tremendous pleasure resort for hundreds of thousands of British factory workers offers amusements on a mass-production basis, something on the order of Coney Island with a Lancashire accent; a stay at the Imperial Hotel offers a chance for some good swimming.

Blackpool to Stratford-on-Avon—176 miles

Leave Blackpool via A-584, following the shore road through Lytham St. Annes and into Preston, a cotton-manufacturing town; then A-59 into Liverpool, where the Stork Hotel offers pleasant, modest rooms. Liverpool, if the local Chamber of Commerce will forgive us, is more for businessmen than tourists, although the miles of docks are absolutely fascinating.

Just outside of Liverpool, at Wallasey, you can take a most interesting ride: boat service by means of a "hovercraft" that travels on a cushion of air over both land and water.

Cross by tunnel from Liverpool under the River Mersey into Birkenshire, where you take route 41 into Chester, and here you must make a short stop (trust us!). The Rows, a series of double-decker arcade shops, are one of Chester's prides and delights, but that's hardly all, for Chester is a perfect town out of the Middle Ages and a place where you'll surely have to buy more color film. Don't miss seeing the red sandstone cathedral and wandering about the colorful old town.

If you have time, examine the two-mile circuit of walls that enclose Chester; it's the only English city completely walled in. If you still have time, take a boat ride to Eccleston Ferry on the River Dee; head down to the river and ask anyone. By now you may be thinking of remaining overnight; not a bad idea if it's a moonlit night, because the walls are best seen then. Put up overnight at the excellent Grosvenor Hotel, or if not there, then in the new wing of the Blossoms. Whatever you do, don't eat anywhere other than at the hotels. This is an official warning, because the local restaurants are not good.

Take route A-483 from Chester to Wrexham, where Yale graduates might like to know that Elihu Yale, founder of their college, is buried. Then to Ruabon, later passing near Chirk Castle, which dates back to the reign of Edward I (thirteenth century). Watch for a left turn onto route A-5 that leads to Whittington and then Shrewsbury, an appealing little town on the Severn. The outstanding single sight is the famous castle built by Robert de Montgomery (no relation to the film star); if you stay over, and you well might, put up at the Raven Hotel, cozy and inviting.

Leave Shrewsbury by A-5 to Oakengates and Cannock; continue along the road for a short while until a right turn comes up (route A-446) toward Coleshill and continue on to Coventry. Although Coventry is not a terribly interesting town since the war (it took a terrific pasting from Nazi bombers), the newly constructed cathedral has become one of England's outstanding sight-seeing attractions. The cathedral is extremely modern, with unusual pleated side walls; it is a very controversial structure, hotly contested by its adherents and detractors. Be sure to see the enormous Graham Sutherland tapestry of the seated Christ, the unusually slim support pillars, the stained glass windows and especially the cross made of nails from the original cathedral destroyed during the war.

Continue the nineteen miles to Stratford-on-Avon. Now admittedly Stratford is something special, but what the "special" consists of is subject to considerable argument. You'll love it or hate it. It will appear to be either the most wonderful re-creation of Shakespeare's life and time or absolutely the nadir of commercialism (and what of all that talk about the crass, money-mad Yanks?). There's a Shakespeare this, and a Shakespeare that, all over town, until one recoils. For example, the home of Judith Shakespeare (his daughter) bears a sign advertising Wimpey Hamburgers. Some effort has been made to stem the tide of rampant commercialism; by local logic it is possible to purchase Shakespeare tea towels, but Shakespeare T-shirts are not permitted. The local residents sincerely believe that if a sign, no matter how commercial, is executed tastefully, and with a sufficient number of curlicues and scrolls and placed on a half-timbered house, it will not detract from the surroundings. They're wrong. Of course, lovers of the Bard of Avon will surely want to see Holy Trinity Church, where Will and his Anne Hathaway are buried; also to poke about Anne Hathaway's cottage. They will also want to attend a performance of one of the master's works at the Memorial Theatre, a perfect example of the wrong building in the right place—far, far too modern for its surroundings. Getting tickets for a performance in season on short notice is *extremely* difficult and perhaps you ought to make arrangements as soon as you're sure of the exact date of your arrival in Stratford, possibly through an accommodating ticket broker in London at the beginning of your tour. You also might write to the Memorial Theatre, enclosing a deposit of $5 for two tickets and ask the box office to hold the tickets until your arrival when you will settle accounts; if not, get to the theater very early in the morning, when a few seats are placed on sale for that evening's performance. Perhaps the management of your hotel can help you out.

When you get to Stratford, head first for the office of the Public Relations Officer at 20 Chapel Street. There you can get free maps and leaflets on the points of interest. There is a "restoration" next door to the Public Relations office called the New Place, where you can buy a ticket entitling you to visit the five restorations. We think it's worthwhile.

Places to stay in Stratford include the Alveston Manor, an extremely attractive converted manor house with lovely gardens; the Shakespeare Hotel, quite nice, all in all; the Falcon, well located near the theater, with nice rooms and a good restaurant; the Red Horse; and the Swan's Nest. Stratford is much better known for Shakespeare than for its cuisine. Just the same, if you do not want to eat at your hotel all the time, try the Mulberry Tree on Bridge Street (closed on Sundays, by the way), which serves continental-type dishes and has a first-rate wine cellar.

Stratford-on-Avon to Oxford—38 miles

From Stratford, take route A-34 to Woodstock, a properous market town with lovely old half-timbered houses; the Marlborough Arms Hotel is quite good. Nearby is Blenheim Palace, once justifiably called a "gigantic pile"; the most pleasing part of this vast estate is the walk through the surrounding park. Even non-walking Americans aren't permitted to drive. A short run takes you from Woodstock into Oxford, the great university city. (See the previous section on Short Trips from London.)

Oxford to London—58 miles

From Oxford, take A-423 through Cowley and Henley and into Slough. Nearby is Eton and Windsor Castle (see Short Trips from London for details). From Windsor, it's route A-4 all the way into London. Good show, old chap!

ᙣ Motoring in Great Britain

First and foremost, traffic drives on the *left*. Don't let this cause you needless concern. Most tourists adjust to left-handed traffic rather quickly. It's the law of self-preservation at work.

Pointer: Cars coming from the LEFT have the right of way. If you're driving an American car, with the steering wheel on the left-hand side, some practice will be required before you're proficient at passing other cars.

The roads are reasonably good, but hardly up to American standards. Some sections of superhighways (motorways) have been opened and others under construction will be opening in the months ahead. Some of these motorways are long-distance highways, such as the one linking London with Birmingham. Others are merely bypasses around heavily traveled areas. Country roads wander about, frequently in what appear to be circles. But you're here for pleasure and are not in a hurry. The main highways are, frankly, inadequate to handle the flow of traffic. But the British are such courteous drivers, you'll seldom be annoyed.

There is a speed limit of 70 miles per hour on the highways, but common sense is expected. Nonhighways are 50 miles per hour; the limit in built-up areas is 30 miles.

The British gallon (Imperial) is larger than an American gallon. For rough computations, you can figure five British gallons as being equal to six American ones. So gas (petrol, as the British say) is cheaper than you first think. Its price is about 85 cents a gallon.

The British highway system is extremely simple: all route numbers beginning with "A" are main roads and those designated A-1 to A-9 are the chief highways. All routes beginning with "B" are extremely narrow; as a rule, barely two small British cars wide. So, care must be exercised. British drivers will almost always signal if it's safe for you to pass on a narrow road. Roads A-1 to A-6 start at London; roads A-7 to A-9 at Edinburgh. The nine roads have the following names: A-1, Great North Road; A-2, Dover Road; A-3, Portsmouth Road; A-4, Bath Road; A-5, Holyhead Road; A-6, Carlisle Road (via Derby); A-7, Edinburgh to Carlisle Road; A-8, Edinburgh-Glasgow-Gourock Road; and A-9, Edinburgh to John o'Groats Road.

In cities, traffic is frequently very heavy. Don't blow horns except in emergencies. Use parking lights (never headlights) when driving American cars in British cities; headlights are used only in the country. In the final analysis, British police are extremely lenient with American motorists. Just don't overabuse the privilege.

The only documents needed to bring your car into the country are the vehicle's registration certificate, your home-state driver's license and the Green Card (the international insurance certificate). Customs people, in clearing your car, will give you a customs notice (No. 115D) that will explain the conditions governing its importation free of duty and excise taxes for a maximum period of twelve months. Keep the customs notice handy, because somewhere along the line it might be requested by an official.

One word of caution: Britain's drunk-driving law (providing for breath and blood tests) is strictly enforced. So if you have been drinking, don't drive.

౨❧ Boat Trips in England

London to Oxford by VERY slow boat

From May to early September, tourists with loads of time and calm, placid natures might enjoy the three-day trip via motor launch from London to Oxford. Boats leave Kingston Pier (near London) at 9 A.M., Mondays through Fridays, and the fare is in the neighborhood of $10. The boats travel slowly and make approximately forty stops en route. You can disembark at any point and pick up another motor launch, as your mood dictates. There are many interesting sights along the river; first, Windsor Castle and Eton, with a two-hour stop for lunch. The boat on the first day reaches Marlow at 6 P.M. At Marlow, during the overnight stop, you put up at a local hotel—at your own expense, of course. Onward the next morning at 9 A.M. and on through to Caversham, where the afternoon and evening are free ashore. On the third morning leave at a luxurious 10 A.M., to arrive at Oxford at 7 P.M. This trip is recommended, but *only* for those who aren't in a hurry and whose patience permits them to enjoy life at a slow leisurely pace.

Oxford to Birmingham via VERY slow boat

During the warmer weather, the famous "narrow boats" ply the canals and rivers from Oxford to Birmingham via Banbury, Leamington and Stratford-on-Avon. En route, passengers travel on small-glass-enclosed boats, with each passenger seated alongside the window. Morning coffee, lunch and tea are served aboard. Stops are made overnight. For details on schedules and tariffs, check with the Fleet Superintendent, Pleasurecraft Hire Office, British Waterways Board, Sampson's Road, North Birmingham 11 (Warwickshire).

ENGLISH CHANNEL AND NORTH SEA
SERVICE FOR AUTOMOBILES

Someone has figured out that there is an automobile-carrying ferry crossing the Channel every ten minutes during the height of the summer tourist season. But don't take this too literally, although the ten-minute scheduling is probably right. The point is, though, that the next ferry shoving off might be departing from a point thirty miles—or more—down the coast, or up it. Thus, it pays to try to have firm reservations before embarking with your car on a trip across the Channel. Don't depend on being able to drive right up to the ferry landing and get aboard. This can work out, but it can also lead to a waiting line of a day or more. Ferries serve Denmark, Holland, Belgium and France. The ones you'll probably be interested in are those between England and France. There are a number of departure and arrival points on both coasts, ranging from Southampton up to Dover and Folkestone on the English side and from Le Havre and Dieppe to Boulogne, Calais and Dunkerque in France. Rates vary with the particular crossing point, the size of the car and the number of passengers. From Boulogne, Calais and Dunkerque to Dover, for example, you can figure on paying about $40 for the average car and two passengers. Actual ferry schedules cannot be shown because they change frequently during the season, stepping up in frequency beginning in April and dropping off during September. For a helpful leaflet with details on Sea Ferry Service, write to British Railways, 9 Rockefeller Plaza, New York, N.Y. It is also possible to ship cars by air. This is expensive, of course. The British Travel Association information offices in London can advise you on airlines currently performing the car ferry service, and the rates.

Pointer: The fascinating *hovercraft* provide speedy service between Dover and Boulogne/Calais, most of the year. For schedules, tariffs or reservations, write Car Ferry Centre, 52 Grosvenor Gardens, London SW1.

MISCELLANEOUS ODDMENTS ¶ Gambling on football games is legal; everywhere you'll hear people phoning in their selections in the complicated betting pools. It's theoretically possible to win vast sums—even if you bet no more than a few cents—if you pick the winners of a series of matches, but you have to be *really* lucky.

When two motorists have an accident, it's customary to get out and apologize for the incident; there's very little name calling in the French (and sometimes American) way.

The English love tradition and won't appreciate your calling attention to the fact that a particular old building needs repairs; this is the British way, and they think Americans place an overemphasis upon modernity.

Everyone is disciplined here and will wait in line patiently for a bus without pushing or shoving; if you don't, you're a bounder and a cad.

An interesting attraction may be observed by getting

to the theater before curtain time; the crowds line up (in orderly British fashion) to get unreserved seats in the top balcony. The "buskers," street players, put on a little outdoor show for them that is one of London's most typical sights.

You'll find an extremely high degree of courtesy, honesty and fair dealing wherever you go. One small exception: the "spiv" or black market operator has to be watched, because he's basically a crook. You'll have to use your own judgment, but it shouldn't be too difficult to tell who's who.

Don't be too shocked at some of the photographs in the London tabloids—they merely reflect the permissive character of the city's contemporary image. Incidentally, they dearly love to run nosy items about the Royal Family, while the editorial pages are simultaneously filled with outcries against those seeking to invade royalty's privacy.

On the same topic, don't try and be humorous about members of the Royal Family. It won't be appreciated. Also, don't try to assign exclusive credit to America for winning the war; the British took an awful pasting during those years and shouldered the burden until we finally got in; many British servicemen served overseas for five years without ever getting home for leave.

If you attend a cocktail party, your hostess will wave vaguely in the direction of about fifty people you've never met and say, "But of course you know everyone," and leave you to fend for yourself. This is the British way, and even when someone introduces himself, he'll only say "Hmgfhth" or "Fasmghrgth" or the like, so you never do learn his name.

FINLAND

National Characteristics

For the Finns December 6, 1917, is what July 4, 1776, is for Americans. That's the date of their declaration of independence. For more than a half century, Finland has been a free and independent state, and the Finns enjoy their independence because they are truly an independent people. Their land, for six centuries, was part of a vast Swedish realm. Then, a century and a half ago, during the Napoleonic Wars, it was separated from Sweden (on the west) and made part of the Russian empire as a grand duchy. So here, in this land that swerves across the Arctic Circle you actually will find East and West meeting, and the encounter makes for exciting sightseeing.

There are many fascinating ways in which East meets West here in this beautiful country of lakes (62,000 of them!). Finland is part of Scandinavia but is a little bit different from her neighbors. There are two state churches here—Lutheran and Greek Orthodox. In Helsinki, the visitor sights the splendid Lutheran Cathedral, all in white, almost side by side with an Orthodox church that is distinguished by the exotic onion-shaped cupola of the East. In eastern Finland, as a matter of fact, there are many Greek Orthodox people, and there are two Orthodox monasteries in the Carelia region.

Finland shares an 800-mile border with Russia, a 335-mile one with Sweden and a 455-mile one with Norway. Russia is literally right next door. The Russian border is only 125 miles from Helsinki, and Leningrad is only another 125 miles farther. Fifty miles across the Gulf of Finland from Helsinski is Tallinn, capital of Estonia, which Russia annexed and made into a Soviet Socialist Republic.

There is also a fascinating link between the Finns and Estonians in language. The Finns speak an almost incomprehensible, extraordinarily difficult language. The only other languages in the world similar to it are those spoken by the Hungarians (away down in the southern part of Europe) and the Estonians, who are just across the Gulf of Finland. How this language connection between Finland and Hungary came about is only one of the many things that will intrigue you in this spell-binding land.

The Finns are warm-hearted, sensitive, very likable people. You'll like them at once and keep on liking them more and more. They are literate. Their literacy rate, if not the world's highest, is very close to it. What they have done in industrial design and handicrafts is known all over the world. They keep doing great things in the social field, too. Finland was a pioneer in bringing into existence the eight-hour day and was the first European nation to grant women equal legal rights with men. City planners in Helsinki are making sure that 30 percent of the available area is maintained as parks and gardens. The Finns concern themselves with making life healthy and pleasant for the family.

The Finns are a mysterious people, too—mysterious in the sense that they seem to be isolated geographically and linguistically from the rest of the world. They aren't, of course. But the touch of mystery rounds out the charm of Finland and her people.

Honesty is the best policy, the Finns believe. The traveler often is made aware of the national passion for honesty. A small coin left behind on the floor of a hotel room inevitably will bring a chambermaid running into the street after a departing guest to announce the find. This honesty is not only individual but national in scope. There are probably few Americans, young or old or in-between, who do not know that Finland alone of all European nations paid back the American loans that were due at the conclusion of World War I. This dedication to meeting one's obligations, individually and as a nation, perhaps more than any other single factor, illustrates the Finnish character and personality.

This is a phenomenal country in the northeastern part of Europe. It is immaculate, beautiful and hardly touched by tourism.

When to Go

Make no mistake about it. The winters here are *cold*. Of course, everything is done to make the interiors of hotels, houses, restaurants and stores completely comfortable. But out in the street on a January or February afternoon it will be (very) cold. It is a *dry* cold, and you may not feel the wintry weather's brunt as much as the thermometer indicates. But it will nevertheless be cold. So, April is a bit too early to head for Finland. May is the very soonest for tourists and even that may be a trifle too early in some years. June is usually fine, but July and August are really the best months for a visit. The weather holds good for a week or so in September and then begins to turn cool; then, in October, cold; then, extremely cold. The summer months are the driest. Always bring warm clothes. Even when the days are warm, the evenings turn chilly. To give you an idea, Finnish weather may be compared roughly with that of upper Maine—pleasant, rather late spring; mild summer; and very early fall. Just to confuse the issue, however, we must add that even in the far north, in Lapland, the summer temperature can—we said *can*—go to 90 degrees.

WEATHER STRIP: HELSINKI

Temp.	JAN.	FEB.	MAR.	APR.	MAY	JUNE	JULY	AUG.	SEPT.	OCT.	NOV.	DEC.
Average	23°	22°	28°	37°	46°	55°	62°	59°	50°	41°	32°	28°
Days of rain	18	16	14	12	12	13	12	16	16	17	19	19

TIME EVALUATION ¶ Helsinki, the attractive capital, should be allowed two to three days. There are few short excursions from the city, although a day in the country just driving about more or less aimlessly will show you the pleasant countryside. A trip through the country, allowing a few days for resort life, could take about five days or so up to two weeks.

PASSPORT AND VISA ¶ As in all countries, you'll need a passport, but no visa is required if you are staying less than ninety days.

CUSTOMS AND IMMIGRATION ¶ A traveler from the United States is allowed to bring in (provided he is 15 years of age or over) 400 cigarettes or one pound of other manufactured tobacco and (provided he is 20 years of age or over) 2 liters (about 2 quarts) of wine or other alcoholic beverage. Also you cannot—generally—bring in more than $100 worth of goods in addition to travel articles and equipment. A visitor may take out of the country $250 worth of gifts without an export license. There is no restriction on money imports, but you cannot take from the country more than 200 marks ($50). This is all theoretical, because there is rarely a customs examination for tourists.

Pointer: There is a quarantine period on pets of four months.

HEALTH ¶ The water is always safe and the milk is delicious. In fact, fresh, cold milk is a national favorite with the Finns. The country is extremely clean, all in all, and is apparently scrubbed up to a high degree of sanitation. The chief concern during your Finnish visit will be to avoid colds, for the temperature often takes a sudden dip in the evening. If you're making an all-day trip, be sure to carry along a sweater or a coat. That midnight sun may be bright, but it doesn't throw off any heat after 9 P.M.

TIME ¶ All through Finland, the time is seven hours ahead of (later than) Eastern Standard Time. When it's noon in New York, it's 7 P.M. in Helsinki. When Daylight Saving Time is in effect in the United States, the time difference is only 6 hours.

CURRENCY ¶ The *finnmark* (written *Fmk.* or *mk.*) is the unit of currency. It is made up of 100 penniä (the singular of penniä is penni).

PRICE LEVEL ¶ The prices run from moderate to high. A single room in a better Helsinki hotel will be anything up to $20, or so; a double, up to $26 or higher. Out in the countryside, hotel prices are somewhat lower, but not too much. A meal in a top restaurant will be somewhat less than the usual New York average. Transportation, in general, is extremely low cost, and Finland ranks among the two or three least expensive countries in Europe in this category.

TIPPING ¶ The tipping situation is a bit different here from that in most European countries. A 12½ percent surcharge is added to restaurant bills, and that takes care of the tipping. You do not have to tip taxi drivers, barbers, hairdressers and some of the other people who perform services for you. That remark does not apply to hotels. The doorman should get a 1 mk. tip, and a similar tip should be given to the porter for each bag he carries. Otherwise, use your own judgment in accordance with the special services done for you. In other words, everyone is not looking for a tip—the way it is some places.

TRANSPORTATION ¶ *Taxis* are numerous, but on the expensive side. The minimum fare is Fmk. 2.30, and fares increase with the number of passengers. If there are 3 or 4 of you using the same cab, the rate is 15 percent higher; for five or more passengers, it is 30 percent higher. Also, between 11 P.M. and 6 P.M. the driver gets an additional 0.50 mk. above the meter reading.

Buses travel an extensive, far-reaching network throughout the country, and travel is inexpensive. To give you an idea, a bus leaves from Helsinki for Porvoo every hour, making the trip in about 75 minutes. The fare is less than a dollar. In the northern part of Finland, the bus usually is the only public means of transportation, but it is still inexpensive. Bus seats can be reserved two weeks in advance by paying the full fare and a small reservation fee. A number of the bus stations have been built in recent years.

There are fine, smooth-traveling diesel *trains* on the principal tourist routes. Rail fares are low, and there is a network of 5,500 miles of track. Round-trip tickets are always a bit cheaper because the longer the distance, the lower the basic rate. The trip between Helsinki and Turku takes three hours. There are eleven rapid trains daily serving Hämeenlinna from Helsinki. The trip takes an hour and a quarter.

Air service by Finnair links almost a score of main tourist points in the country and the rates are really low.

A trip from Helsinki up to the Arctic Circle city of Rovaniemi, for example, costs not too much more than $30. Finnair also schedules special trips to Lapland so that, in polar surroundings, you can contentedly and very agreeably watch the midnight sun.

Waterway travel, what with all those lakes and all that sea, is one of the great ways for getting around Finland in the summertime. There are wonderful short island tours from Helsinki, for instance, to the Western Islands, Eastern Islands and Porvoo. On Saturday evening, at seven o'clock, you can set off for "An Evening in the Lap of the Sea"—a two and a half hour cruise to the islands near Helsinki. From the South Harbor in Helsinki there is passenger-ship service daily to foreign ports during the summer.

Pointer: There is a reasonably priced Holiday ticket which allows unlimited travel by air for fifteen days.

COMMUNICATION ¶ Don't fail to make a few local *phone* calls in Finland, because the charge is less than a nickel. How can you pass up such a bargain? Dial service makes phone calling easy, despite the intricacies of the Finnish language. *Airmail* letters to the United States are expensive. Clerks at the telegraph and cable desks in the post offices almost inevitably speak English, so there will be no language problem.

Pointer: For the day's news and weather forecast, telephone 018 in Helsinki; for information on the day's events and entertainment, telephone 058. The reports are in English.

ELECTRICITY ¶ Just about everywhere in Finland the electricity is 220 A.C., although there are a few remote places that are not yet on the grid and continue to rely on 120 D.C. The higher voltage, of course, is not suited for American appliances without a transformer. In any event, a round two-prong plug is necessary for the Finnish electrical sockets.

BASIC FINNISH

English-Finnish

Waiter: *Tarjoilija*
Bill of fare, menu: *Ruokalista*
Napkin: *Lautasliina*
Bread and butter: *Leipää ja voita*
A glass of orange juice: *Lasi appelsiinimehua*

Boiled egg: *Keitetty muna*
1. soft   1. *pehmeä*
2. medium   2. *puolikova*
3. hard-boiled   3. *kova*
4. egg cup   4. *munakuppi*
Fried eggs: *Paistettuja munia*
Bacon and eggs: *Munaa ja paistettua silavaa*
Coffee, black: *Mustaa kahvia*
Coffee with cream and sugar: *kahvia kerman ja sokerin kera*
Coffee with hot milk: *Maitokahvia*
Tea: *Teetä*
Water: *Vettä*
Ice water: *Jääkylm ää vettä, jäävettä*
Mineral water: *Kivennäisvettä*
Breakfast: *Aamiainen*
Lunch: *Lounas*
Dinner: *Päivällinen*
Shampoo: *Tukanpesu*
Haircut: *Tukanleikkuu*
Manicure: *Käsienhoito*
I want . . . liters of petrol: *Haluaisin . . . litraa bensiiniä*
Change the oil: *Vaihtakaa öljy*
Grease the car: *Voidelkaa auto*
How are you?: *Kuinka voitte?*
Fine, thank you: *Kittos, hyvin*
Please: *Olkaa hyvä*
Thank you very much: *Paljon kiitoksia*
Good morning: *Hyvää huomenta*
Good afternoon: *Hyvää (ilta) paivää*
Good night: *Hyvää yötä*
Yes: *Kyllä*
No: *Ei*
Morning: *Aamu*
Noon: *Puoli—keski päivä*
Afternoon, P.M.: *Iltapäivä*
Evening: *Ilta*
Night: *Yö*
Sunday: *Sunnuntai*
Monday: *Maanantai*
Tuesday: *Tiistai*
Wednesday: *Keskiviikko*
Thursday: *Torstai*
Friday: *Perjantai*
Saturday: *Lauantai*
One: *Yksi*
Two: *Kaksi*
Three: *Kolme*
Four: *Neljä*
Five: *Viisi*
Six: *Kuusi*
Seven: *Seitsemän*
Eight: *Kahdeksän*
Nine: *Yhdeksän*
Ten: *Kymmenen*
Twenty: *Kaksikymmentä*
Thirty: *Kolmekymmentä*

Forty: *Neljäkymmentä*
Fifty: *Viisikymmentä*
One hundred: *Sata*
One thousand: *Tuhat*

HOLIDAYS ¶ Some of the holidays in Finland are the same as ours, and others are different. It is a good idea to know the Finnish ones so that you can do your planning accordingly. Officially, they celebrate New Year's, Epiphany (January 6), Spring Feast and Labor Day (May 1), Midsummer's Day and Finnish Flag Day (the Saturday closest to June 24), All Saints' Day (the Saturday closest to the end of October or beginning of November), Independence Day (December 6), Christmas and Boxing Day (December 26). Other holidays are Easter, Ascension Day and Whit Sunday and days on which student festivals are scheduled.

FOOD SPECIALTIES AND LIQUORS ¶ Lunch is served starting about 11 A.M., because the Finns eat a very light breakfast or almost none at all. Sometimes they will have a cheese or a ham sandwich. Lunch for the average Finn is always light, but guests are expected to join the line at the mammoth "sandwich table," which is called *voilei-päpöytä* (pronounced something like voy-lay-puh-pew-tuh). If you've visited any of the Scandinavian countries and sampled the smorgasbord in its natural habitat, the Finnish version, with its great elaborateness and variety, will not be altogether a surprise. Be sure to comply with the traditional fashion of eating; first, the fish dishes (but always herring, with possibly a boiled potato); second, an assortment of meats; and third, the cheese selections and several of the hot dishes offered in the chafing dishes. You can return to the serving table several times, for the Finns like to eat and admire a hearty eater. Many restaurants feature the wild fowl of the region—ducks, grouse and hazel hens, for example, and as a rule these make exceptionally good eating. There is lots of game meat, too, particularly toward the end of the summer season—including such novelties as bear and elk. Of course, if there is reindeer meat on the menu, someone will suggest that you try it. Reindeer is served in steaks, chops and other cuts. There is reindeer tongue in Madiera sauce, which can be excellent. As an hors d'oeuvre smoked reindeer tongue (delicious!) will be offered on that *voilei-*

päpöytä food extravaganza. Keep your eye out, too, for the salmon. It is lightly salted and is delicious.

Because Finland was once part of Russia, you will find some Russian overtones in the Finnish food and drink. *Stroganoff* is on the menu frequently, and a great popular item is a cabbage roll, which consists of ground meat and rice cooked inside a leaf of cabbage. Bread is most often the dark or rye types. The Finns have a reputation for being heavy drinkers, but this is not always a correct observation, we were told. It is just that they do not drink often, and when they do—well, they do. Foreigners seeing a Finn at a bar apparently do not realize how long an interval it has been since he had his last drink. We were assured of all this, by the way, in a bar, where else? In any event, Finland is one of the largest importers of French cognac. Finnish beer is fine, and delicious. Especially on cold days, a glass of *schnapps* is a real pick-me-up. This can be either the potato-based kind or—not recommended—the type made from wood. This latter version of schnapps is also the least expensive. Vodka is also a popular drink.

Since the country fronts onto the sea with a considerable coastline and the interior has all those lakes, the Finns base a large part of their diet around the preparations of *fish*. During the season, herring is bought in barrels by thrifty housewives and pickled, smoked, fried, baked, and boiled, inevitably to end up in dozens of dishes. There are large parts of Finland where herring is unquestionably the basic food.

Finland's evening meal starts around 4 P.M., believe it or not, but it is possible to be served until midnight in Helsinki restaurants. Some night clubs serve meals until four in the morning.

If there is one single preparation that typifies the local cookery style, it is the *piirakka*, a pastry dough filled with meat and rice, or possibly fish. The Finns like to combine meat and fish in one dish; for example, their favorite *kalakukko*, a sort of fish cake, is made with fresh herring, bacon and pork; don't say anything until you've tried it. Then complain, if you wish.

Fish main courses are popular, too. The crayfish are in season during August, so be sure to try them; their flavor is reminiscent of an American lobster, but more delicate. Another food that has a particular fascination for the Finns is mushrooms, and in this respect they resemble their Russian neighbors, who seem to have developed a cult for the mushroom just two paces short of idolatry.

The best desserts are fresh berries: strawberries of course, but be sure to look for the cloudberries (yellowish raspberries) and brambleberries (like blackberries). Finnish pancakes are the national dessert, although burdened by a tongue-twisting name, *soumalainen pannukakku*. Two interesting and unique after-dinner liqueurs are the *besimarja* (made from the brambleberry) and *lakka* (from the cloudberry).

The principal tourist areas of Finland are Helsinki, the southern lakes district, and Lapland.

Capital City

This is the "White City of the North." That's the impression you get of Helsinki if you approach it from the sea. The buildings along the harbor, such as the Town Hall, the President's Palace, the Swedish Embassy and the cathedral, all make a most impressive welcoming committee for the visitor heading in from the sea, and most of the buildings along the water are a dazzling white. Helsinki has been the capital of the country since 1812, but before that was only a provincial town (the old capital was Turku). Today, the population is about a half-million.

The city is alive and sparkling, with alert people rushing about in the Western fashion. The buildings are clean and attractive, and the overall effect is entirely pleasing. The streets are broad and tree-lined, and the entire city has an open, spacious look as a result of the careful town planning by authorities. Don't misunderstand. Helsinki does not lack the colorful and quaint aspects, by any means. There are such touches in abundance. Yet, unlike neighbors Stockholm and Copenhagen, Helsinki is not overburdened with a sense of living with history. The town is young, fresh and full of vitality. You'll sense this immediately upon arrival. The architecture, for the almost part, is modern in scope and feeling. There is almost a complete break with the past and with tradition, evident by the comparative lack of old buildings, historic sites and narrow, sunless streets. The impression is that of a breath of fresh air—a feeling of all outdoors.

The moderate size of Helsinki is a great boon to the sightseer. Nearly everything may be seen easily. First, a little orientation: The city is mainly built on a peninsula, and also on several islands. The central part is surrounded on three sides by water. There are three harbors, and ships berth right in the center of Helsinki. Facing the middle harbor is one of the city's central points, the Market Square. Come here as early as possible in the morning to see the life and color of the popular marketplace on the waterfront. It is open daily except Sunday from 7 A.M. to 1 P.M., and the women are there selling everything from rugs to baskets—all native products. It is a remarkable scene, because just in the background is the Uspenski Cathedral (the Greek, or Russian, Orthodox church), and the President's Palace is right behind the open market, in all the hustle and bustle. This square is reputed to be one of the most beautiful in the world when covered with snow, and when the snow is on the ground it is probably one of the coldest spots, too. Even during the summer it's extremely colorful.

In the square is the obelisk called the Stone of the Empress, placed there in 1833 when Empress Alexandra Feodorovna of Russia visited Helsinki. From the ferry landing, near the President's Palace, is a boat every hour to Suomenlinna, a group of fortified islands that guard the approaches to Helsinki harbor. On the main island is an old fortress built by the Swedes in the eighteenth century, when Helsinki was part of their domain. There is a series of six islands connected by bridges, and from them there is an excellent view of Helsinki harbor. The fortress is definitely worth a visit. There are fine seaside walking paths, two museums and a delightful restaurant built right into the walls. Lunch here is something you shouldn't miss. The ferry ride to Suomenlinna takes a quarter of an hour. In the winter the entire harbor, as well as a large part of the gulf itself, freezes over. There are no ferries then. But you can get to the islands in the harbor by bus. Yes, by bus! There are people living on the islands, and there is a training center for military personnel. The people have to get back and forth, and when the ice makes ferry transport impossible, the buses take off across the frozen water. Incidentally, one of the main local industries is building ice breakers. The Helsinki yards have built the biggest diesel ice breaker in the world for use in the polar regions of the Arctic. The visitor driving along the harbor front can see some of these ice breakers under construction, and if he happens to be there in the winter, can see them at work. The Finns built Sweden's last three ice breakers and have built at least four for Russia.

Be sure to do some walking about the compact midtown area of Helsinki. Senate Square, lined by buildings a century and a half old, is one of Helsinki's finest sights. The Sederholm Residence in Senate Square by local standards is a real old-timer—over two centuries old. The most interesting streets are the Esplanade, which runs from Market Square westward, and Aleksanterinkatu (the main shopping thoroughfare), which extends from Senate Square to Helsinki's famed department store, Stockmann's, on Mannerheimintie (Street). Other sights to see are the Ateneum Art Gallery, the Parliament, the City Botanical Gardens and the University Botanical Gardens. You'll also want to browse around the Old Town, where the city was originally staked out four centuries ago before being moved to its more convenient location on the water's edge. To get there, take tram No. 6 and get off at the Arabia stop.

From the North Harbor, at the end of Aleksanterinkatu a ferry leaves every hour on the hour, from 9 A.M. until late in the evening, for the Korkeasaari Island zoo. There is also a bathing beach and a restaurant on the island. For a good look at the harbor go to the Stadium Tower, which is open daily from 9 A.M. to 8 P.M. The admission is a half-mark. Another good observation point is Observatory Hill Park, which provides a view of the South Harbor.

If you plan to buy (or just like) Arabia pottery, a great specialty of Finland, take a taxi or that No. 6 Old Town tram to the factory. There are regular tours during the summer for visitors.

By all means you should visit the model garden city called Tapiola, a beautiful development six miles from the center of Helsinki. The name Tapiola was selected from the Finnish national epic *Kalevala*. Tapiola, in the epic, was the imaginary locality where the fabled people lived. But there is nothing imaginary about Helsinki's Tapiola. It is a splendid place, a most representative architectural development. Tapiola was started in 1953 by a group of private organizations—all nonprofit ones, including the Finnish Family Welfare League, the confederation of Finnish Trade Unions, the Society of Civil

Servants and three other national associations. The group's purpose was to demonstrate a way of establishing ideal living conditions in national surroundings. So on 670 acres in the rural district of Espoo, on the outskirts of Helsinki, they built a modern garden city. There are 30,000 people living there. They have their own newspaper, clubs, shops—everything. The central building, thirteen stories high, is the tallest of all the apartment houses. A cafe is on the top floor, and there is an outdoor terrace, around which visitors can walk in the summertime. A fine restaurant is on the twelfth floor, and from the tables is a view of all Tapiola as well as downtown Helsinki and the gulf. The round-trip taxi ride to Tapiola is expensive. But from the bus terminal on Mannerheim Street, you can take a bus (marked Tapiola).

ACCOMMODATIONS ¶ An interesting feature of Finland is the *sauna*, a steam bath. Most hotels have saunas, especially all the newer establishments. Most of the saunas are situated in the basement, but this is not always so. The luxury Palace Hotel, which faces the harbor so marvelously, has an upstairs sauna. What is more, as you (if you're a man) sit in the washing room of this great bath you can look through large picture windows at the scene along the harbor front. (It's just as well the people down on the harbor front can't look into the sauna.) The new Meri Hotel—the name means "sea"—also has a top-floor sauna-with-a-view.

The sauna is very much a Finnish institution. To sum it up succinctly, the sauna is a steam bath with dry heat ranging up to 125 degrees Fahrenheit, or about 55 to 60 degrees Centigrade. If the temperature—and there is usually a thermometer, handy or visible—gets above this level, it's a good time to head for the nearest exit. As if that high-altitude temperature was not enough, it is customary to beat one's self with a birch branch to further induce circulation and perspiration. Just in passing—shy males should be warned that in some establishments a female (of advanced years and extremely muscular) usually acts as an attendant and birch-branch wielder. The whole proceeding is capped off with an ice-cold bath.

Outside of the larger cities, the small hotels are clean and inviting. Naturally there are few luxury services or private baths. Finland already has some motels, but a larger chain of them is now developing throughout the country. At Otaniemi, a short ride from Helsinki, is the big, modern 1,000-bed Summer Hotel, where rooms are inexpensive. There's plenty of parking space, too. Incidentally, never feel hesitant about staying at one of the boarding houses in the lake district. The proprietor and his family will welcome you heartily and make you feel very much at home.

HELSINKI HOTELS

Inter-Continental: Helsinki's leading hotel; brand-new; 285 rooms, several restaurants, and managed by the Inter-Continental chain of hotels.
Palace: Very nice rooms, most of which have a wonderful view of the harbor. A pleasant, quiet place.
Vaakuna: A modern attractive hotel, centrally located, built into two floors of an office building with the lobby on the street floor. Nice rooms, modern décor.
Helsinki: Good, homey hotel with pleasing atmosphere. Rooms are fair in size; hotel is known for good food. Less expensive than the hotels above.
Torni: A well-known hotel, also noted for its fine meals. Not all rooms have private baths.
Marksi: A newish hotel, quite attractive, moderate-size rooms well located in the center of the city.
Meri: A newly completed establishment; the name means "sea" and the hotel is situated about twenty yards or so from the gulf; there's a top-floor sauna, too, with a view.
Seurahuone: A good, moderate-price hotel with a restaurant featuring music with its fine food. Meal prices are reasonable.

HELSINKI RESTAURANTS

Monte Carlo: French and Italian food, quite good, served in pleasant small restaurant.
Savoy: Interesting location atop office building; excellent view from window tables. Often, there are many Finnish specialties on the menu. Moderate to expensive.
Kalastajatorppa: Suburban dining in absolutely charming surroundings. Fair food, pleasant music for dancing.
Vanha Talli: This is in a park along Taivallahti Bay, and you can combine a fine meal with a wonderful view from the terrace.
Linnunrata: This is a top restaurant, finely furnished in Finnish design, with a top view (from the twelfth floor of Tapiola) of Helsinki and the sea and islands.

SHOPPING ¶ The ideal place to start on a shopping expedition is the Finnish Design Center, because you can get a good idea of what is produced in the country. The center was opened in 1960 as a showcase for the presentation of Finnish goods to visitors. It is two blocks from that fashionable promenade street the Esplanade, which is lined with big linden trees. It is also just two blocks behind the Palace Hotel. The exact address is 19 Kasarmikatu. The center is open daily from 9 A.M. to 5 P.M. and on Saturdays from 9 A.M. to 3 P.M. From June to August only, it is also open on Sunday from noon to 4 P.M. There is something like 4,000 square feet of exhibit space and dozens and dozens of items—ranging from furniture to household articles and from machinery to rifles. Recently, at Christmas, for example, 560 individual items were displayed. So that gives you an idea.

There are specialty shops scattered throughout the city and along the main shopping thoroughfares. But Stockmann's, the internationally known department store, has a tremendous selection under one roof. It even has an automobile department. It is the principal sales point for embassies behind the Iron Curtain—for example, it sells Danish furniture to the Danish Embassy in Moscow. Thus, its service, its facilities for shipping and the quality of its goods are excellent.

Products offered the intrepid shopper in Finland follow the Scandinavian pattern, with emphasis upon the *decorative articles* for home use.

Glassware is superb, with smart, clean lines; the etched tableware and vases are just as fine as anything produced in Sweden or Norway. The general price level is quite similar to that of the other Scandinavian countries, with a few exceptions. The very low priced Finnish glassware does not warrant shipment to the United States, because the charge for packaging, shipping and insurance cancels the savings over the prices in the United States. If you do buy, you would be well advised to give thought to the better quality glassware, which although considerably more expensive is more likely to be worth the trouble and expense of shipping.

With *Arabia pottery* and *rice china* the shipping problem is not nearly so acute, because of the superb high-price craftsmanship; many pieces are excellent, others quite (almost too) extreme in design. Although hardly cheap in Helsinki, these are astronomically expensive in New York. Of all the ill-chosen names for a Finnish pottery concern, certainly the selection of the name "Arabia" should win some sort of a prize for confusion making.

Modern furniture is well designed and reasonable; be sure to inquire as to the condition of the articles being shipped. If shipped "knocked-down," their reassembly is none too easy. *Lighting fixtures* and *lamps* are world leaders in modern design; if your home has contemporary decoration, a Finnish lamp or fixture might make an outstanding addition.

Hand-blocked linens and *hand-woven textiles* are noteworthy. You'll find a good selection of drapery fabrics and upholstery materials, but be sure to know your total fabric requirements before you buy, or you may find yourself with insufficient material to cover your sofa.

Stainless steel tableware is well designed and bargain priced, but the selection is quite limited when compared with the other Scandinavian countries. If you see what you like, buy it; if not, there'll be a much larger selection in Denmark (if you're going there).

Souvenirs? Loads of small items made by the Lapps in northern Finland include bone articles, bags, bracelets, pins and similar tourist bait. The *Kalevala brooches* are made in precious metals from designs inspired by the national epic, the *Kalevala*; it is said that no two brooches are exactly alike, but this we cannot guarantee. *Ashtrays, cigarette boxes* and small *vases* make excellent gifts; hand-carved miniature houses and other *toys* will delight any youngster on your list. *Wooden bowls* with a fine grain and high luster are somewhat bulky, but otherwise ideal for gifts.

ENTERTAINMENT ¶ The Finnish State Opera in Helsinki, is a fine one. The season starts September 1, and during a nine-month period there is a presentation of classic *opera, ballet* and *operettas.* The classic operas occupy half of the schedule, and the remaining half is pretty much split between ballet evenings and light operas. These light operas include such modern musicals as *Porgy and Bess* and *West Side Story.* These American shows are very popular with the Finns and even though in Finnish will be pleasant entertainment for a visitor. *Porgy,* for instance, has been presented more than sixty times since its Helsinki premiere in 1964. Because of the language, ordinary *theater-going* will not be interesting to the average visitor. But the National Theater is quite interesting, no matter what. It has three stages, including one with a 900-seat capacity. The smallest of the three stages (only 80 seats in a small Elizabethan-type theater) permits drinking during the performance. Meanwhile, the City Theater moved into a brand new building recently, and the stages are great examples of modern technology at work for the dramatic art.

There is also a Swedish-speaking theater in Helsinki, because 8 percent of the people of the city speak Swedish (from the old days) and 15 percent of those in the countryside are Swedish-speaking. As a matter of fact, Swedish is an official language, and the president of Finland opens Parliament on January 1 in both Finnish and Swedish. (The text on Finnish money is also in two languages.)

Night clubs are not important in the Finnish entertainment scheme of things. They are usually nicely appointed, have a good combo and sometimes present a fair floor show. But it is a weak echo of Broadway, Las Vegas or Paris—so why bother? In case you do, however, try Kaivohuone, which is in Kaivopuisto Park. A real showplace for dining and dancing is Kalastajatorppa, on the shores of a suburban bay. It's worth the trip. A number of restaurants in town have dancing. For afternoon teas, a luncheon, or just a snack, there are many fine cafes just about everywhere in the center of Helsinki.

During the summer months the Peacock presents a ninety-minute *variety show* twice a night (7 and 9) except Mondays; there is also a Sunday afternoon matinee. Quite amusing is the Linnanmaki Amusement Park; it opens in time for the big May 1 holiday and does not close until September 1. The hours are from 6:30 to 11:30 P.M. every weekday except Monday. There is an earlier start—2 P.M.—on Sundays. Admission is 1 mark.

If you are in Finland during early June, go to the outstanding musical event of the country, the *Sibelius Festival*. This event honors the nation's greatest composer and is a real treat for the music lover. If your plans and travel dates are firm, write your hotel *in advance* about obtaining seats for some of the performances. Most times of the year, also, there are concerts by the Helsinki Symphony Orchestra.

SPORTS ¶ The Finns are a sports-conscious and athletic nation. In Sibelius Park, in Helsinki, you can see little toddlers on skis during the winter. You'll also see a fine statue of Paavo Nurmi—remember him? the fleet runner

—with the Olympic Stadium of other days in the background.

So far as we know, the only *golf* course worthy of the name is the one at Tali, in Helsinki. You can play up north in Lapland at midnight for the novelty, but the links are not too good as a rule. There is plenty of *hunting* —particularly above the Arctic Circle—and *fish* are plentiful, both in the lakes and up north in Lapland. The best season for pike is June to October; perch, March to November; salmon, June and July; trout, June, July and August; and grayling, July to September.

By motorboat from the Sea Harbor in Helsinki you can travel to nearby sandy and rocky beaches for a good day of (chilly!) *swimming.*

Skiers should head for Lapland during March and April, when the snow is best and the days are beginning to put in an appearance—that is, there is more daylight than in midwinter.

Goldpanning may or may not be a sport; or it might be entertainment. In any case, gold-panning excursions can be arranged for small groups of visitors in Lapland.

❧ Short Tours from Helsinki

Aulanko

Finland's biggest tourist center is about an hour to an hour and a half by train (depending on which train) through very pleasant countryside. There is a big hotel at the resort, where meals are fine. In case you are interested in a *sauna,* you will be able to indulge in one at the hotel. The setting is superb—a big national park. In snow season, ski equipment can be rented. About three miles from Aulanko is the small town of Hämeenlinna, where Sibelius was born. On the one hundredth anniversary of his birth his home was made into a museum, and it is open all year around. The train stops at Hämeenlinna (not at Aulanko), but a hotel bus usually meets all trains. In any case, there is taxi and local bus service between the town and the hotel.

Turku

The oldest city in Finland, and the country's second largest city, is a little over a hundred miles from Helsinki. There are good train and bus connections. This is a beautiful old medieval city and well worth a visit.

Porvoo

Only thirty miles east of Helsinki is this smallish medieval town with nice restaurants, where you can lunch or dine superbly. Buses leave frequently from the bus terminal on Mannerheim Street.

Rovaniemi

To do this in a day you'll have to fly. Rovaniemi is the capital of Finnish Lapland—or at least the administrative center. The town itself is just a mile or two below the Arctic Circle, but the airport is a little bit north of it. So, when you arrive by plane you will have crossed the Arctic Circle. On the circle itself—you can get to it by taxi—is a hut that is the official circle marker, and alongside the hut is a typical Lapp tent. Rovaniemi is a very modern city; it is newly built because it was destroyed by the Germans in World War II during their retreat. This is Lapp country, as we said, and if you want to learn to drive reindeer, it can be arranged easily by your hotel concierge. You can also obtain a reindeer-driving license —if you qualify. The driver's test includes such questions as "Do you wear sunglasses?" There are both morning and evening flights from Helsinki. The Lapps, by the way, sport bright colors—red, green, yellow and black are favorites. They need such colors because of all that snow. There are something like 200,000 Lapps in Lapland and at least one reindeer for each inhabitant. The reindeer are beautiful but stubborn creatures. Most are grayish, but there are some white ones. If you stay overnight, there's a nice new hotel, the Lapin Portti.

Russia

Yes, we said Russia. Leningrad is only fifty minutes from Helsinki by air; Moscow, one hour and forty minutes. Two trains connect Helsinki and Leningrad daily, and from May to September the two cities are on a twice-a-week cruise itinerary. There are also one-to-four-day cruises between Helsinki and Tallinn, the Estonian capital, which is just across the gulf from Finland's capital.

৯ A Tour of the Country

Helsinki to Turku—109 miles

Leave Helsinki via route 1, departing on the Mannerheim Street, passing through several industrial communities, notably Pitäjänmäki. Seventy miles from Helsinki you come to the small town of Salo, situated on the Uskela River, where the Uusi Hotelli is the best place to stay. The road continues into Turku (also called Åbo), the oldest city in Finland; here you might stay at the Seurahuone or the Hamburger Börs Hotel, both of which can be recommended.

The most interesting sightseeing is in the Luostarinmäki district, with its famous handicrafts museum; here, artisans still make fine Finnish-crafted articles in authentic buildings, demonstrating original techniques. Thirteenth-century Turku Castle stands near Kanavaniemi Harbor overlooking the sea; there is a historical museum within the castle. See also the thirteenth-century cathedral and Cathedral Bridge, which leads into the older part of town. (For those proceeding to Sweden, boat service takes about thirteen hours from Turku to Stockholm, but advance steamer reservations are essential.) An interesting excursion may be made to Naantali, a summer resort with a good beach; the town is tiny but picturesque; the best hotel is in the Lepolinna, open in summer only. If you're in the mood for a pleasant rest at a hotel, drive south just a few miles to Pargas over an interesting road that crosses the sea periodically; the Airisto Hotel, open during the summer months only, is delightful.

If you wish, you can take the boat from Turku to Norrtälje, in Sweden; Norrtälje is just forty-three miles northeast of Stockholm. Boats leave at about 11 A.M. (But either make a reservation or get there earlier than that.) Sometimes there are sailings at night; so inquire. The trip takes about eight hours, but you'll agree that you never had such a ferry ride in your life, what with movies, loads of food, barbershop and beauty parlor and even saunas.

Turku to Vaasa—235 miles

Leave Turku via route 8 toward Mynämäki and Laitila, bypassing Pyhäranta (a fifteen-minute ride to the west),

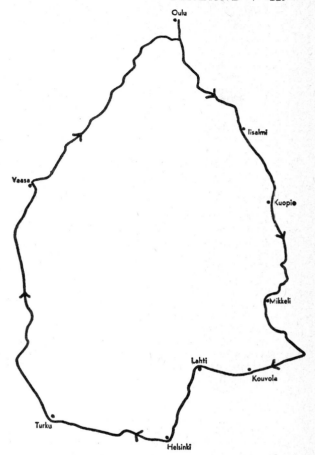

and into the seaport of Rauma, which has the Hotel Rau-
manlinna and its good restaurant. Continue on to Pori,
an old, pleasant town, where the Hotel Juhana Herttua is
the best. The town has several "ports" in the harbor area
that are worth investigating for their natural life and
color. From Pori, proceed through Noormarkku and
Omossa and into the small town of Kristiinankaupunki
(also called Kristinestad), built on both sides of an open
bay that leads into the Gulf of Bothnia; the (hotel) Kau-

punginhotelli is the best available. If you come during the summer months (especially on Sunday), you'll see the women wearing their colorful national costumes.

Further along the route there is a left turn to Kaskö, an island that you might enjoy looking over; its Hotel Centrum has somewhat limited facilities. The main road continues on through wooded countryside directly into Vaasa, where you'll find the Hotel Central and the somewhat more modest Hotel Astor. Visit the open-air museum in Hietalahti Park, just south of the town; the old Vaasa Castle is now a prison. A short excursion outside of the city may be made to Old Vaasa, still interesting although most of the old town was destroyed during a fire in 1852.

Vaasa to Oulu—239 miles

Leave Vaasa via route 8 through Nykarleby and into Kokkola, which has quite good hotels, the Seurahuone and the Grand. Then on through Himanka, Kalajoki and Pyhäjoki and into Raahe; this last town has the Seurahuone and Hansa hotels. There are some rather interesting old buildings surrounding the town's Pekkatori Square. Then on to Liminka, later making a left turn onto route 4 to Oulu, an industrial town facing the Gulf of Bothnia; the leading hotel here is the Tervahovi. The cathedral should be seen; you've surely seen the Merioski Rapids by now; also drive to the end of Kirkkokatu (street) and cross the bridge onto Ainola island, where you'll find an interesting museum devoted in part to the arts and crafts of Lapland; open Wednesday and Sunday 12–3 and 6–8 (no, we don't know who dreamed up those hours).

Oulu to Iisalmi—137 miles

Drive south from Oulu via route 4, retracing your route for a few miles, and then continue on through Rantsila. Be watchful for a subsequent left turn onto route 19 just past Pulkkila; then come Piippola and Pyhäntä and then after a long, fast run, Iisalmi. Here the best hotel is the Seurahuone, which has a good restaurant. In the summer season, interesting boat trips may be made across lovely Lake Porovesi.

Iisalmi to Kuopio—57 miles

Leave Iisalmi by route 5, passing through Onki and Siilinjarvi and into Kuopio, well situated on Lake Kallavesi; the Hotel Atlas can be recommended here. Visit the Market Square (best seen early in the morning) and the fortresslike Kuopio Museum. There are lovely park areas, a restaurant and several beaches nearby on the long Väinölanniemi Peninsula, frequently used to illustrate Finnish travel folders. A diverting boat trip may be made from Kuopio to Savonlinna (via either of two routes, both equally interesting); the excursion takes about eleven hours and motorists not wishing to repeat the return trip by boat can come back by local bus service to pick up their cars. Inquire as to bus schedules before undertaking the trip. The Tott and Seurahuone hotels are the best places to stay overnight in Savonlinna. If the boat schedules here aren't convenient, don't worry, because there'll be other opportunities for interesting lake trips farther along the way.

Kuopio to Mikkeli—126 miles

Continue south on route 5 from Kuopio heading toward Varkaus, an industrial town where the Keskus Hotelli is an excellent place for a stay. Then through Juva and into Mikkeli, where you'll have a choice of two fascinating boat trips on Lake Saimaa. If you're planning to stay here or to take the boat rides, there is the Hotel Mikkelin Pillinki or the less elaborate Hotel Nuijamies. One excursion is to Savonlinna, a ride of almost twelve hours, with service three times a week; you might be well advised to reserve a cabin in case the weather changes en route. There are, as previously mentioned, the hotels Tott and Seurahuone, where you might remain overnight and then take the bus back to Mikkeli, via the village of Juva. The second boat trip is from Mikkeli to Lappeenrauta via either of two routes, one of which involves a change of steamer, but the trips are equally diverting and relaxing. The voyage takes about eight hours and there is almost daily service; for an overnight stay in Lappeenrauta, we would advise the Hotel Patria. On the following day, return by bus to Mikkeli via Savitaipale.

Mikkeli to Kouvola—87 miles

Leave Mikkeli via route 5, making a left turn shortly out of town onto route 13 and passing, amid magnificent lake scenery, through Ristiina, then watch the left turn to Suomenniemi and Savitaipale; several miles along there's a right turn onto route 6. The road continues through Taavetti to Kouvola, a town devoted to the paper industry; the best place to stay here is the Hotel Kymen Kartano.

Kouvola to Lahti—41 miles

Leave Kouvola on route 6, shortly afterward picking up (by a right turn) route 12 to Koria, Nastola and Lahti, a Finnish boom town; the Hotel Seurahuone at Lahti is easily the best. The city is beautifully situated, full of business and excitement and growing by leaps and bounds. Lahti offers the opportunity for taking a long (eleven-hour) all-day trip across Lakes Päijänne and Vesijärvi to Jyväskylä. Should you make the trip, stay overnight in Jyväskylä's Hotel Jyväshovi; return to Lahti the following day by local bus service via either of the two routes offered.

Lahti to Helsinki—67 miles

Leave Lahti via route 5 through Mäntsälä and Järvenpää and into Helsinki.

Pointer: If you'd like to rent a Finnish island of your own for your vacation ask for information from the Finnish National Tourist Office.

৪৯ Motoring in Finland

Your home-state driver's license, the car registration, an identification international registration letter plate (USA for an American-registered car, I for Italy-registered one, etc.) and a Green Card showing you're insured—that's all you'll need for bringing a car into Finland. If you don't have the Green Card, you can buy local insurance, which is not expensive.

Be sparing with your use of the horn. The Finns like the "silent type" on the highways. Exception—if you're overtaking someone, you sound your horn, and that someone acknowledges with a little toot. In built-up areas the speed limit is 30 miles an hour, and during the summer, when traffic is heavy, there are special restrictions on speeds in the open country. Most of the international signs are used. So if you know them, you'll be riding smoothly. But some signs—such as those warning about "loose stones," "local speed limits" and other pertinent motoring matters—are in Swedish or Finnish, or both. So you takes your choice.

Finland is working hard on building up a highway network. Right now only about a fourth of the 40,000 miles of public roads are surfaced or a reasonable facsimile thereof. The country roads (of clay) get pretty slippery, as well as dirty, in a rain. Generally, the main roads in the southern part of the country will be fine, although spring frost plays tricks with them and so does an autumn shower (did we say *shower?*). There is a color system being put into use for the road signs—a background of white for the principal roads, blue for city throughways and superhighways (not many yet, though) and black for private thoroughfares. There are no toll roads.

Gasoline is about 75 cents a gallon; oil, $1 a quart. Gas is available in every town and village. However, if you are proceeding through remote regions or are going to do much driving in Lapland, it is best to fill up the tank in advance.

As in all Scandinavian countries, driving after drinking is forbidden. There are no ifs, ands or buts about it. It is just not done! *Don't drive at all if you've had a drink.*

FRANCE

National Characteristics

La Belle France is the easiest, most accurate and best way to describe this beautiful country. There is no simple, easy phrase to describe the French people. They are so individual that it is almost necessary to describe them one by one. No single person completely understands the French people—least of all, the French themselves. They are idealists and franc-pinchers; they worship the aesthetic, but may rely on eau de cologne rather than baths; they guillotined the aristocracy but never fail to name-drop about their good friend, the baron. They are impossible—they are wonderful—they are French.

These contradictory qualities have their roots in childhood. While American parents concentrate on giving their children material advantages, French mothers and fathers emphasize the importance of home life. Who's right? Well—even despite some *blousons noirs* here and there, juvenile delinquency is not so prevalent in France. Family loyalty and the family unit come first and foremost, even before the material things of life. Walk along the streets of any French city on Sunday afternoon and you'll see *papa* and *maman* out for a stroll with their children, all dressed up and happy just because they're together.

Loyalty to the small unit that is the family naturally exhibits itself in a Frenchman's adult life. You don't live in his *quartier*, his particular neighborhood? Ah, he has nothing but sympathy even if you occupy the grandest suite at the Ritz. You come from Chicago? Imagine residing *anywhere* outside of Paris, the world's only city in the Frenchman's eyes. You live in *les Etas-Unis*? True, it's big, rich, powerful and wonderful—but the United States is not France. And if it's not France—if it's not Paris—if you don't live in his *quartier*, well, you can't be

very civilized or know much about the world. That is
logique. No?

For a long time the Frenchman used to let visitors
come to see his country, but at vacation time he himself
stayed within his nation's borders and rarely went abroad.
Why should he?—was the attitude. France had everything. Frenchmen still think so. In fact, they are more
convinced of it than ever, given the great strides their
nation has made since World War II, both economically at home and politically in the sphere beyond
France's frontiers. But the French also are very human,
and that human instinct to see for oneself what is going
on in other places has been spectacularly at work among
Frenchmen in recent years. About 10 million of them
head for Spain each summer, and many others journeyed
to England last year. Meanwhile, more and more of
them are seeing the United States annually. This traveling
trend by the contemporary Frenchman benefits everyone. With the French becoming "foreign tourists" themselves, they are becoming increasingly aware of ways for
making a visitor's stay more agreeable.

We must remember, too, that France has existed
through two millenniums of history. Most French people
are interested primarily in two basic items: financial
security and individual liberty. The French are often
called parsimonious, skinflint and other uncomplimentary
adjectives—mostly by people who have plenty of money
and aren't too worried about the financial future. But
whatever has been said about the average Frenchman's
love of freedom is probably understated. He will fight to
the death for his right to live as an individual, and, after
all, isn't that the ultimate expression of civilization?

Yes, the French may defy your attempt to fit them
into a neat and cozy niche, a taut epigram or even a
Broadway wisecrack. But they are a people dedicated to
liberty, the enjoyment of life and the right of privacy.

Of course, there's the old cornball about the French
being lascivious, without morals and addicted to dirty
postcards. All untrue—as you'll soon learn. The vast
majority of French women have a stricter code of moral-
ity than equivalent English or American women (ask
any American male who has investigated the subject).
Of course, as you can plainly see on the streets of Paris
and many other French cities, a number of France's
women openly engage in what is usually euphemistically

described as the world's oldest profession—but certainly no more, percentage-wise, than in any other country. The nude girlie shows are patronized principally by tourists.

Is it the inevitable conclusion that the French represent the zenith of achievement in world civilization? Well, maybe. But we doubt it. No nation, it would appear, has a monopoly on that desired state of affairs. Caesar, 2,000 years ago, couldn't understand the Gauls. Today, you won't be able to understand some French gall.

When to Go

Any day, any week, any month, any year. Paris, of course, is a must at any time of the year. Beginning in early April (as the song goes) the chestnuts are in blossom, the mood and air are light, and frivolous and wonderful—although it frequently rains. Now that they have written a popular song about May in Paris, this delightful month is getting its due, because it is actually nicer than April, and has less rain. June is the beginning of the high season (high refers also to prices) and Paris is swamped from then until well into September. The city never gets terribly hot (except for rare, occasional days) and the only comparatively dull time of the year is late August, when true Parisians pull up stakes and head elsewhere. Many restaurants are closed, shops do hasty redecorating jobs and taxis either take to the hills or go underground (we've never found out which it is).

Some contrary people, on the other hand, prefer the August stillness and comparative calm. (No Gallic community is ever truly calm.) Lots of restaurants are closed, but enough are open. Shops are uncrowded, and the streets carry the lightest traffic of the year. October is delightful. November brings rain every other day, but not ordinary rain—rain with Parisian charm, which transmits the pleasure of being slightly chilled and damp, of entering a tiny *bistro* and feeling its warmth, of drinking a cup of execrable, dark, sweet coffee. The winter months are lively and spirited, and actually Paris is at her most chic when the weather is at its comparative worst.

We wouldn't recommend Britanny, Normandy or the chateaux country during the winter months except to moody, brooding soul-searchers. Everyone else will find them cold, raw and damp. Naturally, winter is the ideal time for the ski and ice-skating crowd, the healthy ones

—particularly in the Alps and in the Pyrenees. Along the Riviera, all months are considered in season except November and early December, when it can *really* rain. The remainder of the year is festive and gay. In the Alps, behind Nice, are Valberg and Auron, which are popular with those who like to combine a day on the Rivieria with mountain skiing. The two alpine resorts are only a couple of hours away from Nice by car, and the drive through ravines and valleys is splendid, summer or winter.

WEATHER STRIP: PARIS

Temp.	JAN.	FEB.	MAR.	APR.	MAY	JUNE	JULY	AUG.	SEPT.	OCT.	NOV.	DEC.
Low	32°	33°	36°	40°	46°	52°	55°	54°	50°	44°	37°	35°
High	42°	46°	52°	60°	67°	72°	76°	75°	69°	60°	49°	44°
Average	37°	40°	44°	50°	57°	62°	66°	65°	60°	52°	43°	40°
Days of rain	14	14	14	13	14	12	12	12	11	15	15	15

PASSPORT AND VISA ¶ Merely your passport suffices if you're staying less than three months.

HEALTH ¶ The water is excellent all over France. However, if changes of water upset you, drink the bottled variety. Most milk is pasteurized in this land of Pasteur, but in rural areas exercise care. You can eat everything and anything without fear.

CUSTOMS AND IMMIGRATION ¶ The French customs are undoubtedly the world's easiest. When asked if you have anything to declare, merely say that you haven't and the odds are that you won't even have to open your baggage. If requested, the examination is cursory. The French customs is rather strict on the import of alcoholic beverages, because this is a kind of a home industry. But they won't worry about an American tourist carrying a bottle of his favorite Scotch. Cigarettes are limited to two cartons. Or, instead, you can have 125 cigars or 500 grams (a little over a pound) of tobacco. Women, regardless of their tastes in tobacco, are not allowed to bring in cigars or smoking tobacco free of duty (cigarillos? yes). Two cameras (of different types) are permitted, and also one of just about anything else you can think of —and might have with you—such as a baby carriage (a baby carriage?), portable radio, or an eleven-foot boat (provided it has no motor). There is no longer any restriction on the amount of money, French or foreign, you can bring into the country or take with you on departure.

CURRENCY ¶ The French *franc* has had a succession of ups and downs in the post-World War II era, with each new revaluation or shift in the international money market giving it a new value. One thing that has not changed is that there are still 100 *centimes* in each franc.

PRICE LEVEL ¶ Everybody either knows or has been told that Paris is expensive. What is not generally realized, however, is that some years ago the French government began putting the brakes on rising prices and as a result there has been a general leveling off. Meanwhile, a number of countries during these past years have been automatically boosting their hotel and restaurant prices by 10 percent each year. Thus, although Paris *is* expensive, the price differential between it and some other European capitals is narrowing all the time. Hotel rates are high. That is, for the price you pay for hotel accommodations in the French capital you would get much finer ones in New York. Restaurant prices—especially the places that are *in* at the moment—will also remind you of the New York scene. Certain areas of the country are less expensive than Paris. The Riviera, for instance, can be noticeably less costly, *unless* you use one of those palaces at Cannes, Nice or Monte Carlo as your hotel headquarters and do all your dining and entertaining there.

TIME ¶ France is six hours ahead of Eastern Standard Time; when it's noon in New York, it's 6 P.M. in France. From April through October, when Daylight Saving Time is in effect, the time differential is reduced to five hours.

TIPPING ¶ Almost all hotels add a service charge (roughly 12 percent or 15 percent), which is included in your bill and is, theoretically, supposed to take care of your tips. This is not the case, but you should bear the custom in mind when distributing your hard-earned money. Because there is usually a service charge, your tipping works out something like this: when your taxi pulls up in front of the hotel you've selected in Paris, a porter will take your luggage. Unlike our American system, your baggage does not usually accompany you through the door but is delivered via the service entrance directly to your room. Inside, you'll register and surrender your passport to the clerk. (Make a mental note to pick it up the following morning *without* fail.) Usually someone from behind the desk will show you to your room. In small hotels it might be the owner, the *patron* or another in the family. In larger establishments an assistant manager will be the escort; no tip is expected or required. When the luggage arrives, although you will theoretically pay for service, by custom this does not apply to porters, so give him 1 or 2 francs. In the morning, you'll ring for your morning coffee and croissants, and the waiter should be given an occasional franc, say, every other day. The hotel doorman receives a franc for calling a cab; make it more on a rainy day or when he has to wander for several blocks to flush one—and this will surely happen around the dinner hour when cabs are scarce. About taxi drivers —tip about 15 percent of the meter, not a sizable amount because fares are low by American standards. Regardless of how little the meter reads, don't tip less than 1 franc. Washroom and coatroom attendants should be given a franc and that goes also for the girl who shows you to your seat in a theater—weird and inexplicable, but it's a French custom and when in France . . .

Now we come to a special problem—the hotel *concierge*, who occupies a unique position. You'll see the concierge, usually a man in uniform behind a desk or counter of his own in the lobby; he has nothing to do with the hotel rooms, however. He's the person who gets you train tickets, sends your cables, orders flowers, reserves tables at restaurants and in general makes life easier for you. We would tip the concierge at least 10 francs for a two-day visit and possibly as much as 25 or more francs for a week's stay in a deluxe hotel if he has performed such services. The maid who cleans your room should get something—say, about 10 or more francs per week, depending on the type of hotel. Although the concierge, that one-man wonder, does everything for you, don't call on him to distribute your tips—he's only human and some (or all) of the money might (and probably would) stick to his palms.

TRANSPORTATION ¶ *Taxi* rates in Paris are somewhat like New York's. You can go from one end of Paris to another for $4 or so, but the average fare will not be much more than a dollar. Life is simpler now with the introduction and smooth functioning of radio cabs. The hotel concierge, the head-waiter at the restaurant or a clerk in the boutique where you are shopping will telephone for a cab if none is in sight. The radio cab costs a trifle more—you pay for the phone call, in effect—but it is well worth the convenience. As always, you will encounter Paris cab drivers who'll not be able to pick you up because they are heading either for the garage or for their dinner. Late at night, unmarked private cars for hire frequently line up in front of touristy night clubs, waiting for the over-moneyed, overliquored tourist who will hop in and say, "Hotel George Cinq!" When you arrive and the bandit behind the wheel asks for the equivalent of $10, how can you expect to win the argument? If you *do* decide to take a private car late at night, *always* (repeat, *always*) agree on the price in advance.

The supply of the colorful "rear platform" *buses* continues to dwindle. Double-deckers are now appearing on Paris boulevards. Another new addition is the blue minibus. Buses operate regularly from 7 A.M. until 9:30 P.M., and then there are special late-evening and all-night services. The price of a bus ride depends on the number of zones you travel. For a short ride, the bus is cheaper than the *métro* (subway). But once you start traveling across more than one zone, the tariff increases.

A fast-express *métro* has been added to the Paris subway system, speeding traffic considerably. Meanwhile, the baker's dozen of different lines will get you where you want to go in swift, fairly comfortable subway cars. One car on each train—usually at the center— is for First Class passengers. The other cars are Second Class. The advantage of First Class is that you *sometimes* have a better chance of getting a seat there than in the more popular Second Class cars. But with the affluence of France in recent times, First Class *métro* cars are often more jammed than the Second Class ones. Individual *métro* tickets can be bought, but it is cheaper to buy a book—a *carnet*—of ten at a time. Don't try to enter a First Class car without the appropriate ticket. There is a fine, and controllers ride the cars, continuously checking tickets. For a nice ride on the *métro*, take the main east-west Vincennes-Neuilly line. The train wheels have rubber tires, and it makes for an almost noiseless ride.

The French *railroad* has been doing wonders with its trains in the last couple of years. On main lines, trains travel like bullets or, to be more contemporary in our language, let us say like missiles. Rheims, for instance, is a good hundred miles from Paris, and a nonstop train gets there in a smooth hour and a half. Pretty good, we think. The French railroad makes a point of late-afternoon and early-evening trains, which connect Paris with relatively far-off places (Amsterdam, Toulouse, Avignon, Bordeaux, Brussels, Frankfurt, Luxembourg, etc.) by midnight. In other words, you can spend just about all day in Paris, take a train and arrive in some far-distant city on your itinerary before the day is over. And, as the railroad points out, you'll be arriving in the middle of that city, because that is where the train terminals are. There is sleek, fast overnight service to Nice, and of course also the magnificent fast-flying *Mistral*, which covers the route in the daytime. The one thing to keep in mind about French trains is that everything centers around Paris (like so many other things). If you're going anywhere from Paris, or arriving at Paris from anywhere, train service is excellent and very rapid. But if your itinerary, instead of following a Paris main line, cuts across it—woe betide you. Thus, for instance, if you try to travel by train across France starting at a point like Niort on the Atlantic coast, you'll find that you'll have to change trains a couple of times—or travel in extremely slow ones—before getting to your destination in the Alps or another eastern point.

French *train fares* amount to about 4 cents a mile in Second Class and 50 percent higher than that in First Class, which is fairly expensive. On day trains, for short trips, Second Class travel is perfectly satisfactory. If you are traveling Second Class, you can assure yourself of a seat by reserving one in advance. It's called a *location*. The charge is reasonable, and you can pick your spot in the eight-seat compartment (First Class compartments have only six seats). You can ask for a compartment where smoking is permitted or where none of your fellow passengers indulge in such a habit. You may also specify that you would like a seat by the window, facing forward. To reserve a seat, you must first have your railroad ticket. Seat reservations, except at holiday peak periods, are not needed in First Class cars on day trains.

The *wagons-lits* people have introduced a three-berth

compartment for sleeping-car travel at night, and only a Second Class rail ticket is needed. First Class tickets are required in one- or two-berth *wagons-lits* facilities. The company is also doing a great deal to make the sleeping-car facilities more and more comfortable. A new two-level tourist sleeping car, with nine lower and nine upper compartments, was recently introduced on various Paris to Southern France lines. Each compartment accommodates two people but the lower compartments can be used as one-passenger compartments. A second-class ticket is sufficient for the double occupancy and in addition the double compartment rates are considerably lower than those charged on regular sleepers. In the event you do not want to spend the money for a berth (with sheets, blankets, pillow and a general sense of well-being), you can reserve a *couchette* (resembling a berth) for a relatively small charge. There are *couchettes* for First Class and Second Class travel. Six passengers occupy a Second Class *couchette* compartment; four are in First Class. This is cheap overnight travel, but if you have the choice, by all means take a regular *wagon-lit* berth rather than a *couchette*.

Most trains—let us say that again—all the main liners for the most part will have restaurant cars. But certain little-traveled runs have only a *buffet* serving sandwiches and odds and ends (yes, odds and ends). Check to be sure beforehand on the dining possibilities en route. If there is no dining car, you can buy some fresh-made sandwiches at a terminal food shop before boarding the train.

Trains arrive and depart from a half dozen main stations in Paris. They are:

Gare de l'Est: Eastern France and Germany
Gare de Lyon: The Riviera and points in between
Gare d'Austerlitz: West-central France, Toulouse, Bordeaux and Spain
Montparnasse: The suburbs and Brittany
St.-Lazare: Rouen and the general Normandy region, as well as the boat-train ports of Cherbourg and Le Havre
Gare du Nord: Northern France and Belgium, Holland and points north

The big headache in arriving by train at Paris is the taxi situation; that is, you can't find one on arrival. The French railroad has been working on this problem for years, but it does not seem to be making much headway on the solution. One saving grace is that it is possible to have a taxi waiting for you when you arrive at the Gare de Lyon. You can reserve a taxi at the time you buy your ticket, so don't forget.

Autos may be hired on daily, weekly or monthly rates. But there are no problems in driving your own car. Roads are quite good and well marked, and if you keep out of the heart of big cities, few difficulties should arise. Paris, of course, presents certain special problems because the local drivers display a certain lively sense of daring, of *élan*, a fervent belief that flair is all important—oh well, they drive like maniacs and no use denying it. But you'll hear fewer fenders crumpling here than in your own home town, because French drivers have, along with their *élan*, a high regard for the cost of repairs.

TIME EVALUATION ¶ If you have a month (many people would enjoy spending an entire month), really do a complete tour of the countryside. Of course, on a first visit to Europe, and assuming that you want to see some other countries, allow no less than five days for Paris and its local sights (Versailles, etc.). If possible, visit the two other outstanding regions—the chateaux country (say, about three days minimum) and the Riviera (three days minimum up to a couple of weeks if you want to enjoy the sunshine). If your plans include driving from Paris around the country, you could easily use up an entire month, two months, or even a lifetime sightseeing.

COMMUNICATIONS ¶ French local telephone service is slow and erratic, with about a 50–50 chance of a wrong number. Making a call from a phone booth is calculated to bring on the DTs. Unless you *really* speak the language (and we don't mean one year of college French at Iowa State), have a bar or restaurant waiter make your call and give him a tip and let *him* get the DTs. On the other hand, long-distance calls to the United States often are executed with celerity, if the time is right and the wind is blowing from the correct direction. Just remember that if you wake up at 9 A.M. in Paris and call St. Louis, it will be about 2 A.M. and everyone at home will hate you. And don't forget that the hotel adds a service charge onto the basic cost of every call, local or long distance.

Airmail service to the United States is excellent. A five-gram letter by air costs about a quarter. Stamps are bought in tobacco shops or—we almost forgot—a post office. Post offices are open for a few hours on Saturday morning. They are closed on Sundays. At the main post office in Paris and at a few submain post offices in the city there is limited night and weekend service. In general, however, mailing a letter at a post office on Sundays (if you require stamps) is not possible. But the main post office in any city is always open for long-distance telephone calls and telegrams or cables. Operators usually speak some English. But make things easier all around by having the phone number or the text of the cable written out—preferably typed. Do you want some advice? Give your cables to the hotel concierge.

Pointer: The post office on the Champs-Elysées, just down from Avenue George V, is open till nearly midnight every night in the week.

ELECTRICITY ¶ The electric current in France *all depends*. It can be 110–115 A.C., and then again it can be 220–230 A.C. So be sure you inquire before plugging in. If the chambermaid does not seem certain about the voltage in your hotel room, or if it is not indicated near the bathroom mirror, examine a light bulb in one of the lamps (not a hot one, of course). They will usually be marked with the voltage.

FOOD SPECIALTIES AND LIQUOR ¶ There is more conversation and discussion about food than about sex in France. Well, almost. The French give *very* serious thought to what they are going to eat and drink, considering it a sacrilege to wolf down a ham and cheese on rye with a cup of coffee. At the conclusion of a sumptuous lunch, a true Frenchman immediately devotes himself to the most acute and pressing problem on hand—what to have for dinner? Listen to a young man murmuring to his *petite amie*: My *poulet* [chicken, frequently cooked *à la chasseur*, with tomato sauce and shallots]. You are like *champagne* [a sparkling white wine produced near Rheims]. Your tears are salty like *Marennes* [a special type of oyster]." This French lover is not only making love, he is comparing her to the best thing he knows— French food. He may kiss her eventually, but he is just as likely to eat her up. She does sound delicious at that, although the meal is not well balanced.

If every nation gets the politicians it deserves, then the French have the best food, and we won't say anything about the politicians. With every Frenchman a self-appointed one-man committee to appraise and criticize each restaurant in the nation, it is possible for substandard restaurants to open, but they cannot survive long. It has been said with some truth that you cannot find a bad meal in France; it is equally true that every rule has its exception. In the vast majority of cases, the poor meal is a rare occurrence, the good meal to be expected as routine, with exceptional food found not infrequently.

French chefs are dedicated to their work and take great pride in delighting you with fabulous creations. But it must be admitted that American steaks and chops are of better quality—so it is difficult to understand why tourists travel thousands of miles to Paris, check in at their hotels, drive in a cab to a world-renowned restaurant—and then order a steak. Two forces are at play to nullify the great food resources of France. One factor is the inability of American visitors to cope with a French menu; the other is the fact that French headwaiters, after many years, have become convinced that Americans eat nothing but steak. We occasionally overhear (with acute anguish) snatches of conversation along these lines:

HEADWAITER: "Monsieur, would you like to order?"

AMERICAN: "Er, yes. Would you help us with the menu?"

HEADWAITER: "But certainly, m'sieur."

AMERICAN: "What is this item written in red?"

HEADWAITER: "*Gratin de langoustines.* But if I may suggest, the *bouquet de crevettes?* It is like a shrimp cocktail."

AMERICAN (dubiously): "But . . . Well, all right. Now what is this *filet de boeuf Strasbourgeoise?*"

HEADWAITER: "Very good, the specialty of the house. But monsieur would surely prefer the *entrecôte grillé.*"

AMERICAN: "Why would I?"

HEADWAITER: "It is a favorite with all the Americans. And with it some fried potatoes and some *petits pois*, little green peas?"

AMERICAN (resignedly): "I suppose so. But I did want to have a special dessert."

HEADWAITER: "Ah, yes sir. We specialize in desserts. Special ice cream. *Pêche Melba.*"

And so our American ends up with shrimp cocktail, steak, fried potatoes, green peas and ice cream. It is precisely the same meal that he has eaten a thousand times, in a thousand American restaurants. Not that the food won't be good—it will be very good, although most husbands will say to their wives: "Not any better than Kansas City." Or Phoenix. Or Cleveland. (As the case may be.) And of course, there will be some justice in the remark, for shrimp cocktail, steak and ice cream cannot be too different in Paris or Peoria. But our American almost had a wonderfully unusual meal, beginning with *gratin de langoustines*, shrimp prepared with a marvelous sauce and baked for a moment in the oven with a sprinkling of cheese. How much more would he have enjoyed the *filet de boeuf Strasbourgeoise* (beef baked in a pastry crust) than a plain broiled steak! At least he would have experienced some of the master creations of French culinary art. Tired old ice cream for dessert again, and if the truth be told, not so good as many American varieties. There could have been the first-time pleasure of *fraises des bois*, those unique miniature strawberries, an absolute delight to everyone but the person who has to pick them over.

> Pointer: When the French refer to the "first" floor of a
> building, they mean the second by our understand-
> ing. The first floor of a French building is the main
> floor. If you see "RC" (*rez-de-chaussée*) on an ele-
> vator signal panel, that's the main floor of the
> building.

Most Americans eat a moderate breakfast, have a sandwich, pie and coffee for lunch, and then eat the big meal of the day about seven in the evening. The French, by custom, breakfast only on *café au lait*, coffee with hot milk, plus rolls with butter and jam. They rarely eat eggs, and the Frenchman who would eat Wheatena in the morning hasn't been born yet. Thus (without even a coffee break!), by lunchtime, they are ready for a full meal and aren't the least bit interested in a sandwich or the like. Then, at night, about seven or eight in the evening, they enjoy another complete full-course meal. Now along comes an American tourist into a gourmet's restaurant established in 1879 where the chef spends twelve hours a day creating sublime delicacies. Our American asks for a well-done hamburger, blueberry pie à la mode and coffee. The headwaiter blanches, backs off with gathering speed, finally turning and breaking into a full gallop for the kitchen to confront the chef, who has been patiently stirring a *pâté de maison* for the past two hours. Instantly all is excitement, cries rend the air, diplomatic relations with the United States may be broken off! In the name of Escoffier, did a master chef study for seven years as an apprentice for this? Are three years as *saucier* at *La Bonne Auberg* wasted? It is too much!

It *is* too much to expect a French restaurant to come up with a well-done hamburger, just as it would be to walk into an American diner on route 66 and ask for *tête de veau à la vinaigrette*. It just can't be done and there is no point in fighting nature or French chefs. Give in—you'll enjoy it. Because even if the French don't know much about balancing the national budget, they certainly know all there is to know about eating, and we can learn a lot from them.

Well, let's look at the record, or rather the *menu*. Or do we mean the *menu*? The French make a definite distinction between a *menu* (which refers to a preselected meal at a fixed price) and a *carte* (or single items ordered on an *à la carte* basis). If you're a really well-organized thoughtful type, you will have examined the bill of fare posted outside (before entering) the restaurant.

Most French restaurants have handwritten menus, which they duplicate in red, blue or violet-colored ink on a formidable machine that *grandpère* purchased at the International Exposition of 1889. Unless it is your *bonne chance* day, you will receive the thirty-fourth mimeographed copy, which is practically illegible, unless you have completed a three-year course (with honors) in handwriting analysis with the *Sûreté de Police*. You can risk astigmatism or myopia or ask for a better copy; if you try the latter you'll probably receive the thirty-third imprint. But let us assume that you have finally begun to comprehend the chicken scrawls. The first section is inevitably the *hors d'oeuvres*, the appetizers. Then come the soups, poultry and meats, salads and desserts. Be sure to give serious consideration to any items marked in red (or other distinctive color) because these indicate *spécialités de la maison*, house specialties. By custom, French restaurant reputations are built solidly upon the perfection of a comparatively few dishes. If the specialties are to your liking, be sure to order them; they do *not* mean that the restaurant is pushing the roast beef because it is left over from yesterday.

The French believe in savoring the flavor of each food; for example, they do not approve of meat and vegetables being eaten simultaneously. They may waive a point for potatoes, but never a vegetable with a sauce, like asparagus Hollandaise. They will think you are ready for the booby-hatch if you try to order coffee with your main course and equally demented for trying to have it with your dessert. In the French scheme of things, coffee is served *after* dessert, preferably at some other restaurant or cafe than where dinner was taken. For our part, based on innumerable cups of unspeakable French brews, the coffee course might well be delayed more or less indefinitely or even forever.

Note: Since the invasion of France by Italian coffeemakers, coffee is much better. But not always.

Now about water. There is water in France; this may be stated as a definite fact. We personally have seen rivers and lakes, all filled with water. But at mealtimes, water becomes scarce—first, because the French really don't believe in drinking water; and second, how can you enjoy wine when you're drinking water? So a general conspiracy exists to deny the existence of water during meal hours. Oh well, let's also admit that the restaurants like to sell wine to the customers. However, some restaurants frequented by tourists have, after years of intense questioning under bright lights by ace American private eyes, finally broken down and admitted that water does flow into their restaurant, and have even served occasional glasses to insistent patrons. But ice in water? Now you have overdone it! Pretty soon the service will retrogress so far that even the warm water disappears. Conclusion: sometimes you can get it and sometimes you can't, but when you do it will probably be warm, so is it worth the struggle?

When you've ordered, relax and enjoy life. You're on vacation, aren't you? What if lunch does take an hour and a half? Or two? All of Paris practically comes to a standstill during the midday, with shops, offices and museums firmly shut. By now, the wine steward, the *sommelier*, will have insinuated the wine list into your hand. If you know absolutely nothing about wine, at least know the simplest general rule—white wine with fish, red wine with meat. With chicken or veal, a white wine is also suitable. With duck or wild game, a red. You needn't order more than one wine with your meal unless you're in the mood and at an important restaurant. For two people, a half bottle is usually enough, although not every wine comes in half bottles. A regular bottle is sufficient for three or four diners.

Most Americans don't know a great deal about wines,

having been nurtured as a rule by the Christian Brothers or Manischewitz, but seldom by the *Hospices de Beaune*. Wines, the experts say, are either dry or sweet—so dry actually means not sweet. Don't order any sweet wines with your food or the *sommelier* will grow pale. In fact, we'll let you know just how to handle the situation with the skill and finesse of a British diplomat (in the movies). Merely tell the *sommelier* what you've ordered and let him recommend the wine or wines. Most of these gentlemen are men of integrity, with pride in their work and little desire but to serve you, to have you enjoy your food all the more because of a carefully selected wine, and incidentally to earn a franc or two as a tip. You may rely upon them, but, when in doubt, have the *sommelier* point out, on the wine list, his selections, and if the price seems excessive, register your objection. Now what about all this gamesmanship, about vintage years? The weather varies each year, causing growth and flavor changes in the grapes, and naturally the wine tastes somewhat different from one year to another. Unless you have a marvelous memory or want to carry a wine chart, a simple foolproof system is yours for the reading (of the next few lines). It so happens that 1947, 1949, 1952 and 1953 were just about ideal for *all* French wines; if you select any wine from any of those years, the result must be satisfactory and you are automatically a connoisseur of wines. When the wine comes, a tiny bit will be poured into your glass (the male's, if there is one present) to taste; if you nod your satisfaction, the glasses will be partly, never completely filled. And don't be disturbed, when you've ordered a fine old wine, to see the *sommeilier* discreetly tasting a mouthful—he's merely checking it, not trying to drink up your bottle.

The *couvert* (cover charge), that old fixture of French restaurant bills, has been dropped. So the various items on your bill will be for specific foods and drinks—plus, of course, the *service*. Butter is normally not served in restaurants—except the top ones catering to American clients. Thus, if you ask for it, you can be sure it will be excellent (right from Normandy), but you will also pay extra for it. Coffee, tea, wine, mineral water—anything to drink except plain tap water—will be extra on the average restaurant bill. In certain tourist centers, such as the Riviera, and in restaurants hoping to attract budget-minded tourists, "fixed price" menus are often offered.

Sometimes these all-inclusive menus include everything from the beverage to the *service*. Sometimes they don't (but you don't realize this until you look closely). So, check in advance.

Another pointer: you'll probably have wonderful service in ordering your meal, in selecting your wine and in the presentation of the food—everything, up to the moment you ask for the check (*l'addition, s'il vous plaît*). It is then that the average French waiter avoids your eye. Does he hesitate to let you know the bad news? More than likely it's merely that most Americans want to leave too soon after finishing a meal. It is his way of delaying your departure until you've partly digested your food. (Just a theory.) If you liked the service, it's customary to leave some odd change for the waiter—up to half of the actual *service* charge. A few francs is enough, except in the best restaurants.

Living Off the Land in France

Until the lamentable invention of K-rations, invading armies customarily lived off the land. Not that commandeering food and wine as one travels is recommended, but nevertheless the soldiers of former years knew what they were doing. Why should they carry perishable and tasteless food when delicious local specialties could be had on the road?

Today's traveler to France may also live off the land, eating the special preparations of the particular province where he finds himself. First of all, food is fresher and tastes better in the region that produces it; second, the local citizenry know more about preparing their provincial dishes than many a high-salaried *Cordon Bleu*; and third, food that does not have to be transported is often much cheaper.

Brittany is a good starting point, since it is nearest the United States and is a land of milk, cream and sweet butter. Naturally, almost everything is prepared *à la crème*, that is, with milk, cream and sweet butter. Lobsters, shrimp, crabs and a wide variety of saltwater fish are the high points of the cuisine. With everything, cider (hard, that is) is drunk. For dessert there are *crêpes bretonnes*, excellent sweet pancakes.

FOOD SPECIALTIES OF FRENCH PROVINCES

Food specialties of Brittany: Shellfish, of course, but don't neglect *la cotriade*, the famous fish soup. Potatoes and all fresh green vegetables are exceptional. You'll want to try *mouton de pré salé*, salt-marsh lamb, which has a unique taste and is usually served quite rare by American tastes. Don't miss the *crêpes bretonnes*, the *crêpes dentelles*, the *galettes*, the *pâtisseries*, all sweet confections of the district.

Moving eastward into Normandy, the outstanding specialty of the province is *mouton de pré salé*, lamb which develops an unusual flavor because of the salt marshes where the Norman flocks graze. The French prepare their *mouton* underdone and bloody, much as we enjoy a rare steak. Each town is famous for some one dish. Caen for *tripe à la mode de Caen* (tripe steamed in a casserole). Rouen is known for *canard au sang à la Rouennaise* (duck cooked in its own blood, Rouen fashion).

France's northwest, encompassing Artois and Picardy, lies near the Belgian border and has good, simple peasant food. *Andouillettes* are pork sausages; rabbits abound and are prime favorites (besides costing nothing). One finds rabbit *pâté*, rabbit stew and, possibly a great delicacy, rabbit with prunes. Unlike other Frenchmen, the local folk drink *genièvre*, French gin.

Paris and the surrounding Île de France are the recipients of the choicest national produce. Here there can be no hope of living off the land.

Heading eastward toward the Champagne country, it must be admitted that the region offers little to the gastronome other than the famous drink itself.

Along the German border, Alsace and Lorraine have *quiche Lorraine*, a delicious cheese and bacon pie that is a perfect luncheon dish. Then, too, there are many dishes prepared with fresh goose livers (in season), sauerkraut in the Alsatian style, chicken with Riesling wine, Muenster cheese and the mountain trout of the region. Wines are notably light and drinkable; Mittelbergheim, Riquewihr and Ammerschwihr are good names to remember.

The Burgundy-Bresse area is one of rich food, heavy sauces and great wines. Who could add anything to the praises already sung to renowned Burgundies, famous wines too numerous to mention. Cooking, as might be anticipated, leans heavily on the local wines. Mushrooms are superb—notably *feuilleté aux morilles* (mushroom pastry) and *mousserons à la créme* (creamed mushrooms). The Bresse region is famous for its poultry, the snowy-breasted *poulet de Bresse*, a name that appears on menus all over France.

In the Loire valley, the river yields fine salmon, with which one drinks Vouvray or Chinon wines. The classic *pâté*, *rillettes* (a coarser *pâté*) and pork with prunes are also favored by the local people.

Food specialties of Loire: River fish are highly regarded, particularly pike and carp; try the salmon, too.

Pâtés and *rillettes* (rather coarsely ground *pâtés*) are prepared with pork or other meats; they are a standard appetizer all through the region. Pork with prunes is another dish you'll stumble upon occasionally (if you're lucky). The local cheeses are excellent, although few of them are famous. The wines are unimportant in the world of wines, but make delicious drinking: Vouvray, Chinon, Bourgeuil, for example.

Fronting the Atlantic is Poitou, where the French people, as opposed to the tourists, like to go for a low-cost vacation. Here you can spoon up *la chaudrée*, a soup made with fish right out of the ocean. Marennes supplies the famous green oysters, with their incomparable tang of the sea; with these you eat brown bread and butter. *Torteau fromage* is cheesecake, soft, creamy, luscious and very fattening. And, of course, the little town of Cognac is famous for—oh yes, Cognac.

Preferring to follow the path beaten by thousands of fellow tourists, comparatively few Americans make their way to the southwestern provinces of Limousin, Quercy and Périgord. This is unfortunate, for the roads are almost empty even during the height of the tourist season; rooms are readily available and the food is delicious. Périgord is the land of truffles, those mysterious growths that resemble mushrooms or tubers and are so highly regarded in France for flavoring foods. Truffles are found in just about everything in Périgord except dessert, and one cannot be too sure of that.

In Guyenne and Gascogny, Bordelais cooking is the rule. For uninhibited tourists, there is *tourain Bordelais*, a garlic-onion soup. The aristocratic Bordeaux wines are extensively used by the local chefs in dishes such as *lamproies au vin rouge* (lampreys are long, eellike fish) and *entrecôte Bordelaise* (steak made with marrow, red wine and shallots).

Near Spain is the Basque region, where the people are individualistic; so is the cuisine. *La garbure* is a soup made with ham, goose and local vegetables. A delicious omelette is the *piperade*, a sort of French western omelet made with peppers and tomatoes.

Eastward is Armagnac, producing a type of brandy known for its distinctive, warming quality. The favorite dish of the Toulouse region is the *cassoulet*; basically it consists of small white beans cooked for long hours in a casserole with pork, chicken, duck, goose or combinations and permutations thereof.

Along the Mediterranean (Roussillon and Languedoc) there is plenty of seafood to be had. A good soup is *l'ouillade* (made with eggs and garlic); a fine meat dish is *daube de boeuf*, a beef stew with high qualifications. The *gâteau sec au poivre*, a pepper cake or biscuit, is a true oddity. Roquefort, the king of cheese, is produced in this region.

Auvergne, a region of lovely music, has lovely food, too. The people preserve goose by covering the cooked bird with its own fat; the resulting *confit d'oie* is rich and delicious. Cabbage soup, mushrooms, snails, truffles and chestnuts, regardless of how they appear, are authentic local specialities and far above average.

Food specialties of the Auvergne: From Roquefort comes the world's classic cheese; in addition, there are Auvergne blue cheese, St.-Nectaire and many others. But the basic dish, ideal for a cool evening, is cabbage soup, which may eppear on a menu as *poté auvergnate* or *soupe aux choux*, and even though purists say they're different, we doubt it. *Oeufs a l'auvergnate* are poached eggs with sausage and cabbage; not elegant, but good peasant fare. Mushrooms are delicious in this region. Drink: Chateaugay or St.-Pourcain, near Vichy.

French gourmets are fond of saying, pontifically, that the best food in all France (and automatically, therefore, in all the world) may be had in Lyons and the surrounding area. The city's cuisine is so distinctive that one could live for weeks merely by trying the local specialties. *Quenelles de brochet*, an ethereally light preparation of chopped fish, is served daily and apparently eaten daily by the citizenry. Lyons sausages are also renowned.

In the Alps region, Savoy, there are delicious trout and many unusual lake fish—*féra*, *lavaret* and especially *char* with its delicate flesh. The local honey and cheeses are definitely worth attention.

Provence, that fabled land that encompasses the luxury coast from Marseille to the Italian border, has its own unique style of cooking. Much of the region was formerly part of Italy and the love of tomatoes, olive oil and garlic remains. *Pistou* is a thick vegetable soup, much like its Italian counterpart, *minestrone*, but very garlicky. *Bouillabaisse* and *bourride* are famous fish soups.

Food specialties of Provence: Along the coast, seafood of course, particularly *bouillabaisse*; *soupe aux poissons* (fish soup) is very good, too. A *bourride* is a less complicated, creamy type of *bouillabaisse*. *Aïoli* is a garlic mayonnaise in which you dip boiled fish (if you're brave). *Estouffade de boeuf* is a rich beef stew. The local olives are aromatic and delicious and likely to appear where you least expect them. Good wine country along the Rhône: Châteauneuf-du-Pape, Hermitage and Côte Rôtie are all full-bodied, rich red wines. The white wine of Cassis goes well with fish; Tavel is a pink (*rosé*) wine that is light and pleasant.

Loup, the wolf fish, is prepared in dozens of different ways and is a treat not to be overlooked. *Brandade de morue* is codfish ground fine with olive oil and garlic; a good appetizer. One owes it to oneself to have a *salade Niçoise*, a cold salad of string beans, boiled potatoes, olives, and often tunafish. A *pissaladière* is really the French Riviera's version of an Italian *pizza*, but loaded with sautéed onions.

Except in Paris and the provinces to the north, one should always order the local wines, *les vins du pays*. Attention should be paid to the dishes marked in red or other distinctive colors on the menu. Unlike many of our American "chef's specials," they are truly special, dishes on which the chef has spent years in search of perfection.

Food specialties of Normandy: Anything in the line of shellfish and ocean fish. *Sole Normande* is a classic preparation but try *Sole Trouvillaise* near Trouville. *Moules marinières* (mussels) are good, and cheap, too, which is unusual for something so delicious. The pastry and *brioches* near Rouen are famous. Don't miss sweet butter and the local cheese. Normandy is not a wine producer, but it does well on some other beverages, such as *Benedictine*, which is made at Fécamp, and *calvados*, which is produced far and wide in Normandy. To call *calvados* a hard cider would be an understatement. It is strong, very strong. No matter how long you're planning to stay in Normandy, you won't be there long enough to get used (like the locals) to drinking *calvados* like a tumbler of *vin rosé*. But it is a wonderful *apéritif* or a *digestif*. Try it in your coffee first. When serving a coffee, the cafe waiter in Normandy usually asks: *Avec*? That means: With *calvados*? It has nothing to do with whether you want sugar or cream with your coffee.

BASIC FRENCH
English-French

Waiter: *Garçon*
Bill of fare, menu: *Menu*
Napkin: *Serviette*
Bread and butter: *Du pain et du beurre*
A glass of orange juice: *Un verre de jus d'orange*
Boiled egg: *Oeuf à la coque*
1. soft   1. *peu cuit*
2. medium   2. *mollet*
3. hard-boiled   3. *oeuf dur*
4. egg cup   4. *coquetier*
Fried eggs: *Oeufs sur le plait*
Bacon and eggs: *Oeufs au bacon*
Coffee, black: *Café noir*
Coffee with cream and sugar: *Café avec de la crème (café-crème) et du sucre*
Coffee with hot milk: *Café au lait*
Tea: *Thé*
Water: *Eau*
Ice water: *Eau glacée*
Mineral water: *Eau minérale*
Breakfast: *Petit déjeuner*
Lunch: *Déjeuner*
Dinner: *Dîner*
Haircut: *Coupe de cheveux*
Manicure: *Manucure*
I want . . . liters of petrol: *Je voudrais . . . litres d'essence*
Change the oil: *Changez l'huile*
Grease the car: *Graissez la voiture*
How are you?: *Comment allez-vous?*
Fine, thank you: *Très bien, merci*
Please: *S'il vous plaît*
Thank you very much: *Merci beaucoup*
Good morning: *Bonjour (bon matin)*

Good afternoon: *Bonjour*
Good night: *Bonne nuit*
Yes: *Oui*
No: *Non*
Morning: *Matin*
Noon: *Midi*
Afternoon: *Après-midi*
Evening: *Soir*
Night: *Nuit*
Sunday: *Dimanche*
Monday: *Lundi*
Tuesday: *Mardi*
Wednesday: *Mercredi*
Thursday: *Jeudi*
Friday: *Vendredi*
Saturday: *Samedi*
One: *Un*
Two: *Deux*
Three: *Trois*
Four: *Quatre*
Five: *Cinq*
Six: *Six*
Seven: *Sept*
Eight: *Huit*
Nine: *Neuf*
Ten: *Dix*
Twenty: *Vingt*
Thirty: *Trente*
Forty: *Quarante*
Fifty: *Cinquante*
One hundred: *Cent*
One thousand: *Mille*

Tourist Areas of France ¶ Paris is an area all by itself. Then there are trips to the surrounding countryside, the so-called Île de France. To the northwest are Normandy and Brittany. The southwest has the Basque region, and along the southern coast, there is the fabulous French Riviera. To the east of Paris, tourists head for Strasbourg and the Alsace-Lorraine district. Every part of France is worth visiting, however.

Capital City

Paris is a city that defies description. It is magnificent, probably the most beautiful city in the world. It has charm—but the traffic is intolerable.

Paris is still the favorite goal of the vast majority of travelers, high prices or not. For Paris vies with Caracas and Cairo as the most expensive city in the world. Some people visit Paris with joy on every European trip; others have gone once and never returned. If you've never been to Paris, you must go.

ACCOMMODATIONS ¶ (A list of hotels and restaurants appears later in this section.) The hotel situation is difficult to explain to Americans nurtured in the American way of life. We remodel and redecorate with the seasons, with the birth of new ideas and particularly with change of ownership. In Paris, there is a city law prohibiting the remodeling of exteriors, particularly of hotels located in the vicinity of the Louvre. The hotels in that area were formerly the homes of noblemen attached to the French court and are kept in their original state, as historical monuments. Don't scoff—the New Orleans French Quarter has a similar law. Furnishings are from the turn of the century, halls and corridors are long and windy, bathrooms are spacious and generous of tile but have wheezy plumbing. The elevators are frequently asthmatic, huffing and puffing all the way to the second floor, frequently requiring rest periods in order to recuperate. But the bed linen is immaculate, the room scrupulously cleaned each day and the room service superb. You should have one meal (other than breakfast) served in your room, just to note the improvement over the American room-service method of bringing the entire meal at one time, which causes you to watch helplessly as the ice cream melts while you spoon your soup. Not so in France, where each course is served separately. When registering, check if breakfast is included in the room rate. In any event, breakfast is taken in the room, and, unlike the American custom of phoning for room service, in many hotels you ring for the waiter stationed on your floor.

SIGHTSEEING ¶ To qualify as a tourist, senior grade, you should visit the following "must-see" places:

Arch of Triumph: There is an elevator to the top, from which you can see Paris, and get your bearings; a different view than from the Eiffel Tower.
Eiffel Tower: The absolute must for all visitors. Don't pass it by as too corny; it's worth the trouble. Open from about 10:30 A.M. to 6 P.M.; charge for using the elevator; pick a clear day for a visit; you can lunch there, too.
Invalides: This area contains Napoleon's tomb (very impressive), St. Louis Church, a museum, etc. Tomb open daily from 9:30 A.M. to 5:30 P.M., closed Tuesdays.

Louvre: Probably the world's greatest art collection, small entrance fee; closed Tuesdays. Don't attempt to spend the entire day here, too enormous to absorb in such a large dose. We suggest several visits instead. Wait for a day with poor weather. Hours are 10 A.M.–5 P.M.

Flea Market: The famous market held every Saturday, Sunday and Monday, with miles of stalls and shops featuring loads of junk and some fine, not necessarily inexpensive, antiques—the days of great bargains are just about over. Best time for a visit is Sunday morning.

Gobelins: World's finest tapestries still woven here, plus a historical collection. On Thursdays from 2 to 4 P.M., you may watch an exhibition of the art of weaving.

Nôtre-Dame: Elevator to top, small fee. The church itself is open all day, except on Sundays and holidays. The Sacristy and Treasure may be seen daily except Sundays and holidays.

Sacré-Coeur: High on a hill, offers an interesting view of Paris.

Luxembourg Gardens: The place to take children; has a puppet show on Thursday and Sunday afternoons.

Jardin d'Acclimatation: Variable hours, but always open in the afternoon. A kind of Coney Island plus a zoo; children love it.

Jardin des Plantes: For those who enjoy flowers and gardening. Has a zoo. Open 9–5.

Jardin des Tuileries: Open all day and early evening; near the Louvre and a favorite place to rest your feet after several hours of museum trotting.

Panthéon: An example of classic architecture with famous tombs; open 10–5 daily except Tuesday, but the dome is closed from 12–1:30.

Paris is a city of museums. Some contain conventional, large-scale exhibits. Other collections are housed in former private homes, and the visitor has the feeling of being a guest of some distinguished collector of art.

Unless you are a born museum-goer (and they don't seem to make them any more!), use discretion. Don't go to a museum just because you've planned it several days ahead (unless it is only open on that particular day). Combine your museum-going, if possible, with reasonable quantities of other tourist pastimes. For example, don't try to see the Louvre in one complete day—go for an hour or two on several days. Best of all, save the museums for rainy days. Wear low heels, girls. If your clothes are too heavy, you'll be warm in the airless galleries, where the curators don't care nearly as much about humans as they do about keeping dust and humidity away from their proud possessions. Incidentally, the majority of Paris

museums are closed Tuesdays. And one final word—
Paris museums are remarkable, but for maximum enjoyment, use common sense. Don't overdo it.

The entrance fee for most museums—whether in Paris or elsewhere in the country—is very little. Those outside of Paris are generally closed on Monday. Some, such as the Louvre, have special programs in English. Here are some other Paris museums:

Modern Art/Musée National d'Art Moderne: 9 Avenue New York: a very fine although uneven collection.

Impressionist Art/Musée de l'Orangerie and Musée du Jeu de Paume: both located alongside the Place de la Concorde; superb collections devoted to the painters so much in vogue today; and why didn't your grandfather realize their inherent worth fifty years ago and acquire a few for you?

Eighteenth Century Art/Musée Nissim de Camondo: 63 Rue de Monceau; magnificent collection of furniture and decoration, including minor paintings, ideally housed in a small mansion. Only open 1–5 Tuesdays, Thursdays and Saturdays; 10–12 and 2–5 Sundays.

   Musée Jacquemare-André: 158 Boulevard Haussmann; many fine paintings, both French and Italian, some sculpture; closed Fridays.

   Musée Cognacq-Jay: 25 Boulevard des Capucines; fairly good collection of china, tapestries, paintings; closed Tuesdays.

Miscellaneous Fine Arts/Musée des Arts Décoratifs: 107 Rue de Rivoli; features displays of decorative art of the past 1,000 years.

   Musée Marmottan: 2 Rue Louis-Boilly; various art objects, tapestries and furniture from Renaissance to the past century; open from 1–5 on Thursdays and Sundays.

Sculpture/Musée Rodin: 77 Rue de Varenne; the works of the great sculptor in a magnificent eighteenth-century house, open 1–6 daily except Tuesdays.

   Musée des Monuments Français: in the Palais de Chaillot; the history and development of sculpture; open 10–5 daily except Tuesdays.

Middle Ages and Renaissance/Musée de Cluny: 6 Place Paul-Painlevé; a fine collection from the Middle Ages.

   Musée des Arts et Traditions Populaires: Place Trocadéro; peasant art and folklore, some eighteenth-century specimens.

Oriental Art/Musée Guimet: 6 Place d'Iéna; world-famous collection including many important pieces; open daily 10–6 except Tuesdays.

   Musée Cernuschi: 7 Avenue Velasquez; emphasis on China and Japan; open 10–12 and 2–5 daily, except Tuesdays.

Museums of History/Musée Carnavalet: 23 Rue de Sévigné; a truly *important* museum housed in a former home of Madame de Sévigné; art objects, prints, maps covering the complete history of Paris; open 10–6 daily, except Tuesdays.

   Musée de la Conciergerie: Île de la Cité; the famous prison where Marie Antoinette and Robespierre occupied cells; small, gruesome collection, but interesting; open 10–12 and 1:30–5 daily, except Tuesdays.

Musée des Archives: 60 Rue des Francs-Bourgeois; the story of France, beautifully arranged in four lovely old houses; don't fail to see the bedchamber of Princesse de Soubise; open 10–5.

Music and Performing Arts/Musée de l'Opéra: in the Pavillion d'Honneur, Rue Auber; opera and concert mementos; open daily 10–5 except Sundays.

Musée Instrumental du Conservatoire: 14 Rue de Madrid; souvenirs of important musicians, rare instruments; open Thursdays and Saturdays, 2–4:30.

Miscellaneous Museums/Musée de l'Homme: in the Palais de Chaillot; anthropological exhibits; open 10–5 except Mondays.

Musée de l'Armée: in the Hôtel des Invalides; displays of military equipment, etc.

Musée des Gobelins: 42 Avenue des Gobelins; a part of the Gobelin factory; best visited on Thursday from 2–4 when it is possible to see tapestries being made.

Muséedu Vieux Montmartre: 22 Rue Tourlaque; small, but amusing exhibits of prints, signs and other souvenirs of old Montmartre; unfortunately only open 10–12, first Sunday of each month.

Artists and Writers/Musée Victor Hugo: 6 Place des Vosges; drawings and souvenirs displayed in the home of the famous writer; open 10–12, 2–5 daily except Tuesdays.

Musée Eugène Delacroix: 6 Place Furstenberg; the rather small apartment of the artist, with some of his work, plus occasional special exhibits; open 10–5 except Tuesdays.

Musée Balzac: 47 Rue Raynouard; for lovers of the great writer only; mediocre house, some mementos of an unhappy man who spent much time eluding his creditors; open 1:30–5 daily, except Mondays; closed in August.

MORE SIGHTSEEING ¶ First, the *tours*. With its hundreds of thousands of visitors, Paris offers more conducted sightseeing tours than any other metropolis in the world. Should you or shouldn't you? It's a matter of taste. Many people enjoy doing it the easy way, seeing the sights from a bus, having them pointed out and described by someone—often a pretty Parisian girl—who usually knows what she is talking about. The best sightseeing bus tour anywhere, of course, is the Cityrama, the bubble-type double-decker bus with earphones at your seat so that there is simultaneous translation. This is only a very superficial quick look at just about all the main sights in Paris. The Cityrama buses cover all of them, but only pause at a few of them. But it is a great trip. The rates, depending on the trip, are on the high side but are well worth it.

There are several night club tours that offer a tremendous value, even if the evening is scarcely a gay one. Most of these visit several different night clubs, give you a free drink at each one, a girlie-girlie show or some other "typical Paris night-life scene," a students' basement joint, a strictly phony Apache dive and, best of all, return you directly to your hotel when it's all over. The charges vary, depending on what you get to eat and/or drink, the number of cabarets visited and which particular ones. The lowest-priced tour, for instance, does not get you to either the Moulin Rouge or the Lido. But the top-priced one not only takes you to them but to three others as well and tops off the night with a big bowl of onion soup. So there! For unescorted ladies, the night club tour has the virtue of being just about the only way of seeing Paris night life. Organized, group-style merriment is forbidding, plodding gaiety—but most people would rather take a tour than not go at all. Incidentally, in spite of the guide's efforts to jazz up the evening with the possibility of *danger*, there isn't any. Zero, absolutely zero.

Sightseeing on your own: To a race of Americans who customarily regard walking as something one does to reach an automobile, we hesitate to recommend the obvious and best way of seeing Paris. On foot. You're going to hate us, but it's true. So put on the stout footwear (low heels for ladies) and go.

Trip 1: Take a bus, taxi or *métro* (destination—Cité station) to the Île de la Cité, often regarded as the heart of Paris. Here you'll find, in the early morning, a flower market; on Sundays, a cheerful, twittering, colorful bird market. Let's get our bearings by looking for the Eiffel Tower, which is in the west. Now walk toward it, that is, westerly, and you'll come to the Palais de Justice, the law courts; if you're a lawyer or interested in the workings of French trials, you might inquire about the possibility of seeing one. Walking south (a left turn) toward the south shore of the islands, you'll arrive at Ste.-Chapelle Church, built in the middle of the thirteenth century; it is a superb example of Gothic architecture. Proceeding north along the Boulevard du Palais to the Tour de Horloge is the Conciergerie, the Revolutionary prison. If you're up to it, you can see the grim cells that once housed Robespierre and Marie Antoinette.

Now for the Cathedral of Nôtre-Dame, 800 years old, at the eastern end of the island. After you've walked through it, be sure to circle around outside to see the rear view. Then cross over the bridge onto small, charming Île St.-Louis. The island doesn't have one single important monument or "must-see" point of interest, but there are lovely 300-year-old houses, graceful trees and the placid, slow-moving Seine. At the eastern end of the island, cross to the Left Bank (the south shore) via the Sully bridge. Once over the bridge, turn right, walking toward the Eiffel Tower (what would we do without it!) along the Quai de Montebello and you'll pass the twelfth-century church of St.-Julien-le-Pauvre. Then ahead to Boulevard St.-Michel and turn left to find yourself in the heart of the student or "Latin" quarter, so called because no one studies Latin any more. Three streets up is the intersection of St.-Michel with Boulevard St.-Germain, where the beautiful Cluny Museum is situated. One block away is the world-famous university, the Sorbonne. South from the Sorbonne, you'll reach the Rue Cujas; turn left and walk toward the Panthéon, a magnificent structure in the shape of a Greek cross. Among others, Voltaire, Hugo, Zola and Rousseau are entombed there. Remember, the building is closed Tuesdays.

If you still have any energy left, walk back toward Boulevard St.-Germain and rest up at any student's cafe over a refreshing beverage. Take a taxi to your hotel; or walk to the nearest *métro station* by going east on Rue Clovis, until you get to Rue du Cardinal Lemoine, then turn left and walk until you see the station.

Trip 2: Afternoons only. Off by taxi or *métro* to Avarenne station to see the Rodin Museum, located in the Hôtel Biron. The museum is open 1–5 daily, except Tuesdays.

Then cross the street and enter Hôtel des Invalides, where you'll find the tombs of famous military men, notably Napoleon and Foch. Tour the military museum, enormous and impressive, open daily until 5 except Tuesdays. Coming out, look for your old friend, the Eiffel Tower, and head in that direction until you come to the Avenue de la Motte-Picquet and turn left. You'll soon arrive at the Place Joffre, where you'll have an unexcelled view of the Eiffel Tower. If your legs will carry you, continue walking toward the tower through the Champ de Mars, if not, take a taxi. There you'll find the Swiss

Market (56 Avenue de la Motte-Piquet), a sort of miniature Flea Market, with miscellaneous bargains, scrimshaw, geegaws, antiques and junk—but lots of fun.

Now, about going up in the Eiffel Tower. Many people shy away from the obvious, but sometimes the obvious is just that because thousands of people have enjoyed it. Unhesitatingly recommended; be sure and go all the way to the top. There are bars and restaurants for the weary, and you should be by now or you aren't human. The tower was constructed between 1887 and 1889 by an engineer named Gustav Eiffel. Many thought it wasn't possible to construct a building of that height, others thought it would sink into the ground and other dire predictions were made. It's still there and hasn't settled an inch and you're perfectly safe in riding to the top— but be sure to pick a dry, clear day or you won't see much. As a personal favor to us, promise NOT to buy a replica of the Eiffel Tower. Not only as a favor to us, but also to your friends, who'll never be able to find any conceivable use for it.

If you've the energy, cross the Iéna Bridge to the Palais de Chaillot and wander through its museums— particularly the anthropology museum (if you like anthropology); open 10–5 daily, except Mondays.

Trip 3: By taxi, bus or *métro* (get off at Place du Châtelet station) to Square St.-Jacques. Here is the lovely tower of St.-Jacques. Now face east (your back to the Eiffel Tower) and continue along the Rue de Rivoli to the Hôtel de Ville, or somewhat less elegant in English, City Hall. Across the street from City Hall is the Bazaar de Hôtel de Ville, a department store specializing in household goods, kitchen equipment and other fascinating items; the street behind the department store has shops selling copper pots, culinary equipment and the like. Going east again on the Rue de Rivoli, you'll soon come to Rue Vieille du Temple; turn left to the Rue des Rosiers, the Jewish quarter, and follow that street eastward to its dead end. Turn left on Rue Malher to Rue des Francs-Bourgeois and the Musée Carnavalet, open daily except Tuesdays from 10 to 6. Even if you absolutely hate museums, visit this one. You'll learn about Paris and its history, and it's pleasant and informative. Back once again on the Rue des Franc-Bourgeois, continue several blocks to the Place des Vosges. Henri IV was responsible for this square, an architectural masterpiece, with fine old houses along its edge. The Victor Hugo Museum is located at number 6; open 10 to 12:30 and 2 to 5 daily except Tuesdays. Come out of the Place des Vosges by its far end, the Rue de Birague, then left on Rue St.-Antoine, which leads out onto Place de la Bastille. (This general area from Rue Vieille du Temple toward the Bastille district was known as the Marais, a favorite residential area of the nobility of some 300 years ago; wandering about the attractive side streets you'll see any number of decrepit, but still inherently fine, old houses.) The Place de la Bastille marks the site of the infamous prison, the Bastille, destroyed on July 14, 1789—and July 14, is, of course, the French national holiday equivalent to July 4 in our own country. You can, if you are energetic or drink two fortifying cognacs, climb to the top of the tower in the center of the *Place*; that is, if it's between 10 and 5, and if it isn't Tuesday. Otherwise, you must deny yourself that pleasure. At night, if you're brave and your insurance is paid up, walk eastward away from Place de la Bastille on the Rue de la Roquette to the Rue de Lappe, scene of the *bals*, where the poor people of Paris entertain themselves with dances in the local style to the music of accordions. Actually, you're pretty safe, except that we wouldn't recommend carrying too much money or jewelry, or being too well dressed or looking like excessively rich tourists. On the other hand, if you're timid, don't go.

Trip 4: On a pleasant Saturday or Sunday morning take a taxi or the *métro* (Clignancourt station) to the Flea Market. After you've wandered all over the market, head for the Place du Tertre, and we think a taxi necessary because this isn't very fascinating territory for walking, and besides, it's easy to lose your way. Place du Tertre is, well, shall we say, touristy-picturesque. You should see it, however. Walk through all of the side streets surrounding the square, although if you start your trip late in the day and it's getting dark, perhaps you'd better hurry over and have a look at Sacré-Coeur. It's traditional to walk through the church, coming out onto the steps to find the sobering magnificence of Paris at your feet. And if it's almost twilight, with the lights of the city just coming on—well, that's Paris at its best. You'll find many places to eat and drink in the area.

Now, just let gravity take over and walk downhill from the Place du Tertre. No one street runs downhill more than a few blocks, but if you keep walking downhill, sooner or later you'll arrive at either the Boulevard de Clichy or Boulevard Rochechouart. Head toward Pigalle; if it is necessary to ask directions, just say the magic word "Pigalle" (pronounced Pig-al, not Pig Alley).

This is where Parisian night life reaches either its peak or nadir, depending upon your own background and personality. If it's not for you, walk around a bit, look at the posters and windows and listen to the barkers describing the various attractions. Then go home. If you enjoy night life, here is everything they whisper about in Peoria and Dallas. Everything is obtainable, everything may be seen or done—at a price. Night clubs, strip-tease, music, dancing, champagne, high life, snails and hamburgers, what have you, what does m'sieur desire?

SHOPPING ¶ Just as London is a man's town, so is Paris a woman's town. ("A man's town" means that a city has a masculine personality, caters to men and in general offers more to men.) Turnabout is fair play, so men should be reconciled to comparatively few bargains for themselves in Paris. Still we'll get around to those later.

Pointer: French store hours—Open from 9 or 9:30 A.M. until 5:30 or 6 P.M. Smaller shops often close at noon for about two hours. Most stores are open on Saturday, closed Monday. On the Faubourg St.-Honoré, Paris' most important shopping street, some shops are closed on Saturday during the summer and almost all close by noon.

Perfumes are without question the best shopping value in France. The $10 spent on a French perfume represents a $20 or $30 value back home, and as every woman (well, practically) regards perfume as the number-one luxury gift, you can hardly go wrong. That is, if you purchase recognized, standard brands. If you're a mere male, with little or no knowledge of perfume brands, almost anything put up by Guerlain, Worth, Caron, Rochas, Schiaparelli, Carven and Dior will be welcomed by your donee. (A donee is a person on the receiving end of a gift by a donor.) If you purchase a substantial amount, always ask for a discount over and above the normal price; most shops give it, sometimes willingly, sometimes grudgingly, but don't be shy—it's your money.

Many manufacturers of French perfumes have restricted your purchases to one bottle of each *different* product they make; those presently with restrictions in effect include Guerlain, Lanvin, Chanel and Patou, but the list changes frequently, so be sure to inquire when making a purchase. Now what does this all mean? The restriction refers to one bottle of a particular perfume per person, so a couple could bring back two bottles, for instance, of *Joy* and two bottles of *Moment Suprême* (both of which are packaged by Patou). The restriction is pretty silly because the regulation limits you to one bottle each, regardless of whether the bottle holds one-half ounce or a gallon. Since the protection extends to the *trademark* only, you can scratch off the labels from a dozen Chanel #5 bottles and bring them back home without an argument; the restriction applies only to the label and not to the perfume. In addition, as a rule, the United States customs man couldn't care less about protecting perfume trademarks and will normally not even bother to examine your purchases if you merely list "Miscellaneous French perfumes—$50" on your declaration.

The perfect "small" gift is often a bottle of *eau de parfum* or *eau de toilette*, in lieu of the more expensive perfumes. For a few dollars a very suitable remembrance can be brought back for someone who gave you a book (or something else you left home) as a going-away present.

Handmade suede *gloves*, many of them washable, are an outstanding value and the sort of purchase (and gift) on which you can expect to save 50 percent. The longer six- and eight-button models offer, comparatively speaking, even better values. For gifts, be conservative and buy black or white; pastel shades are not nearly so acceptable to most women. French detailing on gloves is unexcelled—you'll find delicate beading, petit point and beauvais embroidery on many models. Washable leathers are good purchases.

For *lingerie*, girdles, as you might expect, are good buys. Breathes there a woman with soul so dead that she has never coveted a French girdle? *Scandale* is probably the best known, prices are moderate and you should scarcely leave Paris without buying a black girdle. French brassieres are something else, since French women apparently have different figures from their American sisters.

Around the hips, O.K., but to the north, you're on your own. If the brassiere fits, buy it. Another thing, the French delicately refer to a brassiere as a *soutien-gorge*, a throat supporter. (Don't ask why.)

Petticoats, slips and half slips are attractive but do not necessarily represent good value. On the other hand, if you get a thrill out of a slip with a Paris label (or have an aunt who would), it's a good purchase.

Regarding *dresses and haute couture*, most American women arrive in France with the full expectation of bringing back a dress or two with a Paris label. Soon after their arrival, they ask the concierge in the hotel to arrange for a couple of tickets (the second is for the unwilling husband) to a fashion show. The tickets are usually easy to obtain except when the dress houses are closed for vacation or have previews for wholesale buyers only. The fashion show itself is pleasant, although as a rule, at least half of the garments apparently are created with a *Vogue* or *Harper's Bazaar* photograph in mind and would be considered unwearable by most American women. A saleslady is stationed behind each group of potential customers, although she seldom does more than audibly admire various numbers as they are shown. Rarely will the customer be pressed into making a purchase. The reason is obvious—very few Americans can afford to buy them! A typical basic black street dress ranges from $700 to $800; an evening gown varies from $1,200 to $1,500, depending upon the detail and the mood the designer was in at the time he sketched the dress. Why these superlative prices? A simple question of economics. A large Seventh Avenue (New York) dress house can afford to pay French couturiers' prices, copy the garment and sell thousands of copies, amortize the copy of the sample and charge it off as a business expense. *You* can't, unless you're a Hollywood star and presumably require it in your profession. Except for occasional Texas oil millionaires, heiresses to dime store fortunes and others singularly well endowed with worldly goods, Paris originals are out. Well, then, how do French women dress so well at those prices? As a rule, most of them have their dresses made by the so-called "little" dressmakers who copy the big-name designers for a price of about $150 or so. You can, too, if you've the patience to seek out one of these, pursue interminable conversations in colloquial French, have any number of fittings and also (here is the principal problem) be able to wait several weeks for the finished product. Another point to remember with regard to Paris chic and elegance is the fact that American women enjoy a large variety in their wardrobe and Frenchwomen concentrate on a very few outfits—spending a large part of their clothes budget for one "good" suit and one "important" evening gown. The following season, the same procedure is followed, and last year's "best" becomes this season's second best.

For centuries, the French have emphasized handwork in preference to machine work. Although there has been some slight changeover, comparatively little progress has been made toward the American system of mass-produced garments. Other than classic sweaters, blouses and skirts, most French ready-to-wear is not well made. Unlike the fashion jungle in our own country, Paris originals are protected by law for two years; by the time the large-scale copyists can get to it, the style is pretty close to extinction, except, as previously mentioned, for the sort of classic clothes that are never out of style.

Most of the leading stylists, particularly those located near the Rond Point, have tiny shops, *boutiques*, selling dresses and accessories at prices that are still startling, but less than those previously mentioned. For example, a rather good-looking cocktail dress, of the type any woman would want and use, might run to about $250, with several fittings included. (We didn't say this was cheap—but it's better than $750!)

So-called "sample" dresses in the $100–$200 range are frequently advertised in the *International Herald-Tribune*. Buy with care, for many are soiled and shopworn, having been modeled in dozens of fashion shows. Anna Lowe has a shop on the Avenue Matignon, which often has sample dresses and suits from the famous designers at fair prices.

Raincoats are highly styled and a delight to the eye, but highly styled (and expensive) French raincoats are often copied for a fraction of their Paris price in the commercially minded United States. And very quickly, too.

While on the subject of raincoats, we should mention that *umbrellas* are high on the list of good buys. Excellent gifts, too. The very slim models are extremely attractive and if you measure your luggage, you'll find that most umbrellas fit (diagonally) into a large suitcase.

Your mouth will water when you examine the beautiful detailing and styling on a Paris *blouse* creation. Most shops will fit them without extra charge, and they are a joy forever, but the price runs fairly high—a minimum of $25 up to $50 or more, with an average of about $35. Worth it, if you want to spend that much—and remember, the more you spend the more you save. (That's female logic, you know.)

The couturiers have a good selection of *handbags* in their *boutiques*, but prices are high. The French flair for handbags is too well known to require discussion, and the work is particularly impressive in the higher price brackets. Beaded evening bags always make us feel guilty —think of those thousands of tiny beads individually picked up on a slender needle and stitched into place— but who could resist them at half the Stateside prices? Brocaded bags are becoming important again and are equally good values. For handbags at popular prices, go to the department stores; they all carry a Paris label. If you're throwing all caution to the winds, look at alligator bags. Prices are very high, but the skins have the smallest markings you'll ever see. Figure a basic minimum of $100 and a top of about $275, but after all, they last a lifetime, or, at least, a very long time and if the cost is spread out over ten years . . .

As long as anyone can remember, Paris *hats* have had a certain symbolism intertwined with gaiety, Freud and hang-the-expense. This is still the reaction of most women, but don't let yourself get *completely* carried away. It's fun but foolish to buy a chapeau so extreme that you feel self-conscious in it back in Kansas City. Invest in something at least reasonably wearable.

MISCELLANEOUS SHOPPING FOR WOMEN ¶ *Handkerchiefs* are attractive but the prices are high; available all over Paris. *Costume jewelry* is unique—smart lines, well executed and quite low prices. *Pins* and *clips* are French specialties and make first-rate gifts. *Antique buttons* (many from old uniforms) and handmade *compacts* and *lipsticks* are not necessarily cheap but have a distinct "Paris" quality about them. Scarves are often gargantuan in measurement and price.

Now that women have been disposed of (as to shopping, that is), let's give a thought to bargains for men.

French lisle *socks* are about half United States prices. *Ties* are so-so; if you're going to London or Rome, buy them there. Custom-made *shirts* are better in London, but French shirts are topnotch, although quite expensive; avoid the ready-made ones. Men's *suits* are horrible, and that goes for overcoats, too, with the exception of the Montignac coats made with dressy black fabric. *Hats* are passable, but not worth bothering about if you're going (or have been) to London or Rome. *Handkerchiefs,* hand-rolled, are beautiful.

Wines and liquors, for gentility's sake, are classified for men, but women have been seen to make purchases. Just don't go overboard, despite the bargains, because you can only bring in one (only one) regular bottle of wine or liquor without payment of tax. That's per person, so three people can bring back three bottles even though one is a teetotaller. In addition, if you're returning by plane, give a fleeting thought to the weight of your purchase, unless you can put the bottles in your flight bag and sneak them by the eagle-eyed attendants. You needn't have any qualms about sending liquor home in case lots (it hardly pays for less), because the shipment will arrive in good order. Be prepared to rescue your liquor with lots of forms, and pay the tax when the lot does arrive. Cognac, for all practical purposes, represents the best all-around liquor value. It will cost half—maybe, even less—of what it does back home. The saving is increasingly great on twenty-year-old velvety smooth types. Clear white *alcools,* fruit brandies, are worth buying; there is a choice of plum, cherry, and several others, but the best of all is *framboise,* raspberry. It's as dry as a dry martini and equally potent. Not cheap, even in France. If you like champagne, the savings are impressive.

MISCELLANEOUS SHOPPING ¶ Antiques are good values if you know what you're buying. Of course, the Flea Market (in the Marché Biron district) has some marvelous stuff, but since most of the displays come up from Paris for the weekend market, don't look for bargain-basement prices—those disappeared back in the depression days. There are dozens and dozens of small, hole-in-the-wall shops with antiques scattered throughout the Left Bank district in the vicinity of Rue Jacob. Don't neglect the Swiss Village (near the Eiffel Tower) for similar merchandise. Don't forget to bargain—it's expected, and you'll overpay if you don't. On articles over 130 years old (approximately), there is no United States customs duty, so be sure to obtain a certificate of antiquity when making a purchase.

Linens, china and glassware are all specialties of France and represent good value, even though Paris prices are high—but that's because you're buying quality goods. Sevres and Limoges make exquisite porcelain dinner services; the prices will often floor you momentarily, but you'll find them twice as high in your local shop in Seattle. Baccarat crystal is undeniably glorious and although not low-priced, you'll pay considerably more at home.

Pointer: Buy extra glasses instead of just a dozen, so that you won't be heartbroken when you break one. Don't worry about shipping goods, for the china and glassware is insured and usually arrives in perfect condition.

If you know a great deal about *art*, there's nothing we can add. If not, you'll be buying blindly. The fine galleries around the Faubourg St.-Honoré charge hefty prices, particularly for the modern and Impressionist art now in great demand. For all practical purposes, there is no limit on the amount you may be asked. Don't expect to come away with *anything* by an important painter without spending well into several-thousand-plus (dollars, that is). If, however, it's just something with a souvenir value you're after, you might look in on the small shops near the Place du Tertre up in Montmartre, or anywhere else that you see a tiny, unassuming gallery.

Fine and rare *books*, particularly those with illuminated manuscript pages, are a specialty of Paris. Old *prints*, Toulouse-Lautrec lithographs and similar memorabilia of Paris are found in shops throughout the city. However, they specialize in these items on the streets of the Left Bank that lead away from the Seine; just wander about at random.

Oddments: An attractive gift for a dog-fancier (or for that matter for a dog) is an unusual collar. Small diaries and notebooks (also of leather) make excellent small gifts and they don't weigh much or take up space in your luggage. If you have a friend who enjoys being a hostess and giving elaborate dinners, she would probably be pleased with a set of menu cards and menu holders. French stationery is remarkably attractive although quite bulky; better have it mailed. A French poodle can be sent home by plane; be sure the necessary health certificates, etc., are all in order.

Pointer: If you accumulate a large quantity of purchases, take them to Pitt and Scott, Ltd., who make a specialty of packing and shipping and are particularly reliable with antiques and fragile goods.

What not to buy: Although almost anything in the way of women's clothing is recommended, there are two outstanding exceptions—shoes and furs. Prices for furs are stratospheric, and then comes the United States customs duty in addition. You'll do better back home. Ladies' shoes are priced all right, but they never seem to fit— wait for Italy. (This advice goes for men, too.) Men's clothing, especially suits, should be avoided.

The French seem to lack a certain know-how with simple, mechanical things. Avoid locally made fountain pens, typewriters, clocks and watches, which may look attractive but seldom work. Exception to the exception: French butane lighters are good.

ENTERTAINMENT ¶ What is entertainment? To some it represents a chamber music recital, to others a night in a brassy cabaret. To early-to-bedders, 11 P.M. is the end of a big night; to many people, merely the beginning. Then the question of budget: in a small town, a few dollars for a movie and an ice cream soda might seem the limit; big-city expense-accounters might think a $50 check for two very reasonable. Obviously, no single plan for an evening's entertainment is possible. Go through this section and pick and choose according to your individual desires, but note these few comments. If you have never in your entire life been to a night club, Paris, although expensive, is the place to start. *Au contraire*, if the Stork Club was a second home to you, Paris night clubs will provide few surprises except for the nudity in the floor shows.

Unlike New York, *theater* tickets usually can be obtained on a few days' notice, except during the height of the winter season. Don't bother trying to buy your own seats unless you just happen to be passing the particular theater; pick them up at a ticket broker or have the concierge get them; there's only a small charge. First, let's consider the "state" theaters:

To get the bad news out of the way, the famous *Paris Opéra* is closed during August. The remainder of the year, you can have opera almost every evening (no performances Tuesday, and Wednesday is devoted to ballet). The Opéra's performances are erratic, but as a rule the level of performance is well below the standards of New York's Metropolitan or Milan's La Scala, and this might even be an understatement on occasional off nights. If you are an opera lover, you'll go nevertheless to round out your opera experiences. If you never go (or have never been), make inquiry as to whether the Opéra is scheduling a *Gala Performance*, usually presented in connection with a new work or the restaging of an accepted classic. The *Gala* is an unexcelled opportunity to show off a new gown and to see French society, too. Formal dress customarily is worn; usually there will be a uniformed line of guards along the famous staircase of the fabulous Paris Opéra house and the whole setting has a definitely unreal (and exciting) quality.

The *Opéra-Comique* is closed during July, but open the remainder of the year. No performances Monday. The Comique portion of its title doesn't necessarily refer to comedies, however. Operas with spoken lines (as opposed to works that are completely sung) are given at the Opéra-Comique. The Comique is well presented and a pleasant evening's entertainment may be counted upon generally. Not quite so formal or dressy as the much grander *Opéra*.

Ever since high school, you've probably planned to see a presentation of French classics at the *Comédie-Française*. (The newer and more correct name, which no one uses, is the Theatre Français.) To begin with, the Comédie-Française closes down for the summer. Performances are given at two theaters, the Salle Richelieu and Salle Luxembourg; the repertoire is drawn principally from the great classicists—Molière, Corneille, Racine and some few others. Occasionally, after many years of success and acclaim on the commercial stage of Paris, a more modern play is performed. Here is your opportunity to hear French spoken the way it should be—not the way you learned it in school. One warning—if you don't understand *any* French at all, the evening may be wearing.

At lower prices than any of the above is the *Theatre National Populaire*, which exhibits its talents in the enormous Palais de Chaillot. These performances are good, although the acoustics of the theater are spotty, but how can you go wrong at the low prices they charge? Here, in addition, there are occasional Saturday and Sunday specials featuring a concert (with good soloists), then a show (by the Theatre National Populaire company) and later a pleasant, light supper. The price? Not much more than an ordinary ticket. This is a five-star special even if you don't understand French and never go to concerts, because you'll have an unexcelled chance to meet the great mass of French citizenry enjoying themselves under informal circumstances.

So much for state-supported theaters. Now for the commercial stage. To begin with, most dramatic performances begin at 8:30 P.M., musical shows as late as 9. You'll have to plan on an early dinner (or have a late tea and eat again after the show), and taxis are *extremely* difficult to find around theater time. You are unequivocally advised and urged to select a restaurant for pre-theater dining within walking distance of the theater—or you may find yourself making the second-act curtain (not the *first*). Typical prices for a musical show are less than in New York, but more than in London. Dramatic shows are something like half the New York rate. Once in the theater, remember when you're escorted to your seat to tip the usher (most often a woman) 1 franc a person. (No, we can't imagine why this is necessary. But not only is it a custom—the usher will make it an issue if you try to ignore her.)

But should you go to the legitimate theater at all? To be candid, if you don't speak even the high-school variety of French, much of the average play will be lost upon you, although there are a few exceptions, such as spectacles where language is unimportant or performances at the Palais-Royal, which feature boudoirs, cuckolds, lovers in closets, sweethearts under the bed and other similar examples of the finest art of the theater. But with regard to ordinary dramas or light comedy, much of the show will be a waste if even a primitive command of the language is lacking. Exception: the Comédie-Wagram

Theatre has certain seats equipped with earphones, and you'll hear a simultaneous translation (in English) of the play, in the fashion of a session at the United Nations. Be sure to request seats with this equipment. Even if you have language difficulties, you almost owe yourself one French performance, so go here.

Another point to remember is that nudity will crop up unexpectedly. You might be contentedly watching a light comedy, your mind actively coping with *le subjonctif* and *le plus-que-parfait*, when all of a sudden (to your horror or delight) the heroine will disrobe as completely as a peeled onion. And you never can tell when (or even if) the event will occur.

From September through June, the Paris stage is alive and very healthy, indeed. If you've seen French television, you *know* it couldn't hurt the legitimate theater. Getting tickets for shows in Paris is *not* best accomplished by going to the theater in question—it takes time, and you might not be understood. Most leading hotels have a theatre ticket office (the Hotel Bristol, for example) in their lobbies; ticket brokers are also to be found around the Madeleine. Pay the small service charge; it's worth it.

Musical shows in Paris do not demand even a rudimentary command of the French language. As you might guess, this miracle is accomplished by featuring complete stage settings, playlets and routines about the exposure of that unique feature of female anatomy—the mammary glands. Patriotic songs are sung to an almost nude representation of Mademoiselle France; art and science are pictured as two nude girls, one with trailing plumes (that's Art with a capital A) and one with a square head-dress (that's Science, in the mind of the producer). No matter what the variations, after you've seen a few dozen bare bosoms—that's it. For enthusiastic girl-watchers, such constitutes a full evening's entertainment, but for most (especially female) spectators, how welcome a funny line would be! For, truth to tell, the musical shows are long on exposure and short on humour, plot and nuance. Unquestionably the number one tourist-bait is the *Folies-Bergère*, which seems to go on year after year pulling in the customers. Peculiarly enough, not all of the spectators are Americans—but you'll seldom find a Parisian there. It's too corny for the sophisticated boulevardiers, but is the sort of thing the visitors from the provinces, from Montignac and Pau, have to see on their visit to Paris, or what could they tell the folks back home? Close behind the Folies-Bergère in elaborate nudity is the *Casino de Paris*, although not nearly so famous.

For vaudeville with a slight difference there is the *Olympia Theatre*, the equivalent of London's Palladium; here you can get along fairly well without French. Of lesser caliber in the vaudeville field are the *ABC* (occasionally presenting light operettas), *Alhambra* and also the *Bobino* (in Montparnasse). Lower down and strictly from strip-tease are the *Caumartin* and *Mayol* theaters.

Motion pictures are very much in evidence in Paris; they are numerous all over town, particularly along the grand boulevards and the Champs-Elysées. American films are extremely popular and may be seen in their original version, that is, with Elizabeth Taylor speaking for herself. Outside of the theater, if you look carefully at the sign, you'll see "V.O." indicating original version or should we say "version originale." If not, you'll hear and see a dubbed-in affair that might be much less enjoyable. Did you ever imagine Kirk Douglas speaking French?

Concerts are something else again. The French have good soloists and small ensembles, but the hard and inescapable truth remains that the Lamoureux and Cologne orchestras are second rate. The best musical French aggregation, we think, and don't laugh, *s'il vous plaît*, is the *Garde Républicaine*, the band that knocked them dead on a recent American tour and whose hi-fi records are guaranteed to lead to vibrating chandeliers and broken glassware.

Well, what about night clubs? Well, what about them? First of all, and in a sort of class by itself, is the *Lido* on the Champs-Elysées. It features a long (two and one-half-hour) show, often considered the world's best night club spectacle, in a basement that seems the size of Madison Square Garden and just about as noisy as you'd expect. Don't dare go without an advance reservation, and make it a day or so ahead through you-know-who (your concierge, that's right), because if your table isn't fairly close up front, you might as well stay home. The show is fast, elaborate and lavishly costumed, usually featuring American acts, and the girls are nude only from the waist up, although scarcely overdressed in the southerly exposure. Much to the same effect is *Nouvelle Eve* in Montmartre except that it's MUCH more expensive and MUCH more nude (or is it nuder?), and the show is on a stage, revue-fashion.

Fast achieving a fame similar to the Lido's is a special type of Parisian nighttime institution called the *Crazy Horse Saloon*. It is on the lower end of Avenue George V, toward the Seine. The Crazy Horse (whose proprietor, by the way, is a very wise gentleman) is for Americans who want to see what French people think the Wild West would have been like if the French had settled it—and there's not a brassiere in a wagon train of settlers! It is quite a place, and the fun is lively and imaginative.

The *discothèque*, with its pop-rock beat, strobe and psychedelic lights and affable bar, is providing a big part of nighttime entertainment for the *smart set* of Paris. The very *in* place at the present is *New Jimmy's* on Boulevard Montparnasse. The director of this establishment is Regine, whose name is a household word—or at least a familiar one to those who follow the gossip and social columns of the Paris press. She is at all the leading parties and receptions in the city, and it seems that all the leading personages of Paris drop in at New Jimmy's sometime during the evening or early morning.

Castel's in the Rue Princesse, just off the Boulevard St.-Germain, is also a great favorite—what with a pub and a pleasant discothèque. In the same *quartier*, the *King Club* and *Le Bilboquet* are big drawing cards—especially for the younger folks. Up by the Arch of Triumph, on the Right Bank, the *Club d'Etoile* is also *in* —or *dans le vent*, as the French put it. Drinks at such places are not inexpensive. They're expensive. They average about $3 or $4. But no one urges you to "drink up" —and with one drink you can remain in a place as long as you like to. Many of the most fashionable nighttime places are theoretically private clubs. But this is basically a means for giving the establishment a chance to pick its clientele. If you pass muster with the doorman, that's all there is to it. To facilitate your entrance at such places, it is best to go early—around 9:30 or so.

Young people have a lot of good times at the *Bus Palladium* in Pigalle. It is small, noisy and alcohol-free. But despite such ingredients—or, is it because?—the young people like it very much. Send your teen-agers there.

If you are in search of *le jazz*, then head for the *Slow Club* on the Rue de Rivoli, which is on the Right Bank, or go over to the *Riverboat* on the Left Bank.

Maxim's (3 Rue Royale) requires some special discussion. Basically, *Maxim's* is a restaurant serving fine food, but is almost equally famous as a night spot. Open every evening, except Sundays during the month of August; be sure to have a reservation. Dressy, but evening clothes required only on Friday night; dark men's suits and cocktail dresses are suitable other evenings. Lots of celebrities, gay nineties décor, Old Worldish atmosphere with New Worldish prices. Or go late to the upstairs bar, where the crowd is usually pretty glamorous.

SPORTS ¶ The French are crazy *pour le sport*. Among the spectator sports, *auto racing* is a mania, and the *bicycle races* throughout France cause traffic detours for days.

Tennis enthusiasts should contact *Fédération Française de Lawn-Tennis* (French is so simple) located at 3 Rue Volney, in Paris, or call OPEra 4491 to help arrange for games, courts, partners or even admission to private tennis clubs.

Golf is considered an extremely smart social game. For club privileges, get in touch with *Fédération Française de Golf*, 1 Rue Lord Byron, Paris, or phone ELYsées 3842 (closed Saturdays) for all information. There are about ten courses within driving distance of Paris, but only two are outstanding. The nearest of these is St.-Cloud, about six miles out, with thirty-six holes (closed Mondays); a very attractive, well-designed course. In the same category is Mortefontaine, with twenty-seven holes, about twenty-five miles away (closed Tuesdays); by train from the Gare du Nord to Survillier, frequent service. By car via route N-17 through Port de la Villette. Other nearby (to Paris) clubs at Chantilly, Fontainebleau, Lys-Chantilly, Marly, St.-Germain-en-Laye.

If you can be introduced by a club member, so much the easier, otherwise the *Fédération* will help you.

Horse racing switches from one track to another every few weeks; almost all tracks are very close by, and Auteuil is particularly easy to reach. Special races are held throughout the year, and these should not be missed; here is a chance to see Paris society and lots of local color. Follow the announcements in the *International Herald-Tribune*.

Skiing and winter sports begin just before Christmas and finish in mid-March. February is the height of the season, although the snow begins to thin out toward the end of the month. The most popular region is around Mont Blanc, with hotels near Mégève and Chamonix.

MISCELLANEOUS NOTES ¶ The *cafes of Paris* are a world of their own. When you've walked about as far as your feet can carry you, sit down and watch Paris go by—a uniquely European custom and not unpleasant. At odd hours, you can drink an *apéritif*, as the French call it, although their choice of drinks is pretty horrible by American tastes. Most Frenchmen disapprove of hard liquor and imbibe (and that is the only word for taking a half-hour to consume an ounce or two of fluid) light alcoholic drinks intended to whet the appetite. These drinks break down into four groups: those with quinine (Damiani and Byrrh are examples), some with bitters (Campari and Suze, to illustrate), the vermouth types (Noilly Prat and Cinzano are popular) and the absinthe type (of which Pernod is outstanding). The French tell us (with a wagging forefinger) not to drink gin or whisky because they destroy the palate's ability to distinguish foods; so do quinine and bitter drinks, we reply. Try them, but be warned in advance that you probably won't like them. But drink something, even if it's a glass of white wine or a cup of coffee.

The *bateaux mouches*, the excursion boats that have been a hallmark of the Seine for years and years, are in the same class with the Eiffel Tower—a *must!* There are many trips of various types throughout the day—starting early in the morning and capping the day off with a midnight cruise on the Seine. The highlight, probably, is the dinner cruise, which begins at 8:30 in the evening. It is a delightful journey along the river, with the monuments along the banks softly illuminated. There is also a lunchtime cruise and an afternoon-tea one. Rates are surprisingly low. All cruises start from the Pont d'Alma, which is at the foot of Avenue Marceau and of Avenue George V. It is a magnificent way of seeing Paris.

Newcomers to the Seine are the *Vedettes Paris-Tour Eiffel*, vista-domed excursion boats leaving every twenty minutes or so from the Iena Bridge on the Left Bank. It's an hour-long cruise that is not at all expensive. In the evenings there are "Illumination Cruises," at 9:30 and 10 o'clock. The cruise, if you wish, can include a visit to a wine cellar near the Eiffel Tower and a tasting of its various products.

French newspapers are oddities to our way of thinking; you probably won't use them too much. The English-language *International Herald-Tribune* is a gold mine for tourists, listing important events, shows, gala performances, and exceptional financial coverage. A commercial booklet appearing weekly is the *Semaine de Paris*, or Paris Week, which lists in detail all matters of interest to tourists, including 367 (or more!) night clubs.

Attending *church* at a famous house of worship is a memorable experience. There is frequently a small charge for a seat, and two collections are taken. The American Cathedral at 23 Avenue George V (for all Protestants) has Sunday service at 10:45. The American Church in Paris is nondenominational and holds Sunday service at 11 A.M. at 65 Quai d'Orsay. The Liberal Synagogue (Jewish) is at 25 Rue Copernic and holds services Friday evening at 6, Saturday morning at 10:30. The Paris Mosque, 1 Place du Puits-de-l'Ermite, is open daily except Fridays from 2 to 6 and is interesting for a visit if you've never seen a mosque.

When meeting a French lady (if you're a man, that is) don't kiss her hand if she's unmarried. (How can you tell? Look at her hand and see if she's wearing a wedding ring? But if she's wearing gloves? Ah, well, listen carefully when you're introduced.) Although people in France like to shake hands when meeting and departing, don't shake hands with a lady unless she offers you her hand first; this is basically true for a man, not for a woman.

Paris is divided into twenty *arrondissements*, which are something like small boroughs with their own local administration, the *mairie*. The numbers of these various political subdivisions are used in much the same way we put postal zone numbers on our mail. An address bearing a street address ending with "1" or with the French abbreviation for *first* (1er), for example, means that it is in the first, or *premier*, *arrondissement*. Most of the tourism attractions are in the first (the Louvre, Place Vendôme, for example), the sixth (the Latin Quarter) and the eighth (Champs-Elysées, Place de la Concorde).

A *kilometer* is about 62 percent of a mile; for very rough calculations, multiply by 0.6. Thus, 60 kilometers equals slightly more than 36 miles. A *kilogram* (also called a kilo) equals 2.2 pounds. *Grams* are confusing for weight measurements, but 100 grams is roughly equal to 3½ ounces; our pound (16 ounces) equals 453 grams. In fluids, a *liter* equals 0.946 of an American quart. An American gallon (say, of gasoline) equals 3.78 French liters. As a rough yardstick, consider 4 French liters as slightly more than 1 American gallon.

Before investing heavily in *antiques* or *paintings*, take them (on memorandum) to the Chambre Syndicale des Experts, 8 Rue Bonaparte (DANton 4736), Tuesdays through Saturdays, 10–12 and 3–7. Allow twenty-four hours for an expert opinion.

French *banks* are calculated to drive Americans crazy. It takes forever to complete simple transactions, so, unless absolutely necessary, avoid them. Letters of credit, for this reason, are seldom practicable (unless for very substantial amounts of money) because of the time consumed in cashing them. Businessmen who have to deal with French banks receive our deepest sympathy. In Paris, the banking hours are 9 A.M. to noon and 2 to 4 P.M. The banks are closed Saturdays. At the railroad stations, the Invalides air terminal and the airports there are all-day currency-exchange service. On Saturdays, in the middle of Paris, a convenient exchange is the bank (but it takes time) on the corner of Rue Bassano and the Champs-Elysées—just up from Avenue George V.

The *sewers of Paris* (*les égouts*) provide a rather special form of entertainment. If you've ever read Hugo's *Les Misérables*, they may make an interesting trip, particularly if there are children in your party. You'll walk on a sort of shelf above the water; sometimes the attendants take you in boats. The tour groups meets at the Statue de Lille in the Place de la Concorde at 2, 3, 4 and 5 P.M. (from May 1 to July 1) on the second and fourth Thursdays of the month. Same hours every Thursday from July 1 to October 15.

The *catacombs* are a little on the gruesome side, but loads of people like them. Gather at 2 Place Denfert-Rochereau on the first and third Saturdays of the months at 2 P.M. from October 15 to July 1. From July 1 to October 15, every Saturday at 2.

Children in Paris are lucky. It's a wonderful place for them, filled with all sorts of delights. First, there's the Eiffel Tower and the ride up will thrill most (usually to speechlessness). A ride on a *bateau mouche* up and down the Seine is almost inevitable and should be a source of pleasure. For children who want to compare French and American zoos, several are available—the one at Vincennes requires a long ride, but the display is unusually good. There is a small zoo, half-Coney Island, at the Jardin d'Acclimation. A museum is combined with a zoo at the Jardin des Plantes, 57 Rue Cuvier. There are two (count them) aquariums in the Musée France-d'Outremer.

Two *circuses* hold forth in Paris and are definitely worth seeing by adult or child, providing you are in town at the proper time. Cirque de Montmartre (63 Boulevard Rochechouart) gives shows from September through April daily plus matinees except Tuesdays at 9 P.M., Thursdays and Saturdays at 3. Cirque d'Hiver begins in October and quits when the mood strikes the management (or business falls off), with evening performances each night except Fridays at 9, matinees Mondays, Thursdays and Saturdays at 3, Sundays at 2:15.

Punch and Judy shows are a Paris institution. When the weather permits, try the Luxembourg Gardens for performances daily at 4 from July through October. At other times of the year, ask for details, although there are usually performances on Thursdays and Sundays, the French children's holidays, which are apt to be fairly crowded.

The *bird market* (*marché aux oiseaux*) is not so much for the birds as it is for children; Sunday mornings at Place Louis-Lepine (Cité station on the *métro*). The *dog market* (*marché aux chiens*) is open every Sunday from 1 to 4, but can you hold out against a small child who simply must buy every cute dog in sight? Harden your heart or don't go. The *stamp market* is easier to cope with; after all, how heavy can a stamp get? This may be visited every Thursday, Saturday and Sunday almost all day long. The traders meet in the vicinity of Marigny and Gabriel avenues. The *horse market* (*marché aux chevaux*) delights most animal lovers of any age; horses, donkeys and mules are displayed for sale on Mondays, Wednesdays and Fridays, from 9 to 1, at 106 Rue Briancion.

PARIS HOTELS

A series of new, usually large-capacity hotels is beginning to appear on the Paris scene. The current building trend, historians point out, began back in 1966 with the construction of the 492-room Paris Hilton. Until then no new luxury hotel had been built in Paris since the George V in 1933. After the Paris Hilton came the Sofitel Bourbon and, at Orly Airport, the Hilton Orly, the Air Hotel and the Frantel. From then on hotels (and plans for them) expanded—example, the Saint-Jacques, on the left bank, which opened in 1972, and the Meridien, at Porte Maillot. These last two are extremely large hotels, with every facility.

Paris has lots of hotels—1,400 with 60,000 rooms. A baker's dozen or so of these are the tops—four-star deluxe. Some 51 are in the next lower category, four stars; and 141 are three stars. Two-star and three-star hotels make up about two-thirds of the hotel rooms available.

Many factors will dictate your choice of available hotels: price, location, modernity, for example. Let's consider the luxury hotels first; then go on to popular-priced establishments and finally the economy spots for budget travelers. Needless to say, the following are only suggestions because, as we said, Paris has many hundreds of hotels.

Deluxe Hotels

The tariffs vary in the leading hotels, but $50 or higher would not be unusual.

Ritz: Probably the single most famous hotel in Paris, with an international reputation. Magnificent location on the Place Vendôme, but unfortunately only suites face the front. Large, elegant, old-fashioned rooms in the grand style.

Meurice: Located on a quiet side street that is sandwiched between the Rue de Rivoli and Rue St.-Honoré. Well run, excellent, among the least expensive of the luxury hotels; however, most single rooms are not too large and face a court, rather than the front.

Intercontinental-Paris: This well-located hotel has been completely remodeled into a lovely modern hotel, but retains old French atmosphere. Excellent accommodations, several restaurants. Operated by the Inter-Continental hotel chain.

George V: Without a doubt, the most popular hotel in Paris with American tourists; almost all the help speak English. Lively, busy, almost jumping with excitement on occasion. Most rooms are of fairly good size. Very popular with the Hollywood, theatrical and dress designer set.

Prince de Galles: Next door to the George V, but with a

completely different personality. Subdued and quiet as a rule; most rooms are very nice and furnished in contemporary style.

Plaza Athénée: An extremely fine hotel, still preserving its original atmosphere; popular with the French, so that should furnish a clue. Many, but not all, rooms are of good size and pleasantly furnished.

Crillon: A classic luxury hotel located on a tremendously busy traffic circle, the Place de la Concorde. Somewhat run down and vaguely behind times. Most rooms are extremely old-fashioned, but the redecorated ones are pleasant.

Bristol: Centrally located on the Faubourg St.-Honoré, this distinguished hotel specializes in wealthy patrons who can pay its high rates. Most rooms are beautifully furnished, and almost all, even ordinary double rooms, have small sitting rooms. Quiet and elegant *and* expensive.

Lancaster: An excellent smaller hotel located on a mediocre side street off the Champs-Elysées, but the rooms are beautifully furnished; the hotel atmosphere is very pleasant.

Hilton: New, modern, contemporary and equipped with all the time-savers and conveniences—plus interesting restaurants and bars—that are the hallmarks of Hilton everywhere; nicely situated near the Seine and the Eiffel Tower.

Lotti: Very nice accommodations, almost bordering on the luxury type. Good-size, often very large, rooms. Just off the Place Vendôme and Rue St.-Honoré and next door to the Intercontinental.

Royal Monceau: A good hotel, pleasantly located near the Etoile. Most rooms are of comfortable size; a few are quite large.

L'Hotel: A very deluxe small hotel, individually decorated rooms, good service, and of course, very expensive.

Note: Other deluxe hotels include the Majestic, Raphael and Sofitel-Bourbon.

POPULAR-PRICED HOTELS

In this category, many hotels charge almost luxury hotel prices for their best rooms. Figure on about $25 to $30 for a double room. Tariffs can be lower but don't count on that too much; they can also be higher.

Ambassador: A large, bustling hotel fronting onto the busy Boulevard Haussmann. Nice rooms, typical furnishings, conveniently located for businessmen.

Scribe: An extremely busy and popular hotel, also very convenient for businessmen. Rooms are good-size and traditionally furnished.

Castiglione: A comparatively modern hotel (for Paris) located on the Faubourg St.-Honoré, the best shopping street. Rooms are mostly small to average in size, but very pleasant.

Claridge: A large, very popular hotel in the center of everything, facing the lively Champs-Elysées. Rooms are moderate size and only the suites face the front.

D'Iéna: Small, pleasant old-fashioned hotel. Rooms are average size but pleasingly furnished. Popular with airline personnel.

Napoléon: One of the better popular hotels, quite modern, very pleasant atmosphere. Not far from the Etoile.

St. James et d'Albany: An older, but well-maintained hotel on the Rue St.-Honoré. Average to large rooms, traditional furnishings.

California: Near the Champs-Elysées. Rather modern and friendly atmosphere; most rooms are good size and neatly furnished.

Lutetia: On the Left Bank, this block-front hotel is very popular and low-priced. Some rooms are quite nice, others are rather small and old-fashioned.

ECONOMY HOTELS

D'Angleterre: An unpretentious, small hotel. Rooms are none too large but the atmosphere is pleasant.

Du Printemps: Slightly away from the center of town near the St.-Lazare railroad station. Hotel is well maintained; rooms are quite satisfactory.

Grand Hotel du Louvre: Well located near the Louvre. Old-fashioned, but offers good value.

PARIS RESTAURANTS

The biggest breakthroughs in the Paris cuisine scene in recent years have been made by establishments patterned—or, anyway, named—after American and English institutions. The *Drug Store*, near the Arch of Triumph, is one of the most exhilarating places in Paris day or night—and the dishes, drinks and fountain specialties it offers are nothing like those in the corner drugstore back home. A companion of the Arch of Triumph—Champs-Elysées Drug Store has been installed on the Boulevard St.-Germain, on the Left Bank—and that, too, is very successful. Other establishments of a similar nature are now cropping up. The ones at the Opéra and at the Rond-Point are particularly magnificent.

You owe it to yourself, too, to drop in at the *Sir Winston Churchill Pub*, which is in the Arch of Triumph area, also. This is better, and more fun, than any "pub" you're likely to come across in England. There are brass fixtures, comfortable leather banquettes, a variety of drinks and interesting foods (even yogurt and cherry ice cream).

As for Paris' traditional restaurants, there are thousands of them. No list could possibly hope to do more than merely skim the surface. Any Parisian could add a dozen more good restaurants, and no two people would agree on a single list. The list that follows is intended to point out some of the renowned, plus a selection of less-known es.ablishments.

Pointer: It is absolutely essential to phone for a table reservation for dinner at the better Paris restaurants; otherwise, your trip may be in vain. Your hotel's telephone operator or the hotel concierge can make the reservation, or you can do it yourself if you can manage the few necessary words in French. But be sure to phone ahead for a reservation if you're going to an important restaurant.

THE LEADING HIGH-PRICED RESTAURANTS

Lapérouse is often regarded as Paris' outstanding restaurant; with this, we would heartily concur. Over the years, we have never had anything but superb food.

Maxim's: As much a night club as it is a restaurant. Although the food is good, the big attractions here are the Gay Nineties atmosphere, the celebrities, the exciting Parisian atmosphere. Dress on Friday nights.

Tour d' Argent: For oil magnates, Hollywood producers on expense account and other fortunates; prices are often astronomically high. Almost everything is well prepared and served in one of Paris' handsomest dining rooms.

Grand Vefour: Marvelous food, but since the proprietor became a television personality, the service leaves much (repeat, much) to be desired. Just the same, the food should be exceptional.

Lasserre: An elaborate, very expensive restaurant with lovely, elegant surroundings and, we think, Americanized French food. There are those who swear by it. Others think it ordinary.

Allard: Another miniature place, about as simple and unpretentious as a restaurant can get; you must make a reservation. Topnotch food with the best *coq au vin*, chicken in wine, in Paris. For serious eaters.

Lucas Carton: Dining in the great tradition of Paris. Excellent food, high prices, gracious atmosphere, very sophisticated.

Taillevant: Has the same qualities as Lapérouse or Lucas Carton—chiefly because it, too, will only serve the very best.

San Francisco: The best Italian restaurant in Paris, and for all we know, maybe the very best Italian restaurant in the world.

Chez Garini: An exceptional but expensive restaurant; be sure to have the fish soup and the trout.

SEAFOOD RESTAURANTS

Prunier: Serves excellent fish dishes. Far from inexpensive but often remarkably good. Be sure to order their specialty, scallops—if you like scallops.

Drouant: Also highly recommended for all fish preparations. The *bouillabaisse* is Drouant's proudest achievement.

STEAK RESTAURANTS

Let's clear up one point immediately; French steaks are not the same as American. In addition, Frenchmen like their steaks blood rare, and if you don't make a point of specifying exactly what you want at the time of placing the order, that's the way it will be served. For well done, ask for *bien cuit*; for medium, *à point.*

Dagorno: For hungry Americans who want a tremendous cut of steak grilled over a charcoal fire.

Cochon d'Or: More than a steak restaurant, with a good selection of other dishes. A good place for a meat-eating male and a less carnivorous female.

Boeuf Couronne: Pretty good, too.

All three of these restaurants are alongside each other and you could hardly go wrong.

Note: The Paris Hilton is famous—and justly so—for its American-style steaks.

OTHER GOOD RESTAURANTS

Boule d'Or: Slightly out of the tourist area, but the food is extremely good. Worth the short ride to try their *quiche Lorraine*, a custard, cheese and bacon pie.

Au Pactol: On the Left Bank, this is an interesting and good restaurant serving a very complete dinner for a fair price. Offers a good value, all things considered.

Petit Bedon: A small, sophisticated restaurant serving excellent food. Not inexpensive but very pleasant.

La Colombe: A tiny place with loads of atmosphere. The food is good, although not extraordinary, but the atmosphere is absolutely charming—Ludwig Bemelmans' murals, candlelight, with classical music played on a guitar. Particularly recommended for honeymooners and romantics.

Chez Mercier: An unpretentious place, just off the Champs-Elysées. Ideal for a simple lunch or dinner at moderate prices.

Coconnas: At the end of the Place des Vosges, an attractive old Paris square. Food is quite good, not too expensive; try their chicken in a pot.

Rôtisserie de la Reine Pédauque: Perfect for the hearty trencherman. A big, many-coursed meal, all the wine you want; a fixed, reasonable price.

Raffatin and Honorine: Features marvelous hors d'oeuvres and a wide selection of desserts; so much, that it's seldom necessary to have a main course. Moderately expensive.

FINE FOOD REGARDLESS OF SURROUNDINGS

Chope d'Orsay: Extremely tasty food, sometimes simple dishes, sometimes complicated preparations. Eat in the dining room upstairs.

Au Petit Coq: Specializes in seafood, but also has some interesting meat and poultry dishes; delightful atmosphere and moderately priced.

Chez Michel: Serves a very large meal at a fixed price; enormous selection of dishes. A great value providing you're hungry.

Lescure: A family-style, overly crowded *bistro*, but can be loads of fun. Mobbed at lunchtime, because it's just about the only low-priced spot near the Place de la Concorde.

La Grille: Marvelous food at moderately expensive prices, slightly out of the tourist area; meat dishes are particularly good.

L'Oenothéque: Designed especially for wine-lovers. It serves good meat dishes, but primarily those that best accompany wines. Wines can be ordered by the glass or half bottle only. For a wine-tasting party, try to go with four or six people.

Restaurant Lucien: Very small, with only eight tables; well-prepared food at fair prices, pleasant atmosphere.

❧ Short Trips from Paris

The French government and Paris municipal authorities have excellent tourist information facilities. The best all-around information service is the Welcome-to-France office at 7 Rue Balzac (on the right-hand side of the Champs-Elysées as you look toward the Arch of Triumph). They'll be able to give you information on everything from train schedules to where to find a hairdresser that's open on Monday and speaks English. They are open every day in the week—every day—from 9 A.M. to midnight. There is also a French government tourist office at 127 Avenue des Champs-Elysées. For advice on train excursions, reduced fares and ticket buying, the French railroads (SNCF) makes it easy for you by having offices at 127 Champs-Elysées (the same place as the government tourist office) and 16 Boulevard des Capucines. Attendants in these places speak English and are very courteous to visitors. The hours are 8:30 to 6:30, except Sunday.

When visiting cathedrals and churches, visitors are on their own, although there generally are guided tours in English. At museums, chateaux and monuments, it is usually necessary to take the guided tour. You're not allowed to wander about on your own. The guided visits generally last about thirty minutes. In the very popular centers, such as Versailles and the main chateaux of the Loire, guides speak English. Elsewhere, they come close to understandable English—but often not close enough. If the guide has been helpful, give him a tip of a franc or two. American Express has regular excursion trips to the major points in the general area of Paris, although the coverage of the eastern zone (Rheims, Compiôgne, Château-Thierry, etc.) is not quite so frequent as in other zones (Fontainebleau, Chartres, Versailles, for example). On all excursion buses, regardless of the company, there will be a translation in English. The guides on the American Express buses speak *only* English. Day-long excursions generally do not include lunch in their tariffs, so check this. But lunch is usually inexpensive, or a reasonable facsimile thereof. The tour operator picks out some moderately priced, convenient place where you can eat a complete meal inexpensively. If there are small children in your group, check about children's rates; these vary with the tour operator. On the railroad, children's rates are uniform: those from four to ten years old travel for half fare; under four, the ride is free, and you have our sympathy. Oh, yes: If you're following a railroad timetable, keep in mind that schedules can (and often do!) change on the last Sundays of May and September. Any changes are usually small, however, and they are very rarely on the short runs.

Versailles

There is very frequent train service in both directions out of the Gare Montparnasse. By car, you leave Paris by Porte St.-Cloud (in the southwestern part of town) via a choice of routes. N-307 goes through a tunnel and then connects with a main highway (the western *autoroute*), with a subsequent left turn (D-182) to Versailles. Or, take N-10 from Porte St.-Cloud, which passes through Sevres (with an opportunity to visit the porcelain factory). The showroom here is open daily from 9 to 6, closed Saturday afternoons; the factory may be visited from 2 to 5 weekday afternoons.

Versailles is enormous, lavish and unbelievable. Now that boring high school history lesson about the French Revolution that you may have dozed through will come alive, peopled with all the figures of those wonderful and horrible days. There is much to see—the Palace and the Gardens, the Trianons (Grand and Petit), the museums and also the surrounding area. But hours must be watched carefully. The Palace is open every day from 10 to 5; small admission charge. The Trianons are closed Tuesdays; open all other days in the afternoons only, 2–6. Madame de Maintenon's apartment may be seen daily except Tuesdays from 2 to 5. (Confusing, but not impossible.)

Avoid Tuesdays and Sundays; Tuesday is poor because many places are closed, and Sunday is overcrowded. However, the fountains in Versailles Park play on the first and third Sundays in each month at 4:45, so if you want to see this spectacle, you'll have to put up with the crowds. But be forewarned, for trains and roads are often jammed. You might stay overnight at the luxurious Trianon Palace Hotel if you want to do a thorough sightseeing job on Versailles.

EXTENSION TRIP FROM VERSAILLES TO CHARTRES ¶ Leaving Versailles by car via route N-10, the road skirts Rambouillet, but you should turn in and visit Rambouillet, with its interesting chateau and dense surrounding forest. The chateau is the summer residence of the president, but is open to the public when the prez is in Paris trying (desperately) to balance the national budget. Visit the tremendous National Sheep Farm, even if you don't care for lamb chops. Don't plan on staying overnight here; no lodging can be recommended. Leave Rambouillet via N-10 (by getting back onto the highway) or by a more countrified road, N-306, later joining N-154 to Chartres, about twenty-five miles distant. The *Chartres Cathedral* is so impressive and so architecturally magnificent that no visitor, regardless of how casual or calloused about routine tourist sights, should omit it. Its two towers differ in size and design, but the overall effect is homogeneous; the rose-colored glass in the cathedral windows is electrifyingly beautiful. The town of Chartres itself has twelfth- and thirteenth-century houses; the Chartres museum features fine old tapestries and medieval objects. By train, there is passable service from Paris' Gare

Montparnasse and a round trip can easily be accomplished in a day. You could, if you wish, stay overnight at the Hôtel de France; the Vieille Maison is an excellent restaurant.

Leaving Chartres, it is possible to return by an alternate route if time permits. Head north on N-154 to Dreux, which has an interesting chateau, a large forest and many fine, old buildings. From Dreux, take N-12 eastward toward Paris via Versailles.

Fontainebleau

Fontainebleau lies south of Paris. Train service is somewhat erratic, and schedules from the Gare de Lyon should be carefully checked. By auto, leave by Porte d'Italie on route 7; the distance is about thirty-eight miles. You'll soon be driving through the vast Forest of Fontainebleau. The Royal Chateau is, of course, the big attraction in Fontainebleau and, if anything, is more appealing than the one at Versailles. Here is an opportunity for a Tuesday excursion, for unlike almost every other high spot in France, the chateau is open every day from 10 to 12 and 1 to 5. Famous tenants of the chateau included just about every ruler from the twelfth to nineteenth century; Louis VII, Marie Antoinette and Napoleon are among those who lived here. If you want to visit the quaint little village of Barbizon, drive west from Fontainebleau on N-837 until you come to a right turn toward Barbizon. Famous residents of that artistic town included Robert Louis Stevenson, Daumier, Corot, Millet, Rousseau. If you wish, return from Fontainebleau to Paris via Melun, going north via N-5.

The woods around Fontainebleau, by the way, are full of all manner of game. Quail (*caille*) is a specialty on menus in the area. The Gorges de Franchard restaurant is in a nice setting and serves excellent dishes.

Valley of the Marne

In the plains and valleys to the northeast of Paris, American history is uniquely and eternally tied to France. The doughboys of World War I and the GIs of World War II know the area well. Many Americans fought and died there and have made it hallowed ground for their countrymen. Names like Château-Thierry, Belleau Wood, Soissons, Compiègne and Rheims are monuments to America's fighting men.

Trains from the Gare de l'Est serve some of these points on the same line—but not all of them. So it will be necessary, if you're going by train, to break up this visit into two days. Excursion buses are not much help, either. They cover some but not all of these places, and not very frequently, either.

The handiest way to go is by drive-yourself car. Take route 3 at the Porte de Pantin. Just before Meaux there is a roadside memorial to the famous World War I French general who requisitioned Paris taxis to take the troops off to battle. When you get past Montreuil, watch for the signs and the side road that leads to the American cemetery of Belleau Wood. Once you get back to route 3, be on the lookout for another road—this time, off to the right—which will take you to Hill 204, a famous battle-ground in the Château-Thierry phase of the war. There is a fine nostalgic view of the Valley of the Marne. Château-Thierry, aside from its war fame, is remembered also as the home of the fabled writer Jean de La Fontaine. His birthplace can be visited from 10 to 12 and 2:30 to 6:30 except on Tuesday. The fee is 1 franc (20 cents).

At Rheims, the celebrated schoolhouse where the World War II armistice was signed is just across the railroad tracks from the center of town, not far from the railroad station. The *salle de guerre*, its walls covered with war maps, is on the first floor. Seats around the table are arranged the way they were on the day the Nazis put their signatures on the dotted line. Visits are possible from 9 to 12 and 2 to 6 (except Tuesday, again) for 50 centimes (10 cents).

Most of France's kings, starting with Clovis (the first one), were crowned at Rheims. The sumptuous cathedral was the site of the coronation. This is the cathedral, remember, with that "Smiling Angel," who winsomely looks down from the North Porch. There are guided visits of the cathedral, and also the tower, from 9 to 11 and 2 to 5. These are arranged by the local tourist office (the *syndicat d'initiative*) and are usually in English. There is an extra small charge for the tower visit. By the way, something like seventy yards separates the bottom step from the top of the tower—so you have to be more than strong in spirit to make this trip. Strong legs are definitely required.

Rheims, of course, is in the heart of the champagne country. We haven't worked this out on a computer, but as we figure it, there are 25,000 acres of champagne vines in the Rheims-Epernay area, and 18,000 wine growers. The bubbly stuff is stored in caves that wind around (underground) for more than 125 miles. Sampling the vintage at one of the houses is easy, and visiting a typical cellar is just as simple. Just walk right in. Moët & Chandon, Mercier, Veuve Clicquot and Mumm's are some of the find old champagne "names" that will welcome you for a visit. In Rheims an excellent place to eat—you have to do more than just quaff champagne— is the Florence restaurant, across the park from the railroad station.

To round out your visit of this historic area in the northeast of France, return to Paris from Rheims by route 31. At Soissons, take time out to peek in the refectory of the ancient St.-Jean-des-Vignes monastery. Not a meal has been served in the splendid refectory in a very long time, but it is a nice scene to contemplate. This can be done between 9 and 1:30 and 3:30 and sundown. There is no fixed fee, so give a franc or two as a gratuity.

As you approach Compiègne be on the lookout for a turn to the right. It is about four miles from town and will guide you to the open patch in the forest where the armistice for World War I was signed. There is also a replica of the railway car in which the signing was done. (The Germans, when they came back in World War II, stole the original one.) You can visit the railway car just about all day. The actual hours are 8 to 7. The fee is merely a half franc.

Compiègne is crammed with things to see. Its palace, for example, should be close to the top of your list— especially Marie Antoinette's apartment. Guided tours are every half-hour. The city also has an intriguing automobile museum, open from 10 to 12 and 2 to 5. There is a small entrance fee—and even smaller on Sunday (but the place is crowded). The palace visit has the same time and price.

Getting back to Paris from Compiègne is no problem: there are lots of signs. If you are an inveterate watcher of highway numbers, then take route 32 to Senlis, then route 17, and finally into Paris on route 2.

Troyes

This city, not quite a hundred miles southeast of Paris, is off the path that tourists keep beating all the time, but we suggest a visit. Why? Well, first let's tell you how to get there. Train service from Gare de l'Est is excellent. The sightseeing companies don't serve Troyes, so that leaves a choice of either the train or drive-yourself car. By car, leave by the Porte de Bercy and follow route 19. The town of Provins is just about halfway, and this is worth a visit and look-around. Provins is a split-level town right out of the feudal times. The St.-Jean gateway and the miniature houses crammed around the Place du Châtel will fascinate you. We think so, anyway.

Troyes is the old-time knitting center of France, and in the museum there you can see how styles have changed —and fortunately!—in many knitted articles. All manner of knitted articles are displayed, covering (almost!) a century of progress, from 1830 to 1925. Also, the museum presents a stunning selection of men's and women's bathing suits from the turn of the century to more recent days. Possibly the most glamorous items of all, however, are the silk stockings that were a favorite of Louis XVI and other gentlemen of his era.

The Knitting Museum—that is of *bonneterie* (literally, hosiery)—is in the Hôtel de Valluisant, a few blocks from the railroad station. In the same building is the Historic Museum of Troyes and Champagne (not the wine, the *district*). The big item here is a collection of folkloric costumes. The twin museums are open daily from 10 to 12 and 2 to 6 except Wednesdays. The entrance fee is small. If you're a dedicated museum-goer we'll let you in on a little bargain. A combination ticket available at either the Beaux Arts or the Knitting Museum entitles you to visit both at a slight reduction. The Beaux Arts Museum, incidentally, is across town, near the cathedral.

There are nine old churches in Troyes, and each one of them has something of interest. We're not going to give you all those details now. But we will say that very few churches in France still have the old-style chancel screen, or *jubé*, and the one in Ste.-Madeleine's is among the finest in existence.

Troyes has its old quarter, too; an intriguing point of view is the tiny Ruelle des Chats—the Little Street of

Cats. It's not that the place is filled with cats. It is merely that the houses are so small and close together—almost forming a canopy over the street—that the cats can leap from one rooftop to another on the other side without any difficulty. This picturesque street is just behind the Hôtel de Ville.

The pork of the Troyes region is renowned, and just about every restaurant features *andouillettes* as an entrée. They are made from pork tripe shaped like a sausage, are a grayish white, and are roasted or fried. Restaurants also like to use champagne freely in preparing their dishes. The new Café de Paris restaurant serves better-than-average food at fair prices. On the way back to Paris from Troyes you can take route 19 and route 373 to Sézanne, then go home via route 4.

Beauvais

Route 1, starting at the Porte de la Chapelle, will bring you to this northern French city, which is associated with one of the finer things of life: French needle-point. (No excursion buses to Beauvais, but good train service from Gare du Nord.)

Beauvais is only forty-eight miles away on the direct road. If you have time and wish to do some additional sightseeing, take the slower route. You could go to Beauvais, for instance, by way of Chantilly, following route 16 and route 31. As an alternate sightseeing route, on the way back travel via St.-Germain-en-Laye. The roads to follow in that case would be route 327 and route 184. (And if you are detouring in these ways, don't forget to see whether *crème Chantilly*, whipped cream, tastes as good on its home grounds as it does everywhere else. The viewing from the terraces at St.-Germain, too, are magnificent.)

The cathedral at Beauvais is a good starting point for your visit. Cathedral-goers exult about the nave of the cathedral at Amiens, the façade of the one at Rheims and the bell tower at Chartres. But when they mention or think of Beauvais, it is the choir, or sanctuary. The Gothic vault over the altar is the highest in the world—something like 163 feet.

One of the many prides of the cathedral is the collection of twenty tapestries of the fifteenth, sixteenth and seventeenth centuries. For several years, eight of these tapestries (representing Acts of the Apostles) have been removed from the walls while undergoing restoration and minute repairs. But from what the officials told us, they all should be back in place now.

The needlepoint industry of Beauvais was destroyed during World War II, and all the old-time tapestry workers have moved to the Gobelins factory in Paris. But the needlepoint spirit is still alive in Beauvais. It is a very precise art. The experts produce about one square yard of fine point in a *year*.

Just starting on its second century of existence is the cathedral's famed astronomical clock, which was built between 1865 and 1868 by a local civil engineer. From a proud sign on the clock we read that this monumental timepiece reproduces on fifty-two dials the movements of the stars and the tides, as well as the civil and church calendar. It tells you, also, the current time in eighteen cities of the world (including New York), and at the top there is a reproduction of the Last Judgment. From little windows in the façade peek personages of church and state—such as the pope, Napoleon III, the prefect, the bishop, the engineer and the *curé*.

The cathedral *gardien* gives guided tours of the clock (in French only, alas!) at noon, 2, 3, 4, 5 and 5:45. This tour can be followed up, if you wish, by a look at the Treasure Room for a small charge. There are some fine enamel works of the sixteenth century and also some unusual-looking musical instruments—that is, if an instrument shaped like a serpent is considered unusual! The *gardien* will conduct you into the Treasure Room almost any time. Try to be in the cathedral at noon or 6 P.M., because there are carillon concerts then.

Easily the most splendid window in the north of France is the stained-glass panel in the church of St. Stephen. The glasswork, known as the "Tree of Jesse," is a bit hard to find, so be patient. Incidentally, it is only about half of its original size. Part of it was chopped away during the French Revolution to make way for a door when the church was used as a warehouse. The church and the cathedral are open from 7 to 12:30 and 1:30 to 7 P.M.

The Hôtel de Ville is right in the center of town. It is a good-looking building in itself, but it is also a historic one. In one of the big rooms looking onto the square, Marshal Foch was chosen Allied commander in World War I. The square is named Place Jeanne Hachette, we forgot to say. But no one in town will forget to tell you who the distinguished lady was. Some five centuries ago, when a Burgundian army marched on the town, Jeanne Hachette took an ax to a soldier ready to scale the ramparts. This opening symbolic gesture inspired the townspeople, the enemy army was repulsed and every year in June since then the young lady has been fittingly remembered in a lively celebration.

The Pignon Pointu restaurant is right on the square. It is one of those northern France-type restaurants, with a cafe downstairs and a dining room on the upper floor. But even though it does not look superior, you will eat well there.

St.-Germain-en-Laye

St.-Germain-en-Laye is only fifteen miles west of Paris. Good train service out of Paris from St. Lazare station. By car, leave Paris via Porte Maillot on N-13. There is a wonderful terrace in St.-Germain with a remarkable view of the Seine in the direction of Paris. The town has its chateau, but frankly it's just another chateau and unless you have a passion for them, this one might be readily omitted. It's closed Tuesdays in case you don't want to see it anyhow, but maybe you will when you learn that Nazi Field Marshal von Rundstedt had his headquarters here during the war. Actually, the charm of St.-Germain lies in the surprisingly countrified, rural atmosphere of the town. If you have no plans to tour rural France and have never seen a typically provincial Gallic town with an open food market, donkeys, pushcarts and similar bucolic attractions, don't miss the market days held on Tuesdays and Fridays. If you want to see the chateau, Friday is the best day for a visit here, because it combines the market with a visit to the chateau. Incidentally, the Hôtel Pavillon Henri IV is often regarded as one of France's outstanding luxury hotels, being beautifully situated and altogether delightful. It was here that Béarnaise sauce was invented, and don't think that the hotel management will fail to have some delicacy on the menu that features that great creation.

A trip here might easily be combined with a visit to Versailles by driving onward from St.-Germain to Versailles on route N-184, a mere eight miles.

Also worth visiting in the immediate Paris area: Enghien-les-Bains, a pleasing lake region with a thermal spa, with waters known for their restorative qualities, plus a gambling casino and similar attractions; good for a few days' rest and quiet away from Paris. Can you stand still another chateau? There's one at Chantilly (sixteenth century), which is open most of the year daily from 1 to 5; better check if going during winter months. The little town of Bougival has absolutely nothing to recommend it, for as French towns go, Bougival is without a single historic site or monument or any other attraction save one—the restaurant Coq Hardi. The exterior of this formidable establishment is bare and unprepossessing, but the interior is glorious French provincial, decorated in delightful fashion and with an exquisite terraced garden. The food specialties include many superb creations, notably a *gratin de homard*, lobster in a rich, toothsome cheese and cream sauce. Also, their poultry roasted over an open fire is superb as will be almost anything that you select. Hardly cheap, but a delightful experience.

❧ Regional Tours of France by Automobile

NORMANDY AND BRITTANY

Paris to Rouen—47 miles

Leave Paris by the Porte Clignancourt and take route N-14. The road passes through Pontoise, Ste.-Clair-sur-Ept and then Ecouis, with its fourteenth-century church, known for many famous statues. Then on to Rouen, a city that endured a terrible pounding during the invasion of Normandy but is now fairly well restored. Entering the city, turn right on either Rue de la République or Rue des Carmes toward the Notre Dame cathedral, a magnificent structure. A few blocks west of the cathedral, on the Rue de la Grosse Horloge, is the famous old building called the Grosse Horloge and its famous clock (with just one hand), dating back more than five centuries. Only a block away is the partially restored Palais de Justice, severely damaged during the war. Also worth seeing are St.-Ouen and Ste.-Maclou churches. Rouen is the city where Joan of Arc was burned at the stake; a commemorative marker appears on the sidewalk (Place du Vieux Marché) where this unhappy event took place.

If the Joan of Arc story interests you, you might like to stroll casually down the Rue St.-Romain, a little street flanking the episcopal palace. Here, on May 29, 1431, there took place the session of the trial in which she was cited to appear on the following day at the Vieux Marché to be burned alive. One sign on the old palace door records this bit of history. On the other side of the doorway another sign says: "In this archiepiscopal palace on Wednesday July 7, 1456, was rendered the sentence of rehabilitation of Joan of Arc." (That did her a lot of good!) In case you walk down to the bridge where her ashes were thrown into the Seine, look down the river about seven miles to the town of Val de la Haye. It was there, at Val de la Haye, that Napoleon's ashes, on being brought home to Paris, were transferred to another boat for the remainder of the journey upriver. I know it's not a thrilling historical item, but it is true.

You could spend quite a bit of time in Rouen, because there is a great deal to see. The Rouen cathedral has a marvelous set of bells. There are fifty-six of them altogether, and they weigh in at 35 tons. A 9.5-ton one is named *Jeanne d'Arc*, what else? Carillon concerts are given frequently. The timetable is posted near the bookstand in the North Tower wing—inside, not outside.

St.-Maclou's church, not far from the cathedral, is interesting because of the oak doorways sculpted (there's a word for you!) in the style of ancient Florence. Another fine church of Rouen is the fourteenth-century St.-Ouen abbey. Its nave is about twenty feet longer than the cathedral's and ten feet longer than Nôtre-Dame's in Paris. St.-Ouen's is near the Hôtel de Ville gardens, so it is especially convenient and worth visiting.

You can't miss Rouen's big clock, because it arches across the street like—well, like an arch. From Easter to September 20 you can climb into the clock tower for a dramatic view of the town and the outlying countryside.

It is open from 10 to 12:15 and 2:30 to 5:30 except Tuesdays. A combination ticket includes the clock tower, the Beaux Arts Museum and the Iron-works Museum, which features a beguiling array of locks and keys. Beguiling, if you like locks and keys.

Other points of interest at Rouen include the Donjon (which is free) and the Museum of Antiquities (small charge—but free on Sunday and holidays). Youngsters will particularly like the Joan of Arc Museum and its story of France.

Rouen has a fine hotel, the Poste, at 72 Rue Jeanne d'Arc. Wonderful food at Relais Fleuri, notably the sole prepared in vermouth (*sole au vermouth*) and *billi-bi*, the smoothest, most luscious, cold cream of mussel soup ever encountered. The Restaurant Couronne has an extraordinarily attractive interior.

On your way to Rouen from Paris on route 14 you can make a cutoff to the left—when a little over halfway—to Les Andelys. Overlooking the Seine is the very imposing Château Gaillard, which Richard the Lion-Hearted put there to block the road to Rouen for the king of France. Richard, among other things, was Duke of Normandy in those days—apparently, they were some days!

Rouen to Caen—84 miles

Leave Rouen by N-180 directly to Honfleur, an old fishing town with a unique wooden church, Ste.-Catherine's. Honfleur used to be a big port in Normandy until it began to gather too much silt, and François I decided to build a new harbor at Le Havre (which wasn't Le Havre at the time, but Havre de Grâce). It was from Honfleur, too, that Champlain set sail on his famous explorations. Honfleur has the kind of port that delights movie directors. The cafes and little restaurants ringing the harbor are nothing *formidable*, but the view is perfect. There is an absolutely delightful place to stay in Honfleur, the Ferme St. Siméon, a small hotel with rather good food. A good choice for a home base while you explore the region.

Those who like ship models might choose to visit a small chapel above the main town, Notre-Dame-de-Grâce. Continue along the sea on N-183, to Deauville and Trouville, twin resort cities connected by the Toques Bridge over the Toques River. The "high" season begins the end of the first week in August and runs through the end of the month, but actually Deauville-Trouville are worth a visit anytime from April through October. Even the winter months have their own nostalgic, mournful charm. The region caters to the wealthy, particularly in the plush hotels of Deauville; Trouville is lively, more popular, less snooty. For a visit in Trouville put up at the Hotel Bellevue. Restaurant A la Sole Normande has about the best food in town.

Continuing along the shore, you pass smaller, quiet resorts filled with British visitors on their holidays— Blonville, with a fine beach, and Villerville, with a renowned hotel, Chez Mahu, famous for its inviting garden filled with trees and flowers. And you can dine very well indeed at Chez Mahu (open from Easter through September) and, of course, seafood is the thing here—shrimp, mussels, sole. Then comes Houlgate and Dives, the spot where William the Bastard (well, it *was* his name!) embarked in that historic year of 1066 for the invasion of England, which feat is more than can be said of Hitler. Cabourg, a mile or so farther on, is a favorite resort of the French "small" businessman or shopkeeper.

Next comes Caen, a city almost completely demolished during World War II but now largely rebuilt. By some miracle, most of the old churches survived the bombardments. These include St.-Jean's, with a belfry tower that slants precisely in the fashion of the Leaning Tower of Pisa.

Caen to Mont-St.-Michel—122 miles

From Caen, take D-22 to Arromanches, about nineteen miles away. Here you can see the remains of the British landing dock, known during the war as Mulberry. Scattered about are skeletons of battered ships, the pitiful ruins and utter desolation of war. The whole debarkation and liberation operation is graphically described in the exhibits at the Arromanches war museum near the beach.

Farther along the beach near Grandcamp and around the bend near Ste.-Mère church are the memorable Omaha and Utah beaches, where American forces landed on June 6, 1944. From Arromanches to Bayeux is six miles by N-814; Bayeux is renowned as the first town to be freed by the Allies—the historic date is June 7, 1944. The small community is built around an admirable cathedral, but the town's pride is the famous tapestry, an extended, winding affair about 231 feet long, although merely 20 inches high, which depicts in bright colors the Norman conquest of England; it may be seen in the local museum. Walk through the old part of town, notably on the Rue Bourbesneur.

From Bayeux proceed to St.-Lô via N-172, Poor St.-Lô was the center of the fiercest fighting of the invasion and was almost completely destroyed. Go from St.-Lô to Coutances via N-172 and then on N-171 to Granville, perched on a peninsula jutting into the ocean. Continue via N-173 to Avranches, where you'll get your first view of Mont-St.-Michel, best seen from the Jardin des Plantes. From Avranches travel to Pontaubault, then pick up N-176 to the fabulous Mont. This remarkable structure dates back almost a thousand years, although most of the construction took place between the eleventh and fourteenth centuries. "The Marvel," as it is frequently called, may easily be the outstanding single tourist attraction in France, if not in Europe. Cars are parked before you enter, and then comes the climb through the Mont's street. On your left there's the famous Hôtel de la Mère Poulard, and farther along is the Hôtel du Guesclin, both good places to stay overnight. Every visitor is duty-bound to try an omelet in one of the restaurants, this constituting the great specialty of the Mont. Summer days, particularly good ones, find the Mont overcrowded and busy with bustling tourists; at night, all is peaceful and serene and wonderful. The surrounding tides are very impressive at certain times of the month; be sure not to venture out onto the sands without checking incoming tides. In the spring, the tides are most exciting the two days before the new moon and two days after the full moon. Moonlit nights are also a great delight.

If your first visit to the Mont takes place during the summer months, you are destined to feel somewhat let down by the rampant commercialism. The local folk can spot an American at fifty paces and frequently shout, "Get your real American coffee here, folks," plus a few cries of "howdy" and "allo." Everywhere there are would-be guides, color postcards and plastic representations of the Mont, and it is difficult to avoid the feeling that a quick departure might be best under the circumstances. But don't despair; continue upward toward the abbey, and you'll soon arrive at the serenity that makes the Marvel what it is, truly a marvel. Be sure to see the cloister, a thirteenth-century structure, one of the most beautiful buildings anywhere in the world. From the cloister, continue on to the refectory, the monks' dining hall. If possible, try to visit the Mont as early in the morning as possible, preferably before 10 A.M.; as an alternative, stay overnight and enjoy the peace and serenity of the Marvel after the daytime visitors depart.

Or, if you want to play it really safe and sound—with no worries about hotel reservations—stay overnight in Rennes, the capital of Brittany, and take an early-morning drive into Mont-St.-Michel. It is only an hour or so away, and the road is good. You can get a tide table, by the way, at the tourist office in Rennes or almost any of the other towns in Normandy and Brittany. The tide table will tell you what days high tides can be expected at Mont-St.-Michel and also their actual times. Incidentally, both Normandy and Brittany have a running argument over who actually possesses Mont-St.-Michel. It apparently is right on the borderline between the two regions. We can't blame each for wanting it. It *is* fabulous.

And, oh yes. We can't leave the northern corner of France without mentioning the Manoir du Vaumadeuc, a fifteenth-century restaurant and inn, at Pléven, on the north coast. It is well worth a detour from wherever you're going. The Manoir is like a private house, charming, delightful and expensive.

BRITTANY AND THE EMERALD COAST

This region really lives by the sea, with strong, heavy green rollers roaring in swiftly, only to crash along the rocky shore; from the tourist point of view, it offers few "sights" of interest, but for a restful vacation it is unexcelled. Its people are simple and unaffected; most of the hotels, while not primitive, offer few of the luxuries of other resorts. The motorist is best advised to follow the coast roads that follow the sea and stop as his inclination directs.

Mont-St.-Michel to Lannion—103 miles

Drive from Mont-St.-Michel to Pontorsin via N-776, then to Dol on N-797, and on to St.-Malo.

St.-Malo and Dinard face each other across a bay; there is service on small motor launches, or *vedettes*. St.-

Malo is a busy port; Dinard is primarily a British resort, filled with red-faced, retired colonels. Farther along is Sables-d'Or, small and attractive. Continuing on N-786 you come to St.-Brieuc, but it is away from the sea and not worth much time, unless you're there during the week beginning September 29 for the annual fair. St.-Quay-Portrieux is built up and social, but Paimpol is a colorful and fascinating fishing port. North from Paimpol about four miles (via N-786-C), there are boats to the island of Bréhat, rocky, primitive and delightfully low key. Take N-786 to Tréguier, where (at adjacent Minihy-Tréguier) there is the tomb of the patron saint of lawyers, St.-Yves, a favorite saint with the local people. Farther along is Lannion, with a twelfth-century church and the innumerable steps leading up to it. From Lannion, head north to Perros-Guirec, a resort with a good-size beach. From this region to Ploumanach and to Trégastel are unbelievable rock formations, twisted and gnarled.

St.-Yves, by the way, figures in a special Brittany institution, called a *pardon*. It is something like a combined pilgrimage and country festival and is enjoyed by all. There are many *pardons* all over Brittany during the summer—some on horseback, others on foot. Always there is singing and dancing, although the day begins with religious services in the local church. These *pardons* are a colorful hangover from the past and are very interesting. The government tourism offices in Brittany will give you a calendar of *pardons*, and you can synchronize your visit through the region with them. Don't forget that hotel space becomes tight during that period.

Lannion to Paris—294 miles

Going back to Paris is swiftly accomplished by N-167 to Guingamp and picking up N-12 to Rennes; from Rennes to Alençon and back to home base, all via N-12.

THE LOIRE VALLEY AND THE
CHATEAUX COUNTRY

This region is one of the most popular with visitors and deservedly so. Unlike other tourist areas, most of its attractions are within comparatively short distances, and sightseeing is easy and pleasant. During the fifteenth century, the victorious British ordered Charles VII out of his capital, and he retired to a life of exile in Tours. Of course, the court moved with him, and members of the nobility vied to build stately homes and thus built up the chateaux country. Although Charles VII was not thinking of tourists, the net result is idyllic, for you can select one location, unpack and settle down for several days, make daily tours in the district and return each evening. Or if desired, two or three places may be used as a base, with trips fanning out in all directions. How many days for the chateaux country? Not less than three or four, but even a week or as much as two weeks (assuming the weather is good) will be enjoyable. The peaceful Loire valley is a region rich in French history and offers calm, placid scenery and very good food. Because tourists come in droves during the fine weather, don't count on driving haphazardly from place to place and finding satisfactory last-minute lodging; the local hotels are good, sometimes excellent, but usually quite small.

By train, service is not bad. About an hour and a half is required from the Gare d'Austerlitz in Paris to Orléans, about two hours to Blois and a half hour more than that to Tours. In addition, bus tours leave frequently from Paris during the summer months. In almost all of the principal cities of the Loire, you'll find local bus tours circling the principal chateaux of the district, particularly those in the vicinity of Tours. However, unquestionably, the best way to see the Loire district is with your own car; driving is pleasant and distances are moderate.

Paris to Orléans—72 miles

It is only about two or so hours from Paris to Orléans via N-20 (leave Paris oddly enough by the Porte d'Orléans). The route is fast and there is little reason to stop, although Arpajon offers an interesting food market, and Etampes has many medieval churches and houses. The city of Orléans marks the beginning of the Loire district, and you might like to have lunch at the Jeanne d'Arc restaurant; be sure to try the Sauvignon wine.

In Orléans the Hôtel de Ville—the old one and the new one—is a convenient starting point for a look-around and getting the feel of this city that calls itself the heart of France. The old Hôtel de Ville is now the Beaux Arts Museum (open 10 to 12, and 2 to 6 except Tuesdays; entrance, small charge). Every bit as fascinating is the new Hôtel de Ville. The concierge will let you do some sightseeing, even showing you the mayor's office and the room in which Francis II died. This is now the *salle de mariages*. There is a tableau on the wall depicting Francis II's death, thus giving the room a historic verisimilitude (or something close to it). Those sculpted ceilings in the Hôtel de Ville will have you looking upward for hours afterward. Orléans is where Joan of Arc routed the English and delivered the city for her countrymen; they remember her each May 7–8 in a magnificent pageant. A big statue of her (on horseback) is in the main square, Le Martroi. You can admire the seasonal flowers that are bunched around it. There are always flowers. If you would like to see some impressive horticultural gardens, detour for a couple of miles to the junction of route 751 and you will pass some dazzling ones. Provided there is time, drop into the cathedral Treasure Room. Some interesting antique crosses, religious ornaments and medals were unearthed during excavations in the crypt back in 1937, and they are on display. The *gardien* in the sacristy will arrange a visit. The combined fee for crypt and Treasure Room is 1 franc.

At night, some of the castles in the Loire valley are illuminated—a splendid show, with sounds and lights. Check with tourist offices in Orléans, Blois, Tours, Angers and Le Mans about nighttime tours. Also, ask them about river cruises.

Orléans to Tours—135 miles

Two roads lead through the chateaux country. N-152 extends from Orléans to Angers; this is the road to the north (right bank) of the Loire River. The south (left bank) road is N-751, and the area is slightly more countrified. You'll want to try both roads, but most of the sights (although not all) are on the south shore. The following section gives the highlights, but there are, needless to say, many delightful small chateaux, castles and points of interest that you'll stumble across on your own. Best of all, for many people, are the restful and pleasing vistas of the rolling countryside and the gentle slopes leading away from the serene river. Tensions ease and the placidity of the region makes itself felt.

Drive along route 152 (north road) past Meung and Beaugency (known for its wine production), where you might stop for a glass of light and palatable Gris-Meunier. At Mer, cross the river (D-112) to Chambord, the largest and most imposing of all the chateaux. Francis I began its construction in 1519; everything was executed on a fabulous, exaggerated scale. To get a few facts out of the way, there are over 400 rooms and a tremendous park surrounded by a twenty-mile wall. What makes Chambord so extraordinary is not the chateau itself but its fantastic roof, with a bewildering assortment of turrets, chimneys, pinnacles, towers, gables, domes and spires. The amazing staircase in the chateau consists of a series of spirals that never meet; people walking up and down pass each other unseen. The chateau is open from 9 to 12 and 2 to 7 during the season and at night there is a floodlit sound-spectacle, which may or may not entertain you.

From Chambord, continue (via D-112 and D-102) to Cour-Cheverny, which, to many, is more interesting because it is lived in even today and contains wonderful furnishings and decorations. In this countrylike setting, away from the cities, you might want to stay overnight at either the Hôtel des Trois Marchands (noted for its food) or Les Vieux Logis.

Take N-765 to Blois, which has its own chateau. The city of about 20,000 inhabitants has a calm, dignified air. In the courtyard of the Blois chateau is a tremendous chunk of stone that the Druids once used as an altar for human sacrifices. This fantastic piece of the past is twenty centuries old; it was found ten miles from the chateau.

Those salamanders—not the real ones—etched on the chateau's outside walls represent the coat of arms of Francis I, who is closely identified with Blois and its grand chateau. Blois has had a great past. It was the political capital of France for two centuries and the home of seven of its kings. The architectural and finishing touches on the chateau are superb. The Francis I staircase, for instance, curls upward in an unusual way. The guide will get a special kick out of asking you to study the optical illusion in the Flemish tapestry on the wall of the Francis I salon. He also likes to make a big *mystère* about all those wooden panels in the workroom of Catherine de Medici and the supersecret ones that hid her secrets (and she had a few!). The one-time secret panels in the woodwork have been pointed to—and at —over and over so many times that they look more obvious than the plain ordinary panels. Still, it's fun to join in the guessing game with the guide. Take our word for it—because we took someone else's—there are 237 panels in the wall. The guide might ask you, so try to remember that, please.

Here's something else to keep in mind: A two o'clock bus makes a circuit of the Chambord and Cheverny chateaux, leaving from the Blois railroad station. The bus operates only on weekends in April and May, but is daily during the summer. In case you have come to Blois by train, this is a handy thing to remember, because the bus gets you to these other chateaux and gets you back to Blois in time for an early evening train to Paris. The bus fare is reasonable. Entrance fees to the chateaux are extra, but are not high. It is customary to give the guide in the chateaux a tip of 1 or 2 francs to show that you are pleased. Opening hours for the chateaux on this circuit are: Blois, 9 to 12 and 2 to 7; Cheverny, 8 to 12 and 1:30 to 6:30; and Chambord, 9 to 12 and 2 to 6.

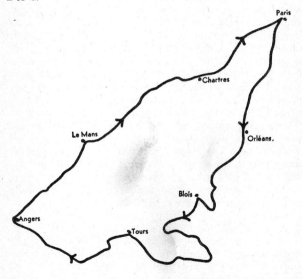

At Blois, lunch at the Rôtisserie Pompadour. Its *poularde* is magnificent. From Blois, via N-751 you proceed to Chaumont, with a not-too-pleasing chateau you might omit. Then to Amboise, serene and restful on the bank of the river. The chateau oversees the town from a high point. Because of its location the only good view of the building is from across the river. Leonardo da Vinci came to the chateau to work and died nearby.

From Amboise to Chenonceaux (via D-31 and N-76) is just a matter of minutes. The latter is probably the most interesting and fascinating of all the chateaux, both architecturally and historically. The beautiful residence was more or less stolen from its former owners by a crafty character named Bohier, whose heirs in turn (as if in retribution) lost it to the king. On his accession to the throne in 1547, Henry II made a gift of this plaything to his mistress, the comely and sexy Diane de Poitiers. When Henry died, his embittered widow, Catherine de Medici, snatched it from her erstwhile rival. The two stories of this loveliest of all chateaux bridge the meandering Cher River and in the most graceful of fashions.

Take D-40 and D-17 to Settes and then N-156 to Valençay, whose local chateau was occupied by Talleyrand, later known as the Duc de Valençay; its gardens are open only from 8 to 9 in the morning.

Heading westward on N-760 through Montrésor brings you to Loches, a fascinating old town, an architectural showplace of the Middle Ages. The castle had its unhappy moments, as the depressing dungeons reveal. There were also gay times when Charles VII's very good "friend," Agnes Sorel, held sway. Be sure to see the Royal Apartments and the Keep. (A *keep* is the strongest and most fortified of all towers, to which the troops could retire in the event of an attack.)

From Loches to Tours on N-143, which leads into N-10. Tours, the capital of the Touraine district, is a comparatively large town, still interesting for a visit although heavily bombed out during the war. There is the Hôtel Métropole (a good base for future trips), with excellent food. This is the place to try specialties of the Loire district and drink Vouvray, a white wine produced only a few miles away. (If you like, drive to Vouvray itself and inspect the cellars and sample the vintages.) Although badly damaged, Tours still retains its cathedral and the Tower of Charlemagne.

Tours to Angers—79 miles

From Tours, cross the Loire River and pick up N-751 to Villandry, with wonderful gardens although the chateau is unimportant. Then on to Azay-le-Rideau, which has led quite a sheltered life with little to relate in the way of murder, political intrigue or infamy, but still full of beauty and quiet delights. The chateau is delicately fashioned, partly thrown across the Indre River and therefore reminiscent of Chenonceaux.

Continue toward Chinon, with its three fortresses guarding the picturesque medieval town. Rabelais, born in nearby La Devinière, spent his childhood here. It was here, too, that a slight, bewildered young girl, Joan of Arc, told Charles VII, then the Dauphin, that he was the real king of France. Chinon is famous for its red wine—light and supposed to have the taste of raspberries, although others say it savors of violets. Regardless, the wines are light and quite drinkable.

On to Saumur, another wine town with a chateau perched on top of a hill. During the last two weeks of July there are displays in the town of Saumur by the Cadre Noir, a brilliant cavalry regiment. A good place for an overnight stay here is the Hôtel Budan. If you wish, a side trip may be made (on N-138) to Montreuil-Bellay, with its miniature chateau. If not, continue on either the north or south road to Angers, situated on both banks of the Maine River. This city has an interesting cathedral and chateau, plus a wine museum. The Anjou is a good hotel; Le Vert d'Eau has excellent Loire River pike, prepared in the classic fashion, with white butter. Try Bourgueil wine—pleasant and flowery and a specialty of the region. From Angers, it is easy to take a short side excursion (via N-161 and N-748) to Brissac, a fortress-chateau with two immense towers. In addition, the interior is beautifully furnished.

Angers to Paris—169 miles (via Le Mans)

From Angers, it is possible to return to Paris by retracing your route (or a similar one) through the Loire valley. For a somewhat different (and faster) route, leave Angers via route 23 to La Flèche, then into Le Mans, Chartres, Versailles and finally Paris.

PARIS TO THE RIVIERA

The itinerary below, which goes from Paris through Vichy, Le Puy, Nîmes and into the Riviera, is a very in-

teresting route, and well worth taking. For those who are in a hurry to reach the Riviera, there is a far more direct route, using the autoroute *(superhighway). You can reach the* autoroute *heading toward the Riviera, by picking it up just outside the Paris city limits, at the Porte d'Orléans, at the southern end of the city. Of course, there's almost nothing to be seen on the* autoroute, *except more cars, but if time is very short, there's no doubt that it's the quickest road to the Riviera. Except of course, on weekends and certain holidays, when the road is jammed beyond imagination. The French government is working hard to complete the road all the way to the Italian border, but the last portion won't be finished for some time to come.*

Paris to Vichy—211 miles

Leave Paris via N-7 (through the Porte d'Italie) toward Fontainebleau, continuing on toward Montargis, an unimportant little town but with the Hôtel de la Poste, known for its fine restaurant. The duckling (*cameton Vallée d'Ouanne*) is superb. Southward to the hamlet of Les Bezards, there is an opportunity for a side trip (turn left onto D-56 to Chatillon-Coligny and its ruined chateau). Otherwise, continue on through Braire to Pouilly, where they produce a fine white wine with a curiously flinty, dry taste. Then on to Nevers, often called the "pointed city" because of its many spires, steeples and sharply angled roofs. From Nevers to Moulins is about thirty-four miles. Moulins was so named because of the many mills built along the Allier River; the chief sight now is the cathedral of Notre-Dame and its fifteenth-century windows. From 2 to 6 it is possible to see the important triptych, a French primitive masterpiece. From Moulins to Vichy; of evil name during occupation days, it is now a city of parks and gardens, famous for its curative (or is it restorative?) waters. You have a choice of several hundred hotels in all price categories. Something is going on all the time (concerts, recitals, the casino) to amuse the many elderly guests, who seek to pass the time while taking the waters.

There is a fine swimming pool at the river's edge, and if you don't care for a plunge, at least you'll enjoy a promenade along the banks of the Allier.

This is cheese country and also the home of the Marquise de Sévigné delights. That's fair warning for those of you who are conscious, or unconscious, about waistlines. But have no fear. The deluxe hotels at Vichy specialize in serving specialties that have a minimum number of calories. Just tell the maître d'hôtel about your diet concern, and he will do the rest.

Vichy to Le Puy—100 miles

Heading southward (on route N-106) from Vichy, you come to Thiers, a town with many fine medieval houses, particularly those near the Corner of Chances (*Coin des Hasards*). There is a Romanesque church, a fifteenth-century chateau and, to be mundane, many cutlery factories. Farther along is Ambert, a one-time paper center but now supporting only a few small plants. The classic rag paper of Auvergne is still made by the old method; see the Mill of Richard de Bas, founded 600 years ago.

The next stopping point is La Chaise-Dieu, with its famous abbey church perched at the highest altitude of any church in France; the fresco of the Danse Macabre is the outstanding feature of interest. Then on to Le Puy (watch for N-106 to change to N-102), a unique spot in the French countryside, having been formed thousands of years ago by volcanic action. The surrounding area is almost level and plainlike, recalling parts of our own Iowa, but the pious folk built (by dint of superhuman labor) the centuries-old cathedral of Notre-Dame du Puy on top of a cliff. To visit the cathedral, it is possible to drive part way up the volcanic peak; then park the car and walk toward the highest point. The big day here is August 15, with a colorful traditional festival. Le Puy is also famous for producing a unique green lentil.

Le Puy to Nîmes—119 miles

Leave Le Puy by N-88, which changes to N-102 after about thirteen miles; approximately seven miles later, be sure to watch for a left turn onto route N-500 in the direction of Pradelles and Langogne—don't miss this turn. Langogne is noted for five enormous medieval towers, which are extremely interesting. At Langogne pick up N-106, passing en route the town of La Gorde-Guerin with more than two dozen fortified houses, built through absolute necessity during troubled days when raids and forays were commonplace.

Then come Villefort, Alès and finally Nîmes, the begin-

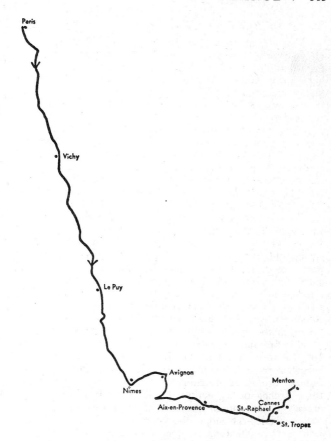

ning of the south, and the tempo of life changes very noticeably here. Nîmes is a busy town, but the pace becomes even livelier late in the afternoon on the streets, in the *zincs* (the small bars) and in the street cafes. Outstanding sights of the town include the *Maison Carrée* (the Square House), a classic temple in the Greek-Roman style, and the immense Roman amphitheater, which is as impressive as the Colosseum in Rome and in much better condition. An overnight stay at the Hotel Imperator is recommended.

Nîmes to Avignon—28 miles

From Nîmes, take N-86 to Remoulins, where you can (if you wish) turn left on N-581 (merely two miles) to Pont-du-Gard, the 2,000-year-old Roman aqueduct bringing spring water a distance of thirty miles to Nîmes; highly recommended. Back at Remoulins, follow N-100 to Avignon, a fascinating place worth a fair amount of sightseeing.

In the latter part of the thirteenth century, papal Italy was being torn apart by various factions. Pope Clement V, in 1305, decreed the removal of the papacy from Rome to Avignon. Five successive popes resided here for the next seventy years, a period during which churches were built, art flourished and Avignon became a sort of international world capital. The festival held during the last two weeks in July features interesting dramatic performances in the famous gardens of Pope Urban V. The Palace of the Popes, often called the most beautiful stronghold in the world, was built partly as a fortress, partly as a residence. Today it remains an impressive sight that no tourist should miss; there are tours lasting an hour at 9, 10, 11, 2, 3 and 4 o'clock, with additional tours at 8 A.M. and 6 P.M. from May through September. Be sure to see the view from the Rock of the Doms, not far from the Palace of the Popes. The old part of Avignon is fascinating, with winding streets, blind alleys and colorful turns, most of which must be seen on foot; the entire town is surrounded by medieval ramparts. The famous bridge at Avignon, Pont St.-Bénézet, extends in three arches partly across the Rhône River; there is a chapel at the end of the first arch. Across the river is Villeneuve-lès-Avignon, the summer residence of the popes; its outstanding sight is the Carthusian monastery. There are good places to establish a home base in Avignon—the Hôtel Europe (known for its excellent food) and the slightly smaller Hôtel Crillon. A delightful place to stay is the Hostellerie le Prieuré, just across the river in Villeneuve-lès-Avignon; in mild weather, it's delightful to eat in the outdoor garden. Eight miles southeast of town (on route N-7) you find, at Noves, the Restaurant La Petite Auberge, one of the great restaurants of France. The duck prepared in a paper bag and the Gigondas wine are particularly worth trying. Incidentally, La Petite Auberge is also a hotel, should you wish to remain overnight; it's very pleasant and popular, so best phone ahead for a reservation.

With Avignon as a base of operations, many fascinating side excursions are possible. Nineteen miles to the east is the Fontaine-de-Vaucluse, or Vaucluse Springs. Follow N-100 to L'Isle-sur-la-Sorgue, a tiny hamlet, and then pick up D-25 to this outstanding tourist attraction. An underground river pours forth water with a almost unbelievable fury—foaming, surging, dashing madly downstream. The ideal time for a visit is during the winter or spring months, when the underground waters are at their highest levels; at other times of the year, the flow, while interesting, may be comparatively tame.

A somewhat longer trip may be made northward from Avignon to Orange, on N-7. Orange, a small town, has two important sights—the Roman theater and the Triumphal Arch. Have a delightful lunch at Le Provençal, which specializes in duck prepared with olives; the local wine is Gigondas. If you like antiquities, drive northeast from Orange to Vaison-La-Romaine, where some marvelous Roman ruins have been excavated, including complete city streets. Return southward on route N-538 to Carpentras, an old town with a fourteenth-century gate and a fine Jewish synagogue, the richest in all France. From Carpentras to Avignon by N-542.

Avignon to Aix-en-Provence—49 miles

Although Avignon is delightful, the time must come for a departure. Leave Avignon to the south by D-570; after crossing the river, there is a left turn onto route N-571, which leads to St.-Rémy-de-Provence. Continue ahead to pick up D-5 to a region of famous antiquities; here are the excavations of Glanum (Les Fouilles de Glanum), including rooms, bath, houses and a temple, all Graeco-Roman, dating back to the second or third century before Christ. Les Antiques, nearby, include a beautifully executed, although partly ruined, municipal arch and a mausoleum. Across the road is the home where Van Gogh spent a year near the end of his life.

Continue on D-5 until it joins with D-27-A, which leads in about three miles to Les Baux. Nearby is one of France's outstanding inns and restaurants; reservations are necessary for one of the limited rooms. The Oustaou de Baumanière has a swimming pool, a terrace and wonderful food; the local wine is called Les Baux de Provence.

Up the hill from the inn stands a sparse, almost deserted village, formerly the stronghold of the cranky, bellicose lords of Les Baux. Only a handful of people now remain there, hard by the deserted shell of a town that once rang with shouts, dancing and pageantry. On moonlit nights, the town walls, the rocks and general atmosphere of desolation are brooding, haunting and romantic.

Les Baux has an outstanding summer festival program. Incidentally, the word "bauxite" comes from this town's name. Aluminumating? (That's a joke.)

Tearing yourself away from Les Baux is a wrench, but you continue on D-78-F, which later changes to D-17, into Arles, with the Hôtel Jules Cesar and the smaller Nord-Pinus, both good. Arles is a small city, ideal for walking about; Julius Caesar founded it in 46 B.C. The "must-see" attractions include the ancient theater, the Arena, the wonderful Romanesque church of St.-Trophime (and its cloister), renowned because of its stark beauty and also because Frederick Barbarossa was crowned there as the king of Arles almost 800 years ago. Near St.-Trophime is the Arlaten Museum, founded by the great poet Mistral; extremely interesting displays of Provençal life and art.

Arles is also a handy take-off point for the vast wide-open spaces of the Camargue, a bizarre land of rice fields, *pampas* and bullrings. It is also gypsy country, especially in May, when the happy wanderers from all over gather at Stes.-Maries-de-la-Mer on the Mediterranean shore. It's crowded and noisy then, but fascinating.

Take the barren road marked N-113 to Salon, known because Nostradamus, the famous prophet of the future, lived and was buried here; then N-572 until it joins N-7 —a fast, straight ride into Aix-en-Provence, with its Cours Mirabeau, a wide, tree-lined street bordered by somnolent old mansions. The outstanding single sight is the Cathedral St.-Sauveur, but there is also the Granet Art Gallery. This was the country of Cézanne, the great painter who was born and lived part of his life nearby. Excellent accommodations and food at the Hôtel Riviera or at the Roy René.

Marseille is known for many things, but for our purposes its noteworthy contribution to civilized life is *pastis*, that licorice-tasting husky brother of anisette and a somewhat less potent descendant of absinthe. At an outdoor cafe, try a *pastis* with water. All along the southern

French coast to the Italian border at Ventimiglia, *pastis* is the drink at *apéritif* time.

SIDE TRIP ¶ If you desire, a side trip can be made via N-8 southward to Marseille, the great seaport of France. Although the old quarters' winding tortuous maze of streets and alleys was dynamited by the Germans, Marseille is still interesting, as seaports always seem to be. The main street, La Canebière, runs up from the harbor, called the Vieux Port, filled with a miscellaneous assortment of ships. High above the city is the fairly modern church of Nôtre-Dame-de-la-Garde; in the suburbs is the interesting architectural design for an apartment house created by Le Corbusier (for visits, apply at the Cité Radieuse, 9–11:30 or 2–5:30; small admission charge). If you like *bouillabaisse*, the wonderful fish soup, this is the place to try it. Dignified old hotels include Grand Hôtel & Hôtel de Noailles (only one place even though it has a double name), the Splendide and the Hôtel de Bordeaux & d'Orient (there they go again). If you're really serious about eating, there are two restaurants we could recommend—Café Brasso and the Brasserie de Catalans. Excellent seafood at both of these establishments.

Aix to St.-Raphaël—72 miles

Leave Aix by route N-7, which passes through St.-Maximin, with a fine old basilica; open 9–12 and 2–6. Then drive through Brignoles and, just past Le Luc, turn right onto N-558 toward St.-Tropez. The town, once a fishing village, has become a favorite resort for the writers and artists of Paris—the bearded ones—and also a few millionaire yachtsmen. The harbor is a semicircle, bordered with deep banks of tables, arranged in almost mathematical precision by the numerous cafes of the town. One wonderful morning—August 15, 1944, to be exact—the Allies landed on the beaches at this unlikely place; the rest is history. Next along around the bend is Ste.-Maxime, which seems to cater to Frenchmen rather than tourists. Here you'll find two good hotels—Chardon Bleu and Le Manoir. Eastward along the coast on N-98 is St.-Raphaël, with a protected beach, popular as both a winter and a summer resort; fine accommodations at the Hôtel Beau Rivage.

If you are headed for Cannes, Nice or Monte Carlo and don't want to dilly-dally along the way, stay on route

7 and travel inland over the new *autoroute* that starts at Fréjus. It cuts hours off your travel time and avoids the slow-moving beachcombers on the coast road. Of course, you lose all those impressive seascapes. So, you make the choice.

Note: The next leg of your tour takes you through the heart of the French Riviera, from St.-Raphaël to Menton, on the Italian border. Certain aspects of the Riviera deserve special mention, so we have included the section that immediately follows. The trip to Menton is resumed after this brief aside.

HILL TOWNS OF THE RIVIERA

Because of the great number of American tourists who visit the southern coast of France, perhaps that area will become known soon as the American Riviera. At present, almost all Americans congregate in the expensive, heady atmosphere of Cannes, Antibes, Juan-les-Pins and Nice. But these luxurious havens are reminiscent of other resorts for the wealthy, although with the addition of a slight French accent. In the hills behind the bikini coastline are the "perched" towns, colorful old villages that literally hang from the cliffs; these represent the quintessence of the history, art and charm of old Provence, and it is possible to stay at a comfortable inn at a fraction of the cost of staying on the coast itself.

Southern France was first settled in the fourth century B.C. by Greek traders. But in the centuries that followed came raiding bands of Vandals, Visigoths, Ostrogoths and Franks who sacked the towns, and stole anything and everything of value, leaving only devastation behind. The local peasantry took to the hills, searching out the highest peaks and most inaccessible cliffs; here, like falcons, they built their homes, narrow and cramped, for space was at a tremendous premium. Around their tiny communities, they constructed ramparts with rocks laboriously transported to the mountaintops.

But the worst was to come in the eighth century, when various groups of Arabs, Moors and Barbary pirates (generically called Saracens) systematically began to move into the Provence area, particularly in the vicinity of La-Garde-Freinet. Even after their forced departure in

975, the Saracens made coastal life almost impossible for the fishermen and peasants for a few centuries, by sporadic forays along the shore. Those were bad times for the common man; protection was lacking; the princes and lords fought for aggrandizement, seldom to protect their vassals.

The temporary falcons' nests became permanent homes for the beleaguered peasantry. Soon, many of the nobility, bowing to practical necessity, moved into the rampart-girt towns, often building miniature chateaux. Generation after generation of the native folk lived their lives within the confines of the perched towns, only leaving its protection to work their fields, drenched in the flat, brilliant yellow sunlight of southern France. During the nineteenth century, the self-imposed banishment came to an end with the gradual disappearance of the raiders and marauders; then there was a progressive movement toward the coast.

The ancient trouble that forced the good people of Provence to seek refuge from their enemies is the good fortune of the present-day tourist. The little hill towns of the Riveria were built to be as unapproachable as possible, but roads have now overcome that difficulty. Each town, by design, has an unobstructed, often breath-taking view of the surrounding countryside. Rolling azure hills drop gracefully down to the bluest of seas—the Mediterranean. Spring brings the gold of mimosa; summer finds wild lavender plants covering the undulating slopes with a cool blanket of purple.

Within the eroding ramparts of each town are narrow, cobbled streets set at impossible angles, each one wandering off apparently at random and by whim. These steep pathways must be explored on foot, and cars should be left at the town's central point—usually a decayed, crumbling fountain. The town is laid out in the medieval fashion, with sloping walks leading to flagged terraces, which in turn drop away to lower levels and covered paths. Each house is cheek by jowl with its neighbor, joined by thousand-year-old party walls. Vaulted archways open into diminutive, flowered closes, the sole source of light and air. Many houses are minute architectural masterpieces; scanty in size, impressive in skillfully executed detail.

Behind Cannes, the darling of American tourists, is

the old hill town of Mougins, with its old gateway; most of the ramparts constructed in the Middle Ages still stand. Farther along is Gourdon, a town perched in rather exhilarating fashion on the very top of a mountain and reached only by a road that zigs and zags its way to the peak in the spirited manner of a drunken roister. The town's pride is in its fourteenth-century fortress, the Seigneurial. To the west are the roosting villages of Mons, Trigance, Taloire, Rougon and Chasteuil. Not far from Nice is Cagnes-sur-Mer. Its heights, Haut-de-Cagnes, are known for the fine museum and chateau; the view from the tower is unsurpassed.

Worth a half-day's excursion on its own is lovely, soulful Vence, like a timid eagle looking down on the world. Be sure to go on Tuesday or Thursday to see the Matisse Chapel, decorated in daring fashion by the great artist. East of the sprawling metropolis of Nice and magnificiently situated on the Moyenne Corniche, the middle mountain coast road, is Eze, truly one of the high points of any visit to this region. The musty streets are a delight merely to wander through; there is still another chateau in ruins and an exotic garden filled with the flora of the Mediterranean region. Eastward along the coast, behind Monaco, is the toy village of La Turbie. This old hamlet rests its claim to fame on the Trophée des Alpes, a famous monument erected in 6 B.C. by the Romans in commemoration of their subjugation of much of France and Germany. It was precisely placed at the highest point where Italy and France (or Gaul, as it was then known) met. The base is more or less intact, but the upper portions are fragmentary except for several columns and a portion of the tower. It still remains an imposing sight. La Turbie is a romantic place at night: the floodlit Trophée, the moonlit view of the Mediterranean, the twinkling lights of Monte Carlo below, the sleeping stillness of the deserted streets of an old town.

Sightseeing may be combined successfully with good living in this general area, for scattered about the hill towns are outdoor restaurants (the weather is almost always excellent) serving the distinctive food of Provence. In lovely old Vence, for example, about fifteen miles from Nice, there is the well-known and excellent Auberge des Seigneurs, where the food is delicious and the atmosphere Provençal. At St. Paul, a fortified village to the west of Nice, are the Colombe d'Or and Les

Oliviers, where *pissaladière* (onion tarts) and *ratatouille* (a cold vegetable appetizer) may be enjoyed, accompanied by Belle, the pleasant *rosé* wine of the region.

There are old abbeys converted into outdoor restaurants, where whole sides of beef and lamb are barbecued in the open and cut to order. One of these is called L'Abbaye, and it preserves the original chapel. There are country inns serving dozens of elaborate and fascinating hors d'oeuvres; there are tiny village stalls where one eats *pans bagnat* (a Provençale "sandwich" of black olives, onions, tomatoes, anchovies—the whole liberally doused with olive oil and vinegar).

For a midmorning snack, all of the local *zincs*, the bars, will serve you a glass of refreshingly chilled white wine and a *tarte au blé*, a bit of pastry covered with cooked white beet tops. Warm, summer afternoons in Provence are best spent in quiet contemplation of the good things of life—the soft, warm air, the incomparable panorama of the Mediterranean, the feeling of well-being.

St.-Raphaël to Menton—66 miles

From St.-Raphaël eastward to the Italian border is one of the most favored spots on earth—the Côte d'Azur. Mimosa, jasmine, carnations, roses and violets fill the air with soft fragrances, the bluish-hued mountains push down to the sea, villas and small chateaux cling to the most unlikely sites. The climate is wonderful most of the year, except during the very late fall. In its small towns stroll international figures and grizzled fishermen. American tourists and French *bourgeois*. This is probably the outstanding resort area in the world.

Moving eastward along the coast on N-98 is a delightful ride; gentle, undulating curves in the road offer seductive views of the placid Mediterranean. Agay is a small spot with jagged colored rocks thrusting toward the coastline; Le Trayas is colorful and pleasing, with a good beach; La Napoule is just the place for those who love flowers; nature and the La Napoule Chamber of Commerce seem to have evolved a working agreement about mimosa and orange blossoms. The Hôtel Beau Rivage is pleasant here for a stay, and one needn't go hungry, for the restaurant Réserve Montana features chicken on the spit, and La Mère Terrats is renowned all along the coast for *bouillabaisse* and indeed for all seafood. The famous restaurant here is l'Oasis, and you'll find it a few blocks inland from the main highway. I find that l'Oasis is a rather good but not great restaurant, and you may consider mine a somewhat negative vote. But go anyhow, for it's worth trying at least once.

Now we come to the most famous resort of all, the chic, fabulous capital of the social set, Cannes. Born a small fishing village, Cannes has become the elegant, superluxurious center of the pleasure-seeking Côte d'Azur. Getting established is easy, for here are a wealth of places to stay, including the Hôtel Martinez (facing the sea) and Réserve Miramar. The Hôtel Carlton is particularly deluxe, filled exclusively with Americans. Under the new owners the Hôtel Majestic is being completely remodeled, and is more luxurious than ever. Cannes is popular all year round, except during November and December, when the winds blow for days at a time. The winter months are particularly smart, with hundreds of people promenading on La Croisette, the avenue that runs along the shore; on one side is the beach, on the other, fine shops, particularly those featuring clothing and jewelry. The older part of town has the charm of the centuries through which it has survived. Incidentally, if you have not been at Cannes for a few years you'll find that La Croisette has been widened and the beach area increased. There is a whole new section of additional beach area with fine powdery sand. In other words, this splendid lily has indeed been gilded.

Several interesting excursions may be made from Cannes. First, there is the trip via N-567 to Grasse, by-passing along the route (to the right) the fine old Roman town of Mougins, with its fortified walls. Grasse, famous for its perfume manufacture, is the center of the flower-producing region. During most of the year, the air is heavy with the almost overpowering fragrance of the blossoms. A visit to one of the perfumeries is interesting when the flowers are being pressed, otherwise not terribly exciting: Fragonard is one you'll see as you enter the city. Be sure to visit Grasse's food market in the center of the old town. Another pleasant day may be spent by taking the boat to the Lerins Islands; service from Cannes at 10, 11:20, 2 and 2:30 P.M., with returning boats at convenient hours from the two islands, Ste.-Marguerite and St.-Honorat. The boats leave from the

Cannes Maritime Station, very close to the Municipal Casino, and you should go if you want to see something unchanged from a century or two ago. St.-Honorat, especially, is worth visiting. You'll be able to eat at a pretty good restaurant here, if you can find it hidden among the trees. There is a monastery on the island, but only men are permitted to enter; the women customarily wait for their husbands in the souvenir shop. The monastery has a small hotel, open to men only (of any religious faith) for an extremely nominal charge. Ste.-Marguerite is famous for the fortress where the "Man in the Iron Mask" was kept as a prisoner. The island has a few simple hotels, to call them by a formal name, where tourists can remain overnight (if rooms are available), and also several places to eat.

The next town along the coastline (via N-7) is Golfe-Juan, famous because Napoleon landed here on his fateful return from exile in Elba. The Restaurant Nounou at the beach specializes in seafood; so does the Tétou. Then comes Juan-les-Pins, to which the French give the full pronunciation, Je-wan. Juan (to be familiar) has several beaches, all pretty well developed and possibly commercialized, but the bathing is very good. The town itself teems with life and excitement, particularly during the high seasons, when the streets are crowded with pleasure-seekers. Traffic is intense, the cafes are filled and all is social bedlam. The Juan-les-Pins night spots are in fragrant gardens, the beaches have real sand and the barber shops are open all night. That gives you an idea, as a starter. It's a lively spot.

Then comes Antibes, an old fortified town with an extremely interesting promenade along its waterfront; the nearby chateau is open 10–12 and 3–6. Be sure to drive on route N-559 to Cap d'Antibes, with its lighthouse and Thuret Gardens (open 8–12, 2–6) and the especially outstanding view from the Plateau de la Garoupe.

Nice is the largest city of this region, with a distinctive, ruggedly individualistic population. A Niçois accent can be spotted easily, even by those who cannot speak French; there is a certain Italianate quality to the speech, for Nice belonged to Italy as recently as 1860. Standard sights include the Promenade des Anglais (the wide boulevard facing the sea), the Place Massena, the lovely flower market with its enticing displays of fruits and vegetables, the narrow, medieval streets of the old quarter of town. The two luxury hotels are Negresco, on the Promenade des Anglais, and Plaza, facing the park just off Place Massena. Other better hotels include Royal, Splendid-Sofitel, Park, Napoleon (he lived in Nice at the Rue St.-François-de-Paule), Westminster.

Unfortunately, the bathing at Nice leaves something to be desired, for the beach is rocky and usually crowded. But don't take our criticism of the Nice beach the wrong way. Practically no one comes to Nice to go swimming. Nice is ideal for snoozing in the sun or for bikini watching, either from a comfortable chair on the Promenade des Anglais or from a cafe table right at the water's edge.

From Nice to the Italian border, there are three roads at varying levels—the Lower, Middle and Upper Corniches. The Middle Corniche is an exciting magnificent drive, but the upper road is more thrilling, with breathtaking views of the sea. The lower road follows the sea closely and is extensively built up, very busy and heavily traveled. First along the seaside route comes Villefranche, a fisherman's salty town with a distinctive flavor. There you'll find the Hôtel Welcome and the Restaurant Auberge du Coq Hardi. For some reason, the French rather than the Americans seem to head for the Versaille Hôtel, a terrace-like series of buildings located *down* from the road and facing the sea. Although the entrance is not terribly prepossessing, the rates are, so this isn't for those who are economy-minded. At the water's edge in Villefranche is a fisherman's chapel decorated by Jean Cocteau. After Villefranche, make a right turn to St. Jean-Cap-Ferrat, a lovely peninsula dotted with delightful homes in an ideal setting. The late W. Somerset Maugham, the noted author, lived here at the Villa Mauresque—what more fitting place for a famous writer?

At the tip end of the cape is the aging Grand Hôtel du Cap Ferrat, perfectly set in a park facing the sea, and, if that weren't enough, renowned for its food. If ordinary luxury isn't enough, there's the much newer and much more luxurious (and more expensive) Hotel Voile d'Or. When the French invented the word *de luxe*, they must have had this place in mind—it's really quite special. Don't count on saving any money here—it's not that kind of hotel. Be sure to take your best clothes and briefest bathing suit. Oh, and did I mention that you should bring money? After Cap Ferrat, the road passes Beaulieu and then Eze-sur-Mer and its nice little hotel, La Bananeraie. High above Eze-sur-Mer is Eze-Village, on the Middle Corniche, a colorful village clinging precariously to the cliffs. Cap d'Ail is a tiny seaside resort with a rather good beach. And then comes what may be the most famous area in the world—Monte Carlo.

Monte, to give it the local name, is in the principality of Monaco, ruled over by the ancient house of Grimaldi, the present titleholder being Prince Rainier, married to an American movie actress named . . . oh, yes, Grace Kelly. The entire state is tiny, consisting of three towns. —Monte Carlo, Monaco and La Condamine. Monaco's outstanding sights include the exotic tropical garden, the oceanographic museum and the palace—all very quaint and colorful. La Condamine holds little interest for tourists, but the same cannot be said for Monte Carlo and its famed gambling casino. Entry is gained on presentation of a passport and payment of a small admission charge. The casino, sad to relate, is not nearly so glamorous as those who have never visited it might believe; the gambling rooms are no longer magnificent, but have a rundown, slightly seedy appearance. However, it is still good fun to join the excitement whether you bet or not. The hotel situation in Monte Carlo is somewhat difficult to cope with, to say the least. The leading place is the Hôtel de Paris, one of the grand old establishments, where rooms are almost impossible to come by during August unless reserved months in advance. However, the Hôtel de Paris caters almost exclusively to the wealthy (not just merely rich millionaires) and prices are quite high; incidentally, its location is not convenient for those who enjoy bathing, and a bus ride is necessary to and from the beach in the hotel's little omnibus. The Hôtel de Paris has a good restaurant, but you'll never get a table on its front terrace unless you're staying at the hotel; the roof dining room is actually more attractive and not nearly so busy. A block away is the Hermitage Hôtel, which is fairly good, although the rooms could be larger. For lovers of beach life, the best choice might be the Old Beach Hôtel, situated directly on the Mediterranean; in fact, the waves are almost under the windows. Although it has no restaurant (which means you must have a car), it's excellent for those who want to spend their days on the stony beach. Nearby is the coast's largest swimming pool.

Assuming you're settled down in Monte Carlo, we might point out some eating places: Bec Rouge is quite good, particularly if you like *beignets des moules*, mussels dipped in batter and something like fried clams. Le Regent Restaurant is worth a visit, too. If you don't mind a little trip, be sure to have lunch or a late-ish dinner at La Chèvre d'Or, a superb restaurant about five miles from Monte Carlo in the unbelievably picturesque community of Eze-Village. Be sure to allow a little time to explore this medieval showplace, and although it's been restored, it's absolutely delightful to wander through. Talking about making trips, and assuming you're a hungry gourmet and don't mind driving over beautiful mountains make a lunchtime excursion to the miniature village of Gattières about fifteen miles northwest of Nice via route N-209; here you'll find the Auberge de Gattières, which serves superb food at moderate prices, especially their hors d'oeuvres and also the meats roasted over vine branches.

Between Monte Carlo and the Italian border there's the coastal region known as Cap Martin sometimes called Roquebrune-Cap-Martin. Anyhow it's the same area and runs together. Up on the Grand Corniche, there's the Hotel Vistaero, with excellent views of the coast, and what's more, good food. The prices are, well, fairly high, although not up in the stratosphere.

If you've never visited the Italian Rivera, you would undoubtedly enjoy driving across the border, just past Menton, and continuing on to the resort town of San Remo (which has a big casino), where you can buy bargains in Italian merchandise. If it's summertime, be sure and get an early start, because traffic can pile up at the border. En route, if you're hungry, there's the Restaurant La Mortola at the right-hand side of the road just beyond the border. It has marvelous hors d'oeuvres, but otherwise the food is mediocre. It used to be a favorite with Sir Winston Churchill. San Remo doesn't have a single really outstanding restaurant, but the Del Casino is quite attractive for lunch. Riviera points, from San Remo to Cannes, are now connected by hydrofoils (*aliscafi*), which zip along with the French name of "flying fishes" (*poissons volants*). A ride in one of them along the

Riviera coastline gives a new dimension to the Mediterranean's beauty. They are also ideal for casino-hopping.

PLAYING ROULETTE AT MONTE CARLO

The game: The roulette wheel consists of a circle with 37 separate compartments, alternately colored red and black—and a number zero, which has no color. In front of each wheel is a table with the 36 numbers plus zero indicated by a series of squares; bets are placed by putting chips upon desired numbers, colors, odd or even, and so forth. When the bets are placed, the wheel is spun, the ball lands in a given compartment, and winners are paid off. Losers, as you might suspect, are not.

The odds: If you bet on a given number and win, you're paid off at the rate of 36 times the amount of your bet; actually the odds against you are 37 to 1, because of that little number zero. That small fraction, say, roughly less than 3 percent, is what keeps the house in business.

Ways of playing: It's possible to bet on odd and even, called *impair et pair*; if your number comes up, you'll be paid even money, but the house still retains a slight edge—yes, the number zero. You may also bet on black or red, but the odds work out exactly the same way.

Another wrinkle, permitting more frequent winners, is a bet on two numbers, that is, on horseback or *à cheval*; if either number comes up, you win, but you'll be paid 17 times your bet, which also gives the house its edge. If you bet on three numbers and any one comes up, you're paid 11 times your bet.

Conclusion: You may win occasionally; you may even win substantial sums of money, but in the long run, the house edge will always defeat you. No system has ever been devised, despite what you may have read, that can beat the house. But don't think that people doubt this; come early some day and watch the "system" bettors, working with notebooks, charts and statistics. They always lose in the long run.

Farther east along the coast is Menton, known for its old lemon trees, old marketplace and old English residents. The town is, by Riviera standards, dignified and comparatively quiet. You may stay at the Hôtel Prince de Galles or Les Colombières and eat at the Restaurant Rocamadour. You'll find the Rocamadour restaurant near the waterfront; it's convenient, if you're going to Italy, to drive along the shore road as far as it goes before joining the main highway toward San Remo.

CORSICA

Corsica, about 115 miles long and 50 miles wide as the crow flies, is one of the largest Mediterranean islands. Its jagged and winding coast, however, is much longer: over 625 miles of large and small bays, gulfs and inlets following one another, mostly below the steep cliffs of towering mountains. Except for a small plain in the middle of the east coast, all of Corsica is mountainous. And these are high and rugged mountains with central ranges very similar to the Alps and reaching over 8,500 feet; the highest peak, Mount Cinto, soars up to 8,860 feet above the sea; and we mean literally *above the sea*, since here you really start going up from sea level.

Wine and olives, which are among the main products today, were brought to Corsica by ancient Greeks who founded their first settlement here in 565 B.C. Eventually the Romans took over and ruled the island for over six centuries of peaceful existence. Later, the Romans founded the principal towns, constructed roads and as the health- and cleanliness-loving *ancient* Romans did almost everywhere, discovered thermal waters and built spas. During the Middle Ages a number of invaders, including the Vandals and the Arabs, came to the island, stayed awhile and left it again. Later the Genoese established their hold over Corsica with the help of the Pope and remained until the 18th century. But none of the conquerors had an easy time with the stubborn, rugged, fierce and proud Corsican population. The Genoese constructed tower-like forts along the coast (which make nice landmarks for tourists today) in order to protect the island from invaders, and themselves from the Corsicans. For the same reasons the Genoese constructed a number of town fortresses, for instance in Bastia, Calvi, and Bonifacio, where they lived in the citadel on the hill above, secluded (and protected) from the Corsicans below. From time to time Corsicans fought for their independence but always failed.

Corsica's turbulent history has quieted down since France took the island over in the late 18th century.

French is the official language of Corsica but most Corsicans speak (among themselves) an Italian dialect which, however, has almost nothing in common with the Sardinian spoken on the neighboring island. Since the French conquest, and more recently since the beginning of the tourist conquest, many French have moved to the island, among them refugees from Algeria. The latter, who include not only Frenchmen, but also various types of Algerians who had thrown their lot in with the French, are not well liked by the Corsicans.

The best way to reach Corsica is by air. Several daily flights connect Nice and Marseilles with Ajaccio, Bastia, and Calvi. The best way to see the island, unquestionably, is by car. You can, of course, bring in your own car (or a car rented on the mainland) by car ferries departing from Nice, Marseilles or Toulon, in France, or from Genoa, in Italy. These ships usually run overnight and are therefore not particularly interesting to travel on (if you don't have to transport a car, of course).

SPECIAL NOTE FOR DRIVERS: Except for such main routes as the one connecting Ajaccio with Bastia via Corte, and the east coast road from Bastia to Bonifacio, all roads are narrow, frequently *very* narrow, and climb up and down the mountains, and run along the shore in innumerable curves, mostly sharp. A flat statement can be made to the effect that except for most of the east coast road (Bastia-Bonifacio) and very few stretches of the Ajaccio-Corte-Bastia road, there are no straight roads in Corsica. Most roads have hard surface, which in some sections, such as between Calvi and Porto, can be in pretty poor condition.

If you don't have a car or don't want to drive, you can take a number of bus tours ranging from half-day up to six days. The best departure points are Ajaccio and Bastia. A certain amount of sightseeing can also be done by train.

Ajaccio (with 50,000 inhabitants) is one of the two principal cities on the island. Napoleon was born here in the Maison Bonaparte, his ancestral house, now shown as a museum. More Napoleonic mementos are on display in Musée Napoléonien in the City Hall and in Palais Fesch, also a museum. A row of pleasant cafés lines the street facing the yacht and fishing harbor between the Citadel and the fish market, which stands at the corner of the park-like Pláce Foch. Hôtel de la Villa (City

Hall) is on this square, as well as a number of restaurants specializing in lobster. Drive up to Promenade de Salario (2½ miles) or to Château de la Punta Pozzo-di-Borgo (2,300 feet, 8 miles) for fine views of the beautiful Ajaccio Bay. The leading hotel in the city is Grand Hôtel et Continental, an old-fashioned palace in a small park. But the best hotels are outside the city. Sheraton du Cap, in a splendid location across the bay at Porticcio, is the top hotel in Corsica; the Campo dell'Oro, at a fine beach near the airport, is more functional but also luxurious. You will find a number of smaller but also modern and comfortable hotels on the road to Cap de la Parata, the northern end of Ajaccio Bay; among them Eden-Roc (above the road) and Cala di Sole (with good restaurant) and the new motel La Parata, both on the beach below the road.

Bastia (with 55,000 inhabitants) is the second of the two main towns and is located near the northeastern end of the island (Ajaccio is on the southwest coast). The most interesting sights include the old town with old narrow streets (but quite dirty and smelly) and with the palace of the former Genoese governors (now a museum), and the old port (now a yacht harbor), surrounded by old Mediterranean-style apartment houses and lined by side-walk cafés. The hotels include the modern Rivoli above the beach in the south suburbs, the new Le Tyrrhenien near the old port and facing the sea, and the Ile de Beauté near the railroad station, furnished in Empire style (made in 20th century). Good food (fish and other Corsican specialties) at Chez Mémé, on Promenade de Quais, near the old port. Next door in a cave is Caveau Marin, specializing in seafood and sometimes offering folk music and dance programs.

You can start a tour of Corsica proceeding south from Ajaccio, up and down the hills to the picturesque town of Olmeto and from there to the gulf of Valinco and the rapidly growing sea resort town of Propriano (the best hotels—all new—include Arena Bianca, standing by itself on the beach south of the town, and Le Miramar, Roc e Mare and Valinco on the main road just north of town and high above the beach). From Propriano you climb up to the fresh breezes of Sartène, an old and typical Corsican mountain town with fine view of Gulf of Valinco. There are about 53 miles from Ajaccio to Sartène and about 35 more to Bonifacio at the southern tip of Corsica.

Bonifacio is a citadel town sitting like a fortified nest on top of the cliffs growing up from a fjord. The port section of the town lies at the feet of the citadel and at the end of the fjord. Here you could stay overnight at Hotel Solemare.

Bonifacio-Bastia (about 110 miles): the first stop is Porto-Vecchio, on the large gulf of the same name, with remains of the 16th-century Genoese town fortifications. (From Porto Vecchio you can take a side road up to the mountain through the beautiful forests called Forêt de l'Ospedale and Foret de Bavella (nearby is a mouflon preserve) and join the main road to Bastia again at Solenzara.) From Solenzara northwest you drive across the only flat plain in Corsica. Just before crossing the Tavignano river you can visit the tiny town of Aleria standing on a small hill with an old Genoese fort (now a museum). Aleria was originally the Roman capital of Corsica and part of the Roman town has been excavated. Further north is the beach resort of Moriani Plage, but the sea is too shallow here to enjoy real swimming. Then comes Poretta with the Bastia airport and Bastia itself.

Bastia—Cap Corse—L'Ile Rousse—Calvi— about 115 miles

The drive around Cap Corse is an exciting experience in the variety of marine-mountain vistas, softer and quieter on the eastern shore with small port towns, and wilder and more rugged with the towns hugging the steep mountain slopes along the western shore. The most picturesque towns on the eastern shore are Erbalunga and Porticciolo; on the western shore Centuri and Nonza. The entire Cap Corse peninsula, as well as much of the rest of Corsica between the sea and the tree line, is covered by the unique green shrubbery of the *Macchia*, a sort of low bush "forest," blossoming in the spring and in the fall and exuding a typical, pleasant, strong scent far out to the sea. From Nonza, the road continues to the very colorful old fishing town of Saint-Florent with an interesting 11th-century Romanesque Cathedral. Between L'Ile Rousse and Calvi on the west coast are some of the nicest beaches on the island. L'Ile Rousse is the port town for the La Balagne region, one of the most fruitful in Corsica. A very pleasant new hotel is La Pietra on the small rocky peninsula beyond the fort, with a crystal-clear rocky beach. The Splendid, near the sandy beach near town, is also quite good. Calvi has the most impressive citadel in Corsica and one of the nicest sandy beaches across the small bay from the town proper. The port, which is filled with pleasure and fishing boats, is lined with attractive sidewalk cafés and restaurants. You bump into romantic corners in the narrow old town streets at every step. The best hotel in town is Grand Hotel. Slightly lower rates are charged at the Palm Beach, completely new, and located in a pine wood at the beach. Ile de Beauté, offering fish and other food, is regarded as the best restaurant in town. Au Comme Chez Soi, next door, is probably just as good but less expensive. Both are located at the port.

Pointer: For additional travel information: Write to the French Government Tourist Office, 610 Fifth Avenue, New York. Request their set of folders for the provinces of France, or any other specific points of information.

ALSACE-LORRAINE, THE BLACK FOREST, SWITZERLAND AND THE SAVOY DISTRICT OF FRANCE

Paris to Nancy—191 miles

When starting at the Place de la Concorde, please be sure to drive carefully around this famous traffic hazard with its milling, snorting cabs. Head eastward (but don't worry, traffic is one-way and you can't go wrong), following the road on the right bank of the Seine. It is hardly possible to lose your way, for the road closely follows the river; after a while, you'll see signs directing you toward the Porte de Bercy, one of the gates (exits) out of Paris. This is route N-4, which you'll stay with all day.

(We made this entire trip in a Renault Dauphine and have nothing but praise for its excellent performance and economy of operation.)

The road goes through Gretz and Fontenay-Trésigny, bypasses Rozay-en-Brie and then becomes a fairly long

run without towns or villages of any size until Esternay
(not that Esternay is any too large). Should you be contemplating food or overnight lodging, direct your thoughts
to the small, sleepy village of Sézanne, about eight miles
ahead. The main highway bypasses Sézanne, so if you
wish to eat well or remain overnight, make a right turn,
at the designated spot, into this town and head down its
main street until you come to the Hôtel France on your
left. The food here is particularly good, notably the
coq au vin, chicken in red wine; the rooms are modest
but clean and comfortable.

Follow N-4 through more miles of open country that
rises and falls gently; a chateau may be seen occasionally
and the road is almost always very good. The next village
of any size is Vitry-le-François; the route bypasses St.-
Dizier, goes through Ancerville, Ligny-en-Barrios, Void
and Toul, and then you finally arrive at Nancy.

Driving into town, you'll find the Hôtel Excelsior on
your left, not far from the railroad station; the accommodations are satisfactory if you get a redecorated room. At
the far end of town is the beautifully situated Grand
Hôtel, fronting onto lovely old Place Stanislas. Louis
XV placed the Polish nobleman Stanislas in charge of
historic old Lorraine, and many of the buildings were
constructed by Stanislas. Nancy, in its older quarters, is
about the loveliest of all the towns of Lorraine. In back
of the square is the Ducal Palace, worth a little exploration. Incidentally, this is a town for good eating; the
Capucin Gourmand serves topnotch food; if you'd like
something special, try the fish wrapped in a delicate
puff pastry.

Nancy to Strasbourg—93 miles

The route number remains N-4 from Nancy all the
way to Strasbourg. Leave Nancy via the Rue St.-George
driving through St.-Nicolas-de-Port, Dombasle, Luné-
ville, Blâmont, Sarrebourg, Saverne and Wasselone and
into Strasbourg. If you should arrive before 12:30 P.M.,
head immediately for the cathedral, which can be identified readily from miles away by its distinctive spire.
The cathedral has a remarkable astronomical clock with
a series of figures that, at the appointed time, move in an
extremely lifelike fashion; the clock actually operates at
12:30 P.M., although it is listed for noon in most guide-

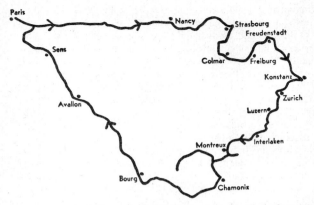

books. Don't miss seeing the cathedral itself, before or after the astronomical clock; then too, the old quarter of the city, called La Petite France, with its network of canals, is definitely worth a visit. The new, modern Sofitel Hôtel is Strasbourg's leading hotel, should you wish to remain overnight. Here's a chance to try some excellent Alsatian food; head for the top (fourteenth) floor of the new building into which the Valentin-Sorg Restaurant has moved. The view is good, but so is the food. Serious eaters also would not want to overlook an eight-mile ride (via route N-68) northward from Strasbourg to Wantzenau, with the famous Restaurant au Moulin. (As this restaurant closes for several weeks during the summer, be sure to phone No. 1 Wantzenau just to be on the safe side.) Incidentally, Strasbourg is the place to buy *pâté de foie gras*, and the largest selection is at the Maison Feyel.

Strasbourg to Colmar—56 miles
(via the wine district)

Leaving Strasbourg heading south on route N-83, but as the road is well marked, there should be no difficulty in finding your way toward Sélestat. Six miles past Sélestat at the village of Ostheim you'll see a right turn onto route N-416 to Ribeauvillé, less than four miles away. This is the beginning of the Alsatian wine country and a pleasant place for a day or two, particularly during the late summer or early fall, when the wine harvest and celebrations are under way. Highly recommended are the Hôtel Ville de Nancy (in town), and just a few minutes' drive into the Vosges forest is the Hôtel Pépinière; both places are well known for their food.

From Ribeauvillé, drive south to Riquewihr, and don't worry about the route number, just follow the signs. Riquewihr, two miles away, luckily escaped being damaged during the war and the fine old medieval buildings still delight the eye. The town itself is charming to wander about in, although it is quite tiny; don't fail to ask for the Maison Liebrich, built in 1535, and don't miss seeing the Dolder Gate, with its clock tower and belfry (the sort from which bats ought to fly). The town itself is just about perfect in its picturesque evocation of the Middle Ages. Unfortunately, there is no suitable hotel or restaurant, but you'll be able to taste the local vintages at Au Tonnelet d'Or, which specializes in Alsatian wines.

From Riquewihr, go on to Mittelwihr, Benniwihr, Sigolsheim and lovely Kaysersberg, with old sloped-roof houses lining the Weiss stream. It is a delightful little spot and you might want to remain overnight or longer at the miniature Hôtel Chambard.

From Kaysersberg, proceed via route N-415 just two miles to Ammerschwihr, which was heavily damaged during the war, but part of the upper town still remains for the sightseer. Then continue on to Colmar, a rather large and attractive city that boasts a world-famous restaurant, the Maison des Têtes, housed in a showplace of a building; don't fail to try the various Alsatian specialties here. Be sure to see the Cathedral St.-Martin, dating back to the thirteenth century; the great museum known as the Unterlinden, with its lovely cloisters and housing the renowned altarpiece "Retable d'Issenheim," painted by Mathias Grünewald; the old Customs House (Ancienne Douane); the Maison Pfister, generally regarded as the finest Alsatian house in Colmar. Even if you're not dining at the Restaurant Maison des Têtes, be sure and see the building in which it is located.

GERMANY

Colmar to Freiburg—32 miles

Leave Colmar via route N-415 heading toward Neuf-Brisach. The road is fairly good, and under ordinary circumstances not heavily traveled. Just before the companion village of Alt-Brisach, you'll pass the French-

German border. Clearing the customs is a matter of minutes if you have your passports, automobile ownership or rental certificates and the necessary third-party insurance. Even if you lack the insurance, it will be issued in short order on payment of a very moderate fee.

The road now becomes route 31 and goes through Gündlingen, Tiengen and St. Georgen and into Freiburg. Although extensively damaged during the war, Freiburg has been rebuilt very much in the modern fashion, and the main shopping street is a treat for those anxious to buy German merchandise. Needless to say, there are marvelous values in cameras, binoculars and sunglasses (including the classic Zeiss lense and the new, cheaper plastic lenses). Also recommended—Rosenthal china; Black Forest liqueurs (such as *Kirschwasser*, cherry brandy, and *Himbeergeist*, raspberry brandy); coffee and tea sets in pewter, brass and copper are also worth buying. In the way of local sightseeing, nothing equals the unusual cathedral (750 years old); also don't overlook the *Kaufhaus* building immediately adjacent. The Kaufhaus is a fascinatingly arched and gabled affair in bright colors that was once a medieval hotel for traveling merchants. In front of the Kaufhaus there is generally an open-air food market in progress, where it is possible to see considerable local color. Should you be hungry, head for the Oberkirchs Weinstuben, also in the Münsterplatz. (Church Square), an extremely interesting restaurant. As to lodging, we're going to suggest two extremes in accommodations, depending upon your mood. For atmosphere and local color, you might stay overnight at the Hotel Zum Roten Bären (The Red Bear), with a history going back to the Middle Ages. If you're looking for the utmost in spanking new modern construction, the Hotel Colombi would be ideal.

Trips from Freiburg include an excursion to Lake Titisee, which is pleasant but not wildly exciting. You might enjoy the forty-five-minute trip by suspended cable car to the peak of Schauinsland Mountain; there are hotels and restaurants at the top.

Freiburg to Freudenstadt—61 miles

Leave Freiburg via route 294, which goes all the way to Freudenstadt. After Waldkirch, you'll be in the heart of the Black Forest, one of the prettiest regions of Europe.

Don't expect, however, to find gloomy stretches of forest, exuding a forbidding, overcast atmosphere. This vacation area is smiling and pleasant, and the heavily wooded stretches of pines, through which sunlight cannot reach, are the only reason for the use of the descriptive name of Black Forest.

From Waldkirch, go on to Gutach and Elzach and begin a fairly steady climb into the mountains, followed by an equally steady descent coming into Haslach. Then to Hausach. If it's Sunday (or if you're fond of the distinctive old Black Forest houses), make a diversionary right turn to Gutach, also called Gutachal (and not the one you've already passed en route); the peasant women wear extremely colorful costumes on Sunday to and from church. Return to Hausach; thence on to Wolfach, which has an extremely good local-style inn, the Gasthof zum Hecht, pleasant for refreshments or an overnight stop. You occasionally see the Kinzig River on the way to Schiltach, then comes Alpirsbach and a climb into Lossburg, a descent and another climb into Freudenstadt, often regarded as the key resort town of the Black Forest. There are two good, large, old-fashioned hotels, both in about the same category of comfort, the Hotel Waldeck and the Luz-Hotel Waldlust. Many rooms have spectacular views of the surrounding countryside. Both hotels also have very good restaurants. About four miles away is Eurotel in Baiersbronn, a large modern hotel with an indoor swimming pool. Many rooms have also kitchenettes and refrigerators.

Although largely destroyed during the war. Freudenstadt today is in good shape physically after extensive rebuilding. The town lives and breathes tourism, without which it soon would lapse into somnolence; but the fresh pine air and the refreshing surroundings are all that are needed to attract visitors. Everyone heads for the town's main square, an enormous open area surrounded by stores and cafes, the natural gathering place for tourists. You'll want to visit the cathedral and walk around the square, gazing into the shop windows under the arcades.

Pay a visit to the local casino, which serves meals, features entertainment and concerts and is generally the town's social center; there is an entrance fee involving an infinitesimal amount.

(Freudenstadt is a good starting point for a side trip to

Baden-Baden, possibly Germany's plushest watering place and resort, only thirty-six miles away over interesting mountain roads.)

Freudenstadt to Konstanz—89 miles

Leave Freudenstadt by the same road, route 294, on which you arrived, heading back in the direction of Wolfach and Freiburg. In about six miles, you are once again at Lossburg; pay careful attention to a left turn in the direction of Sulz. This is an unnumbered road that passes through Leinstetten and Hopfau before reaching Sulz, a colorful and rather pleasing small town on the renowned Neckar River. Make a right turn onto route 14 heading south to Oberndorf and then to Rottweil, and into Tuttlingen.

From Tuttlingen, merely follow the signs toward Stockach, Radolfzell and Konstanz (at varying times traveling over routes 31, 34 and 33). Konstanz, which is called Constance in English, is a lakefront town on the Bodensee, which, for reasons unknown, becomes Lake Constance in English. That doesn't change the lake, which is as pretty in German as it is in English. Be sure to take one of the steamer excursion trips, although on Sundays the boats are apt to be overcrowded. The most typical eating places here are the Stephanskeller and the Engstler Beer Garden. If you want to stay overnight, the Insel Hotel, located on a small island along the shore, charming and comfortable, is the place. It used to be a monastery, and you can still admire the cloisters.

SWITZERLAND

Konstanz to Zurich—41 miles

Leave Konstanz in the direction of the Swiss border (as indicated by the many road markers). The border is quickly reached at the outskirts of the city and here you'll find little to delay you. There is an insurance charge of a few Swiss francs (for those without a Green Card), but it should be clearly understood that this does *not* constitute an insurance policy and is merely a governmental charge for handling insurance claims. Third-party insurance should be obtained *before* entering the country (the Green Card), or if desired it may be secured in Zurich; check with the Zurich governmental tourist office as to which companies issue short-term insurance. You can buy it for one week or more, depending on the length of your stay.

Once in Switzerland, it's route 1 through Engwilen, Müllheim, Frauenfeld and Winterthur, a small town that boasts two excellent art collections, one located in the Fine Arts Museum and the other in the Reinhart Foundation. Then continue on to Zurich, an extraordinarily pleasant city situated at the extreme northern end of Lake Zurich. The leading luxury hotel is the Baur au Lac; the Schweizerhof is conveniently situated near the railroad station; the City Hotel is modern and centrally located. Of Zurich's many good restaurants, may we call your attention to the Zunfthaus Zimmerleuten, a fine eating place pleasingly set in an ancient guildhouse once belonging to the carpenters' craft. Sightseeing in Zurich includes the cathedral and the Fraumünsterkirche, as well as the many museums. For us, the most interesting part of Zurich is the old section of town, with narrow, twisting streets, scarcely wide enough for walking, much less driving in a car.

If time permits, make a twenty-minute excursion to the tiny village of Regensburg, a breath of medieval times high on a hilltop. There is a small inn that has a few rooms; be sure to eat at least one meal here. If you like roses, there is a fabulous collection belonging to the wife of the owner of the inn.

Zurich to Lucerne—41 miles

Leave Zurich by following the waterfront along the Alpen Quai, heading toward Adliswil, Sihlbrugg, Baar and Zug. The lovely lakeshore village of Zug is one of Switzerland's prettiest little towns, with two outstanding sights—the Kolinplatz, a square onto which front many fine old buildings, and the Zytturm, a remarkable clock tower with a tiled roof. Should you wish to eat or remain overnight, we would heartily recommend the City-Hotel Ochsen on the Kolinplatz.

From Zug, take route 25 to Walchwil, later passing Mount Rossberg on the left; then into Arth, Küssnach, Greppen and Lucerne (or Luzern, if you prefer the German version).

Getting settled in this loveliest of all Swiss cities should present no difficulties. Close to the lake, there's the large Carlton-Tivoli, whose rooms have balconies; the Luzernerhof is smaller, compact, new and well located in the center of town; the Wilden Mann is for those who love atmosphere, for the hotel's history extends back several centuries.

In Lucerne, there are loads of things to see and do. The old part of town invites walking at random, for of all Swiss towns, Lucerne has best preserved its medieval aspect. There are covered bridges—notably the Chapel Bridge, with more than a hundred paintings hanging from its roof. Of course the harbor and its lovely waterfront always delight the viewer, but there are also canals and waterways to explore, for the city is not only located on Lake Lucerne, but also on the Reuss River. Drive above the town to see the Musegg Towers, a series of nine structures joined by a medieval wall of fortifications. Of boat rides, Lucerne offers a wide choice, but any one selected will be delightful, for Lake Lucerne has magnificent picture-postcard scenery; if you don't care for extra long rides, take the short trip to Vitznau across the lake.

But we're overlooking the obvious, which of course is the fact that Lucerne is a marvelous place to buy watches and clocks, with an almost unbelievable assortment available for your inspection and choice. Embroideries and laces are other specialties, all very tempting to the female of the species, or to the male who wants to please the female with a typical product of Swiss handicraft. (See the chapter on Switzerland for detailed information on shopping.)

Lucerne to Interlaken—45 miles

The road out of Lucerne for Interlaken cuts through the center of town via the Obergrundstrasse, later becoming route 4. You drive through lovely scenery to Alpnachstad, Alpnach, Sarnen, Giswil, Brienzwiler. At Brienz you begin to follow the north shore of Lake Brienz. Brienz, it may be noted, is the center for the woodcarvers of Switzerland, so if you happen to need a life-sized carving of a bear, Brienz will oblige you (for a price, needless to say).

The trip into Interlaken is pleasant and easy and soon the only question is selecting a hotel, and there should be no problem in getting settled at the leading establishment, the charmingly Old Worldish Hotel Victoria-Jungfrau, which is well run and extremely pleasant for a stay of just a night or even much longer. In point of fact, if you are planning a trip to the Jungfrau, a minimum of two nights is necessary because the journey to the mountaintop is an all-day affair. A more modest place than the Victoria-Jungfrau is the nearby Schlosshotel Wilderswil, in Wilderswil (ten minutes south), also very pleasant.

The big purpose of Interlaken and the reason for the town's popularity is as a base of operations for trips to the Jungfrau, a mountaintop offering panoramas of unmatched beauty—that is, when the weather is clear. If it isn't, the whole trip is reasonably close to a waste of time, because the journey takes several hours in each direction and if, when you arrive, the weather is foggy, cloudly, raining or snowing (all of which can happen even in July), you will be very high up indeed and see absolutely nothing. Just in passing, the fare is not inexpensive; remember that six or more people buying tickets at the same time and traveling on the railroad together are entitled to a substantial reduction, so round up your own party. Take good, strong shoes and a sweater or coat, and don't forget your sunglasses. Camera enthusiasts should have a sunshade and filter for their camera or the pictures will have little definition because of the intense light. If, when you arise on the day of the Jungfrau trip, the weather seems doubtful, have the hotel concierge phone to the mountaintop and ascertain weather conditions at the summit.

If time permits, drive from the center of Interlaken via routes 70 and 71 toward Wilderswil and Lauterbrunnen, where you'll pick up the road for the Trümmelbach Falls. Near the falls there's a hotel, should you wish some lunch or refreshments. These are falls with a difference; instead of a straight drop, the tremendous forces and pressures of the seething waters have carved an irregular circular path through the rocks, the entire effect producing an unusual and exciting display.

Interlaken to Montreux—81 miles

Leave Interlaken via route 20 heading toward Spiez, a pretty little town noted for its twelfth-century castle. Just past the town, watch for a left turn, indicated by signs in the direction of Gstaad and Château-d'Oex. The road from Spiez goes through Wimmis, Latterbach, Erlenbach, Weissenburg and Oberwil; after Boltigen, take a left turn toward Garstatt (not to be confused with

Gstaad). Next continue to Zweisimmen, Reichenstein and Saanenmöser and begin a climb uphill to Schonreid. After a descent into Saanen, there is a left turn toward Gstaad, a run of only a few miles for those who wish to see this famous ski resort. Gstaad's big season is the winter, but the town comes to life once again in summertime, when it plays host to thousands of visitors hungry for Alpine sunshine. There can be no doubts about recommending the Gstaad Palace Hotel, surely one of the finest hotels in Switzerland even though its exterior is not very prepossessing.

From Saanen, it's route 76 toward Château-d'Oex, (how do you pronounce it? Chat-oh d'Ay), but just follow the directional arrows indicating the towns and don't worry about route numbers. At Château-d'Oex, watch for the signs toward Aigle, a route (77) that offers some extraordinary scenery, passing through L'Etivaz and La Lécherette on the way. At Aigle, make a right turn onto route 9 heading for Montreux. Just before the city of Montreux, you'll see on the left-hand side on an island in Lake Geneva, the renowned Château de Chillon, famous as the place of imprisonment of one François Bonivard, a patriot. About 1816, Byron visited Chillon and immortalized Bonivard in his famous poem; the castle is open to visitors.

Montreux is an extraordinarily popular resort, renowned all over the world. The town stretches along the lakefront for a considerable distance and exists almost solely as a tourist's haven. There is a car rack railroad to the Rocks of Naye; there are theatrical performances at the casino; some attraction is scheduled almost daily, and in fact, Montreux is one of the liveliest spots along the lake. The Montreux Palace offers luxury accommodations; more homey, modest rooms may be had at very comforable Elite and Des Palmiers hotels.

If you prefer a larger city, you might continue on along the lake to Lausanne (sixteen miles) an interesting town with both an old and a new section. Be sure to see the famous cathedral and the old buildings in the streets nearby. You will find more than pleasant accommodations at the enormous Lausanne Palace Hotel, or you might consider a small hotel like the Victoria.

There is a marvelous place for a week's vacation (or longer) if you wish, involving luxury on the grand scale. This elegant spot, very popular with French society, is

Divonne les Bains; it may be reached by driving from Lausanne in the direction of Geneva for twenty-three miles until you reach the village of Nyon, at which point you make a right turn to Divonne, a few miles farther. Golfers, attention! Divonne has just about the best course in the country. There is a swimming pool, a casino (with gambling and shows) and good food. Not inexpensive, but the rate includes meals and is not too high, everything considered.

SIDE TRIP ¶ You might also want to drive to Geneva (about forty-two miles from Lausanne), located on a remarkable site at the southwestern end of Lake Geneva. The newer part of town follows the lake shore, and there is a wide selection of hotels, with plenty of restaurants and marvelous watch stores, including the home offices and factories of many leading manufacturers. The largest and finest hotel in Switzerland is the new Intercontinental, with views of Lake Leman and Mont Blanc and with many unusual features, shops, restaurants; the Alba in the central part of town is new and very up to date; La Résidence is in a pleasant residential district; the Hotel Wex is small, modest and friendly. High above the town may be seen the cathedral, and around it cluster narrow streets lined with interesting shops—the entire area is very fascinating to explore.

If you've made Lausanne your headquarters, return to Montreux and pick up the tour. If you're staying in Geneva, you have the choice of returning to Montreux (by way of Lausanne) or of rejoining the tour by taking route 37 out of Geneva and driving along the south shore of Lake Geneva through Thonon and Evian.

FRANCE

Montreux to Chamonix—51 miles

Leave Montreux on route 9 by way of the same road on which you previously entered. Pass the Château de Chillon on your right and go through Villeneuve, Rennaz, Roche and Aigle. Then head for Bez, Evionnaz, Martigny-Ville and Martigny-Bourg. Here you pick up route 115 toward Chamonix; the road is none too good, but not unpleasantly bad, and the scenery makes up for it. You climb into Trient and then descend toward Châtelard. Just before the Swiss-French border, there is a cluster of small restaurants and tiny shops and a railroad station. This is your last chance to buy Swiss articles (at bargain prices) and if you like a *fondue*, Switzerland's classic melted cheese dish, it is very well prepared in the simple dining room of the railroad station.

Crossing into France involves a minute or two of formalities, but seldom more. After the border, there's a climb up a road surrounded by lovely scenery, then another descent into Argentiére, and soon you're in Chamonix. It's no problem at all to find overnight lodgings, for the Hôtel des Alpes and the Carlton are both good —the Alpes being particularly known for its cuisine, and you shouldn't miss trying the local fish prepared in the provincial fashion, the *féra farcie à la Savoyarde*. The Relais du Carlton also is an extremely good restaurant, by the way.

Of course, Chamonix exists solely because of its location at the foot of magnificent snow-covered Mont Blanc. If at all possible, try to obtain a hotel room facing the mountain, for if it is a moonlit night or if you should (fortunately) awaken early enough to see dawn over Mont Blanc, you will experience a never-to-be-forgotten moment of emotion (yes, we mean it). The town itself is touristy, sure, for everyone comes to look at the view. Even if you're the sort who cares little for scenery, Mont Blanc constitutes the exception; we feel certain you'll agree.

The classic trip to Mont Blanc is the two-stage ride by cable car, which leaves the foot of the mountain at the edge of the village of Chamonix. Be sure to wear stout shoes and don't forget to take something warm (sweater, etc.) no matter how pleasant the day, because it's almost always cool at the mountaintop. If extreme altitudes bother you, don't eat much before going and take some smelling salts; sunglasses too. The cable car carries oxygen, so if you feel faint, don't hesitate to ask for it. The little discomfort you might feel is worth it, though, because the experience is indescribable. One exception: heart patients should not attempt the trip.

Chamonix to Talloires—67 miles

From Chamonix, take route N-506 toward St.-Gervais and Megève, this last a famous winter skiing spot. There is a tremendous selection of hotels, most of them small and cozy, but if you're driving through during the summer months, don't be surprised if most are closed. The Hôtel Résidence is, however, open during the summer and is very nice; by all odds, the best place in town to eat is Gérentière, for the dining room is absolutely lovely, and incidentally, they have a few hotel rooms. From Megève, on to Le Praz, Flumet and Ugine, where you make a right turn (on route 508) toward Faverges and Annecy. After a few miles, there is another right turn toward Talloires, and with the lake on your left you soon reach that extremely attractive little village. Head for the lakeshore, if you wish to remain overnight or for a wonderful few days of relaxation, pleasure and good food. The Hôtel de l'Abbaye is delightful; its kitchen is renowned, particularly for a wonderful hot shrimp dish, *chaussons de queues d'écrevisses*, and we want you to raise your hand and promise not to fail to taste this succulent preparation! The almost adjacent Restaurant Père Bise serves magnificent, memorable classic French food, with considerable emphasis upon local specialties; dinner is relatively high, but an experience. There's swimming, boating and water skiing; you can drive around the lake; there are chateaux to visit and explore (the lovely one at Duingt is across the lake). You may gather that we like Talloires and Lake Annecy and you're absolutely right.

Talloires to Bourg—81 miles

Leave Talloires heading toward Menthon and Annecy. The latter is a quaint, good-size town at the north end of the lake; there are several hotels to select from, including the elaborate luxury-style Hôtel Imperial Palace, facing the lake; in town, the Old World d'Angleterre is off the main street and has a pleasant garden. For a vacationlike spot, the Hôtel Regina (just 1½ miles south of town via route N-508) has a marvelous site overlooking the lake. Annecy is at its most interesting during the Tuesday morning market, which spreads and overflows through the old part of town, a region with many canals, waterways and tiny bridges. We'll carefully resist saying that it's like a miniature Venice. If it's just a good meal you're seeking, head for the first-rate Auberge de Savoie, Annecy's best restaurant, located on the Place St.-François. Don't just drive past Annecy without parking your car and viewing the old part of town.

Leaving Annecy, watch the signs directing you to Bellegarde; this is route N-508, which goes on (via N-84) to La Cluse, at which point you could take a shortcut to Bourg via N-79, but may we suggest that you follow the signs directing you to Bourg by way of the main road. It's a little longer but lots more comfortable.

Bourg (-en-Bresse, its more formal name) is a fairly large town and a crossroads for a whole series of highways; for the tourist, the only sightseeing attraction is the church of Brou, which you'll notice on your right as you enter the town, a large structure that is not particularly interesting, although there is some good Flemish art in the interior. Across the street is a superb restaurant, the Auberge Bressane, which features *quenelles de brochet*, pike balls in a shrimp sauce, which are absolutely delicious. The Hôtel de France is by far the best placed to stay here.

Bourg to Avallon—128 miles

From Bourg, it's route N-75 toward Chalon, via St.-Trivier, Cuisery, Tournus; then N-6 toward Chalon, which the road bypasses. If you're hungry or sleepy, drive into the town of Chalon to the Hôtel Royal, where we feel sure you'll enjoy staying overnight, and if you eat there, don't fail to have the trout prepared in a paper bag.

Route N-6 goes on to Arnay-le-Duc and then reaches Saulieu, not a terribly interesting town, but it does house one of France's greatest restaurants, the Hôtel de la Côte d'Or. Dining here is not inexpensive (an understatement!) but the elaborate meal is memorable; the hotel has some bedrooms for overnight guests, but you should phone ahead, calling Saulieu 18, for there are comparatively few accommodations.

The next town is Avallon, a dull town, but this is the home of another great inn and restaurant, the Hostellerie de la Poste, whose kitchen is almost as good (and costly) as that of the Hôtel de la Côte d'Or in Saulieu. The Hostellerie de la Poste has a simple entrance, but after you drive into the lovely narrow courtyard, it will be to find yourself carried back several centuries; the rooms are charmingly decorated—and be sure to ask for those away from the road. Better phone ahead to Avallon 448 for a reservation.

If you're *really* looking for quiet country contentment in beautiful surroundings and with marvelous food, head for the Moulin des Ruats, a country hotel. It's only a few miles to the left of the highway via routes N-444 and D-427 (just before Avallon) in the Valley du Cousin. Don't miss this if you like French provincial inns.

Avallon to Sens——69 miles

From Avallon, go through Vermenton on the way to Auxerre, which isn't too fascinating for tourists although St.-Etienne Cathedral is worth seeing. For overnight stops, the Hôtel Fontaine is not an elaborate establishment but one that is pleasant and homey. For a meal, head for the Restaurant Cerf Volant, where chicken is the great specialty.

After Auxerre, the road widens and excellent time can be made toward Paris (until the immediate suburbs are reached). You go through Joigny and soon arrive at Sens, a historic place dating back 2,000 years, when it was a Roman town. Be sure to see another St.-Etienne Cathedral (Auxerre has one with the same name, too) and the Roman walls. The big hotel here is the Paris et Poste, but you will find the Hôtel de l'Ecu very warm and pleasant.

Sens to Paris——70 miles

From Sens, it's route 5 in the direction of Fontaine-bleau, although the road itself bypasses the town. To see this perfectly lovely place, make a right turn at any one of the several signs on the right-hand side as you near the town. This is a wonderful sightseeing spot that should not be missed by anyone interested in the history or art of France; be sure to visit the great forest and palace of Fontainebleau (especially the Marie Antoinette apartments). If it's late in the day and you don't have a reservation at a Paris hotel, it might be advisable to spend the night in this beautiful town and continue on in the morning. There are two good hotels—the Aigle Noir and the Legris et Parc. About three miles from town in the direction of Paris is the elaborate Restaurant Grand Veneur, which is extremely attractive, and on pleasant days, you'll eat outdoors on a terrace overlooking Fontainebleau Forest.

From Fontainebleau, it's a straight, wide, heavily traveled road (route N-) into Paris. En route you pass Orly Airport, then go through the Porte d'Italie. Eventually, after some slow driving (you're back in Paris now!)

you'll find yourself at the Seine River. If you want to get to a Right Bank hotel, make a left turn just at the river's edge and continue on until (with the Seine on your right) you see the obelisk on the right (on the other side of the river), denoting the Place de la Concorde. Cross the Concorde Bridge and approach the traffic maze; directly ahead of you will be the Rue Royale, at your left the tree-lined Champs-Elysées, stretching out toward the Arch of Triumph—and what a magnificent sight that is!

ᘒᔰ Motoring in France

The only documents you now need to bring a car into France are its registration certificate, your home-state driver's license and the Green Card (*Carte Verte*) insurance certificate. It's best to remember to have your insurance company furnish you with the Green Card before you leave home, or wherever you rent a car.

Roads are, generally, extremely good. France is adding miles and miles of new *autoroutes* (superhighways) all the time, and on all points of the compass from Paris, the main roads are excellent. The highway to the Riviera from Paris—part of it is *autoroute*—is heavily traveled all the time (night and day, winter and summer). During the August holidays it is *extremely* heavily traveled. If possible, always choose alternate routes to main highways. As a matter of fact, the tourist out to see the country will miss much by using the most important roads.

France now has two new traffic regulations. It is strictly against the law to zig-zag, that is, keep changing lanes on the highway. On the *autoroutes*, the superhighways, you are legally entitled to pass on the right, if traffic conditions permit.

In built-up areas the speed limit is 60 kilometers—37 miles—an hour, but it can be less than that. Signs will keep you posted. Similar signs will also advise you of speed limits on highways. If there is no sign on the open road, then you are to proceed prudently, using your own good judgment as to the maximum speed. In 1969, all drivers on French roads who have had their driver's licenses less than one year (including foreigners) were forbidden to drive faster than 90 kilometers—about 56 miles—an hour. Don't blow your horn except when necessary. In Paris, and a number of other places, horn blowing is forbidden. The traffic in Paris, by the way, is often enough to startle an American driver, but a few hours of practice will develop a feeling of confidence. French drivers are frequently reckless, by American standards. Care should be observed on narrow roads and at intersections.

If you see solid yellow lines on the road, be absolutely *sure* not to cross them. Often, when you're behind a slow-moving truck going up a hill, it's very tempting to try to pass, but if there are solid yellow lines on the road, don't try it. The police are very insistent about this regulation.

Be careful about city parking. Parking in restricted parking areas in the center of Paris and most French cities is regulated by a *disque bleu* system. The driver puts a cardboard disk in his window to show the time of his arrival. In setting the movable disk to the time of his arrival, the driver automatically indicates (through a special opening on the face of the disk) the hour at which he must vacate the parking place. This is usually an hour. Anyone cheating on this honor system of parking gets heavily fined. Disks can be obtained from gasoline stations, automobile clubs, hotel concierges, tourist offices, and so forth.

Parking meters are becoming increasingly prominent along French streets. In Paris, particularly, numerous underground parking garages have been constructed, and fees are relatively low.

GERMANY

National Characteristics

After the short and mild recession of a couple of years ago which followed the post-war "economic miracle," the German economy recovered its bloom, and the German *mark* has become the most coveted currency in Europe. The Germans are hard at work in producing the second stage of the *Wirtschaftswunder*. At the same time they also seem to be set on bringing about some assorted political happenings that, if they do not measure up as genuine miracles, at least will have to be classified as minor marvels. For the Germans are reaching out in all directions—East and West, particularly—for cordial relations with one and all.

When World War II ended, editorial writers and scholars had a field day generalizing about Germany, the Germans and how a seemingly civilized nation erupted with regularity into major wars. This was nothing new, for historians have been saying the same thing for some 2,000 years, all the way back to Caesar and Tacitus, who expressed their own opinions (most unfavorable). The Germans have been getting a bad press for centuries, and they're used to it.

Since 1946 dislike has in most cases turned to grudging respect for their hard work, perseverance and astonishing ability to recover from the ravages of war. But an indefinable something seems to divide most Americans from the Germans. What is it?

The Germans take themselves very seriously. In fact, it has been remarked that they are so serious that even their jokes are serious. Even streetcar conductors are so official-looking that a passenger is likely to give a salute before paying his fare or to expect a smart hand-salute after putting down the money for his ticket. Persons in authority, no matter how slight, are automatically accorded an *unwarranted* degree of respect—a phenomenon that always baffles the foreigner. In the United States, anyone is the butt of a laugh or a joke—especially the politicians, although the military come in for their fair share. From ward heeler to President, every American politician feels the barbs and slings of radio and television comedians. This is against the German tradition, where, until recently, politics were regarded as sacrosanct.

Then, too, Germans defy categorization by having produced some of the world's greatest musicians, including Bach, Beethoven, Brahms and Wagner to place them in traditional order. How does a nation of musicians produce the war chords that have laid waste Europe in succeeding generations? The people are neat, industrious, sanitary, hard-working, honest, conscientious and everything else that one could want—although slightly shy on charm. The American who comes today is made welcome, greeted heartily and treated well. West Germany, and West Berlin, have been our staunch allies, backing American foreign policy.

You'll see occasional evidence of war rubble and destruction, but just about every speck of it has been cleaned up. Generally, the people prefer to talk about something else and will, unless you insist. They don't want to think about the war years and the past and would rather concentrate on their future problems—of which they have more than a fair share. What the coming years will bring for Germany, no one can say for sure. But of one thing the Germans are positive: they will be trying the best way they know to preserve their national integrity.

When to Go

Spring more or less follows the Rhine northward. While alpine peaks are still snow-capped, valleys burst into green, and early April flowers pop up everywhere. May and June bring springtime perfection. September and October are the lovely fall months filled with festivals and wine celebrations. July and August are on the warmish side, and often overcrowded in the resort areas. But German resorts—and there are hundreds of them off the beaten path—are leisurely, very agreeable settings for a summer stay of several days or more. In the winter-time from December through March, the ski resorts in the

Harz Mountains and of course the Alps, especially in the Berchtesgaden area, are lively and filled with sports enthusiasts.

WEATHER STRIP: FRANKFURT

Temp.	JAN.	FEB.	MAR.	APR.	MAY	JUNE	JULY	AUG.	SEPT.	OCT.	NOV.	DEC.
Low	26°	28°	31°	37°	46°	52°	55°	54°	49°	41°	34°	29°
High	35°	38°	45°	54°	65°	72°	74°	72°	66°	55°	44°	37°
Average	31°	33°	38°	46°	56°	62°	65°	63°	58°	48°	39°	33°
Days of rain	15	15	15	13	13	13	15	14	13	14	14	15

TIME EVALUATION ¶ Berlin itself, although fascinating politically, has little to offer tourists other than a quick view of the local situation; allow two to three days. Of course, if you're driving through western Germany, at least a week, or even longer, would be appropriate. The Black Forest district and around Lake Constance are resort regions, and a week or two in those areas would be delightful for a luxurious rest. But the main vacation and tourist region is Bavaria, especially Upper Bavaria with its lakes, its Alps and with the city of Munich, the capital of Bavaria and the merriest place in Germany. Allow at least ten days or two weeks, and more if you are a beer connoisseur or a folklore enthusiast.

PASSPORT AND VISA ¶ A passport, but no visa, is required for West Germany and West Berlin. If you travel by train to West Berlin, registration cards will be issued during the trip for entry into the city. Motorists will receive control cards at border crossing points. Air travelers to Berlin encounter no formalities of this type, as they are traveling *above* the Russian zone and not *through* it.

HEALTH ¶ Water and milk are excellent throughout the country. As always, make sure the milk is pasteurized. There is no need for special precautions in food. If you drink too much beer (by too much we mean from three to five quarts on), of course you're on your own.

TIME ¶ Six hours later than Eastern Standard Time. When it's noon in New York, it's 6 P.M. in Berlin. When Daylight Saving Time is in effect in the U.S., the time difference is reduced to 5 hours.

CUSTOMS AND IMMIGRATION ¶ You're allowed two cartons of cigarettes, or 100 cigars or 50 grams of tobacco per person (above 15 years of age). American cigarettes, as well as all kinds of foreign ones, are available, although a bit higher than at home. There is no limit on the amount of German and other currencies you take into— or out of—the country. You can also bring in reasonable amounts of tea, coffee, perfumes and alcoholic beverages. Ninety-nine times out of a hundred, the German custom inspections are the merest sort of formality.

CURRENCY ¶ In the fluctuating international money market the *Deutsche mark* (DM) has become one of the most famous, and valued, currencies around. The number of marks to a dollar has been varying in recent years, and all signs are that there will be more changes in the future. There are 100 *pfennigs* in each mark, but few items cost less than 1 mark nowadays. Many shops, hotels and restaurants will accept American dollar bills as readily as German currency. Besides banks, of course, you can exchange money at all major railroad stations, airport terminals and highway border crossings. The exchange offices in railroad terminals, such as the Hauptbahnhof in Munich, are usually open from 6 A.M. to 10 P.M., or even later.

PRICE LEVEL ¶ Germany used to fit into the middle price range somewhere, but has been gradually drifting (upward) into higher latitudes. There are fixed-price menus in modest restaurants, but by the time you add up the lunch bill it will come to several dollars (without any frills). In general, a meal in a good restaurant—with wine —will be $5 or more. In a top restaurant it could easily cost $10; yes, $10! Hotel prices are a fine bargain. They are relatively low, and you get more than your money's worth. German hotels, for the most part, are either completely new or thoroughly renovated, and everything— even in the most humble big city hotel or in a country inn—is in apple-pie order. Some cities are more expensive than others. For instance, Frankfurt will be more costly all along the line than Munich.

TIPPING ¶ Hotels and restaurants automatically add the service charge to the bill. In hotels it ranges from 10 to 15 percent, and in restaurants it is a flat 10 percent. If you're ever in doubt about whether a service charge has been added to your restaurant bill, merely ask, "*Mit oder ohne Bedienung?*" (With or without service charge?) An easier way to say it—and it will be understood, too—is "*Mit oder ohne Service?*" If the service has been good, you might leave a little extra—up to 5 percent of the bill—for the waiter. Germans do not like to overtip, and the tipping problem is not nearly as acute as it is in France or Austria. At the hotel, tip those people who performed an extra service for you, such as the luggage porter and the room waiter. But do it moderately. Taxi drivers receive 10 percent of the meter reading, somewhat less on very long hauls. If a doorman has gotten a cab for you, he rates a tip of a half-mark (double that, if he has gone to a lot of trouble). Don't forget the hotel concierge, particularly if he has done something that would have been troublesome for you to do; not less than 2 marks, in any event.

TRANSPORTATION ¶ There are plenty of *taxis* generally available. It takes a while, and much blinking of the eyes, to get used to seeing nice big black Mercedeses used as taxis. But this is the land of the Economic Miracle! Taxis in major cities usually click 2 marks on the meter in taking off, and the clock keeps ticking away as smoothly, expensively and efficiently as a Mercedes motor.

Germany has a highly developed *bus* system, which works out well for anyone who wants to see the country and doesn't have a car. Most tour buses are new, or practically new, with sliding glass roofs, snack bars and —one item not to be joked about—toilet facilities. The hostess always speaks English, and fares are moderate. The government post office and the railroads run most of the buses, but there are private operators as well. You will have a wide choice of bus tours. A fine one is along Lake Constance (the Bodensee). Other spellbinders are the Black Forest, the Moselle and Rhine valleys, the trip from Munich to Berchtesgaden, the German Alpine Road (Berchtesgaden—Garmisch—Lindau) and the Romantic Road between Würzburg and the Alps.

Railroads are wonderfully efficient, clean and modern.

Even branch-road equipment, which had been antiquated, has been replaced to a large extent with new rolling stock. The German railroad operates along 20,000 miles of track. In addition, a couple of hundred nonfederal government railway companies (whew!) serve a network of 3,750 additional miles. So there is plenty of trackage for you to travel upon. You'll travel fast, too. Germany has some of the world's swiftest-moving trains (100 miles an hour is nothing at all for them!). One-hundred-fifty-mile-an-hour trains have already been tested. Trains have elegant names. The *Rheingold* (no, not the beer company!), a sleek First Class train, travels between Basel and Amsterdam. Other top trains have such names as *Parsifal, Helvetia, Saphir* (Sapphire), *Diamant* (Diamond), and *Blauer Enzian* (Blue Gentian) which is a day train between Hamburg and Klagenfurt in Southern Austria. The fares per mile vary according to distance, i.e., shorter trips are relatively more expensive than the longer ones. On express trains you'll have to buy a *schnellzug Zuschlag* (fast train supplement) for a small extra charge. Better buy it before you get aboard because it costs more on the train. The sleek TEE trains also are more costly than normal ones. For nighttime travelers, there are the international *wagons-lits* and the German *Schlafwagen* (the latter within Germany and on international lines to neighboring countries), sleeping berths as well as *Liegewagen* (the equivalent of French *couchettes*). The *Liegewagen* rates are not high.

Steamer service on the Rhine is particularly pleasant and is probably one of the outstanding tourist attractions in the country. The service is maintained by (*Achtung!*) the Köln-Düsseldorfer Rheindampfschiffahrt Gesellschaft, an old-time company that has been operating along the Rhine for almost a century and a half. (That long name, by the way, means Cologne-Düsseldorf Steamship Company.) With ships carrying such fine names as *Europa, Helvetia, France, Nederland* and the newest, *Britannia* (entered service in 1969), the company operates long cruises up and down the length of the river between Basel and Rotterdam. The journey (from Basel) downstream takes four to five days, depending on the season of the year; upstream, it ranges from five to seven days and is a touch draggy. The ship is your hotel, and in the evenings it ties up at the berth of some interesting river town. Fares depend on the type of cabin chosen.

Round-trip fares are a bit less than double the one-way tariff, but one-way is enough if you're under eighty years of age. Starting recently, the company for the first time scheduled wintertime service between Basel and Rotterdam. In addition, there are cruises on the Rhine and Moselle, starting from either Rotterdam or Basel and serving Trier. For complete details, get in touch with the Cologne-Düsseldorf Steamship Company, 15 Frankenwerft, Cologne 5, West Germany.

Besides the long, leisurely cruising, short river trips can be taken daily, starting from almost a score of major river towns along the Rhine between Cologne and Mainz. Tariffs are low. As we said, you can use your railroad ticket on the river journeys, in general, if the train route parallels the waterway. The company also operates a driving service, making it possible for motorists to board a steamer and have their car driven between Cologne and Mainz. Check with the Cologne-Düsseldorf Steamship Company at its offices in Cologne about the arrangements for, and the cost of, this service.

Steamers crisscross beautiful Lake Constance all the time. The German Federal Railroads operates more than thirty vessels. It is possible to do some exciting and highly agreeable sightseeing from one international port to another (in addition to Germany, Austria and Switzerland border Lake Constance).

All of Germany's major cities have modern airports and are linked with international *airlines* as well as its own Lufthansa German Airlines. A no-reservation air service, called the air-bus, operates a few flights a day between Hamburg and Frankfurt, and between Cologne and Hamburg. General Air and some other local lines fly from April through October from Hamburg and Bremen to Helgoland and from Helgoland to some other Frisian islands.

COMMUNICATIONS ¶ One place you can still find use for *pfennig* coins is when you are making a local phone call. Long-distance and overseas telephone calls can be made easily, and swiftly, from main post offices day or night. Be sure to reverse the charges when calling the United States. Many (not all, I hasten to add) German hotels make a stiff service charge for long distance calls, and you can generally avoid these unnecessary charges by having the charges accepted at home. Telegrams are relatively inexpensive and are handy for hotel reservations. Special rush telegrams are sent at double tariffs. Cables to New York cost less than those to other U.S. destinations. An air mail postcard to the U.S. costs about a quarter for the first five grams.

BASIC GERMAN

English-German

Waiter: *Kellner*
Bill of fare, menu: *Speisekarte*
Napkin: *Serviette*
Bread and butter: *Brot und Butter*
A glass of orange juice: *Ein Glas Orangensaft*

Boiled egg:	*Gekochtes Ei*
1. soft	1. *weichgekocht*
2. medium	2. *mittelweich*
3. hard-boiled	3. *hartgekocht*
4. egg cup	4. *Eierbecher*

Fried eggs: *Spiegeleier*
Bacon and eggs: *Eier mit Speck*
Ham and eggs: *Eier mit Schinken*
Coffee, black: *Kaffee, schwarz*
Coffee with cream and sugar: *Kaffee mit Sahne und Zucker*
Coffee with hot milk: *Milchkaffee*
Tea: *Tee*
Water: *Wasser*
Mineral water: *Mineralwasser*
Breakfast: *Frühstück*
Lunch: *Gabelfrühstück*
Dinner: *Mittagessen*
Shampoo: *Haarwäsche*
Haircut: *Haarschneiden*
Manicure: *Maniküre*
I want . . . liters of petrol: *Ich wünsche . . . Liter Benzin*
Change the oil: *Wechseln Sie das Öl*
Grease the car: *Schmieren Sie den Wagen*
How are you?: *Wie geht es Ihnen?*
Fine, thank you: *Danke, gut*
Please: *Bitte*
Thank you very much: *Danke schön*
Good morning: *Guten Morgen*
Good afternoon: *Guten Tag*
Good night: *Gute Nacht*
Yes: *Ja*
No: *Nein*
Morning: *Morgen*
Noon: *Mittag*
Afternoon, P.M.: *Nachmittag*
Evening: *Abend*
Night: *Nacht*
Sunday: *Sonntag*
Monday: *Montag*
Tuesday: *Dienstag*
Wednesday: *Mittwoch*

Thursday: *Donnerstag*
Friday: *Freitag*
Saturday: *Samstag* (*Sonnabend*)

One: *Ein*	Nine: *Neun*
Two: *Zwei*	Ten: *Zehn*
Three: *Drei*	Twenty: *Zwanzig*
Four: *Vier*	Thirty: *Dreissig*
Five: *Fünf*	Forty: *Vierzig*
Six: *Sechs*	Fifty: *Fünfzig*
Seven: *Sieben*	One hundred: *Hundert*
Eight: *Acht*	One thousand: *Tausend*

ELECTRICITY ¶ Voltages vary widely in West Germany, but the one in general use is 220 A.C. This means that your American appliances won't work on German voltages without a transformer. At the largest hotels, a transformer is occasionally available. You'll also need an adapter plug with round prongs.

SPAS ¶ Mineral waters bubble throughout Germany, and the country is the home of some famous spas, ranging from Baden-Baden in the Black Forest to Bad Reichenhall over in the eastern corner of Bavaria. There are more than 200 major health resorts. Some are in the mountains; others in luxuriant valley settings. All of them are equipped with open-air and/or indoor swimming pools. Most spas are open throughout the year. They are usually moderately priced, but during the months from October to March there are sizable reductions in rates, both on rooms and on full board. For a complete list of the spas, and the types of facilities and treatments at each one, get in touch with the Deutscher Baederverband (German Health Resorts), 27 Poppelsdorfer Allee, Bonn, Germany.

FOOD SPECIALTIES AND LIQUOR ¶ If you arrive in Germany after a visit to France, the food will be a great letdown; if you're coming from England, you'll be enthralled. If you've come directly from the United States, the classification is a little more difficult.

Germans are basically an outdoors people, fond of exercise and sports—wherever you go you'll see them walking, cycling, rowing and running. Naturally, an active race of people eat hearty fare, and the favorite dishes of the nation are heavy, substantial and stick to the ribs, even on a hot summer's day when you'd rather they didn't. At its best, the food is delicious in the way that a home-cooked meal can be; at its worst, it's likely to be floating in grease and covered with a dark brown sauce.

First of all, let's understand the meal hours and what may be expected. Breakfast, *Frühstück*, when you awake, is the usual continental coffee and rolls, but you can get some sliced ham (particularly if you're in Westphalia) or even a boiled egg, without causing an international crisis. Later in the morning if you're hungry (and you will be) look for a sign in a small eating or drinking place with the word *"Brotzeit"* displayed in the window—that means "Breadtime," or sausages and bread. Just the thing for that hour of the morning, or so the local folk think. In some parts of Germany, particularly in the south, everyone has a little snack, a *Veschperle*, which is traditionally black bread, a large slab of smoked bacon and a tiny glass of *Kirschwasser*, a dry cherry liquor; even if it's called *Z-nuni*, it still means second breakfast. (P.S.— You will like the *Kirschwasser* but you may not like the smoked bacon.)

Along the Rhine you can even have a glass of wine at breakfast. And no one will lift an eyebrow if you soak your breakfast roll in the wine.

Lunch is a ritual, served about 1 P.M., and here you'll be expected to down a large, filling meal of several courses—you know, something dainty like a bowl of thick split pea soup with ham, a platter of pigs' knuckles, sauerkraut and a boiled potato and a tremendous portion of pudding covered with a rich fruit sauce. Also a glass or two of beer and possibly a bottle of wine. (Coffee is postponed until about 4:30, when you have cake or pastry.) It should not be forgotten, however, that the lunch to most of the Germans is actually dinner, i.e. the main meal. If you prefer a light snack, look for a *Mölkerei* or dairy store, where you can have a cheese sandwich and a glass of milk. There's good coffee cake and coffee at a *Konditorei*, a pastry shop, some of which also serve light lunches. A *Bäckerei*, as you might expect, is a bakery, and those with tables will serve you anything you select with coffee. If you like sausages, there are all sorts of small shops selling them, and these will help you avoid the somnolent after-effect of a 2,000-calorie five-course lunch. The evening meal is *Abendessen* and is served from 6 P.M. on, and generally not too late except in the big cities; in restaurants it is the same type of meal as at mid-day, but in most private homes it is a much lighter meal.

There are various classes of restaurants—beginning with *Gaststätte* and *Gasthaus*, the general type. Food is always served at *Bierkeller* (beer restaurants)—usually a large variety of favorite local dishes—and at *Weinrestaurants* (wine restaurants)—the better and more expensive kind. In *Weinstuben* (wine taverns), the food is mostly incidental to the beverage. In the popularly priced dining establishments (but not in more expensive restaurants), you'll frequently find tables for six, eight or even ten people. In Germany, it's customary to share a large table (when the place is busy) and custom requires that a nod or bow be made to those you are joining; it's considered good manners to talk to your neighbors, but it's not absolutely necessary unless you're in the mood.

Herring is the favorite appetizer and it's served in endless variations. So-called green herring isn't really green —it's fresh (as opposed to smoked or pickled) and is generally fried. *Heringssalat*, is, as its name implies, herring salad, usually made with beets. We all know *rollmops* —rollmop herring—pickled herring rolled around sour onions; *Matjeshering* is a delicious style of salt herring, and so on. The soups tend to be on the substantial side —*Kohlsuppe* (cabbage soup), *Erbensuppe* (pea soup), *Gerstensuppe* (barley soup) and the most filling and richest of all, *Ochsenschwanzsuppe* (oxtail soup). One of the most popular in South Germany is *Leberknödelsuppe* (liver dumpling soup).

The German cuisine has exhibited little imagination in regard to fish; too often it is merely breaded, fried and served with a bland stock sauce, of which the chef seems to have an endless supply. Exception: the smoked Rhine salmon is absolutely delicious, particularly with a slice or two of dark bread and butter. Don't look for broiled steaks or chops in the American style except at the leading hotels; the German national cooking style is to roast, boil, stew, sauté or pot the meat and serve it with a thick gravy or sauce.

The big food specialty of Germany is the sausage, and what Germans can do with a pig, including certain unmentionable parts, is simply amazing. Even the porker would be astonished! To start on familiar ground, the frankfurter (our American national favorite) originated here, as did sauerkraut. Then too, we all know liverwurst, the liver sausage. But the Germans go on and on and on. Here are just a few: *Weisswurst*, a whitish-looking sausage; the *Regensburger*, a spicy pork sausage; *Nürnberger*, small, spicy charcoal grilled sausages, a specialty of Nürnberg; *Bratwurst*, a general term for pork sausage, the type depending on region but always roasted or grilled; *Rinderwurst*, a beef frankfurter; even *Blutwurst*, yes blood sausage. (Let's stop at this point.) In one area they're served boiled, in another fried, in some towns they are baked in pastry dough; in another, roasting is the custom. The favorite food expression in Mainz at festival time is *Weck, Worscht und Wein*—a roll, sausage and wine.

Vegetables are quite limited, the national ideal being firmly fixed on a boiled potato and sauerkraut or possibly cabbage. An exception may be made for the delicious Braunschweig and Schwetzingen asparagus, but frankly, this is an exception. Dumplings are a mania in Germany, they'll appear on menus frequently; after two *Knödel*, don't plan on being able to walk for an hour (after four *Knödel*, allow two hours)—but *Spätzle* are much lighter. The breads throughout the country are delicious, making our own pale white product seem innocuous. Look for Westphalian pumpernickel, dark brown and marvelous with sweet butter or cheese. Dark bread is called generally *Schwarzbrot*.

An outstanding pastry confection is the *Baumkuchen*, a towering cake glazed with icing; *Gugelhupf* is a marvelous coffee cake; a *Schwarzwälder Kirschentorte*, Black Forest cherry cake with whipped cream, is delicious. Our personal preference is for the Berlin doughnuts, *Berliner Pfannkuchen*, iced with sugar.

Coffee is variable in quality and always expensive; it is almost never included in the price of a regular meal. If you just order coffee, it will seldom be good. The best coffee is *Mokka*, which is served in a small pot and poured into a demitasse, but it is strong. You can order it *mit Sahne* (with cream). In rural areas, assume that the coffee will be terrible. And it will be.

Now, what about alcoholic beverages, as they are politely called? Let's keep in mind a few terms. *Weinbrand* is brandy; *Schaumwein* or *Sekt*, a sparkling champagne-type wine; *Süsswein*, dessert wine; *Weisswein*, white wine; *Rotwein*, red wine; *Liköre*, liqueurs; *Spirituo-*

sen, liquors (in general), and *Bier*, beer, but of course you knew that. Germany is, of course, a beer-drinking country, but wine is tremendously important, too. Use your judgment. If you're in a fine restaurant, drink wine. At a beer cellar, drink beer. Also, give consideration to the locality in which you find yourself: in the Moselle, Palatinate and Rhine districts, where wine is produced, order wine with meals. In southern Bavaria, around Munich, for example, beer is the thing. No matter where you are in Germany you'll be able to get both wine and beer. But it's fun to try a local product on its home grounds. You don't have to order a full bottle of wine. Just ask for a *Viertel* (pronounced *fear-till*)—a quarter of a liter. It will be served either in a glistening carafe or in a *Römer* (Roman), a large goblet on a straight or cone-shaped stem which supposedly originated with the Romans who planted the first vines in Rhine and Mosel valleys.

There are varieties of beer—you can have the light brew (*helles*) or the dark type (*dunkles*); try both, just so you'll know your preference. Then too, it can be small (*kleines Bier*) or large (*grosses Bier*) all the way up to steins and even tankards, called *Masskrüger* in Munich, which hold a quart! Wherever you go in Germany, you'll find a locally produced beer and you are hereby urged to sample them all, although the outstanding beer-producing regions are Munich, Upper and Lower Bavaria, Franconia, Dortmund, Berlin and Cologne, which last has the pale *Kölsch* beer. In Berlin during the summertime, they'll serve *Berliner Weisse*, a whitish beer frequently taken *mit Schuss*, with a splash of raspberry juice. You might like it, if you like raspberry-flavored beer. Still on the subject of beer customs, in North Germany it's a practice to drink *Schnaps* (a raw, clear, strong spirit) followed by a beer chaser. *Steinhäger* is the word that will bring you a dry, ginlike beverage with a juniper flavor, but each region has a local firewater. Shades of the boilermaker!

Now about wines: German whites are frequently among the world's best, but some terrible stuff is produced too. For example, many Americans almost automatically order a bottle of *Liebfraumilch*, but since this is a generic name, the chances are about equal that you won't necessarily get a fine bottle but the bottom of the barrel. Obviously, your best bet is to consult the wine steward or waiter and get his advice.

The leading white wines include the Rheingau type (you could hardly go wrong with a Schloss Johannisberg or Hochheimer); from the Rheinhessen comes Niersteiner, Bodenheim and Liebfraumilch; the Palatinate puts its wine in brown bottles, but the quality is uneven; you'll probably like Moselle wines (in green bottles) because they're so light and pleasant—order Wehlener Sonnenuhr, Piesporter, Zeltinger or Bernkasteler. Among the Steinwein, you'll find Escherndorfer and Würzburger, but they're a little crude to American palates and take a little getting used to. Most of the better German wines are white, with few good reds being produced. You'll find some passable red wine if you look for Schwaigern, Assmannshausen and Ahrweiler, but they're not in the same category with a great Burgundy or Bordeaux. Now a word of warning: a wine served in a jug or carafe is not going to be a great or important wine, nor will a very low priced bottle prove to be an exhilarating experience—you'll have to pay a fair price, say a few dollars anyway. However, and here comes the big caution, don't necessarily assume that you'll find real pleasure in a $15 or $20 bottle of wine because these are frequently the very rich, sweet (oversweet, we think) varieties that can be too much for our American palate, accustomed to martinis and bourbon.

The German wines are well labeled, and a close examination should help you understand what you're getting. *Originalabfüllung* refers to the fact that the wine was bottled at the vineyard where the grapes grew; *Auslese* designates selected or better grapes; *Beerenauslese* means hand-selected grapes, carefully picked over; *Spätlese* refers to a type made from a later vintage (meaning picking of the grapes) than usual, resulting in a richer and sweeter wine; *Trockenbeerenauslese* is the queen of German wine types, referring to grapes that have been permitted to dry on the vines until they become like raisins; it's very sweet and cloying, not to mention fabulously expensive.

The principal tourist areas are Berlin (in a class by itself), the Rhine valley, the Lake Constance-Black Forest region, the Bavarian Alps and the Heidelberg-Neckar valley district. The most interesting cities (besides Berlin) are Munich, Heidelberg, Nürberg, Bremen, Frankfurt, Cologne, Stuttgart and Düsseldorf.

GETTING YOUR BEARINGS ¶ The West German Republic consists of the following states: Bavaria (capital, Munich), Baden-Württemberg (capital, Stuttgart), Hesse (capital, Wiesbaden), Rhineland-Pfalz (capital, Mainz), Nordheim-Westphalia (capital, Düsseldorf), Niedersachsen, or Lower Saxony (capital, Hanover), and Schleswig-Holstein (capital, Kiel); and the city-states of Bremen and Hamburg.

Capital City

Berlin undoubtedly is one of the most exciting cities in the world for a visit today. In Rome or Paris, one relives history. In Berlin, history is in the making, and you'll surely want to see it yourself so you can tell your grandchildren (or anyone you want to impress!) just how you reacted to the struggle that has been underway here between the East and West for most of the postwar era. Berlin, to be sure, is not the capital anymore; Bonn is West Germany's capital. But for Germans it remains the chief city, the *Hauptstadt*—a showcase. We all remember the wartime story of the Reichstag fire and how this building (which had housed the old German legislative body) had been heavily damaged. Now from the ashes, the building is rising once more. The structure stands just a few feet from the East-West border wall in West Berlin.

West Berlin is completely safe for Americans, and there is no cause for alarm—even for the most timid tourist. The easiest way to reach West Berlin, as already mentioned, is by plane. Pan American Airways has direct service to the city, and the only document you'll need is a passport; no visa is required. Berlin also may be reached by train from Hanover; the necessary papers for passage through communist territory are issued at the local checkpoint. The trip from West Germany to Berlin may also be made by private car. (For particulars, see the section that appears subsequently on automobile tours covering the trip from Hanover to Berlin.)

There are 2.2 million people in West Berlin, about 1.1 million in East Berlin. A heroically executed monument, the Brandenburg Tor (Gate) is now at the dividing line between the East and West, although the gate itself is in Red territory. Near the Brandenburg Gate is the Russian Memorial (or *Denkmal*, as it is called in German), which is in *West* Berlin but guarded by *Russian* sentries. It was constructed from building material taken from the ruins of the Reichstag, which Hitler's gangsters set afire for political purposes. You'll surely want to take a picture of this unusual scene. The heart of the town is the Kurfürstendamm (shortened to "Kudamm" in ordinary conversation); it is roughly comparable to New York City's Broadway, except that Broadway is now more shoddy and run down. The Kudamm begins (or ends) at the Gedächtniskirche (Memorial Church), the famous landmark of Berlin, and across the square is the Europa Center, an involved group of buildings, with scores of shops on several levels and more than a dozen restaurants, taverns, and cafés of different types and classes reaching from the basement level to the twentieth floor of the central building from whose top there is a marvelous day and night view over Berlin and its environs. If you want to see the life and activity of Berlin at its frenzied peak, return here at night and view the modern prosperity that has returned to a city that was a heap of ashes only a few decades ago.

Berlin, even in its prewar heyday, could never compete with Paris or Madrid as a handsome city filled with historic buildings and beautiful streets; it was always something of a second-class city in this respect, and the war completed the picture by destroying many of its more important attractions. But there are a few sights, both old and new, worth visiting. If you come by plane, you'll arrive at Tempelhof Airport, with its remarkable half-mile crescent terminal building, so large that planes can come alongside and discharge passengers under a covered arcade. Outside the airport is the renowned Air Bridge Monument (you could never pronounce it in German), dedicated to those who took part in the airlift that saved West Berlin when the Russians tried (and failed miserably) to blockade the city.

You'll want to see the Rathaus, the Town Hall (no name-calling of politicians, please!), where the Freedom Bell (an American gift sneaked through Russian territory into West Berlin by our ingenious countrymen) sounds every day at noon. Incidentally, this is a good time to mention the fact that of all the peoples of the world to whom billions have been given in foreign aid, the Berliners are the most appreciative. Not far away in Russian territory are the remains of one A. Hitler's concrete bunker where the world and fate finally caught up with him.

One of the truly great sights of Berlin (and of the world) is The Wall, as everyone calls it. This wall, built by the Russian communists, is to keep the East Germans from leaving that unhappy land by the tens of thousands. It's often the scene of demonstrations or excitement, and no one could possibly visit Berlin without seeing The Wall. There's something about it, difficult to describe, that captures everyone's imagination.

We've postponed talking about a visit to the Russian sector because you should do all your West Berlin sightseeing first in order to appreciate the contrast. Don't forget that immediately after the war, both East and West Berlin were on an even footing—both almost completely flattened. East Berlin today has made some strides, but compared to its western portion it is pretty grim and seedy.

Should you visit the eastern part or shouldn't you? More than likely, you are perfectly safe, although occasionally incidents occur to change your mind. If you're at all hesitant, you should inquire locally about immediate conditions, because these change frequently, sometimes from day to day. The safest but least interesting way of seeing the Soviet side is by means of regularly scheduled bus excursions; this is just about as safe as you can get and rather dull. You'll ride along the reconstructed historic buildings in and about Unter den Linden, Berlin's famous prewar street, and to the reopened Pergamon Museum containing some of the finest Babylonian, Assyrian, and Greek antiquities, and then continue across Alexander Square and through the Karl-Marx and Frankfurter Allees (which used to be Stalin Allee) to the Treptow park with one more ubiquitous Soviet war memorial, and you will see functional apartment building rows, the outside of some shops, and a lot of poorly dressed and despondent people. The tour director will tell you when to take pictures and when not to, and in about 3½ hours you'll be back in West Berlin (usually the East border guards will check every passport and picture against the owner).

The more adventurous can visit the eastern portion of tne city by making a few advance preparations. Dress in your most inconspicuous clothes, tuck your passport away securely in your pocket, take just a little money with you and IMPORTANT, leave your camera home. Take the U-Bahn (subway) in the direction of Alexanderplatz. (Incidentally, DON'T take the S-Bahn, because its facilities run all the way past East Berlin into communist Germany, and you might find yourself under arrest.) If you want to hire a taxi in East Berlin, or have a meal, or buy some souvenirs, change your money at the money exchange shop near the subway station. Western money (American or West German) will not be accepted in East Berlin. All visitors must exchange their Western currency before entering East Germany.

There is a third way of visiting East Berlin. Take a taxi to "Checkpoint Charlie" (even the cabdrivers know it by that name), the American entry point to East Berlin. Check in with the American soldiers, show your passport and then walk across into East Berlin.

Use common sense; no matter how militantly anticommunist you may be, just walk about and keep your comments to yourself. Don't try to buy anything, because that's a sure way to get into trouble; another way is to take a picture, but you were cautioned previously not to bring a camera. It would seem advisable also to keep out of bars, and theoretically, in any event, you won't be served without showing your passport. Wander about and draw your own conclusions.

As Berlin is an island city, there are no short sightseeing excursions in the vicinity. Within the city limits at its western portions are extremely attractive lake regions, surrounded by pine woods, and actually lakelike sections of the Havel River, the best known among them the Wannsee and the Tegeler See. They may be visited by combined bus-boat sightseeing tours starting near and at the Gedächtniskirche. You can also reach their shores by taxi (a long ride) or bus and then take various available boat rides from there.

ACCOMMODATIONS ¶ As almost all of Berlin was destroyed during the war, all hotel facilities are just about brand new and very modern. Old-fashioned atmosphere and quaintness are not a part of today's Berlin. German hotel rooms are always, without exception, clean and more than adequate regardless of whether the accommodations are deluxe or simple. Like their Swiss neighbors,

Germans have discovered and practiced the fine art of hotel keeping.

Any establishment designated by the word "Hotel" is generally in the highest category of price and degree of luxury. The smaller places, with limited numbers of rooms, are frequently called *Gasthäuser*, these being customarily found in the smaller towns. The simplest, but not necessarily inferior, type of accommodation is in the pensions, designated by that word or by "*Fremdenheime.*" Of course, rooms with private baths are infrequently encountered in *Gasthäuser* or *Fremdenheime*.

BERLIN HOTELS

Kempinski: A very modern, leading hotel with excellent accommodations, modern décor in all rooms. Very pleasant, friendly atmosphere. An Inter-Continental hotel.

Hilton: A very large establishment of the Hilton chain, much like other luxury Hilton hotels all over the world. Fairsize rooms, modern furniture, several restaurants.

Ambassador: Recently constructed and very modern, with swimming pool on the roof, open fireplace in the lobby and a French restaurant.

Schweizerhof: Over 250 rooms, all with bath or shower and air-conditioned, very nicely decorated; Swiss-style restaurant.

Am Zoo: A somewhat older, but well-maintained hotel, very popular with Germans and tourists alike. Rooms are larger than average, nicely decorated.

Berlin: Excellently located modern hotel, offering all facilities. Rooms are good size with extremely pleasant furnishings; first-rate restaurant.

Palace: At the Europa Center, also one of the newest; comfortable, modern accommodations, medium size, two restaurants, and a pleasant bar.

Savoy: A small hotel near the Opera House. Average-size rooms, all with bath or shower, decorated in traditional fashion.

Three hotels located in suburban, residential parts of Berlin, for those who prefer to be somewhat out of the center of town:

Lichtburg: On the way towards the suburbs; a new hotel, attractively decorated. Average-size rooms, modern furniture.

Schlosshotel Gehrhus: Near the *Grunewald* (Green Woods). A remodeled private mansion about 10-15 minutes from Berlin's center. Spacious, homey and different. Fairly good rooms, pleasantly decorated.

Berliner Hof im Grunewald: Small in size, but all rooms have bath or shower; also has 7 suites and a small indoor swimming pool. Located on a lake.

BERLIN RESTAURANTS

Schlicter: An outstanding restaurant in the German tradition. Fine selection of wines; excellent display of cold appetizers.

Aben: A dignified restaurant, with quiet, old-fashioned elegance. Helgoland lobster, Russian caviar, Rhine salmon and Dutch oysters lead the long list of fish and meat courses accompanied by an even longer selection of wines.

Ritz: A very small place that has caught on with the public; features the food of eight different countries, mostly Asian. Reservations are absolutely essential.

Kottler's Zum Schwabenwirt: Swabian special dishes and wines from Württemberg, served in amusing surroundings; zither music in the evening.

Maître: French and expensive. On Tuesdays and Fridays bouillabaisse made with fish flown in from Marseille.

Alexanders: Elegant rooms upstairs with fine cuisine; in the pleasant downstairs rooms the prices are lower and the selection simpler but equally good.

Café Wien: A popular-priced establishment, with an outdoor cafe and indoor restaurant. Viennese food with rich desserts and a good wine list.

SHOPPING ¶ Shops in general open at 8 or 8:30 A.M. and do not close until 6:30 P.M., Mondays through Fridays. The Saturday closing time is 2 P.M. The exception is the first Saturday of the month. Then, most German shops stay open until 6 o'clock. Some shops close during the lunch hour (12:30 to 2:30 P.M.); others don't. Don't look for a hairdresser on Monday; they're closed.

Pointer: With rare exceptions, prices are fixed and no bargaining is possible. Exception: antiques. Germany is marvelous for shopping, with opportunities for many fine buys.

Cameras are probably the outstanding values. If you're an enthusiast, there is nothing we can add to your fund of information except to mention that cameras, photographic accessories and the whole kit and kaboodle of lenses, filters and related items are significantly cheaper than in the United States. It all depends—but the price differential might be 25 to 33⅓ percent, or more. First, if you have never worked with a "miniature" camera, the kind using 35mm. film, you'd better do some serious thinking about whether this is the kind for you. Comparatively speaking, they require a fair skill to operate with any degree of satisfaction. The Leica is the most important German 35mm. camera. It's hard to quote prices because they cover a wide range, in accordance with lenses and the camera models. There are less expensive 35mm. cameras than the Leica, and they might be just the thing for beginners. A truly miniature camera is the Minox, which fits into the palm of the hand. This is only for experts, because the film is small and, if the picture is not in sharp focus, enlargements get fuzzy. When greatly enlarged, Minox prints show a great deal of grain (a photographer's term that means in plain language that the enlargements are poor). The best and the newest types of reflex cameras are Rollei 66 SL, Contarex Se, Leicaflex SL, all of them "one-eye" reflex cameras, along with the older "two-eye" reflex cameras, such as Rolleiflex and Rolleicord; their prices vary greatly.

Binocular, telescopes and *microscopes* are usually sold by the camera dealers and represent the highest quality of workmanship at good prices, although scarcely given away free. Unless you have a special purpose in mind, don't buy the extralong, extremely heavy glasses, which are apparently used only in Hollywood movies about the German Navy. Much more practical, you'll find, is a comparatively lightweight model, not more than 8-power. Anything in this field made by Zeiss or Leitz will be slightly more expensive than that of some unknown firm, but you are assured of quality.

Optical goods are German specialties. Eyeglasses, sunglasses (particularly with Zeiss lenses) and contact lenses are all worth buying, but fittings might be a problem for the contact lenses.

Part of the "economic miracle" has been the production of *women's clothing*. Young women in Munich, Düsseldorf, Berlin and elsewhere today are among the best dressed in Europe. Berlin, Düsseldorf, Munich and Stuttgart are fashion centers and each features several women's clothing fairs every year. Berlin designers such as Oestergaard, Staebe-Seger, Schwichtenberg are best known, but Oestergaard recently moved to Munich. Whereas the designers' originals are high in price, as elsewhere, the numerous elegant boutiques offer excellent buys for the slim set and mass produced articles can withstand considerable competition, both in style and in price. Handbags and gloves are among the best in Europe. You might want to try the German version of nylon stockings called perlon, about which there seems to be some lack of agreement; try one pair and judge for yourself. If you're planning to buy Bavarian clothes, you'll do best in the Munich-Black Forest region; here you can get loden cloth articles and dirndls. Although Americans think dirndls are only skirts, the Bavarians use the term to designate a complete dress. The surprising thing about an authentic dirndl is that it looks equally good (or bad, depending on how you feel about them) on the young, the old, the slim and the well-rounded. Children's clothes are often marvelous values and are very attractively made.

Men's clothing is principally of the sporting or outdoor type; loden coats are good values, particularly if you live in the suburbs where they'll be useful. With these, you must have an alpine hat decorated with bird feathers which you can buy, or, if you are a hunter, with chamois hair (that is, if you can get that chamois). If you're a mountain climber, a pair of *Lederhosen*, leather pants, will surely last a lifetime (of mountain climbing), which may be shorter than you think.

For *china* and *porcelain* there are two great names: Meissen and Rosenthal. Old Meissen is extremely scarce and bargains are difficult to find. There have been some modern imitations, but they are *not* Old Meissen. The genuine article is not inexpensive and cannot be purchased in typical gift shops. Some nice pieces turn up occasionally in antique shops. Look for the pair of crossed swords in blue at the base of the porcelain article. The actual design of these swords, however, changes in accordance with the year or the period of creation and you'll need an actual chart of porcelain marks to pin down dates and authenticity. Another fine old porcelain mark to look for is KPM (Imperial Porcelain Manufactory).

Rosenthal china has been in existence less than a hundred years; there are, as a result, comparatively few antique pieces around. Since Rosenthal is actually a combine, consisting of a number of Bavarian porcelain factories, sometimes the name appears in full, sometimes it is indicated by a shield, a crown or the label "Johann Haviland." Rosenthal may be purchased in tea sets, odd pieces, complete dinner service for six, eight or twelve or in miscellaneous figurines. There is a tremendous saving over the Stateside prices, and it will be shipped home for you, properly packed and insured, by the Rosenthal shop where you buy it.

Leather goods, principally manufactured in Offenbach, are fairly good; look for luggage and ladies' handbags.

Toys are sensational here; even though you're no longer

a child, there's a marvelous time to be had in one of the toy shops. Particularly noteworthy are the electric trains, selling for considerably less than half of American prices for comparable articles. For girls, the dolls and doll houses (including some with running water) are absolutely amazing. Nuremberg is famed for its toys.

Cutlery, chiefly made in Solingen, and Geislingen, is outstanding. Carving sets, steak knives, penknives, tool kits, manicure sets and similar items like barometers, hygrometers and thermometers, are all worthwhile.

Clocks are available in three principle types: cuckoo clocks, 400-day affairs and alarm clocks. The cuckoo clocks are manufactured chiefly in the Black Forest and are amusing novelties at low prices. For more than 300 years, the peasants of the region have been whiling away long, quiet winter evenings making wooden clocks; the cuckoo part came later. If you *need* a cuckoo clock, this is the place to buy one.

The *400-day clocks* are something else and require a little explanation. They no longer represent a good value, because most of the United States has been inundated with 400-day clocks and prices have gotten almost as low as the retail price in Germany, so little is gained by buying here. *Alarm* and folding *travel clocks* are excellent buys, however.

Wines, liquor and *food* might be considered as gifts or personal purchases. If you've taken a fancy to any particular German wines, you'll save considerable money on these, but unless the wine retails for at least a few dollars a bottle in Germany, it will hardly pay to bother. Asbach brandy is the only German brandy worth considering, the others are quite crude; if you're going to France, buy cognac there instead. An excellent liquor purchase is *Himbeergeist* (a very dry white raspberry liquor) or the Black Forest *Kirschwasser* (clear cherry brandy); the smaller, attractively packaged bottles of these liquors are ideal for small gifts. Wander through a culinary section of a department store and you'll find yourself surrounded by all sorts of interesting canned goods and delicacies; many are worth shipping home.

Automobiles have shot to the fore as an important German export. The best-known name, of course, is Volkswagen. It comes in different models and savings in buying it in Germany can amount to hundreds of dollars. You have to figure on the additional cost of bringing it home and the customs duty, too, when you are doing your comparative shopping. The Porsche, the smooth sports car, is also a favorite with discriminating (and well-heeled) car buyers. The best car produced in Germany, unquestionably, is the Mercedes-Benz. The price differential on some of these models can be thousands of dollars. But they are priced accordingly—well up in the higher brackets. By the way, these foreign cars are so popular, you'll find good parts for them, and servicing facilities, all over the United States.

Novelties and odd gifts can be found everywhere. Look for music boxes, beer mugs, woodcarvings, 4711 cologne, kitchen gadgets, electric coffee makers and water boilers, elaborate candles and hundreds of other small items.

ENTERTAINMENT ¶ The night life in Hamburg, Berlin and Frankfurt is wild, unfettered and definitely not suited to everyone's taste. Much of it is vulgar and crude and tiresome. On the other hand, there are many pleasing restaurants, wine and beer cellars, discothèques and even night clubs with good music and entertainment. Some cities, particularly in the wealthy Ruhr district, have private clubs that are so selective that they are not anxious to have tourists come trotting in to dispel the serene spell. Hamburg's much-famed *Reeperbahn* is on an anything-goes, more-the-merrier basis. One night spot after the other is lined up in a long, noisy row, and all cater to the spender. Sometimes you don't have to spend much. A bottle of beer in one place might be not much more than a dollar, and for that you can sit down and stare for hours at a strip-tease show. That's pretty *cheap* entertainment, no matter how you look at it. At the other end of the country, in Munich, entertainment is always on tap, but really reaches peaks at two specific times of the year. One is the *Oktoberfest*, which gets rolling at the end of September on many acres of meadows that are tranquil at other times of the year. During the festival, all Munich (and large numbers of her friends) joins in. It is a time for free-wheeling beer drinking, sausage eating and hilarity. The other big amusement period is *Fasching*, the pre-Lent carnival time of fancy-dress balls and merrymaking.

But a night out in Germany does not have to be beer

cellars and bars by any means. It is still a country of music and music lovers. There are symphony orchestras from Berlin to Bonn. The Bavarian State Opera in Munich is, possibly, Germany's best.

SPORTS ¶ All of Germany is sports-minded, with athletics and physical exercise forming an accepted part of the national culture. Believe it or not, *walking* may be the favorite activity—you'll see everyone out on foot during the warmer months (no Americans, however!) in famous beauty spots like the Black Forest.

Golf is increasing in popularity, and there are about eighty courses scattered throughout western Germany. You needn't be a member of a German or American club to play; usually permission is granted on payment of a moderate greens fee. Bad Ems has the most beautiful course, but you'll find others in Berlin-Wannsee, Baden-Baden, Freudenstadt (in the Black Forest), Berchtesgaden and Garmisch-Partenkirchen, and most leading cities and resorts have at least one course.

Fishing in Germany's lovely lakes and streams is permitted with a license (fee $3.60), obtainable from the police department. Some private streams may be fished on payment of small weekly fees. For complete fishing particulars, contact the Verband Deutscher Sportfischer (VDSF), located in the Pressehaus, 1 Speersort, Hamburg. *Hunting* is very popular but because of the inroads urbanization has made on the countryside, game has become sparse in certain areas and results are likely to be somewhat indifferent; more details and information from the Deutsche Jadgschutz Verband, at 3 Drachenfelsstrasse, Bonn. Licenses are issued for five days, or for one year, by the Landratsamt, the District Office; annual licenses commence April 1 each year.

Horse racing is becoming increasingly popular, but German horses don't begin to compare with British or French. The biggest race is at Baden-Baden during late August and is worth attending if you're anywhere in the vicinity. *Trotting races* are fairly good, notably the German Trotting Derby at Berlin-Mariendorf, Munich and Hamburg.

Skiing and all winter sports are booming throughout Germany. The most popular ski areas are in the Harz Mountains and of course the Alps, particularly the Garmisch-Partenkirchen and Berchtesgaden zones. The Allgäu district is also popular. In the Kleinwalsertal—which you enter from Oberstdorf—you will be skiing in one of those geographical perculiarities of Europe: a region that is tied to Germany economically but, politically, belongs to Austria. Its geographical position in the mountains causes this. The region can only be entered from Germany.

In the Bavarian Alps are the two leading winter resorts of Germany—Garmisch-Partenkirchen and Berchtesgaden. G.-P. (to be familiar) is overcrowded on weekends but ideal during the remainder of the week except during the Christmas rush; this is the place to come if your spouse doesn't ski because there's so much else to do around here—theaters, concerts, entertainment. Not too far away is Zugspitze Mountain, with the longest skiing season—all year round. Berchtesgaden is well equipped and has many ski schools, in case you're a novice.

MISCELLANEOUS ODDMENTS ¶ When you consider all the American activity in West Germany in the postwar decades and the continuing presence of so many United States troops, it should come as no surprise to you that many Germans speak English—particularly in the tourist hotels, restaurants and shops. But they never do when you're in dire need of information in some small village in the mountains.

The local folk (male) have a habit of removing their hats and bowing when they meet acquaintances—and they don't just lift the headgear an inch from their heads, but a yard.

If you see what looks like the capital letter "B," just give it a double S effect and you'll come out fine. Example: Schlo*B* in German is really Schloss, a castle.

Ladies may smoke in restaurants or hotels but not on the street; just not done.

If you ask for the road to Munich, don't be surprised if the German shakes his head negatively; you've got to learn the German place names, in this case, München. Cologne is Köln, Brunswick is Braunschweig and so on.

Hotel and restaurant keepers are scrupulously honest; there may be exceptions but we've never met any so far. However you should be on the alert in low level night spots, where the lights are so dim that you cannot read

the list of drinks or where you have forgotten to ask for
one, but this is, of course, good advice anywhere in the
world.

ঙ A Tour of Germany

The tour begins at Flensburg, near the Danish border,
on the assumption that you are coming from Copenhagen. The Danish portion is described in the appropriate
section devoted to Denmark.

A tour of the Black Forest, starting from the French
border, is described in the section on France.

Flensburg to Hanover—201 miles

The first stop is at Krusau, the Danish-German border
point, which was arranged by a plebiscite held in 1920.
The road continues on to Flensburg (no longer Flens-
borg), a city worth at least a brief stop for the sake of
seeing the old houses, guildhalls and Gothic church; for
a stay, there are Hotels Flensburger Hof and Europa.
From Flensburg follow route N-76 to Schleswig, then
N-77 through Rendsburg and its very long bridge; the
old town has some fine old structures. Then to Neumün-
ster, not too interesting for tourists; here you pick up
route N-4 and proceed to Bad Bramstedt, a health spa
famous for its mud baths, but if you don't care for one,
continue on to the extremely important city of Hamburg, the second largest city in the country (with 1,850,-
000 inhabitants), on the River Elbe.

Hamburg, a vital industrial area, was heavily damaged
during the war, although some fine buildings remain,
notably the Rathaus (City Hall) and St. Michael's Church.
Most of the city has been rebuilt in very modern architecture. You will find some of the most beautiful sections
of the city along the shores of the two lakes formed by
Alster River: the heart of the city around the smaller
Binnen Alster lake, the lake sightseeing boats take off
from here; and the elegant green residential districts on
much larger Aussen Alster lake. One of the most interesting sights in Hamburg is the great port which can
be visited by several types of sightseeing boats departing
from St. Pauli piers. In the St. Pauli section is the no-
torious Reeperbahn area, famous for its naughty night

life, and perhaps that's an understatement; don't go if you're easily shocked.

The best hotels in Hamburg are Vier Jahreszeiten on the lakefront of the Binnen Alster, and Atlantic on the shore of Aussen Alster; they are among the most luxurious hotels in Germany (and Europe). A top eating place is Weinrestaurant Ehmke, especially for seafood, including the famous Helgoland lobster. Among other good restaurants are Dölle near the Opera, Ratsweinkeller in the vaulted City Hall cellar, and Sellmer out at the fishing port (take a cab), outstanding for fresh fish from the North Sea.

During the summer months you can take an excursion ship, leaving early in the morning, down the Elbe river past the beautiful residential suburb of Blankenese and the port and beach town of Cuxhaven at the river estuary, out to the open sea and to the island of Helgoland, once a sea fortress and now a pleasant and colorful vacation resort and a free duty paradise for liquor, cigarettes and what not. You return to Hamburg late at night.

A side trip from Hamburg takes you southwest to Bremen, another great port city, with a population of about 600,000 (the second German port after Hamburg) and located on the Weser River. The most interesting sights in the old town center are the medieval cathedral, the 12th-century church called Frauenkirche, the famous Renaissance-style City Hall with a big statue of the medieval knight Roland in front of it, and several old guild houses, many reconstructed partially or fully after the holocaust of the World War II air raids. Bremen has the fine luxurious Park Hotel and some good and interesting restaurants, among them the large Rathskeller in the City Hall cellar with the longest wine list in Germany (about 600 types are available), and Essighaus in a former patrician town residence. Downstream at the estuary of the Weser is Bremerhaven, another important port, where you may land if you come to Germany by ship. Bremerhaven is also the port for the U.S. forces in Germany.

Back on our route south from Hamburg, follow the road N-3 through Harburg, Wintermoor and Soltau and into Celle, an interesting place to spend an hour or so of wandering about; there are many fascinating medieval buildings including the town's pride, a ducal castle. Route

N-3 goes on to Hanover, a city of half a million population, which can also be reached from Hamburg directly via the Autobahn in case you are in a hurry.

Hanover (spelled Hannover in German) is a heavily industrialized city with both an old and a new town hall and some few remaining timbered houses. Basically, however, it is a city for business and commercial trade and a very lively place indeed during the industrial fairs. It is at Hanover that plans should be made (if not arranged previously) for an automobile trip through Communist-controlled territory to Berlin, should that be on your schedule. Those motorists proceeding south will find the tour continued immediately after the section that follows. The Intercontinental Hotel in Hanover is supremely modern. For something comfortable, but in the lower-priced field in Hanover, try Esso's Motor Hotel on the Tiergarten.

Hanover to Berlin—174 miles

Leave Hanover via the northeast by route N-3, turning onto the autobahn. This superhighway does not touch any town, but signs soon indicate, as the road continues, that the motorist is passing Peine and later Braunschweig (or Brunswick, in English). Should you wish to turn off the autobahn, this city has some interesting sights, notably Dankwarderode Fortress (on an island in the river), the statue of the renowned Brunswick Lion and a Romanesque cathedral. The next town is Helmstedt; here one can see a ninth-century monastery, many half-timbered houses and the old university of Juleum. Approximately two miles farther along is the border crossing. Appropriate transit papers are issued for a small charge at this point. Motorists are strongly urged not to leave the main highway under *any* circumstances and not to stop unnecessarily from this point to Berlin. *This is important!*

From the border to Berlin is a run of 120 miles; since no diversions from the main route are permitted, it is fruitless to describe anything along the route. Berlin is described separately earlier in this chapter.

Hanover to Cologne—182 miles

Take route N-6 to the west out of Hanover until it meets the autobahn; turn onto this fast road (route N-55-D) heading south. Those who wish to make an

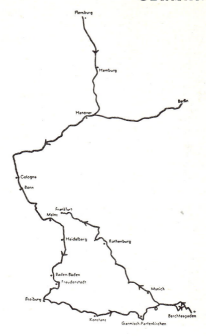

overnight stop may turn off into the interesting old town
of Herford and stay at the Hotel Stadt Berlin; the next
opportunity is at Bielefeld, where there is the Hotel
Kaiserhof. As we proceed, signs indicate other towns
along the route: Gütersloh, Wiedebrück, Hamm, Dortmund and Düsseldorf, where it would be advisable to
spend a little time. In this busy industrial city, the leading sight is the famous shopping street, the Königsallee
(which everyone calls the Kö), but a visit might be in
order to the old Rathaus (City Hall) and St. Lambert's
Church. You may choose one of the two newest and
largest hotels, Düsseldorf Intercontinental (opened in
1969) or the Hilton (opened in 1970), or one of the
older but luxurious and atmospheric ones, Breidenbacher
Hof or Parkhotel, both with very fine restaurants. Düsseldorf has several notable restaurants, among them
Müllers and Fest, rated among the best in Germany and
located in the Königsallee. If you're looking for atmos-

phere in the old town section, the Schneider-Wibbel Stuben is located in the small street of the same name reserved exclusively for pedestrians. The old town district, largely destroyed by air raids during the last war, has been rebuilt in such a fashion that it still exudes a good deal of the original atmosphere. Because of the numerous drinking places ranging from small bars and tiny taverns to enormous brewery restaurants, it's sometimes referred to as the "longest line of bars" in Germany. Here you can sample a special kind of beverage called Altbier (Old Beer), which is produced according to an old German beer recipe used over a century ago. Nowadays, this kind of beer is mostly found in Düsseldorf or Cologne (where it's called Kölsch); it is aromatic, somewhat bitter, usually amber in color, and has a peculiar fruity taste. It's worth a try.

An interesting side trip for shoppers may be made from here to Solingen (south from Düsseldorf via N-8 to Langenfeld, then left turn via N-229); this is the town that makes all sorts of German cutlery—knives, razors, scissors, etc. Don't fail to see the lovely old Müngsten Bridge, between Solingen and Remscheid. Nearby is Wuppertal, another important industrial city and a pioneer in experiments attempting to solve modern city traffic problems. Here you'll find the famous monorail, a suspended railway invented by a local engineer and constructed at the turn of the century. A two-story (one above the other) road tunnel was added in 1970, the first of its kind in Europe; the traffic in the ¾-mile tunnel is controlled from police headquarters (about 4 miles away) via some 20 closed-circuit television cameras installed in the tunnel.

From Düsseldorf, take route N-8 south to Leverkusen, then into Cologne (or Köln, in German), where a stop may be made at Excelsior Hotel Ernst, Dom-Hotel, or Baseler Hof. Cologne has a history dating back to Roman times, but many of her finest structures were damaged during the war years, although the renowned cathedral was spared; the spacious interior is well worth a visit, no matter how hurried. A number of other interesting churches were spared completely or only partially damaged during the war. There's St. Gereon with a pre-Romanesque central section; if you're really an enthusiast of old churches, you could also visit St. Pantaleon, St. Severin, and St. Aposteln. Some fine Roman ruins remain in Cologne, including an aqueduct and a city wall tower.

At the Wallraf-Richartz Museum, there is an excellent collection of modern paintings, plus a good selection of German, Dutch, and Flemish paintings. For dining, the Excelsior Hotel Ernst has a very good menu. Although it's expensive, the Weinhaus Wolff, located in the Komödienstrasse (not far from the cathedral), is a fine restaurant.

Since Cologne is such a popular place with all European tourists (not only Americans), it is possible that you might have trouble finding hotel accommodations. To prevent this, the Municipal Tourist Office operates a very helpful service and will do its best to get you the hotel accommodations you want, or a room in a private house if that is your desire. The office is situated just across from the main entrance of the cathedral. It is open from 8 A.M. to 10:30 P.M. on weekdays and during the summer and on Sundays and holidays from 9 A.M. to 10:30 P.M. The wintertime hours on Sundays and holidays are 2 to 10 P.M. The phone number is 20-38-33-45.

A side trip west from Cologne, either via the Autobahn (about an hour's drive) or route 55 (longer), takes you to Aachen, which once—around A.D. 800—was the capital of Charles the Great (Charlemagne, if you prefer). You can still see his marble throne in the cathedral, whose central, Carolingian-style section was constructed around 800. His remains are in a beautiful sculptured shrine on the main altar. After Charles the Great, who was the first Holy Roman Emperor and who set the pace, thirty-two Holy Roman Emperors of the German Nation, as the full title went, were crowned in the Aachen cathedral, although most of them resided in Vienna.

Cologne to Mainz—111 miles

From Cologne south along the Rhine River to Mainz is possibly the most scenic route in all Germany. (See the section on Transportation for a description of the steamer service on the Rhine River.) All motorists are strongly urged *not to* drive from here to Mainz, if at all possible, because much of the view cannot be seen. The road from Bonn south on the west bank of the river (although better than the east) is quite narrow and, during the summer months, is heavily trafficked. The motorist might find the trip pleasant in April–May or September–October, when traffic is light, but in the busy summer months the trip is difficult, driving is tiresome and the entire run may become a somewhat tedious ordeal. Steamer service from Cologne to Mainz is good and very frequent; it is possible to arrange to have your car driven (or shipped) to a point along the river—this is undoubtedly the ideal method, for you avoid driving south *and* get the benefit of the marvelous river trip.

The ideal way to cover this lovely stretch of the Rhine River is a combination—one way by river boat, one way by car in order to tour the lovely medieval towns that extend along the river banks. If time permits, this is undoubtedly the best method.

If the road is to be driven, leave Cologne via Severinstrasse (route N-9) to Bonn, now the capital of the Federal Republic of West Germany. Music lovers will surely want to visit Geburtshaus Beethovens, Beethoven's birthplace, and the museum. Bonn also offers the Münster (an 800-year-old cathedral), the university buildings, the Bundestag (government building), the colorful marketplace and adjacent town hall and Poppelsdorfer Schloss, an eighteenth-century pleasure castle.

The number of hotel accommodations available in Bonn has increased considerably, but because of government activity and frequently-scheduled conventions, it is still not easy to get a room, at least not at the last moment. I suggest you reserve in advance if you plan to stay overnight here. Among the best hotels are the Königshof on the Rhine River (so be sure to request a room facing the river) and the Steigenberger Hotel Bonn (now that's a mouthful!) located on the top floors of an office building with an indoor swimming pool on its eighteenth floor. Other less expensive places to stay include the Am Tulpenfeld, Schlosspark and Bergischer Hof; this last hotel has very good food.

From Bonn, head south on Koblenzerstrasse via route N-9, a lovely winding road through Bad Godesberg, a summer vacation spot with a tiny colorful place for an overnight stop, the Adler Hotel. Other good hotels are the Park, Insel, and the large Rheinhotel Dreesen situated on the bank of the Rhine. The best food in town is available at the colorful Michaeli Stuben in the Burgstrasse. Then comes Mehlem; the road bypasses Remagen and goes into the ancient village of Sinzig. From here continue on to Niederbresig, where you'll find the Hotel Marianne on the Rhine bank; next, the medieval walled town of Andernach, complete with towers, ramparts and turrets, where the Rhein-Hotel offers Old World hospitality. From Andernach an extremely pleasant side trip of nine miles may be made to the eleventh-century abbey of the Benedictines, Maria Laach, where you'll find, alongside the Laachersee, a fine church of the Middle Ages and a series of extinct volcanoes. The next town on the route is Coblenz (Koblenz in German), where the Rhine and Moselle rivers meet to form what is often called "the German Corner"; a pleasant hotel is the Pfälzer Hof near the main station. Coblenz's outstanding sight is the Feste Ehrenbreitstein (Ehrenbreitstein Fortress), on the east side of the river; open from 10–6 daily. Another important attraction is the Weindorf, or Wine Village, made up of typical taverns representing the different wine districts; don't miss this.

A side trip up the Mosel (which is the German original for Moselle) Valley, winding between steep hills covered with vineyards, will be of great interest to a wine connoisseur, for it is here—especially in the area around the pretty half-timbered town of Bernkastel—that some of the best German wine is produced, which means some of the best white wine in the world. The city of Trier, with the famous Roman-built gate of Porta Nigra, is the oldest in Germany; a Celtic settlement of a Treveri tribe existed here as early as 400 B.C. while the present city was founded by Emperor Augustus in 15 B.C. During the following centuries Trier was the Roman capital of the north from which the ancient Rome ruled over Western Europe and a number of Roman Emperors actually had their main residence in Trier.

At Coblenz, it is advisable to cross the river to Ehrenbreitstein and follow route N-42 south to Niederlahnstein, Oberlahnstein and Braubach, a miniature fortified village that is worth walking through. Farther along is Filsen, where a pleasant ferry trip may be taken across the river to Boppard, a fascinating old town right out of the Middle Ages; June is the month to be in Boppard.

This entire area is wine country, with miles of rolling ground devoted to vineyards, dominated by castles reminiscent of Wagnerian opera and all of the folklore of the Rhine valley. Continue along through Bornhofen and St. Goarshausen, from which point it is possible to see Lorelei, the legendary rock immortalized by the poet Heine. St. Goarshausen also has Katz and Maus (Cat and Mouse) castles; a ferry goes across the river to St.

Goar, an ancient market town dominated by the ruins of Rheinfels Castle, largest on the Rhine. A Ritterschänke (a Knight's Tavern) is very colorful and amusing for a visit; a small hotel was recently added, and it's pleasant for an overnight stay.

Then comes Kaub, a walled town; in the middle of the river stands the island castle of Pfalz, formerly a medieval toll house where all river traffic had to pay a fee—even in those days! Next, on the right (or eastern) river bank come Lorchhausen and Lorch, two old wine-growing towns, marking the beginning of the famous Rheingau wine region where some of the best white wines in the world are produced. From here nearly to the spot where the Main River flows into the Rhine, every village and town is a famous name to wine connoisseurs the world over. Lorch is also a starting point for an inviting side trip into the beautiful Wisper Valley; it's a very pleasant ride to Gerolstein and Bad Schwalbach, from which point you could continue to nearby Wiesbaden. The next town on the Rhine after Lorch is Assmannshausen, the famous old wine center noted for its red wines. Alte Bauernschanke and Weinklause are among several characteristic wine tavern-restaurants in the narrow town streets where loud music resounds in the evening. From Assmannshausen you can drive or take a chair lift to the vicinity of the Jagdschloss Niederwald, a former hunting castle converted into a hotel and restaurant specializing in game dishes. Assmannshausen has the well-maintained 400-year-old Hotel Krone; its guest list included Goethe at one time. It is open from late March until mid-November, and during the warm weather you may dine on the terrace; otherwise the excellent food is served in an elegant, wood-panelled restaurant with large windows overlooking the Rhine; the long wine list is headed by local reds from the hotel's own vineyards. However, because of the proximity of the railroad line, ask for a room on the quiet side.

Next comes the lovely town of Rüdesheim, the center of Rheingau and definitely worth a stay. Here you'll find the first class Parkhotel Deutscher Hof, or the less expensive Traube, Rheinstein, or Aumüller, all in a line flanking the Rhine bank; the rooms overlooking the river offer a beautiful view. Unfortunately a railroad line flanks the river, too, so you'd do well to ask for a quiet inside room. The Rüdesheimer Hof is a good hotel in a quieter location about two blocks away from the river. Most of the

Rüdesheim hotels are closed during the winter, which is not a suitable time of the year to visit this area anyway. In the center of town is the picturesque narrow street called Drosselgasse, lined with indoor and outdoor wine restaurants and taverns, with lots of jolly music and singing. Rüdesheim is famed for its wines, and joy is completely unconfined (and sometimes unrefined) during the wine festival in September. Don't miss the town's old houses, the market square with its parish church and town hall, and the Brömserburg Castle which houses a very interesting wine museum. Take a walk or drive to St. Hildegard Abbey amidst the vineyards and ride on the chair lift to the majestic Niederwald Monument high above Rüdesheim; it was erected in the last century to commemorate the German unification. From the Niederwald Monument you can reach the Jagdschloss Niederwald in about 15 minutes on foot. Wine lovers will also want to visit nearby Schloss Johannisberg, whose white wines are among the best in the world. There is ferry service across the river to the town of Bingen where you can look back at a wonderful view of Rüdesheim.

From Rüdesheim, continue along the Rhine through Geisenheim, Winkel, Mittelheim, and Oestrich to Hattenheim, where a side road winds through the vineyards to the historic monastery of Eberbach, now the headquarters for an important wine estate. Back at Hattenheim, proceed through Erbach to Eltville, where it is possible to visit the champagne (or *Sekt*, as it is called in Germany) cellars of the Mattheus Mueller (MM) Company—an interesting tour if you have never seen the champagne process. Several other champagne producers in Rheingau also keep their doors open for similar visits. An attractive place to stay overnight in this area is the Schloss Reinhartshausen, a castle hotel decorated with period furniture, located on the Rhine bank in Erbach, with fine food and, of course, its own wines.

The city of Wiesbaden is reached via Niederwalluf and Schierstein. Wiesbaden is not only the capital of the German Federal State of Hesse but also one of the leading European spas. The International May Festival with musical and theatrical performances is staged here every year. You'll find a wealth of places to stay, with all the attractions and tourist accommodations of a large city. Hotel Schwarzer Bock, the largest and most luxurious, has a thermal water indoor swimming pool. The runners-up are the Nassauer Hof and Rose hotels. Fine food is available at the Mutter Engel on Barenstrasse 5.

From Wiesbaden, head back to the Rhine. At Biebrich, still part of Wiesbaden, is the baroque palace of the Dukes of Nassau, and at Kastel, a suburb of Mainz, cross the Rhine on a bridge to get to the city of Mainz proper. The top sights in Mainz, which is the capital of the German Federal State of Rhineland-Palatinate, are the imposing 1,000-year-old cathedral and the original Gutenberg printing press which may be seen in the World Museum of Printing, for it was in Mainz that Johann Gutenberg, the inventor of movable type, was born in 1397, lived, worked, and died in 1468. There is, of course, also a Gutenberg Monument on Gutenberg Square. Mainz is a wonderful place to visit during late August and early September when the wine market is in full swing. Should you remain overnight, the Mainz Hilton, located on the river bank, and the less expensive (but also very modern) Europa-Hotel are recommended. There's an interesting restaurant, the Haus des Deutschen Weines ("Home of German Wine"), in the Ludwigstrasse, not far from the cathedral, where you can choose from hundreds of wines from all of the German wine regions.

If you wish to make a side trip, route N-40 goes on to Frankfurt, the financial and industrial center of Germany. It was heavily bombed in the war, but has been completely rebuilt. The ideal choice if you want to remain overnight is the most modern Intercontinental Hotel. The excellent and elegant Frankfurter Hof has an ideal location in the heart of the city. The better restaurants: Brückenkeller, deep under the street level and exuding medieval atmosphere; Kupferpfanne for grill and dishes prepared at the table; Frankfurter Stubb in the cellar of Frankfurter Hof, quite large with 19th-century Frankfurt mementos, musical evening entertainment and local cuisine. Most people want to see Goethe's House and Museum, open on weekdays from 9 A.M. to 6 P.M. and on Sundays from 10 A.M. to 4 P.M. There is a small entrance fee. Also outstanding is the Römer, once the Town Hall, composed of three fine Gothic gabled roofs. St. Bartholomew's, the cathedral, is worth a visit; the entrance fee for the tower is 30 pfennigs. Nearby is the Leinwandhaus, the Cloth Hall, a reconstructed fourteenth-century building of remarkable appearance. In the foyer of Frankfurt's city theater hangs Marc Chagall's *commedia dell'arte* painting. On your shopping tour head for the heart of the city, to the area near the Hauptwache where big department stores are located as well as many smaller shops.

Mainz to Heidelberg—57 miles

If you decide not to visit Frankfurt, leave Mainz by route 28 to Darmstadt (from Frankfurt to Darmstadt, follow route N-3). Darmstadt's sights include the famous porcelain museum, the Porzellanschlösschen. This is an intellectual's town, with many writers and artists and the home of many German publishing houses; a large literary and artists colony is located near the "Wedding Tower," the Hochzeitsturm. From here proceed south by N-3 through the gently undulating hills of the Odenwald, famed for a mild climate due to the sheltered location; spring comes to Odin's Wood earlier than in the southernmost portions of Germany. The road travels by the various "heims," but passes through Bensheim, Heppenheim, Weinheim and Schriesheim.

Then into Heidelberg, the renowned university town on the equally famous Neckar River. (Does anyone remember *The Student Prince*? Every German operetta, it would seem, is set in romantic Heidelberg, but where could a composer and librettist find a more idyllic location?) For here is the dream setting—crisp, sparkling air, a ruined castle above the city, lovely scenery, a colorful student quarter and one of the most charming river valleys to be found anywhere. And is it mobbed during the tourist season? It is! Sometimes it is so mobbed that much of the pleasure is lost. A great hotel is the Europäischer Hof; Esso opened a motor inn recently. Other fine places to stay are the Schrieder, Schwarzes Schiff and Haarlass Park hotels. In case you have not reserved hotel space in advance the chances are very good that you'll need help in getting a room for the night. Help is right there; the local tourist office at the main railroad station (about a mile from the heart of town) will see to it that you are comfortably housed. Perkeo on the main street is the landmark among the restaurants. Some of the historic students' taverns in the university area are Schnookeloch (going back to 1407), Zum Seppl and Goldener Hecht. The university is the thing here: the various buildings, the students' inn and the Karzer Prison, which was used to incarcerate students for infractions of university rules. Heidelberg Castle is almost too perfect. It is probably the loveliest of all German ruins, magnificently situated above the city. The world's largest wine cask is in the town, the Heidelberg Tun, which is twenty-eight feet long and holds almost 50,000 gallons. Even if you don't ordinarily like museums, a visit is warranted to the Kurpfalzisches Museum, with its renowned wood carving, the Twelve Apostles altar.

Heidelberg to Baden-Baden——54 miles

Continue south on route N-3 to Leimen, Wiesloch, Langenbrücken and Bruchsal, which has a remarkable eighteenth-century baroque castle formerly owned by the prince-bishops of Speyer; there is also a lovely old church. The route passes through Weingarten and Durlach, a suburb of Karlsruhe; from here a right turn will bring you into that important industrial city, particularly famous for its Ducal Palace in the classical style.

From Durlach, continue on to Ettlingen and Rastatt, being sure to watch for the left turn toward Baden-Baden, an ultraluxurious resort with a wide selection of hotels and restaurants. Baden-Baden (the double name implies the town of Baden located in the state of Baden—the state of Baden was once a separate state in the German federation, now it is a part of the Federal State of Baden-Württemberg) is a wonderful place to rest for a few days if you're weary and want to break away from the daily routine of motoring. Here you'll find a lovely resort town catering exclusively to visitors: gambling at the plush casino, window shopping, slow walks along the tree-lined Lichtentaler Allee and, if you wish, horrible tasting and smelling waters that are reputed to cure you of whatever you wish to be cured of. August is the height of the season here, with horse racing at nearby Iffezheim, six miles west; unlike most lush, ermine-trimmed resorts, Baden-Baden has charm.

This was the direct route from Heidelberg to Baden-Baden (an even faster version of this route goes via the Autobahn), but you may find another route more interesting although quite a bit longer. From Heidelberg proceed southeast upstream through the beautiful Neckar Valley, passing through picturesque little towns, almost all dominated by medieval castles, among them Neckarsteinach, Hirschhorn, Zwingenberg, Neckarzimmern and Bad Wimpfen. There are a number of castle hotels in this area, among them in the Hornberg Castle in Neckar-zimmern and in the Hirschhorn Castle. A few miles from Bad Wimpfen is the historic Heilbronn, an old imperial town (this means that at one time the town had special autonomous rights and was under the direct jurisdiction of the emperor). Further up the Neckar Valley you pass through Ludwigsburg with the largest baroque-style palace in Germany, patterned after Versailles, and reach Stuttgart, the capital of the Federal State of Baden-Württemberg.

Stuttgart (population about 650,000) is not only an important industrial center (if you own a Mercedes car it was made here, and the same goes for Porsche cars and Zeiss-Ikon cameras, for instance), but also the most important orchard area in Germany, and the third largest wine producing district of Germany. The main historic sights are the Old Palace (Altes Schloss) in Renaissance style, now a museum, and the baroque New Palace (Neues Schloss), once the residence of the kings of Württemberg. Stuttgart, devastated greatly by air raids during World War II, has since resumed its pre-war role as one of the leading cities in modern architecture in Germany and you will see the evidence of it in all sections of the city. Stuttgart is basically a green city for only 25% of its surface is built over, while 75% is parks, gardens, vine-yards, orchards, fields, meadows and woods. The best hotels in the center are Graf Zeppelin and Am Schloss-garten, both very modern and at the main station. Hotel Stuttgart International, in a new twenty-story skyscraper, is in the suburbs near the Autobahn. A wing of the baroque Solitude Castle up in the woods above the city has been converted into a pleasant small castle hotel. Very fine food and wines are served in the following restaurants: Alte Post, Alte Kanzlei and Graf Eberhard.

About 25 miles south of Stuttgart is the old university town of Tübingen, and from here you may proceed west to Freudenstadt in the heart of the Black Forest and then north to Baden-Baden. The more direct route from Stuttgart to Baden-Baden is west via Pforzheim, at the northern end of the Black Forest, and on through Karls-ruhe.

Baden-Baden to Freudenstadt—38 miles

From Baden-Baden, take the road south to Freuden-stadt; this is the lovely Schwarzwald-Hochstrasse, the

Black Forest Highway, which runs through extremely fine scenery. En route, you'll pass Lichtental, Bühlerhöhe, Unterstmatt, Ruhestein, Bad Peterstal and Kniebis and then come into Freudenstadt. Here is an extremely attractive mountain resort in the pine woods. The town is built around a very large square, with an unusual Stadtkirche (church); the two naves of the church meet at right angles, a seldom-encountered architectural feature. The leading places for an overnight or vacation stop are the Luz-Hotel Waldlust, built in the local Black Forest fashion, which is either quaint or a hodgepodge, according to your own personal taste, or the Waldeck, another interesting place, much more modern than the Waldlust.

Freudenstadt to Freiburg—60 miles

Leave Freudenstadt via route 294 heading south through Lossburg, then descend to Schiltach. Next come Wolfach, Hausach and Haslach, then a climb followed by a series of drops toward Elzach. We continue on to Bleibach, Gutach, Waldkirch and Freiburg in Breisgau.

It is with some hesitation, because opinions frequently differ, that we say that you will probably fall in love with medieval Freiburg, a charming town in the midst of the most beautiful portion of the Black Forest. See the Münster, a red sandstone cathedral facing onto a colorful open-air market that operates during the mornings. On the opposite side of this area is the Kaufhaus, a sixteenth-century predecessor of today's department store, and the Wenzingerhaus, an eighteenth-century architectural masterpiece. The very modernistic Hotel Colombi is an extremely fine establishment with every convenience. Freiburg is an interesting town for shopping, with an important main street lined with stores.

Esso has a new motor inn in Freiburg at 27 Sundgauallee. The German Automobile Club (ADAC) in the Karlsplatz will help you with suggestions for pleasant trip possibilities from this capital city of the Black Forest. Office hours are from 8 A.M. to 1 P.M. and 2 to 6 P.M. on weekdays, and 8 A.M. to 1 P.M. on Saturdays. The phone number is 4-54-55.

Freiburg to Konstanz—85 miles

From Freiburg take the extraordinarily scenic ride via route 31 to Ebnet and Titisee, a lovely resort town that unfortunately is very much overcrowded during the summer months. Then to Neustadt, Hüfingen, Donaueschingen (with old Fürstenberg Castle), Geisingen and Engen; here make a right turn via route N-33 to Singen, deep in the Hegau, possibly the most peculiar part of Germany, where flat-topped extinct volcanos rise unexpectedly over the landscape. The Hohenwiel, an isolated mountaintop nearby, has an enormous ruined castle and marvelous views of the surrounding countryside. Then to Radolfzell, a quaint old town with ramparts, towers and medieval walls; from here continue on through Allensbach and into Konstanz, where the Seehotel Hecht is extremely pleasant.

The ravages of war never hit Konstanz (also spelled Constance), on the lake of the same name, and there remains much of the old city to see: the Town Hall (Rathaus), the cathedral and the Konzilgebaüde, the Church Council Building. Excursions may be made to Insel Reichenau, an island in the lake, with several churches built more than a thousand years ago; Insel Mainau has a ruined castle surrounded by lush foliage. Almost all of the sightseeing trips on the lake are delightfully restful, if the weather is good.

A delightful island hotel at Konstanz is appropriately called *Insel.*

Konstanz to Garmisch-Partenkirchen—143 miles (via the ferry)

From Konstanz drive to Staad and take a ferry to Meersburg, or as an alternative, drive around the western portion of the Lake of Überlingen (as the northwestern part of Lake Constance is called) via routes 33, 34 and 31 through Radolfzell, Ludwigschafen, Überlingen and Meersburg, which has hotels Schiff on the lakefront and the small, very atmospheric, half-timbered Brandners Drei Stuben in the old town above; this is a fine spot for a vacation stay. The next town, surprisingly enough, is Friedrichshafen, the "Zeppelin City," where the ill-fated *Graf Zeppelin* was constructed during 1937–1938. (If you aren't planning to tour Switzerland, or if you just enjoy boat rides on general principles, take the ferry across the lake to rustic Romanshorn in Switzerland.) The road continues along the north shore of the lake to delightful Langenargen, adjacent Kressbronn and Nonnenhorn (slightly off the road). Definitely worth the brief detour in Kressbronn is a famous restaurant, Zur Kapelle. Then to Lindau, an island town joined to the mainland by two very narrow bridges; a dreamlike medieval masterpiece right out of a Walt Disney movie, unbelievable and absolutely lovely. As you might expect, Lindau has a Diebsturm, a thief's tower, complete with dungeons, and several nice hotels with terraces facing the romantic, walled-in port; but the most delightful pastime in this fantastic spot is wandering about at random up narrow streets and into flowered courtyards.

If you enjoy boat trips, there are nearly two dozen motorships and various other kinds of passenger vessels from which to choose, some of them Austrian, others German. The scheduled trips are from Bregenz and Lindau to Friedrichshafen, Meersburg, and Konstanz, as well as on the two lower sections of the lake, popularly known as the Untersee and the Überlinger See. I've already mentioned the ferries connecting Staad with Meersburg, as well as Friedrichshafen with Romanshorn in Switzerland. On any of these boat trips you can be sure of a marvelous view of the lake and the mountains (on a clear day, of course).

From Lindau, take route 12 to Isny, more a winter than a summer resort; then through Buchenberg Pass and into Buchenberg and Kempten. This chief town of the Allgau region is known for its cheese production; if you're a cheese enthusiast, try some here. Kempten sightseeing: the Kohnhausplatz, a fine old medieval area and its adjacent Kornhaus and museum (Roman excavation, etc., in the Heimatmuseum). Leave Kempten via route 309 through Durach, Bad Oy and the popular resort town of Nesselwang; after this, there is a left turn onto route 310 to Füssen, a town with unbelievably attractive surroundings, delightfully situated on the Lech River.

From Füssen, head north via route 17 (on what is called "the Romantic Road" because of the many romantic medieval towns and castles along the way) toward Hohenschwangau, an aristocratic castle built by the royal family of Bavaria; then comes the absolutely inconceivable Neuschwanstein Castle, overhanging the roaring Pollat Gorges, which must be visited. (This is the famous castle used as an illustration in many calendars and travel magazines.) The road continues to Steingaden, where a right turn is taken onto an unnumbered route that cuts across the Echelsbacher Brücke, a bridge over the Ammer Valley. Six miles after the turnoff, route 23 is reached; make a right turn to Saulgrub and Oberammergau, scene of the famous Passion Play staged every decade in the years ending in zero. The performances were originally given in thanks for deliverance from the Black Plague some 350 years ago. In a quiet, central location is the Alpine-style Hotel Alois Lang, and be *sure* to have advance reservations during the season. Then on through Kloster Ettal to Garmisch-Partenkirchen, once the scene of the Olympics. Here you'll find dozens of hotels of all categories, among them the elegant Parkhotel Alpenhof, the very modern Alpina and the colorful, Bavarian-style Clausings Posthotel which serves very good food, including special Bavarian dishes.

Garmisch is unquestionably the leading winter resort and sports center of Germany, but the summer season from June through late September is just as enjoyable from the tourist's point of view. The scenery is just short of breathtaking, with lovely mountains to the north and the entire region generally bathed in sunshine. You definitely should make an excursion to the top of the Zugspitze, a two-hour railway journey. Trains leave hourly from Garmisch during daylight, via the Bayer-Zugspitz Bahn to Schneefernerhaus; here you change for an aerial cable car to the Summit Station, where the view is absolutely unsurpassable. It's possible to return by another aerial cable car which descends directly to the lake of Eibsee (or you can go up this way) and view different scenery. Even after you've made the railway trip to Zugspitze, try the cable railway to Kreuzeckhaus, merely a ten-minute ride but a very exciting one.

If you drive to Garmisch directly from Munich, you can use the newly completed autobahn south of Munich as far as Penzberg, and continue from there to Murnau, a lovely old town on the Staffel Lake. Then on to Garmisch on the Olympic Road (so called because it was constructed for the Winter Olympics of 1936). At Oberau, just a few miles before Garmisch, the road from Oberammergau and Kloster Ettal joins the Olympic Road. Kloster Ettal is a reconstructed fourteenth-century Benedictine monastery; the monks produce a fine herb-scented sweet liqueur which you can buy in bottles of assorted shapes and sizes. In a nearby valley is the Schloss Linderhof, or Linderhof Castle, another example of the sort of structures built by King Ludwig II during the last century. However, this one is quite different from the very famous Neuschwanstein Castle; Linderhof is in the rococo style and almost hidden in a quiet park.

Garmisch to Berchtesgaden—119 miles

Leave Garmisch via route 2 to Mittenwald, an absolutely charming village deep in the Isar valley; this violin-manufacturing community has fine old homes, and the streets warrant wandering about. A recently and daringly constructed aerial cable car takes you steeply up over the rocky wall of the Karwendel range to the top from which there is a fantastic view. (Those who are continuing on to Austria should leave Mittenwald via route 185 to Seefeld, Zirl and Innsbruck; pick up the tour of Austria at the appropriate page in the Austrian section.)

From Mittenwald, take route 11 through Krün and Kochel; nearby is the Walchensee power station, which is open for inspection most of the day (guided tours). Next comes Benedicktbeuern, a village beautifully located; there are conducted tours through the former Benedictine abbey, now a Salesian monastery. Then to Bichl, where you pick up an unnumbered road east (right turn) to Bad Tölz, colorful and quaint, with renowned iodide springs (but these are really evil tasting and smelling); here raft trips may be arranged on the Isar River to Munich for those with loads of free time. Then to the Tegernsee (Lake), driving around the lake shore via Bad Wiessee, Rottach-Egern and the resort village of Tegernsee, with another famous former Benedictine abbey on the waterfront. Then north to Gmünd and Miesbach and onto the autobahn; those whose time is limited may omit Berchtesgaden and head directly for Munich. Otherwise, take the autobahn heading toward Prien (watch for the turnoff); this little town is primarily a base for trips across the Chiemsee, the Bavarian Sea, as it is popularly called. Boats make frequent excursions to the islands— Herrenchiemss (which has a magnificent palace in Versailles style built by Ludwig II) and Frauenchiemsee, on which there is a ruined monastery and a good inn for those who like peace and quiet, the Hotel zur Linde.

From Prien follow route 305 to Bernau (first passing the autobahn) and reaching Reit im Winkle, a popular ski resort; then on the same road to Ruhpolding and Traunstein, where everyone (who wants to) takes a mud bath. Next is Bad Reichenhall, known for its brine (salt) baths given in the Salinengebäude, the salt bath house. There are several good hotels here, the luxurious Grand Hotel Axelmannstein with its own park; the new and modern Elite; the Kurhotel Luisenbad; and in case you wish to stay high up on the mountain, take the aerial cable car up to the Berghotel Predigstuhl at about 4,300 feet. From Bad Reichenhall, route 20 takes you to Berchtesgaden, Hitler's old hangout.

Probably one of the most beautiful natural areas in all of Germany, Berchtesgaden is famous the world over as a winter resort; the Hotel Geiger, an extremely comfortable inn, is about the best in town. Side trips can be made to the tiny village of Au (yes, that's it, Au), where the old costumes of centuries gone by are still worn by many of the inhabitants; make a tour through the Salzbergwerk, the salt mines (be sure to wear old clothes); see Hitler's "Eagle's Nest" at Obersalzburg, although the houses of the Führer and his henchmen have been demolished so that they should not become a martyr's shrine; visit the Eis Höhle, the icy grotto at nearby Schellenberg; and don't miss the best trip of all, the fifteen-minute ride by electric railway to the Königssee, a lake surrounded by snow-covered mountains.

Berchtesgaden to Munich—90 miles

Retracing our route back to Bad Reichenhall we pick up the road (route 306) leading to the autobahn in the direction of Munich, then turning off onto route 306 to Traunstein and into Wasserburg, surrounded on three sides by the Inn River, a lovely old town often described as having an Italian character and appearance. Then on via route 304 through Ebersberg and into Munich, or München, as the Germans call it. Or, if you wish, you can simply pick up the autobahn after Bad Reichenhall, and proceed directly to Munich. Be sure to watch for the turnoff signs leading to various parts of the city. In fact, if you know what hotel you're going to stay at, it might be a good idea to inquire en route as to which exit to take for Munich.

You'll surely want to spend some time exploring this artistic and intellectual center of Germany; originally founded by monks (its name *München* comes from the expression *zu den Mönchen*—"at the monks' "), Munich has a remarkably carefree outlook on life, making it the gayest of all German cities. Sightseeing? The Neues Rathaus, New City Hall, has a set of figures (the Glockenspiel) that perform at 11 A.M.; the impressive Our Lady's Cathedral (Frauenkirche, fifteenth century); the old city area and its famous Karl's Gate (named after the 18th-century Bavarian Duke Karl) on the Karlsplatz; the Schloss Nymphenburg, a baroque palace with sumptuous interiors of the period; the Königsplatz, the King's Square; the great technical museum, the Deutsches Museum. On the colorful square called "Am Platzl" stands the famous former royal Brewery (Hofbräuhaus), founded by the Bavarian dukes in the 16th century, and now owned by the State of Bavaria. Nearby is the Alter Hof, now restored after the war damage, the medieval residence of the Bavarian dukes. But the best way to see Munich and learn something of the city and its people is to wander about at random, enjoying sights as they appear, with frequent stops to enjoy the famous sausages and beer; incidentally, you must visit either the Löwenbräuhaus or the Hofbräuhaus, enormous beer-drinking establishments full of bustle and good-natured excitement—the most typical representation of Munich and its pleasure seekers.

For art lovers, one of the great attractions of this city is the Old Pinakothek, or in German, the Alte Pinakothek, which isn't too much in the way of an improvement. It is an enormous structure housing a fantastic art collection, featuring Memling, Rubens, Van Dyck, Düer, and Cranach paintings. The museum is open every day from 9 A.M. to 4:30 P.M. and from 8 to 10 P.M. on Tuesday and Thursday.

While you're in front of the Neues Rathaus, waiting for the 11 A.M. display on the clock tower, look to your left down Neuhauser Strasse, which is now a shopping mall, completely free of auto traffic. It's one of the best shopping streets anywhere in the world, and it's quite fascinating to wander in and out of the stores and buy all sorts of things you could easily do without.

MUNICH HOTELS

Vier Jahreszeiten: This is a leading hotel with a fine old tradition. It is now part of the Inter-Continental Hotel group, and has been renovated and considerably enlarged. Located near the opera house and known for its food.

Bayerischer Hof: Another celebrated hotel noted for old-fashioned luxury and comfort (but not for food). It has a heated rooftop swimming pool. Not far from the cathedral.

Continental: Also a luxury establishment with a good restaurant. Located just off the Maximiliansplatz in the center of the city.

Sonesta: In a pleasant location at the English Gardens near the river, but a bit away from things. Very modern.

Sheraton: A part of the well-known U.S. chain. The largest in Munich, it also has ample convention facilities. The Sheraton stands at the Effnerplatz in the Bogenhausen suburb.

Hilton: A new, large, and very typical Hilton hotel with pleasant bedrooms and public rooms. It's located in the suburbs, at the English Gardens.

Esso-Motor-Hotel: Not far from the Sheraton but much smaller and more modest albeit also new and quite modern.

Holiday Inn: At the northern end of Schwabing, a franchise of the well-known U.S. chain. Locally it has become best known for its extravagant night club "Yellow Submarine," where sharks imported from Florida swim behind thick glass.

MUNICH RESTAURANTS

Humplmayr: At the Maximiliansplatz. Considered by the international set to be the top restaurant in Munich. Elegant and expensive. Reservations needed.

Zur Kanne: On the Maximilianstrasse, near the View Jahreszeiten Hotel. Very good, medium-to-expensive food served in atmospheric surroundings. Quite pleasant, and they serve fine wines by the glass.

Schwarzwälder: Near the Cathedral. Tradition-filled, it was family-run for many years. It has the best wine cellar in Munich but the food has become less reliable under the new ownership. Reservations needed.

Boettner's: On the Theatinerstrasse, in the center of town; excellent and very expensive. Marvelous but very very high.

Halali: Not far from U.S. Consulate. Game is served here amidst hunting décor and zither music (in the evening). Medium-priced.

Spatenhaus: Across from the opera house. A large and comfortable beer and wine restaurant serving well-prepared and tasty food. Very reasonable.

Ratskeller: As the name implies, it's in the Rathaus (Town Hall) cellar. Very colorful old interiors and good food. Reasonable prices.

MUNICH BEER HALLS

Munich, which is undoubtedly the beer capital of the world, of course has its historic beer halls. These establishments, annexes of the breweries themselves, do not consist just of one room but rather of a series of halls, rooms, gardens and terraces on the ground level, on upper floors and sometimes even underground. All of them offer restaurant service, and while the quality of food and beer is the same in all the halls or rooms of such an establishment, the make-up of the guests sometimes varies.

Hofbräuhaus: On the Platzl Square. The most famous establishment in this category and a sightseeing landmark of Munich, it belongs to the Hofbräu Brewery.

Salvator-Keller: Across the river on Nockherberg. It becomes the center of Munich during two weeks of the Lent period when the dark, strong Salvator beer is served.

Löwenbräukeller: On Stiglmaierplatz in the neighborhood of the main station. As the name implies, it belongs to the Löwenbräu Brewery.

Hacker-Keller: Above the Theresienwiese (where the Oktoberfest takes place) and near the exhibition grounds, it belongs to the Hacker Brewery.

Augustiner-Keller: In the neighborhood of the main station. In winter somewhat small, but during the summer it has the largest beer garden in Munich.

Munich to Rothenburg—130 miles

From Munich, take the autobahn to Augsburg; here you can stay at the historic Palasthotel Drei Mohren, newly rebuilt since its wartime destruction. This ancient town, stronghold of the fabulously wealthy Fugger and Welser families of medieval times, has many architectural masterpieces. Be sure to visit the cathedral (whose origins go back to the year 994); the Renaissance-style Town Hall; St. Anna's church and its Fugger Memorial Chapel; the "Fuggerei" in the Jakoberstrasse, a miniature medieval community, given to the municipality by the Fugger family in 1519 for the use of needy families. In the Fugger city palace (on the Maximilianstrasse) you can dine fairly well and drink Fugger beer in the recently opened restaurant. These are ancient premises indeed, and people have been drinking Fugger beer for some four centuries. You'll surely want to attend (during summer months) the open-air opera performances presented near the Rotes Tor, the Red Gate.

Leave Augsburg via route 2 through Meitingen and Mertingen and into Donauwörth, an old town whose main street is the Reichsstrasse; many of the fine old houses lining this street were damaged or destroyed during the air raids of April 1945. The town walls, some timbered houses and the Town Hall remain. From Donauwörth take route 25 to Harburg, a town overlooked by impressive Harburg Castle, the largest preserved medieval fortress in southern Germany, with very rich museum collections, especially tapestries, wood carvings and old books. Next comes the quintessence of charm—wonderful old Nördlingen, where customs of the Middle Ages are observed and the peasants frequently still wear the old costumes of bygone days; the classic sightseeing requirement is a walk around the old city walls, which still seem to breathe with the romance of another era. After Nördlingen, route 25 turns right and heads north to Öttingen and then Dinkelsbühl; this somnolent old town, dreaming of the past, is the medieval center you've always envisaged but rarely seen—a perfect replica, intact and preserved for the twentieth century, with gabled houses, towers and moats. Be certain to walk down Segringerstrasse, the outstanding museum street of the town, particularly noting the Teutonic Knights' House. St. Georgskirche (fifteenth century) is a fine example of late Gothic architecture.

Next comes Feuchtwangen, a quiet town famous for its handcrafted articles and the old marketplace; the road continues to Rothenburg ob der Tauber, which was formerly an imperial free city during its heyday of power in the Middle Ages. You can stay at the Eisenhut, a hotel with extraordinary personality. For less expensive and more personal atmosphere try the Haus Bi, located directly behind the Goldener Hirsch. You enter through an unbelievable gate in the city wall. In your sightseeing, you'll visit the Town Hall (Rathaus) and the Protestant church, St. Jakobskirche; the Spitalor (Hospital Gate) is a good starting point for a walk alongside the edge of the town walls. Whether you remain overnight or merely pass through Rothenburg, be sure to eat a meal at the Eisenhut, one of Germany's best restaurants. Not inexpensive, we regret to say.

Rothenburg to Frankfurt—123 miles

From Rothenburg head north onto an unnumbered road, being careful to take the route along the Tauber River to Creglingen, Röttingen, Weikersham; upon reaching route 19, make a left turn to Bad Mergentheim. Here, once again, is a reincarnation of the spirit and times of the Middle Ages; this historic old town was headquarters for the Teutonic Knights and their wild, spirited exploits, until Napoleon brought the organization to a sudden end. Next take route 19 north through Giebelstadt to Würzburg, where the Mozart Festival is a treat for eye and ear during June and July, with outdoor recitals being given in the lovely old Residence Castle. See also the bridge over the Main River and the Marienburg (a thirteenth-century fortress) high above the city. Among the best available hotels, all of medium quality and very reasonably priced, are the cosy Lämmle near the main square, the new Rebstock near the cathedral, the rather impersonal Excelsior at the station, and Walfisch at the river. From Würzburg, highly agreeable boat rides can be made along the Main. Departures are at 11 A.M. and at 1:30, 2 and 2:45. Boat decks are covered, and facilities are comfortable.

SIDE TRIP ¶ From Würzburg proceed east on route 22 across the undulating plateau of Steigerwald to Bamberg, which harbors some of the greatest architectural and sculptural treasures in Germany: the four-spire and two-choir Romanesque cathedral containing works by two famous German wood sculptors of the Gothic period, Tilman Riemenschneider of Würzburg and Veit Stoss of Nürnberg; the world-known equestrian statue, called the Bamberg Rider, sculpted in stone by an unknown master around 1230 and which also stands inside the cathedral; the Old Residence (Alte Hofhaltung) and the New Residence (Neue Residenz), palaces of the prince-bishops; the old patrician houses, especially the Böttingerhaus; the Old Town Hall standing in the middle of a bridge on the river. Continue east of Bamberg on route 22 to Bayreuth, the city of Richard Wagner, where a Wagner opera festival is staged each summer in the Festival Theater, which was designed by Richard Wagner himself. South of Bayreuth and reached by the Autobahn or route 2 is Nürnberg (about 500,000 inhabitants), the most important city of this region which is called Franken (Franconia) but is a part of Bavaria. Nürnberg, which was hard hit by bombs during the war, has been meticulously restored and once again has a medieval atmosphere. The most important sights include: the city walls; the fortress; the 13th-century St. Sebaldus Church with sculptures by Peter Vischer and Veit Stoss; the main square with the Gothic fountain and the Gothic Frauenkirche (church); the old wooden Hangman's

Bridge (Henkersteg) across the Pegnitz river which halves the old town; the Gothic St. Lorenz Church with the beautiful Rosetta stained glass window, the Tabernacle by Adam Kraft sculptured in stone and the Angelic Salutation carved in wood by Veit Stoss. The St. Lorenz Church was severely damaged by air raids during the war and its rebuilding and restoration was financed partially by Rush Kress of New York; the ancestors of Kress emigrated from the Nürnberg area to the United States in 1752. Albrecht Dürer, probably the greatest German painter (1471–1528), was born and also died in Nürnberg. The Albrecht-Dürer-Haus, where the master lived from 1509 until his death, is shown today as a museum. First class accommodations are offered by Grand Hotel near the main station. Among good restaurants are the medieval-style Böhm's Herrenkeller, the deep Nassauer Keller in the cellar of an old patrician house, and Goldenes Posthorn near St. Sebaldus Church. The Nürnberg specialty, for lovers of good food, however, is small sausage taverns with open charcoal grills where the famous, small and spicy Nürnbergerbratwürstl are grilled. From Nürnberg you return northwest to Würzburg either via the Autobahn or on route 8. The circuit Würzberg-Bamberg-Bayreuth-Nürnberg-Würzburg covers about 210 miles. If you wish to relive history and see more of the great old architecture you can drive southeast from Nürnberg on route 8 to two other cities filled with old atmosphere, both of which were also governed at one time by powerful prince-bishops; Regensburg on the Danube with the famous Gothic cathedral, and Passau on the German-Austrian border at the confluence of three rivers (Danube, Inn and Ilz), with a 15th-century cathedral which contains the largest organ in the world. From Passau you can drive to Munich on route 12, if you do not wish to go all the way back to Würzburg in one day.

Continuing our original tour from Würzburg, we proceed northwest to Aschaffenburg via route 8. The road passes through the thickly forested hills of Spessart. Aschaffenburg was severely damaged during the war, but the city has been reconstructed. The interior of the squarish, imposing Schloss Johannisburg burned out during the air raids of April 1945, but it has since been restored so that it now houses a collection of paintings. Near the Schloss is the Pompeianum, constructed in imitation of a Pompeian house by King Ludwig I, in the days when a king's wish was quickly fulfilled. Be sure to see the Stiftskirche, dating back almost 1,000 years, and the adjacent Museum der Stadt Aschaffenburg, with fine examples of early German primitive art. The town is also proud of its famous gardens in the lovely Park Schönbusch; for those remaining overnight, the Hotel Stadt Mainz offers pleasant accommodations.

Another lovely way to reach Aschaffenburg from Würzburg is to drive alongside the River Main, going through the medieval towns of Wertheim and Miltenberg, both fabulous examples of half-timber architecture. At Wertheim, visit the Kittstein Tower and the impressive castle of the Wertheim counts. At Miltenberg, you'll probably recognize the market square surrounded by half-timbered houses, because the government tourist office has used this scene for magazine ads and tourist folders. Miltenberg is also proud of having what's believed to be the oldest hotel in Germany; it's the handsome half-timbered (you weren't expecting modern architecture, were you?) Gasthof Zum Riesen. There are records going back to 1504, although the present structure goes back "only" to 1590.

Then on to Frankfurt. Here at this central point the tour terminates, permitting the motorist to return to any desired point.

৪৯ *Motoring in Germany*

The formalities for bringing your car into Germany—and driving there—are relatively few. You have to have a nationality-registration plate for it (USA for the United States, F for France, etc.) and the registration certificate. There is a theoretical requirement that you must have either an international driver's license or an officially German-translated copy of your home-state driver's license. As a practical matter, your regular state driving license will ordinarily be sufficient, but it's best to have the international driver's license, to be on the safe side. Oh, yes! You'll need the Green Card covering third-party liability in case of accident. Temporary insurance can be obtained at the border in case you do not have the Green Card with you.

German roads may be divided into three categories: *Autobahn*, *Bundesstrasse*, and *Landstrasse*. The autobahns are the famous superhighways of Germany, there are more than 2,500 miles of them. They permit extremely fast travel. Unless one is in a hurry, their use is not advisable because little can be seen of the countryside. (But remember, an autobahn is the only road you can use through the Russian zone to Berlin.) As on our own superhighways, entrance to and exit from the autobahns are permitted only at specified points along the route. There are (believe it or not) no tolls. The *Bundesstrassen* (national roads) are mostly in excellent condition and always paved. Numbers are marked by signposts—yellow with a black edging—and motorists should experience little difficulty in following the routes. Don't count on making too much time on these roads, because in some sections they are quite narrow and passing is difficult—particularly when you're behind a wide truck and trailer. The *Landstrassen* (state roads) are occasionally unpaved—dirt or gravel—and require careful driving. However, many of these *Landstrassen* lead to the most interesting medieval communities and prettiest scenery. They should be used by the tourist who wishes to do real sightseeing.

Drivers keep to the right. There is no speed limit on the open highways or on the autobahns. In built-up areas, the speed limit is 31 miles an hour (50 km.).

Pointer: In traffic circles cars approaching from the left have priority over those entering from the right.

GREECE

National Characteristics

The Greeks are no strangers to us. As school children we learned about the Battle of Marathon; the Golden Age of Pericles; and Socrates, Plato and Aristotle. That was the Greece of twenty-five centuries ago. We know it from closer experience, too. In the late 1940s America, with men, money and supplies, helped the Greeks put down a communist insurrection that threatened to wreck the country. We, the Greeks and the world have a word (or three) for that timely, helpful aid: the Truman Doctrine.

Greece is now being "discovered" by tourists. More than a million tourists visit the country every year, about 20 per cent of them American. Soft skies, friendly, hospitable people and the "glory that was Greece" are sure-fire magnets luring travelers to this gracious land and making them happy they came.

The Greek man in the street apparently spends most of his waking moments there. A bold and fearless time-waster—at least, in comparison to high-pressure Americans—he devotes endless hours to any one of his favorite occupations: sitting outdoors in a *kafeneion* (an outdoor cafe), talking politics, drinking coffee or *ouzo* or having his shoes shined.

It is not difficult to detect the gentle, warm-hearted friendship extended freely by the vast majority of Greeks. Are you lost? They will lead you to your destination. Are you tired? Why not sit in the shade and rest with them? If you inquire at a villager's home in the country about directions they are more than likely to invite you into the house to have a little snack or a glass of something with them. They are hospitable people in the great tradition of the Mediterranean.

The past decades have been shattering indeed to the

average Greek—the long war years; the occupation by the Germans and the Italians, during which people died of starvation by the thousands; the subsequent civil war. Who can blame the average person if, emotions worn bare, nothing seems important to him except the pleasures of sitting in the brilliant sun and talking about the past glories of his wonderful country.

When to Go

Athens *can* be warm and agreeable, and sunny, even in January, but in places above sea level the weather can be nippy and cloud covered. March through September is the best time, however. This is the principal season for tourists. Those who can should come during March, April and May, which are actually the very finest months. June through August are bright, brilliant, comparatively free of rain and . . . hot as Hades during the middle of the day! To cheer you up, it should be quickly stated that the evenings are generally pleasant and much cooler, because of the combined influence of the high mountains and Greece's physical situation—a water-surrounded peninsula. This—we have been told—causes air currents to travel across the country as soon as the sun sets. It seems that the moist air from the sea hits the mountains and—well, anyhow, it cools off at night. The fall season, September to October, offers pleasant weather. But the days are shorter and there is more chance of rain. Greek winters are raw and unpleasant generally; and if the local Chamber of Commerce hates us, at least, we've told the truth!

WEATHER STRIP: ATHENS

Temp.	JAN.	FEB.	MAR.	APR.	MAY	JUNE	JULY	AUG.	SEPT.	OCT.	NOV.	DEC.
Low	42°	42°	46°	51°	60°	67°	72°	72°	66°	60°	52°	46°
High	53°	56°	60°	68°	77°	85°	90°	90°	83°	74°	64°	57°
Average	48°	49°	53°	60°	69°	76°	81°	81°	75°	67°	58°	52°
Days of rain	12	11	11	9	7	4	3	3	4	9	12	13

TIME EVALUATION ¶ For Athens itself, three days would be about right. If you're using Athens as a base for sightseeing (trips to Delphi, Cape Sounion and Mycenae), then a week would be ideal. Add another week if you're planning to make a circuit to Rhodes and Crete. Inter-island travel to the smaller islands would also take about a week. Of course, if you are headed for Mykonos or one of the other resort islands, the sky is the limit.

PASSPORT AND VISA ¶ You will have to have a passport, naturally, but for stays of up to ninety days no visa is needed. If you wish to remain longer than ninety days, you'll have to register with the Athens Alien Department, Chalkokondili Street, Athens. Elsewhere in the country, you can register at the nearest police station. You'll have to bring along three photographs (passport size) for this.

CUSTOMS AND IMMIGRATION ¶ The Greek customs inspection keeps getting simpler and less complicated all the time. It is now virtually only a formality, but there are limits, nonetheless, on tobacco and liquors particularly. The official limit on cigarettes is one carton. You are also permitted through customs with a bottle of liquor. In general, reasonable quantities of items that a traveler normally carries—film, toilet articles, etc.—will be allowed in duty free.

CURRENCY ¶ Happily, gone are those old days when Greek currency was quoted in figures as long as a telephone number. The problem of inflation has been licked, and the Greek currency is stable. The currency is the *drachma* (plural, *drachmae*). The actual value of the *drachma*, in relation to the dollar, varies in accordance with changes in the world money market. The drachma is divided into 100 *lepta* (singular, *lepton*) but generally the prices you'll come across will be quoted only in drachmae. Foreign currency can be changed at hotels, major restaurants and many shops—as well as banks; banking hours are 8 A.M. to 1 P.M. The Agricultural Bank of Greece, at 23 Venizelos Avenue in Athens, however, is also open in the afternoon. A visit to a Greek bank is likely to induce high blood pressure and is about the most certain known way yet devised for killing time. For some reason the hotels and travel agencies can change your money quickly (you don't usually get quite so good a rate, of course, but your blood pressure will also be lower). Now what happens when you're traveling around the country and run out of money? You must take time out and change your money at the local bank, although major hotels can help you. Be sure to have sufficient Greek money with you when setting off on a day's trip—and on weekends—because you can't count on cashing your checks or American dollars into drachmae as easily as you can in Athens, particularly on Sundays.

HEALTH ¶ Milk is potentially dangerous here and should generally be avoided unless it has been (positively) boiled. Use milk sparingly—if you must—in coffee. You're usually safe in Athens and the major cities when in principal tourist hotels—but you can never be absolutely sure. As to drinking water, Athens is perfectly safe, and so are Corfu, Rhodes and Crete. But elsewhere call for bottled water, or drink the local wines. And above all, stay away from ice in your drinks. When out in the countryside, don't even use tap water to brush your teeth. Among the leading bottled mineral waters are Nigrita, Sarza, Lutraki and Suroti. Melons and fruits with a thick skin, such as oranges, are all right. But such greens as lettuce and celery and raw fruits without peels should be avoided or eaten very sparingly—and only if previously washed in potassium permanganate. Raw shell-fish (oysters, particularly) are likely to cause trouble to the sensitive traveler. So beware! Cooked shellfish is much safer.

PRICE LEVEL ¶ Were you in Greece last year or the year before? Prices won't be the same this year. They keep going up and up! It is no longer the bargain paradise it was, but prices are still fairly reasonable. Deluxe hotel rooms run about $25 a day, but around half that in the countryside. In general, for a comfortable but not deluxe way of life in Greece, figure on about $25 a day. Restaurant meals will average out around $3 to $4 each. If you obsolutely insist, you can spend $5 or more for dinner, but that is exceptional. Local cigarettes are 25 to 50 cents a pack and up (American ones are available, but more expensive than at home). An espresso, 20 cents; a haircut, 65 cents; a "set," about a dollar.

TIME ¶ Greece is seven hours ahead of (later than) Eastern Standard Time. When it's noon in New York, it's 7 P.M. in Greece. When Daylight Savings Time is observed in the U.S. the time difference is cut to six hours.

TIPPING ¶ Although a service charge is added to your hotel bill, naturally you'll still have to tip the baggage porter (5 drachmae for each bag) and certain other people. The chambermaid, for instance, should be given 10 drachmae a day if she has been particularly good about fixing your room. And, of course, if the concierge has helped you, he should get 50 or more drachmae at the end of your visit. In restaurants you'll find that a service charge (usually 10 percent) has been added to your bill, but it is customary to leave an additional 5 percent (more or less) in change for the waiter. If there is a busboy, give him 5 drachmae too. Don't forget that almost everyone lives on his tips. If you are in a guided tour, it is customary to give something to the guide—10 to 20 percent of the tour fee. If you have hired your own guide and have set a flat rate in advance, there is no need to tip him unless he has really performed above and beyond the call of duty and/or your expectations. Tipping taxi drivers is not necessary as in other countries, but most tourists do.

TRANSPORTATION ¶ There are plenty of *taxis* in Athens (and most other tourist points) with fairly good drivers. The rate is relatively low. Most drivers speak some English, but it is best to have the address of where you're going printed on a piece of paper in *Greek* characters to make sure you'll get there. The hotel concierge can do this for you. Of course, if you're headed for the Acropolis or some other landmark (American Express, for example) this paperwork will not be necessary. If you hire a car for an excursion out of the city, agree *in advance* on the price. *Self-drive* cars are quickly and easily hired. All you need is your American driver's license. Rates combine a daily charge for the use of the car plus an extra charge for each kilometer. Naturally, the rate is proportionally more expensive for shorter than for longer periods.

Greece's national *railroads* are not a usual form of travel for the tourist, unless he is interested in going north to the Salonika area or south to the Peloponnesus.

You will, of course, be interested in the fast electric sub-waylike train that connects Athens and the city's port at Piraeus. This handy, inexpensive and fast service is highly recommended to those who do not have their own cars. Tourists will not, as a rule, enjoy railroad travel even in First Class. By all means use the tour buses, airlines, steamships and private cars—or even walk.

Bus travel is well organized. Buses connect Athens with all major cities and archaeological sites. Throughout the year there are one- to five-day guided bus tours starting out from Athens. The classic trip is from Athens to Delphi, with halts en route at Thebes, Arachova and Levada. Another all-day trip goes to Corinth, Argos, Nauplia, Epidaurus and Mycenae. A five-day bus tour is a wonderful way of seeing the country, if you don't mind riding on buses. Rates are not bad at all. Bus travel in the city of Athens is very inexpensive—a matter of pennies. The fare is a drachma or two, depending on routes and whether you're on a trolley bus or a motorized bus.

Steamer trips through the Greek islands are among the most satisfying excursions available to visitors. During the summer there are many special cruises, of varying lengths (two days, three days, etc.) to the Greek islands and along the coastline. The cruises also include visits to points of archaeological and sightseeing interest. The port of Piraeus, at Athens, is the starting point for these boat trips. The vessels range from mammoth ferries to comfortable cruise ships. The excellent Sun Line, for example, makes a number of different cruises ranging from three to seven days. Their newest ship is the *Stella Solaris,* which is quite luxurious, and charges from $45 up per day for the cruises. There is also the very good Epirotiki Line, which has a number of medium-sized ships, offering a number of short cruises through the Islands. Some of the vessels have cruise stops in Turkey, which offer an added dimension to your cruise.

There is, as mentioned before, regularly scheduled cruise service from just outside of Athens to almost all of the islands that make up this partly maritime nation. The charges for the ferries are reasonable, but often the boats are *extremely* crowded during the summer months, and often they're *really* crowded, often uncomfortably so, being loaded with what looks like the entire sophomore class of some twenty different American colleges.

Greece's national *airline*, Olympic, services a score of domestic points from Athens, including Corfu, Crete, Rhodes, Salonika and Samos. There are also a number of inexpensive air excursions to great points of interest. There is a one-day trip to Crete, daily, and also a fine three-day air excursion to Crete and Rhodes. Several dozen main international airlines serve Athens.

COMMUNICATIONS ¶ A five-gram airmail letter to the United States costs about a quarter. For calls outside of Greece, dial 16 and ask for an English-speaking operator. Long-distance calls can be made from post offices. Athens has a special office for telephone calls and telegrams (OTE) near the Central Post Office, which is in the Omonia Square area. The hotel concierge or the clerk at the telegram counter will help you with cables. It is always best to have the cable text *typed out*—and have a duplicate for your own peace of mind and/or records.

BASIC GREEK ¶ As you know, the English language developed a different alphabet from the Greek one, and the individual letter characters are written in an astonishingly different way. Greek names, even when written with English-language letters, can be spelled differently because of pronunciation variations.

FOOD SPECIALTIES AND LIQUOR ¶ Breakfast is taken in your hotel room or in the dining room any time you awaken, but usually not later than 10 A.M. Lunch may be served at 1 P.M., but 1:30 is the more frequent starting time. Some of the tourist hotel dining rooms open as early as 8:30 P.M., but the Greek people wouldn't care to be seen dining that early as a rule, preferring to wait until 9:30 or 10:30, or even 11:30 P.M. in the summertime.

Most better hotels and restaurants serve what is generally known as "international hotel" style food, that is, basically French with some vague local undertones. Sometimes, rather on the occasional side, you'll be served something worthy of a fine French restaurant, but as a general rule the mixture of Greek-French cooking will hardly be calculated to make food the reason for visiting Greece.

But the food in the local restaurants of the interior

and the *tavernas*, the colorful local cafes, have quite good fare for the more intrepid diner. While you're in Athens, wend your way by cab or on foot (it's just ten minutes or so from Constitution Square) toward the old quarter of the city, the Plaka, directly below the Acropolis. Get out and walk about and select any *taverna* that suits you, or where the music sounds good. If it smells good, that's also encouraging; go in, because you'll find the best of all ways to have a good dinner with lots of wine and listen to pleasant Greek music in a most pleasing atmosphere. Almost anywhere you go, you'll find olives, usually black and wrinkled. To begin with, everyone orders *ouzo*, the clear white anise-flavored liquor; into this, one pours a little water and observes the cloudy effect. At first the taste is that of a combination of cough medicine and licorice candy; several drinks later the taste is still that of a combination of cough medicine and licorice candy, but you somehow care less. Also available are *mesticha* (a type of brandy) and *tsipouro*, which isn't but should be against the law. With any of these, you'll be served some kind of appetizer, such as tiny pieces of grilled, spiced meats, the *mezes*. Sometimes you'll be offered *taramosalata*, the fish roe appetizer that is a sort of poor man's caviar and can be quite good, but meals in Greek *tavernas* usually begin with a soup; as a rule this is *soupa avgolemono* (lemon and egg soup) and is fairly good. The Greeks use red mullet, *barbounia* extensively as a fish course, a rather tasty item when well prepared. Octopus? Well, when very small, these aren't (gulp!) bad at all—taste them, you'll be pleasantly surprised, or maybe you won't. The local clawless lobster is fine and that goes for the shrimp, too. The meat course may be a roast lamb dish, sautéed lamb, lamb on a skewer, grilled lamb, lamb stew or possibly the less attractive mutton. Vegetables are inevitably cooked in olive oil, the kind of preparation known as "*à la Grecque*" the world over; good, if you don't object to the olive oil. The salads are appetizing, too, if you feel up to trying them (don't, in small towns or villages); they'll be served usually with big chunks of lemon. If you want something interesting, ask for a piece of the local *feta* cheese (whitish and with an astringent flavor) and crumble a little into your salad. As a rule, Greek meals of the people end with bowls of oranges, which are considered the perfect conclusion (why, we'll never know). Occasionally you'll be served some of the oversweet, calorific, honey-laden pastries of the Near East. A few bites are delicious, but more than that can be cloying. Coffee is served black, with or without the grounds, with or without an excess of sugar—better ask for it *metrio*, or medium. Greece has some fair wines, although none of them are in the same classification as the better French and Italian varieties. The whites are fresh and pleasant, particularly the *King Minos* and *Tour-la-Reine*; the reds are a trifle too heavy, but you should find the red *Naoussa* satisfactory. Pay a little attention to the wines and select a couple that please your palate because, as previously mentioned, outside of Athens and the resort islands, you shouldn't drink the local water. Greek beers are fair, but not remarkable. *Caution*: the Greeks are fond of wines that have been flavored with *resin*; most Americans don't like *retsina*, resinated wine. Be sure, when ordering wine, to specify *aretsinato*, that is, without resin. The Greeks prepare an excellent after-dinner drink called *Metaxas*, a type of sweetish brandy almost as rich as a liqueur, which makes a good ending to a meal and is a good beverage to order in a night club.

WHAT TO EAT IN GREECE

Elies: Ripe olives
Soupa avgolemono: Soup prepared with lemons and eggs
Dolmadakia: Vine leaves stuffed with rice and meat
Spanakopeta: Spinach and cheese prepared in a pastry dough
Tsiri: Dried fish, not usually appreciated by tourists
Mussaka melitzanes: Ground meat and eggplant baked in a casserole
Entrather: Lamb and artichokes
Kokoretsi: A dish of sheep's intestines; not too appealing
Souvlakia: Small pieces of lamb or beef, roasted on a spit, much like the familiar Turkish shish-kebab
Yuvarlakia: Meat balls in tomato sauce
Pilav: A steamed rice dish, sometimes made with shell-fish or other ingredients
Feta: The white, astringent cheese of Greece
Kasseri: Yellowish, dry cheese
Melachrino: A cinnamon-flavored cake
Kourambiedes: A rich pastry confection
Karidopita: A good walnut cake

HOTELS ¶ The Greek government has been greatly encouraging, sponsoring, and supporting the construction of new hotels. The tourist trade has become one of the most important income items in the Greek economy.

The number of hotels keeps rising, with now well over 2,500, which is a lot for a small country like Greece.

TOURIST OFFICES ¶ Each city, resort and large town in Greece has a local tourist office, which will provide you with free information and brochures on sightseeing and excursion possibilities in the area. Special tourist police, uniformed, also are available in areas frequented by visitors. These policemen speak English and can be helpful in a hundred and one ways. In addition, the Greek National Tourist Organization has information offices in the following cities: Athens, 6 Karageorgi Servias, 35 Akti Miaoulis in Piraeus and the Hellinikon airport; Salonika, 2 Komninon; Rhodes; Epirus, Igoumenitsa; Kerkyra (Corfu); Heraklion and Chancea (Crete).

SPAS ¶ Greece has some well-known thermal springs that are said (I don't really know) to be helpful for specific ailments. As always, in the case of "taking the waters," it is wise to do so only under a doctor's instructions. Thermal resorts are at Vouliagmeni, Ikaria, Loutraki, and Kallithea (Rhodes).

CASINOS ¶ The palace built on the island of Corfu by the late Austrian Empress Elizabeth is now used as one of Greece's two casinos. The other casino is in the Grand Hotel Summer Palace on Rhodes.

The principal tourist areas in Greece are the city of Athens and the surrounding region, much of the Peloponnesus, the Cyclades Islands and the resort islands of Rhodes, Corfu and Crete.

CAPITAL CITY ¶ Athens (which the residents pronounce *Athen-ay*) has been a center of civilization for thousands of years. The first inhabitants settled there around thirty centuries before Christ, and in 1300 B.C. it became known as the City of Theseus. From then on, Athens was at the very hub of Western civilization and was the prize sought after by many less civilized countries. The Romans, Franks, Catalans, Turks and Venetians have been among those who have occupied the city. Since 1834 Athens has been the capital of the kingdom of Greece. Athens ruled the world and was at the height of its power about twenty-five centuries ago. Its government, writers, sculptors and architects were the vanguard, the intellectual leaders, of Western civilization as we know it today. All previous civilizations were in the Eastern world, and Greece was the very first important Western culture. The monuments, theaters and buildings that remain are thrilling (and they are!) reminders of the greatness and importance of ancient Greece. The modern sections of the city are reasonably attractive, but carping critics have found its general layout something less than magnificent. In truth, the rectangular—even monotonous—streets seldom delight the eye of the beholder. The principal charm of Athens lies in its ruined reminders of the past and the gesticulating, passionate personality of its present-day citizenry.

Athens is situated in an incomparably beautiful setting, surrounded by a group of mountains with such romantic sounding names as Parnassus, Hymettus and Pentelikon. From the city the eye is inescapably drawn toward two above-eye-level sights—the Acropolis, a 512-foot-high rock upon which stand some of the foremost antiquities of the world, and Mount Lycavitos, on whose crown is the Chapel of St. George. It is possible to visit the Acropolis any day of the year. During the summer, it is open from 7:30 A.M. until sunset, and in the winter the opening time is 8:30 A.M. (The closing time is the same as in summer.) On nights with a full moon, the Acropolis can be visited from 9 P.M. to midnight. Needless to say, this moonlight viewing of the Acropolis is spellbinding and I hope you're lucky enough to be there at that time. The Acropolis is far and away the number-one attraction of Athens—and of all Greece, for that matter. Ambitious, moderately athletic tourists (with stout footwear) can easily walk from the center of town up the gentle slopes. If not, you can ride up by taxi in a matter of minutes.

Acropolis, by the way, is a combination of Greek words meaning the upper part of a city. In Athens, the Acropolis was the high area on which the Parthenon was built. The Parthenon, the temple built in the fifth century B.C., is the outstanding monument still standing on the Acropolis. It is often considered the world's most perfect structure, its architectural design is the classic Doric. Not nearly so well known is another superb building, the Erechtheion, the temple of Athena Polias and Poseidon-Erechtheus. You'll be able to wander about and see the

Temple of the Wingless Victory, the Unfinished Propylaea and also the old Athena Temple. Along the slopes of the Acropolis are two remarkable outdoor theaters —the Odeon of Herodes Atticus (remember how many American movie theaters used to be called the Odeon?) and the Dionysos Theater. Both are extremely interesting. How long to spend on the Acropolis? Any length of time from an hour to several days, but you'll enjoy it most if you can break your visit into two (or more) shorter parts—possibly once during daylight and once by moonlight. Incidentally, the Acropolis is best seen before 11 A.M. or after 4 P.M. because the light is more flattering from an angle rather than directly overhead.

The Greeks dearly love gathering in crowds. The solitary Greek philosopher of centuries gone by, who spent decades in meditation, is little known today. The most intriguing pastimes in modern Athens are wandering about in its colorful markets, shopping in the small stores and loafing in the coffee houses crowded with men (no women). Standard sights of modern Athens include the National Library, the Royal Palace and the Academy. None of these buildings is terribly interesting, however, and the tourist would do well to devote his time to the glories of the ancient world of Greece. One exception we would make is the Parliament building, which is the old palace; it is quite a handsome structure. Near the Parliament building, by the way, the colorful *evzones*, the Greek soldiers in native costumes, execute the changing of the guard at the Tomb of the Unknown Soldier each Sunday morning at eleven o'clock. Here's a tip to camera fans: They don't mind having their picture taken. In fact, they love it.

MUSEUMS ¶ The museums of Athens are indeed worthwhile in this land of antiquity and antiquities. Here is the schedule:

National Archaeological Museum, 1 Tositsa Street: Open daily except Mondays from 8 A.M. to 2 P.M. and 3 to 6 P.M. Sunday hours are from 10 A.M. to 2 P.M. Thursdays and Sundays are good days because admission is free. There is a small entrance fee at other times.

Museum of Numismatics, in the same building as the National Archaeological Museum: It is open daily from 9 A.M. to 2 P.M., but is closed on Sunday and Monday. (Small admission fee.)

Benaki Museum, 1 Koumbar Street: The Benaki has a dazzling collection of Byzantine icons, religious ornaments and articles and a variety of Coptic, Moslem and even Chinese art objects. It is open daily from 9:30 A.M. to 1:30 P.M. and 4:30 to 7:30 P.M. But it is closed on Sunday afternoons and all day on Tuesdays. (Small admission fee.)

Byzantine Museum, 22 Queen Sophia Avenue: As the name implies, this museum has a far-ranging collection of Byzantine art and provides a fine review of the artistic world of the Near East of olden times. There are icons and a variety of religious items. It is open daily from 8 A.M. to 6 P.M.; except on Monday, when it is open only in the afternoon from 2 to 6 P.M., and on Sunday, when it is open only from 9:30 A.M. to 1:30 P.M. Thursdays and Sundays are free; other times, small admission fee.

Acropolis Museum, on the Acropolis: Open weekdays from 9 A.M. to 6 P.M. The Sunday hours are 10 A.M. to 2 P.M. It is closed on Tuesday mornings. (Small admission fee.)

Museum of the Agora (Marketplace), at the Stoa of Attalus: Hours are, daily, from 9 A.M. to 4 P.M. except Sunday, when it is open from 10 A.M. to 2 P.M., and Monday, when it is closed in the morning. (Small admission fee.)

Keramikos Museum, at Keramikos: The hours are daily from 8 A.M. to sunset to see the excavations and 9 A.M. to 5 P.M. for a visit to the museum. The Sunday hours are 10 A.M. to 2 P.M. It is not open on Monday morning. (Small admission fee.)

Note: You should also see, if you're a *real* tourist, while in Athens, the Temple of Zeus, the Theseion (also called the Temple of Theseus), Mars Hill near the Acropolis, Hadrian's Library, the Tower of the Winds (also known as the Water Clock of Andronikos) and . . . there are so many things. Those we've mentioned are only suggestions, for ancient Athens is filled with many other marvelous sights.

TOURS ¶ There are, of course, sightseeing tours by American Express and other travel agencies. Taking one of these might provide a chance for a quick, superficial look at the scene so that you can get your bearings. Then, you can return to individual sites at your own convenience later. There is a daily three-hour sightseeing tour in the mornings and a similar-length but different-itinerary tour in the afternoon. These tours, as we said, give you a quick once-over-very-lightly look, but you do get an idea of the beauty and great scope of Athens' wonders. There is a more detailed morning tour that includes the Acropolis. It lasts four hours.

ठ~ Short Trips from Athens

Cape Sounion (Sunium)

The trip to this delightful point on the seashores of Attica can be easily managed in a half-day excursion. The distance is only about forty-five miles each way—going by the inland road and returning by the coastal highway, which is a bit longer. Go by the inland route through Lavrion. At Cape Sounion there is the Sanctuary and Temple of Poseidon, the God of the Sea. These magnificent ruins, which are deeply moving, date back to the fifth century B.C., and their location is unique. There is an unparalleled view of the sea. At Cape Sounion there is a nice restaurant at the Green Coast Hotel, where you can have a good lunch. You can even stay for a day or two—at very reasonable rates. However, if you'll take our advice, have lunch at one of the simple seaside eating places along the shore. Be sure to order *mereda* (tiny fish fried to a crisp, golden brown). They are so good that we wish we had some right now. Return from Cape Sounion along the coast following the shores of Attica. The road is extremely attractive and runs almost entirely alongside the sea. In case you do not have a drive-yourself car, you can take a pleasant afternoon excursion by bus to the cape. The tour can include dinner if you wish. The departure during the summer is at 4 P.M. (an hour earlier in the winter months) and the bus swings along the Bay of Athens and follows the coastal road. You will visit the Temple of Poseidon on this tour, and if you wish, you can take a dip in the sea. The bus gets back to Athens around 9 P.M.

Marathon

Another half-day trip from Athens is the pleasant run through Kifissia to Marathon, scene of the great battle fought in 490 B.C. in which the Greeks defeated the Persians against overwhelming odds. The messenger bearing the glad tidings raced on foot to Athens and subsequently dropped dead from exhaustion. To this day, the "Marathon" races held all over the world involve what experts regard as the precise distance from Marathon to Athens—26 miles, 385 yards. If time permits, continue on from Marathon to Kalamos and visit the Sanctuary of Amphiareion, including the temple and altar.

Delphi

It is a 200-mile drive to visit Delphi and return to Athens, over fairly good road. The trip is not difficult, if you make a reasonably early start in the morning, do your sightseeing and have lunch at one of the local hotels or restaurants. There are more details later in this chapter, under the description of the Motor Tour of Greece.

Hydra and Spetsai

A hydrofoil boat (that is, one that rises above the surface of the sea and lessens the possibilities of seasickness) makes these two ports within easy reach of Athens. The hydrofoil *Express* leaves from Passalimani (near Piraeus) and takes just a little over an hour to Hydra, an artists' colony and a pleasant small town built up from the sea into the hills. If you wish, you can continue on to Spetsai, twenty minutes farther along. At either of these places, it's fun to wander about slowly, have a pleasant lunch with wine and relax. The hydrofoil returns the same day. If you want to make a reservation or get information, get in touch with Express Argossaronicos Co., 4 Acadimias Street, Athens.

Other short trips from Athens: *Daphni-Eleusis*, with wonderful examples of Byzantine architecture at Daphni and excavations at Eleusis; *Varibobbi-Tatoi–Scala Oropou*, visit the king's country home at Tatoi, the royal tombs, and have a meal at Scala Oropou, a village known for its seaside restaurants; *Penteli*, the famous monastery and the Church of Aghia Tris; *Kaisariani*, to see the monastery and its murals, also nearby Asteri Monastery; *Piraeus*, the old port city of Athens, principally to observe the bustling waterfront. Piraeus is also the starting point for boat trips to the outlying islands. One of the closest islands is *Aegina*, only 1¼ hours from Piraeus. Aegina itself is a small port, but just to its east are the excavated remains of a prehistoric community. A drive about the island is rewarding for those who wish to see historic ruins and the primitive life of the islanders.

🐟 Other Trips from Athens

Besides the Greek mainland itself, the other chief tourist interest of the country is its many fascinating islands.

Rhodes is a favorite, followed closely by *Corfu, Mykonos* and *Crete*. If time allows, by all means visit Rhodes and one or two of the other islands. Air travel, of course, is the fastest, but the most delightful way is the longer sea voyage.

Rhodes

There is frequent plane and ship service to Rhodes. During the peak of the tourist season—in summer—there are as many as three flights a day from Athens (other times, one or two). The flying time is ninety minutes. There are also three flights a week that include Crete (Heraklion) on the itinerary. Every day in the week except Sunday, ships from the Athens port of Piraeus leave for Rhodes, either directly or via other islands. From spring to fall there are scheduled cruises to Rhodes and other ports of call. Sailing time between Athens and Rhodes is about twenty-four hours. In or near the town of Rhodes itself are several luxury hotels. The best hotel is surely the Grand, located on the beach; it has large, bright, attractive rooms, good swimming and a casino to dispose of your excess currency. Also very good indeed is the Golden Beach Hotel, consisting of low buildings on the beach; on a clear day (no joke) you can see Turkey. Most of the Golden Beach's accommodations consist of two-room suites, fairly high in price and quite delightful. On the north coast, at Rhodos Bay, there's a 300-room hotel built into the side of a mountain. It has regular double rooms, but also an assortment of split-level apartments and bungalows; rates are moderate for the regular double rooms, and more expensive (quite naturally) for the special accommodations. The Oceanic is a new hotel situated on the road from the airport, about eight miles from Rhodes; it is on the beach and has a swimming pool. Not quite so expensive as the Grand or the Golden Beach, it represents good value and is almost in the deluxe category. The Belvedere is another new hotel located just as you enter the city; medium-size rooms, medium prices too. If you like beach-front cottages, there's the Hotel Miramare, which is nice but has mediocre rooms; if you like isolation, there's the Eden Rock (sic) on the other side of town. A very simple mountain inn is the Hotel Elaphos, located right in the forests—but be forewarned, there's nothing to do except relax. The island has passed through many different hands during its checkered history. After the time of the Crusades, notably in the fourteenth and fifteenth centuries, it was under the control of various groups of knights from different countries. If you have time to see anything outside of Athens, don't miss lovely Rhodes. Be sure to visit the old walled city built by the knights during medieval times; the order of knights was organized according to countries of origin and for this reason there are within the walls various "nationality inns"—of Castile, Aragon, Provence, Auvergne, France, Germany, Italy, England—and the Palace of the Grand Masters, the local Acropolis and the famed theater. There are conducted tours around the medieval fortifications of Rhodes every Tuesday and Saturday afternoon. Also on the island: *Petaloudes*, famous for its swarms of butterflies; *Kamiros*, with ruins of an old city; *Lindos*, with a castle, theater and temple. Using Rhodes as your headquarters, you may make a number of local boat trips on the small steamer *Panormitis* and visit many of the Dodecanese Islands. For example, every Wednesday the boat leaves Rhodes at 9 A.M. and goes to Castellorizo, returning at midnight. For those who haven't visited Turkey, a one-day excursion (available only on Thursdays) is worthwhile. The boat leaves Rhodes at 7:30 A.M. and heads for Marmaris (in Turkey). A bus meets the boat and takes you to the town of Mougla, which has a sort of bazaar; you'll return to Rhodes at 8 P.M. But these are just samples of the possibilities available.

On the Turkish mainland, too, is the ancient city of Ephesus, with its Temple of Diana, main street, library and other glistening-white ruins.

Corfu

There is frequent service, often several times daily during the season, from Athens to Corfu. By all means go, for it's a lovely green island. Although it lacks the antiquities of many other Greek islands, it has its own charm, and is worth three days, unless you're looking for a beach vacation, in which case, a week or two would be delightful.

There's boat service from Athen's port city of Piraeus, taking 18 hours. However, you can fly over in slightly over an hour. Next, where to stay. There are several luxury hotels: close to town is the Corfu Palace, all rooms with terrace, and with lovely gardens and a swimming pool; don't take rooms near the noisy end adjacent to an orphan's home. If you don't want to be near a beach, there's the Hotel Castello; and if you like bathing, there's the Corcyra Beach Hotel. At Canoni, you'll find the very good Xenia Palace, which has restaurants, night clubs, swimming pools, tennis, golf, and everything else; the hotel is connected to the beach area by a funicular. However, at the other side of the island, I'd recommend the Miramare, particularly if you stay in their cottages. But there are many new hotels under construction right now.

The town of Corfu (which has the same name as the entire island) is exceptionally interesting to wander through, both during the day, and then late in the evening. For variety, take your bathing suit and drive to either Glyfada Beach, or Paleocastriza, where you can have a swim, and eat a seafood lunch. Incidentally, at Paleocastriza, the lobsters are giant-sized, delicious, and fairly expensive; ordinary fish is reasonable in price.

Mykonos

Probably the most renowned of all Greek islands, Mykonos has quite a lot in its favor, and a fair amount against it. From the point of view of a visitor, arriving and leaving during the same day on a cruise ship, the problems are minimized. However, it's different for other visitors.

First of all, the island has been adopted by any number of hippies, and what used to be called beatniks. Next, where to stay is a bit of a problem. The Hotel Leto, informal and unassuming, has an excellent location facing the harbor; but it's terribly noisy at night, with a nearby discotheque which quits at about 4 A.M. Probably the best bet is the Hotel Xenia, at the edge of town. At the extreme end of the island, there's the Aphrodite Hotel, on the beach; the rooms are anything but attractive. You can eat at the hotels, or at any of the waterfront restaurants; you'd better like fish.

There is regular ferry service from Piraeus to Mykonos, taking a scheduled five hours; but don't be surprised if it takes eight hours during the summer months, when the north wind, the *vorias*, is blowing. It can be very choppy indeed. But there's good news, because a new helicopter service makes the trip from

Athen's airport to Mykonos in about 40 minutes; the fare isn't low, but it's worth it. The hydrofoil service is erratic; sometimes it's in full swing, sometimes it's canceled.

Mykonos, famous for its windmills, is an island of rocks and stones. However, it's atmospheric, moody, and exceptionally interesting. The town itself isn't large, and is constructed of brilliantly whitewashed, squarish houses, with little space between. The streets are narrow, winding, and diverting to wander through. There are small shops selling knick-knacks and nonsense, plus high-style, and also handmade sweaters, which are probably the best value on the island. There are hundreds of small churches, often attached to the homes.

From Mykonos, there's frequent boat service, usually in the morning, to the nearby island of Delos. There's a great deal to see there, and it's surely worth at least one visit. The island is now uninhabited, but there's a Tourist Pavilion, which serves refreshments and meals.

For many people, an overnight stay in Mykonos is enough; others might want to stay on for weeks.

Crete

This island is 175 nautical miles from the port of Athens and a trip of something less than fifteen hours by boat. The flight by plane is 75 minutes. Heraklion, the chief city, has a population of 65,000. The Old Town is a delight, for it was once under the control of the intrepid seafaring Venetians, whose fine buildings are still in evidence. There's one luxurious hotel, the Minos Beach, with individual bungalows, and fairly high rates, but it's worth it. The Minos Beach isn't in town, but it is a very nice, quite luxurious place at which to stay. There are also two first-class (but not deluxe) hotels which are less expensive, and rather nice; these are the Astoria and Atlantis. I must say I don't think too much of the Astir Hotel, which is barely passable.

The first item on the agenda is a visit to the Heraklion Archaeological Museum, which is most attractively arranged; it is better to see the museum first before going on to the ruins. Some twenty minutes away by auto are the ruins of the palace of Knossos, the home of King Minos. At one time, it is said, over 100,000 people lived in the vicinity; the palace was probably destroyed by fire about 1380 B.C. Be sure to see the restored rooms, the grand staircase and the enormous jars in which food was stored for the Minoans. You'll surely want to drive to Phaestos, another ruined palace (about thirty-eight miles away and taking about an hour). The drive itself is lovely, often quite exciting, and there is a tourist pavilion overlooking the ruins where a fairly good lunch is served.

Salonika

The bewitching coastal city of eastern Macedonia has been part of Mediterranean history for twenty-five centuries. Once it was, after Constantinople, the second capital of the Byzantine Empire. It remains a major metropolis today and is Greece's second largest city. It is 320 miles from Athens; there is a daily bus from Athens, and Olympic Airways makes several flights a day. The major international express trains (Orient Express, Balkan Express and Yugoslavia Express) connect Salonika and Athens. Also steamships regularly ply between Athens and this fine port city.

About an hour's drive from Salonika is Mount Athos, a community of a score of monasteries in an extraordinarily impressive setting. It is the only monastic state of its kind in Europe. A nine-century rule bans women from setting foot anywhere near the monasteries. Even men visitors have to get permission in advance from the Ministry of Foreign Affairs in Athens. On the road from Polygyros to the Mount Athos settlement is the ancient city of Olynthus. Thanks to the intercession of Demosthenes (the great orator), Athens and Olynthus buried their differences in the fourth century B.C. and, shoulder to shoulder, forces from the two cities withstood the onslaught of Philip of Macedonia. American archaeologists, in their patient, skilled diggings, have uncovered most of the original city. In Salonika, don't miss the Arch of Galerius of the (A.D.) fourth century—relatively new! It is a memorial to a victory against the Persians.

ACCOMMODATIONS ¶ In the larger cities, First Class hotel rooms are available, although even the best hotels somehow seem to have a few rather mediocre rooms facing dark courtyards. Accommodations are extremely variable in size and décor, with many fine front rooms beautifully decorated only to be contrasted by some minute chambers apparently decorated straight out of the Early

Alaskan Renaissance. For all Athens and Greece, advance reservations are essential during the season.

When motoring through the country, don't count on finding excellent little off-the-beaten-path hotels or inns, because these just do not exist. Plan your day's trip and be sure to reach your destination as scheduled or you might find yourself sleeping in some dark airless cubbyhole on what looks like a mattress but feels more like a board. Although this restricts the freedom and scope of a motor trip, during the summer months advance reservations are not only important but absolutely vital; ask the concierge or someone at each hotel to phone ahead and reserve your next evening's accommodations.

ATHENS HOTELS

Athens Hilton: Extremely attractive, fairly good-sized rooms, moderately expensive. About five minutes from center of town by taxi. Several good restaurants; swimming pool.

Grand Bretagne: One of the leading hotels; long, excellent record with tourists. The newer wing has extremely attractive accommodations; most rooms are now air-conditioned.

King George: Much smaller than the adjacent Grand Bretagne. All rooms are air-conditioned; most bedrooms are average size, pleasantly decorated.

King's Palace: A medium-size, very attractive modern hotel with an excellent location near Constitution Square.

Athénée Palace: A very modern hotel near Constitution Square; the best accommodations, on the top floor, have fine views. A good restaurant is located on the second floor.

Within easy commuting distance of Athens are four suburban hotels with resort features:

Hotel Parnis: A luxury hotel, atop historic Mount Parnis, with attractive rooms, good food and an incomparable view. About forty-five minutes by car from Athens. Delightful for a few days' rest.

Astir Palace: A deluxe hotel, fifteen miles from Athens Ultramodern, all rooms with a view of the sea; lots of marble, plenty of luxury. Boating facilities adjacent to the hotel.

Astir Beach: A large-scale hotel and bungalow colony at Astir Beach; about ten miles from Athens. Good beach and bathing facilities plus restaurants; excellent for those who want to combine a rest with their sightseeing. Minimum stay: two days.

Pentelikon: Also ten miles from town, at Kifissia, is this pleasant, soothing resort hotel on the side of Mount Pentelikon. Accommodations are quite satisfactory and summer temperatures are inevitably lower than in Athens. Not too many rooms have private baths.

ATHENS RESTAURANTS

Papakia: Small, attractive place with European and Greek food; very good and not too expensive.

Ta Keria: Very interesting small place, pleasing atmosphere, good food. European and Greek dishes; moderate prices.

Platanos: Just the sort of very good Greek restaurant you're looking for—first rate food at moderate prices. By all means visit this simple place.

Gherofinikas: An ideal place for a very pleasant lunch; excellent tasty home-style food, medium prices, very pleasant surroundings. Located two blocks behind King's Palace Hotel.

Dionysos: Very good food, moderately expensive, with a remarkable view of the Acropolis; indoor and outdoor dining.

Le Bistro de Paris: One of the better restaurants serving French-style food; in the downtown area.

L'Air de Paris: Near the race course in the suburbs; French-style food is good here, too.

ATHENS TAVERNAS

Vacchos: A delightful *taverna* with good food served both indoors and outdoors; pleasant music; friendly atmosphere. You'll enjoy it.

Kakoyiannis: Extra large, but it's a friendly and worthwhile place. Tremendously popular with the local people, bustling, but still recommended. If you can't find an English-speaking waiter, point at what you want.

Geros Toy Morea: An excellent *taverna* with wonderful music; very enjoyable to have dinner and spend several hours.

Zambeta: If you're a real enthusiast for *bouzouki*, this *taverna* is said to have the best one in Greece. In any event, the food is good and the atmosphere most pleasant.

Vrachos: A popular *taverna*, with Greek dishes at moderate prices. Pleasant music.

Palaia Athena: An interesting *taverna*, closed during July and August. At other times, be sure to go. Greek show, dancing, music, good food.

Seven Brothers: A pleasant place to have a good dinner and hear some Greek music. Moderate prices.

Xenos: An extremely pleasant, rambling place with a garden; delightful atmosphere, Greek specialties, guitar music.

SUBURBAN ATHENS

Salmatanis: A trip of only seven miles (to Kiphissia) brings you to this family-style garden restaurant featuring roast suckling pig prepared on a spit. Inexpensive and very pleasant.

Vassilena: Only six miles from Athens is this much-publicized ex-grocery shop turned restaurant; an enormous meal half poor, half good, moderate-priced and a good value.

Psaropoula: Attention, fish lovers! A very good fish restaurant located on the city's outskirts in the direction of the airport. The lobster, although expensive, is excellent; also good is *barbounia*, a local fish.

Soupies: Not too far from the Psaropoula Restaurant (above) is this family-style establishment. A good place for those who want to see Athenians enjoying themselves. The food is good and low-priced, but don't fail to have their specialty of assorted appetizers, *mezedakia*.

SHOPPING ¶ Athens' main shopping district is busy Stadiou Street, where anything and everything can be found. Elsewhere, particularly on the Greek islands, buy articles as you see them, because local handicrafts are best purchased at the point of origin and the same opportunity may not arise again. Sometimes you'll see particular objects displayed at one shop or stall and never again. If you're going to Rhodes, do as much shopping as possible while there, because this island has a special tax deal with the government (to assist in its financial recovery), thus permitting substantially lower prices.

Earthenware and ceramic art objects are extremely attractive and not too expensive. Particularly worthwhile are the copies of classic Greek designs, extremely well executed.

Blouses and skirts, usually hand-embroidered, are reasonably priced, but be sure to avoid the overly decorated styles, which may blend into the background in Greece, but won't at home in St. Louis. Also, and this is very important, make sure they fit, because Greek women are shorter and somewhat broader than long-legged Americans.

Slippers, sandals, shawls, handbags, wallets are all worthwhile if you're looking for samples of Greek handicraft. The workmanship is usually painstaking and the craftsmanship evident, although the designs are frequently on the precious side.

Gift articles: a wide choice is available, including the national *dolls, cigarette boxes*, intricately designed *brooches* and *earrings*, small *silverware* articles, *copper* items, costume *necklaces* and *bracelets*.

Carpets and rugs, chiefly made in Kastoria and Arakhova, are not bad values although air travelers will have to arrange for shipment. Another worthwhile island handicraft is the *lace* produced by the peasant women in Hydra and Aegina.

Greek wines and liquors: undoubtedly the best bet is the *Metaxas* brandy, providing you've worked up a taste for it; be sure to buy the better quality brandy. The duty-free limit, as you know, is five bottles per person.

Ready-made dresses have improved in styling over the years. Extremely worthwhile are the *Tsekle-Nis*. Furs are extremely poor and should be avoided, because the furriers apparently do not know how to work the pelts.

Antiques are worthwhile, with good values available to the canny shopper; bargaining necessary. You'll find most of the best shops in Athens on Philhellinon, Argentine Republic and Pandrossu streets, the last of which is particularly interesting for odd items. Elsewhere throughout the mainland and the islands, you'll frequently see antiques for sale in small odd shops.

ENTERTAINMENT ¶ The *night clubs* in Athens cater to large numbers of tourists and servicemen, and frankly the prices are enough to shock even a tourist who has thought himself shock-proof. Considering Greece's otherwise low prices, $2 or $3 per drink or $15 for a bottle of third-class wine is slightly excessive. But that doesn't discourage night life, for Athens is filled with night clubs offering more or less elaborate shows. We do think you'll find more local color at one of the *tavernas*, where you can hear good music and singing and have a pleasant, friendly evening.

Don't go out for the evening before 9:30 or 10 P.M. (You'll be starved until then? Of course, so have some tea at 5:30 to tide you over.) Visit a *taverna*, if you want to have music and singing with your dinner, and the atmosphere will be friendly and informal. Let's assume that you're going to the Palaia Athena (unless it's during July or August, when it's closed). (If so, choose Vacchos —Bacchus—that is pronounced Vac-hus). When you enter, go into the kitchen and select your dinner from the display, then go upstairs to your table. Don't look for American or European food—even if available, it will never be as good as the Greek dishes. By now, dinner concluded, it should almost be midnight; get a cab and drive to Phaleron, ten minutes away, and head for a *bouzouka* place to see the stylized dancing, performed largely by the men guests. Very, very interesting, and not to be missed. Women seldom get into the act, but may, if requested by their husbands. Go, and see for yourself.

During summer the Athens Festival of Music and Drama stages outdoor opera, drama, and concert performances at that ancient theater, the Odeon of Herodes Atticus, on the slopes of the Acropolis. Even if you never cared for opera, you'll surely want to see this. Watch for performances of Greek *drama* during the Athens Festival, also at many of the resorts during the tourist season.

Melina Mercouri and Anthony "Zorba" Quinn have spearheaded interest in Greek films or films about Greece. There are plenty of *movie* theaters in the cities and tourist areas, and the majority of them are American and international (British, Italian, French, Yugoslavian—as we said, *international*). During warm weather, by all means attend an outdoor performance. In Athens there must be almost two dozen theaters that show English-language films. Movie prices are low, too.

SPORTS ¶ Greece is a land of sea and sun, and thus sports have a definite open-air, down-by-the-beach flavor. The Greek National Tourist Organization has done magnificent work to provide international-type sports facilities for visitors. Along with building hotels, motels, inns and restaurants (these are frequently referred to as *Xenia* establishments, by the way), the government tourist authorities have laid out splendid *beaches* and installed superb *boating* facilities. On the road to Vouliagmeni, ten miles from Athens, is the new Glyfada *golf course*, an eighteen-hole championship layout that is administered by the government tourist organization. It was at Vouliagmeni, too, that the tourist officials set up and equipped the first beach in its big program. Similar beaches are throughout the country—especially interesting are the ones at Salonika, Kavala, Loutraki, Patras, Mykonos and Aedipsos. The National Tourist Organization also has more than four score marinas for *yachting* and small-boating sportsmen. Practically speaking, every tourist center has a yachting club. In some cities you will come across surprises in sports possibilities. On Rhodes, for instance, besides *tennis* and *yacht* clubs, there is a *basketball* club. On Corfu, you will want to investigate, anyway, the Byron Cricket Club.

ঝ A Motor Tour of Greece

It is not possible at the present time to make an interesting circular tour of the country on good roads because enough suitable accommodations are not as yet available to motorists.

Athens to Argos—83 miles

Leave Athens, following the signs for Eleusis and Corinth, in a westerly direction. The first town of interest is Daphni, noted for its eleventh-century Byzantine church, with some unusual mosaic work in the interior. Six miles along the road is Eleusis, then the road goes beside the Saronic Gulf, where the Greeks defeated the Persians in a great naval battle in the year 480. Next comes Megara (somewhat inland), but the road returns to the sea shortly afterward. You will then reach a bridge. Please get out, and look down toward the water, about 275 feet below; quite impressive. This is the renowned Corinth Canal, which connects the Aegean and Ionian seas; construction was originally begun in A.D. 66 by none other than Nero, but the work was not completed until 1893, which is a pretty long time, anyway you look at it! A few miles along comes New Corinth, and immediately afterward, Old Corinth; it was here that St. Paul wrote his Epistles to the Corinthians. The ruins are very worthwhile, notably the Fountains of Peirene and the six columns that remain from the Temple of Apollo. A few miles farther along, there is a left turn toward Mycenae. You must leave the car and climb a short distance, entering through the renowned Lion Gate. This is antiquity at its greatest, and worth all the time you can spare. Please don't miss climbing up to see ancient Mycenae.

From Mycenae, back to the main road, and a short run into Argos. Here, too, there are some ruins (the Agora, a museum and theater), if you're still up to it. The hotels at Argos are nothing special, but there is a fine Xenia hotel (remember, Xenia is a government tourist organization establishment) at Mycenae.

Argos to Kalamai—59 miles

From Argos en route to Tripolis—you pass through Miloi, Mousmouli and Stenon, then come into Tripolis, with a choice of the Arkadia, Mainalon and Semiramis Hotels.

From here, a side trip may be made to Olympia (eighty-two miles), birthplace of the Olympic Games and site of some of the most impressive ruins in Greece; the Hotel Spap located on a hillside is the best here.

From Tripolis, continue through Franko Vrisi, Marmaria and into Megalopolis, which has some interesting excavations. Later the road goes through Paradhisia (which it isn't), Dervenia and Allagi and then into Kalamai (which has the Hotel Rex); here you could visit the Kastro (also known as Villehardouins Castle) built in 1206. Kalamai is the starting point for an optional side trip to nearby Mavrommati (Messena); be careful *not* to wind up at Messini, which is five miles west of Kalamai. At Mavrommati you'll find some remarkable ruins of ancient civilization. From Kalamai, return to Athens.

ATHENS NORTHWARD TO SALONIKA

Athens to Delphi—99 miles

For this run, leave Athens by the Eleusis road; after Eleusis, take a right-hand turn to Mandra. Approximately fifteen miles past Mandra you reach Eleftherae Fortress, whose ruins date back to the fifth century. Then on to Thebes, also called Thivai or Thíve, but regardless of the name there is no suitable hotel. The principal sights here are Electrai Gate, Proetides Gate and the town's famous museum.

From Thebes to Livadia (twenty-nine miles); here the sightseeing attraction is nearby Hercyna Gorge, particularly impressive during the spring, when the waters are at their most violent. Leave Livadia by the southwestern road heading to Keresi and Arachova (famous for its hand-woven carpets and rugs) and into Delphi (about thirty miles from Livadia). The Hotel Amalia is new and deluxe. If you recall, this was the site of the famous Oracle of Pythian Apollo, where important questions were asked, the ambiguous answer being given on the seventh day of each month if all the preliminaries and sacrifices had found favor with the gods.

Delphi sightseeing: the Sacred Precincts, the Tholos, the Temple and Shrine of Athena, the theater and the stadium. Castalia Spring is where, prior to entering the

Sacred Precincts, those who wished to ask questions of the oracle washed themselves in accordance with rite and custom.

Delphi to Larissa—131 miles

Leave Delphi, continuing on to Amfissa and Gravia and, at Brallos, joining the main road; then through Kallidhromon Mountains toward Lamia, which, although of not unpleasing aspect, holds comparatively little interest for today's tourist.

From Lamia to Larissa is a run of about seventy miles over good roads in central Greece's province of Thessaly. The route passes through Xinia (located on Lake Xinia), then Dhomokos, which boasts an ancient castle and ruins. The road begins to drop down until you reach Pharsala; there are ruins of an old marketplace nearby. A half-day excursion may be made southward to the local Acropolis; the renowned Battle of Pharsala (48 B.C.) between Caesar and Pompey was fought here, resulting in Caesar's outstanding victory. Next comes Khalkiades, Zappeon, Neai Kariai, Nikaia and Larissa; although it is scarcely luxurious, an overnight stay is possible at the Hotel Olympia, Larissa's best at the present time.

Larissa to Salonika—162 miles

(Approximately fifty miles may be saved by taking the new toll road from Larissa going through the Vale of Tempe to Katerini and then into Salonika. The road is asphalt, and the trip is extremely pleasant. If you're tired of slow driving, the toll charges will be well worthwhile. If you choose to follow the old route, follow the section below for a route description.)

Leave Larissa for the trip to Elasson (thirty-seven miles) heading for Tirnavos, where the road changes direction, heading westward for several miles. The way leads through a quite narrow pass in the valley, through several small villages, including Molopousta, Domenikon, Stefanevounon and Elasson; here you will be interested in seeing the old monastery located in an extremely rugged and quite unlikely setting.

Note: From Elasson to Salonika is a run of 129 miles, and since good hotels are extremely scarce en route, the entire mileage must be completed in one day.

After leaving Elasson, the road climbs, levels off and

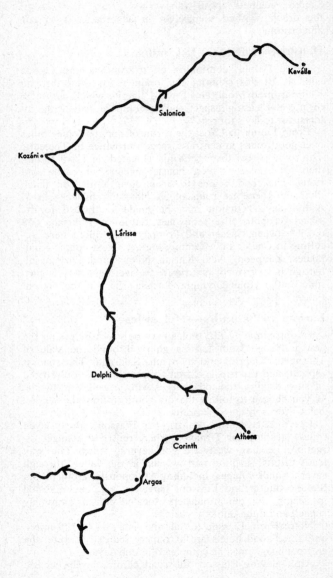

then descends until it reaches (at about thirty-two miles) the quaint town of Servia, originally established by the Serbians, from whom it reputedly gets its name. At Petrana, be careful to take a right turn (the left turn brings you into Kozani, an uninteresting town). The right turn subsequently joins the road leading away from Kozani to Kiladha, Levendis, Polimilon and Verroia (also called Verria). Unfortunately, there are no satisfactory hotel accommodations, but Verroia warrants a visit. The big attraction is the unbelievably picturesque setting of the houses in the Jewish quarter of the town, the buildings seemingly perched on the very edge of a ravine. It may be, although proof is lacking, that St. Paul once preached beside a local mosque.

Verroia is also known for its churches, but because they were intended to be hidden from the invading Turks, the exteriors do not reveal their identities; these include the Ayios Christos, Ayios Kirikos, Ayios Nikolaos and Ayia Paraskevi. You'll require a guide for identification.

SIDE TRIP ¶ From Verroia, head north to Naoussa, a small town, where there are some lovely old houses.

Leave Verroia, passing through Microgouzi, Stavros, Kambokhori, Nea Khalkidon. At the latter point you take a right turn into Yefira. Then it is on to Lakhanokipos and into Salonika (sometimes spelled Salonica; in Greek phonetic spelling, Thessaloniki). Here the leading hotel is the Mediterranean, facing the sea. King Alexandros Palace is one of the newest. Another fine one is the Olympic, which is air-conditioned, incidentally.

Salonika is next in size to Athens and is a vital city in the Greek economy. The great fire of a half century ago unfortunately destroyed many of the town's buildings, but Salonika has grown accustomed to surviving disasters over the centuries.

SIGHTSEEING ¶ The Archaeological Museum, containing many fine pieces, mostly excavated by Americans; Arch of Galerium; many Byzantine churches, notably St. Sophia, St. George and St. Demetrius. But most tourists will not want to linger overly long here, for the town holds little of interest, being devoted chiefly to the tobacco and leather trades. It is at Salonika that motorists from Yugoslavia can enter Greece for a tour of the country.

Salonika to Kavalla—123 miles

The next part of the tour is from Salonika to Kavalla. Leave Salonika by taking the first right turn at the end of Vardar Square heading toward Assyro, Xylopolis, Lakhanas, Evangelistria and Leucona and into Serrai (also spelled Serres or Serre); there is no suitable hotel here, nor is the town of any great interest to the tourist, although commercially important. From Serrai, proceed through Pandapolis, Nea Zichna, Mesoraki, Alistrati, Sytagri and Drama, all without suitable hotels. From Drama, head toward Kavalla, passing Dhoxaton. Here, you approach Philippi, an extremely important tourist area; the Acropolis may be recognized by three immense towers visible on the heights. The old town's history begins with its founding about 356 B.C. by Philip of Macedonia, but renown came to Philippi because of the great battle fought there in 42 B.C. between opposing Roman forces—one army being led by Brutus and Cassius, the other by Anthony and Octavius. Brutus, the murderer of Caesar, died here. Furthermore, Philippi is the site where St. Paul reputedly gave his first sermon in Europe. Wandering about the ruins is extremely interesting; be sure to look for the various basilicas, the theater and the old ramparts of the ancient city. After leaving Philippi, the road passes many old monuments and markers, finally leading into Kavalla.

The best hotels in Kavalla are Tosca Beach on the shore and Astir, with rather good accommodations. About the most interesting sight here is the former old Muslim quarter of the city and the monastery built by Mohammed Ali. From Kavalla, there is boat service (approximately 2½ hours each way) to the island of Thasos, an absolutely delightful out-of-the-world spot; because of the boat schedule, it is not possible to make the round trip in one day from this point. If you are anxious to take the trip in one day, drive to nearby Karamoti, where there is irregular motorboat service (taking less than an hour) frequently, permitting a one-day excursion. The delightful island of Thasos is difficult to classify, except that it exudes peaceful, rustic Greek village charm. Sightseeing: the Agora, the Shrine of Hercules, the ramparts and the theater.

Note: Unfortunately, it is not possible to drive back to Athens by a different route over satisfactory roads offering worthwhile sights and good hotels. The return route must therefore be substantially the same as the original one.

🏵 Motoring in Greece

In order to bring your car or a rented one into the country, be sure to have proof of ownership or of rental; the *carnet* or *triptyque* formerly required is no longer needed. However, your state driver's license is sufficient, no international license being required, although it will be accepted. The green insurance card is now obligatory in Greece.

There is no speed limit on the open road, although you'll be expected to use reasonable care; within cities, the speed limit is 18 miles per hour, but like every other place in the world the taxis seem to go considerably faster. The main roads, such as the highway from Athens to Salonika, are well paved and in generally good condition. Almost all secondary roads are questionable, some good, some very poor. If you venture off the regular routes, be sure to inquire locally about road conditions, and even then use roads only if you have very good tires and at least one spare. Many Greek peasants use horses and donkeys, and it is not unusual to pick up several horseshoe nails in one's tires. Puncture-proof tires are indeed a blessing here. In Athens, up-to-the-minute road conditions may be ascertained from the Automobile and Touring Club of Greece (ELPA) at 7 Odos Amerikis (open 8:30–1 and 4–6).

Drive to the right as usual, and pass to the left. On most roads, extreme care must be exercised because of cattle, donkeys, meandering pedestrians and other road hazards. Don't blow your horn within city limits except in emergencies, although it is permissible on highways. *Benzini* (gasoline) is obtainable in almost every moderate-size community, but nevertheless care should be taken to ensure a full tank at the beginning of each day's journey or prior to venturing into comparatively remote areas. You'll have to either learn the Greek alphabet or memorize the Greek words for the various towns on your route, because highway markers (when they do exist) are in Greek and frequently are almost incomprehensible. If you belonged to a fraternity or sorority in college, it may be possible, with some effort, to translate Greek place-names.

The Greek automobile club, by the way, patrols the roads with service cars, so you can feel sure that in case of a breakdown, help will be on the way shortly.

In Athens parking is made easier by the designation of nearly a dozen special tourist parking areas. Ask a policeman or the hotel concierge about the nearest one when you arrive.

HUNGARY

National Characteristics

An Iron Curtain country, but one that seems to be doing better than most of the others, economically and politically. People on the streets seem reasonably well-dressed, the shops have fairly good merchandise (much of it imported), and there's plenty of food and wine to go around. Of course, no one should come to Hungary expecting to live in the lap of luxury, although if you stay at the Duna Inter-Continental, and never go out of the lobby, you actually can. However, Hungary is an extremely interesting country, and you'll enjoy a visit here.

When to Go

The weather is best from late April through early October. Winters are raw and cold.

TIME EVALUATION ¶ Allow several days for Budapest, and several more for Lake Balaton, if you want to spend a few days relaxing.

PASSPORT AND VISA ¶ You'll need a valid passport, and also a visa, which may be obtained in advance in the United States, or upon arrival at the airport in Budapest, or at the border, if you're driving. Be absolutely sure to bring along two passport-size photographs. You may be delayed in receiving your visa. There's a small fee for a visa.

CUSTOMS AND IMMIGRATION ¶ Don't bring any Hungarian money with you, but you can bring as much American money as you wish, including cash or travelers' checks.
Official currency exchange offices are located in the lobbies of tourist hotels. Keep the receipts for all ex-

change transactions. Do not cash your money at any other place but an official exchange.

HEALTH ¶ Don't worry about anything, except that it's generally not advisable to drink tap water, except possibly at the leading hotels. Bottled water is generally available at low cost wherever you go.

CURRENCY ¶ The local currency is called a *forint*. There's a special tourist rate, but this often changes, so don't be surprised. On departure you can change your remaining Hungarian money back into American if you have kept your exchange receipts.

TIPPING ¶ Tips are expected in restaurants, say about 10% of the check, even though a service charge has been added. In your hotel, only tip the baggage porter; about 5 *forints* should be enough for several bags. Cabdrivers are tipped liberally, in relation to the fares which are low.

ELECTRICITY ¶ The outlets are unsuited for American appliances, and the current is equally wrong. Exception: the Duna Inter-Continental has American-style outlets and current.

FOOD SPECIALTIES AND LIQUOR ¶ You'll be absolutely astonished at how good the food is in Hungary. Wherever you go, you'll find delicious, tasty, home-style cooking. Don't look for American-style steaks, because they just don't cook that way. Meats and chicken are typically prepared with paprika (that red spice which can be mild or sharp), and made into all sorts of stews, typified by that famous dish *gulyás*, which we know as goulash.

With many dishes, in fact with most, they like to serve noodles or dumplings, which come in a wide variety of shapes and forms. There's *gombóc*, *metélt*, *csipetke*, *tarhonya*, and *galuska*, to mention a few.

The soups are absolutely superb, and I would particularly like to single out *gulyásleves*, a goulash soup, filled with meat, potatoes, sausages and other delicious ingredients. Second best, I think, is the bean soup.

As to desserts, this will be paradise for those who don't count calories, for the strudels (*rétes*) are typically prepared with apples, cherries, cheese, or poppy seeds. And of course, the *dobos torta*, a type of chocolate cake, is marvelous.

You'll find the local wines very pleasant and not expensive. The white wines, usually from Lake Balaton, and also the Tokay, range from dry to very sweet. Hungary has only one good red wine, I think, that being the *Egri Bikavér*, which is fine with meats.

Capital City

Cutting through Budapest is the Danube River, and that makes for a majestic setting. One side of the river is called Buda, and the other Pest. Along the banks of the Danube, you'll see castles and fortifications and old churches, and reminders of days gone by, when the Hungarians controlled much of Europe. Away from the river, the city tends to be somewhat drab and unimposing, but it is pleasant to wander through the streets, and look in shop windows, and if you should get lost, all that's involved is an inexpensive taxi ride back to your hotel.

ACCOMMODATIONS

Duna Inter-Continental: This is an extremely fine hotel, and indeed would be outstanding almost anywhere in Europe. For Hungary, it's almost unbelievably luxurious. Rooms are pleasant, and all have terraces facing the broad Danube. The lobby is attractive, and there are excellent restaurants, shops, etc.

Gellért: At one time, this was Budapest's leading hotel, but since the opening of the Duna Inter-Continental, the authorities seem to have let it get somewhat seedy. It's still satisfactory, but certainly not in the same class with the Duna. Rooms are good-sized, and old-fashioned. The hotel's location is somewhat inconvenient, quite far out on the Buda side. Rates about the same as the Duna.

Royal: Situated on a noisy main street, this is a pretty good hotel, all things considered, but far from luxurious. The hotel dining room serves good food. The rooms aren't terribly attractive, but they're passable. Slightly less expensive than the Duna or Gellért.

Margitsziget: A charming old-world hotel, located on an island in the middle of the Danube. Large, old-fashioned rooms; peaceful and quiet at night, but rather inconvenient for sightseeing or shopping. Slightly less expensive than the Duna or Gellért. Fairly good food in the hotel dining room.

BUDAPEST RESTAURANTS (all are moderate in price)

Csárdás Room: This ground floor restaurant in the Duna Inter-Continental, in my opinion, is the best all-around place in the city, and all of Hungary. It's exceptionally attractive, there's delightful gypsy music, and the food is truly exceptional and authentic, plus moderate prices. Service is excellent, although perhaps a trifle slow. Don't order too hastily, because the menu is quite fascinating, and at those prices, you can afford to experiment.

Gundel's: About 15 minutes from the center of town, near the zoo, this is a fine place for an outdoor lunch, or perhaps tea and cake in the late afternoon, in the delightful outdoor garden. At night, dining is indoors, with marvelous gypsy music, and excellent food.

Mátyás Pince: A busy, noisy and very typical Hungarian restaurant, located not too far from the Duna Hotel. It's hectic and bustling, and the food is first rate—if you can manage to catch the waiter's eye and order your meal. Fine gypsy music, if you can hear it above the noise level. Lots of fun, all things considered.

Hungária: A very interesting, spacious, grand-style restaurant, which has fine service. The food is good, although not necessarily better than those listed above, and prices are moderate.

SHOPPING ¶ There's little indeed to buy, other than some of the food and wine specialties. A package (or can) of that remarkable spice, paprika, costs very little, and comes in both sweet and hot types. This is a good small item to take home as a gift to gourmet friends. A few bottles of local wine are also worthwhile, and inexpensive. As to clothing, almost everything worthwhile is imported, as you'll find if you read the labels carefully.

ENTERTAINMENT ¶ If you check with the hotel concierge, he'll tell you what's available in the way of live theater, including opera, and musical shows. (I'm assuming that you can't understand Hungarian.) Also, there are a couple of seedy nightclubs in town, featuring such entertainment as the strip-tease. On the roof of the Duna Hotel, there's a standard nightclub show, for those who want to see a group of imported acts, and have dinner music, plus dancing.

৯ A Tour of Hungary

Theoretically, you could enter Hungary by car through Russia, Yugoslavia, Bulgaria, or Czechoslovakia. But the chances are, based upon statistics, that you'll be coming from Austria, the way the vast majority of American tourists drive to Hungary. Driving from Vienna to Budapest is easily accomplished in no more than 5 hours, or somewhat less at certain times of the day. Of course, the border crossing into Hungary always presents a small problem, because you never know just how busy it will be at the border, and how long it will take to get your visa (assuming you haven't previously obtained it).

Lake Balaton

Although Hungary is a lovely country, there really isn't too much to see in the countryside, with the exception of Lake Balaton. Some people make trips to the wine region, but unless you're particularly interested in wines, and it happens to be late September or early October, I don't think it's worthwhile.

Lake Balaton is a large, long lake to the southwest of Budapest, and easily reached in 2½ to 3½ hours, depending upon your particular destination on the lake. Driving out from Budapest, there's a superhighway for a portion of the way, and it's worth taking. As to the lake itself, I suppose you should see it, if only to eat a *fogas*, the very unusual and delicious fish caught in the lake, and generally served in the hotels, if you're lucky. (Sometimes it's out of season, or the fishermen had back luck, and so on.)

You'll have a choice of several small resort villages, dotted around the lake, at irregular intervals. The best known resort area is called Siófok, which has the Europa, Balaton, Hungária, Lido and Venus Hotels. In the smaller village of Tihany, there are the Kistihany and Tihany Hotels. Now a word or two about the hotels at Balaton. They're quite modern, and many of them are tall. The lobbies are attractive, the dining room serves really excellent food (as a rule), and the rates are exceptionally low. However, the elevator service is inevitably erratic, to say the least, and the rooms are *very* small and unattractively furnished. But, I would admit that it's satisfactory for a few days. The lake itself is good for swimming and boating, and there are several boat rides to be taken. It's generally pleasant, although far from thrilling. But, if you need a few days of rest, Balaton is fine. There are small wine cellars in the area, where you can sit at night with the local people, drink a glass or two of wine, and sing songs, and spend an astonishingly small amount of money.

IRELAND

National Characteristics

Green is the color traditionally associated with the Irish. But Ireland is a rainbow of dozens of shades of green. One green is more enchanting than the other. The warm effect produced by the country's color scheme is reflected in the people. You will be enchanted by them —by their manner of speech, but mostly by what they have to say. Often, a few words of comment from a shopkeeper or the man on the bus next to you in County Kerry sound like poetry. It might be just a greeting or an observation on the day's weather. But tumbling from the mouth of an Irishman, the words have the soft ring of poetry. The Irish are a poetic people.

Life has never been easy for the Irish—at least not in recent centuries. Times seem to be getting a little better. In the past few years a number of new factories and manufacturing plants (American, German and others) have been established in Ireland—attracted by the Irish government's program of tax relief and other fringe benefits. Everyone *knows* that the Common Market is going to mean all manner of good things for Ireland.

Also on the good side is the drop-off in emigration. The outflow of the young has pretty much halted. Those who go abroad nowadays—and today it is chiefly to England—come back home after a few years, carrying a cozy nest egg that accumulated while they were working in their foreign jobs. The unity of Ireland, long a dream of every Irishman, is a major topic of discussion everywhere Irishmen (and their friends) meet ever since the start of the civil rights activity in Northern Ireland (the six partitioned counties).

It is an undeniable fact that marriage in Ireland is postponed far beyond the norm for other countries. The average man weds at thirty-five; the average woman at

442

about thirty. It has been said that the cause lies with the Irish system of matriarchy—the overwhelming dominance of the mother in the family. The young men, held under close restraint by well-meaning but powerful mothers, hesitate to take a wife. To an outsider, the sexes seem to be warring constantly. At most social gatherings, the men and women automatically separate by sex into groups—even into different rooms.

Yet the people are happy. At least they seem to be. Almost everyone, man or woman, is delighted to help a traveler and to extend the kind of friendly hospitality that comes so rarely in this day and age, and particularly to engage in spirited, lively conversation. The Irish dearly love to talk (at great length) and expound on anything and everything, the small and the large. And talk they will! But don't look for a Yeats or a Shaw in every farm boy in Kerry or Galway—or any other place. That kind of brain power is seldom encountered, even in Ireland, home of the literary mind.

In this damp land, Irish wit and fantasy have worked up a whole realm of the supernatural, for the country people do have their superstitious side. Do you know the difference between a banshee and a pooka? Between a fairy and a leprechaun? And if you do know these folks, then who or what is a dullaghass? Ireland is a bewitched country—bewitched by nationalistic pride, by the lovely countryside, by the reputation for liquor and words. Americans speak in black and white. The Irish speak in Technicolor, with each phrase carefully turned, polished and full of hues.

When to Go

Anytime from April until early October is best for a visit, but be prepared for rain almost any day. Ireland's location—near the Gulf Stream—means milder weather than its latitude warrants. But there is also considerable condensation. Although the Irish Tourist Board might not agree with us, it is definitely true that some rain may be expected on an average of two days out of three. But don't let this damp fact discourage you, because the rain seldom lasts very long (we hope). In truth, changeability is the word for Irish weather. Temperatures are seldom excessive—80 degrees is regarded as a very hot summer day. During April, May and September, the days are fairly mild, the nights on the chilly side. July and August are, of course, the busiest tourist months and the warmest. The southwest corner of Ireland has a reputation for being relatively mild in the winter. In any event, houses, hotels, restaurants and shops are always snug and comfortable.

WEATHER STRIP: DUBLIN

Temp.	JAN.	FEB.	MAR.	APR.	MAY	JUNE	JULY	AUG.	SEPT.	OCT.	NOV.	DEC.
Low	35°	34°	35°	37°	42°	47°	51°	50°	46°	41°	38°	35°
High	46°	47°	49°	53°	58°	64°	66°	65°	62°	55°	50°	47°
Average	41°	41°	42°	45°	50°	56°	59°	58°	54°	48°	44°	41°
Days of rain	21	18	19	17	16	15	18	19	16	19	19	21

TIME EVALUATION ¶ Dublin, being a small city, can easily be covered in a day or two. Local sightseeing outside of Dublin (but returning each night) could be managed in another two days. A complete tour of the countryside would take from seven to ten days—or longer, if you are bemused by the lush green scenery. A short trip, cutting across the country from Dublin to Shannon, would take about two to three days each way, figuring leisurely travel.

PASSPORT AND VISA ¶ A passport is required, but no visa.

CUSTOMS AND IMMIGRATION ¶ Each person may bring in five cartons of cigarettes or 200 cigars or any assortment of tobacco products that does not weigh more than two and a half pounds. Also allowable are a quart of liquors and cordials, two bottles of wine and one pint of toilet waters or perfume. If you're bringing gifts for your Irish friends or relatives, the limit is about $50 per person. Above that, you'll have to pay duty. Normal traveling articles—camera, film, portable typewriter, transistor and the like—are also allowed duty-free. But Ireland does have a list of prohibited or restricted goods, which include arms and ammunition, butter, contraceptives, fireworks and "indecent or obscene books, pictures, etc." You can bring in with you any amount of currency of any country.

HEALTH ¶ The water is now completely safe all over Ireland, including both urban and rural areas, so you can drink it right out of the tap, if you wish. Nowadays, the milk is almost always pasteurized, except in occasional rural areas, so it's inevitably safe. The countryside is quite damp (when the sun isn't out). Sweaters or other warm clothes are recommended for off-season visits.

CURRENCY ¶ Ireland's monetary system traditionally has followed that of Britain in a general fashion. When England switched to the decimal method of calculation, Ireland did so as well, and here's how it works: The Irish pound is the basic unit of currency. The pound is divided into 100 new pence. Six decimal coins are in circulation. Three of them (the 50 new pence, 10 new pence, and 5 new pence) are made of cupronickel, which resembles silver in appearance. The 2 new pence, 1 new penny, and new half-penny coins are in bronze, and have the appearance of copper. Bear in mind that British notes and coins circulate freely in Ireland at face value, so don't be surprised to receive them on occasion; also, if you're coming from Britain, don't bother to change your British money to Irish, for it's not necessary.

PRICE LEVELS ¶ One of the lowest-priced countries in Europe—and isn't that delightful news? Of course in Dublin, it's possible to spend well over $5 for a superb meal. But this does not happen too often—or does not have to happen. Even a steak dinner in the city will ordinarily run under $5, and in the country you'll have very good meals for a couple of dollars. Hotel rates follow the same pattern. A double room in the hotels popular with American tourists will average out around $20 (maybe less, maybe more). Usually, breakfast is included. And what a breakfast! Once out of the capital, the rates will drop somewhat—especially in small towns. But don't count on this always. Car rentals are also inexpensive. They are about the lowest in Europe and a real bargain off season.

TIME ¶ Ireland is six hours ahead of (later than) Eastern Standard Time. When it's noon in New York, it's 6 P.M. in Ireland. When Daylight Saving Time is in effect in the United States, the time difference is reduced to 5 hours.

TIPPING ¶ Taxicab drivers are tipped 10 to 15 percent of the meter—but never less than 10 pence. Otherwise, the basic tip throughout Ireland is 10 percent, with few exceptions. In the best restaurants, particularly in big cities, about 15 percent is expected. In hotels, a service charge ranging from 10 to 15 percent is usually added to the bill. If not, be sure to give the chambermaid at least 10 pence for each day of your stay at the hotel. The porter who carries your baggage should get about 10p a bag.

TRANSPORTATION ¶ *Taxis* are relatively inexpensive, and most tourists use them in preference to local buses because of the convenience. One word of caution: it is hard to find a taxi at night because Irish cab drivers do not cruise about. It's advisable to get the card of a radio-cab company and keep it handy. In an emergency, you can telephone for a taxi.

Trains are operated by the Coras Iompair Éireann. That's Gaelic for Ireland's Transport Company. You'll see the Gaelic abbreviation for the company (CIE) frequently, so better get used to it. It's easier than trying to pronounce the Gaelic name. Rail service is good. But don't expect trains to be leaving every five minutes for the place you want to go to. And don't look for any speed records, either. Remember, this is a leisurely country. There is usually a good morning, afternoon and evening train between any two major cities. There will be others, too, but often you'll have to change somewhere along the line.

Rail rates are on the high side, so if you're going to use trains to any extent, you probably should investigate the *Overlander* ticket. It gives you unlimited travel by train or bus from one end of Ireland to the other—including Belfast—on scheduled services of the CIE or the UTA (the Northern Ireland rail line). You can travel in provincial buses on this ticket also (but not, of course, sightseeing or city buses). It's lots of fun to take an all-day ride on a radio train to some scenic spot. It's a happy-go-lucky, holiday-spirited trip in a train that has piped music, commentaries and other features to make the journey highly pleasant, and meals and sightseeing are included in the fares. These trains operate during the tourist season—May through September—and there is one almost every day to some major point, such as

Killarney, the Glens of Antrim and Connemara. The fare, as we said, includes the train ride, lunch and tea on the train and local sightseeing tours. During the busy summer months it is best to reserve a seat when you are buying a rail ticket. Make the reservation the day before you intend to travel. You can reserve a seat at the CIE office at 59 Upper O'Connell Street in Dublin or at any of the city's railroad stations. On the way back to Dublin, or at other points in the country, you can make seat reservations at stations in Cork, Mallow, Limerick, Waterford, Tralee, Killarney, Galway, Sligo, Westport, Ballina, Wexford, Rosslare Harbor, and Belfast. There is a small reservation fee. Meals are served on most of the secondary trains, and snacks are available on most of the secondary trains. To get help on train schedules, call 47-911 in Dublin.

CIE also operates a number of tours that range from a day to twelve days. They are all deluxe—as a matter of fact, the word "sumptuous" is used. The buses used are modern, roomy and comfortable.

You'll probably notice right off that the names of the train stations in Dublin have changed since the last time you were there. Here are the names of Dublin stations and the areas they serve:

Heuston (formerly Kingsbridge): Cork, Limerick, Waterford, Killarney and points in the south and southwest of Ireland

Connolly (formerly Amiens Street Station): Belfast, Derry and points north of Dublin, including Howth, Skerries, Mosney and Balbriggan

Pearse (formerly Westland Row): Wexford, Rosslare Harbor and points to the southeast

Local bus service in Dublin is on double-deckers, in general, and they move swiftly. You have to know in advance the number of the bus needed for your destination, for the buses do not tarry long enough at bus stops for you to engage in a conversation with the conductor about itineraries and routes. The CIE has a network of buses that crisscross Ireland, covering the towns and cities. They are slower than trains, but often they are the only link to a particular point.

Aer Lingus (Irish Air Lines) is the national *airline*. In the summer it operates daily flights between Dublin and Cork and the international airport at Shannon. In the winter, service is not quite so frequent. Aer Lingus also serves many points in Europe and of course has a fine international flight to New York. The airline office in Dublin is at 40 Upper O'Connell Street, and the City Air Terminal is on Store Street, at the Central Bus Station.

COMMUNICATIONS ¶ Local *telephone* calls are 2 pence, which is very close to an American nickel in value, and represents a bargain when compared with our own 10-cent calls. You'll be able to use Irish or British pennies in the phone slots. The General Post Office on O'Connell Street in Dublin is open daily from 8 A.M. to 11 P.M., and branch offices around the city—and the country—usually are open on weekdays from 9 A.M. to 6 P.M. An *airmail* letter to the United States costs the equivalent of about 30 cents.

BASIC GAELIC ¶ Everyone speaks English, of course, but as a result of a government program and encouragement —and a strong feeling of national pride—the use of Gaelic is becoming increasingly widespread. Gaelic is used in all official communications, and you will see it side by side with English on many occasions. Students at school are required to learn it. The Gaelic alphabet contains only eighteen letters. Some of these are written the same as the English-language equivalents, but A, D, F, G, L, R, S and T are written differently. Gaelic, just in case you're planning to study it, has five declensions for nouns, four declensions for adjectives, two conjugations for verbs (in three forms), double terminations—but, cheer up! only two genders (no neuter). Nouns precede adjectives, and verbs are followed by their subject. Gaelic, anyone?

ELECTRICITY ¶ Throughout the country, you'll find that 220 is the standard voltage. However, at most tourist hotels, there will be an outlet for electric shavers only in the bathroom. This means, of course, that your other appliances won't work without a converter.

BANKING HOURS ¶ In Dublin banks are open weekdays from 10 A.M. to 12:30 P.M. and from 1:30 P.M. to 3 P.M. The Saturday hours are 9:30 A.M. to 11:30 A.M.

INFORMATION POINTS ¶ The Irish Tourist Board (in Gaelic, Bord Failté) has an office at 14 Upper O'Connell

Street in Dublin. The phone number is 44-718. Branch offices are located in Cork, Killarney, Belfast, Derry, Limerick, Galway and Sligo. It also has offices at Shannon Airport and at Dun Laoghaire (pronounced *Dun Leery*), where the ferry from England arrives.

Throughout the country there are regional offices working in conjunction with the national tourist board. These regional offices in turn have branch offices in all the major towns and tourist spots. By all means, don't hesitate to visit them for information, because that's precisely why they're there.

FOOD SPECIALTIES AND LIQUOR ¶ The Irish like to eat well, and why shouldn't they with the wonderful meat, dairy products and fish they have? On arising, a cup of tea. A little later, a substantial breakfast (no orange juice) of hot cereal, farm-fresh eggs and marvelous crunchy bacon, thick slices of homemade bread and butter, jam and a choice of good tea or miserable coffee. About 11 in the morning, some coffee and a wee bite of pastry. Near 1 P.M., the main repast of the day, usually a complete six-course meal. In the late afternoon, a teatime snack might consist of just a plain cup of tea, tea and sandwiches or cake, or tea and several hot dishes. About 7:30 or 8 P.M., most local folk have a light cold supper or another complete six-course meal just like lunch.

The food is plain, simple and usually delicious. Your very best bet is with something like roast beef or steak —just about as good as it can be, usually. Among the appetizers, Dublin Bay prawns (large shrimp), oysters and smoked salmon are excellent. Of course, you must try Irish potato soup, cockle (a variety of shellfish) soup, clam soup and one of the classic Irish broths. Lobster isn't too plentiful, but delicious when you do encounter it; trout is very good and the salmon is absolutely marvelous. Ocean fish aren't cooked too well, sorry to relate. Avoid the meat puddings, black or white; they're an acquired taste. We've already mentioned steaks, but don't forget lamb chops and roast baby lamb, both of which are fine eating indeed. Irish stew is made without carrots as a rule; and other vegetables are an American addition. The breads are particularly good—soda bread is the national favorite (made with buttermilk); you should also try a variation—currant soda bread. Treacle bread is made with molasses, potato bread is fluffy and tasty and the brown breads are particularly good with butter or cheese.

Potatoes are, as you might anticipate, the number-one vegetable here, and the favorite method of preparation is mashed with milk, commonly called *champ*. Then there are natural variations on the same theme, like chive champ (also called "thump"), pea champ, parsley champ and best, of all, Colcannon champ—made with cabbage and onion. It's traditional to make a depression in the center, insert a large glob of butter and begin eating from the outside, dipping the champ into the melting butter. With all this, you drink fresh milk or buttermilk.

There are many interesting miscellaneous dishes: *boxty on the pan* is something like hot potato pancakes; *boxty on the griddle* is a type of potato bread. *Fadges* are the name for another kind of pancake, usually made with whole wheat flour. If you come in the shooting (never say hunting) season, menus feature partridge, wild duck, pheasant and many other kinds of game. Salads and desserts aren't too important here, nor are Irish cheeses remarkable except for their freshness and purity. Coffee, as a rule, is pretty, pretty awful. *Irish coffee* is a fairly recent invention: it consists of strong coffee and a slug of Irish whiskey served in a glass with whipped cream on top. Not authentic, but not bad. Not for breakfast, either.

The favorite indoor sport is drinking. Bourbon and rye are scarce, but there's plenty of Scotch. Of course, the national drink is *Irish* whiskey (and please note that whiskey is spelled with an "e" in Ireland and spelled "whisky" in England); it's good with water, and the experts frown on soda. *Poteen*, actually meaning "little pot," is a type of home-brewed whiskey, illegal and not too common. *Irish Mist* is the liqueur or after-dinner cordial of the country; it's made with whiskey and honey and you might like to try it. *Guinness stout* is the brew of the men of Ireland; it's a fine beverage, rich and nourishing and full of hops. It comes in several styles— porter (the lightest and most appealing to Americans), extra and foreign export (far too heavy for most of us). The combination of stout and Galway oysters is considered heaven on earth as a snack by Irish gourmets, and hungry American tourists, too.

At one time, the liquor laws in Ireland were absolutely

mad, with fantastic and complex restrictions on who could, and could not, be served liquor. However, that's all in the past. The new drinking hours are from 10:30 A.M. to 11 P.M. (in the summertime to 11:30 P.M.), except during the hour from 2:30 to 3:30 P.M. (so that they can clean up the place?). The Sunday hours have been changed, and the public house hours are now from 4 P.M. to 10 P.M. on Sundays. Incidentally, if you want to really see a bit of Irish life, while you're in Dublin why not pay a visit to a Pub (that is, a Public House)? They're best in the evening, after dinner. Here are some of my suggestions: Abbey Tavern (a pub with a seafood restaurant and ballad music in a separate area); Bartley Dunne (with the widest selection of drinks in Ireland); Davy Byrne's (mentioned in James Joyce's *Ulysses*); and O'Meara's Irish House (usually quite lively).

The principal tourist areas include Dublin and its surroundings, the counties of Wexford and Wicklow, the Sligo-Donegal region, the southwestern corner (County Kerry and County Cork) and around Galway Bay.

Capital City

The geographer Ptolemy made a few remarks about Dublin eighteen centuries ago, and so has every traveler since then. The Danes and Anglo-Normans are among those who made it their stronghold for varying periods of time during Ireland's long, often dark and difficult days. In the past three-quarters of a century Dublin has been the center of Ireland's political and cultural rebirth.

It is a city of charm and grace, with a population of slightly over 700,000. The name is derived from the Gaelic for "dark pool." Even today, the River Liffey is black, brooding and dark. Dublin is a compact, easily explored city. Visualize it as cut in half horizontally, from west to east, by the Liffey. The north and south shores are connected by nine bridges. Trees line the river banks, the houses are set well back and the atmosphere is quiet, dignified and gracious. O'Connell Street is the main street, and double-decker buses swirl (if that is the word) along it majestically. It cuts across the Liffey at right angles, and the view *toward* the bridge is a fine one. O'Connell Street is as broad a boulevard as any street in Europe. The impressive thoroughfare is lined with statues. Up until fairly recently the most famous statue on the street was the one honoring Lord Nelson, the British hero. The statue topped a tall column in the middle of the street in front of the General Post Office and was a major landmark and convenient meeting point (like "under the clock at Grand Central"). But just before Easter 1966, someone (during the night) dynamited Nelson's Pillar. The dynamiting happened to coincide with the fiftieth anniversary of the famous Easter Rising (rebellion). The General Post Office, across the street from Nelson's Pillar, was a headquarters of the Irish Volunteers during the uprising, and it was fired upon by the British and set afire.

Walk down O'Connell Street, toward the bridge, and cross over to the south bank, continuing straight ahead down another short street, Westmoreland. On your right is Parliament House, which now is used by the Bank of Ireland. If you enter during regular banking hours, a liveried attendant will show you through the building. The general area in front of the bank is the College Green, a handy meeting point in Dublin. On the eastern edge of College Green is what used to be called Trinity College, originally founded by Queen Elizabeth in 1591. It was called TCD (Trinity College Dublin) by everyone and had an extremely high social and scholastic standing (even with Oxford and Cambridge men!). In 1967, the Irish government merged Trinity College (originally British and Protestant) with University College (Roman Catholic). The merger resulted in a new name—the University of Dublin. None of the buildings is of any great age, but the quadrangles are interesting to wander about in. Permission must be requested (at the porter's lodge) to enter the interior. You might spend a little time in Trinity College Library, with its outstanding collection of manuscripts and ancient books. The library's prize is the Book of Kells, often called the world's most beautifully illuminated manuscript, dating back to the eighth century. Unfortunately, displayed under glass as it must be, a page at a time, the book looks much less impressive than it otherwise might. The library is open weekdays from 10 A.M. to 4 P.M. and until 1 P.M. on Saturdays.

Walk west from College Green into Dame Street to City Hall. (Just in passing we should state that the local vote has it that the oysters and Guinness are at their peak of perfection in the places that dot Dame Street.) Hard by the City Hall is ancient Dublin Castle, built from 1208 to 1220, the classic center of the city (Dublin subsequently grew up around the fort). It's interesting to see the Throne Room, St. Patrick's Hall and Bedford Tower. (By the way, if you've ever yearned to have your family tree traced, the genealogical staff of the Heraldic Museum in Bedford Tower will undertake the research for a moderate fee. Here's your chance to discover whether you really are descended from one of the Kings of Ireland!) The castle yard is always open for a look-around. Guided tours of the state apartments are usually made at 10 A.M., noon and 3 P.M. There is a small fee for the tour (give the guide accompanying your group a 10p tip). The Heraldic Museum is free and is open during the week from 9:30 A.M. to 1 P.M. and 2:15 to 4:30 P.M. On Saturday the hours are 10 A.M. to 12:30 P.M. The Church of the Most Holy Trinity is open to visitors during the week from 9 A.M. to 6 P.M.

Continue along Dame Street to its end, and begin ascending Lord Edward Street to Christ Church, founded in 1038 by a gentleman named "Strongbow" when Ireland was under the domination of Danish raiders. The church was rebuilt in 1172, and little remains—if any —of the original structure. The imposing interior is dark, by modern standards. During the tourist season the visiting hours are 9:30 A.M. to 5 P.M. (From October to April, it closes to visitors at 4 P.M.)

Turn left into Nicholas Street until you come to St. Patrick's Cathedral. This imposing structure was dedicated in 1191. The towers and the spire were built in succeeding centuries. Jonathan Swift, the writer, was Dean of St. Patrick's from 1713 to 1745 and is buried here. It is open to visitors daily from 9 A.M. to 5 P.M. There are choral services during the week at 10 A.M. and 5 P.M.

If you're in a secular, as distinguished from a religious, mood, walk back toward Christ Church and up High Street (which becomes Thomas Street) and into James Street, where you'll find the Guinness Brewery, which is the largest establishment of its kind in Europe. It spreads across sixty acres. You'll be taken on a tour through the plant, and it's all very interesting and diverting. At the end, a goodly drink of Guinness is offered. There are hourly tours from Monday to Friday, from 10 A.M. to 3 P.M.

Other must-see Dublin sights include Leinster House, in Kildare Street, where the *Dail* (Chamber of Deputies) and the *Seanad* (Senate) meet. When the legislators are not meeting, Leinster House is open to visitors on weekdays from 10 A.M. to 4:30 P.M. and on Saturdays from 10:30 A.M. to 12:30 P.M. The Four Courts is an imposing structure in Corinthian style and is the home of Ireland's law courts. The building is well located on the northern side of the Liffey. Nearby, on Church Street, is St. Michan's church. The church is only 250 years old, but it is said that a portion of the building is an earlier structure dating back to the Danish occupation. Those of a macabre turn of mind frequently ask to see the bodies in the vaults. They have remained well preserved over the centuries because of certain peculiar atmospheric properties of the surroundings. The church and vaults are open from Monday through Friday from 10 A.M. to 1 P.M. and 2 to 5:30 P.M. (5 P.M. in winter). The hours on Saturday are 10 A.M. to 1 P.M. The vaults are not open on Sundays. There is an admission charge of 1 shilling (12 cents). To become secular again, walk around behind St. Michan's to see the Jameson's distillery, whose whiskey you may have tasted already.

The collections at the National Museum include a good display of Irish antiquities. It is open from 11 A.M. to 5 P.M. on weekdays and from 2 to 5 P.M. Sundays. The National Gallery and National Portrait Gallery, in the same building, have a rather mediocre collection with few outstanding works. Phoenix Park, which covers an area of 1,760 acres, is worth a leisurely visit. There is a zoo too, open daily from 9:30 A.M. to 6 P.M. (in winter, to sunset) and on Sundays from noon to 6 P.M. (in winter, to sunset). There is an admission charge.

ဖ Short Trips from Dublin

North of the city, beginning with Howth, is a stretch of fine bathing beaches. From the Hill of Howth may be seen the city of Dublin, probably the best view possible. Visit Howth Castle and Corr Castle, open Sunday afternoons only. About a mile from shore are the sharp rocks of Ireland's Eye, a small island that can be reached by boat. Continuing north, you come to Portmarnock, slightly off the road, with a stretch of white sand almost three miles in length, although in point of fact, the entire coastline is almost completely bordered with beaches and sand dunes. Malahide, farther along, is another popular seaside spot, particularly known for its castle and the ruins of Malahide Abbey. From here, drive three miles west to Swords, an old history-laden town with an ancient ruined castle and round tower. This entire excursion is pleasing, but not essential for the visitor whose time is limited.

If you're interested in Irish antiquities, visit Glendalough, the Glen of the Two Lakes. Drive south from Dublin on route T-43 through Dundrum and Enniskerry to Kilmacanoge; then route T-61 to Roundwood and Laragh. Two miles west (via L-107) is Glendalough, one of Ireland's holiest spots. St. Kevin founded Glendalough of the Seven Churches during the sixth century and, although in ruins, there is much to see, including the oratory known as St. Kevin's Kitchen (Church). Return to Dublin by going back to Laragh, next to Rathdrum, the country town of Wicklow, then through the resort of Bray and back into the capital.

Arklow

Some forty-five miles south of Dublin and seven miles from the Vale of Avoca, which Thomas More celebrated, this is one of the beauty spots of Ireland, with lovely beaches and resort areas. Late spring is a really excellent time to visit in the vale, because the flowers are then in bloom. There are frequent train and bus services from Dublin. It is only a short drive from Dublin via Bray, Glen of the Downs, Rathnew and Ballynapark.

Bray

This is considered one of the main seaside spots in all of Ireland. Its beach is more than a mile long, and one of its great assets is its proximity to Dublin. You can get there by train, if you wish, but it is just a short bus ride, only about fifteen miles from Dublin, depending on the route you take. By bus there is a wide choice according to the starting point of your trip. From St. Stephen's Green, take St. Kevin's bus. If you are at Dun Laoghaire, take No. 45A. By car, the shortest route (thirteen miles) is by way of Donnybrook, Stillorgan, Cabinteely and Loughlinstown. A scenic route (sixteen miles) is through Blackrock, Dun Laoghaire, Dalkey and Killiney.

Greystones

Five miles south of Bray, Greystones is reputed to be the driest region in Ireland. That alone is plenty of distinction (in a country like Ireland!) meriting the attention and visits of tourists. But it also has two fine beaches, a top-flight eighteen-hole golf course, the ambiance of a genial holiday resort, plus woods, tree-shaded roads and many excursion possibilities in the neighborhood. Train and bus connections with Dublin are frequent by way of Bray. At College Street in Bray, take bus No. 84. Just a mile and a half from Greystones is Delgany, another fine resort area of County Wicklow.

ACCOMMODATIONS ¶ The hotel situation in Ireland requires some explanation for the first-time visitor. The Irish have not had as much experience as some continental nations in the fine art of entertaining overseas tourists on a large scale. Until recent years Ireland was more or less overlooked in the plans of American tourists, but it was "discovered" not too long ago. In Dublin, hotel service is as efficient and organized as it is in the best hotels of America or Europe. As a matter of fact, in a handful of the leading Dublin hotels practically the only guests there in the summer are Americans. The same goes for a number of other establishments in tourist areas, including the various hotels in the Great Southern Hotels chain at Killarney, Mulrany, Galway, Kenmare, Parknasilla, Bundoran and Sligo. In some parts of Ireland, however, hotel service is slow, good-natured, forgetful and altogether charmingly erratic, although well-meaning. Private bathrooms—a necessity for those peculiar Americans—are few and far between in the smaller hotels and inns and almost unobtainable during the height of the season without advance reservation. Most hotels do not have central (steam) heating but instead rely upon fire-places. It is difficult to convince the hotel staff that an indoor (not outdoor!) temperature of 50 degrees calls for a fire! Even if you offer to pay for it, they'll dilly-dally and postpone laying on the fire unless you indicate you're on the verge of frostbite. In hotels with central heating, the management hesitates (an understatement of colossal proportions!) to give heat unless it's December, with snow on the ground. All this is beyond the comprehension of coddled American tourists. (None of this applies to Dublin, where the whims of tourists are quickly catered to.) Some efforts to convince hotel owners to adopt a less rigorous policy have been made by the Irish Tourist Board, and results have been starting to show up. Many hotels, however, have electric heaters, which will be produced after numerous requests. The staff usually stands on a point of honor to deny their existence, at first. A joke or two—not an argument—will bring them forth.

Another peculiarity of smaller hotels is that dinner is not served in the evening, the heavy meal being the midday one. However, even simple country hotels will serve a high tea or "meat tea" after 5 P.M., and such repasts usually include at least one hot dish. However, as the number of tourists increases, this condition is being changed and often a real dinner will be served at country inns. Needless to say, none of this applies to the larger tourist hotels. It occurs primarily in the small, family-style inns where you pay only a few dollars for a room.

All the above is offered in a spirit of constructive criticism. In fairness to Irish hotels, it should also be said that anywhere you go, the beds will be comfortable— with fresh (Irish) linen. Most rooms have running water, the atmosphere is friendly and the welcome hearty— completely different from the casual reception extended in larger, tourist-overladen cities. Irish hotel staffs are often recruited from the locality and quite naturally are unfamiliar with the professional niceties of First Class hotel service to be found, for example, in London or Paris. But be patient with them, and never order the help around. Politely worded requests will do more for you. Eire, as Ireland is known in Gaelic, is a young country, although inhabited by an ancient people. They have had their independence as a nation for only a comparatively short time.

DUBLIN HOTELS

The leading hotel is undoubtedly the Intercontinental, about ten minutes south of central Dublin by car or taxi. The Gresham and Shelbourne are fixtures on the Dublin scene and have clienteles that return season after season.

Intercontinental: Fairly new, attractively situated. Good service, choice of restaurants. Rooms are well decorated and have pleasing views.

Gresham: Centrally located, with somewhat old-fashioned rooms; pleasant service, good restaurants. However, most rooms are extremely noisy, because of street traffic in front and machinery in the rear.

Burlington: A very modern hotel located slightly outside of town. Nice rooms, all with TV. All facilities; several restaurants.

Shelbourne: An old, well-known hotel with a peaceful location on St. Stephen's Green. Some rooms are attractive, others somewhat drab.

Royal Hibernian: Somewhat old-fashioned rooms, but very homey, Irish atmosphere. Many, but not all, rooms have private baths.

South County Motel: If you have a car, it might be pleasant to stay at this motel on Stillorgan Road, four miles south of Dublin on the Dublin-Bray road. Swimming pool.

Russell: A quiet, small hotel beautifully situated on St. Stephen's Green. Rooms are about average in most cases; the remodeled rooms are far more attractive. Many, but not every hotel room, has a private bath.

Moira, Landsdowne, Jury's and Wynn's: All of these are small and cozy and have that certain Irish atmosphere, but don't look for luxury or skilled service. Very few rooms have private baths.

DUBLIN RESTAURANTS

Beaufield Mews: A very popular suburban restaurant, less than a half hour outside of town, in Stillorgan. They serve a complete dinner in delightful, atmospheric surroundings, and the food is generally good. Prices are a trifle high, but not excessively so. Be sure to have a reservation before you go.

Gresham Hotel Grill: A pleasant, attractive restaurant with very fine food; also serves some innocuous international hotel-style dishes. In the hotel basement, there's the Hunting Lodge, which is quite nice, and not terribly expensive; good, basically simple food.

Bernie Inn: Several different restaurants and bars, each specializing in a different dish. The main dish determines the price of the meal.

Russell Hotel Restaurant: Their menu offers a tremendous selection of dishes. Several of the French dishes seemed uninspired, but the grilled chicken and steaks are excellent.

Snaffles: An interesting restaurant featuring pretty good food, particularly game dishes. Moderately expensive.

Shelbourne Hotel: Good, although not exciting, hotel-style food; pleasant, sedate atmosphere.

Bailey: A very old, very popular restaurant. Good for simple dishes like roast meats. Draws a literary, bookish crowd.

SHOPPING ¶ For all practical purposes, the best shopping street for tourists is Grafton Street. There are specialty shops galore, but for general, one-stop shopping, there's Switzers, and also Brown, Thomas. Here, they're prepared to ship your purchases, and know all about customs charges, etc. *Tweeds* are Ireland's best value for the shopping enthusiast, and this is no wonder because hand-woven tweeds are a traditional specialty of the Irish. Women can order tweeds made up into suits at ordinary tailoring establishments for $30 or $40, but the styling should be carefully watched or the finished garment may be disappointing. Dublin has a half-dozen important dressmakers, or couturiers, who charge much more ($100, and up), but the results are probably worth it to fashion-conscious women traveling without budgetary restraints. Sybil Connolly, with a showroom on Merrion Square, is probably the leading women's dress designer of Ireland.

Irish *lace* is world-famous, but lace isn't too important in the fashion whirl right now, except for wedding gowns or lingerie trimmings. *Linens* are another story, for linens are high fashion, and they are available by the yard or made up into sports dresses or separates at low prices. Linen tableclothes are good values, ranging in price around $20. Place mats and napkins for eight cost somewhere around $15 and are worth it. Linen sheets with pillows to match, for a double bed, are quite expensive ($30 and up) and are marvelously cool for summer use. But, alas! they crease rapidly.

Men's accessories are good values. In addition to the sports jackets and tweed suits previously mentioned, sweaters, sports vests, raincoats, ties and shirts are all bargains. Don't buy the mediocre ready-made shoes; custom-made are the best buy, but only if you're staying several weeks. If you smoke a pipe (or have a friend who does), a Peterson pipe may be the thing; prices range from as little as $2 to what-have-you, but anything you buy would be at least twice or three times as expensive at home. Irish linen *handkerchiefs*, hand-rolled, are beautifully made and retail for 50 cents to $2 each; not necessarily cheap but bargain-priced for merchandise of this quality.

Women's clothes in the ready-made field are not remarkable in styling, as a rule. An exception might be made for Aran sweaters and wool suits; the linen blouses are also quite attractive. Excellent clothes may be made to order at one of the finer couturier shops located on little streets running to the east of Grafton Street; the styling, fabrics and smartness of these shops is unimpeachable; figure at least $125 for something simple, $275 for an elaborate outfit.

Liquor is, of course, an excellent buy—especially Irish whiskey, which is priced relatively low. (Note: If you've arrived or are departing through Shannon Airport, there's a tax-free shop about as big as the main floor of a department store, where you'll be able to buy any number of items at low prices.)

Glassware is worthwhile if you purchase Waterford Galway hand-cut crystal; not cheap even in Ireland, but much much less than at home. You may have it shipped with full confidence, but buy about fifteen of each item instead of twelve, because individual replacements are difficult and expensive. *Belleek china* is delicate, light and appealing; you'll find a good selection in Dublin. *Old silver* is as good as in England and certainly cheaper, although no fantastic bargains are obtainable today, when everyone knows the value of truly fine antique pieces.

Food should also be considered, for Irish specialties are quite delicious. At Shannon Airport, they have a special food section, where you can buy, just prior to departure, such items as smoked salmon, cheese, brown bread, and Irish bacon. All of these are permitted by U.S. Customs, and the only problem presented is that your baggage is all checked in, and you'll have to carry them in your flight bag. But, if you've developed a taste for a particular Irish food, you can continue your feeling of being in Erin, by bringing back the bacon.

Important Note: Although Ireland restricts the export of certain items, the articles usually purchased by the average visitor are not on this list. If you have any doubts, ask the nearest Irish Tourist Board office and they will show you a copy of the complete restricted goods list.

Pointer: Irish store hours—in large cities, shops are open from 9:30 A.M. to 5:30 P.M. Shops throughout the country have what they call a half-day, in which they close on one afternoon during the week. In Dublin, it can be Saturday afternoon or Monday afternoon, but shopkeepers usually pick Wednesday for their half-day. In the countryside, it is generally Wednesday or Thursday.

ENTERTAINMENT ¶ The Irish Tourist Board offices have on hand a calendar of events, and with a copy of this you'll have a good idea of how to spend your free hours. All the evening newspapers carry complete coverage of the doings, from concerts to circuses, and the Irish Radio

(Radio Eireann) news broadcasts will round out your knowledge of goings-on. Dublin has a relatively large number of theaters, including some amateur ones as well as what might be called semiprofessional companies that turn out first-rate productions. But, of course, the Abbey Theatre—no matter what is on the playbill—has something you will want to see. If you aren't one of the first ones out of the theater, you may find it difficult to get a cab, especially if it's raining. Arrange for transportation to your hotel in advance; be on the safe side, by telephoning beforehand to a radio cab (Tel.: 61-111 or 72-222) or to a nearby cab stand through the main switchboard (Tel.: 66-666). Radio cabs are a bit more expensive and thus are easier to get (generally).

There isn't a really first-class orchestra playing during the tourist season in Dublin; the Radio Éireann Symphony Orchestra is fairly good, particularly with Irish music, but performances are generally given only during the winter months. For some reason, probably because Irishmen love to sing, choral groups are found wherever you go—some very good, some not so very.

There's the new Abbey Theatre, and I'm afraid that it isn't more than a mediocrity, as theaters go, being somewhat sterile and unappealing in décor. It is air conditioned, however, often chillingly so. As a rule, the second company holds forth during the tourist season, but even so, a visit is inevitably worthwhile. Ticket prices are low, around a couple of dollars; your hotel porter can get them for you and will smile happily when you give him a tip of 35 cents or so. If you have a drive-yourself car, you can go directly to the theater about twenty minutes before curtain time and leave it in front of the theater—attendants will find you a parking space nearby.

Now what about the public houses, "the pubs," favorite gathering place of the Irishman of wit and humor? Drinking, and lots of drinking, is the favorite evening's pastime for the men of Dublin, and most of the country for that matter. Women are accepted, on occasion, in the city pubs but seldom in country spots. In Dublin, the famous pubs include the Pearl Bar in Fleet Street for the literary and journalistic crowd; McDaid's is very popular with writers, too. O'Meara's Irish House and the Palace are all worth a visit at one time or another. Here, it is said, you'll hear the cream of Irish wit and conversation flowing at its best, but although you're always welcome, unless you've got remarkably good hearing, you're just a visitor and not a member of one of the groups. If at all possible, try the pubs with some Irish friends or acquaintances.

Pointer: A number of Dublin pubs feature singing groups, known as Balladeers, once or twice a week. There is usualiy an admission or cover charge on such evenings.

SPORTS ¶ *Horses* and *horse racing* are tops in Ireland; try to visit Dublin during the horse show (August) when everyone (who is anyone) comes for the big social event of the season. There's racing all over Ireland from March through November, both flat and steeplechase. Don't fail to go to a race meet, which even the clergy attend; the atmosphere is carnivallike, full of fun and offbeat. No mutuel machines, totalizers or fancy equipment—bet with the "Turf Accountant" of your choice, and isn't that a wonderful description for a man who takes bets?

Golf may be played all over Ireland, for there are at least 300 courses scattered about the countryside and over two dozen in the Dublin area alone. In most places you'll be welcomed and only have to pay the moderate greens fees; to be doubly sure, phone the club's secretary for permission.

Fees are very moderate. For a few dollars, you'll be able to pay the greens fee and the caddy and have lunch in the bargain, generally.

Fishing season usually begins January 1 and ends October 31. Some waters are free, others belong to hotels (which permit their use if you're a guest) and still others are privately owned. Salmon fishing is best from March through June; sea trout during July and August. A license is needed. However, there is no license requirement for any other kind of fish, including pike, brown trout and perch.

A *hurling* match is worth seeing, if you can get a ticket; fifteen on a side, vaguely like hockey but with loads of variations and legal mayhem. *Gaelic football* is like soccer, but is played with a smaller ball. There is considerable *shooting* for small birds in the center and west of Ireland; for particulars and permissions, communicate with the Irish Land Commission, Merrion Street, Dublin.

&~ *A Short Tour of Ireland*

If only two to three days are available for sightseeing in Ireland, it would make an extremely pleasant trip to drive from Dublin to Shannon Airport. The vast majority of tourists who leave Ireland do so by air, from Shannon. On the way home from the continent, fly from Paris, London or wherever you happen to be into Dublin. Arrange for a rented car at Dublin and leave it at Shannon Airport, for which you'll pay a service charge, but inasmuch as Irish auto rates are otherwise low, the total figure will not be too large. Suggestions for a longer tour of Ireland appear after these recommendations for a two-day trip.

Dublin to Cong—165 miles

Leave Dublin by driving from the General Post Office down O'Connell Street until you reach the River Liffey. Do not cross the bridge, but turn right, following the north bank of the river straight out. Follow the signs for Sligo, Athlone and Galway. The road goes through Lucan, Maynooth and Enfield, and, at Kinnegad, be on the lookout for a left turn, which could be easily overlooked, toward Mullingar. Then comes Kilbeggan, Moate and Athlone. Here, we suggest the Shamrock Lodge Hotel for lunch, or indeed for overnight should you wish to stay over. Drive from Athlone to Ballinasloe and Galway, where there is a sharp right turn toward Cong. Ashford Castle, at Cong, is a castle remodeled into a deluxe hotel situated in its own attractive park; but be sure to phone ahead for a reservation. Around Cong, *The Quiet Man* was photographed. The entire day's trip is only 165 miles.

Cong to Shannon Airport—155 miles

The next day, drive from Cong to Leeane, Clifden (this region being known as James Joyce Country) and Ballynahinch, where lunch should be taken at Ballynahinch Castle Hotel, another reconverted castle. Then continue to Galway, Gort and Ennis, and then, just before Limerick, watch for a right turn to Shannon Airport. This day's trip covers about 155 miles and inasmuch as most

flights leave Shannon Airport late in the day, you could have a pleasant day's sightseeing driving from Cong and make your plane easily. The auto renting companies have their offices at the airport, which is a great convenience.

SIDE TRIPS FROM SHANNON ¶ Should your schedule allow for one extra day, by all means stay overnight at Shannon Shamrock Motel, near Bunratty Castle, on the road from Shannon Airport to Limerick. The following day, drive from Limerick down to Killarney, a run of about eighty miles, sightsee around the famous lake and drive back to Shannon Airport in the afternoon, making a total of about 160 miles for the day.

If you want to enjoy an interesting, luxurious vacation of the kind that cannot be duplicated in the United States, there is Dromoland Castle, located in a 350-acre estate some seven miles from Shannon Airport near the hamlet of Newmarket on Fergus. The seventy guest rooms have been recently decorated; there is a golf course adjacent, plus fishing, riding, etc. Dromoland Castle is situated in lovely grounds, and makes a pleasant one- or two-day stop. The food is only so-so, the atmosphere is delightful and soothing. The rates are high—not for Miami Beach perhaps; but for Ireland, definitely. Not too far from Dromoland is the Clare Inn, which is a good place to stay, although scarcely so elaborate or expensive as Dromoland. The food here is not much to write home about.

The Shannon area is a good one for tourists, particularly if they have a drive-yourself car. There are several castles, including Bunratty, where, at modest prices, you can have a pleasant evening of medieval-style food and music. One day you can drive to the Cliffs of Moher, in about an hour and a half, going through Ennis, Lahinch, and to the coast. At the Cliffs, you'll find an exciting spectacle of the high, rock-bound Irish coastline, the cliffs filled with birds' nests, and the ocean rolling in, its first landfall. Incidentally, don't fail to have lunch at the Aberdeen Arms, a small hotel in Lahinch, famous for its marvelous seafood, especially the lobster broth, as they call it; it's a chowder to my way of thinking.

On another day, or the same one if you make an early start, you might want to see the new tourist cottages in Ballyvaughan, on Galway Bay. You can continue from Lahinch to Ennistymon, and go on to Lisdoonvarna, and then reach Ballyvaughan. (If you drive directly from the Shannon area, ahead for Ennis, and once past there you'll see signs pointing out the road to Ballyvaughan.) The scenery en route is often strange, indeed weird, for the rock formations are almost unique; many botanists say the plant life here is rarely found anywhere else. At Ballyvaughan, a small seaside village, there are quite a number of thatched cottages in the Irish countryside style. They are quite well equipped inside, with good bathrooms and kitchens, and mostly with three bedrooms. They rent by the week only, for very modest rates, and are fantastic bargains for a family, or for two or three couples. Don't plan on doing any sea bathing, because the water is usually too cold. If you're interested, you'd better make reservations as far in advance as possible through the Irish Tour Office.

ꝗ❧ A Tour of the Country

At the outset, it should be emphasized again that hotel rooms with private baths are extremely scarce, particularly during the summer months. Be *sure* to phone ahead for reservations.

Dublin to Waterford—101 miles

Leave Dublin by crossing the O'Connell Street bridge southbound to College Green; past College Green turn left onto Nassau Street, then Merrion Mount Street, Northumberland Road and route T-44. The route follows Dublin's shore resorts; first comes Dun Laoghaire, where the steamers arrive from England, then Dalkey (which is called Dawkey) and Bray, possibly the most popular of all, with an esplanade and the usual seaside attractions. After this, you pass Greystones, Kilcoole and Wicklow, a small town facing the sea. Then sixteen miles to Arklow, a picturesque fishing port; west of the harbor is a pleasing, picturesque region called the Fisheries, full of thatched cottages.

Continue onward, via route 7, passing Ferns and Enniscorthy, after a not particularly interesting stretch of road, compared with the section you've previously covered.

From Enniscorthy, turn left onto route T-8 to Wexford, one of the most interesting towns of the area. Wander through the extremely narrow, twisting streets to the ruins of ancient fortifications; nearby is Johnstown Castle, well worth a visit. The Talbot Hotel is quite good here. (If you wish, make a ten-mile side excursion farther on to the seaside resort of Rosslare, with steamer service to Fishguard, Wales. The best hotel here is the Strand, located on the beach.)

From Wexford take route T-12 through Camaross and into New Ross, then route 7 into Waterford, another town with steamer service to Fishguard; the appealing old Bridge Hotel is the only one with private baths. Eight miles south of Waterford is the Majestic Hotel at Tramore, a seaside resort, particularly lively during the horse racing season in mid-August. Waterford is worth a brief sightseeing tour, colorful and attractive as it is; you'll hardly avoid seeing Reginald's Tower, dating back to 1003. If you're interested in fine glassware, Waterford crystal is, of course, made here.

Waterford to Cork—79 miles

From Waterford, take route T-12 through Kilmacthomas into Dungarvan, a beautifully located old town; ˙n the immediate surrounding area you'll hear only Gaelic spoken by most people. (If time permits try an interesting side trip from Dungarvan via route T-30 to Cappoquin, with its fine old castles and abbeys; colorful Lismore, site of Lismore Castle; Ballyduff and Fermoy; then back to Dungarvan. The entire trip passes through extremely beautiful scenery; enchantingly placed castles and ruins combine to make an entirely pleasing excursion.) The road continues with sharp, hairpin turns from Dungarvan toward Youghal; en route there is a left turn to Ardmore, very charming and attractive, where a stay may be made at the Cliff House Hotel (no private baths). Youghal (pronounced Yawl) on the Blackwater River is a pleasant town; look for Myrtle Grove, where Sir Walter Raleigh lived for some length of time. For an overnight stop, the Devonshire Arms Hotel is the best available, although there are no private baths.

From Youghal to Middleton; immediately afterward there is a left turn to Cobh, where the transatlantic steamers arrive, but Cobh has little to offer the tourist. On to Cork (Gaelic for "Swampy Place"), an important manufacturing area, scene of much destruction during 1920, when great sections of the city were burned out. Little remains of the old town after the "Troubles" of that unhappy year. The outstanding structure in Cork is St. Finbarr's Cathedral, about 200 years old. The famous Bells of Shandon may be heard at St. Anne's Church on the hour, but the trip is barely worth the effort. There is the fine, new Intercontinental Hotel here, the ideal place to stay. Also the pleasant Silver Spring Hotel.

Cork to Killarney—103 miles

Of course, everyone feels duty-bound to visit Blarney ("The Plain" in Gaelic) Castle. Leave Cork via Blarney Street for the castle, where the famous kissing stone is located. Those who kiss the stone are said to become endowed with the gift of blarney, the gift of persuading others by talk; to wit, the gift of gab. To accomplish this, however, you must lie on your back, feet firmly held by an attendant, and kiss the Blarney stone (at a lower level) upside-down, a procedure that is vaguely like standing on your head. The entire affair is now somewhat commercialized, with photographs, entrance fees and souvenir stands, but it is Irish commercialism, lightly laid on.

Leave Blarney and pick up the road westward toward Dripsey, where you rejoin route T-29 through the Lee valley into Macroom, a pretty town in a lovely location; there is a castle that dates back to King John. Right after Macroom, look for a left turn to Inchigeela and Ballingeary; at Ballingeary, watch for a right turn to Gougane Barra, also called St. Finbarr's Hollow, where the River Lee begins its course under idyllic surroundings. The entire area is particularly attractive and should not be overlooked; the Hotel Gougane Barra is here, should you wish to stay.

The road continues through the scenic beauties of the Pass of Keamaneigh, past the ruins of Carriganess Castle and then into Ballylicky on Bantry Bay; turn left (route 65) into the village of Bantry, beautifully situated on twenty-mile-long Bantry Bay. The Ardnagashel House is suitable for a vacation stay.

From Bantry, return via route 65 along the bay to Glengariff, the "Rugged Glen," which it isn't at all; instead, you'll find Glengariff to be one of the outstanding beauty spots in the nation, having a mild climate, subtropical plants and extravagant flowers during the season. Just in passing, we should mention that Glengariff has been "discovered" by the Irish and British, who flock here in considerable numbers during the summer season. The leading hotels are Eccles (the largest), Casey's and the Glengariff Castle. Just in passing too, G. B. Shaw wrote a large part of *St. Joan* while staying at the Eccles Hotel, if that matters to you.

From Glengariff to Kenmare, by route 65, there is a winding road that twists and turns about with exuberance; the route presents no serious difficulty, except for the driver who tries to enjoy the scenery and watch the road at the same time. Kenmare is situated in a superb location, but the town is fairly dull most of the week, coming alive only on Wednesday, the market day.

Kenmare calls for a decision: you can take the direct route (T-65) to Killarney, or make a left turn (route T-66) toward Templenoe and into Waterville for a tour of the Iveragh Peninsula. Route T-65 features about twenty miles of lovely scenery and then you reach Looscaunagh Hill, which has a world-famous view of the Vale of Killarney and three lakes.

SIDE TRIP ¶ The alternative coast road (T-66) from Kenmare passes through Parknasilla, a seaside resort; the village of Sneem; the vacation playground of Waterville, which has a very good hotel, the Butler Arms, known for its clublike facilities. A boat trip might be arranged to nearby Church Island for a visit to the ruins of the circular house of St. Finian. From Waterville to Cahirciveen, passing en route a left turn (at Inny Bridge) toward Ballinskelligs and Portmagee: this road is not good (in fact, it's bad) but the trip is rewarding for those who like offbeat, lonely spots. Should you decide to turn off, at Portmagee there is a ferry to Valentia Island, with its two tiny villages of Coarhabeg and Knights Town. At Portmagee, it is also possible to hire a motorboat to visit Skellige Rocks, the breeding place for thousands of wild seabirds, as well as a lighthouse, and ancient ruins of a monastery. Cahirciveen (called Care-see-veen) is beautifully located; from here ferry trips may be made to Knights Town on Valentia Island. The circular tour continues through Glenbeigh and Killorglin into Killarney.

Killarney is, of course, famous for the natural loveliness of its surroundings, but the town itself is extraordinarily dull. To get yourself settled, the best place to stay is the newish Hotel Europe. Next best are the International, the Dunloe Castle and the Great Southern. The Lake Hotel has an attractive view of the waters of Lough Leane. There are two new motel-like operations, quite nice, called Ryan's Hotel and the Great Southern Inn; they're on the road to Cork, about five minutes outside of town. It is displeasing to relate that Killarney has become overcommercialized during the tourist season; there are conducted tours, large-scale groups, would-be guides and many petty annoyances. It is also our regretful duty to tell you that independent trips around Killarney are difficult, so it is necessary to join an organized tour. Everyone wants to take an excursion on the lakes and boatmen are scarce in season, when they are reserved for the group tours, and also scarce out of season. Perhaps your hotel can arrange for the necessary boat and boatmen should you wish to make the excursion on your own.

The classic trip through the Gap of Dunloe is quite difficult for the independent traveler, because you have to make several connections. It's worthwhile, all things considered, unless it rains. I suggest taking along a lightweight raincoat, because it always can rain in Ireland, as you'll probably notice. Transportation from your hotel to Dunloe is inevitably provided by the tour companies.

It is inconvenient to take your own drive-yourself car, because the excursion starts at Dunloe and ends at another part of the lake. At Dunloe, there's an inn, called Kate Kearney's Cottage, which is a sort of bar, tourist spot, and local landmark. Sometimes, tours proceed a little further along to a place called Arbutus Cottage, the final point for automobiles. Here, you board (if that's the word) a pony trap or Jaunting Car (horse-drawn small carriages, often with the passengers facing the sides, not the front). You ride through lovely scenery, and then are rowed across the lakes, and it's all delightful—if it doesn't rain! It's best to have a raincoat along, as mentioned above—unless you're *positive* it won't rain.

Killarney to Limerick—86 miles

From Killarney, take route 29 to Tralee, a charming, quiet town. Benner's Hotel is the only place for a stay, and the Dingle Peninsula to the west is worth exploration.

SIDE TRIP ¶ Take route T-68 from Tralee to Dingle, the most westerly town in Europe, remembering always that many of the people here speak only Gaelic. From Dingle continue to Dunquin, where boats may be hired to the Blasket Islands, possibly the most primitive settlement in Ireland. Returning to Tralee, come through Dingle again, turn north through rugged Connor Pass and head for Castlegregory, an absolutely magnificent spot, practically isolated and very charming; there is a small hotel. Then return to Tralee.

From Tralee, take route 68 through Listowel and Abbeyfeale; then route 28 to Newcastle West and into Limerick, the "Bare Spot" in Gaelic. Here you'll find an attractive, fairly new Intercontinental Hotel, which is excellent for both rooms and meals.

Limerick has three sections—Irish Town, English Town and the shopping and hotel center called Newton Perry (also spelled Newtown Pery). It's an ancient settlement having the oldest city charter in Ireland and is filled with fine old tradition-laden Georgian houses; don't expect everyone to spout limericks on request (except possibly the hotel clerks, who have been egged on beyond endurance). You'll surely want to see Mungret, with its ruins of an abbey, the Castle of King John and St. Mary's Cathedral.

SIDE TRIP ¶ May I strongly urge you to consider a trip to the Aran Islands? It's easily and not too expensively accomplished by flying, on a small plane, from Shannon Airport; usually there's an all-inclusive one-day package trip, as well as those which include a few days on the islands. If you have any taste for unusual islands and a different way of life, a trip to Aran is strongly recommended. (You can also reach Aran by boat from Galway, where there's a daily boat service in season, the trip taking three hours each way.) The flight over takes a matter of minutes, and travels along the coast, passing the spectacular Cliffs of Moher, then cutting northwest to pass over the two smaller of the Aran Islands (Inisheer and Inishmaan) to reach the main island, called Inishmore. From the air, you'll note that Inishmore is long and narrow. Its chief village is the community of Kilronan. This island, as are the others, is composed chiefly of carboniferous limestone, which is a technical way of saying the land is rocky beyond all belief; this makes ordinary farming and agriculture very difficult. However, sheep raising is possible, although the amount of grazing land is quite limited.

The tiny settlement of Kilronan is nothing less than charming, built as it is on sloping land reaching down to the harbor, which is really the lifeline of the island. There are a few stores selling handmade Aran sweaters (now made largely on the mainland and brought to Aran), as well as other handmade articles, such as mittens, gloves, shawls, and so forth. You'll find a few general stores and more than a few bars, many of them quite atmospheric, and, if you have the time, which offer an excellent chance to talk to the local people, particularly if you offer them a glass of Guinness.

It's a good idea to take a walk along the coast, or perhaps even better, hire a rickety taxi to see such local sights as exist here. There are also many pony carts for hire, and they're lots of fun, and certainly fit into the local scene more than automobiles do, although their number is very limited. Although Aran does have telephones, so far it has no central power system, but many people do have their own private power plants. If not, it's kerosene lamps at night. The outstanding sight is an old fort, said to date back some four thousand years, which is in ruins (quite naturally) but worth a little exploration. You'll note the small houses, many still using thatch for the roof, and some of the houses may be rented by the week, for a marvelous Irish vacation. Aran has no hotels, but there are several guest houses, where the rooms are small, and the bathrooms anything but private; nevertheless, for those who don't require comfort, a vacation in Aran will be a marvelous, unforgettable experience. Incidentally, there are a few small bathing beaches. More than the sights, more than the feeling of isolation, the chief reason for coming to Aran is the people, who are extremely friendly and gregarious. By all means, plan on spending at least one day on Aran.

Limerick to Galway—63 miles

Leave Limerick via route T-11 to Newmarket-on-Fergus to Ennis, where you should park your car and wander through the fascinating streets, straight out of the late Middle Ages. At Ennis, there's a real Irish country inn, the Old Ground Hotel, which you'd probably enjoy, should you wish to make a stopover. If time permits, make a side trip from Ennis to the Cliffs of Moher (less than twenty-five miles) via Ennistymon. The Cliffs of Moher are rocks that have been eroded by the action of the pounding sea and constitute really exciting scenery. Between Limerick and Ennis, near Bunratty Castle, there is a new motel, the Shannon Shamrock, an interesting innovation for Ireland; it's a pleasant place to stay overnight or as a base of operations for sightseeing in the area. Inquire at the hotel if they're having a medieval dinner at the nearby Bunratty Castle—definitely worth attending. Incidentally, Bunratty Castle is worth a short stopover at any time, just to walk through. Then to Cursheen, Gort and Galway on the River Corrib; the Great Southern Hotel is easily the best in town. The city has quiet, winding streets; the architecture is frequently in the Spanish style (this town once had heavy commerce with that country and travelers brought back Spain's architectural influence).

Places to eat? The Great Southern has a rather good top floor restaurant (the one on the main floor is pretty bad), where some of the local fish specialties of the region may be had. These include oysters (in season, of course), scallops, prawns, sole, and lobster (which is quite expensive). Across the square from the Great Southern Hotel is probably the best restaurant in town, called Lenihan's Tavern; the food is generally first rate in the dining room to the left as you enter. On the right hand side there's an atmospheric bar, where you can get simple snacks, sandwiches, etc.

If you aren't going to Aran, and I do hope you manage to squeeze it into your itinerary, you should drive west from Galway, through Salthill, Barna, Spiddal, Inveran, and up to Costelloe. Here you can see something resembling the Aran Islands, with their Irish farmhouses and rocky fields, and the sidetrip is quite worthwhile. If you can spare another couple of hours, continue on from Costolloe to Carraroe and the general area, which offers a somewhat different type of coastal scenery, or through the adjacent Lettermore Islands.

Galway to Westport—120 miles

From Galway, take route 40 north to Headford; make a left turn toward Cross on an unnumbered road. Approximately a mile and a half farther along the road are the ruins of old Ross Abbey. Continue on to Cross, where there is a left turn to Cong, a strip of land between two lakes, which furnishes Cong with its name, Neck of Land. The area is pleasant; there are caves to visit and excellent opportunities for all sorts of sport. Ashford Castle is located here and is possibly the most inviting place in Ireland for an extended vacation stay; the old castle has been remodeled very successfully into a modern resort-style hotel with twentieth-century amenities and good food. Be sure to have an advance reservation, however, and note that the management is not partial to those who wish merely to remain overnight.

Leave Cong by route L-101 through Clonbur and Cornamona into Maam and Maam Cross, then westward (via T-71) to Recess and Clifden, the last a lovely resort town. The two best places here are the Clifden Bay Hotel and the smaller Ivy Hotel. Next drive to Cleggan, where the mailboat may be taken for a pleasant excursion to Inishbofin Island and its old Christian ruins. From Clifden or Cleggan, continue on route T-71 through Letterfrack and Aasleagh to Westport.

Westport is a city with a continental design, rare in Ireland, for it was laid out by a French architect employed for the purpose by the Marquis of Sligo; the streets run out from a central area, and the overall effect is unlike any other town in the nation. But the great days of trade with overseas countries are gone, and Westport is somewhat down at the heels, its prosperity and fine airs long since vanished. From here a pleasant day's excursion is a trip to Clare Island; at Roonah Quay, take the mailboat to this exceedingly picturesque spot. Another outing may be made from Westport via route T-71 to Newport, Mulrany and Achill Island, where it is possible to make purchases of rough amethysts from the local folk.

Westport to Donegal—115 miles

From Westport, take route 40 to Castlebar, Bellavary, Foxford, Ballina and Easky to Sligo, where the leading hotel is the Great Southern. Sligo is an active town, not itself a tourists' haven but the center for day trips into the surrounding regions. Be sure to see what is left of Sligo Abbey, founded 1252, if you are not tired of old ruined abbeys by this time, which fact is within the bounds of possibility. Be sure to drive around the lake, Lough Gill; at Dromahair, there is yet another ruined abbey.

Leave Sligo via route T-18, a road that travels through exciting scenery, wild and desolate, with tumbling sand dunes and a green and white seascape. The road passes Drumcliff, Grange, Castlegal and Bundoran, a resort town with a very highly regarded hotel, the Great Southern. Then head for Ballyshannon, from which a side trip may be made to the little village of Belleek (where the pottery is made) and to see lovely Lough (Lake) Erne. Route 18 goes on to Donegal (which must be pronounced Dawn-nee-gawl or the residents won't know what you're talking about), a busy place, filled with people occupied with one principal trade, weaving, so we'd continue onward after buying the Donegal specialty, locally made tweeds.

Donegal to Londonderry—120 miles
(via the coast road)

(If time is short, route 18 [later A-5] may be followed through Ballybofey directly to Londonderry, but this road cuts inland and cannot be compared with the far more interesting coastal highway.)

To tour the Donegal peninsula, leave the town by route T-72 to Mount Charles, Inver, Dunkineely and Killybegs, a village that specializes in making carpeting. At Killybegs, go north to Ardara, a vacation spot where

tweeds are produced and are generally available for purchase directly from the makers. From here through
Glenties and Maas into Dungloe (be certain to drive
this curving road with care).

From here extends the remarkable wild area called
the Rosses, with rough boulders, peat soil and an un-
trammeled air of secret and romantic desolation. The
coastal road goes on to Gweedore, Middletown, Brinlack
and Gortahork. Here, trips may be taken to Tory Island,
but unless the weather is fine, the water may become
very rough and unpleasant, so make careful inquiry beforehand as to wind conditions and the state of the sea.

From Gortahork continue on to Dunfanaghy, a resort
town where an overnight stop could be arranged at Ar-
nold's or the Carrig Rua Hotel. The road continues to
Creeslough, Carrigart and Rosapenna, where there is
a fine hotel, the Rosapenna, pleasant and inviting. On to
Milford, Rathmelton and Letterkenny, then T-59 into
Londonderry, passing the North Ireland customs on the
way; as a rule, this is merely a formality for American
tourists.

Londonderry, which everyone calls Derry, is so named
because the region was controlled by a London merchant company during the seventeenth century; it is now
a busy commercial city of about 50,000 people. It is also
a center of the civil rights movement and the accompanying violence that began reemerging in Northern
Ireland in the late 1960s. The most important sights are
the old city walls, built in 1617 and still in fair repair
although much is now hidden from view by buildings.
The City Hotel is the place to stop.

Londonderry to Belfast—85 miles
(via inland road)

Leave Londonderry by route A-2 to Limavady and
Coleraine, then route A-26 to Ballymena and Belfast; or
if time permits, the motorist has a choice of driving the
renowned marine road along the coast (via A-2). However, regardless of the route selected, everyone will want
to visit the Giant's Causeway; take route A-29 from
Coleraine to Portrush (a lovely resort), then A-2 along
the coast to Bushmills and toward Port Ballintrae, just
before which there is a left turn to this famous tourist
spectacle. Here, through some prehistoric volcanic action, are more than 40,000 vertical columns in hexagonal

shape, about a foot and a half in diameter, placed by nature in a fantastic arrangement. The sight is spectacular and should not be missed (even on a rainy day).

Assuming you choose the coastal road, follow A-2 to Cushendall and Carnlough; the route passes through the famed nine Glens of Antrim into the coast village of Ballygally, where a stop could be made at the attractive Candlelight Inn. The next town is Larne, where steamers maintain a service to Stanraer, Scotland. Then on to Belfast, with two good hotels, the large Grand Central and the smaller Midland.

Belfast to Dublin—101 miles

Take route A-1 from Belfast to Lisbon, Hillsborough, and Banbridge into Newry, so-called reportedly because of a yew tree (popularized into New-ry) planted by St. Patrick. From Newry to Dundalk, passing the Irish customs, the route changes from A-1 to T-1; Dundalk is known for its copy of Cambridge's King's College Chapel, a handsome edifice, here called St. Patrick's. From Dundalk continue south to Dunleer, after which you come to Newton Monasterboice, with its fine High Crosses and Round Tower, going back to various dates in the sixth century. If ruined structures interest you, continue on to Mellifont, with very interesting remains of a twelfth-century abbey and also a restored chapel.

Continue on to Drogheda (pronounced Draw-ee-dah), where the White Horse Hotel is the best available; you'll be interested in seeing the old gates, which once were the only openings through the old walls of the town. Then to Gormanstown (a bathing resort) Balbriggan (a hosiery town) and Swords (an old community with much historical background). The Round Tower, the Archbishop's Palace (in ruins) and the picturesque general area make a stop worthwhile. Then to Dublin, where the trip terminates. Sure, and it's been a lovely journey.

ࣘ Motoring in Ireland

Formalities for bringing a car into the country have been simplified to the point that all you need is the car's registration, your home-state driver's license and the Green Card certifying that you are insured. Car rentals (within Ireland) are remarkably inexpensive—the lowest-priced period is winter, the next lowest is fall, and the highest are spring and summer. But even then rates are comparatively low. It is possible to bring your car to Ireland from England by air or sea, but unless you are going to do lots of driving in the country over a period of some time, the transportation rate would be more than a rental would cost.

Mountain roads are often gravel-surfaced, and these should be traveled slowly, but in general highways are quite good. Look out for country roads, though, because they are frequently bumpy and narrow. Outside the larger cities, the roads are sparsely traveled—sometimes almost deserted. Traffic keeps to the left as in England, but this should present little difficulty because of the light traffic. There are no speed limits outside cities; in built-up areas, speed limits are always well displayed and these should be followed. Why speed through Ireland in any event?— the charm and quiet of the country are the chief attractions for tourists.

Gasoline stations are plentiful near cities and towns; be sure to have a full tank when touring the country. Don't forget that five Irish gallons equal six American, so the price per gallon is actually cheaper than it seems. Filling stations are frequently closed on Sunday, so gas up on Saturday if you intend to do any Sunday driving.

An Irish mile is not the same as an American; eleven Irish miles roughly equal fourteen of ours, although this should cause little inconvenience, for distances are generally quite short. Don't rely on road conditions or travel information furnished by a rustic—he's thinking in terms of his horse and cart, not your automobile.

MISCELLANEOUS ODDITIES ¶ Profanity is seldom used in Ireland and is considered in very bad taste.

Irish may disagree among themselves about every possible question under the sun. But to a man they agree that the six partitioned counties of Northern Ireland should be reunited with the rest of the country.

Certain subjects are, as a rule, taboo in polite conversation: sex, dirty jokes and the church, for example. For one person who will converse about those subjects, a hundred others will not. However, recently, people have shown a tendency to joke (somewhat gently) about the church.

Don't tell the Irish that there aren't enough bathrooms

in the hotels; they know it and are trying their best to remedy the situation. But *do* tell them about the lack of heat, because they aren't doing enough about that.

As previously mentioned, the hotel and restaurant staffs are good-natured and well-meaning, but simply do not have the professional experience of continental Europeans.

Except in tourist hotels, don't expect to find mixed drinks or American cocktails. The Irish like to drink their whiskey straight.

The Irish speak English with what we usually call an "Irish brogue." However, students of the subject believe that English was so spoken during the Tudor era, and therefore the brogue is actually the historically correct way of speaking.

Ireland has roughly the same area as Maine; the entire country can be toured in a few hurried days, but the charm of the countryside will reveal itself only on a slow, unhurried journey.

ITALY

National Characteristics

What are the Italians like? you ask. We ask, Which ones do you mean? Those from Genoa? The people of Venice? The Romans? Neapolitans? Milanese? All of them are Italians, but each regional group in Italy is spectacularly, wonderfully different from another, even though living in adjacent areas on the same crowded (but beautiful!) peninsula. To get one view of what the Italians are really like—or, more specifically, a particular regional group of them—put the question to an Italian about a part of the country other than his own. A Venetian's description of a Torinese would be very (very!) interesting, just as the capsule comment of a Milanese would be equally fascinating about someone from Sicily, or Sardinia, or the toe of Italy—or from anywhere but his own Lombardy.

And all of them—north, south, and central—have their own pet opinions about the Romans.

We have our views about Italians, too. There's no need to describe them region by region, from Piedmont to Calabria. Let's just sum them up this way: Italians are completely wonderful. *Basta!* Which means Enough! That's it!

If any qualities specifically characterize Italians, they are love of family and a deep religious nature. No matter how the members may quarrel among themselves, the family is a closely knit unit. Even after his marriage, a son still owes strong allegiance to Mother (with a capital M). Generally, marriages are still approved by a family council, which gives more regard to the financial standing of the prospective bride or groom than to love and romance, because, as all sensible people know, a "suitable" marriage is far more important than one based on mere physical attraction. Fun and pleasure, to most Italians, occur when the entire family meets as a unified group (including aunts, uncles, third cousins, nieces and nephews)—preferably around a bountifully laden table, with much wine and lots of songs. Which isn't bad, either.

In addition to adhering to the matriarchal family system, nineteen out of twenty Italians are Catholics. Some are devout (notably the women), others are not (notably the men). Americans are sometimes startled at the behavior of Italians in church—their casual manner, conversation and general attitude of making themselves at home in houses of worship. Well, the Italians are *at home* in church in a manner that Anglo-Saxons find incomprehensible. The in-a-hurry impression-gathering American tourist must keep in mind, too, that the religious sites he visits are usually the ones filled with tourists like himself and not with the local people. St. Peter's, the Duomo in Milan, St. Mark's in Venice and the cathedral in Siena —to name just a few—do not give a sharply accurate or comprehensive portrait of the religious life and church-going habits of Italy's men, women and children.

One thing that confuses many tourists who have been in Italy before is that the Communist party has a strong foothold there. As a matter of fact, Italy's Communist party is the largest in the Western world. The Catholic Church maintains a firm line against communism, yet the Italian Communist party is strong. No one in Italy finds this hard to understand or to reconcile—except a poor confused American.

This American, by the way, is even more confused by the charming manners and hospitality of the people he meets in the villages. Italy's defeat in the war has been completely forgotten, and we are welcomed not as conquerors but as friends. As a matter of fact the average Italian family inevitably has a relative or close friend in the United States, and to mailboxes in tens of thousands of homes throughout Italy the mailman regularly brings checks or cash sent by loved ones from abroad.

Contrasted with the warmth of the Italians is petty larceny involving hub caps stolen from parked cars, taxicab drivers who overcharge and small, annoying rackets involving only a few cents, for example. Not in defense of these practices—for theft and dishonesty can never be successfully defended—but only in mitigation, may one small voice be heard? Can the average tourist, who spends $10 or more for overnight accommodations, possibly realize the grinding poverty of so many Italians, to whom $10 might represent a small fortune—the total of a year's earnest savings?

There is, unhappily, a good deal of systematic crime directed at tourists, particularly in the Naples area, including the theft of money from hotel rooms, rental cars and luggage out of cars. These criminals have extended their activities into the international trains going to Switzerland, Germany and Austria. Their favorite victims are women traveling alone. Even the North Italians are stirred up by this activity of the *Gigis*, as they call the Neapolitans, who are swarming into the north, looking for prey. During the past year, American tourists reported to the American Embassy in Rome thefts of money amounting to $1,500,000, and the Embassy estimates that another $500,000 or more was probably unreported. So, be careful, lock your luggage, and the trunks of automobiles, and don't carry around too much cash. At least if travelers' checks are lost, the amount can be recovered.

In the north of Italy, people earn good wages in the many plants and factories and are frequently inclined to vote the Communist party line. In the agricultural south, people are easy-going, poor as church mice and almost irreconcilably anticommunist. Does this all add up? And if so, to what? The result somehow produces a charming people in a fascinating country.

When to Go

During the winter months, the area with the consistently warmest weather (not always, though!) is the south—Calabria, on the lower end of the peninsula, and the islands of Sicily and Sardinia. The Italian Riviera (adjacent to the French), from Ventimiglia down the coast past San Remo, has sunny but often nippy days in the winter after the late-autumn rains have stopped. Rome usually has a serene winter—sunny, a bit frisky at times, with a touch of rain or a big cloud cover now and then. Some years ago—in 1963—some of you possibly were in Rome when it had a real snowstorm that few Romans have forgotten yet. But that was freakish. Most of Italy is suitable for a visit anytime from April through October, but the really perfect weather is from April until mid-June and during September and October.

July and August are crowded and frequently quite hot. But it's better to visit Rome or Florence on a steamy, humid day than never at all. If you're planning a trip, bear these facts in mind and arrange your schedule accordingly. If arriving in May for a complete tour of Italy, begin your travels in the south and proceed northward in order to take advantage of the warming climate. If you arrive in Italy in September, start your trip in the north and work your way south.

WEATHER STRIP: ROME

Temp.	JAN.	FEB.	MAR.	APR.	MAY	JUNE	JULY	AUG.	SEPT.	OCT.	NOV.	DEC.
Low	38°	40°	44°	49°	54°	61°	66°	65°	61°	54°	46°	40°
High	52°	55°	59°	66°	73°	81°	87°	86°	80°	70°	60°	53°
Average	44°	48°	52°	58°	64°	71°	77°	76°	71°	62°	53°	47°
Days of rain	10	10	9	9	8	5	2	3	6	11	12	12

As of the last couple of years the biggest problem about when to go to Italy has not been the weather but the frequent strikes, which are so numerous that a strike information bulletin has been introduced by the Italian TV. You never know when you will be delayed at the border or inside Italy because airline, railroad, gas station attendants, hotel personnel, restaurant people, and even customs officers, not to mention post offices, telephone, banks, etc. will go on strike. Strikes may last anywhere from a day to a week or longer; and then to crown it all, there's a general strike from time to time.

TIME EVALUATION ¶ On a month's vacation trip, don't plan on less than ten days for Italy, unless only Rome is on your itinerary, in which case a minimum of five days should be allowed. An automobile trip (as outlined in this book) covering Florence, Perugia and Venice would take from ten days to two weeks; the same time allowance should be made for a trip south (Naples, Sicily, etc.). Even on a brief trip to Italy, allow a bare minimum of four days to a week or more for a quick visit to Sorrento, Capri, and the Amalfi coast. Needless to say, Italy is such a large and varied country that your entire month's vacation could easily be spent there.

PASSPORT AND VISA ¶ A passport is needed but, unless you're staying for more than ninety days, you will not have to have a visa. If you are planning to remain longer than ninety days, either apply for a visa—before leaving home—at the nearest Italian consulate or make an application with the police (Office of Foreigners) when you are in Italy.

CUSTOMS AND IMMIGRATION ¶ Italian customs are particularly interested in knowing whether you have cigarettes or liquor in your baggage because these are high-tax items. You are theoretically allowed to bring in two cartons of cigarettes, one quart of liquor and two bottles of wine, but Italians are extremely hospitable to Americans, and it is likely that they will limit their customs inspection to a big welcome smile. In any case, if they do look, two hand cameras, a record player, a portable typewriter, a movie camera, a pair of binoculars and, of course, a transistor radio are among the items a tourist is allowed to have with him duty-free. Theoretically, too, export of more than 50,000 lire is not allowed, but we haven't heard of anyone bringing this regulation up for years and years. Also, if you make a point of announcing the presence of a portable radio in your baggage—such as by playing it during the visit of the customs men—you are possibly going to be reminded that there is a radio-use tax in Italy, and even though a transient, you will have to pay a slight fee. So a word to the wise radio owner should be sufficient. *Capito?* Which means, so to speak, Quiet Please!

HEALTH ¶ From Rome northward, have no fears, because a high set of public health standards exists. From Naples to Sicily, however, the opposite is true, and sanitation is often primitive in the rural areas. Of course, these statements are general and do not apply to large tourist hotels. Water may be safely consumed in all of the large northern cities, but should generally be avoided in the south. This applies to milk, too. It is seldom pasteurized, by the way. Drink bottled water in the south—that is, if you're not substituting water with the very low priced wines of the country. There are plenty of mineral waters —the gassy and nongassy kinds are available everywhere.

Be a little cautious of shellfish, particularly raw ones. The cooked kind is comparatively safe. Are we scaring you? We don't mean to. The chances are you'll be perfectly O.K. Just take care about the drinking water in the more rural areas of the south.

TIME ¶ Six hours ahead of Eastern Standard Time. That is, when it's noon in New York, it's 6 P.M. in Italy. BUT —as those of you who have been in Italy in the last couple of years know, the spring now brings not only beautiful flowers but Daylight Saving Time, called in Europe Eastern European Time and so defined in the summer air and train timetables dealing with traffic connections with Italy. The time differential remains the same.

CURRENCY ¶ The *lira* (plural *lire*) is the Italian currency. The number of the lire to the dollar has been varying with the variance of the international monetary situation. If you cash traveler's checks and dollars at your hotel, you might get a noticeably lower rate than at a bank. This is because the concierge or other nonbanker middleman takes a slight cut for his services. But there is no black market in currency, and the only advantage of changing money at your hotel is the convenience. The best rate—because it is the *official* rate—will be given by a bank. Exchange offices generally do not pay so high a rate as the bank does. On a few dollars, the difference of 10 or 15 lire (per dollar) does not amount to much. It can be substantial, however, with large sums.

PRICE LEVEL ¶ The prices have been climbing again— and that goes for hotel and restaurant prices, particularly. In any event Italy is no longer a bargainland, but prices on certain things (restaurant meals, for example) are still more or less fair. An *espresso*, in its homeland, is always inexpensive. Generally, the areas frequented by *foreign* tourists (especially Americans) have high prices. These include Venice—perhaps we should say *headed* by Venice—then Florence, the Naples-Capri-Ischia-Pompeii-Sorrento complex and leading lake and seaside resorts (Como, Amalfi, Portofino, etc.). You'll notice we didn't say anything about Rome. The reason is that Rome, perhaps surprisingly, is not so expensive generally as many other cities of Italy. In small cities and towns, and in resorts frequented primarily by Italians, prices will be even lower.

TIPPING ¶ Be ready with a pocketful of small change wherever you go in Italy. You'll need it. In taxis, tip 15 percent of the meter, but not less than 100 lire. A service charge of up to 15 percent will be added to your hotel bill. But, in addition, give the chambermaid 100 lire for each day you're at the hotel and about the same for the concierge unless he has done something really special for you. The hotel porter gets 100 lire a bag but in railroad stations the minimum *official* fee is 150 lire for the first bag and 100 lire for each additional one. Restaurants will add 15 percent to your bill as *service*, but leave 100 to 300 lire extra for the waiter if he has been attentive. The usual tip for checkroom and washroom attendants is 100 lire. The waiter who serves breakfast in your room is entitled to a couple hundred lire—for two people. If in doubt, remember that 100 lire is equivalent to 16 cents and may be given with the same overall effect as a quarter tip back home.

TRANSPORTATION ¶ Italian train service is quite good, and the trains run on time (supposedly a carryover from Mussolini). The top train is the *Settebello*, a luxury extra-fare train that connects Rome and Milan, with stops at Florence and Bologna. There are also a number of Trans-European Express trains—First Class, reserved seats only, extrafare—that link Milan, Italy's industrial hub, with such far-off continental points as Lyons, Marseille, Munich, Paris, Geneva and Zurich. The names for the types of trains in Italy all connote speed. But there are degrees of speed, so it is a good idea to know the classifications. In that way you can tell which of the speedy-seeming trains are really so, or not so. The fastest is the *rapido* (some runs are First Class only, and seats have to be reserved; in any case, a supplement is always charged). Next in speed is the *direttissimo*, a long-distance express. After that is the *diretto*, a standard express train; and at the bottom of the speed chart is the *accelerato*, a local train that makes all stops on the route. It's like olives— the smallest size is called jumbo. Italian trains are *always* crowded. It is advisable—even in First Class—to reserve a seat in advance. The reserved-seat fee is slightly higher at a travel agency than at a railroad station. On a number of fast through trains a seat reservation is obligatory. For lots of train travel, the special tourist season tickets are a money saver. Dining-car prices in

Italy tend to be high—close to $1, for instance, for a continental-type breakfast and $5 or $6 (with wine and coffee) for lunch or dinner. (Note: the train meals are not worth the price.)

Airplane service within the country is good, although it is not used to anywhere near the extent used here at home Because of the country's great length and comparative narrowness, air travel is mainly practical in north-south directions, rather than east-west. The largest number of flights is between Rome and Milan—fourteen a day. Sardinia and Sicily are also in frequent air contact with Rome and Milan. The domestic flights are by *Alitalia* (which also has extensive European, North and South American, African, and Middle Eastern service); by ITAVIA, ATI and *Alisarda* (the Sardinian Airline). Round trip fares are double, usually with no reduction. If you are going to be traveling around Naples—and the chances are you will—keep in mind the helicopter service from the Naples airport, Capodichino; from the city's harbor to Capri, Ischia, Sorrento and Positano; and between the airport and the harbor. The rates are very reasonable. Round trips are double the regular price except if they are made on the same day; then they are quite a bit cheaper. There are four or five helicopter trips a day on these runs to the islands in the Bay of Naples. In addition, over on the Adriatic coast (and to the north), there is helicopter service between Rimini and the independent republic of San Marino. It is a pleasant fifteen-minute flight.

A good way of seeing the Italian countryside is to use the *bus* (pardon, motor coach) service of CIAT, which, during the tourist season (generally April–May to September–October), operates along classic itineraries on day-long runs. Milan, Genoa, Florence, Rome, Naples and Venice are starting and destination points on the CIAT bus lines. The trips leave in the morning around 8 or 9 A.M. and reach the destination point somewhere between 6 and 7 P.M. It is a longer ride than the train, but you see lots more. The bus service is not expensive either. Besides the CIAT service, local buses operate from main cities to regional points of interest. There are, in addition, low-priced bus tours of Sicily and Sardinia that are worth looking into.

Taxis are plentiful (and fairly expensive) in the larger

cities. They charge about 30 cents for the first third of a mile and 10 cents for each additional third of a mile. This tariff can (and does) differ somewhat from place to place. Cabs in Rome and many other cities post rates clearly (and in English, as well as other languages). At night an extra charge is made. Drivers also collect additional lire for baggage. In some cities, especially Rome and Naples, taxi drivers love to take the innocent tourist for a ride, driving him around in circles or "forgetting" to start the meter and then claiming an amount to their liking. Chauffer-driven cars (including late-model Cadillacs) are available at surprisingly low rates.

If you plan to do any *automobile driving* in Italy, it might be advisable to join the Automobile Club d'Italia (ACI). Annual dues are extremely reasonable, and are even less for members of an affiliated automobile club. There are all kinds of benefits (besides road maps and itinerary advice), such as reduced prices (or none at all!) on a range of things, from parking space to museum and art gallery admissions. You can join the ACI at one of its offices at the border when you enter, at an office abroad or at the Membership Section (*Servizio Soci*) of its office at 8 Via Marsala in Rome —a few steps from the main railroad station. Remember! if you remain in Italy with your car for more than six months—without driving it out of the country at least once in that time—it will be subject to taxation. *Rented cars* are available everywhere, literally. Be sure that you get comprehensive insurance on the rented car, including personal liability coverage for yourself. It costs a bit more, but is infinitely worth it.

There is frequent service by *ships* of the Tirrenia line between the Italian mainland and the main islands of Sardinia and Sicily and between Sicily and Malta. For instance, there are daily sailings between Naples and Palermo (Sicily), between Civtavecchia (forty miles northwest of Rome) and Olbia (Sardinia), between Civitavecchia and Cagliari (Sardinia) and between Genoa and Porto Torres (Sardinia). Twice a week ships connect Naples and Cagliari, and three times a week Syracuse (Sicily) and Malta.

ELECTRICITY ¶ Voltages range from 115 to 220, but the current is usually A.C. The cycles, meanwhile, vary from

42 to 50. All of this means that you'll probably need a transformer for your electrical appliances. You will also have to have an adapter plug, because only plugs with round prongs fit Italian sockets. The flat-pronged plugs we use won't work no matter how hard you try. So don't try.

COMMUNICATIONS ¶ *Cables* can be sent (in small towns) from post offices. Simplify things, and save confusion all the way around, by having the text typed out and addressed so that all you have to do is hand it to the clerk at the telegram counter. The easiest way of all is to give it to your hotel concierge. You can—theoretically—dictate the texts of cables and telegrams over the telephone. But this is the best way yet devised to lose your mind. Remember! Cables to the New York area cost less than those to other U.S. destinations. Seven words is the minimum. Sixteen-word (minimum) telegrams within Italy are about $1.

Telephone service is not so bad on local calls, and neither is it too bad on overseas calls. Public telephones are everywhere—coffee bars primarily. They are indicated by a disk representing a telephone dial. To make a public telephone call you use a *gettone*, a coin that is purchased from the coffee bar or whoever has the phone. In railroad stations you can usually get the tokens for the telephone at one of the newsstands. Long-distance calls between a number of cities in Italy can now be dialed directly, but you have to know the area code number, of course. To *airmail* a letter to the United States, the cost is about a quarter. Please don't ask us why it costs somewhat less to airmail a letter from the United States to Italy. That's one of those things that baffles us. (It might have something to do with the prevailing winds.) An airmail postcard home costs about two thirds of the postage for a letter. You theoretically buy stamps at the post office, but it is usually easier (and much quicker) to get them at a tobacco shop (identified by the letter T on a sign outside). Or, you can get them from the concierge at your hotel. If there is not enough postage, the postal people don't send the mail back to you for more stamps. They just send it on its way by ordinary mail—and that takes *extra*ordinarily long (a couple of weeks, anyway).

Basic Italian

English-Italian

Waiter: *Cameriere*
Bill of fare, menu: *Lista delle vivande, menu*
Napkin: *Tovagliolo*
Bread and butter: *Pane e burro*
A glass of orange juice: *Un bicchiere di succo d'arancio*
Boiled egg: *Uovo bollito*
1. soft: 1. *poco*
2. medium: 2. *giusto*
3. hard-boiled: 3. *sodo*
4. egg cup: 4. *portauovo*
Fried eggs: *Uova fritte*
Bacon and eggs: *Pancetta affumicata e uova*
Coffee, black: *Caffè nero*
Coffee with cream and sugar: *Caffè con panna e zucchero*
Coffee with hot milk: *Caffè e latte*
Tea: *Tè*
Water: *Acqua*
Ice water: *Acqua ghiacciata*
Mineral water: *Acqua minerale*
Breakfast: *Prima colazione*
Lunch: *Colazione*
Dinner: *Pranzo*
Shampoo: *Shampooing*
Haircut: *Taglio dei capelli*
Manicure: *Manicure*
I want . . . liters of petrol: *Vorrei . . . litri di benzina*
Change the oil: *Cambi l'olio*
Grease the car: *Ingrassi l'auto*
How are you?: *Come sta?*
Fine, thank you: *Benissimo grazie*
Please: *Per favore*
Thank you very much: *Molte grazie*
Good morning: *Buon giorno*
Good afternoon: *Buon pomeriggio*
Good night: *Buona notte*
Yes: *Si*
No: *No*
Morning: *Mattino*
Noon: *Mezzogiorno*
Afternoon, P.M.: *Poweriggio*
Evening: *Sera*
Night: *Notte*
Sunday: *Domenica*
Monday: *Lunedi*
Tuesday: *Martedi*
Wednesday: *Mercoledi*
Thursday: *Giovedi*
Friday: *Venerdi*
Saturday: *Sabato*
One: *Uno*
Two: *Due*
Three: *Tre*

Four: *Quattro*
Five: *Cinque*
Six: *Sei*
Seven: *Sette*
Eight: *Otto*
Nine: *Nove*
Ten: *Dieci*
Twenty: *Venti*
Thirty: *Trenta*
Forty: *Quaranta*
Fifty: *Cinquanta*
One hundred: *Cento*
One thousand: *Mille*

FOOD SPECIALTIES AND LIQUOR ¶ First a word or two about Italian restaurants. Heading the list, there is the topnotch place called the *ristorante*, and when you see that word you can usually be assured it's a first-class establishment. A *trattoria* is one step down the scale, generally. But that doesn't mean you won't get good food. There are several classifications of *trattorie*. Some are excellent and rank with top restaurants. Others are family operations, with Mamma in the kitchen, Papa acting as the host and a relative or two serving as waiters or helping in one way or another. A *rosticcería* is a combination delicatessen and stand-up snackbar (a few have tables) where you can get a good range of hot and cold dishes. There are no frills, but quality is usually high and the service is speedy. The *rosticcería* is not bad when you're in a hurry or just want a snack.

Italians have their own dining customs, eating merely coffee and bread or a sweet roll for breakfast. Lunch at about 1 P.M. or thereabouts is usually the big meal of the day for most people, and, from Rome south in particular, that means a leisurely two-hour meal. In the industrialized north (Milan or Turin, for example) businessmen are shortening lunch hours in the time-is-money American tradition. But in Rome, there is none of this sandwich-and-a-cup-of-coffee routine. In the evening, dinner begins about 8:30 or so, and even 10 or 11 isn't considered too late. In a garden restaurant in Rome on a summer evening people arrive as late as midnight for dinner. Dining at this hour, however, does cut one's appetite for a bedtime snack! The most difficult problem for early-rising Americans hungry for lunch in mid-morning is solved by a visit to a coffee bar. There you can have a *cappuccino*, coffee and milk *espresso* style, with cake or tiny sandwiches, which should tide you over until lunchtime.

Most Americans think Italians eat nothing but spaghetti with tomato sauce. With the same lack of logic, some Italians think Americans eat everything out of cans. In southern Italy, a dish of spaghetti or macaroni usually comes with a heavily garlicked tomato sauce, but this is native only between Naples and Palermo. Rome isn't fond of garlic or tomato sauce, and in the north, spaghetti dishes aren't terribly popular. Not only that (this is the day we destroy all your illusions!), but olive oil isn't used too much in the north, butter being the preferable ingredient. Garlic is just about as popular in the north as it is in the United States. Italian cooking styles are varied, the food is good, often marvelous, and if you don't gain weight, it's because you're lucky or careful.

If you want to live and eat like an Italian, here's the way: Before meals, no cocktails or whiskey; try a vermouth, a Campari and soda or an Americano or Negroni (though at first you probably won't like them). Your meal might commence with an *antipasto* (assortment of appetizers), sometimes very elaborate, sometimes limited to a few items. Then comes *pasta asciutta*, a generic term for all of the endless variations on the spaghetti theme. These are delicious and always well prepared, but don't limit yourself to the inevitable spaghetti. Why not try *maccheroni* (macaroni), *fettucine* (noodles), *cannelloni* (stuffed baked noodles), *lasagne* (layers of noodles with sauce) or *linguini* (very narrow noodles) to name just a very, very few. A big favorite on Thursday in Rome is *gnocchi* (cornmeal or potato balls), which you might learn to enjoy.

Soups are substantial: *minestrone* is so filling that it's been the downfall of many tourists. If you have a *pasta*, don't have soup, or vice versa. Chicken is the standard poultry dish; there is some turkey, but little in the way of duck. Broiled steak, as we know it, is comparatively rare and may be seen only in the tourist restaurants, where it is a recent addition and not authentic. (Exception: Florence has fairly good steaks.) Veal is the meat of the country, sometimes tiresomely so. You'll surely try *saltimbocca*—veal and ham combined, and very good. In fact, ham (usually *prosciutto*, the smoked type) is frequently combined with various other meats such as sweetbreads or served as an appetizer with iced melon, *prosciutto e melone.* Just for your information, whenever a menu offers *scaloppine*, it refers to thin cuts of meat, which is inevitably veal. And we're probably not doing you any favor to mention that the word for veal is *vitello*, because you'll never see a menu without it.

Don't fail to try *risotto* at least once, particularly up north; basically it's a type of sautéed and steamed rice prepared with bouillon and whatever the chef has handy —mushrooms, truffles, seafood, onions, and so on, far into the night. *Polenta* is the cornmeal dish popular around Milan and particularly in Veneto and Friuli regions but also frequently encountered elsewhere: Maybe it's not thrilling but try it once. By the way, many restaurants hesitate to serve simple peasant dishes like this because they feel it isn't high class or upper crust. In the same line of reasoning, a fancy New York restaurant will not serve hominy grits.

The Italians aren't too fond of rich desserts as a daily diet and save the very fancy cakes and pastries for special occasions (birthdays, holidays and family celebrations). When the average restaurant comes to the dessert course, it will offer cheese and fruits—or, at the most, a *crema di caramella* (a kind of custard). The luxury tourist restaurants, however, knowing the sweet tooth of Americans, have a big variety of desserts—just like those in an Italian restaurant back home! *Gelato* is the Italian word for ice cream or sherbet. It's not the same as American ice cream—but in a top place, such as one of the Motta or Alemagna bars, it can be excellent. Only the tourist restaurants will serve coffee as a matter of course. Italians usually go to a nearby bar for an after-dinner or after-lunch coffee. However, any Italian restaurant, no matter how small, will send a waiter out for coffee for you if you wish to have it at the *end* of your meal.

Everyone drinks wine, and you'll find yourself an amateur expert within a few days. The Italians, unlike the French, make little or no fuss about wines, just drink and enjoy them. You should have white wine with hors d'oeuvres, fish, chicken, turkey and veal; just as a suggestion we'd recommend Frascati, Verdicchio, Orvieto or Soave. Red wines are naturally better with red meats; Valpolicella is light and most people like it immediately. Barbera, Bardolino and Barolo are others you'll surely want to try. For a liqueur, a favorite orange-based cordial is Strega, with a biting aftertaste; also Ratafia, made from fruits and nuts; Cerasella is a cherry liqueur. Grappa is a strong Italian brandy that GIs used to like because nothing else was available. You probably won't, unless you were a GI.

SPAS ¶ Among Italy's many riches are its mineral springs. Great resorts have been built up around some of them, such as the fabulously beautiful one at Montecatini in Tuscany. Others are in a completely undeveloped stage and are popular with local people who know how helpful the waters are for a person's well-being. Among the noted ones are Acqui Terme, near Turin; San Pellegrino, north of Milan; Sermione, at Lake Garda; Abano Terme, not far from Padua; Salsomaggiore, in the Parma area; Fiuggi, not far from Rome; Castellammare, near Pompeii; and Sciacca, on the island of Sicily. These spas are always nice places to visit even if you have no intention of "taking the waters." But, remember! please don't decide by yourself which waters, and how much, are for you and your particular ailments. Always get a doctor's advice.

CASINOS ¶ If you're over twenty-one—and not many seem to be in these days of the youth explosion—you will be welcomed at one of the four casinos spotted around Italy. All you need to do is show your passport and pay an entrance fee (relatively stiff, too!). The most noted casino, probably, is at San Remo, especially during the winter months, when the Italian Riviera's sun attracts people so that they can gamble *indoors*. That's the way people are, though. Venice's casino is also very famous, but it moves from one place to another during the year. Confusing? In the winter it's at the Ca' Vendramin; starting April 1, it transfers to the Lido. The other casinos are at Campione, in the Lake Lugano enclave and at St. Vincent, in the Aosta valley.

The principal tourist areas are Rome, Florence, Venice, the Dolomites along the northern border, the lake region, the Italian Riviera, Naples and the south and Sicily and Sardinia.

Capital City

Rome—the Eternal City, the Timeless City or whatever you choose to call it—is undoubtedly the number-one American favorite of all cities in Europe, having supplanted Paris within recent years. (Two reasons—Paris became too used to tourists and too expensive.) Picture a city 3,000 years old, with monuments, ruins and relics from every period of those thirty turbulent centuries, today inhabited by about 4 million busy, gesticulating people who love life and enjoy every minute of it. To tread the streets of Rome is a genuine thrill for most of us, products of a mechanized twentieth century. Even the manhole covers bear the legend SPQR (*Senatus Populusque Romanus*, the Senate and People of Rome); everywhere one turns there are mementos and traces of the glories of past civilizations. When Rome's subway was being constructed, the excavators uncovered many old buildings and monuments, and the route was changed so as not to destroy the antiquities. Today, the subway twists and turns, but the ruins remain undisturbed.

Sightseeing in Rome depends upon the individual. Much can be accomplished in two days of intensive effort; it *could* require several years of more leisurely viewing. First of all, decide what you want to see. Rome's attractions may be broken down into categories: Religious Rome, the Vatican and the historic churches; Ancient Rome, the ruins and museums; the Tourist's Rome, which consists of shopping, eating, drinking in cafes and having a wonderful time. (A fourth Rome—the Social—is for those with Roman friends who will welcome them into their homes and introduce them to their friends.) As a rule, most people enjoy a little of everything—they want to see the Vatican, the churches, the Colosseum and the Forum, but they also enjoy shopping, eating, drinking, the cafes *ad infinitum*.

To get acclimated, one of the natural centers of the city is the Piazza di Spagna, which is reached by the famous stairway located not far from the Hotel Hassler. The name "Spanish Steps" is derived from the fact that the Spanish Embassy has been the principal building on this square for centuries—and is still there. The Via Sistina, one of the streets on the upper level leading to the Spanish Steps, is filled with chic shops (mostly for women). Chic means expensive, it would appear. Going down the flight of 137 steps is easy (up is difficult); at the bottom are the flower vendors and a famous Bernini fountain. Romans are crazy about fountains and you'll see them all over the city. Near the foot of the steps is the house where John Keats died in 1821, now the Keats-Shelley Museum. From the base of the steps, walk directly into Via Condotti, the main shopping street of fashionable Rome, and the downfall of many a true-blue red-blooded American woman! If you don't have a will of iron, beware of the Via Condotti. To get back from this area to the principal hotel district, which branches off from Via Veneto, unless you want to have a charley horse the next day, take a taxi.

On another trip, head for the Colosseum, completed in A.D. 80, the most publicized ruin in the world. Here the Romans held the famous entertainments to amuse the citizen of nineteen centuries ago and divert his mind from the stark poverty of his daily existence; gladiators struggled and were killed, thousands of beasts were sacrificed for a few hours of diversion, Christian martyrs perished and the band played on. (No, Nero didn't fiddle while Rome burned; it's all been proved untrue, a mere fairy tale.) The massive structure fell into disuse until about the twelfth century, when smart contractors realized that here was a wonderful source for ready-cut travertine (marble) and carted away wholesale quantities to construct homes for the nobility. The Palazzo Venezia was constructed largely of materials from the Colosseum. And that, readers, is why the Colosseum is in ruins.

The Colosseum is open during the summer from 9 A.M. to 7:30 P.M. There is a small entrance fee for the upper section. Upon leaving the Colosseum, you'll face the entrance to the Foro Romano, the Roman Forum, a quarter-mile treasury of archaeology, open daily except Tuesday throughout the year. The summer hours are 9 A.M. to 7 P.M. (winter, till 5:30 P.M.).There is a small entrance fee. Here, in the Roman Forum, was the fabulous center of ancient Rome, with its old streets, markets, statues, arches, temples and buildings. Here history truly comes alive. You—yes, you!—are walking in the steps of all the great Romans; perhaps, the very spot where you stand was trod by Julius Caesar, by Antony, or by one of the great rulers of Rome—Augustus, Trajan, Titus.

At one time or another, you'll surely see the Pantheon (in the Piazza del Pantheon), a wondrously designed architectural masterpiece; don't fail to see the interior; fascinating shrines and statues, as well as the tomb of the great painter Raphael. Nearby is the Piazza Navona,

one of Rome's most attractive old squares, where circuses were held with wild chariot races à la Ben Hur. Although today the area is slightly rundown and vaguely
seedy, it's still not difficult to imagine the chariots screech-
ing around the turns with togaed drivers urging the
horses onward. (No pari-mutuels.) On a pleasant, moonlit night, what could be more delightful than to sit outdoors at the Restaurant Tre Scalini, gazing soulfully at
the Navona fountain and downing a wonderful *tartufo*
(a giant chocolate ice)?

Not far away lies another marvelous old square, the
Piazza Colonna, with its imposing column in the center,
erected in the year 195 (no, nothing is missing from the
date).

Vatican City, a foreign state completely separated from
Italy, is the high point of a tour of religious Rome. No
present-day European monarch has anything resembling
the power of the Pope, within the confines of the Vatican,
to proclaim laws, control currency and issue stamps.
Approximately 2,200 residents live in 108 acres of Vatican City State (the official name). But most of the area
is occupied by official buildings, the radio station, gardens, and other facilities. Housing for Vatican employees
is at such a premium that many live in Rome. The square
in front of St. Peter's is extraordinarily impressive, if
only for its tremendous area, more than 1,100 feet in
length and almost 800 feet in width. Around the piazza
are about 300 columns, and the entire effect should impress the most indoctrinated Russian atheist. St. Peter's
itself, the mightiest house of worship in the world of
Christianity, was constructed on the original site of a
basilica built in the year 319 over the tomb of St. Peter.
In the fifteenth century, work on the present structure
began; the dedication took place in 1626. The interior
of St. Peter's is truly awe-inspiring, and any amount of
time may be spent there examining the art work and
architectural details. St. Peter's is almost always filled
with group tours, ranging from ten to a hundred persons, being lectured to by guides giving hackneyed talks
consecutively in several languages. The great size (160,-
000 square feet) and the height of the dome (over 400
feet) give pause to the viewer and are the principal
sources of interest, for the interior of St. Peter's is not
quite so harmoniously executed as one might have hoped.

An elevator goes to the roof (a small fee is charged

for the ride) from 8:30 to 4; but from the roof, there is a small matter of 700 steps to the copper ball at the top. (No advice is offered; *you* know whether or not you want to climb 700 steps.)

The Vatican Palace, adjoining St. Peter's, is partly the Pope's residence but is occupied chiefly by a series of museums and libraries. Incidentally, from the entrance to St. Peter's to the museum entrance is quite a distance and in the interest of saving your legs for wandering about the galleries, a taxi is advised. (As with taxis all over the world, the drivers would rather not take you to the museum entrance if they can talk you out of it, because it's difficult for them to pick up a fare at that point.) The museums (you'll find the entrance on the Viale del Vaticano) are open daily from 9 to 2, except on Sundays and religious holidays. There is an admission charge except on the last Saturday of every month when it is free. Incidentally, be sure *not* to go on the free day unless you enjoy enormous crowds of people, something like a subway crush. The content is stupendous, with particular emphasis upon sculpture and Etruscan and Egyptian art; the oil paintings are generally limited to religious subjects and the overall picture collection is somewhat less than great. By order of the officials in charge, all nude sculptures of male figures have been covered with fig leaves. The Vatican Library contains some remarkable manuscripts, including works by Petrarch, Virgil and Boccaccio.

Within the museum, arrows direct one toward the Sistine Chapel, so-called because it was constructed by Pope Sixtus IV. Almost every inch of the walls and ceiling is lovingly decorated, almost overdecorated by modern standards. The walls include work by Botticelli and Ghirlandajo, but everyone's eyes are naturally directed toward the ceiling, painted by Michelangelo, who spent four uncomfortable years at work on the renowned frescos, while lying on his back. After twenty years, Michelangelo returned to paint the Last Judgment on the altar walls, a task that took eight more years, from 1534 to 1541. Unfortunately, the Sistine Chapel is a goal for every tourist and sightseer to Rome and is inevitably overcrowded and stuffy; fortunate indeed is the lucky person who finds the chapel comparatively uncrowded and so can contemplate its magnificence in peace and thoughtful quiet.

WHAT TO EAT IN ROME

Fettucine alla Romana: Thin egg noodles served with melted butter and cheese

Fettucine al burro: Thin egg noodles served floating in butter, sometimes with cream added

Gnocchi alla Romana: Potato or cornmeal dumplings with a light tomato sauce

Spaghetti alla carbonara: Spaghetti prepared with egg, cheese and ham

Spaghetti alla matriciana: Spaghetti with tomatoes and bits of pork

Abbacchio arosto: Roast baby (really infant) lamb, a wonderful specialty

Saltimbocca: Ham and veal flavored with sage leaves

Trippa alla Romana: Stewed tripe with a thick sauce

Carciofi alla giudia: Deep-fat fried tiny artichokes, very delicate flavor

Pisellini al prosciutto: Young green peas cooked with ham

The local cheeses include *mozzarella*, which is soft and bland. A good Frascati wine can be excellent, but make sure the waiter picks out a really fine one for you. In general, the local wines, like Frascati, from the Castelli Romani are quite good.

ᛒ Short Side Trips from Rome

Villa Adriana

Only a brief ride (about forty-five minutes) from Rome brings you to the Villa Adriana, the palace of the Emperor Hadrian, now in ruins. Farther along is the Villa d'Este, also in ruins, but with its famous fountains still in operation. Allow about a half day for this trip and lunch in Tivoli, which has a few sights of its own—the Temples of Vesta and Sybil and the cascades.

Tarquinia

One of the most interesting all-day excursions out of Rome is to the little Etruscan village of Tarquinia. The Etruscans had a remarkable civilization, dating back to about the seventh century B.C., and were believed to have emigrated from Asia Minor. If you are interested in art, by all means make this trip; it is easily undertaken in a rented car. The trip to Tarquinia is only fifty-six miles; drive westward on the Corso Vittorio Emanuele and watch for a left turn onto the Via Aurelia in the direction of Civitavecchia. At Tarquinia (thirteen miles past Civitavecchia), head for the National Museum of Tarquinia and hire a guide (absolutely necessary). He'll take you to see the Etruscan tombs. Don't visualize anything depressing, the tombs were robbed centuries ago, and all that remains are the rooms themselves, beautifully decorated; bring (or wear) walking shoes. Afterward, have lunch outdoors at Tarquinia's little Hotel Le Rose, then visit the museum and later wander through the old town.

Anzio

Anzio is a word that remains with any American soldier who served in Italy during the invasion, and many ex-soldiers may want to see the old battleground. Its beaches have been cleared and only memories remain. Service by bus is preferable to the train, but a private car makes the thirty-three miles in less than an hour.

Lake Bracciano

A short ride from Rome is this large body of water whose basin had its origins in an old volcano. Now bordered by several small, pleasant villages, it is the largest lake in the Rome area and a very pleasant place for lunch on a warm day, because for some reason it is rarely flooded over with crowds. Prices are very reasonable, too, at the shoreside cafes and restaurants.

Castelli Romani

The Castelli Romani (plural) themselves should be visited. It is not possible to visit all of these delightful towns tucked in the hills around Rome, but you should pick out one or two of them anyway. The wine at Frascati, as we already pointed out, is good, and the town itself is very agreeable. So is Grottoferrata, Genzano, Albano—well, as we said, there are many of these wonderful little places only a short bus (or train) ride from the city. Nemi, for instance, is only twenty miles from Rome. These hill towns of the Roman district also include Castel Gandolfo, the summer residence of the Pope.

Ostia

Ostia is the beach area of Rome and is just a *subway* trip from the main railroad station in Rome. You can get to it on a fine highway, too. But, on summer weekends, the roads—especially on the way back in the evening—develop American-style traffic jams with lots of Roman-style horn blowing to make it even more nerve frazzling. Avoid the road then—just not worth it on weekends.

ACCOMMODATIONS ¶ Rome is short on hotel space from May through September, and advance reservations are not only advisable but imperative if you don't want to end up with an airless room over the kitchen. The better hotels, among the older ones, are almost all located in the "tourist area" between the Spanish Steps and the Via Veneto. The tendency recently, however, has been to build new hotels away from the downtown zone. Many of the newer ones—and some very fine hotels, too—are in the fashionable Parioli district. Most Americans find Roman hospitality quite satisfactory, with good food and service. Deluxe hotel rates range up to $20 for a single, $30 for a double. This is an all-inclusive tariff covering taxes and service, not meals. Everyone tends to breakfast in his bedroom (press the waiter's buzzer, which is indicated by a symbol of a man carrying a tray). It's advisable to bring your own soap, although a miniature cake may be furnished (sometimes on request). You can buy a bar of Palmolive, Lux, Camay or some other standard make in a tobacco shop. To the *basic* hotel room rate about 20 per cent is added for service, taxes and such appropriate items—when available—as heating and air conditioning. The better hotels usually, but not always, include heating and air conditioning in their all-inclusive rates. I know that's not very helpful, but that's the way it is.

ROME HOTELS

Grand Hotel: Rome's classic hotel, quiet and dignified. However, it is slightly out of the main tourist district, although only five minutes' walk away. Rooms are moderate to large, pleasantly decorated and air-conditioned.

Cavalieri Hilton: A very modern hotel, about ten minutes by taxi from downtown Rome. Every bedroom has a beautiful view; spacious setting, swimming pool, several interesting restaurants.

Excelsior: Centrally located on the Via Veneto, this has been extremely popular for many years with theatrical personalities and upper income bracket tourists. Hums and buzzes with excitement all day long and far into the night! Rooms are nicely furnished; air-conditioned.

Parco dei Principi: A rather new, excellent deluxe hotel in a beautiful setting—at the edge of the lovely Villa Borghese Gardens, in the smart and tranquil Parioli district. Very good, restful.

Flora: Key location on the Via Veneto and near the Villa Borghese; an attractive good-size hotel with rather good rooms, recently redecorated. Somewhat quieter than the Excelsior; completely air-conditioned.

Hassler: A small First Class hotel at the top of the Spanish Steps, probably the outstanding hotel site in Rome. The hotel is efficiently although somewhat stiffly run. It has a delightful roof restaurant with a marvelous view.

Holiday Inn: A brand new hotel with 350 spacious rooms, swimming pool, restaurants, and lots of fresh air; located in a residential area and very practical for motorists; bus service is provided to St. Peter's Square.

Bernini-Bristol: A rather modern hotel situated in the busy Piazza Barberini; ideal for businessmen. Rooms are none too large, but the hotel is well run and pleasant.

Ambasciatori: A moderate-size hotel on the Via Veneto; rooms are extremely variable, some small, some rather large. A favorite with tours.

Metropole: A rather new and quiet modern hotel, located near the railroad station. Almost American in scope, service and atmosphere. All rooms air-conditioned.

De la Ville: An older, conservative, but very pleasant hotel located on the Via Sistina, just a few hundred feet from the Spanish Steps. Rooms are good size, traditionally furnished; homey atmosphere. It has recently been redone.

Majestic: This is a good moderate-price hotel for those who wish to be on the Via Veneto, but want a small, quiet, dignified hotel. Rooms are pleasant, but slightly old-fashioned.

Eden: A good, moderate-size hotel just a few minutes from the Via Veneto and the Spanish Steps. In a quiet location, ideal for those who wish to be close to the center of things.

Boston: On a side street, quiet and old-fashioned. Many rooms are quite large, some have balconies facing the Borghese Gardens.

Quirinale: A luxury hotel in a convenient, busy location about midway between the main railroad station and Via Veneto; rates are good, too; very handy for opera-goers.

Palatino: A new, modern and fairly large hotel in the first-class (but not luxury) category. Not far from the Roman Forum and Colosseum.

Forum: As the name implies, near the Forum. It's a comfortably furnished pleasant place, although the rooms are small—the single rooms are ridiculously tiny. Pleasant rooftop restaurant.

Rome Restaurants

Hostaria dell'Orso: Rome's outstanding luxury restaurant, serving excellent food in extraordinarily handsome surroundings. Large, elaborate menu; almost anything selected will be excellent. Fairly high; reservations essential.

Passetto: First-rate food served in excessively modern décor. Beautiful display of specialties as you enter; outdoor dining in season.

La Fontanella: Excellent food in rather simple surroundings. This Tuscan restaurant has some of the best home-style cooking to be had in Rome.

Giggi Fazi: On Via Lucullo, a few blocks from the Via Veneto and the American Embassy. Lamppost signs indicate the restaurant's whereabouts (as if it were a secret), but everyone in the vicinity knows it. Very pleasant interior, ideal for good-weather outdoor dining. Excellent *pasta.*

Capriccio: Ideal for lunch, just a minute or so from the Via Veneto. Excellent food, particularly specializing in *abbacchio*, baby lamb. Their outdoor dining terrace is lovely.

Galeassi: Have a wonderful meal, Roman style, on tables placed on the street's cobblestones, on Piazza Santa Maria, in Trastevere; very good, not too expensive.

Alfredo all' Augusteo: This is the place to go for one special dish, *fettucine all' Alfredo*, homemade noodles served with plenty of rich cream and butter (slightly fattening).

Romolo: Lots of Trastevere atmosphere, music and singing and very pleasant. Food is fairly good, prices moderate; don't dress.

Alfredo in Trastevere: Local, informal atmosphere. At its best when the weather permits you to dine outdoors. Not dressy; rather inexpensive.

Tre Scalini: Located in lovely old Piazza Navona facing the Bernini fountains. If you haven't had dessert, come here after dinner on a fine evening and try the house specialty, *tartufo*, a magnificent chocolate ice.

Biblioteca del Valle: Pleasant, touristy and atmospheric. The food is fairly good, too.

Scoglio di Frisio: Perhaps the most typical Neapolitan-style restaurant in Rome, specializing in seafood and pizza; located at Via Merulana 256.

Da Meo Patacca: This is a popular Trastevere establishment that captures the color of Rome in a happy-go-lucky way that makes a hit with tourists; recommended, it's lots of fun.

George's: A top-notch and expensive restaurant located behind the Excelsior Hotel, operated by an Englishman, specializing in international cuisine, with a French-Italian accent; quite elegant.

Ranieri: A well regarded restaurant near the Piazza di Spagna; generally very good food at moderate to high prices.

L'Osteria da Marcello: An interesting atmospheric place located at Via Calabria, 23. Specializes in pasta and grilled meats.

Il Fedelinaro: Located on the square adjoining the Trevi fountains; despite that fact, the food is first rate. If you visit the fountains, it's convenient for lunch or dinner.

Al Moro: Located on a tiny side street near the Trevi fountains, the restaurant is larger than the unprepossessing entrance might suggest; the food is typically Roman and rather good.

Da Carlo in Trastevere: Located at 16, Via Cardinale Merry del Val, this is one of the best of the Trastevere restaurants and usually off the tourist path. Food is good and not expensive.

SHOPPING ¶ Rome is making a valiant effort to win the *haute couture* leadership away from Paris; notable strides have been made, but Paris still seems to retain an edge. Who knows about the future? Prices at the leading couturiers run in the vicinity of $375–$400 (or more) for suits or simple dresses; evening gowns are very high, or should we say even higher? The *boutiques* have some ready-made clothes at lower prices, or, in any event, lower by couturiers' standards. One Roman specialty is *knit goods*—sweaters, skirts, blouses and coats—and these are very reasonably priced; if they don't have your style, something suitable usually can be made up in a day or two.

Shoes are good at the more expensive shops where they are custom-made; the ready-made shoes are unsatisfactory because the last is wrong for American women, or rather for the feet of American women. If you're going to Florence, postpone shoe purchases until you get there; Florentine bootmakers offer a wide selection and better prices. Leather and suede handbags are good, although the price differential between Rome and New York for the identical article is not more than about 25 percent; again, if you're going to Florence, wait. Gloves, *small accessories* like compacts and lipstick cases are good values.

Table *linens* and placemats are exquisite; prices are high, but bear in mind that it's all hand work. Silk, available in lengths for dress materials, is a big specialty, but be sure to look for the label *pura seta*, to make sure you're getting the genuine article.

Men's clothing represents an outstanding value in Rome. Tailor-made suits run from $150 up—much less than the Stateside price for similar workmanship. Remember that delivery takes about a week, anyway, because at least two fittings are required. So place your order as soon as you arrive and then do your sightseeing. By the time you are ready to leave Rome the suit will be ready. Don't be talked into having a custom-tailored suit made up in a hurry. It just can't be done. *Shirts* are excellent values. Custom-made ones average $20–$25, but ready-to-wear shirts can be almost as good and much less expensive—about $12 and up. *Ties* are exceptional for gifts, and so are robes, dressing gowns and sweaters. They are approximately half the price—or even less—than at home.

Men's *shoes* are now being retailed all over the United States at reasonable prices and while there is some saving to be made, don't bother about shoes unless you're returning by ship. Excess baggage charges on planes will remove the price differential. Most men want to buy a *Borsalino hat* but hesitate because Italians prefer wider brims; these will be cut down for you on request at the better shops. Only buy the more expensive hats—the cheaper ones aren't as good a value.

Antiques may be purchased along the Via del Babuino, a busy street leading away from the foot of the Spanish Steps; but don't invest heavily without *expert* advice, for the phony art racket still flourishes in Italy. It's possible to be misled if you don't have the required knowledge, and even if you do, be careful if your purchase involves more than a nominal amount. While on the subject of What Not to Buy, avoid fountain pens, perfumes, toilet water, cotton yard goods, clocks and almost anything mechanical except a Fiat automobile, which is an excellent small car. Another approved exception is the Olivetti portable typewriter, which sells for about $20 less than in the States.

There is a special opportunity for women to indulge in a day of roman luxury, beauty-parlor style. If you are female and longing to be pampered, make a reservation at a beauty shop called Eve of Rome, located on the Via Veneto. If nothing else, have your hair done here and get that special Roman look. If money is still plentiful, get the works—massage, facial, manicure and pedicure, leg waxing, eyelash dye, etc. Many smart Roman women think nothing of taking off an entire day, once a week, and getting the full treatment. Or, if you're having a special evening on the town, have them put on your make-up for you. No wonder Nero fiddled!

Pointer: Shops open at 8:30 or 9 A.M. and close at 1 P.M. In the afternoon they reopen at 3:30 or 4 P.M. and remain open till 7:30 P.M. or, in sum-

mer, till 8 P.M. The time schedule varies a bit in
northern cities, where people take shorter lunch
hours and go home earlier.

ENTERTAINMENT ¶ What would Italy or Rome be like
without opera? In the winter, indoor performances; during the summer months, outdoors in the atmospheric
ruins of the Baths of Caracalla. Outdoor classical concerts in the Roman Forum, a superlative setting, should
not be missed by any music lover. The Italian legitimate
theater may be completely disregarded unless you speak
the language and possibly even if you do. An interesting
but little-known fact about the cinema (or moom pitchers
as Americans call them) is that Italian films featuring
the swelling torsos of nubile female stars are made
twice—once for Italian-European consumption and once
again for export to Puritanical Americans. As you have
probably guessed, the Italian version is much more torrid
and with considerable epidermis in evidence on what
used to be called the silver screen. If you are a connoisseur of the female form divine, a visit to at least one
Italian cinema might be in order.

Italian night life doesn't amount to very much. The
few leading places (an outstanding example being La
Cabala, above the Restaurant Hostaria dell'Orso) are
luxurious, with pleasant dance music, urbane and sophisticated. One of the most popular and elegant dine-and-
dance places in Rome is La Pergola, the rooftop night
club of the Hotel Cavaliere Hilton, with magnificent views
of the Eternal City. During the summer months, it's pleasant to drive to the outskirts of town to the Belvedere delle
Rose, on the Via Cassia Antica, where you can dine
delightfully and see a floor show of sorts.

Whether you were last in Rome ten years ago or ten
months ago, the night life situation has not changed
very much. Despite all that talk abroad about *La Dolce
Vita*, Italian night life doesn't amount to a great deal.
In the back streets off Via Veneto there are some slick
bars, discothèques and even a Pub (with a capital P)
where the members of the international movie set, and
others, gather. There are a couple of night clubs with
floor shows, but these are mostly for sailors on leave
and other unwary, or even wary, tourists. The big nighttime activity, for entertainment's sake, is sitting in a sidewalk cafe on the Via Veneto and watching the passers-

by. In summer, the rooftop bar and dance floor of the Hilton is splendid. Visit one of the suburban garden restaurants on the Via Cassia on a balmy evening in summer. That's what the Romans do, and there is usually some pleasant music to go along with a fine meal. Trastevere—"across the Tiber"—the picturesque, antique section of Rome, has some popular places where old and new folk songs are sung throughout the evening. The Fiammetta in downtown Rome and the Archimede in the Parioli district feature English-language films in their original version (no dubbing, no subtitles, no nonsense). In these inflationary times, the better movie theaters charge about $2.50 and up.

Pointer: Another theater showing English-language films is the Pasquino, in Trastevere. Its prices are very low but the seats—I warn you—are not upholstered.

SPORTS ¶ *Golf* is not at all the popular sport that it is in the United States but is more of a top social activity. The golf courses, therefore, reflect this high-level tone. There are some crackerjack courses, such as those in San Remo and the Lido of Venice. Most of the top ones, it seems, are concentrated in the northern area, where all the big business is located. At Rome, the Circolo Golf Olgiata—about twelve miles from downtown—has an eighteen-hole course and a nine-hole one. For full details on golfing possibilities, get in touch with the Italian Golf Federation (Federazione Italiana Golf) at 70 Viale Tiziano in Rome. Just in case you are a *bowler*, there are alleys on Viale Regina Margherita in Rome—and a real big place it is. For *swimmers*, Ostia (although crowded) and Fregene are a half-hour drive from Rome, and less crowded and equally fine beaches are only a little farther away. The Foro Italico, on the edge of the Tiber near the Ponte Milvio, has a splendid open-air swimming pool that was built for the Olympics some years ago.

≥ *Some Other Tourist Spots*

Florence

The world was saddened in the late fall of 1966 when flood waters from the Arno swamped this magnificent city and for some perilous hours threatened the priceless works of art that make the city a storehouse of Western culture. Happily, damage was kept to a minimum, and by the following spring Florence was once again able to receive visitors in its traditional, gracious way. If you can manage, come to Florence anytime except July and August, which are *extremely* hot. April–May and September–October are, in fact, the best periods for a visit. Nevertheless, the busiest months are June, July and August.

For almost three medieval centuries, the world looked to Florence for its cultural expression; governments came and went, but, for some obscure reasons, Florence produced the greatest writers, painters, sculptors, scientists and architects, who have left for our pleasure what has often been called a "museum city." During World War II, Florence escaped major damage although every bridge was destroyed with the exception of the Ponte Vecchio. Don't tear through Florence in a day, sightseeing everything at high speed but in fact seeing nothing; several days should be allotted even on a hasty trip. Here's a brief check list: Palazzo Vecchio, Uffizi Gallery, Duomo, San Michele oratory, Palazzo Medici-Riccardi, Santa Croce, San Lorenzo. Only two blocks from the Medici palace is the Gallerìa dell'Accadèmia, with the statue of Michelangelo's David, considered by many one of the world's greatest pieces of sculpture. After crossing the Arno River by the Ponte Vecchio, still lined with shops, you should visit Palazzo Pitti and the Boboli Gardens, Santa Maria del Carmine (for its frescos) and up on the hillside, San Miniato al Monte.

Florence also has two modern pastimes: shopping and eating. The city is noted for antiques, old jewelry, gloves, straw handbags, leather goods (including purses, wallets, ladies' shoes) and all sorts of small handicrafts like marble articles and wood carvings. Next to Bologna, Florence offers the best food in Italy, and there's nothing more delightful after a day of sightseeing than a wonderful dinner accompanied by a bottle of local Chianti wine.

WHAT TO EAT IN FLORENCE

Minestrone: A thick home-style vegetable soup
Funghi alla Fiorentina: Mushrooms prepared in the local fashion, with a little olive oil
Gnocchi: Cornmeal dumplings served with a thick sauce
Triglie alla Livornese: Fresh mullet in a tomato and olive sauce

Fagioli all' uccelletto: A bean and tomato stew
Pappardelle: Thick noodles, served with a heavy sauce
Lasagne alla cacciatora: Large, flat macaroni with meat sauce
Arista: Roast loin of pork, usually flavored with herbs
Bistecca alla Fiorentina: Plain broiled steak, but very good, a specialty of Florence
Stracotto alla Fiorentina: Thick, rich beef stew
Manzo girato al fuoco: Beef grilled on a spit
Panforte: Cake filled with candied fruits and nuts

This is the region where Chianti is produced—both red and white. Instead of the usual straw-covered bottles, try the *classico* Chianti, which comes in a traditional wine bottle and is much finer.

Venice

The tourist season covers June through August, during which months Venice can be very hot. It's best to try for May, September or October. If you do come during the warm weather, allow time for cooling off at one of the beaches outside Venice, perhaps on the sands of the Lido—and schedule your sightseeing very early or very late in the day.

Venice is accessible by plane, train or car. Let's consider each of these methods in order, because a little explanation is necessary. By plane, you'll arrive at the new, imposing international airport. Whether you are staying at the Lido or around Piazza San Marco, take a motorboat. If you don't mind the cost, hire a private motorboat, but *please* ask the price first. When arriving by train, you'll find porters to carry your bag directly to the dock, where you'll transfer to a motorboat or *vaporetto* (a baby steamboat). The official porter's tariff nowadays is 150 lire for the first bag and 100 lire for each additional one. Arriving by car involves leaving your vehicle at the giant AGIP garage at the end of the mainland highway, because there is no driving within Venice; porters carry your bags to the motorboats for the same tariff as mentioned above. The porters are noted for complaining, but don't pay more. A special island, which will provide parking space for 5,000 cars, is under construction near the Maritime Station because the present parking facilities are not sufficient. It may be completed by the time you read this.

Four centuries ago, Venice was a great world power; today it is a romantic tourist favorite, completely unreal except for the shouting of the gondoliers on the canals, the put-puts of the motorboats and the throngs of tourists everywhere. The only substantial open piece of real estate is Piazza San Marco, filled with cafes, flying pigeons and Americans taking pictures of each other feeding the pigeons. Nearby is the Grand Canal, the principal "street" of Venice; branching off are hundreds of important but smaller canals, and even the narrowest of alleys are water paths. The city's 120 islands are subdivided by slow-moving water and connected by stylized bridges, raised in the center. There are dozens of eye-filling attractions: the Piazza San Marco, the Cathedral of St. Mark, the Campanile (a copy of the original, which just got tired of it all, leaned over and collapsed in 1902), the Bridge of Sighs, the Ducal Palace (also called the Doges' Palace), plus famous art galleries, churches and many rococo palaces. Most fun of all, perhaps, is wandering about on foot through narrow streets, across bridges, into court-yards, along the waterways until finally you're hopelessly lost; then into the nearest *vaporetto* or gondola (to signal one, cry out, "*Ho, gondola!*") and back to your hotel. If you tend toward beach and resort life, you might stay at a Lido hotel, and even if you do not, plan on taking a boat from Venice to see this internationally known length of sand.

If you've come to Venice by auto, a car ferry can take you and your vehicle to the Lido. Ferry boats depart from Piazzale Roma (Tronchetto) at 7:50 A.M., 9:30, noon, 1:40 P.M., 4:10, 5:50, 7:30 and 9:10. In summer, there is an extra evening sailing at 10:45. Rates for cars are reasonable. There are roads on the Lido and you'll get some use out of your car. The Lido is luxurious and smart, but somewhat inconveniently situated for intensive Venetian sightseeing. Although there's a chance to gawk at celebrities and gamble at the casino, the general atmosphere isn't too different from Palm Beach or any other international resort.

See the local islands: close by is San Michele (boats leave the *Fondamenta Nuove*), which is interesting only if you like old cemeteries; continue to Murano, a group of islands famous for glass blowing (before disembark-ing, be sure to ask when the next boat returns to Venice or you might have a longer wait than you want). If you're in the market for glassware, buy it here because it's slightly cheaper than in Venice proper. Caution:

select your glassware, *watch it being packed* and then *take it with you*. Many people have complained about not getting what they purchased; at your hotel, the concierge will arrange for the shipment home.

Not to be confused with Murano is the lace-making island village of Burano (boats depart from *Fondamenta Nuove* and take about forty-five minutes). Burano is a fishing village, old and colorful; pick up a subsequent boat and continue on to marvelous old Torcello to see the tiny church dating back to the seventeenth century. Have lunch and wander about this medieval miniature island.

On a pleasant day, you'll probably enjoy a boat ride to Chioggia, a village loaded with the atmosphere of the Middle Ages. The trip is rather long, about two hours, and small steamers leave from the Riva degli Schiavoni, returning later in the day.

From Venice, there are many interesting short trips: Padua (about twenty-five miles away), a university town that was at its height of fame in the twelfth and thirteenth centuries; roughly twenty miles farther along the same road is Vicenza, a city famous for the buildings designed by Palladio, a renowned sixteenth-century architect. Another hour by car (say, thirty-five miles) brings one to *Verona* (*Two Gentlemen of*, by one William Shakespeare), today a large, thriving city; Verona is chockablock with marvelous old buildings and is a great art city, second only to Florence; art lovers will want to remain for days, weeks, years. The well-preserved Verona Arena is the third largest Roman amphitheater (the Colosseum in Rome, and the Amphitheatre in Capua are larger). It still seats 22,000 spectators (the number was 25,000 during Roman times); open-air opera performances are scheduled during the summer. You can also visit the well-preserved Roman dramatic theater, not far from the cathedral. The powerful fortress of Castelvecchio (Old Castle) on the river houses a well-arranged art museum. The hub of the old town of Verona is the Piazza dei Signori with its marvelous old palaces; the Piazza delle Erbe is adjacent, and this ancient area is still used as a market square. The best hotel here is the Due Torri, located near the Church of Sant'Anastasia. Another good, less expensive hotel is the Colomba d'Oro. An outstanding restaurant is the Twelve Apostles, situated at Corticella San Marco, not too far from the Piazza delle Erbe.

Another good eating spot is the Re Teodorico, situated at Castel San Pietro with a fine view of the city and the river. (Verona is at the eastern edge of the lake region, an area you'll surely want to visit if time permits. This lake area is discussed in some detail subsequently.) Nonart lovers will enjoy several hours just absorbing the general atmosphere of the colorful city. Incidentally, the tomb and residence of Juliet (from the play of the same name) are only suppositions. No one seems to care about Romeo and where *he* was buried. Except us.

Now, how long to allow for a stay in Venice? Not less than two or three days even on the most hurried trip. Not more than a week or ten days on the most leisurely excursion. Venice, wonderful and dreamlike, suddenly can become tedious. The charm of riding a gondola is lessened when you're frequently overcharged by the gondolier; the romance of gliding down a canal is diminished by the miscellaneous garbage floating alongside. The heat and humidity, ordinarily bearable, are subject to magnification when wafted on a sewage breeze. For most people, Venice is a fairyland to be seen and heartily enjoyed—once; the percentage of returning travelers is quite low.

WHAT TO EAT IN VENICE

Pasta a fagioli: Thick soup of beans and *pasta*
Brodetto: Fish soup, often containing many unexpected types of seafood
Gnocchi: Potato or cornmeal dumplings, usually served with a thin tomato sauce
Polenta: Yellow cornmeal
Polenta e osei: Yellow cornmeal with very small game birds and served with a sauce
Baccala mantecato: A Friday specialty of boiled codfish and garlic
Risis e bisi: Rice and green peas, sometimes as a vegetable, sometimes as a thick soup with pieces of meat
Fegato alla Veneziana: Sautéed calves liver and onions prepared with a little wine
Broada: Compote of turnips, for those who like a compote of turnips
Scampi: A Venetian first cousin to shrimp, but better, served grilled or prepared with olive oil and garlic
Granceole: Large crabs, a Venetian specialty and very good
Radicchio: Large radishes of the area

The local cheeses are Pecorino and Montasio. Drink Valpolicella, one of Italy's best light red wines; Bardolino is good with spaghetti dishes. You could never go wrong with Soave, a dry white wine, whenever having fish or veal. Prosecco is so sweet that it's really better with desserts, unless you're unused to dry wines and like sweet types.

The Dolomites

From Venice to the Dolomites, a marvelous area of mountains, snow and small resorts almost due north, is only a matter of three or four hours by car or bus. CIT runs a special bus service from Venice, which leaves Piazzale Roma parking lot at 8 each morning; the bus passes through all the Dolomite high spots and returns in the early evening. If you're planning a stay, remember that the time of the year is important. At Cortina, a leading winter sports area, the winter season runs from December 15 into March, the summer season from June through September; at other times of the year, many (although not all) hotels are closed. But the Dolomites are worth seeing at any time of the year, even during the off season. If you are driving, the route winds through Belluno and Pieve de Cadore, a trip of about 120 miles, but the mountainous roads are open only during the summer. When the highways are impassable, a combination train and electric railway service will take you to Cortina, and it's not a bad way of going; your concierge can get train tickets.

Cortina d'Ampezzo, to use the full name, is an outstanding winter ski resort situated in an incredibly beautiful location and equally ideal for a visit during the summer months. The high summer season from late July well into August is extremely popular, so make reservations.

If you wish to continue onward into the Dolomites, the road from Cortina to Bolzano is twisting and winding, and traffic is very slow, but the view is worthwhile. Driving into Bolzano, the tourist might think himself in Austria, having crossed the border in an absent-minded moment. But don't be misled by the boys in lederhosen and the signs for *Gasthaus* or restaurant. Much of this area formerly belonged to Austria and was involved in the World War I power-politics land shuffles. For this reason you will see bilingual signs (German and Italian) everywhere.

Bolzano has several worthwhile sightseeing possibilities. Most interesting, I think, is the Laubengasse, a narrow arcaded street in the heart of the old town, lined with medieval houses and now Bolzano's main shopping street. Also worthwhile are three fine old churches; these you can spot by their bell towers and walk to them directly. If you like heights, try one of the several cable car rides; the most interesting is the Rittner Cable Car which lifts you high up to the plateau of Oberbozen overlooking sloping vineyards. In town, the best hotel is the Park Hotel Laurin, but it's open only during the summer season. The Hotel Greif, on the main square, is quite comfortable, although not luxurious, but it does serve the best food in town; the Hotel Mondschein is not bad and has the added convenience of a garage with direct access to the hotel. Above the city, with a marvelous view, is another hotel, the Reichrieglerhof, about 1½ miles from the center of town.

This area, known as Alto Adige by the Italians and the Süd Tyrol by Austrians, in recent years has been a real trouble spot. There have been bombings, shootings and fatalities. The Italian-Austrian state of relations is quite delicate in this zone, so please do not get involved in proclaiming your own opinions on political matters. Recently the situation has calmed down considerably. Italy has agreed to give a more realistic degree of self-governing autonomy to the region. However, relations between the German-speaking population and the Italian authorities are not quite perfect, to say the least.

Not far from Bolzano (Bozen in German) is Merano (formerly the Austrian city of Meran, to which the Italians added a final vowel). This favored spot, known for its mild, even climate, has a local panacea—the "grape cure," a custom merely sixteen centuries old. In the autumn, when the Merano grapes are harvested, people still come to take the cure, eating nothing (but nothing) except grapes, grapes, grapes. This would surely cure us of one thing—eating grapes. The famous landmark in Meran is called the Schloss Tirol (Tyrol Castle); this medieval fortress was the headquarters for the Counts of Tirol as early as the 12th century. The leading hotels in Meran are the Grand Hotel Bristol and the Grand Hotel Emma. Don't bother looking for restaurants here; dine at your hotel.

What to Eat in the Dolomites

Gnocchi: Famous dumplings made with cornmeal or potatoes (or even both) served with a sauce and grated cheese

Ravioli: Boiled dough pockets stuffed with cottage cheese, vegetables or meat and served with a thick meat or tomato sauce

Leberknödel: Liver dumplings, an Austrian specialty popular in this region

Tiroler Speckknödel: Dumplings made with bacon and pork, served with sauerkraut.

Selchkarree mit Kraut: Smoker pork chops with sauerkraut.

Tiroler Speck: Literally Tyrolean bacon, but actually a sort of cross between bacon and ham, often served as a snack food with farm bread and a glass of red wine.

Trelaner, Riesling and Traminer are the best of the white wines. Among the red, which are mostly light red in this area, look for Sankt Magdalena, Lagreiner, Teroldego and Kalterer See, which is the best known wine of this region.

The Italian Lakes Region

Somewhat like Switzerland, the various lakes in northern Italy offer charm, lovely restful scenery and comparatively nothing in the way of excitement. At best from April through September, the lake region is delightful, but is this Italy?

Untamed and exotic Lake Garda is east of the main district, making it a sort of orphan—a beautiful orphan with an unusually mild climate for this part of the world. Its western shore is mostly rocky with the road running through tunnels and galleries. But in the southern section where the lake is widest, there are some important resort places: Gardone Riviera on the west shore (the best hotels here are the Grand and Fasano) and Garda on the east shore. At the top (north end) of the lake is the fascinating old town of Riva with a large array of hotels (Sole, Lido Palace, Grand Hotel Riva and many others in less expensive categories). You'll find a string of picturesque little towns along the east shore, and they're pleasant to wander through. Remember that most of the hotels along the shore of Lake Garda are open only from April through September or October. Continuing westward on route 11, you come upon Brescia, a large city with a varied assortment of museums, monuments and churches. The main highway continues on toward Bergamo, a town with upper and lower sections. Bergamo Alta, the heights, has fine old fortifications and ruins. You can, if you wish, continue on to Milan and its many hotels and restaurants or cut across to Como. Among the top hotels in Milan are Principe e Savoia, Continental, Palace, and Excelsior Gallia and the newest Sonesta (350 very comfortable rooms, all air-conditioned), located at the city air terminal and owned by the Hotel Corporation of America. Savini (in Milan) is one of the best restaurants in North Italy. Another good and much less expensive restaurant in Milan is Bagutta, located on the street of the same name; during the warm weather season it has a nice garden area. The main sightseeing stops in Milan include the ponderous but nonetheless graceful Duomo (cathedral) executed in the Gothic style; the painting of the Last Supper by Leonardo da Vinci is in a former monastery hall attached to the Church of Santa Maria delle Grazie; the Sforza Castle, an old fortress that now houses several museums. Of course, you simply must spend an hour in the Galleria Vittorio Emanuele II, just off the Duomo square, where everybody meets; it's the largest and best known of Milan's famous arcades, lined with shops, cafes and restaurants. If you're an opera fan, you should take a short walk from the Galleria to the Teatro della Scala, or La Scala if you prefer, just about the most famous opera house in the world. Performances are given only from December to May. When you sum it all up, Milan is really not a major stop for tourists, although it's pleasant enough for a brief visit.

Como, a resort town, is the starting point for a long (four-hour) boat ride that is almost compulsory for first-time visitors; absolutely delightful and magnificent —if the weather is clement. Lake Como also may be encircled on its shore road by drivers with stamina—the trip is well over 110 miles and worth it for the passengers, but the driver sees comparatively little while concentrating on the many turns.

From Como, go on to Lake Lugano, the neglected lake. Possibly the neglect is justified, because Como and Maggiore have overshadowed it on most counts; so you might as well continue on to Varese (a popular vacation spot with the Milanese) and then into Stresa, which merits some explanation. Stresa (on the east shore of Lake Maggiore) affords all that a plush resort should— luxury hotels, night clubs and even a cog railway to the top of a mountain, conveniently located nearby. But Stresa is much more—maybe not paradise but, at least, the peaceful place to write that great novel, to do some real relaxed planning and to savor delicious coffee and cake at an outdoor cafe, while gazing across the lake and dreamily wishing you could spend the rest of your life here. If you're in the mood to visit Switzerland, take a low-flying excursion plane from Stresa to Locarno.

There's boat service from Stresa to three of the Borromean Islands, and the trip can easily be accomplished in a morning or afternoon excursion. You are cordially urged to make the trip. The Isola Bella has a palace and several small hotels; there are formal gardens and do you know who once slept here? No, not George Washington, Napoleon! Another island, Isola dei Pescatori, is, as its name implies, a fisherman's island and is quite simple and unspoiled and has a quiet little inn where you can get away from it all, particularly at night when the sound of a dropped pin would awaken the populace. Isola Madre, Mother's Island, is wild and tangled and has a famous botanical garden. (The fourth island, the former home of Arturo Toscanini, cannot be visited, for it is privately owned.) It's possible to drive from Stresa to Pallanza and into Intra, where there is ferry service across the lake to Laveno (which shortens the sightseeing time).

West of the lake region, in the northwesternmost corner of Italy, is Val d'Aosta (Aosta Valley) nestled alongside the highest peaks of the Alps at the edge of the Swiss and French borders. Although geographically part of Piedmont, Val d'Aosta is a self-governing autonomous region because of its French-speaking population. The small city of Aosta (about 35,000 inhabitants), the capital of this region, has some important Roman relics, such as the Arch of Augustus (Aosta was founded in 24 B.C. by Augustus), the remains of an amphitheater and city walls, as well as several towers and gates; the early medieval Cathedral of Saint-Ours has a beautiful 12th-century cloister. But the most interesting aspects of this region are the numerous spectacular side valleys leading to summer and winter mountain resorts clustered under the high peaks, such as Gressoney under Monte Rosa, Valtournanche and Breuil-Cervinia under the Matterhorn (Cervino, in Italian) and Courmayeur under Mont Blanc, the highest mountain in Europe. From Courmayeur you can drive through a 7-mile tunnel to Chamonix, the famous French resort and climbing base for Mont Blanc; or you can cross over to Chamonix by means of a spectacular aerial cable car system which takes you 12,000 feet high through the Mont Blanc scenery.

The best gateway to the Aosta region is the city of Turin, the capital of Piedmont and the home of the Fiat automobile. The factories are located outside the city, and Turin's center is marked by beautiful straight streets crossing at right angles; the architecture shows considerable French influence. Some of the outstanding architectural monuments, mostly from the baroque period, include the Palazzo Madama, the Royal Palace, and the Palazzo Carignani where the first Italian Parliament met more than a century ago (at the time of the political unification of Italy). A funny-looking structure and a landmark of Turin is the Mole Antonelliana, built in 1863 by an architect named Antonelli; it's a palace topped by a steep cupola, which is further topped by a needle-like steeple reaching to a height of over 550 feet. Turin is also known for its production of vermouth; Turin is the home of the Martini family, the famous vermouth producers. There are several good hotels available, the best having the grandiose name Excelsior Grand Hotel Principi di Piemonte, located in the center of the Via Gobetti and close to everything. There are also several fine restaurants, among them the historic Cambio (on Carignano Square) and the Villa Sassi (about 2 miles out of town) with a nice garden. The breadsticks you see in every Italian restaurant (*grissani*) originated here.

WHAT TO EAT IN THE LAKES REGION

Minestrone: The famous thick vegetable soup with beans and pasta

Zuppa alla pavese: Soup with eggs and toast

Risotto alla certosina: Rice with seafood and mushrooms

Risotto alla Milanese: Rice, colored and flavored with saffron and cheese

Costoletta alla Milanese: Fried breaded veal cutlet or chop

Osso buco: Braised veal knuckle, usually served with *risotto*

Agnolotti: A local version of ravioli—stuffed envelopes of dough

Fonduta con tartuffi: A melted cheese dish served with truffles, which are in season during the fall

Gnocchi alla fontina: Small dumplings made of semolina flour and fontina cheese

Camoscio in salmi: Chamois (a kind of deer) cooked with oil, garlic, wine, anchovies and herbs

The cheeses in the Milan region and to the north include Gorgonzola (usually eaten with a pear), Fontina, Stracchino, Robiola and one of the very best in Italy, Bel Paese, mild and delightful.

Wines: Inferno, Sassella (about the best red in this region). Chiaretto del Garda is a rosé wine that is so light and pleasant that it can be drunk with just about everything. The best red wines of Italy are produced in this general area of Piedmont; these include Barbera, Barolo and Barbaresco. The Italian version of champagne, Asti Spumante, is made here; it's all right but pretty sweet.

The Italian Riviera

Extending east and south from the French border, this is the Italian coastal extension of that fabulous playground the Côte d'Azur. It's divided into two parts—the Riviera di Ponente (from the border to Genoa) and the Riviera di Levante (from Genoa southeast to Viareggio). Here the Italians have modified the French notion of what constitutes an international pleasure coast. In France, life is superluxurious, expensive and *très gai*; on the Italian side, life is quieter, less expensive, slower-paced and considerably more individualistic. The Italian answer to the French Riviera is a long series of beaches, a coastline literally swarming with people and flowers and a social life toned down to comparative moderation. Come anytime to the Italian Riviera and you'll find fairly good weather; during the winter months, days are mild (although swimming temperatures are improbable); the summers are warm but rarely hot. Rain comes on occasion, notably during the late autumn. Start at the border and continue along the coastline; if you've driven down from Paris, cross the French-Italian line at Menton and at Ventimiglia, continuing on in the direction of Rome. Ventimiglia is famous for its outdoor market, held on Fridays, on a street lined with palms, just behind the main street of the town. You can buy a wide assortment of surprising and routine objects here; do a little bargaining first. There is a good flower market (except that it does not operate during the warm months from the middle of June until late September), which gets under way at 2:30 P.M. daily. The old town across the river, with two churches from the 11th century, is interesting.

From Ventimiglia head on to Bordighera via route 1, the modern counterpart of an ancient Roman consular road, the Via Aurelia. Bordighera is a town where flowers grow the way weeds flourish for most amateur gardeners. A large bouquet of sweet-smelling posies sells in the out-door market for less than a dollar. If you wish, send a bouquet to anyone in Europe for a couple of dollars or so—the price includes shipping *and* the flowers. San Remo, famous for its climate, is the exception on the Italian Rivera—a large resort town with all of the paraphernalia of its French equivalent: fancy hotels, expensive restaurants, a gambling casino and a golf course.

Alassio is a small resort with a good beach, largely occupied by retired British government officials and former colonels in the Bengal Lancers (or so it seems). Farther along is Albenga, a small community with several medieval showplaces and a Roman bridge; at Finale there are some famous caves; little Spotorno is pretty and in-viting for a beach holiday, but don't bother with Savona, because it is too industrialized for tourists. Here is where you run upon the new *autostrada* (superhighway) di-rectly to Genoa, a city of about 700,000 people.

Genoa is a busy, hustling seaport, and most of the city's active life and color naturally center about the har-bor. The old part of town is seedy and down at the heels but very interesting for meandering about, preferably on foot, for most of the streets are extraordinarily narrow. If time permits, visit the Cathedral of San Lorenzo; see also some of the remaining mementos of Genoa's great maritime history—notably the Rosso, Dogi and Doria Pamphili palaces. Nothing will be lost, however, if you pass up all of Genoa's stock sights and concentrate in-stead on wandering about on your own and absorbing local color. Not to mention drinking a glass of wine and consuming a large bowl of Genoa's famous fish soup, *buridda di pesci.*

From Genoa on, the coastal region is known as the Riviera di Levante, and instead of the quiet seascapes to the west, the coastline now tends toward the unruly and unusual, which is all the more interesting from the traveler's viewpoint. The first town heading eastward is

Nervi (see the marvelous exotic garden), followed by Bogliasco, completely unimportant but very colorful. Recco can be disregarded, but Camogli is agreeable for a short stop, principally because of its picturesque location, crowded against a mountain and arranged around a small bay. Then comes the important resort town of Rapallo, world famous for its charm and color and deserving of a few days' stay, or in any event, a visit anytime you happen to be nearby. If you're feeling romantic, take a *carrozza*, a horse and buggy, or drive your car to Santa Margherita Ligure, a nearby, quiet seaside resort. Farther down the peninsula one comes to the gem of the area, Portofino, about as picturesque, delightful and physically attractive as any fishing village has a right to be— and perhaps Portofino overdoes it, at that. It borders on the verge of being just a shade too perfect, too precious, almost like a stage setting. If you do stay for a few days, take a short boat trip to the end of the point to see San Fruttuouso, a little fishing port blocked off from communications by the mountains; there are several other boat services to odd little spots you won't want to miss if time permits. There is a delightful hotel in Portofino called the Splendido, an imposing name indeed for this pleasing place, which has gardens all about it. Rooms are attractive, prices are high, but it's the best in Portofino.

On the way once more (if you can tear yourself away from Rapallo and Portofino), you'll pass Chiavari, which has a fine bathing beach, and arrive at La Spezia, an important port. You'll want to drive to the point of the cape, Porto Venere, an extremely attractive fishing village. Even better than driving is the boat trip; at Porto Venere, occasional boatmen may be prevailed upon to take you to the Palmaria Islands to see the Grotta Azzurra (Blue Grotto) and Grotta dei Colombi. (There is also boat service from La Spezia to Lerici, another attractive resort, which has several medieval houses.)

Back on route 1, the road travels through Sarzana; nearby are the ruins of Luni, an old Etruscan village; if you're not in a hurry, a side trip like this can be very rewarding, and it gets you off the main road. Farther along on route 1, you'll see a left-hand turn to Carrara, home of the famous marble; there is an opportunity to visit the quarries and watch the sawing and polishing of the marble. The next town is Massa. The last stop on the Riviera is Viareggio, a resort particularly popular with the Italian equivalent of Paris' Left Bank intellectuals. But that's being unfair to Viareggio's snowy white sands and the pine forests nearby. If you're fortunate enough to arrive at the time, you'll find a marvelous carnival just before Lent.

Viareggio is where Shelley drowned in a shipwreck, and his ashes were scattered along the beach by his friend Byron. A monument has been erected at the spot where it is believed his body was washed ashore. You'll notice, perhaps, that the pines along the beach have a burned, scorched, dark-brown look. They say that the ill winds from seaward bring with them some element (a few say diesel fumes; others, just plain salt) that has been turning the pines brown.

From the roof of the Palace Hotel (which, incidentally, serves some of the finest food in Italy), there is a magnificent view of the sea-front promenade. The landscaping on the sea boulevard varies from block to block, making a different pattern in each street. The Viareggio area gets as many as 120,000 (!) visitors on a very busy day, but there is plenty of room. The visitors spread out along a fourteen-mile strip of sand, called the Versiglia Riviera, because the Versiglia River sweeps into the sea near here.

Viareggio has night life aplenty. The most elegant "night" (the Italian word for night club) is the Oliviero —a wide terrace of palms and lanterns (yes—it is as romantic as it sounds), restaurants, dance floor and, in a restored villa, a comfortable bar furnished the way you wish your living room was. The Oliviero is operated by the same folks who have the Club 84 in Rome's Via Veneto zone. It is open for two months in the summer only.

The Sporting Restaurant looks out on a private small-boat harbor. It is excellently furnished—a sit-down bar, discothèque, and other sparkling amenities. It is open for about three to four months during the summer. The Sporting is right on the beach, so you can come directly from a swim or a sunbath to the lunch table. A fabulous lunch will await you, too. It is on the expensive side. Bussala means "compass," and when a top attraction (of international standing) is being presented at the Bussala, the folks come from all points (of the compass). It has a big dance floor, plus several other rooms—upstairs, downstairs, everywhere (and something is going on in each of them all the time). The Bussala packs them in by the thousands. It is not inexpensive, but it is very enjoyable.

While in Viareggio, treat yourself to a ride on one of the double-decker dark-green buses that operate along the seafront as far as Forte di Marmi. The buses are imperiously called *imperiali*, and the hightop view is a royal one.

Aliscafi (hydrofoils) now operate between Viareggio, Elba and Bastia, located on France's Corsica (and Napoleon's birthplace). Each summer the feature is an international boat race (usually in July) between Viareggio and Bastia. Americans invariably win (that's a fact —we're not just boasting), and they seem to come from the Miami area (the Nassau races, apparently give them a chance to train).

Looking for a place that's a little off the beaten path? Why not give a thought to the island of Elba, where Napoleon spent some time, and where you can get away from it all? From Viareggio, it's only a matter of about seventy-five miles to Piombino, reached by driving southward to Livorno (also called Leghorn in English, for reasons that escape us), and then through Cecina, turning off for Piombino at the village of San Vincenzo. There is good boat service, taking about 1¼ hours, running about four times a day and taking you and your car to Elba's leading town, Portoferraio. Here, the best hotel is the Darsena. For car reservations on the ferry, wire ahead to the steamship company, the Navigazione Toscana, at Piombino or stop at the company's office in the Piazza Micheli in Livorno. Hotels are springing up all over Elba now. If you like the beach, there is a nice hotel at Procchio, a beautiful spot. Don't look for night life or excitement, but a marvelous, low-pressure rest. Another village, Poggio, has a good hotel favored by artists and writers.

WHAT TO EAT ON THE ITALIAN RIVIERA

Zuppa di diattero (also *pesce*): Seafood soup or chowder
Trenette al pesto: Noodles flavored with *pesto* (garlic, basil, oil, nuts, cheese)
Pasta: Almost any sort of spaghetti dish will be good in this region; near Genoa, inevitably served with *pesto* sauce
Ravioli alla Genovese: Squares of dough, stuffed with various mixtures and served with a thick sauce
Fritti misti: Assorted fried seafood
Funghi trifolati: A chopped mushroom dish

Torta pasqualina: Cottage cheese, green vegetables and eggs baked between layers of dough

Stoccafisso: A dried codfish dish with anchovies, olives and walnuts

Antipasto di mare: Mixed seafood salad with squid, clams, mussels, shrimp and oil and lemon juice dressing

Cappon magro: A fish salad with vegetables and olives

No important cheese produced here. The wines aren't too memorable either. Cinque Terre is a sweet white wine; Coronata is a metallic, dry white wine.

MISCELLANEOUS ¶ If you have questions or require any information about Italy, contact the Italian State Tourist Office (ENIT) at 2 Via Marghera in Rome. It is only a block or two from the main railroad station. The bureau is most obliging and will give you full details about fairs, festivals and special events, in addition to run-of-the-mill tourist matters. National and/or provincial tourist offices are in all major cities, and each town and city has an official tourist office as well. These offices are usually right in the center of town.

It may come as a surprise to learn that Italian women are still (sometimes) dominated by their husbands; don't comment on this (even humorously), because it won't be appreciated. Married women rarely attend the theater, or even go to a restaurant without their husbands or at least some male member of their immediate family.

In the same vein, if a young lady sits alone at a cafe, according to Italian custom, this constitutes an open invitation for local young men to come over and start a conversation. Young women traveling alone should bear this in mind—if they do, or don't, want to attract the attention of the local conversationalists.

Do your shopping in places where the product is manufactured; for example, leather work in Florence is cheaper than anywhere else in Italy and there is a wider selection.

Take along as many American cigarettes as you'll need; they're fairly expensive throughout Italy.

Most cities have *alberghi diurni*, day hotels, where the weary sightseer can find (at a reasonable price) all sorts of facilities he needs (and without paying for a hotel room)—hot baths, pressing service for suits or dresses, refreshments, shoe shine and so forth. It's a genuine pleasure to freshen up during the middle of the afternoon on an all-day sightseeing trip, particularly when the weather is hot.

Most Americans automatically order Chianti wine in Italy; don't, unless you're in the Chianti district (near Florence). There are dozens of better wines your waiter will recommend if you can't remember the names.

About before-dinner drinks: while the smart folk in Rome drink expensive Scotch, it's scarce elsewhere and the Italians don't believe in drinking hard liquor before dinner anyway. If you want to go along with the Roman way of doing things (almost said, "When in Rome . . ."), try their version of predinner drinks. An Americano is made with vermouth, bitters (Campari) and soda; it is exactly like cough medicine. If you don't like that, try Cinzano (say chin-sano) and soda; it tastes exactly like cough medicine. If not, try Rabarbaro and soda; it tastes exactly like rhubarb-flavored cough medicine. All are tastes you'll get to like. Or not.

Beauty parlors and barber shops are very good and represent marvelous values. Permanents are an outstanding buy for women.

Don't bargain at large department stores, important shops and the like. However, be sure to haggle a little at small places, particularly the souvenir shops. If you buy a substantial amount, ask for a discount.

As mentioned, tap water is safe in most large towns, but you might exercise a little care in a primitive village. Call for bottled water, and remember that Fiuggi and San Pellegrino are both good.

Many drugs that require a prescription in the United States are sold without this requirement in Italian pharmacies; bring the empty bottle with you and the druggist may be able to cater to your needs.

As in France, the price for breakfast is unwarrantedly high. In most First Class hotels, you'll pay about a dollar for rolls and coffee, which is much too much, but it's the Italian way of charging slightly less for the hotel room and making it up on food. If you should order fresh orange juice, watch the bill shoot up. Eggs, ham and other American breakfast items are expensive extras.

No matter how well intentioned, jokes or unfriendly comments about the Pope are unappreciated. If your host says anything critical, he may object to your joining in. (You can criticize your own family—but strangers better stay out!)

When using older model public telephones, you have to press a button when the person you're calling answers. Otherwise, your party won't be able to hear you, and you won't be in communication.

ॐ A Tour of North Italy

FLORENCE, PERUGIA, VENICE, ETC.

(If your time is limited, you may want to take the superhighway, the autostrada, which runs from outside of Rome to just above Terni. Obviously, if you take the autostrada, you will see other autos on the road, and not too much else, whereas the route described below is far more interesting, but slower. Of course, the autostrada can get very jammed, particularly on weekends or holidays.)

Rome to Spoleto—79 miles

Your starting point from Rome is at the foot of Piazza di Spagna, the Spanish Steps. Head north on the Via del Babuino (a narrow, one-way street running in the desired direction) and at the Tiber watch for signs pointing to Terni.

The road is often heavily traveled but as a rule the mileage to the first town, Civita Castellana, should be easily accomplished although the going is slow at first. The next town is Narni, located beside fields of olive groves; there isn't any place worth stopping at for a meal (hungry so soon?) until Terni, which has the more than acceptable Restaurant Allegretti. After Terni the road widens encouragingly, only to narrow down heading into Spoleto; although the highway skirts the town, it's worth a visit, what with more than 3,000 years of history behind it. The Gian-Carlo Menotti festival is held here during late June and early July, should you be in the vicinity about that time of year. There are two good (and quite new) hotels in Spoleto—Dei Duchi and Clarici; during the festival, it's best to have a confirmed reservation. Just outside of Spoleto, strategically located on a hill, is another new hotel, the Del Matto. Don't worry about food—the town is filled with restaurants, some simple and unpretentious and others heavily encrusted with modern eighteenth-century décor, including frescoes on the ceiling (still damp). About festival tickets: you'd do well to get them in advance through CIT, the Italian travel organization, in Rome. After the theater, there are loads of places (even night clubs!) with music, for those who like to stay up late.

Spoleto to Perugia——43 miles

The next town is delightful Trevi, beautifully situated slightly off the road on the side of a hill in a terraced effect and constructed almost completely of cut stone in a definite medieval style. Next comes Foligno, whose principal attraction is its magnificently designed cathedral; Spello is a miniature masterpiece of Italian architecture, if you're in the mood to inspect it. Most tourists hustle on (via route 75) to Assisi (a short distance to the right off the main road), the town made famous by St. Francis, who befriended not only the birds but also the beasts. The town is peaceful, drenched (when it isn't raining!) in hot sunshine and meditative silence most of the time, conveying a feeling of relaxed timelessness. Bus tours arrive, disgorging people who visit the Basilica di San Francesco and are gone within a matter of minutes. If time permits, wander about the almost silent streets of Assisi, absorbing its peacefulness and thinking of the saintly man who brought it fame. Possibly the gentle quality of Assisi will hold you; if you wish to remain overnight, there is the Hotel Subasio, by far the best in town for a room and a good dinner.

The next town is one of considerable importance—Perugia; this is a chocolate manufacturing town and the delightful aroma is frequently encountered. Here the leading hotel is the Brufani Palace (some of whose rooms overlook a valley resembling the classic paintings of the Italian countryside to be seen in local museums); rooms facing the front are inclined to be noisy, because the populace likes to gather until late at night in the adjacent park. The town's best restaurant is located on the main street; La Trasimeno has the air of a place that knows its food is good, and it is. Ask if they have any local specialties of the mountains when you're there—trout, mushrooms, cheese.

Perugia to Rimini——123 miles

Leave Perugia by the Via 14 Settembre, route 3-*bis*, (*bis* merely referring to a division of route 3) to Bosco and Umbertide (although the signs frequently point to Gubbio, another town on the way). At first the road is quite good, but it deteriorates before Città di Castello; the castle for which the city is named may be seen on the left side as you enter the town. At San Giustino, there are a series of right turns (watch for them!) onto route 73-*bis* heading toward Urbino. The road turns to gravel, although it's not too bad for traveling; there is a steep ascent leading to the saddle of the mountain, the Bocca Trabária, where there is a small inn, should you wish some refreshment. The descent is fairly steep, too, but

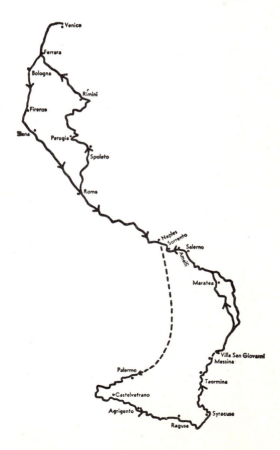

not troublesome. A few miles before the village of Borgo Pace, the road is paved once again and quite straight. Don't turn left into Borgo Pace, for the main road (which we want) bypasses that small community. At Urbánia (not to be confused with the next town, which has a similar name), the road begins to climb once again until you reach Urbino, where you enter through the town gates and climb up the hill. You'll see a sign directing you to the house of the great painter Raphael. For the moment, proceed to the right toward the Ducal Palace and the National Gallery of the Marches, with its remarkable art collection. The Ducal Palace is definitely worth visiting; it was here that Duke Federigo held court and gathered about him all of the talented artists and writers of that prolific era in which he reigned. The results of his support of artistic endeavors and his superb palace may have to be seen somewhat hurriedly, because there is no satisfactory hotel for an overnight stay. The Restaurant Raffaelo is more than adequate for lunch, though quite simple. Much of the city's original medieval wall still stands, and Urbino, we think, has been unfairly neglected, principally because of its lack of a suitable hotel—and how did the Jolly Hotel people (with their chain of new hotels in the south of Italy) ever forget about Urbino? Just outside of town at San Bernadino is the mausoleum where the renowned duke lies (just a short detour off the main road). The next town is Pesaro (on the Adriatic Sea), where a stay could be made at the small Hotel Royal. For those not planning a stopover in Pesaro, watch for a sharp left turn on the outskirts of town, directing the motorist (via route 16) to Rimini, the Atlantic City of Italy. Here you'll find literally hundreds upon hundreds of hotels, but the Internazionale and Villa Bianca may be recommended; the Grand Hotel is the great lady of the Old World hotels. There is an excellent restaurant in the center of the older part of town (away from the sea) called Vecchia Rimini, which is extremely good. However, if you should find yourself on the seashore (off the main road, however), you might head for the long breakwater that points out into the sea. There are several restaurants on the breakwater, none too remarkable, but satisfactory if you want fresh grilled fish; besides, eating on a terrace facing the Adriatic with the ripple of the waters at your feet is delightful. Yes, this is the Adriatic, and from here on better think in terms of seafood. The *scampi* are like shrimp, but are twice as good; if you see *coda di rospo* on a menu, try it; it's an unusual Adriatic fish with a heavy spine but no bones.

SIDE TRIP TO SAN MARINO—29 MILES ROUND TRIP ¶ By all means, take off a few hours for an extremely worthwhile trip to San Marino, still an independent republic, although dozens of conquerors have made unsuccessful efforts to conquer this miniature stronghold.

Drive southwestward (away from the sea) from the center of Rimini on route 72, a road called the Via San Marino. Driving from Pesaro into Rimini, it's a left turn a few blocks after you see a large stadium on your right hand. The road is well paved and level but soon begins to climb to the heights of San Marino, a picturesque picture-postcard of a town, surrounded by its original fortified walls. San Marino, to be blunt, exists today solely because of tourism, but tourists can't change San Marino, which is fascinating and worthwhile. Don't stop at the first parking area, unless you want to admire the view, but continue up the narrow road some 200 feet higher to a large open area, which is closer to more interesting sights.

You'll want to climb to the heights and wander through the old town and buy some of San Marino's postage stamps at the local post office (they're so used to tourists requesting stamps that they have an assortment in a cellophane envelope, costing about a quarter). Try San Marino's sparkling white wine (not much more than a dime a glass); very refreshing, but stop at three if you're doing the driving! The best accommodations are at the Hotel Diamond, with a marvelous view of the countryside; the best food is probably at the Restaurant Diamond. (Return to Rimini by the same road.)

Rimini to Ferrara—81 miles

Leave Rimini on route 16 heading toward Ravenna; on the way you'll pass Cesenatico (with its colorful fishing fleet) and Cervia. Ravenna, with its long history, is a pleasant little town, although the outskirts are a bit grimy; of course, our old standby, a Jolly Hotel, very modern but with small rooms, may be found on the right-hand side coming into town. But the big attraction here is the famous series of mosaics, tiny bits of colors arranged with unbelievable skill and artistry, which attract art lovers from all over the world. First you'll want to head for an extremely lovely and graceful building, the Basilica of San Vitale; the mosaics here are probably among the finest to be found anywhere. Nearby is the Mausoleum of Galla Placidia, which from the exterior is unimpressive, but where you will find more remarkable mosaics. The mausoleum contains the Empress Galla Placidia and two emperors, the interior quickly suggesting the tomb scene from *Romeo and Juliet*, with daylight, the only source of illumination, filtering in, softly hued, through thin sheets of marble and alabaster. Don't expect to enjoy these mosaics fully until your eyes have been accustomed to the dim light, a matter of five minutes or more.

From Ravenna to Ferrara there is a flat, level road where fast time may be made if the trucking isn't too heavy (tip—it's often lightest from noon to 2 P.M.). At Ferrara, the outstanding attraction is the Castello Estense, the remarkable survival of a medieval castle with all the atmosphere of those terrible and wonderful times. In Ferrara, the route passes through the center of town, alongside some fascinating outdoor markets. Worth exploring, too, if you like pushcart bargains. Ferrara has the Astra Hotel and the somewhat smaller San Giorgio Hotel. The Touring Hotel is very modern, something like an American motel; try the Grotta Azzurra for local food specialties.

Ferrara to Venice—69 miles

(If you wish, there's an autostrada, *which may be picked up just to the west of Ferrara, which runs just to the outskirts of Mestre.)*

From Ferrara head (route 16) for Rovigo; if you're hungry, the Restaurant Granatiere in Rovigo is the place at which you'll want to dine. Then into Padova, or Padua as we (for unknown reasons) call it in English. Padua is a town renowned for its food; to uphold its reputation, Padua boasts the grand-style Toscanelli Restaurant and the simpler, but really remarkable, Dotto Restaurant, where you should have a *risotto*, rice with seafood, the great specialty of this region. Or, if you're not watching your weight, try a *polenta*, the classic cornmeal dish. Padua is a town frequently bypassed by tourists anxious to hurry on to Venice, but if it's early in the day, spare at least an hour or two for Padua and its sights. The most notable attraction is the Cappella degli Scrovegni, with frescoes by none other than the great master Giotto. In the center of town, there is a lively piazza worth wandering around.

From Padua a superhighway (*autostrada*) leads into Mestre, a rather dull town from a tourist's point of view. However, for those arriving in the very late afternoon or evening who would prefer to enter Venice bright and early the next morning, an overnight stay could be recommended at the new Hotel Tritone in Mestre. If it's raining heavily, better delay your arrival into Venice, because transportation in that waterbound city is somewhat difficult when the weather is bad.

From Mestre, there's a good wide road leading toward Venice; at land's end, you'll see a large garage on your right hand. At this building, the AGIP garage, you'll have to leave your car. (If you're staying at Lido, it may be ferried over. Lido is just about the only stretch of land near Venice where there are automobile roads.) First, drive into the garage and deposit your luggage at the center island; everyone but the driver can remain in the waiting room. An English-speaking attendant will tell you on which floor to leave your car; drive up the circular ramp to the designated floor, select any vacant space and lock up. An attendant on that floor will give you a ticket; ride the elevator down to the street level, present the ticket to the cashier and obtain a receipt for your car.

A porter will then carry your luggage, held together with a series of straps, down to the canal. You'll have to readjust yourself to the fact that you're at land's end and just about everything from here on in the line of transportation requires a boat. You'll have your choice of a gondola (for romantics), or a motorboat which is more expensive (but worth it on rainy days).

Venice's most elegant hotel is the 100-room Gritti Palace, closely followed by the larger, popular Bauer Grünwald, Danieli Royal Excelsior and Grand hotels, all four with fabulous locations on the picturesque canals. Smaller and more modest are the Continental and Splendid-Suisse hotels. Venice has many good restaurants, but we'll single out for special mention Taverna La Fenice for its marvelous food and Quadri for its elegance and location on the Piazza San Marco. A few minutes off-shore, there's the excellent Cipriani Hotel, which has nice rooms and top food.

One way to combine a beach vacation with a visit to Venice is by staying at Lido, or Venice-Lido as it is sometimes called. At Lido, there is a good beach and a large selection of hotels. The elaborate, palace-style hotel is exemplified in Lido by the Excelsior Palace, an enormous establishment with very large rooms. The Excelsior is often filled with celebrities, especially during the film festival, otherwise by tourists who don't mind paying its fairly high prices. The Italians seem to prefer the Grand Hotel des Bains, which is much less expensive. One advantage of going to Lido, as mentioned previously, is that your car can be taken along, which avoids the necessity of a baggage transfer.

Lovers of good food would surely enjoy an excursion to Torcello on a sunny day. Boats leave from in front of Harry's Bar (not far from San Marco), and the speedy motorboats take about forty-five minutes to the peaceful little island. It's advisable to make a reservation at Harry's Bar and be sure to show up just before noon, when the boats leave. At Torcello, you'll find a charming inn, the Locanda Ciprioni, where the food is extremely good. There are even a few rooms for true lovers of peace and quiet, but be forewarned—there's nothing to do here but eat and sleep and relax.

(There are more details about Venice in the main section on Italy.)

Pointer: There is a new car-plus-passenger service running between Venice and the Israeli port of Haifa, with stops at the Greek ports of Piraeus and Rhodes and at Cyprus. This service is operated by the Epirotiki Lines, using the good ship *Hermes*; the American agents are the Greek Line, 10 Bridge Street, New York. The voyage takes about three days to Piraeus, about six days to Haifa.

SIDE TRIP ¶ About 100 miles east of Venice, jammed between the sea and the Yugoslavian border, is the historic port city of Trieste. Trieste belonged to Austria for almost five centuries (prior to 1918), and was the chief port of the old Austrian Empire. Trieste once had been an independent maritime republic and voluntarily joined Austria back in the fourteenth century, by petitioning the Emperor to take it under his protection. This action was prompted by Trieste's fear of the more powerful Venice (then a separate city-state with its own government and navy). It was a good situation for both Trieste and Austria, and Trieste became the Empire's chief port, the greatest in the entire Mediterranean. During the power politics of World War I, Italy was promised Trieste if she would enter the war on the side of the British and French; she did so, and received Trieste as a prize in 1918. However, after Italy took control, the port traffic ebbed to almost nothing. It picked up somewhat after World War II but never returned to its former eminence. After the war Trieste became a free territory, from 1945 to 1953. By an agreement entered into in 1953 by Britain, the United States, Italy and Yugoslavia, the city was returned to Italy while most of the surrounding area was given to Yugoslavia. The port area is a sort of promenade these days for the local citizens; the downtown area still has an Austrian appearance. The best place for an overnight stay is the Grand Hotel de la Ville facing the port; there is also a Jolly Hotel, but it could stand a little refurbishing. Trieste's cuisine is a strange but interesting mixture of the various nationalities which have made it their home over the centuries. But whatever you select, put your trust in the local seafood, which is superb. Now, where to dine? Al Bragozzo, on the waterfront, is exceptionally good; nearby, you'll find the Nastro Azzurro.

Venice to Bologna—104 miles

(As you'll recall, there's an autostrada *which may be picked up outside of Mestre, which runs to the outskirts of Bologna. Not much can be seen on this superhighway, but it's usually a faster trip than the one described below. It can become very crowded, however, on weekends.)*

To leave Venice, you'll have to go back to the mainland and the AGIP garage; pay your auto storage bill (which is quite moderate) at the cashier's office on the ground floor, get a receipt and take the elevator to the proper floor, drive down the circular ramp, load your baggage and take off in a matter of minutes. The route is a duplicate of the one used entering Venice; at first you ride back to Mestre, then to Padua. After Padua, it's route 16 heading back to Rovigo and Ferrara. At Ferrara, take route 64 to Bologna, but don't even bother looking for the route number, because there are dozens of signs to set you in the right direction. The road is quite fast, and the thirty miles between Ferrara and Bologna shouldn't take very long.

Getting settled for the night in Bologna involves three pleasant choices. To begin with, there is the very large, old-fashioned Hotel Majestic Baglioni, but be sure to ask for rooms away from the heavily trafficked main street, the Via dell Indipendenza, that is, if you're one of those soft, coddled Americans who likes to sleep at night. Smaller and very modern is the Hotel Cristallo, with very satisfactory accommodations; and of course, need we mention that our old friend, the Jolly Hotel, has a new place here?

Bologna is a town of thinkers and eaters. The thinkers are in the city's renowned university, historically a center of learning and culture for many centuries. For some reasons, and a good problem for psychiatrists, just as the French are the epicures of all Europe, so the Bolognese citizens are the epicures of all Italy. A walk through the marketplaces, particularly those leading off that lively open square the Piazza Maggiore e Neuttuno, are calculated to make the eyes open wide, the mouth water. Was there ever such an assortment of salamis and sausages, or fancy shapes of spaghetti and other pastas—who had the patience to arrange the fruits and vegetables so lovingly? Of course, you'll probably want to tear yourself away from all this long enough to see the Garisenda Tower, which leans alarmingly, much like the more famous one in Pisa; several of the famous churches are worth inspecting, too, although none of these is truly outstanding. To be crude, people come to Bologna to eat, and eat they do. There is a wide choice of restaurants, but may we mention the Restaurant Sampieri, a turn-of-the-century establishment where the high quality of Bolognese cookery is kept not only alive, but wide awake. Just order any one of the featured spaghetti or noodle dishes and you'll know why people come to Bologna to eat. Also renowned is Al Pappagallo, a famous restaurant. The local folk, however, strongly urge visitors to have a meal at a simple place called Nerina, where they say the food is truly in the Bolognese style; to this we can only add our note of agreement. But be sure to go hungry—in fact, very hungry.

Bologna to Florence—67 miles

(There's an autostrada *starting just south of Bologna, which runs to the outskirts of Florence. The* autostrada *is an alternate route to the one described below.)*

Leave Bologna via the Via Santo Stefano, a straight road that later becomes route 65 heading due south toward Florence (or Firenze, as it is called in Italy). You'll see many signs directing you there, so there's no need to worry about route numbers. Once out of town, the road begins to wind and climb, and although you'll find yourself averaging rather low speeds because of the hilly turns and the difficulties of passing other vehicles on an upgrade, the local countryside is more than worth glancing at; every view suggests the sort of Italianate landscape paintings you've seen before and will see afresh in Florence. After passing the observatory, the road begins a gradual descent intermixed with a good number of brief ascents. Once in Florence, don't follow the directional markers, because these will take you to the outskirts of the city, and you do want to get settled in your hotel. Most of the hotels are near the Arno River; ask a policeman for directions to the river. (If it's the main season, we sincerely hope that you have made an advance reservation, because Florence is in the heart of the tourist country and rooms are inevitably scarce.)

The two largest hotels are the Grand and Excelsior-Italia, across the Piazza Ognissanti from each other and fronting onto the Arno River. Just a trifle smaller is the Baglioni e Palace on the very diverting Piazza Unità Italiana; at Santa Maria Novella square, not far from the main railroad station, is the smaller Minerva Hotel. Two nice smaller places, fronting onto the Arno River, are the Mediterraneo and the Plaza Hotel Lucchesi, situated to the east of the center of town. For light sleepers (and Florence can be very noisy on summer nights), and also for those who want to stay somewhat out of the main part of the city, give thought to a place called the Villa Belvedere, located on a hill called Poggio Imperiale. This hotel is a remodeled private house, with gardens, a swimming pool and quite good food. Near the south exit of the Highway of the Sun is the new Esso Motel. The restaurant situation is quite good here, for the food in Florence is usually extremely well prepared and you should dine well wherever you go. Between noon and 3 P.M. almost everything else is closed, so take a long luxurious lunch hour (or hours); in the heat of summer, most tourist attractions are locked tight until about 5 P.M. May we intervene only to point out one luxurious dining spot where the food is likely to be memorable—Sabatini, in the center of town. If you don't mind sharing your table with strangers and do enjoy a great deal of informal, pleasant chatter, you owe yourself a lunch (but go early) at the very unfancy Trattoria Sostanza (25 Via del Porcellana), just up a side street from the Excelsior Hotel. The food is absolutely superb, particularly the hot chicken livers on toast, the bean dishes and, well, just about anything. In this region (Tuscany) everyone drinks Chianti, usually of a better quality than you've previously experienced.

Florence, the mecca of all tourists, has so many attractions that you'll find it difficult to see them all unless you stay for at least a week. During the late Middle Ages, for reasons not completely clear even now, this remarkable city became the center for great architects, sculptors, poets and painters. The two great art galleries, Uffizi and Pitti, could involve days of straight sightseeing for the ardent lover of Italian art. By all means begin with the Uffizi, and if you'll take our tip, *ride* to the top in the small elevator and walk down.

The unexpected translation of the word "Uffizi" is "Offices," for in point of fact, this building was the administration center for the government of Duke Cosimo I. Later, his son created the present picture gallery. For centuries, the powerful Medici family had bought, borrowed, bribed for and stolen works of art on a gigantic scale. When the last member of the Medici family, Anna Maria Louisa, died in 1737, all of these priceless paintings, statues and jewelry were given to Italy. Additional items have been added, but basically the Uffizi is known for its paintings created during the so-called Florentine Renaissance.

The Uffizi fronts onto the Piazza della Signoria, where you can refresh yourself and rest your tired feet after the gallery has been visited. Next to the Uffizi are the Medici Monumental Apartments; it's definitely worth paying a measly 10 lire to ride up and down; the apartments are something you shouldn't miss (and they're something we'd like to rent for a few years!). Within walking distance is the Ponte Vecchio, the ancient bridge that was the only one over the Arno not destroyed by the Germans during their northward retreat during World War II. Today, it is a show piece closed to all but pedestrian traffic and lined with jewelry shops. Across the bridge, a few minutes' walk brings you to the Pitti Palace and the renowned, fantastic gallery. In the rear of the gallery are the classic Boboli Gardens, surely worth visiting. Before leaving Florence, you should also visit the Duomo (Cathedral), the nearby Campanile (originally begun by Giotto) and the Baptistery. If you can manage to arrive when the famous Door to Paradise is not completely blocked by busloads of tourists, you'll see this famous masterpiece by Ghiberti. But Florence, being a museum city, is filled with buildings and monuments of all sorts, evocative of the fourteenth to sixteenth century, when the city was a center of culture, learning and art for much of the world. In a way, it still is.

At night, head for the Piazza della Repubblica, a large open area filled with outdoor cafes. One features an orchestra and assorted vocalists, and everyone leans back and listens to Puccini (which might be expected), followed by rock 'n' roll (which might not).

If you're looking for an offbeat gift, or if you're just curious, inspect a seventeenth-century pharmacy that first opened its doors in 1612 under the operation of an order of monks. Head for the Officina Profumo Farmaceutica at 16 Via della Scala. Here you'll find such items as powdered iris root (ideal for lending fragrance to linen closets), virgin milk (for removing freckles) a baldness cure made from new leaves gathered in the springtime and even antihysterical water (made from aromatic plants and very soothing to the digestion), plus a complete assortment of perfumes (here called "essences").

Florence to Siena—45 miles

Leave Florence by the Della Vittoria bridge, heading south on route 2. The road is quite good and rather fast, with some moderate rises and descents, none too extreme or troublesome. It should not take very much more than an hour or so to make the trip under ordinary circumstances. Soon you'll come into the little town of Poggibonsi (which sounds as if a child had selected the name); here you have an opportunity for a side trip to the most perfect medieval village of Italy, San Gimignano. It's only a few miles to that charming reminder of the Middle Ages, and we urge you not to bypass San Gimignano.

SIDE TRIP TO SAN GIMIGNANO—16 MILES ¶ At Poggibonsi, after crossing the railroad tracks, there is a right turn directing the motorist toward San Gimignano a mere eight miles away. The town seemingly has altered but little over the centuries and should delight everyone, particularly camera enthusiasts. Although there were once sixty-two towers, only thirteen remain of these strange, square architectural curiosities. Drive your car up to the Piazza della Cisterna, a centrally located spot from which you can base your walks through the old town. See the Palazzo del Popolo (once a fortress), then the Piazza del Duomo, but for maximum enjoyment just walk through the streets at random. If you're hungry or want to remain overnight, there's a small hotel and restaurant with a hyphenated name, the La Cisterna–Le Terrazze, with its charmingly decorated dining room. Return by the same route to Poggibonsi.

From Poggibonsi, it's just a short run through Staggia and Fontebecci to Siena, loftily situated on three large hills overlooking the surrounding plains. Better plan on spending several hours here (if you're not remaining overnight), looking over the enormous central square, the Piazza del Campo, which somehow reminded us of the Yale Bowl, with its scooped-out center. At one end of the piazza is the Palazzo Pubblico, with a marvelous clock tower; the interior is worth seeing.

Uphill from the Piazza del Campo is the magnificent Duomo (the cathedral) covered in black-and-white marble stripes, except for the ornate façade which is executed in white marble. Inside, the cathedral floor is nothing short of fantastic, consisting of inlaid marble divided into 49 different designs, most representing scenes from the Bible. The most highly regarded are available for viewing only from August 15 to September 15. Siena, you may recall, is where the city's famous pageant called Il Palio takes place twice yearly, on July 2 and August 16. The central event is a horse race, in which each of the city's 17 wards has an entry. It's very colorful, exciting and also mobbed with enthusiastic people. The best hotel in Siena is the Excelsior, with a roof garden restaurant open during the summer. Less expensive, and pretty good, is the Continental, the remodeled palace of a nobleman. If you'd rather stay outside of Siena, there's the Park Marzocchi, in an old building in a park (on the Via di Marciano); also the Villa Scacciapensieri (now there's a catch name!) with a fine view of the city. Both of these last two are open only from April to October. For good food, you might try Al Mangia, on the Piazza del Campo; the Da Mugolone restaurant, on the Via dei Pellegrini is not bad, by the way.

Siena to Rome—145 miles

It's a half day's drive straight through (on route 2) to Rome, with little to attract the motorist en route. The highway is fairly good, although the surface changes frequently every few miles. The road is well marked, however, for as everyone knows, all roads lead to Rome. This one goes through Monteroni d'Arbia and climbs into San Quirico, only to be followed by a gradual descent.

There are a series of curves and climbs around Radicofani, where there is an old fortress (with a restaurant in the fort itself), but you no longer have to ascend the mountain highway to the top. A valley road now passes below Radiocafani. Just before Acquapendente, the highway again twists, turns and climbs. Later, you'll see Lake Bolsena on your right side (very beautiful) and come into Bolsena, Montefiascone (great wine country!) and Viterbo. Then you drive through Vetralla, Cura and Baccano and ultimately into Rome by way of the Via Cassia. (Along here you might keep an eye out for some pleasant-looking garden restaurant to return to on a subsequent warm evening.) As you enter the Eternal City there are a series of signs directing you toward a group of landmarks like the Piazza di Spagna (site of the Spanish Steps) and the Via Veneto (where most of the hotels are located). From here on, just follow the signs and watch out for those little 500s and 600s (the Fiat automobiles), which, in the relatively affluent Italian society of the last few years, have been putting the Vespa and Lambretta scooters on the sidelines. You'll probably agree that the little cars scoot around you just as much as the scooters did on your last visit in Rome. *Arrivederci!*

NAPLES, SORRENTO AND THE AMALFI COAST

Note: The superhighway, the Highway of the Sun (*Autostrada del Sole*), now extends to Naples and south to Pompeii, Salerno and beyond. The stretch between Rome and Naples is 126 miles long, and there is no speed limit outside city boundaries. Thus, Naples may be reached within three hours, including getting to and from the centers of the cities. This, needless to say, is a toll road. However, it should be remembered that nothing of the countryside may be seen on a superhighway. Unless time is of the essence, please drive on the old route, set forth below. If you do take the *autostrada* to Naples, at least stop off at Cassino and visit the famous Monte Cassino monastery, now completely redone since its wartime damage.

Rome to Naples—143 miles

(If you wish to take the autostrada *from Rome to Naples, the road may be picked up to the southwest of Rome, and it runs to the northeast of Naples.)*

Using the Colosseum as a starting point, drive down the Via Labicana, turning right on the Via Merulana, which runs into Piazza San Giovanni in Laterano. Follow the traffic around the square, turning off on the Via Appia Nuova, which later becomes route 7 and continues on to Albano. (Getting out of Rome can be very difficult during the morning, midday and afternoon rush hours; if possible, make your start very early in the morning or at off hours. Should you lose your way, there is one Italian sentence that will help you get on the right road. It's *"Dove la strada per . . . ?"* or "Where is the road to . . . ?")

Driving about in Italy is best accomplished with a Fiat, for all local mechanics have every possible spare part and know this excellent car inside out. We have driven a Fiat on several different occasions with complete satisfaction.

The road down to Naples is often heavily traveled, but under ordinary circumstances the trip is quite pleasant, proceeding through rolling countryside, and the highway itself a good one. Velletri is the first town of any size, a good place for an in-between-hours cup of coffee, preferably a *cappuccino*, the favorite coffee and milk combination that may be had almost anywhere along the road. Next comes Cisterna di Latina, and shortly you reach the sea at Terracina, where there are a fair number of restaurants; should you wish to make a halt for lunch, you'll find the Hotel Tunisia Palace and the Restaurant Scoglio delle Sirene. Continue on from Terracina to Findo, Itri and Formia. After Scauri there is a choice of roads, but route 7-*quarter* (a subdivision) is far more interesting, because much of it is along the seashore, particularly the stretch near Mondragone. Proceed through Castel Volturno, a little village, and through a number of pine forests, then Lake Patria on the left side and into Naples via the Autostello, a fairly fast road when not overloaded with local traffic.

Now what about lively, gesticulating Naples? If you're staying overnight, the Hotel Continental is right on the sea and quite nice; the Royal has a view of the Bay, but is often noisy and commercial. The Hotel Excélsior is extremely good and has the great advantage of being air-conditioned. Most tourists have been advised to visit the Restaurant Zi' Teresa, and here you'll find lots of excitement, noise and not a little gaiety, but the food is just so-so. Much better food may be had at Da Angelo, a short ride up to the Vomero; in town, on the waterfront, there is the Transatlantico, a highly regarded place for serious eaters. The choice of restaurants is wide and most of them specialize in seafood, usually well prepared if you don't mind a touch (!) of garlic. If the Chamber of Commerce will forgive us, we're prepared to state that Naples has comparatively few standard tourist sights, although you will want to look at the Castel Nuovo, built on a miniature island in the bay. Next most interesting is the glass-enclosed *Galleria*, filled with shops, something like a supermarket in a hothouse. But the chief sights of Naples are the people themselves, thousands living in closely packed quarters on narrow streets, and far too many of them out of work.

Naples is a tremendously busy port and industrial town and therefore not suitable for prolonged stays by the average tourist, and although from here the boat may be taken to Capri, should you wish to do so, the ride is excessively long and better undertaken from Sorrento, farther down along the coast.

Don't forget the island of Ischia, either. Some prefer

it to Capri. The lesser-known Bay of Naples island of Procida is also worth a visit if there's time. There are dozens of vacation spots fronting the Gulf of Naples, beginning with Sorrento and continuing along to Amalfi, where most American visitors will find ideal places to stay. Positano is one of these many superlative places that Italy has in such great abundance. It is not a bad idea to establish a home base and do all of your sightseeing from one particular point, because distances are not great and there is a wide choice of attractions within a short radius.

WHAT TO EAT IN NAPLES

Pizza was created in Naples, so you'll have to sample it in a *pizzeria* here. There are many types of pizza, and all have names (Capriciosa, Margherita, etc.). Try them all! Other Neapolitan dishes are:

Maccherone alle vongole: Macaroni with clam sauce, a great favorite
Spaghetti al pomidoro: Spaghetti with tomato sauce
Cannelloni all' Amalfitana: Large sheets of noodle dough, rolled and stuffed with meat and cheese, covered with tomato sauce
Minestra martita: Meat soup with pieces of sausage
Zuppa di vongole: Soup made with tomatoes, garlic and steamed clams
Peperoni imbottiti: Peppers stuffed with bread crumbs, olives and capers
Melanzane alla parmigiana: Eggplant baked with cheese and tomato sauce
Fritto misto: Assorted pieces of deep-fried fish
Spumoni: The classic ice-cream dessert with pieces of nuts and fruits

The outstanding local cheeses are provolone, a semi-hard white cheese with an interesting smoky taste, and mozzarella, a rather mild cheese used principally in cooking. Lacrima Cristi (the Tears of Christ) is the well-known white wine, but it is fairly sweet. Gragnano is fruity and quite delicious, an excellent all-around red wine. Falerno is another good red (also comes in white). Capri has a moderately good white that is a trifle sweet.

From Naples to Sorrento—29 miles

From Naples head eastward through Pórtico, Torre del Greco and Torre Annunziata, then south to Castellamare and along the coast to Sorrento, which might be given some serious consideration as a central sightseeing point. Sorrento is located high on a bluff overlooking the sea and is quite charming, on a somewhat larger scale than the other and smaller towns of this district. In Sorrento there are two large hotels facing the Gulf of Naples— the Excelsior-Vittoria and the Europa Palace, whose front rooms offer exciting views. Much newer and more modern is the Hotel Carlton, extremely attractive, but not on (although close to) the waterfront. Slightly outside town is the agreeable Hotel Cocumella. The restaurant situation is limited, however, and your meals are best eaten at the hotels, although della Favorita o'Parrucchiano is satisfactory.

The Amalfi Coast

Continuing on from Sorrento, the road traverses that famous stretch of coastline the Amalfi Drive, generally agreed to be the most spectacular bit of scenery in all of Italy, and that is really taking in a good deal of territory. Now what about the Amalfi Drive—is it all that it has been claimed to be? The answer must be a mixed reply of yes and no. Yes, for the scenery and natural beauty. No, because of the problems of enjoying the drive. The Amalfi Drive *is* magnificent; the curving hundred-year-old road is truly remarkable and a memorable trip, all things considered. From the driver's point of view it is somewhat less so, because of the problem of dividing one's time between the difficulties of negotiating the narrow, trafficked road and catching glimpses of breathtaking vistas of the sea on the one hand and of the vine-terraced land on the other. On weekends, the Amalfi Drive is so overladen with traffic that the pleasure is considerably diminished, to put it mildly. Heavy buses, loaded with packaged tourists, ply the road from 9 A.M. to 5 P.M., the only break occurring during the lunch hours. The bleating horns of these monsters, sounding notice of their approach on each turn (and the Amalfi Drive is largely a series of turns), is not only annoying, but worst of all, it means that if you should get behind one, you'll have to crawl at a snail's pace the entire length of the road. After considerable observation we are in a position to offer anyone who is disturbed by the buses a few words of advice. Make the trip early in the morn-

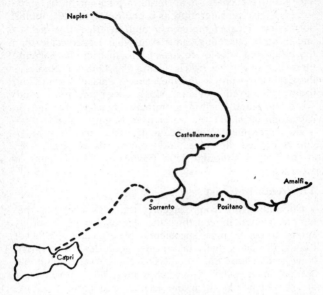

ing, preferably before 9 A.M., when traffic is light, or after 5 P.M., when it isn't light but at least most of the buses have gone. Another good opportunity is afforded during the lunch hour from 12:30 to 2 P.M.

The first town, or rather village, of interest on the drive is lovely Positano, the perfect fishing village you've always dreamed about; Positano almost overdoes its attractiveness. Surely you've seen it before on a Pan Am calendar; if not, then in an Italian movie. You'll definitely like it and possibly may even fall in love with it. To be more prosaic, the Hotel Le Sirenuse can be highly recommended on all counts; the Miramare is cozy and small, but very much in order for those who like an intimate hotel with an exciting view of the sea.

Farther along is Amalfi, snuggled into a cove and backed up by mountains—all in all, a lovely place for a stay. Looking down on Amalfi from the heights is the Hotel Cappuccini-Convento, reached only by elevator and featuring a sensational view of the Gulf of Salerno. Smaller but very suitable are the hotels Miramalfi (slightly out of town) and the Residenza Punta.

Ravello is absolutely lovely—small, sleepy, almost somnolent, but loaded with scenes that cry out for a camera or easel. There can be no problem here about hotel accommodations, for both the Rufolo and the more elaborate Caruso Belvedere offer good quarters and pleasing food.

To reconstruct the entire problem of selecting a place to stay along the coast, we may summarize by saying that you could hardly go wrong anywhere in the area. However, of them all, Sorrento offers less in the way of charm, quaintness or picturesqueness (because after all, Sorrento is a fairly good-size town), but is actually the best base of operations for several days of sightseeing in the area. Excursions to Vesuvius and Pompeii as well as boat trips to Capri are best undertaken from Sorrento. If it's a pure vacation and rest, with little emphasis on sightseeing, by all means think seriously about Positano, Amalfi or Ravello.

Capri

Once settled, you'll surely want to see the local sights. Let's start with Capri, a perfectly delightful spot, although somewhat (well, considerably) overcommercialized by tourism. Nonetheless, most people enjoy it immensely and no visit to this area is complete without seeing Capri. If you wish to remain a few days at Capri, the luxury hotel is the Quisisana, but the small Villa delle Sirene and Tirrenia are both extremely pleasant. The Gatto Bianco is centrally located and, believe it or not, every room has a bath; prices are moderate. Prices are high at La Canzone del Mare, a very interesting restaurant and by far the best in Capri; well worth a visit if you don't mind spending some money. La Canzone also has a swimming pool and beach cabins; you could spend the day having a swim and then eat lunch or dinner. At the far end of the island is the restful upper town of Anacapri, and there is a handsome hotel that has the finest physical location of any we know—the Caesar Augustus, perched high above the Gulf of Naples. For a nice, friendly hotel with attractive rooms, the Europa Palace at Anacapri is very worthwhile for a stay.

Excursions from Sorrento to Capri can easily be made in a one-day round trip, if you wish. (Helicopters, as we already mentioned, considerably reduce the travel time between points in the Bay of Naples. So do the *aliscafi*, the fast-moving hydrofoils.) A number of conventional-type boats cross between Sorrento and Capri daily, in each direction, and as a rule the voyage is fairly smooth; naturally, it is best to undertake the sea journey on a fine day.

Arrive at the pier, located on the waterfront in the lower part of Sorrento, about a half-hour or so before sailing time and buy your round-trip tickets, then get in line so you'll be able to get a good seat aboard the vessel for the ninety-minute trip. (Incidentally, tour tickets are on sale all through Sorrento and the surrounding vicinity offering a packaged price for the boat, visit to the Blue Grotto, lunch and taxi at Capri. You may buy them if you wish, but there seems to be no conceivable reason why you can't do all of these things on your own and save much of the price.) When purchasing your round-trip ticket to Capri at the Sorrento pier, you may also buy one for the Blue Grotto, but it really isn't necessary, for there are dozens of boats to take you there from Capri's Marina Grande. The trip from Capri to the famed Blue Grotto involves a change from a motorboat to a rowboat; don't go if the sea is choppy, for you'll get soaked by the spray.

In Capri, head for the funicular, which carries you to the top in exhilarating fashion. To see the island a taxi may be engaged or, if you choose, the local buses go from Capri to Anacapri about every ten minutes. Be sure to have lunch on the outdoor terrace of the Hotel Caesar Augustus, where you have to force yourself to eat—the view is so unbelievably devastating.

Ischia

If you find you enjoy the atmosphere of Capri and Anacapri and have the time for it, take the boat from Naples to Ischia, a lovely island much like Capri but much less crowded and unspoiled, meaning much less commercialized. The trip takes about an hour and a half, and then you'll find yourself on an island where life flows by smoothly and peacefully. You can also take the beneficial thermal baths here, if you like thermal baths. Accommodations may be had at the Hotel delle Terme, a large, quite elaborate affair. Much smaller, but very good, are the Excelsior, with its marvelous view, and the Parco Aurora.

Pompeii

Even if you don't care for ruins, make an excursion to Pompeii, located on the roads from Naples to Sorrento. It is an overwhelming experience to see this remarkable Roman city, destroyed by a volcanic eruption of Mount Vesuvius in A.D. 79. You'll be able to inspect the shops, restaurants, temples and amazing everyday details of a very civilized town of 2,000 years ago. Unfortunately, when you drive toward the entrance to Pompeii, you'll be overwhelmed by a flood of what may, in all good conscience, be described as plain unadulterated pests, offering unwanted services, selling useless knicknacks and in general, seeking a fast buck. But disregard these pests and visit Pompeii, because you'll find it extremely enjoyable and if we may say a dull word, educational. There is a restaurant *inside* the ruins of Pompeii, should you get hungry.

The entrance fee to Pompeii is 150 lire (about a quarter)—cheap enough. But the guide fees are indeed stiff. Guides point to a sign to show that the tariff is official. If split among three or four people it is not bad—but it *is* still expensive. But these are the Pompeii ruins—and it is being ruined again, this time by the tourist exploiters. They are so used to American tourists that they accept not only American bills but also American silver change. If you order fresh orange juice at one of those stands blocking the entrance way, be prepared to pay a relatively high price in this land of oranges.

Vesuvius

If time permits (or possibly on another day) when you've seen Pompeii, drive from there on the *autostrada* (in the direction of Naples) about nine miles and make a right turn off the highway toward Vesuvius as indicated by the sign marked "Vesuvio." A fifteen-minute drive consisting mostly of a climb toward the heights brings you to a fork in the road where you'll have a choice of a chairlift or of walking to the top of Vesuvius. The right-hand turn takes you to the chairlift, which brings you effortlessly to the crest of Vesuvius in a matter of minutes. If you take the left turn, you'll have to leave your car in a parking place and walk and walk through crushed molten lava (slightly cooler now, of course) and struggle to the top, a half-hour's climb. Hardy, athletic folk will enjoy the walk; all others best take the chairlift. Looking into the crater of Vesuvius discloses first and foremost a great big hole, but for some it has the secondary value of permitting one to view in person something he has read about for many years.

After leaving Vesuvius, drive down the mountain road and watch for signs to Herculaneum, or Ercolano as the Italians call it. It's just a short ride—say, ten minutes—to this remarkable place, which was buried under a flow of volcanic lava when Vesuvius blew its top in A.D. 79. This was a sort of summer beach resort for the rich people of Pompeii, and the excavated ruins show the fine style in which many lived.

And so, having visited the Amalfi coast and seen its sights, you can return to Rome via Naples, taking the same route used in driving down. Or, if you wish, take the trip southward to Sicily.

AN EXTENSION TRIP FROM NAPLES TO SICILY AND SOUTHERN ITALY

Naples to Sicily by Steamer

Pointer: The tour described in this section begins with an overnight ferry trip from Naples to Palermo, Sicily. It is therefore essential that tickets for passengers and the automobile be engaged in advance, either through your local travel agent, your hotel concierge or the ferry company itself, Tirrenia. Tirrenia's Naples office is at 2 Rione Sirignano. The telephone number is 380-200.

To locate the Naples pier, head for the waterfront road, the Via Caracciolo, where you'll find the pier you're looking for, the Molo Beverello. Although the steamer does not leave until 9:30 P.M., it is advisable to present yourself and the car at the pier about 7:30, but, in any event, not later than 8:30 P.M. When you drive into the pier enclosure, proceed directly to the side of the ship and wait; in a few minutes, a representative of the steamship line will approach, ask for your tickets, passports and certificate of automobile ownership (or rental). Better remove the bags you'll need in your stateroom during the overnight passage. When the ship is ready to load, you'll have to drive the car aboard yourself and park and lock it (with no remaining baggage in it, if at all possible). Space aboard the vessel (for vehicles) is very limited, and you'll have to maneuver a good deal to squeeze your car into place.

On board ship, you'll be pleasantly surprised at the attractive white vessel that makes the crossing in about twelve hours; the First Class cabins are adequate, although not very large, and private baths are not available. A fair dinner is served soon after sailing. The voyage is sometimes a little choppy, but seldom enough to disturb your sleep.

After an early breakfast, the ship enters the harbor at Palermo, largest city of Sicily. To the west of town is the gracious, luxurious old Hotel Grand Villa Igiea. The more modest Hotel Sole is in the center of town and the Hotel Jolly is out in the suburbs facing the sea. Since there are going to be many more Jolly Hotels scattered through Italy, we might tell you what to expect. This hotel chain has grown phenomenally in recent years, by providing modern accommodations in areas that previously had no satisfactory hotel rooms for discriminating travelers. The interiors are all similar, quite modern and clean, although as a rule the rooms are small; the Jolly chain is to be congratulated for opening up areas that would, in many cases, be completely unsuited for travelers because of the scarcity or even lack of hotel rooms.

Palermo is a rather attractive town, interesting to wander about in; its outstanding single sight is probably the famous cathedral, a truly imposing structure, although many people might rate the Royal Palace first. See the cathedral first, because the Royal Palace is on the road leading out of the city.

The Royal Palace, also called the Palace of the Normans, is a short walk from the cathedral. The Sicilian Parliament (Sicily is a self-governing region) is located in the Palace of the Normans. Nearby is the very old Church of San Giovanni degli Eremiti, with an oriental garden, one section of which dates from the period of Arab rule over Sicily, at which time the church was a mosque. If you want to swim in Palermo, there's a fine beach at Mondello, in a pretty bay about 7 miles west of the center of the city. There are two fine hotels—the Mondello Palace and the Splendid Hotel Torre—both open only from April through October. The fish restaurants located in Mondello are excellent. From Palermo, you can also visit the island of Ustica by regular boat (it takes about 3 hours) or make it faster by hydrofoil (about a little over an hour). By hydrofoil, you can also visit the more distant (3 hours) Lipari Island; the main town is also called Lipari and is dominated by an impressive medieval citadel. All of these islands are particularly interesting to fishermen, for the fishing is generally quite good, and so are the seafood restaurants.

WHAT TO EAT IN SICILY

Caponata di melanzane: Chopped eggplant relish
Scacciata: A slight variation on pizza
Pasta alle sarde: Spaghetti with cooked sardines; also served with other kinds of fish
Calzone: Ravoli (square of dough) stuffed with anchovies
Cuscusu: Steamed semolina (like a cereal) served with a spicy sauce (very much like the Algerian *couscous*)
Cassata: A type of rich ice cream

The local cheeses are only so-so; the best are caciocavallo and provolone. Corvo is an interesting dark, purple-violet red wine; the white type is good. Zucco is a sweet white wine, high in alcohol. The local specialty is Marsala, a rich, sweetish yellow wine. Etna wines are worth trying, although slightly biting to the taste.

Palermo to Castelvetrano—108 miles

Leave Palermo by the Corso Vittorio Emanuele, the main street extending away from the waterfront which, after passing the cathedral and the Palace of the Normans (through the Gate of the Porta Nuova), becomes the Corso Calatafimi and finally becomes route 186 in the direction of Monreale. The road climbs precipitously, with a series of sharp turns. In a short while, Monreale is reached, and you should watch for the town's square, make a sharp right turn and park the car in the open area. Across the road is the famous Cathedral of Monreale, built during the twelfth century and one of the greatest buildings of its type in the world. The mosaics are superb, but it is the unusual Norman architecture that delights the eye. Don't fail to wander through the lovely old flower-filled cloister adjacent to the cathedral; no two of the many columns are identical. After exiting, look for the sign marked "Chiostro dei Benedetti" nearby; walk all the way out for a wonderful panoramic view of Palermo, which may be seen from the broad terrace.

Leave Monreale, driving through its narrow streets,

after which the road twists and turns its way through the mountains in the direction of Alcamo, passing through Pioppo; at this last village watch carefully for a comparatively inconspicuous sign directing you to Trapani. Go on by a road that hugs the mountainside, with a great number of turns, finally coming into Borgetto. (Incidentally, even though it rains in the mountains, it's usually clear once out of them. That's just a general rule and is not absolutely guaranteed.) Borgetto and Partinico are almost twin cities; at Partinico, the route becomes 113, although you can only tell by looking at the highway kilometer markers, for the Italians direct you along your way by arrows pointing to towns; seldom are the route numbers indicated by the arrows. On the same subject, it's always a good idea to look ahead on the map to learn the names of the next few towns, because frequently the highway arrows will show directions only to a town a great many miles distant, rather than the next nearest village. (Oh well, we might admit that occasionally the entire procedure is vice versa.)

The road climbs into the town of Alcamo; as the heights are reached, watch for an extremely sharp left turn leading through the center of town via its main street. As if to make things equal, at the far end of town, there is a very sharp right turn. The road goes through some fine, well-kept farmlands; watch (at the end of roughly nine miles, about fifteen kilometers) for a right turn off a main road to the ruins of Segesta; this little side trip of three miles is definitely worthwhile. Here you'll find a 2,400-year-old Greek temple of unbelievably graceful proportions, built when the Greeks held sway over this part of the world. Through the centuries, it would appear, almost everyone in the Mediterranean attempted to take over control of Sicily. It was tough on the local inhabitants of those days, but wonderful for the twentieth-century tourist, who finds a tremendous range and variety of ruins, monuments, cathedrals and remembrances of cultures gone by.

After returning to the main road from Segesta, continue on toward Trapani. The road begins to level out and there are many straight stretches where good time can be made. Finally Trapani is reached, a rather large but basically dull commercial town. The only suitable place to eat is the very good Ristorante Russo, in a secluded location on the Via Neve, a little difficult to find, but worth the trouble. Also very good is the Firenze, on via Santa Elisabetta.

(From Trapani, a worthwhile ten-mile side trip may be made to the fascinating old medieval town of Erice, with some remarkable old ruins; there are pleasant accommodations here. If you remain overnight in Trapani, you'll find a new motel at the far end of town. There is boat service from Trapani to the nearby Aegadian Islands, where the inhabitants live under somewhat primitive but not unhappy conditions.)

After Trapani, drive toward Marsala, leaving town via route 115. Although the road is poor at first, it soon improves. Marsala, the home of the famous sweet dessert wine, offers little of touristic interest, but a stop should be made at some local bar to taste the syrupy wine. The wine firm of Florio welcomes tourists and, besides, gives samples! The road goes on to Petrosino, bypassing Mazara; then there is a fast, smooth road into Castelvetrano. Here you'll find the new Jolly Hotel, the only suitable place to stay overnight, and to have dinner, for that matter.

Castelvetrano to Agrigento—72 miles

About five miles after leaving Castelvetrano, there is a turnoff to the wonderful remains of Selinunte, a city founded about 620 B.C. The side trip involves a drive of only ten minutes or so, and you'll never regret the time it takes to reach these fabulous ruins of a Greek outpost of civilization dating back thousands of years. The site of three old temples magnificently fronting onto the sea is extremely moving, in fact thrilling, and that's a word that doesn't appear too often in these pages.

Proceed back to the main road and head for Menfi, then Sciacca. At Ribera, be sure to look for a sharp right turn on a side street that hardly seems as if it could be the correct road, but it is, in point of fact. Next comes Montallegro, where you turn at a dead end at the extreme edge of the town. Then to Siculiana, Porto Empedocle and Agrigento, a fascinating old town with a world of history. Here you could stay at either of the two Jolly Hotels or at the Hotel della Valle, located on the road to the valley of the temples. You can have dinner at your hotel or at the Restaurant Giugiu, where you can taste local Sicilian food.

Sightseeing in Agrigento could involve days, if you like old temples, for the scope and size of the ruins are indeed impressive. Our two favorites are the Temple of Concord and the Temple of Castor and Pollux, but this is a matter of choice and other buildings may appeal to you even more.

From Porto Empedocle (which is the port for Agrigento), you can make a boat trip to the islands of Linosa and Lampedusa, and even to the very offbeat island of Pantelleria. But you have to have plenty of time for these side trips, because the vessels run only a few times a week. During July and August, there's hydrofoil service to Pantelleria, although not every day.

Agrigento to Ragusa—84 miles

Leave Agrigento heading for Palma, Licata and Gela, a historic old town, once of great importance but now just a bathing spot for vacationers. The next town is Vittoria, where you'll have to maintain a sharp lookout for the road signs, which have been placed in the most unlikely spots anyone could imagine; keep watching for directions for Ragusa and Modica, and you'll manage to find your way out of Vittoria. Then on to Ragusa, picturesquely located in a mountain area. Here you'll find that trusty old standby the Jolly Hotel, and a good place to eat, the restaurant La Lucciola.

Ragusa to Syracuse—55 miles

Leave Ragusa heading for Modica, an attractive town built on two levels. At the end of town, go left around the circle and watch immediately for a right fork to Syracuse (or Siracusa, if you prefer the Italian name). Proceed to Ispica, where you must watch for a sharp right turn down a steep grade. The road then passes through Rosolini, Noto, Avola, and Cassibile, then reaches Syracuse. Here you have a fine choice among the new Jolly Hotel (and we hope that a directional sign from the road to the hotel has now been erected), the Grand Hotel Villa Politi, or perhaps the Park Hotel and the Albergo Bellavista. If you want to sample the best in Sicilian food and wines, proceed into the older part of town to an extraordinarily fine dining spot, the Dell'Orologio, just off the Piazza Archimede. Did you know that it was here, in Syracuse, that Archimedes cried out, "*Eureka*," and dashed out into the street (minus his clothes) after discovering the principle of the displacement of water?

The ruins of the old city of Syracuse are about five minutes by car from the modern town. A pleasant couple of hours may be spent enjoyably wandering about the ruins, even if you aren't greatly interested in archaeology; there is a restaurant located immediately adjacent. For reasons known only to the authorities, you must walk through a prescribed path until you finally reach the Greek theater, one of the best of the ruins remaining. Be sure to see the echo chamber called the Ear of Dionysius, famous for its remarkable acoustical qualities. If you are truly interested in Greek ruins, days could be spent profitably in exploring Syracuse.

Syracuse to Taormina—75 miles

Leaving Syracuse, the road soon becomes fairly level and reasonably wide. After Priolo Gargallo, the route descends steadily, but climbs again going into Carlentini. Two streets within the town, there is a sharp right turn, inconspicuously indicated, in the direction of Catania. But don't relax, because there is another sharp turn, this time to the left, a few streets farther along. By now, you *may* (if the weather is clear) be able to see impressive Mount Etna, over 10,000 feet high; on cloudy days you'll have to just imagine it's there. Soon, you reach Catania, a town that unfortunately is not well marked (within the city limits) from the motorist's point of view. If you should get lost, head for the waterfront and just ride alongside the wharfs in the direction of signs indicating Acireale, Taormina and Messina.

Catania has, of course, a Jolly Hotel, as well as a luxury establishment, the modern Excelsior. There is also a good choice of restaurants, most of them serving the classic fish soup of the region. But on to Taormina!

(*There's a superhighway, an* autostrada, *which runs inland from Catania to Messina. It's alright if you're in a hurry, but otherwise not recommended, because you'll miss Taormina, and you really shouldn't.*)

Continue to Aci Castello, Acireale and Fiumefreddo, and finally reach the gem of Sicily, the perched town of Taormina. The climb from the seashore road to Taormina must be negotiated with some care, because should you meet a wide bus, the road is almost too narrow for both of you. An outstanding hotel is the San Domenico Palace, housed in a remarkable thirteenth-century (former) monastery, with corridors smelling of incense and gardens that are absolutely ravishing. Other suitable, although not luxurious, and less elaborate places include the hotels Bristol Park, Jolly Diodoro, Excelsior Palace, Miramare Grand, Timeo and Mediterranée. There are also scores of lower priced hotels and pensions from which to choose. Among the new modern hotels at the beach, below the town, the terraced Atlantis Bay with a swimming pool and the lovely new Mazzaro. The swimming problem at Taormina, which once required a 10-minute trip by car or bus on a steep and curving road, has now been solved; there's a cable car which operates frequently throughout the day and takes you to and from the beach in minutes. The cable car takes you to Mazzaro, an attractive but somewhat stony (by American standards) sort of beach, which can get very crowded. Not too far away there are other less crowded beaches, such as Lido di Isola Bella, Baia delle Sirene and Lido Mazzeo. Don't fail to make the short climb (by foot, if you're strong and athletic, by car if you're lazy, like us) to the ridiculous and unbelievable mountain village of Castel Mola, sitting like an eagle's nest, high up in the hills above Taormina. Here you can taste the oversweet almond wine sold in the local shops or buy handmade blouses (at infinitesimal prices) or just admire the view.

From either Taormina or Catania you can drive up the slopes of Etna to the mountain lodge called Rigugio Sapiena; from there you can take the aerial cable car to another spot closer to the top, with marvelous vistas (if it's clear, of course).

(Before starting the next part of the journey, please read carefully the introductory part that follows.)

Taormina to Messina—31 miles

In order to head for northern Italy, it will be necessary to take the ferry at Messina for the mainland; inasmuch as the ferry operates only five times a day in each direction, it is necessary to do a little advance planning and decide on the next scheduled destination. It's perfectly possible to stay overnight at Messina (at the Jolly Hotel, where else?), get the early morning ferry and continue on. But it certainly is not advisable to arrive at Messina in the late afternoon, make the crossing in an hour to the mainland and then have to search for a place to stay. Incidentally, there are comparatively few hotel rooms to be had on the mainland (suitable for luxury-loving Americans) before Gioia Tauro; if you don't phone ahead and secure a reservation there, it may be difficult to obtain a hotel room elsewhere. Now, are we all set? Then, reluctantly, tear yourself away from Taormina, descend the hill to the shore road and drive the thirty-one miles to Messina.

The ferry terminal may be reached by heading for the waterfront (on the right-hand side) as soon as you enter the city limits; follow the wharfs and piers to their end and just before the harbor road takes a left turn, you'll see the steamship pier. As a rule, there are a group of English-speaking young men standing about who will offer their services (tip expected) to non-Italian-speaking motorists; this is helpful but not absolutely essential. Park your car, enter the terminal building and go to one of the ticket counters; the clerk will want to see your automobile ownership or rental papers and after a pause (averaging ten minutes!), while the clerk looks for his forms, the tickets for your automobile and passengers will be forthcoming. Then back to your car and exhibit the ticket to the pier attendant, who will show you where to park until actual departure time across the Strait of Messina to Villa San Giovanni.

Villa San Giovanni to Gioia Tauro—29 miles

(*From Villa San Giovanni, there's an* autostrada *which runs all the way north to Salerno, Naples and Rome. It's a good fast road, but runs generally inland, starting about an hour above Pizzo. It's difficult to make a choice of routes because the* autostrada *is quicker, but of course, you won't see very much on the way.*)

After the ferry docks and everyone scurries wildly off in complete disorder, the motorist should have no difficulty in finding the desired road (route 18), which is marked to indicate Scilla, Palmi and Vibo Valentia. If in doubt, keep to the left (on main streets of course), and you'll soon find yourself on route 18 heading northward.

The first town reached is picturesque old Scilla, whose miniature harbor for fishing boats might be worth a picture or two. Scilla (Scylla in Greek), if you remember your mythology, was the famous rock across the strait from the violent whirlpool of Charybdis. In between the two hazards swam a monster that swallowed sailors. Thus, we have retained the expression, denoting being placed between two evil choices, as being between Scylla and Charybdis.

The road starts its wandering route, following the coast toward Bagnara, then to Palmi; on a clear day (and may there be many of them for you!) if you look back at Sicily, it's often possible to see Mount Etna. And so, you continue to Gioia over a road that soon ceases to turn and twist and becomes somewhat straighter. At Gioia, those who wish will find sustenance and a pleasant place to remain overnight at (you knew it all along) the Jolly Hotel.

Gioia Tauro to Maratea—160 miles

It will not be possible to make good time from here to Maratea, so if it is after 2 P.M. or it is raining, the 160 miles may take much longer than your estimate. On a bad day, therefore, it might often be best to remain overnight in Gioia and make an early start the next morning. (Another alternative is to head through the mountains for Nicastro or Cosenza, which are only 65 and 115 miles respectively from Gioia. If you do decide to go through Nicastro and Cosenza, continue on routes 18-*bis* and 19, rejoining this tour at Sapri.) Although the shore road is not without its difficulties, the mountain roads involve a good deal of climbing and descending and it is difficult to maintain a fair rate of speed. However, if it is fairly late in the day or the weather is unsatisfactory, better take the inland route, stopping at Nicastro or Cosenza, both of which have (of course!) their Jolly Hotels.

Leave Gioia heading inland toward Rosarno, Mileto and Vibo Valentia. Then the road begins its return to the coast toward Pizzo. Shortly after Pizzo, there is a fork in the route; the left-hand road is a continuation of route 18 following the shore, whereas the right-hand road goes through the mountains toward Nicastro and Cosenza, as discussed above.

Assuming you're taking the shore road, however, proceed along the coastline toward Almantea, Fiumefreddo, Paola, Scalea and Maratea. The route that follows the shore is extremely beautiful; the sea has a color shading that defies description, all of which is lovely for the passengers, but the driver must pay strict attention to the road, whose construction engineer apparently disliked anything resembling a straight line.

At Maratea, be careful not to follow the signs to the main part of town, but head toward the water, where you'll find the charming Hotel Santavenere, with attractive rooms facing the sea, an ideal place for a night's stop.

Maratea to Amalfi—114 miles

Leave Maratea, heading for Sapri, a waterfront town with the pleasant Hotel Tirreno. After Sapri, the road is straight, flat and ideal for traveling for some distance, but inevitably begins to climb again as it circles Mount Scuro on the right-hand side. After Vallo della Lucania, the road begins its descent toward Rutino and Ogliastro, and then finally, some miles farther along, you come to the marvelous ruins of Paestum on the left side. Don't just drive by lovely Paestum, for even the hurried traveler should spend an hour here, walking about the remains of the great city once called Poseidonia.

At Battipaglia, the mountain road rejoins the coastal road and both head toward Salerno, a name engraved in the minds of many Americans who landed there during the days of the invasion of Italy. Salerno, once reached, discloses itself as a pleasant city perched high on a cliff overlooking its beach. You, too, in company with hundreds of thousands of invading military personnel, will wonder why this unlikely spot was selected as the point of invasion, for the heights of Salerno are not easily climbed. For an overnight stay, there's a Jolly Hotel and the Hotel Grand Diana Splendid. For a good meal, you could hardly do better than La Rosetta, an unpretentious restaurant that serves first-rate local food.

Past Salerno, the road (now route 163, although you need only follow the directional signs to Amalfi) begins to hug the rock-girt coastline. After Maiori comes Minori and then Ravello, a delightful little coastal town, largely overlooked by tourists in favor of the delights of Positano, Sorrento and Capri. At Ravello, the best place is the Hotel Caruso Belvedere. Then continue on to Amalfi along the beginning of the famous Amalfi Drive, surely the finest stretch of scenery and coastline in Italy. Amalfi is a pleasant place for a stay, with several good hotels and restaurants, and is a fairly good center of operations for local sightseeing, although possibly not quite so convenient as Sorrento, some miles ahead, which is more centrally located. (There are more details about this area in the section that describes the trip from Rome to Naples and the Amalfi coast.)

Amalfi to Rome—191 miles

Leave Amalfi heading for Castellamare and continue through that busy port until just before Pompeii, where you pick up the *autostrada*, the superhighway, for a short run into Naples.

The *autostrada* enters Naples just a block from the main railroad station, so it will be easy for you to get your bearings. The toll from Pompeii to Naples is about a quarter, but it is worth many times that. After a little sightseeing in Naples, or possibly a snack or so, you can return to Rome via route 7 (along the coast, part of the way) or via route 7-*bis* (inland). Either way, the road is good, and mileage goes by swiftly. Coming into Rome, you will see directional signs for the Via Veneto and Piazza di Spagna (remember the Spanish Steps?). They are reference points that will orient you swiftly.

৯ *Motoring in Italy*

Italian gasoline is now a dollar or so a gallon, but gasoline coupons will cut the price by about 40 percent, very roughly speaking; we suggest you stick to super and avoid the regular. At the border customs will issue you a tourist gasoline card (Carta Carburante e Turistica —CCT) which also serves as a six-month entry permit for your car. With this card you can purchase at the border office (or any other) of the Automobile Club d'Italia (ACI) the tourist-rate gasoline coupons which are issued in units of five liters (about one and one third gallon) at the rate of fifteen liters a day for a maximum of fifteen days. That adds up to 225 liters. If you need more when the fifteen-day period has expired, you can buy them through the Automobile Club d'Italia. Unused gasoline coupons have to be turned in at an ACI office before you leave Italy or at the border. If you want to buy your coupons before leaving home, you can do so at the Banca Nazionale del Lavoro, 25 West 51st Street, New York City, but you have to have them stamped at the border.

Another purchase you should make at the border is a general ticket for all *national* museums in Italy. This is something new. At the border it costs a bit less than if purchased abroad. See how we save you money? Not much, in this case. But keep in mind that this is a ticket for national museums and that Italy has a large number of private museums (including the Vatican one), for which this ticket is not valid.

Still another new feature of Italian tourism is an insurance policy against baggage loss and theft. You can buy this coverage at the border also. The cost is very moderate.

Be careful about horn blowing within cities, unless it is an emergency. There are fines for noise-makers. But outside the cities, always blow your horn when going around blind curves, entering intersections and overtaking other cars at high speed.

Italians drive very fast—too fast for most Americans. They will frequently take chances; so be cautious and let the local people have the right of way. Bear this in mind —the car on the right hand has the *absolute* right of way, even if he's coming onto a main highway.

Italian roads are fairly good, although side roads often are extremely narrow. Most roads are paved and quite smooth. More than two dozen *autostrade*, superhighways, radiate throughout Italy, linking up the major cities and points of interest. They are toll roads, and the toll depends on the distance traveled and the size (cylinder capacity) of the car. When a car enters an *autostrada*, the driver is handed a ticket. When the car leaves the *autostrada*, the driver turns in the ticket at the toll booth and the cost for the journey is swiftly determined. The longest of the superhighways is the *Autostrada del Sole* (Superhighway of the Sun) which streaks across the length of the Italian peninsula, starting at Milan and passing through Bologna, Florence, Rome and onward to Naples. Another superhighway continues southward from Naples to Reggio Calabria. The superhighways are designated by the letter "A" and numerals. Thus, the *Autostrada del Sole* from Milan to Rome is the A-1; from Rome to Naples, A-2. During the summer, on the *Autostrada del Sole*, the superhighway (A-11) between

Florence and the sea, and other much-traveled *auto-strade*, information booths are set up. Oh yes—in case you want to bypass Rome, Milan or Bologna there are traffic interchanges on the outskirts of each of these cities. The one for Rome is called the *Gran Raccordo Anulare;* the ones for Milan and Bologna are known as a *Tangenziale.* Sprinkled along the Highway of the Sun is a chain of "Auto-Grill" restaurants. They are chromy, modernistic to a fault, flashy and thoroughly un-Italian. In other words, they are fine places to stop for a meal if you are wasting away with hunger. But, in any case, avoid the *autostrade*, unless you have to make time, there's more to see on other roads.

Note: There are plenty of gasoline stations on the *autostrade*, as well as repair facilities. Nevertheless, fill your tank with gas (*benzina*) and don't take chances. There is no speed limit, but don't let that encourage you. Police can levy fines on the spot for other offenses.

Sad to relate, Italian truck drivers are the most unmannerly in Europe. Passing them is difficult—occasionally, dangerous—for they will not pull over when you sound your horn. Please be careful.

Yes—your home state driver's license is acceptable in Italy.

NETHERLANDS
(HOLLAND)

With a Motor Trip Through the Benelux Countries

National Characteristics

Whether you have visited the Netherlands many times or whether your closest contact with the Dutch has been a car ride to Holland, Michigan, the people of this country by the sea will not seem like strangers. They won't greet you like one, either. All of us from childhood have heard about the windmills and the wooden shoes, the bikes and the dikes, the tulips and the princesses, the cheeses and the pottery, and dozens of other pertinent features of this land of only 12,600 square miles and 12½ million people. We know, too, that the Dutch keep things spic-and-span and that they are very industrious. What delights a tourist is to see confirmation of these notions. Last year, last century—in fact, you could say "forever" —the Dutch have been battling the sea and reclaiming land from her, their ancient enemy. That's a pretty good example of stick-to-itiveness, determination and industriousness. It is a handy way of pointing out, by example, the basic character of the Dutch people, too.

The Dutch take things seriously—to an extent. But in a country of windmills, pretty girls, flowers, canals and bicycle paths, life is not grim by any means. How could it be?

It is a land with tradition and a sense of the picturesque. The farm products—eggs, butter, milk—are among the world's best. So are the electronic products. It is that ability to do both the old and the up-to-the-moment technological task with equal skill and success that helps make the Dutch so interesting and their country so pleasant for the visitor.

About half the people are Calvinists or Protestants of other sects. A little more than one third are Roman Catholics. But the tourist will rarely notice any signs of religious divisions.

Home and family life mean everything to the Hollander. And home means bountiful meals with too much food and with children urged to finish everything on their plates. Many young girls tend to be overweight, and this almost national characteristic is encouraged after marriage by the indulgent husband, who wouldn't for a moment dream of putting himself (or anyone else) on a diet. Possibly even more than a Frenchman, he thinks about food—but with none of a Frenchman's nonsense about sauces, soufflés or the like. He dreams of thick soups, rich stews, raw herring and cheese. The Frenchman has a word or two for the creamy, calorie-filled (but extremely tasty) Dutch cuisine: *Hollandaise sauce*.

No, the Dutchman might be serious-minded, but he is not a stuffy, dull person. In addition, the typical Dutchman has a wonderful sense of fair play, honesty and basic kindness. If you don't find him bubbling with fun and radiating happiness just to be alive, give a moment's thought to what it's like to be living in a tiny country constantly threatened by the sea and by giant neighboring countries.

When to Go

July and August are actually the best weather months because Holland can be fairly cold. April through September (or early October) usually are satisfactory. It is possible to find ideal, sunny weather in February in

WEATHER STRIP: AMSTERDAM

Temp.	JAN.	FEB.	MAR.	APR.	MAY	JUNE	JULY	AUG.	SEPT.	OCT.	NOV.	DEC.
Low	31°	31°	35°	39°	45°	51°	54°	54°	49°	43°	37°	33°
High	41°	42°	47°	54°	62°	68°	70°	70°	65°	57°	47°	42°
Average	36°	37°	41°	47°	54°	60°	62°	62°	57°	50°	42°	38°
Days of rain	10	8	11	8	9	9	11	11	10	13	11	13

Amsterdam. But you can't count on it. The summer ends quickly in September, and October can be raw and damp. There is a heavy percentage of humidity all year around. Assume that it will rain at least every third day. Bring a raincoat.

TIME EVALUATION ¶ Schedule Amsterdam for two to three days; if you want to do some local sightseeing (Volendam, Marken, the bulb fields), add another two to three days. You could easily drive across the Netherlands in a day, but it would hardly permit you to absorb the country's charm. Allow four days to a week.

PASSPORT AND VISA ¶ You do not need a visa for a stay of less than ninety days, but you will, of course, have to have a passport.

CUSTOMS AND IMMIGRATION ¶ Dutch customs men are a little fussy about tobacco and alcoholic items (booze). You can have two cartons of cigarettes, 100 cigars, 200 cigarillos or a total of 500 grams of tobacco (a bit over a pound) in one form or another. One bottle of hard liquor (or two liters of wine) is the maximum allowed duty-free. You can also have a bottle of eau de cologne (a quarter liter), five ounces of perfume and the usual traveler's articles, including movie and still cameras (and film).

HEALTH ¶ Health conditions are excellent here. No need for special precautions about water or milk.

TIME ¶ Six hours later (ahead) of Eastern Standard Time. When it's noon in New York, it's 6 P.M. in Amsterdam. When Daylight Saving Time is in effect in New York, the time difference is 5 hours.

CURRENCY ¶ The *gulden* (also called *florin*, and abbreviated as *f.* or *fl.*) is the official unit of currency. Its value in relation to the dollar changes in accordance with the way the international money market fluctuates. The gulden (or florin) is divided into 100 *cents,* and there are a number of coins—six in all—that you will have to get used to. Remember, now, that the Dutch use the word "*cents,*" also. So if something is quoted in cents, the chances are that they are referring to the Dutch ones and not the American variety. The biggest Dutch coin is the 2½ gulden piece; then there is a silver gulden. They also have a quarter-gulden piece, called a *kwartje*. The three other coins are 5 cents (Dutch), 10 cents and 1 cent. The paper money comes in notes of 2½ gulden, 5, 10, 25, 100 and 1,000. Banks are open from 9 A.M. to 3 P.M. Monday through Friday, but exchange offices are in railroad terminals, as well as at the airports and in-town air terminals. *Gulden* in English, by the way, is guilder.

> **Pointer:** One interesting wrinkle on Dutch currency export controls is that you can take out of the country as much money as you want, except for silver coins. You're limited to 25 gulden.

PRICE LEVEL ¶ This was one of those "sleeper" countries insofar as prices are concerned. Although prices have risen lately hotels and restaurants are still mostly reasonable, but the top establishments are expensive, particularly restaurants, for what they have to offer.

TIPPING ¶ The magic figure is 15 percent. It will see you through any problem that may arise. The hotels will levy a 10 to 15 percent service charge, and this is always shown clearly, and separately, on the bill. The restaurant service charge is generally 15 percent, but occasionally in small, inexpensive lunchrooms 10 percent is normal. If the waiter or waitress adds up the bill verbally—rather than writing it down—you will be told "inclusive." The word "inclusive" means that the service charge has been figured in. The taxi tip ranges from 10 to 15 percent of the meter, but never less than a half-gulden. Railroad porters at the stations expect a little extra in addition to the flat official charge for each bag.

TRANSPORTATION ¶ *Taxis*, as in Paris, seem to disappear just when you want them, although there are plenty around at any other time. You will (almost) always be able to get one at a railroad station. There also are "hack stands" or cab ranks, and it is a good idea to keep an eye out for one near your hotel. Rates are not bad. Amsterdam taxis get a slightly higher rate at night. Taxicab drivers are just short of being ruthless in their demands (if they think you don't know), so be careful.

Railroad trains operate with such frequency on main

lines that you could almost think they were subways. To go from Amsterdam to The Hague or Rotterdam, for instance, don't even worry about a timetable. Just show up at the station and a train will be along very shortly. Because of the relatively short distances between most places in the Netherlands, train service is fast and relatively inexpensive. It is also very good, and it is perfectly satisfactory to travel in Second Class. It is possible to save money on rail travel by buying an eight-day subscription ticket. But these are only worthwhile if you're going to be riding the trains quite a bit. In fact, quite a lot. It is advisable in that case that you buy a timetable for a small charge.

Buses also travel between many cities and towns and are a good way of seeing the countryside. Rates are low.

Within cities the local transportation consists more and more of buses, as the old-time trolley cars are being retired. Fares vary, but average about a half-gulden.

Roads are excellent and well surfaced, and for this reason you will find that *drive-yourself cars* are ideal for sightseeing. They are also inexpensive.

Distances are short, and you'll seldom have need for local *airline* facilities within the country. The big airport, Schiphol, of Amsterdam is only twenty minutes from downtown and about an hour from The Hague. Rotterdam also has a large airport, which serves many neighboring cities such as Brussels, Zurich, Cologne and the English cities of London, Liverpool, Birmingham and Manchester.

Here are some sample highway distances from Amsterdam: The Hague, 35 miles; Rotterdam, 45; Groningen, 125; Arnhem, 63; Utrecht, 24; Eindhoven, 75; Maastricht, 135; Alkmaar, 23; Den Helder, 50. It is 75 miles from The Hague to Arnhem, and 19 miles to Gouda.

COMMUNICATIONS ¶ *Airmail letters* to the United States cost around a quarter, but you can save money by buying V-mail-type stationery—one sheet, or two, or however many you want. The airmail rate then is about half. Local *telephone calls* are very inexpensive —less than half of what they cost us at home. The service —locally, nationally and internationally—is excellent. The Dutch phone system is automatic, and you can direct-dial all over the place, including to many parts of adjoining countries (Germany, Belgium and Luxembourg). Make international calls from your hotel room or from a post office. In either place it will be easy, and there will be no language problem.

ELECTRICITY ¶ Almost everywhere in the country the current is 220 A.C., but in a few places, including a section or two of The Hague, is is 127 A.C..

BICYCLES ¶ As you will quickly observe, bicycling is still a major means of transportation in Holland. It is also a principal way of keeping fit, of relaxation and of taking a jaunt into the countryside. There are 6 million bicycles in Holland—in other words, enough bikes for everyone in the country if one person rides on each of the handlebars. Don't worry about driving problems with all these bikes. The Dutch cyclist is a seasoned traveler, and besides, there are special bicycle paths that are followed by young and old. In northern Drente, Utrecht, Groningen and Guelders—as well as some other places— official tourist organizations arrange lively bicycle tours. If you want to see how the bicycle of tomorrow will look, drop into the Technical University at Eindhoven. Designers proudly show their idea of how the bicycle should be updated in this fast-moving space age. Bicycle renting is no problem. Dealers are everywhere. You can also get one for rent at many of the railway stations, and the stations also have racks for parking bikes. Some of the stations that have bike rentals are Alkmaar, Breda, Endhoven, Delft, Dordrecht, Groningen, The Hague, Haarlem, Hengelo, Hilversum, Middleburg, Rotterdam, Tilburg, Utrecht, Weert—and all of the railway stations in Amsterdam.

FLOWERS ¶ Holland says it with flowers all the time. All the towns and cities have flower markets in a main square the year around. One of the loveliest is at Maastricht. The famous tulip bulbs do their colorful flowering from the end of March to the middle part of May—depending on the weather. Fine places to see them at their best are in the area of Enkhuizen, and along the coast between Alkmaar and Leiden. The flower shows at Lisse and at Linnaeushof are quite dazzling.

Pointer: Here are some blossoming schedules—daffodils, tulips and hyacinths: end of March to middle of May; rhododendrons: May; lilac: middle of July to end of August; gladioli: middle of July to end of August; heather: August and September.

INFORMATION ¶ Official tourist offices throughout the Netherlands will be able to help you with plans as well as with hotel accommodations. Every town and city has a tourist office, identified by the letters VVV (Vereniging Voor Vreemdelingenverkeer—Tourist Association). For a small charge they will call up a local hotel and reserve a room for you. In Amsterdam, the VVV hotel service is in a booth just in front of the main railroad station. Principal offices of the VVV are at 5 Rokin in Amsterdam; 19 Stadhuisplein in Rotterdam; and 38 Parkstraat in The Hague. The VVV offices will also get sightseeing and boat-ride tickets for you *without* any extra charge.

BASIC DUTCH
English-Dutch

Waiter: *Kellner* (when addressing him: *ober*)
Bill of fare, menu: *Menu*
Napkin: *Servet*
Bread and butter: *Brood met boter*
A glass of orange juice: *Een glas sinaasappelsap*

Boiled egg:	Gekookt ei
1. soft	1. *zacht*
2. medium	2. *halfzacht*
3. hard-boiled	3. *hardgekookt*
4. egg cup	4. *eierdop*

Fried eggs: *Gebakken eieren*
Bacon and eggs: *Eieren met bacon*
Coffee, black: *Koffie, zwart*
Coffee with cream and sugar: *Koffie met melk en suiker*
Coffee with hot milk: *Koffie met warme melk*
Tea: *Thee*
Water: *Water*
Ice Water: *Ijswater*
Mineral water: *Mineraalwater, spuitwater*
Breakfast: *Ontbijt*
Lunch: *Lunch*
Dinner: *Diner*
Shampoo: *Shampoo* (product); *Haar wassen* (instruction to hairdresser)
Haircut: *Haarknippen*
Manicure: *Manicure*
I want . . . liters of petrol: *Mag ik . . . liter benzine*
Change the oil: *Olie verversen*
Grease the car: *Wagen smeren*
How are you?: *Hoe is het met U?*

Fine, thank you: *Uitstekend, dank U*
Please: *Alsublieft* (used also when offering something)
Thank you very much: *Dank U vriendelijk*
Good morning: *Goede morgen*
Good afternoon: *Goede middag*
Good night: *Goede nacht* (or) *welterusten*
Yes: *Ja*
No: *Nee*
Morning: *Morgen*
Noon: *Middaguur*
Afternoon, P.M.: *Middag*
Evening: *Avond*
Night: *Nacht*
Sunday: *Zondag*
Monday: *Maandag*
Tuesday: *Dinsdag*
Wednesday: *Woensdag*
Thursday: *Donderdag*
Friday: *Vrijdag*
Saturday: *Zaterdag*
One: *Een*
Two: *Twee*
Three: *Drie*
Four: *Vier*
Five: *Vijf*
Six: *Zes*
Seven: *Zeven*
Eight: *Acht*
Nine: *Negen*
Ten: *Tien*
Twenty: *Twintig*
Thirty: *Dertig*
Forty: *Veertig*
Fifty: *Vijftig*
One hundred: *Honderd*
One thousand: *Duizend*

MUSIC ¶ Holland's big festival goes from the middle of June until the middle of July and its happy notes are struck all over—especially in The Hague, Rotterdam and Amsterdam. The main concert season is from September to May. The Concertgebouw (which needs no introduction) performs at Amsterdam on Wednesday and Thursday evenings and on Sundays. The Hague orchestra is heard on Wednesday and Saturday evenings and on Tuesday afternoons.

PUBLIC EVENTS ¶ The now-familiar "Sound and Light" shows are produced throughout Holland. Arnhem, which has a special role in war history, presents a military parade in June, and Delft has something similar in August. If you want to get in on the celebration of the start of the year's new herring season, then head for such herring high spots as Katwijk and Scheveningen. These ceremonies usually take place in May. Utrecht has a big industrial fair in April and another (the fall fair) in September. In February there's the automobile show at Amsterdam. For the opening of Parliament in September, you encounter a colorful parade in The Hague.

BOATS ¶ You can do plenty of touring of the waterways of Holland, and it will be of the enjoyable kind, we assure you. For a journey along Amsterdam's canals, check with the boat service down the street from the main railroad station, at Rokin street where the canal begins and near Leidseplein.

FOOD SPECIALTIES AND LIQUOR ¶ The food is good, but seldom as exciting as French or Italian repasts. When it's good, it's very very good, but when it's bad—you can guess the rest. Most of the Dutch national dishes are not the sort that appeal greatly to Americans— broccoli, mashed potatoes, red cabbage, sausages and fat pork. But don't despair, a few items are really superb. *Erwtensoep* is the classic Dutch split pea soup and is very good indeed, particularly when the weather is raw. If the soup is designated as *garni*, small open-faced sandwiches are served with it. Then there are the local cheeses— Gouda and Edam, both mild. Herring, herring—they prepare it with everything but whipped cream and who knows. . . . "New" herring is available from May until September, when it is eaten (gulp!) raw. Surprisingly tasty, once the mental adjustment has been made. The local seafood is good, particularly the sole, prepared in almost any fashion. Lobster is no longer a Holland specialty; too expensive. Other local dishes to try include *hutspot*, a beef stew; *boerenkool met rookwurst*, broccoli or cabbage with mashed potatoes and sausages; or *rodekool met rolpens*, rolled meat with cabbage and apples.

But the most interesting feature of Netherlands restaurants are the Javanese specialities; *nasi goreng*, fried rice with chicken, meat, etc.; *bahmi goreng*, fried noodles with pork and eggs; the *sambals*, accompanying relishes, intended to cool the palate. Then of course there is the *rijsttafel* (pronounced rise-tafl), the classic Indonesian rice dinner, which is probably the outstanding and most fascinating dish in Holland (although it's hardly a "dish," since it consists of more than thirty items, all eaten with rice). Plan to be good and hungry or you'll never manage.

Dutch breakfasts are ample: tea or coffee (which will be served on request), slices of meat and cheese and lots of bread; sometimes a boiled egg augments the spread. Then comes a coffee break at about 11. Lunch, known as *koffietafel* or coffee table, follows, and believe it or not, it's a continuation of breakfast—more bread, sliced meats and cheese and a cup of coffee. Dinner is early, and a quite, quite substantial meal. Quite. If you've been in a Latin country and developed the habit of eating dinner at 10, don't try. You're likely to find almost every restaurant closed, for the Netherlanders dine early. Before going to bed, or anytime you feel like a snack, the item to order is *uitsmijter* (pronounced out-smiter), which means a meat sandwich with a fried egg on top. You can get this just about anywhere.

Beer, notably Heineken's, is excellent. The other national drink is the local gin, *jenever*, which is peculiarly dry and not at all pleasing at first. Its musty taste can be quite disturbing to most Americans; but, who knows, you might learn to like it before you leave Holland, I did. In any case try the old (aged) one (*oude jenever*) which is milder and mellower (with age, you know) than the unaged. In a restaurant, order a *borrel*, the slang term for a gin, always served cold. No local wines; all are imported and sold at high prices.

You never have to worry about going hungry in Holland. One of the colorful features of Amsterdam, for instance, is the sidewalk stand, which serves all kinds of tidbits (yes, herring, of course!) and even provides a towel for after-eating tidying up.

The most important tourist areas are: Amsterdam, Rotterdam, The Hague, the cheese towns, the costume district (Volendam and Marken), and the flower regions.

Capital City

Amsterdam is one of the two official capitals of the Netherlands. The Hague is the other. The government and foreign embassies are at The Hague, and it is a much more dignified type of place than bustling, bright Amsterdam. Incidentally, Amsterdam is a city with two faces —the old and the new. If you enter from the airport, the suburbs present row after row of ultra-modern apartment buildings—all spotless and sanitary, well executed in modern design and with the recommended open areas, but frankly uninteresting from the tourist's point of view. Once you are in the center of the city, Amsterdam is touristically rewarding, with canals, green vistas, medieval houses, narrow alleys, pushcarts, vendors and everything else dear to the heart of a visitor who wants to see something "different."

The city has been called the "Venice of the North," an irritatingly incorrect name. It isn't a bit like Venice except for its canals, any more than Bangkok, Thailand, is like Venice except that it, too, has canals. To get an idea of the layout, visualize a strip of water running across the top of an imaginary map; that's the River Ij (pronounced eye). Alongside the river (to the south) is the Central Railway Station and the usual conglomeration of piers and docks. Below the station is a complete series of concentric canals, which head south from the river, change their minds and come about to the north, finally ending up facing the River Ij (still pronounced eye). In addition, and to make it more complicated, there is another set of canals that crisscrosses the concentric series of canals.

But it's important to get started and there's no place to begin like the Dam Square (no jokes please), a large open area in the center of town. On the western edge is the Palace, the New Church and the National Monument to those who died during the last war. On the south side of the square is the beginning of Kalverstraat, a busy, commercial thoroughfare. One block to the east is the Rokin Canal, headquarters for the boats making water trips around the city, something you should not fail to do. Extending northeast from Dam Square is the wide Damrak, a canal that leads toward the railroad station. You'll pass the Stock Exchange Building, on which is inscribed *Beidt Uw Tijd*, Bide Your Time, not from the song of the same name. Almost at the end of the Damrak, cross the bridge on your right hand and you'll see St. Nikolaas Kerk, which is readily translated into St. Nicholas Church. From the church, walk south (away from the waterfront) on the Zeedijk, a famous old street with queer, tilting buildings. This street leads into the Nieuwe Markt, originally erected in 1488 as a gate (boasting five towers) to the medieval part of town. At the south end

of the New Market is the gracious old canal, the Klove-
niersburgswal. On the east side of the canal at No. 29,
you'll find the Trippenhuis, that is, the Trips' house (it
seems there were two brothers named Trip), built in
1660–1662. Now head westward, crossing one canal and
yet another until you come to the Oude Zijds Voor-
burgwal, a lovely, placid waterway; wandering alongside
this canal and looking at the local sights is low-pressure
pleasure, if such suits your mood. Turn right and continue walking (beside the canal) until you see the Oude
Kerk, the Old Church, on your left. Cross over and explore its interesting thirteenth-century interior; then back
to the hotel and take your shoes off.

For another interesting walking tour from the Dam,
follow either the Rokin or Kalverstraat southward (away
from the waterfront) to its end, which is the Muntplein
(an open square), with its Mint Tower built in 1620.
Now head east (on Reguliersbreestraat) to Rembrandtsplein, named, naturally, for the great painter. South of
Rembrandtsplein (via Utrechtsestraat) you'll come upon
Herengracht, a canal lined with fine old homes and very
pleasant for a slow back-four-centuries amble into the
main part of town.

Of course, under no circumstances (unless you hate
art), should you miss the Rijks Museum and its marvelous display of the painting masterpieces of the Netherlands. There are many Rembrandts (the most famous of
which is "The Night Watch"), several good pictures each
by Vermeer, Hals, Steen and Ruisdael and a fair sprinkling of Italian artists' work. If you enjoyed the Rijks
Museum, don't neglect the Stedelijk (City) Museum,
which places emphasis on modern art.

The Rijks Museum is open weekdays from 10 A.M.
to 5 P.M., and on Sundays and holidays from 1 to 5 P.M.
The entrance fee during the week is one guilder, on weekends 0.50 fl. (that is half of a guilder). Except for
opening a half-hour earlier on weekdays, the hours of
the City Museum are the same. The entrance fee is
always a half-guilder.

Then, if museums still suit your fancy, the Royal
Institute of the Indies (now that Indonesia is no longer
Dutch-controlled, the memories here are rather unhappy) is a tremendous place filled with mementos and
examples of the art and culture of Java, Bali, Sumatra
and the other islands. What else to see in Amsterdam—

well, the botanical gardens if you like botanicals, the zoological gardens if you like zoologicals.

You will want to visit two celebrated houses of Amsterdam—Rembrandt's and Anne Frank's. The painter spent happy days in the Amsterdam house, in contrast to the sharp years of terror during World War II for little Anne Frank when she lived secretly with her family at 263 Prinsengracht to hide from the Nazis. The house has been restored, and a guide will take you around it. Rembrandt's house is at 4 Jodenbreestraat.

There's no way of seeing Amsterdam to match a boat ride through the canals. All along the Rokin and Damrak (canals) you can find the pleasant glass-enclosed craft that slowly wander through the waterways. The sightseeing boats leave frequently, and you could hardly invest a half-dollar and get better value, except by spending the same amount on 100 shares of U.S. Steel.

The Bols liqueur people have set up an interesting art museum and restored a three-century-old tavern on the Rozengracht in the 100s block. There are guided tours daily, except on weekends, at 10:30 A.M. You will also be invited to "take a glass" with your hosts.

AMSTERDAM HOTELS

Okura Amsterdam: The newest, tallest, and possibly the best hotel in Amsterdam. Slightly outside of town, 23 stories tall, good-sized guest rooms, several restaurants. Outstanding service. Fairly expensive. For motorists, there's an underground garage.

Amsterdam Hilton: Quite new, and a showplace hotel; good rooms, choice of several restaurants, beautifully located on a canal. Far away from the center of town, however. Expensive, but this is an outstanding Hilton hotel.

Amstel: A grand old place, and the leading hotel before the Hilton and Okura opened. Well run, charming and, of course, more Dutch in atmosphere than the Hilton. Some rooms are quite large, others rather small. On the Amstel river bank, a bit away from the center.

De l'Europe: A pleasing hotel, situated in a fascinating spot on the Amstel river (which looks like a canal here) across from Muntplein square. Although furnishings are dark and traditional, rooms are reasonably attractive and of fairly good size. Elaborate glass-enclosed *Excelsior* restaurant with fine food, a canal view, and a separate entrance.

Doelen: Old-fashioned homey hotel but quite comfortable. One side faces a quiet canal which is unfortunately crossed by a busy bridge. Good food in the hotel's *Savarin* restaurant. Central location.

Victoria: An older hotel that has been largely remodeled. Excellent service, friendly atmosphere. The majority of rooms are pleasant and spacious; some few are on the small side. During the summer, guests must stay on demipension, that is, eat at least one meal at the hotel in addition to breakfast.

Krasnapolsky: A fairly large hotel (for Amsterdam), fronting onto Dam Square. In the modern wing, rooms are attractively furnished. Demipension is required during the tourist season.

Alpha: A new, very large hotel. Has a series of restaurants and bars.

Apollohotel: In a suburban residential section at a unique junction of several canals, including Amstel (canal, not river). All rooms have baths. Very good restaurant.

Esso Motor Hotel: Ultra-modern, 260 rooms; opened in 1969; located in the surburbs.

Howard Johnson Hotel: A surprising delight! Old, restored, typical Amsterdam façades provide a front for 230 very modern rooms.

AMSTERDAM RESTAURANTS

Vijff Vliegen (The Five Flies): Probably Amsterdam's outstanding restaurant, a delightful group of rooms comprising one establishment. Old World surroundings, perhaps just *too* much atmosphere, but the food is surely the best in town. Not too expensive, all in all.

Dikker & Thijs: This is for the serious, dignified gourmet who knows and appreciates the finest; the accent is on French cuisine. Rather high prices, but excellent quality seafood, particularly shellfish.

Port van Cleve: Here is the place for every American to attempt to satisfy that craving for a steak. Prices are moderate and the restaurant draws a large crowd. First floor is popular price; the better dining room is upstairs.

Old Courtyard: An offshoot of the Five Flies; touristy, but amusingly decorated. Exactly the same bill of fare and prices as in The Five Flies.

't Swarte Schaep (The Black Sheep): Beef, veal and seafood with the French accent; a long wine card with the French commodity prevailing. Candle-lit and cozy, expensive, but one of the best restaurants in Amsterdam. Reserve if you want a table next to a window (on second or third floor) overlooking the Leidseplein square.

Havenrestaurant: On the top, the 13th floor, of the Port Authority building behind the main station. Magnificent view of the city and the harbor through the large windows, actually almost a glass wall. Reasonable Dutch fare and moderate prices but rather slow service. One floor below there is a bar and a comfortable modern café—same view.

Indonesia: An extraordinary restaurant, partly a boutique, but serving the best Indonesian food in Europe. The 16-dish rijsttafel, that is, dishes eaten with rice, are exceptionally well prepared, and not too expensive.

SHOPPING ¶ *Diamonds*, often identified as a girl's best friend, are a specialty here, because Holland is a diamond-cutting center. But are you a diamond expert? It's a blind article and you might make a good buy but also might not. Purchases made at reliable shops should, however, represent sound value, if not outstanding bargains. There are two places worth seeing even if diamond buying is further from your mind than a trip to the moon —the diamond-cutting establishments of Moppes & Zoon, and Asscher's (have your concierge phone for permission). Fascinating and educational, but unfortunately no souvenirs are distributed.

Edam or Gouda *cheeses* are fine for gifts, and the export versions are sealed in tins; ideal for taking with you (although slightly heavy) or for shipping. The local candy, particularly *hopjes*, the coffee candy, also Droste's, all worthwhile. The local *gin* (if you've taken to it), or if not, Bols and Fokking *cordials* are excellent. Don't try to bring back *flower bulbs* with you without a health certificate; it's far easier to have them shipped by local export firms who are specialists. *Delftware* is risky to buy; loads of cheap imitations are on the market, so make all purchases in recognized shops. Old *tiles* are attractive, particularly if you can round up a set. You'll be surprised to learn that clothes are very reasonable here, but don't just buy a souvenir; make sure the article is the sort of thing you'd wear back home.

Pointer: Stores in Amsterdam open at 9 A.M. and, in general, close at 6 P.M. six days a week. BUT: hairdressers close at 5 P.M. and cigar shops remain open until 7 P.M. Department stores and many shops are closed Monday mornings. Hairdressers are closed on Tuesdays.

ENTERTAINMENT ¶ American GIs on duty in Germany consider Amsterdam a "good liberty town." Also, it has become the favorite Continental city with American youth. Furthermore, it has acquired a noticeable permissive quality, and municipal authorities seem bent on encouraging this. So that might give you a fair idea of the range or limits of entertainment possibilities in the city. A good beginning, according to an old Dutch axiom, is the important thing. So far as Amsterdam's night life is concerned, we shall at least give you an idea of a good place to begin. It would be the Leidseplein. From this square there are many streets of night spots that might be of interest. Night clubs in Amsterdam (and other large towns) generally stay open until 4 A.M. and serve just about any kind of drink you could possibly dream up. Along the street leading to the municipal theater you'll find any number of bars. Another good starting point is the square named after a famed painter, Rembrandtsplein. In case you still are seeking afterdark picturesqueness, you should be able to find it by the scoopful in the Zeedijk neighborhood, the hangout of sailors and their friends and hangers-on. There are lots of canals, winding and narrow streets and other pitfalls in this zone.

There are loads of motion picture theaters about, with no dubbed films; so, if the production is American or English, you're safe. There are usually a couple of shows in the afternoon and a couple more in the evening. (In places smaller than Amsterdam, however, movies might be shown only once an evening or only a few evenings a week.) The Dutch legitimate theater isn't for you, unless you have a command of the language. Which I doubt.

SPORTS ¶ In this country of inland waterways and exterior coastlines, aquatic sports predominate. They are marvelously varied, too—from rowing and canoeing to swimming and water skiing. *Walking* is also a great sport (and costs very little!). Some towns, such as Nijmegen, have regular walking contests, and in many places "walking marches" are arranged for the general amusement. The local tourist office—anywhere—will be able to let you know what sports are in season at the time of your visit. It is necessary, in case you wish to hire a boat bigger than a rowboat or canoe, to get your reservation in as early as possible. The country is crazy about *soccer*, and you might enjoy seeing a match. Quite a few *golf courses* around, and if you belong to an American club, that's (usually) the only introduction needed. Get details from the Netherlands Golf Comite at 109 Herengracht in Amsterdam. Plenty of *tennis* courts! Ice skating (and ice hockey matches) is the big sport during the winter. (Do you recall reading *Hans Brinker or The Silver Skates*?)

ʒ✎ Short Trips from Amsterdam

Aalsmeer

One pleasant day's excursion involves getting up early in the morning and heading for Aalsmeer, about twelve miles southwest of Amsterdam on route E-10. The flower auctions are active between 8 A.M. and noon (except Sundays and holidays), but after 9:30 you'll miss the best of the sights. There is a worthwhile tourist attraction, the Minicorso, a miniature reproduction of the Aalsmeer Flower Festival displayed inside a glasshouse; very beautiful. Then a short ride into Haarlem, an extremely interesting town. In the center is the Grote Market, the marketplace, where ten streets meet. On the south side of the open area is the Vleeshal, an outstanding Renaissance building dating back to 1602. Alongside is the imposing Grote Kerk, where Frans Hals' body is interred. Walking south from the marketplace on Grote Houstraat, you'll come to the canal; turn left on Gasthuisvest until you reach 62 Groot Heiligland, site of the Frans Hals Museum, with its outstanding painting collection.

The Frans Hals Museum is open six days a week from 10 A.M. to 5 P.M. and on Sunday from 1 to 5 P.M. From early April to mid-May there are candlelight displays of the pictures during the evening, from 8:30 to 10:30 P.M. The candlelight showings are generally repeated from mid-July to early September. The entrance fee for them is 1.50 guilders.

Of course, if you are fortunate enough to be here during April and early May, the major attraction is the bulb fields. The crocuses bloom in early April, then come daffodils, narcissuses (or do you prefer narcissi?) and hyacinths. Tulips are at their very best from late April to the middle of May, as one tulip species after another comes into flower, and naturally there is some climatic variation each year. To see the flowers, drive south from Haarlem toward Hillegom and Lisse (where you can visit the Keukenhof Flower Show and its beautiful gardens from 9 A.M. until sunset during the season; admission charge). Then Sassenheim and Voorhour. Return by a slightly different route. (During the summer months the gladiolas bloom and may make up for your failure to be here during the spring.) To the west of Haarlem is

Zandvoort, a seaside resort, with good hotels and restaurants and lovely sand dunes to stroll over, if you don't mind sand in your shoes.

Volendam and Marken

This is the classic tourist circuit, and most visitors would feel they haven't seen Holland if they didn't make it. You can go by car, train, bus or boat. The boat leaves from the back of the Central Railroad Station, but it's a long trip, and you'll have comparatively little time left for sightseeing.

If you use a private car, cross the River Ij by the ferry (also at the railroad station). The road commences on the opposite bank toward Broek and Monnikendam, and both are very interesting. Next comes Edam, the cheese town with the "floating cellar." You can't miss seeing it. Point toward the coast to Volendam, and now we're going to have a little talk. This town and its too-enterprising inhabitants, together with those of Marken, have become aware (in the commercial sense) of the monetary value of their costumes and the colorful customs of their communities. The result is a brazen commercialization of what was once a charming group of villages. The entire setup has turned into an almost vulgar and displeasing combination of nonsense, Coney Island and honky-tonk. There is nothing more ludicrous than the sight of a matron from Lincoln, Nebraska, taking the picture of a villager (in a fifteenth-century costume) who advises her on the correct camera exposure and then charges her a florin for posing.

If you want to, as a matter of fact, you can even have your own photograph taken in a Volendam costume. As long as you're in the place, you might want to visit another of its "unparalleled" attractions—the House of the Cigar Bands. And if it is a Monday that brings you to this quaint—and we do mean *quaint*—place, there is a special routine about the morning's wash on the line. The local tourist office, by the way, is at 33 Weversstraat.

Peculiarly enough, Volendam *is* an attractive Roman Catholic village; the height of local excitement occurs at churchtime on Sunday, when the villagers do everything but stage a ballet in the fashion of the chorus line at the Radio City Music Hall.

From Volendam, you can take a half-hour ride by

motorboat to Marken, which is similar, only doubled and redoubled. Fortunately, in Marken you can wander through the narrow streets and avoid the hustle and bustle at the tourist docks. You'll see the church and inside, a herring boat in full sail hung from the vault. Along the waterfront, note the dike that protects Marken from the cruel sea.

Gooiland

No, not Disneyland, Gooiland. Leave Amsterdam, in the direction of Bussum, a pretty village filled with flowers and gardens; then on to Hilversum, very progressive and modern. Go from here toward Bearn; if you wish, turn toward Soestdijk, where Queen Juliana resides, but you can't see too much there. Better than that is the trip north to the twin villages of Bunschoten and Spakenburg, where you'll find an uncommercialized and pleasanter version of Volendam and Marken; the villagers' costumes and local customs are at least equal to those in the more highly publicized centers. On the way back visit Laren, an artists' community, and then continue past Bussum to Naarden, whose proudest possession is a very fine old fortress constructed in the shape of a star. Naarden was the scene of considerable medieval violence, for the fortress frequently bore the brunt of attacks by invading hordes of Spanish.

Alkmaar Cheese Market

You must go on Friday—the market day, a truly colorful sight. Boat trips (Friday only) leave from opposite 60 Amstel. By car, leave Amsterdam by the northwest, and head toward IJmuiden, the road running parallel to the North Sea Canal; near IJmuiden cross by ferry and continue on to Alkmaar.

The cheese market, held from late April through September, runs from about 9:30 to noon, so that means you'd best get an early start from Amsterdam. Admittedly, the entire proceedings are now a reproduction of the old cheese market customs that have more or less disappeared, but this is none the less interesting. The cheeses are juggled, shifted and later transferred for shipment by porters wearing the ancient costume of the cheese guilds. The selling procedure, executed by hand clapping, reminds us for some obscure reason of the chant of the tobacco auctioneer in our own southern states. At either 11 A.M. or noon, hurry to the Bath Bridge (opposite the Weigh House) and watch the mechanical pageant in the old clock when the hour is struck. Then comes the carillon concert. If you enjoy organ music, there's a concert at the Grote Kerk on Fridays from 11:15 A.M., lasting a half-hour.

By *steamer* from Amsterdam (Botel Cruises, De Ruyter Kade, Steiger [Pier] 4) you can cruise on inland waterways across Holland and across the heart of Europe. There are eight-day cruises along the flower fields, with visits at Arnhem, Dordrecht, Gouda, Leiden and Haarlem. You have your meals aboard ship and live there. A number of excursions are included in the price, such as those to Rotterdam, Volendam, Keukenhof and the flower market at Aalsmeer. A few are not included, such as a couple of museum visits.

ಽ‿ *Motoring in the Netherlands*

Formalities for bringing a car into the Netherlands are simple: registration certificate, the Green Card (affirming insurance coverage) and your home-state driver's license. You should also have an identification letter at the back of the car for the country in which it is registered (F for France; USA for the United States, etc.).

Don't get the wrong impression about Holland's size. It may be small, comparatively, but there is plenty of room and good roads to travel upon. From Amsterdam, for instance, it is 175 miles to the country's southern border, 150 miles to the one in the north, 120 miles to the eastern one and just 20 miles to the sea on the west.

The precedence (right of way) in driving along Holland's roads is, as usual in Europe, to the car coming from the right. However, Holland has one special rule that is not followed in all countries. In Holland, fast traffic takes precedence over slow-moving vehicles, such as bicycles and motorcycles. But, traffic from the right, whether it is slow or fast, has the priority all the time. Near the German border—or if you see a German car bearing down on you—pay special attention. Germany follows different rules of traffic precedence, and the German driver while in Holland might not remember that he is abroad.

Pedestrians have rights, too—don't forget that. Places

for pedestrians to cross are painted on the street with a patchwork of lines resembling the markings of a zebra (thus, these crosswalks are usually referred to as "zebra crossings"). Cars must let pedestrians have the right of way at such crossings. However, pedestrians themselves are not allowed to jump out into a zebra crossing so quickly, and unexpectedly, that it is not possible for the fast-moving automobile traffic to stop prudently. In built-up urban zones the speed limit is normally 31 miles an hour. At times, this is raised to about 43 miles an hour, and a sign will indicate this (70 kms.). It is possible, also, that you might come upon other signs advising particular speed limits. They'll always be in kilometers, so you'll have to do your own calculating. (A rough rule of thumb is to chop off the last figure in the kilometer reading and multiply by six.)

One of the prettiest routes to travel is from Amsterdam to Leiden to Utrecht. It follows fields, canals and those windmills you have heard (you have, haven't you?) about. The route is about a hundred miles long. Any local tourist office (VVV) will gladly point out some sights for you to watch for on this itinerary and even give you a map to guide you.

The Royal Netherlands Touring Club (ANWB) patrols main highways by car and motorcycle to assist motorists whose automobiles have broken down or are causing them trouble. The service is free to foreigners if they have a card showing membership in an automobile club back home. If you are not already a member of a club in the United States, you can get a membership in the Royal Netherlands Touring Club upon payment of a relatively small fee which entitles you to road assistance. Some main highways are patrolled night and day all year around, while others have this service only in the daytime. In case of any difficulty on the highway, telephone the nearest government tourist office or call the Touring Club in Amsterdam by dialing-direct (02) 22-44-66. On the main highways and in the larger cities, service stations are generally open around the clock. Regular gasoline is not expensive, compared to what it is in most other places on the Continent. Parking rates are usually posted; they are reasonable—an average of a half-guilder an hour. Parking meters have been installed in most cities.

❧ A Motor Trip Through the Benelux Countries

As you know, Belgium, Netherlands and Luxembourg are joined together in an economic union called Benelux, a contraction of the three names. Because of their geographic proximity, a very rewarding trip may be made through these three countries. For convenience, the starting point selected is Amsterdam, but actually, the trip could begin anywhere along the line—Luxembourg City, Antwerp or Brussels, for example.

Amsterdam to Arnhem—52 miles

Leave Amsterdam, starting from the Mint Tower and heading southward on the Vijzelstraat and later the Ferdinand-Bol-Straat until you join up with the main road, the *autosnelweg*, which is a fast but uninteresting highway. Point for Utrecht. Turn off the highway at the sign for Utrecht; undoubtedly the city will be overcrowded during its semiannual fairs (March–April and September), otherwise not too busy. The town itself is completely encircled by the Singel Canal, and the Old and New Canals cut through the city in charming fashion. It's interesting to explore the old town, with its gabled houses, cobbled streets and the Cathedral of St. Michael (called the Dom), whose tower was blown down in 1674.

From Utrecht, pick up route E-36 and turn off at the indicated right turn toward Driebergen and Doorn, where the late Kaiser Wilhelm of Germany lived in exile after the end of World War I. From there the road continues on to Amerongen, which is quite attractive. Go eastward through Wageningen into Arnhem, a town that took a terrific battering during World War II but is now largely rebuilt. Just north of the city is the fascinating Open Air Museum, representing Dutch folklore and country life with old farm buildings, artisans' workshops, and such, brought here and set up for exhibition; open April 1 to November 1, 9 A.M. to 6 P.M. on weekdays, 11 A.M. to 6 P.M. on Sundays and holidays. Admission fee: 1 guilder. The fascinating shopping area covers three downtown squares closed to auto traffic during the day; there's everything from shirts to antiques. Most shop-keepers speak English.

Arnhem to Maastricht—93 miles

From Arnhem, head south to Nijmegen and don't worry about unnumbered roads, for the country is small and the chance of getting lost is equally small. Nijmegen has its Grote Markt in the center of the older quarter of town; otherwise there is not too much to see. Now south from Nijmegen to Gennep and Arcen, the latter having an interesting chateau. Then on to Venlo, via route E-9, passing through Roermond and Sittard. Maastricht is worth a brief visit, because of its Servaaskerk (church) and St. Servatius Bridge. Just five minutes south of town are the labyrinthine quarries of Petersberg; these are 2,000 years old and have been excavated a total of about 200 miles in length and are interesting to walk through if you don't have claustrophobia.

If you remain overnight at Maastricht, a fine place to stay is the Dominicain. It is in an excellent location and has a wonderful cafe furnished in comfortable Old World style.

Maastricht is another place where the shopping is good. Not only does "everyone" speak English, but whatever currency happens to be in your pocketbook will be accepted by the shops without a qualm, quiver or moment's hesitation. It is truly an international city, situated just a matter of a few miles from Germany, Belgium and Luxembourg.

Maastricht to Liège—21 miles

To drive from Maastricht to Liège, head south to the Belgian border; continue on (the road is now marked 43) to Liège. The outstanding attraction at Liège is the imaginative Sound and Light exhibit in Bouverie Park, a superb setting, where the Meuse and Ourthe rivers meet. Here, if time is limited, you can omit Luxembourg from your itinerary and join the tour later at Namur. If this is the case, take route 43 out of Liège (it changes subsequently to route 17) and follow the Meuse River to Namur.

Around the corner from the Hôtel de Ville is one of the antique, narrow streets of Liège (which heads in the direction of the waterfront) that has been converted into an intriguing shopping street. There are no automobiles permitted, and window shoppers can browse tranquilly. Shops are identified by antique-type insignia that have been given a modern, whimsical touch. Even if you don't buy a thing, you'll enjoy this shopping street.

On the way to Namur, along the Meuse River, exciting scenery will greet you at every bend. At Huy, a cable car, swinging from one side of the Meuse to the other, will transport you on a unique ride from the riverbank to the lofty citadel. The banks of the Meuse, too, are excellent locales for the would-be fisherman—or for watching local fishermen fish.

Liège to Luxembourg City—125 miles

If time permits (and you are urged to see that it does) visit Luxembourg, the tiny Grand Duchy, which is either 999 square miles in size (if you are a public relations man looking for an angle) or 1,000 square miles, if you prefer round figures. Take route 32 out of Liège, to Theux, Spa and Malmédy; Malmédy to St.-Vith by route 23, then route 26 until just after Beho; later take a left turn on route 33, which leads to the border of Luxembourg and Belgium. It's route 16 now south toward Ettelbruck, with a right turn onto route 27 about five miles before reaching that little town. Continue on either 7 or

7-A (both rides are about the same) to Mersch, an attractive little spot. Then comes Luxembourg City, capital of said Grand Duchy. I guess the Hotel Cravat is the best.

The city has charm, make no mistake about that; it is winding and hilly and has moats and castles and arched houses and picturesque views and is loads of fun to wander about in, providing you're on foot. By riding about, you'll see only the main streets and not the interesting blind alleys and colorful courtyards with overhanging balconies. You won't want to miss the Grand Duke's Palace, a sixteenth-century castle. Near the City Hall is the Place Guillaume, with a fascinating market during the morning. Not far from Luxembourg City is the American military cemetery where General Patton is buried.

The Luxembourg railroad operates some very attractive excursions from main points of interest in the Grand Duchy, every day from July to September. There are tours from Luxembourg City, Echternach, Diekirch, Ettlebruck and Larochette.

Luxembourg City to Namur—96 miles

Leave Luxembourg City on route 6 toward Arlon and the Belgian border; the road then becomes route 4 and continues to Bastogne, a very old town. Bastogne has a new fame, as well. This is the place where the Nazis, thinking they had the Americans surrounded and defeated, called upon them to surrender. The American General McAuliffe's reply was one word: *"Nuts!"* McAuliffe and his men continued the fight, and you know what happened to the Nazis. They lost. From Bastogne go on to Namur, which is situated at the junction of the Meuse and the Sambre rivers. Namur is a lively place and a popular Belgian resort center. It is an attractive town, but many of its old streets and buildings are gone, destroyed in one or another war, siege or invasion. Don't forget, it has a casino. You will find that the very charming Hôtel Comtes d'Harscamp is the ideal spot if you remain overnight.

Namur to Ypres—114 miles

Out of Namur, route 22 heads toward Charleroi, an industrial town. (From Charleroi, if you have the time, there are a range of pleasant excursions, such as to Loverval, and its lake country; Jamioulx, famous for its

landscapes; the hills and dales of Biesmelle; and the famous battlefield at Fleurus.) From Charleroi, proceed
to Binche, which is famous for its Shrove Tuesday festival.
The Binche festival involves oranges—tons of them.
We advise seeing it, but we also urge you to try to stay
out of the line of fire. Orange juice is best taken internally,
and not externally. It is quite a sight to see the oranges
being tossed about and rolling down the streets during
this vibrant fete. Any other day of the year at Binche
(after all, the odds are 365 to 1 against your getting there
on Shrove Tuesday), visit the chateau, almost completely ruined, and wander about the old town walls—
ruined, too. If you don't like ruined chateaux and ruined
town walls, on to Mons.

As you might expect, Mons has a chateau and a
church, St.-Wandru. What comes as an unexpected surprise is the lovely interior of the church. If you missed
Shrove Tuesday at Binche, could you possibly manage to
be here on Trinity Sunday, when a local dragon meets
with a local knight in combat? (With two possibilities
out of 365 days, the odds of hitting one festival or the
other are down to 182½ to 1.) Mons is also the gateway
to the Borinage, which Van Gogh painted, and the city
is circled by green-mossed mountains that are actually
piles of slag and refuse from the coal mines. At Mons'
doorstep, too, is the brand-new headquarters of SHAPE,
which moved from Paris in the spring of 1967, when the
North Atlantic Treaty Organization had to find a new
home.

All of the Mons museums are open daily except Monday from 10 A.M. to 12 and from 2 to 6 P.M. You might
like to take a look at the community swimming pool—
a heated covered affair. There is a very small entrance
fee if you want to look around, and a slightly larger
one for actually taking a plunge. The pool is on Avenue
Victor Maistriau and is open from 8 A.M. to 1 P.M. and
from 3 to 7 P.M. on weekdays; 8 A.M. to 1 P.M., Sundays.

Leave Mons on route 22, which later (at Hornu) picks
up route 61 into Tournai, with its old cathedral. Sound
and Light displays are presented in front of the cathedral
from time to time (they put them on when groups of
forty or more persons request such a show, in advance).
This cathedral, by the way, is the only Belgian church
that was built to be a cathedral. (Fascinating information
at no extra charge.) Then, from Tournai, continue on

route 71 to Kortrijk (in French, Courtrai). Now route 9 through Menen to Ypres, or Ieper (or even Wypers, as the British soldiers used to call it). Ypres demands a little time, for its medieval and modern history have been noteworthy; during the twelfth and thirteenth centuries it was a center for clothmaking, and the rich citizenry erected a marvelous medieval building, the Lakenhal, or Cloth Hall, in the Grote Markt, in the center of town. Other important buildings nearby include the reconstructed Cathedral of St.-Martin and the Vleeshal, the Meat Hall. Follow the Menensteenweg (a street) eastward to the Menin Gate, a memorial to the British dead of World War I; there is a ceremony in their honor each evening. On the outskirts of town are British and German cemeteries. The hotel situation here is only fair; the best available is the Old World Hotel Splendid Britannique. While the hotel situation is poor, it would be very pleasant to have lunch at the Hostellerie St.-Nicholas, a charming country-style inn; poultry and game are your best bets here.

Ypres each year features a light-hearted Cat Festival, which involves a long procession and winds up with the tossing of toy cats from the bell tower. The tossing is done, naturally, by the town jester. For the exact dates of this and other bits of folklore, get in touch with the government tourist office in the Hôtel de Ville (in Flemish, Stadhuis).

Ypres to Ostend—34 miles

Leave Ypres via route 69 to Ostend, a seaside resort on the general order of Atlantic City, almost completely reconstructed after wartime bombing and later inundated when dikes broke nearby during a 1953 storm. The dikes that protect Ostend are a sight in themselves. But a big attraction for most visitors is the Kursaal, the gambling casino featuring low-priced bets; you'll be admitted on presentation of your passport.

Ostend is a highly agreeable place. The hotels are excellent, and because the food is Belgian, it is magnificent. North of Ostend are smaller, but ultrafashionable, seacoast resorts. Between Ostend and the French border the entire littoral (all right, coastline) has dozens of pleasant places in which to relax and enjoy life—and Brussels is only 90 or 100 minutes away by car.

Ostend to Brussels—80 miles

From Ostend to Bruges, there's a choice of rural route 10 or the superhighway, 10-*bis* (but watch for the exit). Bruges is a lovely old town with a medieval aspect and, along with Ghent, is one of the most delightful places in Belgium. In the center of town is the usual Grote Markt with open-air stalls; the nearby belfry tower has carillon concerts on Monday, Wednesday and Saturday from 9 to 10 P.M. and on Sunday from 11:45 A.M. to 12:30 P.M (from June 15 to September 30; during the rest of the year, on Wednesday, Saturday and Sunday at 11:45 A.M.). Go east on Breidelstraat (a street) to the open area known as the Burg and the Chapel of the Holy Blood, the Palais van Vrede and the Stadhuis or Town Hall. Also, there's St. John's Hospital (yes!), which has a museum of paintings by Memling. But none of this explains Bruges, why it is such a favorite with American tourists or why everyone seems to leave with regret. There are canals (yes, Bruges is another Venice of the north!), but there is peace, calm, quiet beauty and serenity. If time permits, visit the Béguinage, a most unusual convent situated near a lovely little lake, the Minnewater, "the love lake" of a romantic saga. It's truly another world, filled with peace and tranquillity. Please believe us, and visit the Béguinage to soak up the quintessence of Bruges atmosphere. Also, take a sightseeing boat through the canals.

A promenade along the canals is suitable from sunrise to sunset; and on the evenings when the town monuments are lighted up the boats also sail. The trip lasts forty minutes, but its memory will be of much longer duration. The charge for the motorboat ride is relatively small. A sightseeing trip by horse and carriage is also possible. The main tourist office is at 1 Markt, and during the tourist season (April to end of September) it is open every day, including Sundays and holidays.

Continue on from Bruges on route 10 to Ghent, and you'll find another fine old town, a veritable museum of life as it must have been 500 or more years ago. The architecture is wonderfully medieval, the classic buildings rising three stories and then coming to a point two stories higher. In the heart of the town is the Cathedral of St.-Bavo and the Stadhuis. As previously mentioned, it's a close race as to which is the more delightful spot—Bruges or Ghent. A big event at Ghent (French, Gand; Flemish, Gent) is the Floralies, a tremendous flower fair. This occurs, however, only every fifth year—in the years divisible by five—and it is truly something to look forward to. If you would like to see a typical European fair (a trade fair, that is), stop by in Ghent between the second Saturday and the fourth Sunday of September for the annual International Fair. The Community Tourist Service at Borluutstraat 9 will provide you with details on the goings-on in Ghent.

If you want to remain overnight, the Cour St.-Georges is an extremely atmospheric thirteenth century hotel. For dinner you could eat there or head out towards the edge of the town to the Patijntje Restaurant, which serves very good food and has a lovely view of the river. From Ghent, pick up route 10 or 10-*bis* and proceed to Bruxelles (French), or Brussel (Flemish), or even Brussels (English). Brussels and its hotels are discussed in detail in the section on Belgium.

Brussels to Antwerp—30 miles

From Brussels, take route 1 toward Mechelen (French, Malines), leaving the city via the Avenue de Vilvorde. Mechelen is an extremely interesting place for a pleasurable walk, offering a cathedral and a fine old church, plus loads of local color. Mechelen is known everywhere for its fine carillon school. Many of the world's great (are you ready?) carilloneurs (including American ones) were trained here. It is wonderful to walk through the antique streets of the town and to hear the carillons sounding high up in their towers. Then on to Antwerp, Belgium's great port. There you'll find the Town Hall, with some notable murals; St. Jacob's church has the Rubens Chapel, and the cathedral has other fine paintings. Yet basically Antwerp is a busy commercial port city with little to hold the tourist. The largest and most important hotel in town is the Century. Very pleasant and much less expensive is the Antwerp Docks Hotel a bit over a mile away from the center of town. The town boasts two good, fairly expensive restaurants: Cigogne d'Alsace and La Rade, the latter being the better and more expensive of the two.

Many visitors spend a very pleasant few hours—and even an entire day—in the Antwerp Zoo, right next door to the railroad station. It is an extremely agreeable setting, and the manner in which the birds and animals are presented in cageless sanctuaries is fascinating.

Antwerp to Rotterdam—60 miles

Leave Antwerp by the Italielei (a street) to route 1 to the Belgium-Holland border; it's route E-10 in Holland. Just before Breda, pick up the *autosnelweg* (fast auto road) in the direction of Rotterdam. Rotterdam lost most of its old buildings and tourist attractions when Hitler's air force gave the city a completely unwarranted bombing attack *after* the Dutch had signed an armistice, and don't for a moment think the local folk have forgotten or forgiven one iota. The entire city has been rebuilt in modern architectural style and can be seen by car, by bus or, best of all, in one of the little boats that leaves the Willemsplein for a tour of the dock areas. Rotterdam has a new Hilton Hotel, easily the outstanding place to stay, since it is centrally located and boasts several interesting dining rooms. Less expensive, but very modern and attractive is the Park Hotel, located on a canal. Also first class but reasonably priced is the very modern Rijn Hotel. Among the restaurants, the Old Dutch and the Coq d'Or are very good, but quite expensive.

One unique attraction in Rotterdam is its Eiffel Tower-like Euromast, with restaurants and observation balconies. It rises more than 350 feet in the air and is a thrilling viewpoint. There is an admission charge. Incidentally, in case you are interested in that tunnel under the Meuse River—the first one built under a river in Holland—you can arrange a visit by getting in touch with the tunnel people at 27 Charloise Hoofd.

Rotterdam to The Hague—15 miles

Take route E-10 out of Rotterdam, exiting at Delft, where the famous earthenware is being made once again. The town is slow-moving, delightful and pleasant for strolling about; little commercial activity or movement except in the Grote Markt. Boat rides through Delft's canals are relaxing and low-priced.

Leave Delft via the Buitenwatersloot toward the Hoek van Holland, a bathing resort. The name works out to be the Hook of Holland in English. Then route E-8 to The Hague. And this is a place that has many names: 'sGravenhage or Den Haag by the Netherlander, who can't quite decide; La Haye by the French, who are definite; Hague or The Hague by English-speaking people, who are also indefinite. The Hague (we all have to take a stand sometime!) is a pleasing, although basically dull city, inhabited by staid folk who pass the day under the lovely trees that line most of the main streets (but who can blame them). The canals are attractive, but so they are in just about every Dutch town.

A couple of miles north along the coast is Scheveningen, the favorite seaside resort of the country. Driving along the route you'll pass the Madurodam, which is open from mid-April until early October (hours: 9:30 A.M. to as late as 10:30 P.M. in the middle of summer. There is an admission charge. The Madurodam represents, in miniature, a fairly complete Netherlands countryside with buildings, railroads and so forth. Scheveningen is much more amusing for tourists than The Hague and has all the usual beach attractions and many festivals, but is dead as the renowned dormouse during the winter months. The Hague is filled with museums, and most of them are interesting. If you have a hankering to see a variety of old-time instruments of torture, for instance, it can be easily arranged. Just drop by 33 Buitenhof from April to October between 10 and 4. There is a slight admission fee. For general tourist information, or help on accommodations, visit the VVV office at 38 Parkstraat. It is open daily till 9 P.M. The Hotel Wittebrug, opposite the Scheveningen woods, is quite nice. Its hairdressing salon for women and barbershop for men are tops. The Hôtel des Indes is very luxurious; loads of atmosphere at a remodeled chateau in suburban Wassenaar, the Kasteel oud Wassenaar. Be sure to have a meal at the Saur restaurant in The Hague, expensive but good.

Don't pass up the old quarter of Scheveningen, where the people still wear traditional costumes. Not far away from The Hague is the old university town of Leiden. Less than three miles farther on, near the main The Hague-Amsterdam highway, is the new 200-room Holiday Inn Hotel.

The Hague to Amsterdam—39 miles

Take route E-10 from The Hague to Amsterdam, our starting point. If you haven't seen Haarlem, there is a left turn toward Lisse and Haarlem about eleven miles along the way. Haarlem, of course, has the famous Frans Hals Museum. The bathing beaches are excellent at IJmuiden, Bloemendaal and Zandvoort. The latter spot has that famous automobile circuit, as well. If you have not had a chance to do all the fast driving you'd like to along Europe's freeways, you can do some practice runs on the Zandvoort course. The VVV (the tourist office, remember?) will give you all the details. It's in the middle of things at 1 Stationsplein in Haarlem.

And so we arrive back at our starting point.

MISCELLANEOUS ¶ Lots of women still wear the traditional costumes in Holland. On the beaches, though, women (possibly not the same ones) are as modern as anywhere else, with their two-piece bikinis.

Meal hours: Breakfast, any time you get up. Lunch from noon to 2 P.M. Dinner starts as early as 6 P.M. but not much later than 7 P.M., except in tourist hotels. Don't order too many dishes at once; Dutch portions are often kingsize and too large for most Americans.

If you're planning to spend more than a few days in Holland, bring a raincoat. If it doesn't rain, it'll surely be misty or foggy or damp or something requiring a raincoat.

The Dutch are among the few European nations that haven't forgotten the American war effort and you'll often be thanked as if you were personally responsible. Americans are in great favor at present, and let's hope we remain so in this wonderful country.

On being presented to other people, most local folk will announce their names instead of saying "hello." Not a bad system for people who get embarrassed and can't remember names when making introductions.

You know that old gag about "Dutch treat"? It's true, no kidding. The general practice is to divide restaurant checks and the like. You'll see people figuring who had what and how much was it, wherever you go. That doesn't apply at home, of course, nor does it mean that a Hollander won't invite you some place at his own expense, but the practice is often a little difficult for an American to follow. For instance, an invitation to "join" someone for lunch might well mean a divided check. However, an invitation to be someone's "guest" for lunch means just that. Can't help you any more than that; just listen carefully and if in doubt, suggest splitting the check and see if any protest is forthcoming.

Be prompt for appointments; it's a highly regarded virtue in all of Holland. Particularly true in business meetings.

Stay out of all kinds of public transportation during the morning and evening rush hours. You'll get mashed to a pulp, or nearly so, although otherwise the local folk are quite polite.

ACCOMMODATIONS ¶ Spic and span, comfortable, but old-fashioned might be the generic descriptions to encompass most Netherlands hotels. A widespread modernization plan seems to be called for, particularly in Amsterdam, where several large and modern hotels are now under construction. During late April and May (when the bulbs are in bloom) and again during summer months, space is at a premium in almost all the hotels. Expect to find solid comfort, a gracious reception, but in rooms that might well be redecorated. Please make advance reservations if you plan to visit during the heavy tourist season.

Figure on spending between $20 and $30 for a double room with a bath in a top Amsterdam hotel, although you might find accommodations somewhat less expensive.

Pointer: The official tourist office in Amsterdam makes possible person-to-person contacts between visitors and residents through a Get-in-Touch-with-the-Dutch program. Tourist offices in some other cities also do the same thing.

NORWAY

National Characteristics

The word for the southernmost tip of Norway is "Nose." If you take Norway by its *nose* and turn it around like the hand of a clock the northernmost point of the country would reach Rome. Don't try doing that, of course. But it gives you an idea of the size of Norway. The rugged country of the Norwegians is filled with fjords and forests, plus mountains and harbors. Because of all the twists and turns around large, medium-sized and small bodies of water, the Norwegian coastline is 12,500 miles long. But there are fewer than 4 million people in Norway.

Those of you who have previously seen Norway were probably incredulous at the first sight of the country's unbelievable scenery. The west coast of Norway, extending all the way to the North Cape, has some of the greatest scenery in the world. Perhaps the greatest.

Nature has been kind, and unkind, to Norway. Much of the country (a good two-thirds) consists of mountain ranges, and many of these are snow-covered a large part of the year. These magnificent mountains make Norway a prime tourist attraction. On the unkind side, nature has—by giving Norway its natural wonders—crowded the inhabitants into a narrow strip running north and south along the coast. The mountains rush downhill and halt just short of the cruel sea. Only 4 percent of the land in the entire country is under cultivation. Thus, Norway has naturally turned to the sea for its subsistence, and Norwegian ships and sailors sail all the waters of the earth. But, then, when their sailing days are through, they return to Norway and settle down—because, they feel, it is the most wonderful place in the world. (Note: They think the United States runs a close second.) Although conditions have changed for the better in recent years, life has not always been easy for the Norwegians. At the end of World War II, for instance, the entire northern, above-the-Arctic Circle, region of Norway—the zone called Finnmark—was completely burned by the retreating Nazis as they carried out a scorched-earth policy. Some of you, possibly, were in Oslo in the early postwar period. You will remember how it used to tug at your heart to see almost completely empty counters in department stores three, four and five years after World War II ended.

The Norwegians are healthy outdoor people, delightful to be with. But underneath there is a sense of seriousness. Their constant battle for survival apparently breeds a strong sense of self-reliance and determination to win out over all odds. Of all the countries invaded by the Germans during the war, the consensus is that thinly populated Norway put up the bravest resistance, perhaps because of an almost-forgotten incident that preceded the invasion. The hospitable Norwegians had, some two decades before, invited into their homes thousands of German youth orphaned during World War I. Shortly before the second holocaust began, these same befriended youths returned—seemingly of their own volition—to visit, en masse, their Norwegian benefactors. And also, as it later developed, to spy on Norway's defenses as a prelude to the German invasion.

When to Go

It may come as a surprise to you, if you have only spent summers in Norway, that the winters are not so bad as one might think. There is plenty of snow on the ground in Oslo during the winter months, and the days are short—yet the Gulf Stream, which nudges Norway along the west coast, takes quite a bit of sting out of the Arctic Circle atmosphere. Summers are quite mild, similarly, and the hottest July weather might be generally compared with the month of May in the northern half of the United States. Even during the summer months, evenings are cool, with temperatures usually in the low 50s.

Norwegians celebrate Constitution Day on May 17, and this is the start—officially and formally—of the brightest, happiest season of the year. So this is a logical date for you to figure as the start of your vacation trip in Norway.

On Constitution Day a holiday mood is everywhere. Students dress up in picturesque clothes, parents dress their youngsters in a stunningly luminous rainbow of colors and brass bands join in the festivities. The royal family and the Norwegian people wish one another the happiest holiday time possible. That will apply to you, too.

The tourist season—for the summertime visitors—comes to an end almost exactly on September 15. The only months when swimming is possible are July and August, if then. Quite naturally, this is the rush season. Reservations aren't merely suggested—they're absolutely essential. Of course, Oslo Fjord has water temperatures almost identical to those of New York's Jones Beach, but the air will be cooler.

Oslo has some rain about every third day. But you'll find that your plans are seldom disturbed, because the rainfall is usually not of all-day duration. Unfortunately, however, this is not the situation along the west coast, where the rain seems to come down in buckets with unnecessary regularity. Even a beautiful fjord can seem pretty dismal when it rains three days straight. But this condition occurs only if your luck is running unusually bad because, on the average, it rains annoyingly only every third or fourth day. The main thing is to dress for Norway's weather, and then you can enjoy yourself. That's especially important in the wintertime—wear boots, stretch pants and a warm coat.

Norway's ski season is a long one—starting early, and in some places continuing well into May. The high points are Christmas and Easter, and at these times you'll need to make advance reservations just as far ahead as you can.

WEATHER STRIP: OSLO

Temp.	JAN.	FEB.	MAR.	APR.	MAY	JUNE	JULY	AUG.	SEPT.	OCT.	NOV.	DEC.
Low	21°	21°	26°	34°	43°	50°	56°	53°	46°	37°	30°	24°
High	28°	30°	38°	48°	59°	65°	71°	66°	59°	46°	36°	29°
Average	25°	26°	32°	41°	51°	58°	64°	60°	53°	42°	33°	27°
Days of rain	12	12	13	10	11	10	12	15	11	12	12	15

MIDNIGHT SUN ¶ One of the most fascinating features of a visit here is the fact that north of the Arctic Circle the sun never sets for long periods—as much as five months —starting from the middle of spring to very late summer and early fall. South of the Arctic Circle (below Trondheim) the sun sets for a very few hours around midnight, but there is still enough light to read a newspaper outdoors. (The problem is to find a recent edition of your favorite newspaper to read in this off-the-beaten-path area!) Sleeping in daylight (even when you're tired) is difficult, so bring sleep shades or other eye coverings. The hotels have curtains and shades, but closing them tightly means a loss of ventilation.

Here is a handy timetable to indicate the areas where the sun is visible twenty-four hours a day:

From May 14	North Cape
From May 17	Hammerfest
From May 18	Vardø
From May 21	Tromsø
From May 26	Harstad
From June 5	Bodø

Note: On the island of Spitsbergen you can see the sun around the clock after April 21. On Bear Island the Midnight Sun makes its appearance on May 3.

TIME EVALUATION ¶ Oslo itself is entitled to two days; allow about the same time for Bergen. If you're driving up north, no fewer than ten are required. Boat trips through the fjords and up to the North Cape take from seven to twelve days on the average. Driving from Bergen to Oslo (or vice versa) can be done in two days, but three days would be better and you'd get much more out of the trip. If you really enjoy scenery and want to see Norway, allow about two full weeks.

PASSPORT AND VISA ¶ A passport is all you will need for a three-month visit. For longer than that, you'll have to get a visa.

CUSTOMS AND IMMIGRATION ¶ Customs formalities are not complicated at all. There are certain restrictions, as is customary throughout Europe, on tobacco and alcoholic products. You can bring in duty-free two cartons of cigarettes or 500 grams (a little over a pound) of any assortment of tobacco products; one bottle of liquor and a bottle of wine, two bottles of liquor or two bottles of wine. One interesting wrinkle in Norwegian customs regulations is that the visitor is allowed to take into the country, without paying duty, two packs of playing cards! That's novel. Also, of course, you can have the usual accouterments of a classic traveler—transistor, binoculars, camera, film and so forth.

There are some *theoretical* restrictions on currency, but this is no problem for the ordinary tourist. For instance, you can bring in a maximum of only 1,000 Norwegian kroner (and the denominations of the bills cannot be more than 100 kroner). On leaving, you cannot take with you more than 350 Norwegian kroner. As for other currencies, there is no limit on how much you can bring into the country.

CURRENCY ¶ The *krone* (English, crown) is the Norwegian unit of currency. The plural of *krone* is *kroner*, and you'll quickly get in the habit of referring to prices in kroner. The value of the krone varies with variations in the international exchange rate situation. One krone equals 100 *øre* (pronounced *or-uh*). The paper money you will be confronted with comprises five different denominations: notes of 10 kroner (usually written 10 kr.), 50 kr.; 100kr.; 500 kr.; and 1,000 kr. The coins are 5 kr., 1 kr., 50 øre (a half-krone), 10 øre, 5 øre, 2 øre and 1 øre.

PRICE LEVELS ¶ Norway is no longer the travel bargain it used to be. In Oslo, hotel rates are now up to $30 or so for a double room in a top hotel, but elsewhere you can spend much less than that—especially in towns not overrun with visitors. Even in Bergen (a busy place), for instance, several hotels charge upwards of $25 for many of their double rooms. Meal prices are high also, if you have in mind a complete meal with appropriate drinks. Sandwich meals and similar food are of course still very reasonable.

HEALTH ¶ The water is not only safe but delicious. Milk is excellent, although not always pasteurized. The only health problem likely to be encountered in Norway is seeing that you don't catch a cold. This means keeping dry. It might be a good idea to bring along rubbers as well as a raincoat (and in the winter, as we said, make sure you have boots). As even the summer evenings are inevitably cool, bring the necessary clothes. Whether it is winter or summer, be sure to have a good sweater. In the northern part of Norway, particularly in June and July, the insects (although not disease carriers) can be annoying. So bring along some good insect repellent.

TIME ¶ Norway is six hours ahead of (later than) Eastern Standard Time. Daylight Saving Time goes into effect during spring and summer.

TIPPING ¶ The service charge in hotels ranges from 10 to 15 percent. In the larger cities this is usually automatically included in the overall tariff; other places, it is a supplemental charge. Thus, in hotels, you need to tip the maids and the staff only if they have done something special for you (shining your shoes every night, getting an extra pillow and the like). The baggage porter, however, should get an average of 1 krone for each bag. Restaurants will include the service charge in your bill. Norwegians usually leave a little extra—enough to round out an odd sum to an even amount (such as 20 kr. if the bill comes to 18.75 kr.; 10 kr. if it comes to 9.10 kr., etc.). It is customary to give taxi drivers about 10 percent of the meter as a tip, but never less than 1 krone. Hat-check and washroom attendants generally are tipped either 50 øre or 1 krone, depending on the establishment. In some public places, such as the opera, the hat-check tariff will be indicated on a sign in the cloakroom. This will be a minimum fee, and it is the custom to give something additional.

TRANSPORTATION ¶ *Taxis* are still none too plentiful in Oslo (or most other large cities), especially during the summer months. It is generally a good idea to phone the concierge sometime before you are ready to leave the hotel for the evening and have him arrange for a cab. It is even wiser to have a cab reserved for bringing you back to the hotel after your evening out. Taxi rates are not high. The trip to Fornebu Airport, for instance, costs only a couple of dollars or so. *Public transportation* by buses and trams is efficient. But stay out of them during the morning and late-afternoon rush hours, please. (You can save a few cents on your bus and tram fares by buying a carnet of tickets, called a *trikkekort,* but it's hardly worth the effort.) There is good *long-distance bus* service to and between major points. The fares can vary somewhat, but are no expensive. *Airline* travel within the country is on the bargain side and is very good. During the summer there are some wonderful nighttime flights, especially to Midnight Sun points. There are now more than a score of airports in Norway, and even the uppermost reaches of the country are served by regular day and night flights throughout the year. A *train* trip, especially across the mountains, is a spectacular way of seeing the country, and for this type of sightseeing a good starting point is Bergen. The mountains along the route east of Bergen reach near 4,500-foot heights at certain points. This is not terribly high as some alpine mountains go, but the trackage in Norway remains at high levels for a longer distance, probably, than elsewhere in Europe. Rail fares are reasonable.

But the *steamer* trips along the west coast are the greatest of all Norwegian tourist attractions. Bergen is a convenient departure point. Trips vary from a day to more than a week, and you will be pleasantly surprised how low tariffs can be. But buy your tickets before getting on the boat. They are cheaper that way. (More later.)

COMMUNICATIONS ¶ The use of dial *telephones* has been expanded in recent years. If you're making a local call, deposit the amount of coins indicated in numerals on the front of the telephone instrument, either before or after receiving a dial tone. You can't go wrong, because if it doesn't work one way, just try the other. When your party responds, push the button to complete the call. *Airmail* to the United States costs around a quarter for a letter of five grams. The service is excellent, with letters delivered within two or three days to New York and, by the polar route, to California in about three days on the average. Letters sent by ship may take anywhere from two to three weeks. Or four. National, as well as overseas, *telegraph services* are excellent throughout the country.

KNOW THE NORWEGIANS ¶ Without any formality whatsoever, you'll be meeting and knowing the Norwegians very fast because they are so friendly and hospitable— particularly to Americans. Many tourists like to visit the home of a typical family in a country in which they are traveling, and this is easily arranged in Norway. There's an active Know-the-Norwegians program through the official Travel Association offices in Oslo, Bergen and Stavanger. These offices will make it possible for you to meet and visit with a family that has interests similar to yours. But get in touch with one of these offices as soon as you arrive. Better still, write in advance and tell them of your desires and your schedule. The address of the Oslo Travel Association is 19 Rådhusgaten. Don't be bashful.

GUIDE SERVICES ¶ Guides are available through Travel Association offices in major cities, particularly Oslo. The rates are not high.

HOLIDAYS ¶ New Years, Maundy Thursday, Good Friday, Easter Monday, Labor Day (May 1), Ascension Day, Constitution Day (May 17), Whit Monday, Christmas, Boxing Day (day after Christmas).

ELECTRICITY ¶ The voltage in general use throughout Norway is 220 A.C. and 50 cycles, so you will have to have a transformer for your appliances. In Stavanger, however, the current is 110 A.C.—just right for American appliances.

BASIC NORWEGIAN

English-Norwegian

Waiter: *Kelner*
Bill of fare, menu; *Meny*
Napkin: *Serviett*
Bread and butter: *Bröd og smör*
A glass of orange juice: *Et glass appelsinsaft (rå)*
Boiled egg: *Kokt egg*
1. soft: 1. *lite kokt*
2. medium: 2. *blötkokt*
3. hard-boiled: 3. *hårdkokt*
4. egg cup: 4. *eggeglass*
Fried eggs: *Speilegg*
Bacon and eggs: *Egg og bacon*
Coffee, black: *Kaffe uten flöte*
Coffee with cream and sugar: *Kaffe med flöte og sukker*
Coffee with hot milk: *Café au lait*
Tea: *Te*
Water: *Vann*
Ice water: *Isvann*
Mineral water: *Mineralvann*
Breakfast: *Frokost*
Lunch: *Lunsj*

Dinner: *Middag*
Shampoo: *Hårvask*
Haircut: *Hårklipping*
Manicure: *Manikyre*
I want . . . liters of petrol: *Jeg skal ha . . . liter bensin*
Change the oil: *Bytt olje*
Grease the car: *Smor vögnen*
How are you?: *Hvordan står det till?*
Fine, thank you: *Takk, godt*
Please: *Vaer så god*
Thank you very much: *Mange takk*
Good morning: *God morgen*
Good afternoon: *God middag*
Good night: *God natt*
Yes: *Ja*
No: *Nei*
Morning: *Morgen*
Noon: *Middag*
Afternoon, P.M.: *Ettermiddag,* E.M.
Evening: *Aften*
Night: *Natt*
Sunday: *Söndag*
Monday: *Mandag*
Tuesday: *Tirsdag*
Wednesday: *Onsdag*
Thursday: *Torsdag*
Friday: *Fredag*
Saturday: *Lördag*
One: *En*
Two: *To*
Three: *Tre*
Four: *Fire*
Five: *Fem*
Six: *Seks*
Seven: *Sju*
Eight: *Otte*
Nine: *Ni*
Ten: *Ti*
Twenty: *Tjue*
Thirty: *Tretti*
Forty: *Förti*
Fifty: *Femti*
One hundred: *Hundre*
One thousand: *Tusen*

FOOD SPECIALTIES AND LIQUOR ¶ Breakfast (*frokost*) begins about 8 in the morning for the tourist—and earlier than that, of course, for the Norwegian. Breakfast will be varied. You can order the American-type breakfast in any hotel (with juice, toast, coffee, eggs), or request the continental-type as a matter of course (only coffee, rolls, marmalade and/or butter). On ships and in certain hotels (such as the Viking, in Oslo), you will be able to partake of the traditional Norwegian breakfast, which has as many different items as a food exhibit at an international fair. This will come as a great surprise to the American, who, at breakfast time, thinks in terms of orange juice, toast and coffee. You're expected to wander over to a large table in the hotel dining room and make your own selection from what appears, at first blush, to be a tableful of herring dishes. However, by the exercise of patience, you'll find sliced ham, cheeses, butter, various cold meats and smoked salmon, and—all in all—you shouldn't do too badly, once the momentary first shock passes away.

Many Norwegians, especially those who work, will have only a couple of open-faced sandwiches at their desk at noontime, or thereabouts. Or, they will drop into one of the many inexpensive restaurants (in Oslo, the Travel Association has a list of several dozen low-priced restaurants, ranging from cafeteria-style to long-established traditional eating places, where a full meal will come to a couple of dollars). The heavy meal of the day is generally taken as early as 4:30 or 5 P.M. (by the Norwegians) so that they can have the rest of the evening free. Most Norwegian restaurants start serving a hot meal starting at 11 A.M. and going right on through to midnight. Tourists, however, can stick to their regular dining-hour habits, and the leading restaurants usually serve dinner (for tourists) between 8 and 9 P.M.

There are two good reasons for the somewhat special eating-hour pattern the Norwegians follow. One is that they like to get the evening meal over with early so that they can enjoy the marvelous light and sunshine of the latter part of the days in summer. Another reason, apparently, is the liquor law situation. In licensed restaurants and in a number of cafes it is possible to get beer and wine throughout the day. But there are *very* strict rules on hard liquor. It cannot be served before 3 P.M. during the week and not at all on either Saturday or Sunday. And no liquor can be served after 11:45 in the evening. About fifteen minutes before that, the waiter will come around and ask if anyone wants a last round (you can guess what the answer to that question usually is!). But, with no liquor allowed until 3 P.M. in the day it is only logical then that the "dinner patrons" begin showing up in restaurants at exactly that moment, or as soon thereafter as possible.

Both at lunch and at dinner, you will probably first be served a hot soup and as a fish dish, possibly some boiled salmon. (You'd better learn to like boiled salmon, because you'll see an awful lot of it during your Norwegian stay.) Then, there will be a meat dish and finally a bland blanc mange-type dessert hidden by a reddish-purple fruit sauce, unless you're fortunate enough to be in Norway when the delicious berries come into season—strawberries, for example, and (far more interesting) cloudberries. Fish is a specialty, but there are all kinds of fish, ranging from dried cod (*lutefisk*) to smoked salmon. A word of warning about the *lutefisk*. It is served with potatoes, and it is possible that you will like nothing but the potatoes; what we mean is that *lutefisk* is an acquired taste. In the winter, boiled fresh cod is a great specialty. It is caught in the North Sea, landed by the fishermen at Bergen and then rushed by air transport to Oslo. If you order a sea trout, the entire fish will be served on a tremendous platter —like in one of those still-life paintings. The magnificent *pièce de résistance*, of course, is the smoked salmon. A great type of this salmon is the *gravlaks*, which has been prepared with a skill and tenderness (going back to the days when such fish were buried in sand banks along a stream as a means of preserving them in the prerefrigeration era). Smoking salmon is an art somewhere on the same lofty plateau as the process of champagne making. In cleaning the fish, for instance, you never use water, brandy is an acceptable cleansing agent, we have been assured. The salmon is flavored with dill, eventually, and is often called "dilly salmon." We're serious.

Beer in Norway does not compare well with the product of her neighbor, Denmark. Don't be surprised to find ice-cold milk served with most meals. It's a Norwegian custom. Aquavit is, of course, the national strong drink. In Norway, there is nothing colorless or drab about this beverage's looks. Depending on the herbs and spices used in it, aquavit can be a golden color or perhaps pale yellow. The Norwegian aquavit is made of potatoes and this is one time when the Norwegians consider the potato as being vital for life and well-being. The quality of aquavit varies, and so does the price therefore. (And there really is a difference in quality. Linie brand aquavit is the most famous label—and deservedly so.)

Because of the restrictions on the sale of liquor—and the complete weekend ban—the solution for a thirsty traveler lies in buying liquor at a Government Monopoly Store and taking it back to the hotel with him. The stores are open weekday afternoons and for a short interval on Saturday mornings. These "package stores" are indicated by the large letter "V" outside.

The Continental Hotel in Oslo meets the no-liquor problem in a pleasant way on Saturday afternoons by opening its cafe bar and serving a special concoction called "Saturday's Drink." What this consists of is their secret, but in the absence of anything else, it hits the spot. The ambiance is splendid, too. The walls of the bar are filled with paintings and drawings by the famed Norwegian artist Edward Munch, and the whole atmosphere is extremely smart and agreeable.

Please do not do *any* driving after drinking in Norway. The laws are extremely strict. Most Norwegians going out to dinner for the evening where liquor might be served will prudently leave their car at home and take a taxi. That could be a good rule for visitors to follow, too.

The most important touring areas include Oslo and vicinity, the fjord country and the Arctic Circle region.

Capital City

Oslo is a cheerful, immaculate city of about 475,000, worth several days of anyone's sightseeing time. Visualize a sparkling, small metropolis facing onto the water with a fjord to the south, bright green hills encircling to the north. In land area, metropolitan Oslo is unbelievably enormous, with tremendous city limits undoubtedly encouraged by such long-range planning as that of Los Angeles.

The leading street is Karl Johansgate, which cuts through the city to the Royal Palace, and most of the important shops and hotels are situated along or adjacent to it. The leading monument of the city, and a sort of central marker, is Oslo's modernistic Town Hall (the Rådhus), which may be reached in a few minutes by walking south toward the waterfront from the Hotel Continental. At a distance, the Town Hall bears strong resemblance to a large furniture factory or possibly to Stockholm's equally stark equivalent; closer inspection reveals a much more pleasing façade. But the interior is absolutely magnificent, with fascinating, brilliantly executed murals, including what is said to be the world's largest, measuring 85 by 43 feet (you'll just have to take our word). Open weekdays 10–2, Sundays 12–3, and please don't miss seeing this.

Oslo cathedral (by European standards) is scarcely ancient, being less than 300 years old—and restored, at that, in 1949–1950. The big attraction here is a giant organ with 6,000 pipes, all of which work (although not at the same time!). The organ is about 240 years old. You'll have to check locally as to organ programs, but the church is open (between June 1 and August 31) from 9 A.M. to 3 P.M., Monday through Friday, and till noon on Saturday; it is closed on Sundays and holidays. You should, if you like sculpture, visit Vigeland's Museum at 32 Nobelsgate. Gustav Vigeland is Norway's greatest sculptor, and his works have been extravagantly praised as well as vehemently damned. The museum is open daily except Monday from 1 to 7 P.M.; admission is free. If you approve of the master's works (or are just curious), visit Frogner Park, a seventy-five-acre area where 150 of his sculptures are on display; in any event, aye or nay, the park is worth a visit. It is always open, and admission is free. Akershus Castle, which can be seen from the Town Hall, was built by King Haakon V in the year 1300. It's open for leisurely inspection (between May 20 and September 15) from 11 A.M. to 2:45 P.M. on weekdays and from 1 to 2:45 P.M. on Sundays. Admission is 1 krone. The National Gallery isn't too remarkable, although there is a representative sprinkling of great European painters, including French Impressionists. It is open (between May 16 and September 16) from 10 A.M. to 4 P.M. Monday through Friday and to 3 P.M. on Saturday. It is also open on Wednesday and Friday evenings from 6 to 8 P.M. and on Sundays from noon to 3 P.M.; admission is free. The Museum of Arts and Crafts (worth seeing, too!) has been selected to house a remarkable collection of tapestries right out of the Middle Ages. It is open daily except Monday from 11 A.M. to 3 P.M. and on Sundays from noon to 3 P.M. Admission is free.

You'll find the most interesting sightseeing in the Oslo area on the nearby peninsula of Bygdøy. (Note: All museums in Oslo are free except those on the Bygdøy peninsula.) There are the authentic Viking ships, the Polar expedition ship *Fram* (the name means "Forward"), a replica of the famous raft *Kon-Tiki* and the Norwegian

Folk Museum. You have a choice of taking a ferry or a bus departing from in front of the Town Hall. However, we recommend the ferry ride (summer only), which you catch at Pier C in the Town Hall Square. From June 20 to August 16 the ferry leaves every quarter of an hour during the day and every half hour 15 and 45 minutes past the hour during the evening. During the rest of the season (from mid-April to mid-September), the boats operate only in the morning hours. In case you prefer the bus, it is a fifteen-minute ride on No. 30, which leaves on the hour and 20 and 40 minutes past the hour. You'll visit the good ship *Fram*, which has gone farther north *and* south than any other ship in the world; then, the *Kon-Tiki* museum, housing a perfect copy of the balsa raft on which the author Thor Heyerdahl and five others who had a lot of spare time floated from Peru across the Pacific. The hours for the *Fram* (between May 15 and September 1) are 11 A.M. to 6:45 P.M. daily. Admission is 1.50 kroner. The *Kon-Tiki* hours (during the same period) are 10:30 A.M. to 7 P.M. Admission is 1 krone. The Norwegian Folk Museum, another attraction on the peninsula, is outdoors, situated in a pleasant park area, and has representations of Norwegian farms, wooden buildings, and peasant homes of today and of years gone by (same timetable as *Kon-Tiki* museum, admission fee, 3 kroner). Then, on to see the three Viking ships, one of which (the *Oseberg*) is in marvelous condition and extremely interesting (same timetable and entrance fee as the *Fram*).

Another trip, particularly fascinating for skiers in the winter (and for sightseers at any time), is to Holmenkollen, the site of the famous ski jump, northwest of Oslo. The Ski Museum there includes polar equipment used by famous explorers. The trip is best made by an electric railway, which leaves from a station at the National Theater. It is a thirty-minute ride (three minutes of it is through a tunnel) and costs 2 kroner. Trains leave every quarter of an hour. Sit on the left side of the car on the way up and on the right coming down. You will get a full-scale view of the Oslo fjord and of the valley. The ski jump is at the 1,300-foot level, but the last stop of the train, Frognerseteren, is at 1,500 feet. A few minutes downhill (walking) from the Frognerseteren station is a cosy restaurant where you can have some nice snacks of open sandwiches, smoked salmon or whatever—and a glass of beer—to tide you over till mealtime. The view from the Holmenkollen is undeniably breathtaking and is a classic late-evening trip in Oslo during the summertime.

In front of Town Hall are the piers generically called the Piperviken; from here a varied and miscellaneous assortment of ferries, boats and launches leave for various points in the vicinity; you could almost make your selection at random and have a lovely ride and a chance to mingle with the Norwegian people. Merely for your guidance, here are some of the boating possibilities: a 1½-hour trip through Oslo harbor and surrounding fjords; a 2½-hour excursion through the Westerfjord district; a trip to Ingierstrand or Hvalstrand, the very popular bathing beaches, which aren't even overcrowded on a Sunday. If you like sightseeing on your own instead of taking the tour launches, get on any one of the regular ferries and wander about as your mood dictates. Those who enjoy sea voyages will surely relish a trip from Oslo to Stavanger or Bergen, returning by a particularly fascinating train ride through magnificent scenery; be sure to check the type of steamer and accommodations available because several of the ships are quite outmoded.

The railroad trip from Oslo to Bergen is great. Beginning amid fairly ordinary scenery, the train darts and turns inquiringly past snow-capped mountains, wooden cabins and sparkling waterfalls. Travelers should make connections at Myrdal to visit the little town of Flåm along the coast. There is a very exciting ride downhill on this run that lasts about an hour; at Flåm you'll find the Fretheim Hotel, old but satisfactory.

For motorists with just a day to spend driving about Oslo and its surrounding country, the following circular sightseeing excursion is recommended: Leave Oslo going eastward on Karl Johansgate (avenue), which joins Bispegata (street), and then onto route 1 through Hølen and into Moss; take the car ferry across to Horten (a forty-minute trip and very beautiful). If time permits, head south to Sandefjord, a fishing town with a famous whaling museum; on the road from Sandefjord south to Larvik, you'll be able to see (at Tjølling) the excavated old town of Kaupang, frequently mentioned in the classic sagas. At Larvik, it's possible to visit nearby Nevlunghavn, a fishing port with lots of color and life when the boats return with their catch.

If time is limited, after the ferry crossing from Moss to Horten, proceed to Holmestrand, Sande, Drammen and Oslo via route 40.

ACCOMMODATIONS ¶ The hotel situation in Norway during the summer months is often chaotic. Be *sure* to have advance reservations for July and August unless you want to end up in a small rear bedroom on the outskirts of town. In outlying regions, the rooms are often furnished with Spartan simplicity, but the general atmosphere is inevitably homelike, pleasant and hospitable. You'll probably be annoyed by the feather beds (quilts), which the Norwegians obstinately prefer to blankets. Insistent hotel guests have been known, on occasion, to prevail upon the housekeeper to produce some light blankets. The trouble with the feather beds is that no way has yet been devised to tuck them in. If you don't mind your toes sticking out, you may be able to make some sort of compromise and sleep under them.

Here's an interesting thing to remember. Some Norwegian hotels charge 1 or 2 kroner extra if you remain only one night. It's supposed to cover the extra laundry charge. Also, in some resort hotels, there is a small charge for luggage. We know it's silly, but it's a custom.

OSLO HOTELS

Grand: A dignified, Old World establishment with a fine reputation. Some accommodations are average in size and décor, but most bedrooms are spacious and extremely attractive. Perhaps the most expensive hotel in Oslo.

Continental: An excellent hotel, with rates that run on the high side (a double room will—if it has a bath—cost more than $30). It is centrally located, well run. The modern part has exceptionally nice, well-decorated rooms. Most rooms have private baths.

Bristol: A very popular hotel, where rates are in the upper bracket. Good accommodations in most rooms, although some are only average in size. Dining room is known for its food.

K.N.A.: This is the Royal Norwegian Automobile Club's hotel. It is in the west end of Oslo, not far from the royal palace. Simple, unelaborate accommodations; rooms are variable in size and décor.

Ambassadeur: Situated somewhat away from the downtown section; not a large hotel, but a pleasant one; rates are fairly moderate.

Viking: A modern, large but compact hotel across the square from the East Railroad Station. Most rooms are extremely small, but adequate; comparatively few rooms have private bath but all have toilets.

Stefan: A good, moderate-priced hotel built by the local Mission society; no liquor, not even wine or beer served on the premises. Modern décor in average-size rooms.

Holmenkollen: On a wooded mountainside overlooking Oslo, about twenty minutes from town. Ideal for those who want to combine a resort stay with local sightseeing. Nice, attractive rooms, some with terraces.

OSLO RESTAURANTS

Freggatten: A new restaurant with wonderful view of the harbor, excellent seafood specialties, well prepared.

Bagatelle: Small, cozy place featuring continental food. Pleasant spot; not expensive.

Continental: In the hotel of the same name on the second floor is a first class restaurant frequented by actors and writers; piano music. *Theatercaféen* downstairs is primarily a café, but also popular for food (prices are lower here than upstairs) and very lively (National Theater is across the street).

Kongen: Marvelous location on a pier in the yacht harbor. Well-prepared dishes; dance orchestra during dinner.

La Belle Sole: A small, sophisticated spot specializing in seafood. Quite expensive.

Ekeberg: Lovely location overlooking Oslo, only a short ride from town. Good food, fairly high prices.

Blom: An amusing, offbeat restaurant catering (simultaneously) to the local arty crowd and American tourists. Sandwich table at moderate prices during lunch; dinner is moderately expensive.

Dronnigen: Beautifully situated restaurant at the end of a pier in the yacht harbor on the Bygdøy side. Several sections: good food in the "Captain's Cabin," dancing on the terrace of "Bootsdeck" and in "Sextant."

Frascati: Popular, busy restaurant serving very good food; interesting wrought iron décor.

Frognerseteren: A log-cabin restaurant, built on a mountain in Norwegian rustic style. Almost a half-hour ride, but worth it for the marvelous view. The moderate-priced food is fairly good.

Najaden: Modern first class restaurant in the Museum of Shipping on Bygdøy. Seafood features among specialties; dancing in the evening.

Folkemuseets Restaurant: On the Folk Museum grounds on Bygdøy, open mid-May to mid-September. Norwegian country food and on summer evenings programs of Norwegian folk dancing.

SHOPPING ¶ *Glassware* is outstanding and very reasonably priced. The stemware is good, but does not seem as well made or as attractive in design as the Swedish or

Finnish equivalent. The small vases and art pieces are well executed and make marvelous gifts.

Metalwork in *silver* and *enamel* is displayed in many of the shops along the Karl Johansgate. The *silverware* is extremely smart in design, particularly the silver dishes and candelabra; the flatware seems to be less distinguished than the work produced in Denmark, although that is not to say that it is unattractive. At considerably lower prices, there is a selection of *enamel* worked on less important metals such as copper, aluminum and stainless steel; the best pieces seem to be in the jewelry field— pins, brooches, earrings, etc.—and the sets of small dessert or coffee spoons are interesting, too. Incidentally, *pewter ware* is extremely popular in Norway and the hand-worked articles are quite intriguing.

Glassware is another Norwegian specialty. The Hadeland factory at Jevnaker, about a ninety-minute drive from Oslo, is well known. Visits to the factory can be arranged by the Oslo Travel Association.

Note: If you would like to see artisans practicing the enamelwork technique in their workshops, drop in at the Oslo Travel Association office. They will arrange a visit for you as part of a small group.

Sweaters and *knitwear* articles are reasonably priced and feature peasant designs. The heavy sweaters are ideal for skiers, although the prices are not low—say, $25 for a man's sweater; the workmanship is apparently first rate and the designs unusual. Mittens and caps make fine gifts if you have any friends living in snow-swept North Dakota or Minnesota; they also make excellent gifts for children.

Ceramics and *pottery* have extremely original and appealing designs, but the workmanship in the other Scandinavian countries is of higher order as a rule; Norwegian prices are moderately high, all things considered.

Woodwork is a great specialty here. Highly recommended are the salad bowls, salad servers and cheese boards; these are beautifully worked and are very inexpensive compared with American prices. The same cannot be said for the wooden carvings of churches and animals, which are intended purely for the tourist trade and as such are patently in the junk classification.

An interesting arts and crafts center has been set up in the old-time stables that ring the cathedral. The municipality has made the area available to artisans and craftsmen, and they have responded to the invitation. A weaver, knife grinder and basket worker are among the individuals plying their antique callings. A few steps from the cathedral's arts and crafts center is the big open-air flower market, which is ready for business winter and summer.

Shoppers also should head for the "Bay of the King's Pipers" area in the City Hall district. Several blocks of old-time slums have been cleared and converted into a bright, modern shopping place.

While you are browsing around the city, you might like to visit the Industrial Design Center (near the American Embassy) at 40 Drammensveien. A food section has just been added, which displays equipment and processes of the food industry. Admission is free and the opening times are 10 A.M. to 7 P.M. daily and 1 to 6 P.M. Sundays.

Furs are one instance in which the Norwegians fall down; the pelts themselves are superb, the resulting fur pieces far less satisfactory Stoles are satisfactory, but fur coats are not. In brief, furs are not recommended on two counts: skins are not properly worked and the United States customs duty is extremely high should you run over your $100 limit. Don't buy Norwegian clothing at all—that goes for suits, dresses and shoes but doesn't apply to ski togs. *Kitchen gadgets* are marvelous—low in price, very useful and ingenious. Pots and pans, in a wide assortment of metals and pottery, are beautiful and ideal for casserole suppers back home.

Important: There is the possibility of saving an additional 12 percent on your shopping purchases—over and above the savings in prices compared with those in the United States. If you buy more than 100 kroner in goods, articles or what have you—and if the purchases are sent directly to the airport or border station from which you'll be departing—you can get a 12 percent reduction. This takes a bit of time, however, so do your shopping early. Don't wait until the morning of your departure.

Pointer: Norwegian shops open at 8:30 A.M., or at the latest 9 A.M. The afternoon closing hour is 5 P.M. often earlier on summer Saturdays.

AIRPORT SHOPPING ¶ There is a large tax-free shopping area at Fornebu, the Oslo airport. Not only Norwegian products, such as furs, silver and enamelware are on hand, but also Swiss watches, French perfumes and a variety of liquors.

ENTERTAINMENT ¶ There is comparatively little in the way of night clubs and formal entertainment throughout Norway. Oslo's leading hotels have dining and dancing most nights during the summer months, with fairly good food served in a rather dignified, sedate atmosphere. A dozen Oslo restaurants have dancing until 12:30 A.M. (Remember that the liquor supply shuts off at 11:45 P.M.) Orchestras come from many parts of the world, particularly Italy and Yugoslavia, and this makes the music more interesting. (Warsaw musical groups are occasionally among the entertainers.) The Grand Hotel, during the off-season, presents a "Cinderella Evening" on Saturday nights, a nicely arranged dinner-dance. It's a young people's affair and very attractive to look at.

A busy musical season starts in September and goes on until May. The Oslo Philharmonic Orchestra presents about 150 concerts during the season in the University Festival Hall. Tickets are inexpensive but are raised slightly if there is a special guest. The opera season in the fall is from September 10 to December 10. The "spring" season starts about January 10, and the last performance is on May 17, Constitution Day, and the official start of holiday season. Artists from various countries appear as guests at the opera. Often, too, there are concert soloists. It might be a Swiss pianist one evening, Isaac Stern another, and Irmgaard Seefried the following night. October is a particularly busy month, with a concert almost every day.

One of the nice attractions of Oslo's Fornebu Airport is the Caravelle Restaurant. It ranks high in food, ambiance and service. There is dancing every night in the week except Sunday. One of the interesting cafes to visit—and you can dine nicely there, too—is the Cafe Engebret on Bank Square. The establishment celebrated its 110th anniversary recently, and it has been in the same family from the start.

The leading dramatic offerings are at the National Theater, and if you've always yearned to hear Ibsen in Norwegian (and there are hardly any of us left!), here's your opportunity. Probably you'll be much better off, all things considered, to see a Norwegian performance outdoors at the Frogner Park open-air theater. Then, if the going is too rough, you can walk out easily. Cabaret revue shows can be seen at Chat Noir and during summer (June 20 to August 31) at Casino Non Stop Show which caters mainly to tourists.

The *cinema* is the big common denominator of Norwegian entertainment; luckily, American and British films in their original versions are featured. However, if you do go, remember that all seats are reserved for scheduled performances, customarily beginning at 5, 7 or 9 P.M., and if you arrive late, you won't be seated (positively). May we suggest you give consideration to attending the 5 P.M. showing, because it comes at the end of the day and works out just right for a late dinner; your hotel porter can have reserved seats picked up in advance.

During the season, many tourist hotels give *folk dance* recitals performed by the staff; naturally, these are variable in quality but almost always worth attending for the spirit of the dancers. Be sure to watch for local celebrations and festivals, colorful and charming as a rule.

Note: The Karl Johans theater in Oslo makes a specialty of presenting a cavalcade of old films, such as a Greta Garbo Fortnight. If the films are in English, this is fine entertainment.

SPORTS ¶ *Golfers*, so far as we know, will have to manage with only three worthwhile courses in the entire country—at Trondheim, Bergen and Oslo. *Hunters* might like to try for a moose during the season (October 1–10), but the fees are on the high side. Licenses to hunt reindeer, on the other hand, are not too high by comparison.

Mountain climbing is great sport in rocky, hilly Norway; the best regions are around Narvik, Romsdal, Jotunheimen and the Lofoten Islands. *Swimming* in the southern fjord waters, particularly around Oslo, is not nearly so cold as you might expect; the bathing season runs from June through August, of course depending upon the weather. Swimming in the west coast fjords is *sometimes* possible but often the weather is colder than a pitcher filled with ice cubes, or so it seems to tourists.

Trout fishing in Norway's south central mountain regions is often phenomenal; up north the results depend upon many extraneous factors, but when the trout are biting, you'll really catch something worthwhile. In the southern part of the country, the fishing season in lakes situated 1,500 feet up does not begin before June 15; higher than 2,500 feet, the season runs from July 15 through the end of August.

The Norwegians learn to *ski* right out of the cradle, and after all, they ought to know the proper time to begin to learn because (they say) skiing was invented by them. Not too many ski lifts in this country, where they think that everyone who wants to ski down should walk up; hardly in line with American thoughts on the subject. Important ski areas: Oslo has a series of trails and slaloms; Lillehammer is the center for a whole group of well-equipped sports areas, particularly Hamar; Voss is outstandingly popular and has a good ski lift; Trondheim is perhaps best known for its bobsledding and tobogganing facilities, but the ski facilities are excellent at nearby Bymarka. Geilo, famous for its remarkably mild weather, is an outstanding winter resort area with a chair lift and excellent skiing conditions during most of the winter.

In the Oslo area, there are 1,200 miles of marked ski trails, and four or five of them are flood-lighted for evening skiing (which is very popular). Three slalom hills are within a half-hour of Oslo by train or car, and a fourth one is about an hour's drive (or train ride) away. Ski equipment can be rented without any trouble. Oslo has sixty-one outdoor ice rinks, and skating costs about 50 cents an hour. Figure and ice-hockey skates can be rented. Oslo has four indoor swimming pools, complete with sauna. The fee is around a half dollar.

Note: The Municipal Labor Office in Oslo operates a baby-sitter service. Make arrangements through your hotel concierge or through the Oslo Travel Association.

Pointer: If you're visiting Norway during May–July, bring along a sleep mask—a cloth gadget to cover your eyes—particularly if you find it difficult to sleep in bright daylight, of which Norway has more than its share. It's light almost all night long.

ᘛ Sightseeing in Norway

Even if scenery doesn't ordinarily interest you, Norway is something special, and ordinary preparations for a trip, executed at the last moment, will not be satisfactory.

There are cruises through the fjord districts and up to the North Cape, most of which leave from Bergen (on Norway's west coast) and for these trips reservations would have to be made well in advance, usually the winter before you plan to go. In making your plans, hills are within a half-hour of Oslo by train or car, remember that the ideal time to visit northern Norway is from May 14 to July 30, when the midnight sun can be seen—the sun shines twenty-four hours a day, a great experience. I wouldn't plan on going before May 15, but there is no great harm in going anytime from then up to August 15, although during the last two weeks there will be a slight dimness around midnight, rather than complete light.

The Bergen Line steamship company, 576 Fifth Avenue, New York City, operates "Meteor Cruises" of from eight to seventeen days. The M/S *Meteor* is a comfortable, 3,000-ton vessel that cruises through the fjords, to the North Cape and into the Pack Ice region at 80-degree latitude (just look that up on the map and get a thrill). The Clipper Line, 1 Rockefeller Plaza, New York City, runs longer cruises that leave from Harwich, England (the company arranges transportation from London to the ship.)

The Bergen Line also has regularly scheduled twelve-day trips out of Bergen that cover the western and northern coastlines of Norway. This is a bargain-type journey, but of course the ships are not superluxurious cruise vessels—although they are snug and comfortable. The staterooms are not large and have running water; there are none with private baths. The boats hug the coast of Norway, making a stop or two every day, all the way up past North Cape and to Kirkenes, next to the Russian border; the ship then returns to Bergen, making different stops. Of course, twelve days of sitting aboard ship is not for everyone, but it is a marvelous rest, and we're sure you'll enjoy the trip.

An interesting, shortened variation on the above (highly recommended) is a seven-day air and sea trip to the North Cape, offered by the Scandinavian Airlines System. The trip is best made between May 15 and August 15, as previously mentioned, and leaves from Oslo almost every day; the all-expense price, including plane and boat fares, meals and excursions, is relatively inexpensive. On this trip, you fly from Oslo to Bardufoss; here a connection is made with a bus that takes you through some remarkable scenery into Tromsø. There is an overnight stay at a local hotel; the next day you board your ship northbound to the North Cape. If the weather is good, you'll be able to climb to the top of the cape, where fortunately there is a refreshment stand. If not, the ship proceeds to Honninsvag, and a bus will take you in comfort to the North Cape. Then on to Kirkenes, adjacent to the Russian border. The ship turns homeward, going back past the cape and heading southward. There are five nights aboard the ship, and with good weather, you'll see scenery that you never thought existed. On the last day aboard ship, there is the really exciting trip through the Trollfjord, a narrow channel through which the ship proceeds with caution. This will be one of the truly great experiences of your life—please have faith in us; this is no exaggeration. You'll leave the ship early in the morning at Bodø and later catch a plane for Oslo. It's a great trip. (If you have three extra days, drive back to Oslo from Bergen. Arrange in advance to fly from Bodø to Bergen and then drive to Oslo—it makes a marvelous round trip.)

Pointer: You can have twenty-hour-a-day viewing of the entire disc of the Midnight Sun at Spitsbergen from April 21 to August 22; at the North Cape, May 14 to July 30; Hammerfest, May 17 to July 28; Tromsø, May 21, to July 23; Harstad, May 26 to July 19; Bodø, June 5 to July 9; and Grimsey, June 19 to June 23.

Bergen to Oslo

If you can manage an extra few days, by all means drive your own car from Bergen to Oslo, or vice versa. You can fly or take the train from Oslo to Bergen, spend a day there, rent a car and drive through unbelievable scenery to Oslo. The rental companies permit you to leave the car in Oslo, on payment of a moderate charge. The roads are not superhighways, but they are adequate and there is no danger involved for an average driver. The trip, as outlined below, involves three days, and although the mileage is not great, three days is the ideal length of time to make the trip.

Bergen to Ulvik—98 miles

The entire trip is made on route 20, with one slight exception, so it is easily followed. Leave Bergen, heading for the suburbs, by following the trolley car tracks; when they turn off, continue on the main road, until you see a left turn indicating route 20 toward Norheimsund. The road goes through Trengereid, and begins to follow the Sørfjord, a beautiful ride. There are a number of tunnels, but the driving is easy. Arland is at the far end of the Samnanger Fjord, then comes Tysee, Kvamskog, and Tokagjel where there is a remarkable gorge. At Norheimsund, there is an extremely pleasant hotel, the Sandven, where you could stay overnight if you've made a late start from Bergen. Then the road goes to Øystese, over the Fykesund Bridge, and into Ålvik, and Kvanndal. This is a ferry crossing, but don't make it—we have better plans for you. Continue on from Kvanndal to Eide and Granvin; at Granvin there is a right turn to Ulvik—watch for it. There is an eleven-mile road through the forest, most enjoyable; even though the road is not paved, it's still quite good. At Ulvik, head for Norway's leading resort hotel, in our opinion, the Brakanes, with very attractive rooms and grounds. Your room will face the Hardangerfjord, one of the loveliest in the country. You can easily make it from Bergen to the Brakanes Hotel in a morning, have lunch there, and spend the day on the lake. If you're planning an early morning start the following day, walk over a few hundred feet to the ferry landing and make a reservation for either the 9:10 or the 10:50 A.M. boat.

Ulvik to Geilo—68 miles

The next morning, even with a reservation, drive to the pier about fifteen minutes before the scheduled time. Drive aboard, and then visit the ticket office and pay your fare. Hurry out on deck as quickly as possible and see the greatest scenery in the world while riding down the fjord from Ulvik to Brimnes; this ferry trip may well be the world's greatest (forty-minute) boat ride. At Brimnes, where the ferry stops, turn left, and head for Eidfjord and then a pretty exciting drive through the Måbo valley, featuring hairpin turns, tunnels and the like. On to Fossli, where you can stop and look at the Voringfoss waterfall, an exciting drop of some 600 feet. Then to Dyranut, the highest spot on the road, just over 4,000 feet. Part of this trip resembles nothing so much as the face of the moon, as visualized in science-fiction thrillers. The road continues to Geilo, a wintertime skiing resort, which is very pleasant in the summer. Here, the leading hotel is the Holms, just a minute off the main road. We hope you're fortunate enough to come on a Wednesday, when the Holms Hotel features its magnificent display of food on the *koldtbord*, the cold table.

Geilo to Oslo—153 miles

This is a straight, easy drive most of the way, and the trip should take about four to five hours. The road drops, on its way down to Hol and Ål, and at Torpo there is a classic example of a twelfth-century stave church. Then come Gol, Hønefoss, Sandvika and Oslo.

Pointer: Don't plan on driving more than 125–150 miles per day through Norway. Ferries take time, the scenery is magnificent and the roads are often none too wide. Part of the time, you'll find yourself averaging about 20 miles an hour; don't rush.

૨ A Tour of Norway

Oslo to Bergen—312 miles

Note: The following trip is slightly different from the route previously described and, of course, is in the opposite direction.

Leave Oslo by heading westward on Karl Johansgate (avenue), which leads into Drammensveien (route 40), passing the Royal Palace in its great park on the right-hand side. The road follows along the fjord and into Sandvika, where there is a right turn onto route 20 toward Hønefoss, passing the Tyrifjord on the left. Then, through Noresund and Gulsvik and into the valley of Hallingdals to Nesbyen and Gol.

The road now becomes quite narrow toward Ål and into Geilo, an attractive tourist region with a good place to stay, the Holms Hotel. The route continues its climb to Haugastøl, Fagerheim and Dyranut. Shortly afterward, you'll be able to see the impressive outlines of the Hardangerjøkulen, the great glacier, on your right side to the north. Here, you begin a sharp descent, calling for considerable attention on the part of the driver, although this somewhat unfairly deprives him of views of stupendous scenery.

(After Maruset, there is an optional right turn to

Fossli and Fossli Tourist Hotel, reached by an amazing road consisting of a complicated series of turns, each rising to a higher point. The hotel is pleasant for an overnight stay, and the view of the gorge and surrounding scenery from the observation platform is unsurpassed. In all of this region, should you be fortunate enough to be driving through on Sunday, you will find the local folk wearing their native costumes.)

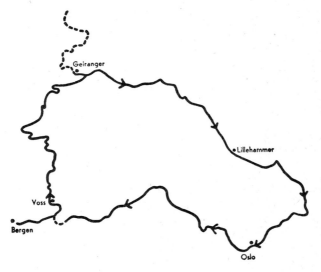

Continue on to Eidfjord, then to Kinsarvik, with the beautiful fjord on your right. There is a ferry from Kinsarvik to Kvanndal, which takes approximately one hour, and, if it isn't raining, you'll enjoy the trip (if it's raining you'll still enjoy it, but visibility is limited). On the north side, take route 20 to Ålvik, an industrial community; then over the Fyksesund Bridge, the longest suspension bridge in Norway. Continue into Øystese, a very attractive little place with good swimming facilities and the comfortable Hotel Øystese. Another nice spot for a stay is at the next town, Norheimsund, which boasts the Sandven Hotel. Then on to Tysse, Arna, Nesttun and Bergen.

This magnificently placed city has a quite modern aspect, for a large portion of the old area was burned out during the fire of 1916. However, much of the old charm is to be found in many colorful little streets still remaining. In selecting a place to stay, there is no question but that the new Hotel Norge, about as modern as a hotel can get, nine stories tall and air-conditioned throughout, is the city's leading hotel. Also quite new is the Orion Hotel, although the rooms are somewhat on the skimpy side.

There's no use denying the fact that it will probably rain during your stay in Bergen, and why shouldn't it? It rains almost every day because the warm air of the Gulf Stream blows across the nearby icy mountain slopes and condenses into solid moisture, that is, plain ordinary rain. So—be sure you have a raincoat with you. Sightseers will want to visit Bergen's famous fish market, the Fishetorvet, but if you'll take a tip from us, don't go too soon after breakfast (or don't eat too much breakfast) because, as you know, fish (even when fresh) have a tendency to smell; but don't miss seeing the fish market anyhow. You should also wander through the Bryggen, an atmospheric waterfront street, once headquarters for the Hanseatic merchants, and the famous German Quay. Other sights worth seeing include Fantoft Stave Church, the Bergenhaus Fortress and famous Upper Street (Øyregaten in Norwegian), the narrow alleys and flights of stairs. Take the funicular railway to Fløyen, where there is a lovely view (if it isn't raining); there is frequent service from Vetrlidsalmenning. A pleasant excursion is a visit to Troldhaugen, the home of composer Edvard Grieg; another short trip is to Elsero, where there is an open-air museum. Bergen, of course, is the starting point for a complete series of cruises by steamer along the west coast of Norway through the fjords; if time permits, this is highly recommended for a delightful scenic holiday.

Bergen to Voss—107 miles

From Bergen, you partially retrace your steps back through Nesttun, Arna, Tysse, Norheimsund, Øystese, Ålvik and Kvanndal; then proceed via route 60 into the resort town of Granvin, which has a pleasant, modest hotel called the Melands.

(From Granvin, there is a right turn that leads, in twelve miles, to Ulvik. The road is particularly attractive in the late spring, when the fruit orchards are in bloom; at Ulvik you'll find a luxurious resort hotel, the Brakanes. From Ulvik, there is a road directly to Voss.)

If you don't drive to Ulvik, proceed on to Voss, where the leading hotel is Fleischers, which has a new wing with private baths; the local sightseeing includes visiting the Finneloftet, the oldest house in Norway (thirteenth century) and the Folk Museum.

Voss is the starting point for an interesting tour that warrants a day's stay; leave Voss by bus to Gudvangen, then by ferry through Nerøy and Aurland fjords to Flåm, from which you take an electric railway up to Myrdal on a truly exciting trip, passing through a series of tunnels and climbing a seemingly impossible gradient. At Myrdal, change for the railroad back to Voss.

Voss to Geiranger—239 miles

Leave Voss via route 60 to Vinje; at Vinje take route 550 to Vik and Vangsnes, where there is an enormous statue of a Viking king (and don't try to say that fast!). Here, take the forty-five minute ferry trip to Dragsvik, picking up route 170, then go into Balestrand. This tourist town has the large resort-type Kvikne Hotel; two miles from town is the Esebotten Hotel, small, isolated and located in almost a dream spot.

From Balestrand take route 170 northward to Vik (this is *another* Vik), where the road begins a sharp climb. As the plateau is reached, there are fine views of the Jostedal glacier; continue on to Moskog, where you pick up route 580 to Skei. Farther along there is a left turn to Sandane, an interesting salmon fishing port where you could get away from the world at Sivertsens Hotel. The main road continues on to Olden, whose best hotel is the Yris; next is Loen, another tourist spot, with the Hotel Alexandra, where the rooms in the newer section are quite nice. Then on to Stryn; those who wish can make a side trip to the west via route 160 to Måløy, a herring fisherman's port with canneries; there is the Hagens Hotel for those who want to stay overnight (and let's hope, for your sake, that the wind isn't blowing off the canneries). At Styrn, pick up route 160 eastward through Hjelledal, a road almost breathtakingly beautiful. Then to Grotli, making a left turn on route 180 toward Djupvass; there is an interesting diversionary trip of five miles to the top of Dalsnibba, 4,950 feet high. The road from Djupvass descends in circles, zigzags and swift drops past the Flydal gorge in a region of overpowering loveliness, finally reaching Geiranger. There is a good hotel, the Union, should you wish to make a stay. Geiranger has several fine waterfalls in the vicinity and also offers a base from which to see Norwegian farm life and the rugged independence of the local people, many of whom are skilled craftsmen.

SIDE TRIP ¶ Those who wish may make an interesting tour to Åndalsnes. Take the ferry from Geiranger northward; the trip lasts slightly less than three hours as a rule, although as little as two hours on occasion. Arriving at Valldal, take route 610, climbing through Gudbrand gorge to Trollstig, where there is a hotel; here a narrow path leads to a platform, which offers an exhilarating view. Then a rapid descent, on a road literally hewn from the rock, into Åndalsnes, another resort town, with the very nice Hotel Bellevue. From here, even further trips may be made: such as to Molde by driving on route 185 to Vikebukt, then taking the fifty-minute ferry trip to Molde, a modern city reconstructed after the old town was destroyed by the Germans during the war. You'll find the Alexandra Hotel or the more modest Romsdalsheimen. The return to Geiranger is via the same route.

Geiranger to Lillehammer—173 miles

Leave the resort of Geiranger via route 180 to Grotli, route 160 through Lom, known particularly for its stave church; there is a pleasant place for a stopover, the Hotel Fossheim. Then you pass Lake Otta, Otta; then to Sjoa (the road changing to route 50), Vinstra, Vålebru, Tretten and Lillehammer. Here you'll find a wealth of hotels, although the Nevra, about ten miles from town, seems most pleasant. Fifteen miles from Lillehammer is the Sjusjøen Hotel, a resort facing the lake. It has many sport facilities. The big attraction in Lillehammer is the Maihaugen, undoubtedly the best of all of Norway's outdoor museums. A wonderful boat ride may be made on the famous paddle steamer *Skibladner*, over a hundred years old, to Gjøvik, from which there is bus service back to Lillehammer; at Gjøvik, there is a truly excellent hotel, the Strand.

Lillehammer to Oslo—180 miles

Leave Lillehammer via route 50 through Brumunddal and into Hamar, where there is a ruined cathedral; the Astoria Hotel is best here; two miles away is the nearby and pleasant Høsbjor Hotel, ideally suited for American motorists. From Hamar, take route 100 to Elverum, a small town surrounded by forests; the local sight here is Christiansfjell Fortress, dating back to the seventeenth century. Then take route 80 south to Flisa and Kongsvinger, where a stop could be made at the Grand Hotel. Those who are proceeding on a tour of Sweden will take route 101 to Magnor, crossing the border and heading for Arvika (pick up the description section from Arvika onward in the Swedish portion of this book). Motorists returning to Oslo leave Kongsvinger by route 101 heading westward to Skarnes, later making a left turn at the junction with route 50 and continuing back to Oslo.

৪৯ Motoring in Norway

Formalities for bringing a car into Norway are simple. You need its registration papers, the Green Card (affirming insurance coverage) and your home-state driver's license. Your state driver's license is sufficient if you wish to hire a car in Norway.

As a rule, you'll find that only the main highways are paved. Outside the areas approaching large cities, you may expect to find gravel and dirt roads where high speeds are unwarranted. In the western part of the country, from Bergen northward through the fjord country, the builders have performed miracles even in creating a road, much less a good one, and sometimes the going is slow and difficult. Mountain passes are often extremely narrow and great care must be taken when meeting another car. Frequently, one of the cars will have to maneuver carefully so as to permit the other to pass. Don't plan on making more than 125 to 150 miles a day as your absolutely top limit in fjord country, and even then you'll find days when 100 miles is all that can be comfortable covered—and what of it, in this wonderful land of unbelievable scenery?

Driving is on the right; overtaking on the left. Gas

prices vary somewhat according to the zone. So look for the price on the pump each time. Gas stations are frequently few and far between in open areas. So always be sure that your car is well supplied with *benzin* (gasoline) before heading off into remote areas of the country. The speed limit is 80 kilometers (50 miles) an hour on the open road and 50 kilometers (31 miles) in built-up areas. In cities, the rule is complicated, requiring the driver to be able to stop within a specified distance. For all practical effect this means you *must* drive slowly through cities. Incidentally, please remember that we said that driving under the influence of alcohol is a very serious offense in Norway. Don't drive after you've had *anything* (repeat, anything) to drink.

If you're heading north during May, better check as to snow conditions on the roads and passes; from June on there should be little delay. In making your travel plans, don't fail to allow for time on the ferry and waiting for it, but don't fret; the ferry trips are delightful. If you're really thoughtful, you'll pick up ferry schedules and plan your trip to match the ferry schedules (and during the summer season, ask your hotel to make reservations on the ferries). A comforting thought is that repair crews often tour the roads looking for motor breakdowns; this is particularly valuable on the mountain routes.

Here are some driving distances from Oslo to major points: to Bergen, 301 miles; Bodø, 760; Kristiansand, 210; North Cape, 1,324; and Stavanger, 396.

PORTUGAL

National Characteristics

Five centuries ago explorers from Portugal roamed the New World and returned home with very enthusiastic reports. In recent years tourists from the New World have been exploring Portugal, and they couldn't be happier about their discoveries. If you were one of those Americans who included this sunny corner of the Iberian Peninsula on your last visit to the continent, then you know what we mean. Most Americans have returned home also with very enthusiastic reports (about Portugal).

It's difficult to put into one word a description of the people of Portugal. One word that fits, however, is *saudade*, a kind of yearning or nagging nostalgia. The Portuguese are always nostalgic about something—themselves, their country, their family, the things they did (or didn't do).

In the bygone years of explorers such as Prince Henry the Navigator and Vasco da Gama and Magellan, Portugal reached great heights of prestige and importance. The country attained its zenith in the sixteenth and seventeenth centuries, but since that time Portugal has sadly (and nostalgically) watched many other countries pass it by in wealth, power and importance. This can only lead to more nostalgia, more singing of fados, the sad tearful stories of unrequited love or unhappy events.

Such, in essence, is Portugal—it feels that its love (of the world) is unrequited. Doubly sad, because it is not true, we say.

Americans find the Portuguese delightful people, extremely hospitable and with marvelous Old World manners. Americans frequently praise the Portuguese above all others, finding them and their country a constant source of enjoyment. The Portuguese are not demonstrative people—that is, they are not dancing in the streets and singing at the top of their voices all the time. As a matter of fact, they often look anything but happy. Yet all it takes is a word or a cheerful "Hello" and they and their spirits burst forth with warmth and friendliness. Liberal-minded critics, however, usually object to the Portuguese emphasis upon the class system. On occasion employers speak to their help as the lord of a medieval manor might have commanded his vassals centuries ago.

Women, the touchstone of social progress, have been gradually emerging from the background, where they have been basking in the shadow of their menfolk since time immemorial. The next generation may see Portuguese women close to being on an equal footing with men—or, at least, daring to being there.

When to Go

Even at New Year's you can expect to have sunny, if a bit nippy, days except in the mountainous areas near the Spanish border in the north. Spring comes in pleasantly just about everywhere. But April and May bring truly marvelous weather (usually, of course) and a countryside covered with flowers. The summer months can be hot on occasion, but seldom oppressive. Still, the long hours of bright sunshine have a tendency to scorch the soil, giving a brown, barren effect. There is the alternate compensation of very little rainfall in summer. Beginning with September, the long autumn season finds all of Portugal delightful. This is just the right time for a visit to the Douro-Oporto district in the north, for the entire region is filled with harvesttime excitement and the weather is (or should be) superb. During winter months, from December through February, you might have to take your chances with the weather at points from Lisbon north. But in the Algarve region, at the southern end of Portugal, the climate will be extremely mild—nearly idyllic—in the wintertime.

WEATHER STRIP: LISBON

Temp.	JAN.	FEB.	MAR.	APR.	MAY	JUNE	JULY	AUG.	SEPT.	OCT.	NOV.	DEC.
Low	46°	47°	51°	54°	58°	63°	65°	67°	64°	58°	53°	47°
High	54°	56°	59°	63°	66°	77°	75°	76°	73°	68°	61°	58°
Average	50°	52°	55°	59°	62°	70°	70°	72°	69°	63°	57°	53°
Days of rain	13	12	14	12	9	5	2	2	6	11	13	14

TIME EVALUATION ¶ Lisbon should be scheduled for not less than four days; this includes local trips to Estoril, Sintra and the opposite side of the Tagus River. If you're driving through the countryside, allow at least a week extra. Needless to say, two weeks would be better, assuming that you wanted to make a stop or two at some of the Portuguese resorts, such as the one at Buçaco.

PASSPORT AND VISA ¶ No visa is required for a visit of less than two months, but you will have to be in possession of a passport, of course.

CUSTOMS AND IMMIGRATION ¶ As a practical matter, the tourist does not have to concern himself with what he can bring into Portugal duty-free. The customs inspectors are extremely cordial and, on the average, will merely wave you onward without the slightest question. Technically, there are limits on certain items, such as no more than 10 packs of cigarettes (or 50 cigars or 250 grams, a half-pound, of tobacco), a bottle of wine, a small bottle of liquor (about a third of a quart) and a tiny flagon of perfume—plus, of course, the usual traveler's articles, including a portable typewriter, transistor, camera, and reasonable amount of film. But, as we said, don't worry about all this too much. As far as money is concerned, there are no restrictions on how much you can bring into the country or take out with you when your vacation is over.

HEALTH ¶ With such a pleasant, warm climate—and that 500-mile Atlantic coastline—there should be no special health problems for the traveler. Water is definitely good in all of the large cities, notably Lisbon, Oporto and Coimbra, and in the Estoril resort area. It is almost as good in the rural areas, too. But if you have any doubts, there are many types of bottled mineral water available at extremely low cost. Salads and green vegetables are well scrubbed in restaurants, so there is no need to hesitate about eating them. The Portuguese do not believe in icing shellfish, on the theory that it damages the flavor. Be careful of shellfish with a doubtful taste, particularly during the summertime. Check if the milk has been pasteurized, or boiled, before you start drinking it.

TIME ¶ Portugal is six hours ahead of (later than) Eastern Standard Time. Thus, if it's 5 P.M. in New York, it's 11

P.M. in Lisbon. However, when we have Daylight Saving Time, there's only a 5 hour difference. Portugal has daylight saving time all year.

CURRENCY ¶ The *escudo* is the currency, and it is broken down into 100 *centavos*. Portuguese represent the escudo by what looks like a dollar sign ($) that is placed between the escudos and the centavos. Thus, an item that is priced at 95 escudos and 50 centavos would be written 95$50. This has been known to disconcert American tourists who at first glance assume the item is priced at $95.50. There is a big difference, because the escudo is worth only a small fraction of the dollar—a few cents. The exact value in relation to the dollar varies with changes in international exchange rates.

PRICE LEVEL ¶ Portugal's prices are still moderate, although as everywhere they keep rising all the time, not getting lower. But, all in all, they are not too high except in Lisbon, where the level is a bit high. A single room with bath can cost as much as $15 in Lisbon, but there are good hotels also where the rate will be half, or even less than that. Away from Lisbon, and out in the country almost anywhere (but especially in the south, the Algarve), prices of everything are wonderfully and refreshingly low. However, in Lisbon meal prices can range from a couple of dollars for a good lunch or dinner up to $4 and $5 in top restaurants and hotel dining rooms. You can spend more than this, though, especially if you have some good wines.

TIPPING ¶ Hotels add a 10 percent service charge to the bill, and that theoretically takes care of the tipping. (A 3.1 percent tourism tax is also tacked on.) But if hotel personnel are helpful in special ways, give them something extra. The baggage porter should be given between 5 to 10 escudos for each piece of luggage. Give the chambermaid an average of 10 escudos for each day you're in the hotel. Perhaps somewhat more in a deluxe hotel. It is customary to give restaurant waiters 5% of the check, in addition to the service charge depending on the size of your bill. Taxi drivers should receive tips ranging from a couple of escudos to 15 percent of high fares.

TRANSPORTATION ¶ The local *airline* (Transportes Aéreos Portugueses) has service between Lisbon and Oporto, Faro, Funchal (on Madeira), Azores as well as between Portugal and New York, South America and many cities in Europe. TAP flights are scheduled several times a day between Oporto and Lisbon. In general, as Portugal is a small country, most tourists will be traveling by road.

Train service is not bad, but nothing to rave about either. There are some top express trains and on these everything will be smooth going. But on the regular trains, the ride can be subject to sudden and unexplained halts at stations and delays of one kind or another. The *Foguete* is a top-flight express, and by all means try to take this; it travels twice a day between Lisbon, the railroad station of Fátima, Coimbra and Oporto. On the international trains, sleeping-car service is available, but reservations in advance are advisable during the summer season. The international trains leave from the Santa Apolónia station in Lisbon, not the Rossio (which is in the center of town), so keep that in mind and budget your getting-to-the-train-on-time schedule accordingly. If you are making a long train trip—especially on an international train—inquire beforehand if meals or snacks will be served en route. This can be very important, because not all trains have food service. Rail rates are low. There is a special weekend rate that cuts rail tariffs about 20 percent both in First and in Second Class. The shuttle service between Lisbon and Estoril is fast and efficient, should you wish to stay at the beach resort and come into Lisbon daily for sightseeing. And shopping.

There are hundreds of *taxis* dashing (and that is the word!) all over Lisbon. Any trip is guaranteed to raise your blood pressure by dozens of points, but somehow you always seem to make it safely. Rates are extremely reasonable. For trips outside of Lisbon (or any other city's limits) be sure to arrange your fare in advance with the driver.

Subway service in Lisbon is excellent and brings you from the center of the downtown area to some interesting outlying points. The cost of the subway ride will remind you of those long-ago days of the five-cent fare on New York's underground.

Buses scoot swiftly and smoothly through Lisbon.

Fares vary, ranging from 1 escudo on short runs to several escudos. *Paragem* is the magic word to look for, because it indicates a bus stop. In the cities buses are numbered according to the routes they serve, and these numbers will be listed on the appropriate bus-stop sign. Out in the country, or in small cities where there is only one bus line, the word *Paragem* will be posted without an adornment. There is very good bus service between all important points. This is an excellent and inexpensive way to sightsee in Portugal, except when the buses are overcrowded—as they often are on weekends and holidays. Service by bus between Lisbon and various Spanish cities is also operated. If you're taking a long-distance bus in Lisbon make *sure* you find out exactly where it leaves from. Some buses depart from the Cacilhas terminal at the ferry station on the *other* side of the Tagus River. This is the kind of information you will be in no mood to acquire at the last minute.

The presence of the Tagus River at Lisbon's front door, among other things, mean that *ferries* will help get you from one side to the other (whether you're on foot or driving a car). Some ferries, however, only carry passengers, so check on this beforehand. Most leave from the area between the Cais do Sodré (a tumultuous, picturesque area) and the Praca do Comércio. A short way downstream from the ferry landings something new has been added to the riverscape: the Tagus River Bridge. Plans for this essential link have been drafted for almost a century, and in the spring of 1967 it was completed. It has an American accent, too. In 1960 there was a competition for its construction and the award was made to the U.S. Steel people. It is quite a bridge, and holds all kinds of records—the largest in Europe, longest continuous trusses anywhere on earth, highest bridge towers in Europe, etc. It is also the longest bridge in the world that can accommodate trains as well as automobiles. The passageway for the railroad, however, is not going to be added until sometime in the future. The only other highway bridge in the area is at Vila Franca, fifteen miles upstream.

Boat rides on the Tagus are possible from May to October. The cruise gets underway at the wharf in front of the big square, the Praca do Comércio, and lasts an hour. Usually there are a couple of cruises in the morning, several in the afternoon, and one late in the day.

Longer cruises along the coast are scheduled on Sundays, Wednesdays and Fridays. They begin at 9:45 A.M. Cruise prices are very reasonable.

Numerous bus sightseeing tours are available by several companies and will take you not only to the main city sights but also to the important points in the vicinity, such as Cascais, Sintra, Estoril, Sesimbra, Arrábida, Setúbal and Palmela. Several night tours of Lisbon are also a daily feature. More distant one-day tours take you to Évora, Fátima, Nazaré and some other places. You can get information on them (as well as on anything else in Lisbon or Portugal) from the Government Information Office at the Praça dos Restauradores, not more than a couple dozen steps from the Rossio railroad station.

COMMUNICATIONS ¶ *Airmail letters* to the United States cost under a quarter. Postcards are 3$30 by airmail—about 12 cents. Surface mail to the United States is 2½ escudos (close to 9 cents), but it can take three (four? five?) weeks for your letter to reach its destination. Here we must say an unkind thing: it has been the experience of many tourists in Portugal that letters left with the concierge (in some hotels) are charged at the airmail rate and then sent by ordinary mail—the concierge apparently pocketing the difference. The solution to this practice is to insist on affixing the stamps and mailing the letters yourself in the hotel. Stamps can also be purchased at post offices, of course, and at tobacco shops (*tabacarias*). Let us say a kind thing: the post office clerks are very helpful and there is no problem about mailing your own letters. Furthermore, main post offices of Lisbon are conveniently located and, what's more, don't lock up early the way most continental ones do. They have a "permanent" service at the main post office on Praça dos Restauradores and at the airport.

Telegraph service, as elsewhere on the continent, is operated by the government and is quite efficient and not too expensive. To telephone telegrams dial 10 and ask for an English-language operator. Better, have your hotel concierge send it. Long-distance *telephone* calls can be arranged by the hotel operator, and this is the most convenient way to do it generally.

Pointer: To get a radio taxi, when there is not a cab in sight, telephone 83-33-38 or 83-44-38 in Lisbon.

BANKING HOURS ¶ In general, banks are open from 9:30 A.M. to noon and 2 to 4 P.M. On Saturdays the hours are 9:30 to 11:30 A.M. There are also many official money exchange bureaus. What is helpful is that a number of the banks maintain evening hours for changing money on weekdays (not always Saturdays). Two conveniently located branch banks with evening service are the Banco Pinto & Sotto Mayor at 11 Praça dos Restauradores (hours—6:30 to 10:30 P.M.) and Banco Português do Atlântico at 66 Praça dos Restauradores (Monday to Saturday, 6 to 11 P.M.).

BASIC PORTUGUESE

English-Portuguese

Waiter: *Gração*
Bill of fare, menu: *Lista, menu*
Napkin: *Guardanapo*
Bread and butter: *Pão e manteiga*
A glass of orange juice: *Un copo de laranjada*

Boiled egg: *Ovos quentes*
1. soft: 1. *moles*
2. medium: 2. *meio duro*
3. hard-boiled: 3. *duro*
4. egg cup: 4. *oveiro*

Fried eggs: *Ovos fritos*
Bacon and eggs: *Bacon (touchinho) e ovos*
Coffee, black: *Café simples*
Coffee with cream and sugar: *Café com crême e açucar*
Coffee with hot milk: *Café com leite*
Tea: *Chá*
Water: *Agua*
Ice water: *Agua gelada*
Mineral water: *Agua mineral*
Breakfast: *Almoço*
Lunch: *Lunche*
Dinner: *Jantar*
Shampoo: *Lavagem*
Haircut: *Cortar o cabelo*
Manicure: *Mancura*
I want . . . liters of petrol: *Quero . . . litros de gasolina*
Change the oil: *Tenha a bondade de trocar o oleo*
Grease the car: *Engraxe o carro*
How are you?: *Como está?*
Fine, thank you: *Bem, obrigado*
Please: *Tenha a bondade*
Thank you very much: *Muito obrigado*
Good morning: *Bom dia*
Good afternoon: *Boa tarde*
Good night: *Boa noite*
Yes: *Sim*
No: *Não*
Morning: *Manha*

Noon: *Meio dia*
Afternoon, P.M.: *Tarde*
Evening: *Tarde*
Night: *Noite*
Sunday: *Domingo*
Monday: *Segunda-feira*
Tuesday: *Terca-feira*
Wednesday: *Quarta-feira*
Thursday: *Quinta-feira*
Friday: *Sexta-feira*
Saturday: *Sabado*
One: *Um*
Two: *Dois*
Three: *Três*
Four: *Quatro*
Five: *Cinco*
Six: *Seis*
Seven: *Sete*
Eight: *Oito*
Nine: *Nove*
Ten: *Des*
Twenty: *Vinte*
Thirty: *Trinta*
Forty: *Quarenta*
Fifty: *Cincoenta*
One hundred: *Cem*
One thousand: *Mil*

ELECTRICITY ¶ The voltage, in general, is 210 or 220 A.C., which means that your appliances, unless they have adapters, will not work. A very few installations are 110 A.C. so inquire locally wherever you happen to be. In any event you'll need special converter plugs (the international type) for the outlets.

FOOD SPECIALTIES AND LIQUOR ¶ The Portuguese cuisine is basically appealing to most Americans, with a few exceptions. To generalize, it would seem that Portuguese cooking is vaguely similar to Spanish food, but with Italian and French accents, because Portugal actually does not have a truly definite and distinctive cuisine. But let us quickly add that there are any number of regional and local specialties, and the methods of preparation of the same dish can change from one town or area to another. Thus, for example, Vila Real is celebrated for its *alheiras*, a sausage of pork, hare and white bread. But sausage from some other region will be recognizably different. The typical Portuguese dish, if there is such a dish, is prepared with garlic, olive oil, tomatoes and onions. When you are served a green salad, you will not get a small plate containing a few lettuce leaves. Instead, you'll receive a large bowl of greens, all spiced and spruced up with slivers of onions. Unfortunately, for the curious gastronome, the average Portuguese restaurant or hotel, in its endeavor to please an international clientele, serves comparatively few national dishes. Regional dishes, however, can readily be obtained while on the highways.

Breakfast in your hotel room can be—let's say, will be—the continental type (rolls, butter, jelly, coffee and hot milk), but it does not have to be. Many Portuguese rushing to jobs and offices stop at stand-up coffee bars and have a cup of coffee with one or two sweet rolls or cakes of some kind. We say "two" advisedly, because when ordering cakes at a coffee-bar counter, the barman always puts two on a plate for you—even if you have only asked for one. It apparently is a courteous gesture. You don't have to eat the *two* cakes. But, of course, you probably will. That's only courteous, too, isn't it? Hotels will not have this variety of cakes for breakfast, because it is simpler to serve standard-type rolls or bread. Incidentally, although you may not believe it at first, Portuguese coffee is the best in Europe, because Portugal is a sort of uncle to coffee-producing Brazil, from which coffee comes (you'll see the Brasilian coffee-town name of Santos, for instance, frequently in the place-names throughout Portugal). At first, the coffee will seem a trifle too strong. But after a day or so, you'll begin to enjoy it fully. Lunch is anywhere between noon and 2:30 P.M., but 1 P.M. seems to be the high point. Early in the afternoon, local outdoor cafes are filled with people eating innumerable calorific concoctions—thinly layered pastries, rich cakes, almond-paste confections—all consumed with a cup of the country's excellent coffee. In a cafe, don't just order coffee—specify the type you prefer. A *carioca* is coffee with hot water added and is not so strong as the usual blend; a *garoto* is coffee with milk; *bica* is just plain coffee. You may also have your coffee served in a glass if you prefer that to a cup. Barmen in most center-of-town coffee bars are familiar with the international terms for the variations of coffee, so use another language (even English!) if you don't know the exact word in Portuguese.

You'll notice, too, that the Portuguese have a mania for sweet things, and the figures of most women show it, unhappily. You'll have to hurry your cake and coffee because as evening draws on—and shops and offices close —the cafes are again crowded. This time it is the aperitif drinker who holds forth. The Portuguese avoid strong liquor, but they drink light wines instead and accompany them with infinitesimally small olives or a handful of nuts. The dinner hour might begin at 8 P.M. or 9 P.M., but in the larger cities any time up to midnight is considered reasonable.

Because of the 500-mile Atlantic coastline that wraps around the western and southern sides of Portugal, fish is naturally a basic item in the daily diet of the average person. As we already remarked, shellfish should be eaten with caution, because the Portuguese do not believe in refrigeration. But freshly caught shellfish, naturally, is safe to eat.

The local clams (*ameijoas*) are very tiny and absolutely delicious; the same cannot be said about the oysters, which are rather flat and poor in flavor and texture. Don't miss the local crab, *santola*, which is extremely tasty. If you can bear their repulsive appearance, try the *percebos*, a local shellfish vaguely resembling a miniature elephant's foot (or possibly a barnacle) and secreting within an incomparable morsel of delicious seafood. The *lagostas*, *clawless* lobsters, and *camarões* shrimp, are also exceptionally good. The favorite dish of the fishermen is herring, but the fresh-cooked herring, sad to say, looks better than it tastes. To us, it tasted—well, fishy, if you know what we mean. The other favorite of the Portuguese is *bacalhau*, codfish, which tastes exactly like codfish does in Boston (when it's fresh). But the local folk prefer it dried, and in many country inns it appears on the menu every single day in one from or another: *bacalhau à Gomes de Sá* is with garlic, onions and eggs; *à Portuguesa* means with a spicy tomato sauce; *pasteis de bacalhau* are small fried croquettes, and so on and on and on. The national soup is *caldo verde*, a green vegetable soup that is good but not wildly exciting; *caldeirada* is a very good fish soup. The meat soup, *ensopada*, is pretty heavy fare except for a crisp cold day; *canja* is a rich, fatty chicken soup.

Don't expect to find good steaks or rare roast beef in Portugal except in a very few specialty places; even then it will not approach the quality of American beef. The best recommendation we can make—and it's only a substitute—is to try *bife na frigideira*, which is not beef in a refrigerator but beef in mustard sauce, customarily served on an earthenware plate. The *cosido à Portuguesa* is a national dish, a type of boiled dinner with meat and vegetables; this is sprinkled with oil and vinegar. A great favorite that you'll see on menus all over the country is *iscas*, or sautéed calf's liver. The Portuguese like to combine two dissimilar items, pork and clams for example, and produce a dish that is surprisingly good, *carne de porco à Algarvia*, also known as *porco à Alentejana*. Tripe and beans or *dobrada*, which you may or may not like, is a local peasants' favorite.

Of the cheeses, the number-one selection might be *queijo da Serra*; absolutely delicious, too, is the fresh cream cheese from Azeitão, called *queijo fresco*. Good salads are scarce, although the situation shows some signs of improvement. Among the desserts, you'll always encounter a dull, uninspired custard with caramel sauce. You'll do well to look for local cake specialties in your travels—particularly the *quieijadas de Sintra*, the local cheesecakes. The favorite Portuguese *pudims* taste slightly insipid; of them all, *pudim Português*, the orange pudding, is the most passable.

The local beer is quite good and almost all types are palatable, although the Imperial brand is considered topnotch. Local wines (except port) are generally undistinguished but certainly drinkable. Incidentally, you should know that included in the price of most restaurant meals is the *vinho da casa* (wine of the house), and if it isn't offered, ask for it. Of course the wine served in open carafes cannot (as a rule) compare with the bottled product. The best dry whites, perfect with seafood, are called *vinhos brancos secos*; look for Bucelas or Colares. In the reds, *vinhos tintos*, you'll find Dão and Colares. Americans take quickly to *vinho verde*, which translates into "green wine" in English but isn't; the green quality refers to its youth—it's extremely drinkable and thirst-quenching and unbelievably inexpensive.

Of course, Portugal is renowned for its port wine, produced in the Oporto district to the north. There are hundreds of different types, but they are classified into five principal varieties: ruby, tawny, crusted, vintage and white. Of them all, only the white (not really white, but pale yellow) is taken before a meal. The others are reserved for drinking with cheese or dessert, or after dinner.

Ruby port is blended and bright red; the tawny is left longer in the cask and loses some of its redness. Crusted port is a type that throws up a good deal of sediment in the bottle and is far better than ruby or tawny, but the bottle must be handled and poured with care or the sediment will become dislodged. Vintage port is the greatest of all, the only one bearing a date (for the others are blended), the height of perfection and seldom put on the market until it is at least 20 years old. To get some idea of the wide variety available, visit the **Port Wine Institute** in Lisbon and sample some of the many types.

To wrap up the Portuguese wine situation, don't ever order Portuguese champagne, *espumante*, because it's horrible. Madeira, produced in that island, isn't terribly popular with tourists, but is worth trying; of these, *Sercial* is dry and makes a fair enough appetizer drink, while *Malmsey* is rich, sweet and cloying.

If you wish something stronger, especially as an after-dinner drink, a wide and powerful range of regional brandies is available.

WHAT TO EAT IN PORTUGAL

Filets de peixe recheados: Fish fillets fried with shrimp in tomato sauce
Bacalhau à Portuguesa: Dried cod with tomatoes and garlic sauce
Tortilha de mariscos: Omelet stuffed with shellfish
Caldo verde: The favorite green vegetable soup
Sopa de camarão: Shrimp soup
Canja de galinha: Rice chicken soup
Sopa de batata e agrião: Potato and watercress soup
Sopa à Portuguesa: Fish soup served with a slice of toast in each soup plate; actually more like a stew
Caldeirada: The fisherman's soup, like French bouillabaisse
Tripas à moda do Porto: Tripe prepared with chicken and ham
Vitela assada: Roast veal made with garlic and white wine
Lombo de porco assado com batatinhas: Roast pork and small potatoes
Iscas: Sautéed calf's liver prepared in wine
Carne de vinha: Pickled and spiced pork
Leitão assado: Roast young suckling pig
Porco à Alentejana: Cubes of pork cooked with baby clams
Frango guisado: Stewed chicken with tomatoes and onions
Galinha recheada: Capon stuffed with olives and eggs
Galinha grelhada: Fried chicken
Vaca estufada: Beef stew
Pato com arroz: Duck prepared with rice
Vinho tinto: Red wine
Vinho verde: Slightly sparkling young wine

Pudim d'ovos: Egg pudding customarily served in the north
Creme de leite com farófias: Very much like our own "float-
   ing island" dessert
Sangria: Fruit punch made with sugar and red wine

The *principal tourist areas* are Lisbon and the nearby
Estoril (with its sunny coast) and the inland town of
Sintra; the coastline facing the Atlantic on the western
shores of the country; the north region, particularly the
area of Oporto. In the wintertime, the Algarve district
at the southern end of Portugal is popular with sun
worshipers.

Capital City

A ship is the classic symbol of the city of Lisbon, and
you will spot this on lampposts, restaurant menus and
many other places. The ship, of course, is a reminder that
this is an old-time seafaring nation and has been responsible for a great many discoveries of and in the New
World. Appropriately, the capital city of Lisbon is situated on the water. It is on the banks of the Tagus River,
not far from where this great stream flows into the Atlantic. Lisbon is a lovely city of about a million inhabitants and is one of Europe's most delightful capitals. The
famous earthquake of 1755 wrecked the city, but it was
soon rebuilt, possibly more beautiful than ever. From the
shores of the Tagus, the city at first rises gently—then,
steeply—with the town spread across seven separate hills.
Lisbon may be considered as a city of two parts: the
Baixa, or lower town, and the *Bairro Alto*, the old part
of the city, or high quarter.

Beginning at the river front, we find the fishing boats,
the women with baskets filled with fresh herring, the
general nervous excitement of a marketplace. Crossing
the river are small, crowded ferryboats; the entire harbor
is alive with motion and excitement. As the government
has decreed that everyone must wear shoes, it's not unusual to see the fishwives, walking barefoot, but carrying
shoes knotted about their neck, in case a policeman
should spot them. The central square at the waterfront
is the Praça do Comércio, a tremendous open area of
impressive dimensions. Walking away from the waterfront you proceed by the broad Rua Augusta to the natural center of town called Praça de Dom Pedro IV, or
Rossio Square. Rossio's history goes back so far, no one

can be quite sure of its origins, but at various times, it was a marketplace, then later used for horseracing, for pageants and spectacles, even as an animal market; today it is the heart of Lisbon, its streets covered with intricate mosaics similar to those seen in Brazil's Rio de Janeiro.

Leading away from the Rossio and climbing uphill is the Avenida da Liberdade, 300 feet wide, which goes straight up to the Edward VII Park, an extremely attractive green area. Incidentally, in the northwestern corner of the Edward VII Park is something quite unique—the *Estufa Fria*, a tropical garden of several acres enclosed, not by glass, but by wood lath, which admits light and air. By all means be sure to see the Estufa Fria, even if you are not ordinarily a gardening enthusiast. Along the Avenida da Liberdade are the leading hotels and shops in town, although in recent years the city has tended to build farther north into the suburban area.

Lisbon's regular attractions for sightseers include: the Carmo, a convent-church, near the Rossio; the Castle of St. George (Castelo de S. Jorge); the "Sé," the renowned cathedral of Lisbon; the many, many architecturally interesting churches scattered throughout the city.

Far more diverting is the old quarter of town, situated high above the business section, called *Alfama*. The streets are so narrow that it is a place for walking and strolling and not for driving a car. It is the old quarter, all right, but everything looks so clean you would think it was brand new. For a pleasant look at the life and habits of the people, drop into one of the wine shops and at the bar ask for a glass of *tinto* ("red"). It will cost about a couple of escudos. It will not be the greatest glass of wine you ever had, but your visit in the neighborhood wine shop will probably make a happy memory. The people won't know English, but you'll be able to communicate. Women should be sure to wear flat shoes for strolling in this area, as the cobblestones make high heels impracticable.

Some of the most interesting sights of Lisbon are in the nearby suburb of Belém. It is a historic area, too. Great explorers set out from the port of Belém on the sea lanes toward their celebrated discoveries, and it was here that they were welcomed as heroes on their return. Belém can be reached either by electric train from Cais do Sodré or by bus from the waterfront at Praça do

Comércio. Allow a half day for the round trip, or plan to have lunch in Belém. Don't miss seeing these attractions: the Tower of Belém, a superb example of what the Portuguese call Manueline architecture (it was from this very spot that the explorer Vasco da Gama set sail); the Museum of Folk Art, featuring peasant artifacts; the Convent of Jerónimos with beautifully carved cloisters; the Coach Museum (open 11–5, closed Mondays), housing a fascinating collection of regal coaches, most of them decorated in unbelievable fashion.

No visitor should fail to have a drink at the Solar do Velho Porto, the Port Wine Institute, at 45 Rua S. Pedro de Alcântara; the little building is extremely attractive and you can, for a very small charge, sample some of the greatest of Portuguese wines. Don't leave Lisbon without hearing the *fado*, the nostalgic songs sung in the little night clubs; more about this in the entertainment section.

১ Short Trips from Lisbon

Across the Tagus River

A fifteen-minute ferry ride takes cars and passengers across the Tagus River, from the Cais do Sodré pier in Lisbon. The boat trip alone is a memorable experience, for it provides the best possible view of Lisbon, with its pastel-colored houses forming a charming crazy-quilt pattern as they appear to be tumbling down the side of the famous seven hills, almost into the river itself. One can see, too, the majesty of Black Horse Square, the popular name for the Praça do Comércio, a large area, surrounded by imposing government buildings on three sides and bordered by the Tagus River itself on the fourth. Another memorable sight is the ancient Castle of St. George, which crowns one of Lisbon's hills and stands as a mighty sentinel, just as it has since the days before the Moors conquered the city.

The newly completed Tagus River Bridge, just downstream, looks particularly splendid from the deck of the ferryboat as you cross over from Lisbon's harbor. Usually there are some large trans-Atlantic passenger and cruise ships in the harbor, and these add to the beauty of the setting. At the ferryboat landing of Cacilhas on the other side, the traveler proceeds on to Sesimbra, Arrabida or even Setúbal.

Sesimbra is a quaint fishing village with a wonderful combination of beautiful beaches, rocky cliffs and verdant farmland at its doorstep. Fine swimming here and skin diving, too, but even more important, Sesimbra is "off the beaten path" for tourists and so the visitor can feel the pulse of everyday life of the fisherfolk who live here.

Arrabida is a beautiful scenic spot handsomely situated in the Serra de Arrabida, an impressive mountain range bordering the Atlantic, with unusual grottoes, wild vegetation, palm trees (the area here looks very Mediterranean, even if it is on the Atlantic). At one point along the road that runs across the crest of a mountain, you can see over miles of valleys and rivers, as far as Lisbon itself, while in the opposite direction, there are vast stretches of the purple-blue Atlantic.

Setúbal is an ancient town, one of the largest in Portugal and the principal fishing port of the country. Here are the many sardine canneries, and fishing boats are built in the shipyards with fine handcraftsmanship. Interesting side trips can be taken in this area—one, for instance to the castle of Palmela—a twelfth-century structure that displays some of the finest examples of the art of medieval military architecture. Palmela Castle boasts a fantastic view in all directions, and on clear days, you may even see the castle of Beja, some eighty-five miles away. If you want to stay overnight, or even for a few days, there's the lovely Estalagem de S. Filipe, built in the old Castelo do S. Filipe, which was a fortress perched on the heights over Sesimbra. Naturally, the view is magnificent, the food good, and the prices low.

The classic all-day excursion from Lisbon is the trip to Estoril, Cascais, Sintra and Queluz. The complete excursion can be made only by automobile or bus, but the link between Lisbon and Estoril, or between Lisbon and Sintra, can be easily accomplished by the subway-like electric train. There is very frequent service to Estoril from the station at Cais do Sodré.

By auto, leave Lisbon from the waterfront, heading westerly on the Avenida Vinte e Quatro de Julho, later the Avenida da India, with the Tagus River on the left hand; this is route N-6. It is just a run of seventeen miles along the excellent road to Estoril, the resort headquarters of the international set. Estoril, it has been said, is the home of more ex-royalty than any other community in the world; certainly if you stay for a few days, you will not fail to note a surprising number of barons, earls, counts and even princes and princesses. Here you might stop over at the very large, luxurious Estoril Palace. There is a famous but small bathing beach, and the casino has gambling, entertainment, dancing and frequent, spectacular gala events. There's a much better beach at nearby Praia do Guincho, which also has several interesting seafood restaurants. Continuing on from Estoril via route 6, it is eight miles to Cascais (pronounced Cash-kay-eesh, if we get it correctly), an old fishing town that recently has become quite popular. If possible, try to attend the unloading of the fishing catch and the colorful *lota*, the fish auction, which follows. Some of the overflow of royalty from Estoril is here; among them are former King Umberto of Italy and the Count of Barcelona. Cascais has a new and very good hotel, the Cidadela, with attractive rooms, apartments and suites, all with terrace or balcony, and there is also a large swimming pool and some shops (in the apartments with kitchenettes you can do a little cooking yourself). It's very nice, rather luxurious and not too expensive. It might make a nice place to stay if you want to be near the beach and away from Lisbon. From Cascais, follow the shore road (route 247) to Boca do Inferno, Hell's Mouth, where the sea has worn openings through the rocks. The road continues through the Guincho, an extremely rugged stretch of shoreline facing the ocean. Here is the Cabo da Roca, the most westerly point on the European continent. At Guincho there is a remodeled hotel, the Hotel do Guincho, formerly a fortress, perched picturesquely on a cliff overlooking the sea. Then comes the villages of Malveira, Colares and Sintra, a charming small town in beautifully wooded surroundings. You could hardly do better than to spend a few days at the extremely elegant Palacio de Seteais, one of the best hotels in Portugal, or, at least, have lunch there. Lord Byron once called this town "a glorious Eden," and who are we to question such an expert?

From Sintra, head toward the suburb of San Pedro to see Peña Castle, high on a rock; the castle is only a hundred years old but has a wonderful fairy-tale look about it, with indescribably exotic combinations of architectural styles, the whole effect being completely and devastatingly charming. Continue to Rio de Mouro, then to Cacém and turn off to Queluz, a small village with a famous old pink wedding cake of a chateau built in imitation of Versailles; there is an interesting restaurant in the old kitchen of the chateau. From Queluz (via route 117) it is only eight miles back to Lisbon.

The Algarve, Portugal's Warm Southern Coast

This doesn't qualify as a short trip from Lisbon, but it's a region worth investigating if you enjoy lazy beach life. Drive down to Lisbon's waterfront, and take the Salazar Bridge across the Tagus, arriving in Cacilhas. Follow the signs toward Setúbal; here you'll find a great place for lunch, the Pensão Naval Setúbalense, featuring hors d'oeuvres. Keep driving toward Alcácer do Sal, through Grândola and into Santiago do Cacém; here is another ideal place for lunch (if you're hungry): the very charming Pousada de São Tiago, but the only sign directing you there is a tiny one marked simply "Pousada," so watch for it carefully. The distance from the bridge to here is about 85 miles; it's another 75 miles to Sagres, but don't count on making fast mileage.

From Santiago do Cacém, head toward Cercal, Odemira, Aljezur and Sagres. Sagres has a delightful place to stay, the Pousado do Infante, which has a fine location overlooking the sea; it serves interesting food and the prices are very low. Nearby is the new Da Baleeria Hotel, which has a swimming pool and is more expensive. Visit the enormous lighthouse at Cape St. Vincent; visitors are welcome.

From Sagres, drive to Lagos which has the new, first class but very reasonably priced Hotel de Lagos with swimming pool. Then continue to Portimão, turning off to Praia da Rocha, which has a marvelous beach with weird red rock formations. There is, of course, the Hotel Algarve and also Miramar and Jupiter and the Estalagem São Jose. At Praia da Rocha if you don't find any hotel space, try the Globo or the Estalagem Miradoiro at Portimão. About 2½ miles west of Portimão is the large Golf Hotel de Penina, which has several restaurants and bars and is located at an 18-hole golf course. Nearby is the luxury resort hotel Alvor Praia, directly on the ocean at Alvor. This is a complete resort. From Portimão con-

tinue on to Lagôa (no, not Lagos) and then to Alcan-
tarilha. About a dozen miles farther on, watch for a right
turn to Armação de Pêra, a coastal village, which has
the luxury establishment Pensão Residencia Cmar. Vila-
lara is a new complex of luxury villas, which have a
restaurant, club, and swimming pool on the grounds.
It's good for a long visit. The Hotel do Garbe, located on
the rocks directly above the beach, is also very attractive.
At Vale do Lobo there is a magnificent new hotel, Dona
Filipa. At Albufeira, the lovely white fishing town, is the
fine and modern Hotel Sol e Mar, right on the beach; a
bit out on the Maria Luisa Beach is the luxurious, new
Hotel da Balaia, with swimming pool and also some
family-size bungalows.

The new airport at Faro has made communication between Lisbon and the Algarve district simply a matter
of a couple of hours, and the great new Tagus River
Bridge in Lisbon has also shortened the traveling time to
this delightful area. Buses leave on regular schedules from
Lisbon (Barreiro and Cacilhas) daily, and in addition
two express trains speed into the Algarve daily from
Lisbon. Remember! This area is called the garden of
Portugal, and spring starts somewhere around Christmas
or New Year's.

ACCOMMODATIONS ¶ Lisbon has some fine hotels, including the very luxurious Ritz. Several of the lesser hotels
are not always as well run as might be desired, but as
tourism has increased, there has been a general improvement all the way around. The 10 percent service charge
and a tourism tax in resort areas boost hotel prices a bit.

LISBON HOTELS

Ritz: One of Europe's most famous hostelries. Beautiful, modern and all that a hotel should be, the Ritz is an excellent
place for a day, a week or until you can finally tear
yourself away from Lisbon. The rates are on the high side,
but the Ritz is without a doubt the most luxurious hotel
in Lisbon.
Lisbon-Sheraton: A new luxurious hotel in a convenient and
excellent location. Rooms are available in standard,
superior or deluxe categories, with corresponding prices.
Several restaurants, including one serving Portuguese
specialties. Tall, 29 stories. In general, a fine place to stay.
Tivoli: A very good, modern, attractive hotel, air-conditioned,
on an important main street; good view from rooms.
Mundial: A fairly new hotel, centrally located and rather

noisy. Somewhat commercial; good, but not excellent, accommodations.

Embaixador: A very pleasant, modern hotel situated in the residential section of Lisbon about ten minutes from the center of town. Nice rooms, well furnished, quite attractive.

Eduardo VII: Quite new, on a main street in central Lisbon. Rooms are only moderate size, but furnishings are pleasant.

Flórida: A rather small, cozy hotel with a friendly atmosphere. The location is convenient and rooms are better than average.

Avenida Palace: A large, Old World hotel in the heart of things, fronting one of Lisbon's busiest squares. If you choose a front room, plan to retire late at night, because the streets are lively until well after midnight.

Fénix: A new, modern hotel, quite pleasant, but located on an extremely busy traffic circle.

Imperio: A very small (30-room) hotel, beautifully situated in a lush, tree-lined area. Pleasant, quiet and dignified; rather good-size rooms.

York House: Possibly Lisbon's best pension; ideal for a lengthy stay if you plan to eat all your meals at one place and want to learn Portuguese.

Other new First Class hotels are the Dom Carlos, Díplomatico, and Lutecia.

LISBON RESTAURANTS

Aviz: A series of attractive rooms make up what many people regard as Lisbon's best restaurant. Very good food and wine; fairly expensive.

Tavares: Sophisticated, smart and very good French food, with overtones of Portuguese and Italian. Fairly high-priced.

Chave d'Ouro: Another serious restaurant for people who appreciate excellent food. Quite high tariff; pleasant fifth-floor location.

A Quinta: At the top of the famous elevator in the center of town; marvelous views of the city and pretty good food, too.

O Lacerda Cortador: A steak restaurant (you select your own cut) that is quite good, although the meat cannot equal prime American beef.

Gondola: Very good Italian food and game dishes served outdoors in a lovely garden; near the popular fairgrounds, which are definitely worth visiting after dinner.

Belcanto: A new restaurant opposite the San Carlos Opera House, with quite good food. Piano music 10 P.M.; dance orchestra thereafter.

Folclore: Lisbon's most elaborate restaurant with entertainment; an ideal place to have a meal featuring Portuguese dishes, hear fado music, and see folk dancing; reservations necessary. Fairly expensive.

Varanda do Chanciler: A lovely restaurant in the Alfama, with a marvelous view of the harbor, and dancing in the evening.

Taverna do Embucado: The decor is that of an old Portugese wine cellar. The food is quite good, and the fados sung late at night, very good.

Gambrinus: In the center of Lisbon, and a meeting place for the society crowd. It's open for lunch and dinner, and even after the opera.

Note: The A Quinta also has a fine tearoom, and the Tágide not only features dancing with your dining but also has a floor show.

SHOPPING ¶ Of course, everyone thinks of *cork* when in Portugal and the shops are filled with hundreds of cork items, some of which are quite sensible or imaginative, others completely ridiculous. Coasters, cork-soled shoes and insulated containers seem good values; the knick-knacks and touristy figurines made of cork are the sort of thing that take up considerable baggage space and get thrown away back home, or should.

Because 18-karat *gold* is the minimum requirement by Portuguese law, small gold articles are worth purchasing. Pins, bracelets and the charms that dangle from them, wristwatch bracelets, brooches and the like are excellently worked.

Women's clothes are made to order by the local dressmakers at unbelievably low prices; about $30 is the typical charge, although you can pay more for finer work at the leading couturiers. Don't undertake custom-made apparel unless you have time for several fittings. Pay *after* the final fitting.

If you aren't going to Switzerland, Swiss *watches* should be bought in Portugal because prices are quite reasonable, about a third less than in the United States. The same percentage applies to purchases of German *cameras*, if you aren't planning to visit that country.

Port and *Madeira* wines are exceptionally good values; they make excellent gifts or you can drink them yourself. *Pottery* and *tiles* are other examples of the local handicraft, although these are quite bulky. *Leather goods* are fairly well made here, but are better and cheaper in Spain. If you've taken a fancy to fado music, why not buy some *fado records* and re-create Portugal and its nostalgic mood when you return home? *Madeira embroideries* are remarkable, but the prices are hardly low; if it's any consolation, they're more than doubly expensive in New York.

One of the increasingly fashionable places to shop in Lisbon is called the *Chiado* quarter. Glassware, ceramics and women's clothes are among the articles featured in the shops and small boutiques.

Pointer: Shops in general are open from 9 A.M. to 1 P.M. and after a siesta start working hours again at 3 P.M. and go on until 7 P.M. But don't expect the shops to open on the dot of nine in the morning. They can be a little slow about getting the day started.

ENTERTAINMENT ¶ Lisbon, and all of Portugal for that matter, has comparatively little night life, except for what may be found in the "typical" restaurant-night clubs of the people. Within Lisbon, the only night club of any importance is the very pleasant Tágide, where, in addition to a regular floor show, there are occasional folk dances, local music and provincial ballets. The other important spot is the Casino at Estoril, which is worth the short trip one late evening. The floor show is fair enough, and there is gambling in an adjacent salon, where you can lose whatever excess money you have with you.

The other way to spend late evenings is to visit the local cafes in the Bairro Alto district to hear the hauntingly sung fados (pronounced fa-dush). There are more than a dozen fado cafes in Lisbon, such as O Faia, Timpanas and Folclore (this last having a long, elaborate show). Others are in Coimbra, and Oporto has a few. *Fado* means "fate," and the renditions are performed by hollow-cheeked, bosomy, intense girls (occasionally by equivalent males, but without the bosoms), who usually sing (sigh!) sad, sad, songs of love, backed by two talented instrumentalists. The fados associated with Lisbon are light-hearted and usually feature stories of love. Those from the fado center at Coimbra are more serious and have a nostalgic tone. In some of the popular cafes where fados are sung, entertainers often also present traditional dances. One of the most famous ones is the *verde gaio*, a dance from the Ribatejo region. It is a cross between a square dance and a reel and is executed in a fast, bright tempo and spirit. Often, there is an accordionist providing the lively music. Most fado songs are tragic, so tragic that the tears will flow like water into your glass of port. A typical fado singer will recite (in detail) about how her boyfriend went to sea and the ship went down, and although 5,000 miles away she knew it all the time, and just as he was being rescued, a tornado came up and swamped the lifeboat and everybody was drowned. Or about how her sister was happily walking down the street and lightning struck her, and *her* boyfriend dashed to help and a horse ran over him. Actually, those are the more cheerful ones, because a good fado is more tragic than sixteen consecutive hours of a daytime opera. But it's all great fun, the singing is most interesting and the cost for an evening's entertainment very low. Inquire locally if Amalia Rodrigues is singing; she's considered tops. Don't be surprised if the audience joins in on some of the better known fados, or if some of the guests request permission to sing—and don't leave Lisbon without going at least once.

During the summer months, be sure to visit Lisbon's outdoor *Feira Popular*, something resembling, but not exactly like, Coney Island; it's an extremely pleasant evening's entertainment and you can watch the local citizens enjoying themselves, have a drink at an outdoor cafe and maybe try one of the grilled fresh sardines.

Motion picture performances are usually given at 3:15, 6:15, and 9:30 P.M. It is best to check about the 6:15 show, because sometimes that one is omitted. For the most part films are shown in their original version, so when it comes to English-language ones you will be all set—or ought to be! There are also some fine legitimate *theaters*, but a knowledge of Portuguese is needed for full enjoyment. The *circus*, if it is performing, speaks an international language and that will be a happy evening. Tune your transistor into a daily 8 to 10 A.M. radio broadcast that is intended to keep tourists informed of what is going on. The broadcast is in both French and English, so if you hear some French words when you tune in, be patient and the English will soon start flowing.

SPORTS ¶ Those who have shied away from the gore of a Spanish *bullfight* are in for some good news here— the bull isn't killed! Actually, the whole proceeding is more of a sport spectacle than in Spain, with the emphasis placed upon engaging the bull while the *rejonador* is mounted upon a horse. The bull's horns are tipped with protecting balls, and the proceedings end more on a sense of the comic, rather than with the tragic, climax of the Spanish bull ring. The bullfighting season begins on Easter Sunday and goes on until October. At Lisbon the contests are usually held on Sunday afternoons and on Thursday evenings. The top bullfights are usually in June, during the Santarém Fair and at the festivals in Vila Franca in July.

Plenty of *tennis* courts. *Golf* is popular in Portugal, and there are several courses, including the Clube de Golfo do Estoril, and on the Algoive the 18-hole championship courses—Penina Golf, Vilamoura, and Dona Filipa.

Just about any point you go to on the west or south coast will be a fine beach. Moledo do Minho in the north is a first-rate *beach*. Foz do Douro, not far from Oporto, is a popular resort. West of Leiria the beachfront is excellent, and of course the long stretch from Lisbon to the westernmost tip of Portugal (and Europe) is particularly delightful. Underwater swimming and aquatic sports are especially good at Sesimbra, Peniche, and Lagos. All-year-around swimming in the Lisbon area is not possible, of course, but if you yearn for a dip in the winter months, then proceed to the beaches of the Algarve.

MUSEUMS ¶ Museums in Lisbon close on Mondays. From Tuesday to Sunday they are open from 11 A.M. to 5 P.M. The admission fee is only a few escudos.

Note: St. George's Castle, atop the highest hill in Lisbon, is one of the great antiquities of the continent. It was founded apparently by the Romans when they were in Lisbon—or maybe even by their predecessors. In any case, it is very old. The moat is filled with flowers and the gardens around the castle are splendid. The gardens are open from 8 A.M. until sunset.

ᘔ A Tour of Portugal

Lisbon to Tomar—88 miles

Leave by the Avenida Almirante Reis, later entering the Aeroporto Road (route 1), continuing on to Sacavém, Alverca, Alhandra and then Vila Franca de Xira, famous as a bullfight center and training area. After leaving the town, you cross the magnificent Marechal Carmona Bridge (toll), passing Arruda Dos Vinhos, then Carregado, where you make a right turn onto route 3 heading for Azambuja, Cartaxo and Santarém; this last city was originally conquered by the invading Moors in the seventh century and recaptured by the Crusaders in the twelfth century. There is an interesting covered market; nearby is the Praça de República, a bustling open area.

Leave Santarém via route 3 toward Pernes, Parceiros, Tôrres Novas and Entroncamento, where you make a left turn onto route 110 to Tomar, a city of extraordinary physical beauty. This town was made famous by the Order of Templars (founded 1119); just outside of town, be sure to see the Templars Monastery. Also, visit the Convento de Cristo (open 10–5 daily), a wonderful opportunity to see the best in Portuguese architecture of the Middle Ages.

Tomar to Nazaré—51 miles

Leave Tomar via route 113; about fourteen miles later there is a left turn onto route 356 to Fátima, the sanctuary that—after Lourdes in France—is the most famous Marian shrine in all of Europe. The Apparitions took place in 1917. The main pilgrimages are on the twelfth and thirteenth of each month (especially during the six-month period between May and October), and the largest-attended pilgrimages are in May and October. Even non-Catholics will find Fátima extremely interesting at any time of the year. It is still, basically, a settlement of farmers and shepherds, and although an extensive amount of construction has been done in the area of the shrine, the surrounding towns retain their pleasant, old-time aspect. A busy windmill, grinding grain for bread, is on a hill at the entrance to the sanctuary area. If you should come here on the twelfth or thirteenth of any summer month, be forewarned that last-minute accommodations are absolutely (well, almost absolutely) unobtainable, and even the few hotels and boarding houses in neighboring towns will be crowded. At other times of the year, and especially during the winter months, good rooms may be had at the Hotel de Fátima, a small establishment that provides fine meals and service.

Continue on route 356 to Batalha, a rather mediocre village, but in it you will find the fourteenth-century monastery of Our Lady of Victory—now a parish church —which was erected by John I to commemorate his defeat of the Spaniards. The monastery is said to be one

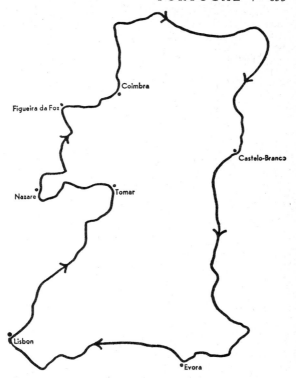

of the finest examples of Gothic architecture. It consists
of a number of cloisters (no longer used) and includes
a small museum of military objects. The Unknown Soldier
is buried inside the monastery, and two soldiers form a
permanent guard of honor. The acoustics in this room
are perfect. If a sound is made, the echoing tone will be
very impressive. In a corner of the room where the
soldiers are on guard—looking down from a small niche
—is a representation of the architect whose handiwork
constructed this massive, columnless, vaulted chamber.

Just past Batalha, there is the juncture with route 1;
make a left turn heading toward Cruz de Légua and
Alcobaça. (Four miles north of Alcobaça is the very
pleasant inn called Estalagem do Cruzeiro Aljubarrota,
well worth the few extra miles of driving, because Alcobaça has no satisfactory hotel.) Alcobaça has a fascinat-

ing outdoor market; be sure also to visit the monastery of Santa Maria of the Cistercian Order. From Alcobaça, take route 8-4 to Nazaré, beloved of American tourists.

Nazaré is one of those rare, perfect fishing villages that the National Geographic dearly loves to write about and has illustrated frequently in color photographs; surely you've seen all of Nazaré before in your dentist's office. (If your teeth ache sympathetically as soon as you look at this colorful port, you'll understand.) The fishing boats, the brilliant tartan costumes, the white-washed houses are all so perfect as to resemble a Hollywood production; you momentarily expect a director to call out, "Quiet on the set!" But its own perfection has been partly Nazaré's undoing, and during the summer months, American tourists and (even!) Portuguese vacationers come in great numbers. Off-season, absolutely delightful. There are now two rather pleasant small hotels; the Don Fuas is extremely attractive and not too expensive. Almost as good, but not quite, is the hotel Da Nazaré. The entire life of the town is at the beach, and this is the place to look for local color. Attention all husbands! Has your wife been complaining about all the work she does at home? Have her watch the fishermen's wives hauling up the boats on the beach. It might slow her up for an hour or two.

If you plan on staying overnight you can try the new Hotel Nazaré, with a pleasant terrace roof bar-café and the restaurant just below, or Hotel Praia, also new. Both are medium small, and are located in the lower town, not far from the beach.

Nazaré to Figueira da Foz—55 miles

From Nazaré, proceed north on route 242 to Martingança, Marinha Grande and Leiria, which has two sights: its women, wearing their round velvet hats, and the castle of King Diniz. (Tourists might consider these as three sights, but we consider the women and their hats together as one "must.")

Some really high-level banquets are held from time to time in the heights of the Leiria castle during official visits of such VIP's as the President of Portugal and Haile Selassie. On such occasions the room at the top is closed in, and the view for the guests around the banquet table is quite spectacular. The regular admission fee to the castle—at nonbanquet times—is only a couple of escudos. From Leiria, take route 109 to Várzeas, Monte Redondon, Guia, Gala and Figueira da Foz (pronounced fega-ru-da fosh). Here you'll find the very modern Hotel Grande, ideal for a stay in Portugal's leading seaside resort. This important beach spot has all of the usual seaside attractions—a gambling casino, miles of fine beaches, occasional gala events and a general air of informal liveliness.

Figueira da Foz to Coimbra—30 miles

Take route 111 from Figueira da Foz through Montemor-o-Velho, Tentugal, and Geria into Coimbra, Portugal's university city. (If you should have occasion to ask directions, it's pronounced koemb-ru.) Although the town is in two parts—the old and the new—the authorities have mistakenly removed much of the colorful old upper town, replacing many fine, ancient buildings with modern structures, architecturally extreme and more or less out of place in this ancient seat of learning, founded in 1290. Sad to relate, the authorities have limited to a considerable degree the once-colorful university customs, thus somewhat lessening tourist interest. Surely you're willing, however, to forgo a little local color in favor of improved conditions for students, who are now beginning to live in far more adequate and sanitary accommodations.

SIGHTSEEING ¶ Students in their robes; the university, notably the glorious library, which never seems to have very many readers; Santa Cruz Church, with the tombs of Portugal's first two kings; Portugal dos Pequeninos, a child's fairyland of miniature homes, castles and churches.

The Hotel Astoria has First Class accommodations for those who wish to remain overnight. Another good hotel is the Bragança. The Residência Almedina is all new and smart looking, but it is on an extremely busy street, and the trafficky location seems to be a disadvantage. In strolling about Coimbra you'll have to walk, or drive, to the *Penedo da Saudade* (remember our little talk about nostalgic Portuguese?). This is a superb viewpoint, atop a high hill overlooking the Mondego River. It is a pine-filled craggy chunk of rock, set in several tiers. There are little paths, stone benches and nooks where the old, the young, nursemaids with babies, schoolgirls—anyone who is or is not nostalgia-filled—like to sit in the after-noon and look out upon their beautiful city.

Note: If you come to Coimbra by train, please remember that it has two railroad stations: the old one, called Coimbra B (about a mile and a half from the center of town), and the new one, which is right in the midst of everything. Please don't get off at Coimbra B.

Coimbra to Castelo Branco—198 miles

Leave Coimbra by route 1 (sometimes marked on maps as route 11) to Mealhada.

SIDE TRIP ¶ Here you can make a right turn to Luso, a famous place for drinking medicinal waters. From Luso it is only a few miles via routes 235 and 547 to Buçaco (also spelled Bussaco), not really a city but a mountain-top and forest boasting Portugal's most luxurious resort hotel, the Palace; this is a wonderful spot for a few days' rest, because the forest area is magnificent.

From Mealhada, continue on to Malaposta and Agueda and at Albergaria-a-Velha, make a right turn onto route 16 through Ribeiradio, Oliveira de Frades and Viseu. Here you have an opportunity to see what is often called Portugal's finest painting, "Saint Peter Enthroned" by Grão Vasco, an example of primitive art and an authentic medieval masterpiece. Viseu is particularly interesting on Tuesday, the market day, when the streets are lively and colorful. Follow route 16 from Viseu to Mangualde, Fornos de Algodres, Celorico and Guarda, where you can make an overnight stop, if you wish, at the Hotel de Turismo. From Guarda, take route 18 south to Teixoso and Covilhã, famed for its steep, extremely narrow streets. Then to Fundão, climbing steeply (please exercise care in driving these sharp, turning roads) until you reach the Vale de Prazeres, then a steep descent and later into Castelo Branco. Here, too, the best stopover place is the Hotel de Turismo. *Sightseeing*: the former bishop's palace (now the Lyceum) and its formal gardens; behind the praça Luis de Camões, a narrow road-way goes through an old arch into a lovely old square surrounded by many ancient buildings.

Castelo Branco to Évora—124 miles

Leave Castelo Branco via route 18, driving almost thirty miles before you come to the village of Nisa; then on to Alpalhão (turning onto route 245), after which you reach Sousel and Estremoz. This latter is a delightful area, particularly in the spring and fall seasons; the town itself seems to be constructed principally of white marble, and the overall effect is quite pleasing. Visit the old castle, high on a hilltop, surrounded by its seventeenth-century walls; the fortification's gateways are particularly lovely.

Leave Estremoz by route 4 to Borba, where you take route 255 to Vila Viçosa; here you should see the immense Bragança Palace. Then route 254 to Bencatel, Redondo, San Miguel de Machede and Évora, for one of the highlights of Portugal. The town is a fascinating conglomeration of architectural styles covering various periods in its checkered history—Roman, Moorish, Renaissance, Gothic, Romanesque. Évora is a town to walk through because of the remarkably irregular, narrow streets; the fortifications, Roman ruins, white-washed buildings all evoke thoughts of the unbelievably colorful events that have occurred in this small community. *Sightseeing*: the Chapel of São Brás, a fortified church; the twelfth-century cathedral; the Roman ruins of the Temple of Diana, dating back some 1,800 years; the quaint colorful streets in Évora devoted to various ancient trades; the unusual Church of San Francisco whose chapel walls are gruesomely lined with human bones. Several fine places to stay have been built at Évora. The Pousada dos Loíos is quite luxurious. The Hotel Plancie is also very nice.

Évora to Lisbon—93 miles

Leave Évora by route 114 to Montemór-o-Novo; there take route 4 to Vendas Novas, watching for a left turn onto route 10 about nine miles from Vendas Novas. Continue on route 10 through Aguas de Moura to Setúbal. This is the center of the sardine industry, and is beautifully located, but the smell of the canneries is often overpowering. *Sightseeing*: the Church of Santa Maria de Graça, dating back to the sixteenth century, has a set of interesting Passion canvases oddly executed in the Chinese style. From Setúbal, take route 10 through Vila Fresca de Azeitão, then to the wine-producing village of Vila Nogueira de Azeitão, Tôrre and finally the port of Cacilhas, where you take the bridge back to Lisbon.

ঌ Motoring in Portugal

Although the old requirements have been abolished for a *carnet* or *triptyque* (customs documents that guaranteed that your own, or a rented car, would be taken out of the country at the end of your visit), the Portuguese still love paper work and red tape. If you're taking your own car, be sure to have *everything* in order before you ship the car. (On rented cars, be careful about obtaining all of the necessary documents before driving into or out of Portugal.) By all means, have your car cleared by the Portuguese AAA if it is arriving by ship, because the paper work is tremendous. Your state driving license is valid here, although naturally an international driving license is acceptable.

Drive on the right and overtake on the left, as usual. The roads are generally first rate, although there are no superhighways except between Lisbon and Cascais. The minor roads are usually quite good, but don't be disappointed to find an occasional very poor one in the mountain districts. On workdays there are no speed limits in the country, although you're expected to be able to come to a halt within a reasonable distance. On weekends there is a speed limit of 90 km (about 56 miles) on all roads. In built-up areas, the limit is 38 miles per hour, but no taxi ever goes that slow (or so it seems).

There seems to be little we can do but admit that the Portuguese are lovely people and the worst drivers in the world. The dodging in and out of line, the haphazard technique of driving in traffic, the overtaking on blind corners is enough to scare the daylights out of any American motorist. The only solution is to take it easy and not do as the Romans do; accidents can be very troublesome on a vacation trip, so let the natives drive in their uninhibited, carefree (yes, even nutty) fashion. It's sporting (so the Portuguese seem to think) to see how close they can come to making contact, then veer away swiftly. Don't blow your horn (it's against the law) except in emergencies, of which you'll have many.

There are plenty of gas and repair facilities all over the country, so no need to be concerned. You ask for *gasolina*, and you will find good, familiar brands.

Gasoline is one of the items that *is* expensive in Portugal. It costs well near a dollar for *super*. Regular is about 10 percent lower in price than the *super* variety.

Note: Automobile insurance is not necessary in Portugal. Let's rephrase that; it is not *obligatory*. As a matter of fact, we think it is *absolutely* necessary, and it would behoove you to make sure you are well covered when you take to the wheel on the Portuguese roads.

ROMANIA

National Characteristics

This is almost surely the most unique of all Iron Curtain countries, mostly due to the individualistic nature of its people. They seem to have a love of life not found in Russia, a somber country which is typically grey in mood and not a little gloomy, whereas everyone seems to concentrate on enjoying life in Romania. Quite naturally, this is a generalization, and as such, subject to the usual exceptions. But no one seems to work too hard, hours are quite short, and in the late afternoon, the streets are thronged with strollers, and window-shoppers, who've obviously nothing further to do but spend a pleasant few hours.

When to Go

The period between early April through late October is fine for a visit, although July and August can be very hot indeed. Along the Black Sea coastline, although it's hot, there's usually a breeze, and the summer evenings are quite pleasant.

TIME EVALUATION ¶ Allow at least 1 or 2 days for Bucharest, plus several days for the Black Sea resort area. If you can manage a visit to Braşov, in the Transylvanian Alps, and to the nearby winter and summer resort community called Poiana Braşov, you'll surely enjoy a few extra days.

PASSPORT AND VISA ¶ Of course, you'll need a valid passport, but the visa is issued free, upon arrival at the airport, in a matter of minutes.

CUSTOMS AND IMMIGRATION ¶ Don't take in, nor take out, any Romanian currency. You can bring in as many U.S. dollars or travelers' checks as you wish.

660

HEALTH ¶ The water is probably satisfactory, but you would be better off, all things considered, to drink bottled water. It's available everywhere and costs just a few cents.

CURRENCY ¶ The currency here is called *leu,* for just one unit of Romanian money. The plural form, which you'll typically use, is *lei.* The exchange rate between the dollar and the *leu* varies with fluctuations in the international money situation.

TIPPING ¶ It's usual to tip an extra 5 percent to 10 percent of the restaurant check, even though a service charge has been added. Because restaurant checks are so low, it scarcely ever amounts to more than a matter of small change. In a hotel, be sure to tip the baggage porter about 5 *lei.* Cabdrivers expect a few *lei* above the meter charge.

ELECTRICITY ¶ The Inter-Continental has current and outlets which are suitable for American appliances. Outside of that hotel, the current varies from 110 to 220, but even where it's 110, the chances are that the plug will be unsuitable, unless you've brought a special plug attachment.

FOOD SPECIALTIES AND LIQUOR ¶ I suppose the basic food of Romania is undoubtedly *mamaliga,* a very firm type of cooked yellow cornmeal, served instead of potatoes. Don't be surprised to find it appearing with a wide variety of dishes, even when not ordered. It's also eaten with cream, butter, grated cheese, eggs, or whatever, and is really good.

Some of the local appetizers are quite tasty. *Ikra* is something like caviar, although light instead of dark in color, and made from carp eggs. Small sausages and meatballs are also delicious to start a meal. As to soups, these are typically home-style, filled with all sorts of ingredients. One favorite, from Russia, is borscht, served in a wide variety of styles.

The national soup of Romania is called *chorba,* which is a sour soup, based upon some sort of fermentation agent, such as lemon, vinegar, or sauerkraut juice. There are meat and fish *chorbas,* in good selection. Speaking of fish, the chances are that most menus will feature carp, in one form or another.

Romanian meat preparations tend to be quite simple, usually just grilled over a charcoal fire. One national dish, not always encountered, is *ghivetch*, a mixture of vegetables cooked together, and very tasty indeed. Desserts tend to be quite simple, rarely outstanding. If you see *clatite* on the menu, order them—they're dessert pancakes.

The favorite before-dinner drink is *tzuica*, a light type of plum brandy, with a pleasant aroma, often served in small water-glasses for just a few cents. The local wines are fair, but not terribly distinguished. If you like strong coffee, the Turkish version should satisfy that desire.

Capital City

Bucharest, surprisingly, is not terribly ancient as Balkan cities go, being only some 500 years of age. It's exceptionally attractive, with large and open areas, broad boulevards lined with trees, roses growing everywhere, and many small park areas. All in all, it's one of the most pleasing of east European capitals. A majority of the structures seem to date back to the last century, and are not too tall, typically about four or five stories in height. Walking about at random is a delightful diversion, for there are really no sightseeing "musts" which simply cry out to be seen. Actually, that's part of the charm of Bucharest, a slow-paced, leisurely city, quite soothing to the nerves of tourists.

Of course, you shouldn't miss seeing some of the fine old churches, many with painted walls, which are definitely worth a visit. Outside of the city there are several castles worth a visit, and all of this can be arranged through Carpati, the national tourist office, located directly across the street from the Ambassador Hotel. Be sure to see the remarkable housing developments, just outside of Bucharest, consisting of scores of high-rise apartments which create an almost complete urban area.

ACCOMMODATIONS

Inter-Continental: Without any doubt, this is the leading and newest hotel of Bucharest and all of Romania as well. It has an excellent location, on Bucharest's main street, convenient to almost everything. Rooms are good-sized, nicely furnished, and there are many restaurants and shops.

Athénée Palace: A very good hotel, perfectly acceptable to American tourists. Rooms are moderate sized, passably furnished, and the service is fine. It has a good location, and the lobby is spacious and attractive.

Lido and Ambassador Hotels: Both of these hotels are located on the main street, and by American standards are just so-so, not terribly good. On the other hand, for one or two nights, they're not impossibly bad. Don't eat in the Ambassador dining room, but the Lido has rather good food, and in warm weather, you can dine on their outdoor terrace.

BUCHAREST RESTAURANTS (all are quite moderate in price)

Bucaresti: In my opinion, the best and most consistent of all Bucharest restaurants. The menu includes a good selection of local specialties plus international food. Don't fail to have their house specialty, a rich dessert which is a cross between ice cream and a mousse.

La Doi Cocoşi: About 20 minutes outside of town, this is a country-style inn, serving excellent Romanian dishes in the pleasantest of surroundings. The food is inevitably excellent, and there's a little music.

Pescarul: This is Bucharest's best seafood restaurant, almost everyone says, and I'd certainly agree. Their carp dishes are superb, but almost everything is quite satisfactory. Located opposite the Inter-Continental Hotel.

Carul cu Bere: The name means The Beer Wagon, and as you might expect, it serves beer, together with simple food, such as sausages, grilled meats, and so on. Everything is quite good, simple, but tasty, and very inexpensive. The surroundings are somewhat barnlike, but the atmosphere is pleasant.

SHOPPING ¶ Just about nothing to buy, except for some regional handicraft. There's a group of so-called Consignment Shops, where antiques and oddities are sent for resale, on a consignment basis. You might possibly see something you like, if you're lucky.

ê❧ A Tour of Romania

You can drive into Romania, typically from Hungary, if you wish. Alternatively, cars may be rented on a drive-yourself basis, and inasmuch as the roads are well marked, you shouldn't have any difficulties. It's only getting in and out of Bucharest that you may experience some difficulties because the roads aren't too clearly marked, but even that is quite a minor problem.

In my opinion, there are two areas worth seeing—the Black Sea Coast, and also the Brasov region, northwest of Bucharest. You can easily drive from Bucharest to Mamaia (pronounced Mam-eye-yuh, by the way) in half a day. The roads are good and uncrowded, and your only problem will be crossing the Danube by ferry, which usually involves a short wait, say 20 minutes, EXCEPT on holidays or Sundays. Then it can take much longer. Mamaia is really just a long stretch of sand, with some fair hotels, from which you can choose. The best hotel, by the way, is the International, which is classified as deluxe. Some of the other hotels along the beach look— and are—more modern, but the rooms tend to be small and quite narrow, and inadequately furnished. The food is usually good at any hotel, however.

Nearby is the town of Constanta, the chief port city on the Black Sea for all of Romania. Constanta has a long history, dating back some 2,500 years, and inasmuch as it's only 3 miles from Mamaia, you'll probably have a good chance to inspect it. Constanta itself isn't suitable for a stay, not having a good hotel, although the Continental is generally quite passable. There are quite a few ruins to see, plus the Archaeological Museum, the Aquarium, and so forth.

Stretching southward from Mamaia and Constanta are a whole series of resort towns, including Eforie, Costinesti, Neptun, Jupiter and Venus. The only truly good hotel is the Europa Hotel, at Eforie. But there's one problem involved—they have a Geriatrics Institute in Eforie, and that means a good many sick people stay at the hotel, which can be a little depressing. Speaking of the Institute, Professor Ana Aslan has been working extensively on work which involves combating the problems and ravages of old age. Patients from abroad are welcomed, and the rates (at least at the moment) are quite moderate. Dr. Aslan has developed a product (in pill form) called Gerovital H-3, which may be purchased at some drugstores, along the Black Sea Coast, and also in Bucharest. These pills, retailed at moderate price, are really a form of high-potency vitamins, and are good for people over 40 years of age. At least, that's what they say.

The other worthwhile region of Romania, from the point of view of automobile sightseeing, is the trip of about 105 miles from Bucharest through Ploeşti (pronounced Ploysht) to Braşov (pronounced Bra-SHOV). Braşov still has an old-world look about it, and is spacious and attractive in appearance. The mountains in the background are the Transylvanian Alps, (you remember Count Dracula, don't you?) and they're almost like a stage setting. The Carpati Hotel here is outstanding, and you'll be astonished at its size and elegance; incidentally, the dining room serves the best food in this part of Romania, so don't miss having a meal. In the evening, at about 9:30 or 10, you might pay a visit to a cellar spot called the Cerbul Carpatin, where you can have a passable, but not great dinner, and listen to local music, and see a show, combining Romanian folklore with typical nightclub nonsense. Not expensive, however, so it's worthwhile.

Be sure to drive along the mountain roads to Poiana Braşov, a lovely resort town about 10 miles from Braşov. There are several passable hotels including the Poiana and the Sport Hotels. They're all right, but not very luxurious. Be sure to eat at one of the various atmospheric restaurants in the vicinity, which are very unusual indeed. The Sura Davilor specializes in traditional Dacian food, and has lots of charm. Very close by is the Coliba Haiducilor, more easily remembered in English as the Outlaws' Hut, located in a sort of rustic villa, featuring foods cooked on open fires, including homemade bread. Both places are quite charming.

If you have a few extra days, one of the nicest trips imaginable is a visit to the famous painted monasteries of Moldavia. The mechanics of making the trip are quite simple, but because almost no one speaks English in Moldavia, it's best to make travel arrangements (at a surprisingly moderate cost) with the government tourist office. You fly from Bucharest to Suceava (pronounced Su-chava) in about an hour and a half. Suceava is the starting point for your trip, and it's best to make your headquarters at the Archers Hotel, which is quite new and passable enough, although the rooms are rather small; the food here is quite good. You can allow a day or two for visiting the monasteries that are scattered about the countryside, separated by only moderate distances. (For this reason, you'll surely need a car and driver in addition to your guide.) The monasteries, which date back to the 15th century, have marvelous frescoes painted not only inside but outside as well. The colors are in amazingly fine condition even now, some 500 years later. Obviously, this is not a trip for everyone; but for those with artistic and architectural interests, it can be very worthwhile and rewarding. At one of the monasteries now run by nuns, there is a small inn where you can remain overnight and where meals are served. Incidentally, the food is first rate. *Special note:* Dr. Ana Aslan, who runs the Geriatrics Institute in Bucharest, has developed a complete course to assist those who wish to resist the ravages of time. A complete examination costs about $30, which is quite moderate. Thereafter, the charge for additional visits is about $5 a day. Dr. Aslan, a remarkable woman, has developed Gerovital H3, a pill which is used in the treatment, and there are those who swear by it. Some very famous people reportedly have taken the treatment, including such notables as Konrad Adenauer, Nikita Khrushchev, Lillian Gish and Kirk Douglas. In any event, thousands of people from all over the world come to the Institute in the hopes of staying the changes that the years bring.

RUSSIA

National Characteristics

Russia is a land of obvious contradictions—a country with atomic bombs and substandard housing; of jet planes and insufficient food; of moon rockets but no refrigerators. These seeming contradictions are readily explained, for the government has bent every effort to catch up with the West (particularly the United States) scientifically and militarily, at the cost of consumer goods.

The good people of Russia are truly that, with almost the identical hopes, fears and desires of their American equivalents. The Russian, too, yearns for a happy marriage, a home and education for his family. Education and culture, in point of fact, have become an absolute mania with him—he literally worships at the shrine of art, regardless of its form—music, painting, ballet, opera, literature. Only a generation away from illiteracy, in most cases, he pays open homage to the literate, articulate artist.

A Special Note about Travel in the Soviet

The one country in which independent, spur-of-the-moment travel is impracticable is Russia. *Intourist*, the official government tourist office, will issue visas only to those who book their trip in advance through travel agents. If this sounds arbitrary, remember that hotel space and transportation are quite limited, and the Soviet tourist people want to know your schedule in advance. Once you are in Russia, it is frequently (although not always) possible to make changes in the itinerary. By all means, however, try to arrange a schedule that you can adhere to, because otherwise there will be considerable effort involved in altering your basic plans.

Your travel agent will obtain your visa, good for thirty days. Should you wish to remain longer in Russia, it is again sometimes (but not always) possible to extend the stay for an additional thirty days. Before your departure, your travel agent will hand you a small book of coupons valid for hotel accommodations and meals, marked "breakfast," "lunch" and "dinner." Coupons must be surrendered for each meal after it is consumed. Don't discard any unused coupons, as they may be exchanged for caviar, chocolates, etc.

The deluxe rate, while apparently high, does have the mitigating factor of being quite inclusive. In addition to meals, including a more or less limitless choice from any hotel menu (but not wines or liquor), all necessary local transportation is provided in private cars. For sightseeing, a guide-interpreter is furnished in addition to the chauffeur. From October 1 to April 30, the rate is reduced by 15 percent, but remember that although this offers a price reduction, the weather around Moscow and Leningrad is bitterly cold; in the Black Sea area, the weather will be much more temperate. It should also be borne in mind that all transportation between various points in the Soviet Union is extra; there is one exception, however—travelers remaining for more than eight days in either Moscow or Leningrad are entitled to free transportation (usually by railway) to the other city. This type of travel is described as *"Deluxe"* and includes a bedroom plus some sort of sitting-room arrangement, private bath, and as previously mentioned, almost unlimited choice of menu. In practice, this means you could theoretically eat caviar three times a day!

Only recently there has been a significant change regarding travel in Russia. The individual travel facilities have been extended to include a new reduced rate during the off-season. It includes single or double rooms and bath with full board (although there will not be an unlimited choice of menu) and transfers to and from the airport. Guide service and cars are not included in the rate; guide-interpreters and cars with drivers are available for an extra charge.

"Tourist Class" is also available, only to those traveling in groups of fifteen or more. Rooms are inclined to be small, but a private shower, occasionally a tub, is included in the rates. The menu, however, is fairly set and is not likely to be more than barely adequate. Needless to say, all local transportation and sightseeing are by motor coach, or would you prefer to call it a bus? There is a 25 percent reduction in the rate during the off months.

When to Go

For Moscow and Leningrad, June through August are the best months. April and May are often chilly but otherwise suitable and the cities are less crowded with visitors. From late August through October, days are usually very windy and cool, nights quite cold. From November through March, the weather is very cold and bitter, and days are short. For visits to southern Russia, such as the Black Sea coast, May–June and September–October are the ideal months; July and August can be extremely hot.

WEATHER STRIP: MOSCOW

Temp.	JAN.	FEB.	MAR.	APR.	MAY	JUNE	JULY	AUG.	SEPT.	OCT.	NOV.	DEC.
High	14°	19°	29°	43°	60°	67°	71°	68°	56°	44°	28°	17°
Low	5°	8°	15°	29°	42°	50°	54°	51°	42°	33°	21°	10°
Days of rain	14	13	12	12	12	13	12	15	12	13	16	15

PASSPORT AND VISA ¶ Since October 1955, Americans have been permitted by the State Department to visit Russia. However, a Russian visa is required, valid for thirty days. As a rule, this should not be secured on your own; the procedure is far too complicated. Your travel agent will make all arrangements, and it is suggested that you allow an absolute minimum of three weeks in order to obtain the necessary visa, although in an emergency, it may be secured in one week.

CUSTOMS AND IMMIGRATION ¶ Russia's customs officials are extremely liberal; the chances are excellent that your baggage will not be inspected on either arrival or departure. Don't bring any Russian *rubles* with you; there is no limit, as a rule, on other foreign currencies. Bring all the tobacco you'll need for your stay, because American brands are unobtainable and the Russian brands are not only expensive but execrable. A bottle or two of bourbon or Scotch may come in handy, for these are unobtainable. By all means, bring all the film you'll need for your still or movie cameras.

HEALTH ¶ The water in all large cities (such as Moscow, Leningrad and Kiev) *when served in your hotel dining room* has been boiled and is quite safe; if you visit outlying regions, bottled waters (such as *Narzan*), beer or tea might be the cautious thing to use. *Avoid tap water at all times.* Don't drink unpasteurized milk, of course; milk is fairly safe in the cities, less likely to be so in the rural regions. It's always a good idea to get typhus and typhoid shots before leaving for Russia.

TIME ¶ Moscow is eight hours later than Eastern Standard Time; when it's noon in New York, it's 8 P.M. in Moscow. When Daylight Saving Time is in effect in the United States, the time difference is reduced to 7 hours.

CURRENCY ¶ The *ruble* is the official unit of currency, and its value in relation to the dollar fluctuates in accordance with changes in the world money picture. There are 100 kopecks in each ruble.

PRICE LEVEL ¶ Astronomically high, so be prepared to be shocked. Your hotel accommodations and meals are prepaid, so at least many of the basic expenses are covered. But if you choose to break away from your regular hotel meals, be prepared to pay a minimum of $10 per person for a respectable dinner with a drink or bottle of wine; at a better restaurant, it might run much higher. Theater tickets for the Bolshoi averages $5 per seat, taxi rides are quite expensive, souvenirs and apparel are sky high. Don't expect to find any low-priced bargains here, but with a degree of reasonable caution, you needn't spend too much money beyond your basic expenses.

TIPPING ¶ The government forbids tipping as lowering the dignity of the people, but unfortunately a degree of tipping is still prevalent. In checkrooms, a 20-*kopeck* tip is still expected; be prepared to surrender your coat and hat in every theater, public building, restaurant before you enter—it's the custom. Waiters are tipped roughly

5–10 percent of the check, and this can be no laughing matter, for restaurant prices are high. American cigarettes and lipsticks are often regarded as more desirable than cash tips by many Russians.

TRANSPORTATION ¶ Almost all of your transportation will be furnished by Intourist, the organization that supervises your trip. Turn to them for transportation whenever you need it. However, if you're going to the theater, *taxis* are available in front of your hotel; rates are about 20 cents a kilometer, roughly 30 cents a mile. The *metro*, Moscow's famed subway, is all right except during morning and afternoon rush hours, but most tourists won't use it except for the one, almost compulsory, sightseeing visit. *Railway* and *plane* trips will be arranged by Intourist; service is quite good between principal cities, considerably less so on minor routes.

COMMUNICATIONS ¶ *Telephone* service is erratic; sometimes fair but often none too good, with about two wrong numbers for each correct one being par for the course. Your hotel telephone operator will have to get your numbers for you, so forget about telephone booths. You must know your party's telephone number, for there are no telephone directories available. *Cablegrams* may be sent from your hotel with little difficulty; they are fairly expensive for straight messages, less so for delayed cables.

BASIC RUSSIAN ¶ The Russian alphabet is Cyrillic, based principally upon Greek, Roman and Hebrew letters. There are many points of similarity but a great many differences that make it quite difficult to even pronounce a Russian word, much less understand it. Unless you're a true student, just learn a few phrases phonetically that will assist you in getting about.

ELECTRICITY ¶ You'll encounter both 120- and 220-volt A.C. in your travels throughout the country. Of course, the 120-volt electricity is suitable for American appliances, but be sure to make inquiries first. A regular European-type plug is necessary, however, for any appliance.

FOOD SPECIALTIES AND LIQUOR ¶ Meals are served in the normal pattern—breakfast, lunch and dinner, although occasionally dinner will be served in the middle of the day. Breakfast is almost American except for the lack of fruit juice, but eggs with ham, toast, jam and horrible coffee are standard. Don't look for orange juice, because oranges are extremely expensive, say 75 cents each! Lunch and dinner are almost identical meals except that most lunches do not include soup, so remember not to give up a dinner coupon when you merely have lunch; at the end of your stay, as we said, any unused coupons may be turned in for fresh caviar, chocolates or other goodies, and dinner coupons have greater trade-in value.

Appetizers in Russia are marvelous—you'll be able to order *ikra* (caviar) at almost any meal, and it's delicious, although in all honesty the portions are modest and the quality could readily be duplicated in New York. Another good choice is salt salmon (much like smoked salmon), an excellent way to begin a meal. Soups are fairly good, particularly one of the *borschts* (beet soups); these come in varying styles, including Moscow style, Kiev fashion, etc. They're all hearty and satisfying, especially those unusual ones made with tongue, olives, etc.

Unfortunately, we have now reached the stage at which the meal not only goes downhill, but drops disastrously off a precipice. In other words, from here on, the food is definitely bad, with a few exceptions. Steak (or any type of beef) is tough, elastic and shoe-leathery. Veal is mediocre. The lamb is fairly good, particularly when served as *shashlik* (cubes roasted on a skewer) or as *kavkaski shashlik* (in larger pieces). The chicken, too, is fairly dull going and the dark meat frequently has a strong, gamey taste. Salads are just about nonexistent except during the middle of the summer, and even then not remarkable. Vegetables are extremely routine, but you'll never starve because everything is served with potatoes, and the Russian breads are absolutely delicious even though the butter isn't. Local cheeses are fairly ordinary, although not inedible; they have the same mediocre quality as our own mass-produced process cheeses, with their synthetic tastes.

Desserts inevitably feature *marujinah*, ice cream, which is only fair, because the butter-fat content is too low for a quality product. Fruit compote tastes like fruit compote does in Kansas City, Kansas. If you're lucky, you might encounter *blinis*, the tasty buckwheat-flour dessert pancakes.

You've undoubtedly gathered that Russian coffee leaves

much to be desired. Let's try that again: it's too weak and cloudy. No, we haven't quite caught all the nuances of the situation: it's just terrible. Because coffee must be imported, at the cost of considerable cash reserves, the brown bean is dispensed with less than a lavish hand; a reasonably good brand of coffee (for Russia, that is) retails in a local shop for about $6 per pound. Small wonder that Russian coffee is horrible. A fore-warned coffee-loving traveler brings his own supply of the instant variety and adds it to the watery beverage at the table or orders *kipyatok* (boiling water) and makes it from scratch.

Incidentally, and this may shock you, Russian tea isn't too good either. Not bad, you understand, but definitely not as good as you can get in England—or in the United States, for that matter.

Russian wines are erratic. White wines are dull and lacking in subtlety; the reds are better, but that is only a matter of degree, and the wine producers of Burgundy and Bordeaux can still relax. The wines are numbered, rather than named, so you order Red No. 2, or White No. 3. Avoid Russian champagne at all costs; it's ridiculously sweet, averaging almost 10 percent sugar, and is just short of being 100 percent undrinkable.

Vodka, of course, is the national strong drink. It is, too. Strong. With vodka's enormous American popularity, it's hardly necessary to describe the clear, white, almost tasteless variety. It might be interesting to learn that it is now seldom made from potatoes, various grains being substituted; the liquor passes through charcoal filters, which remove the coloring and produce the clear liquor we know. Don't look for Bloody Marys or Screwdrivers; the Russians drink it neat, slightly chilled. The ideal combination is caviar and vodka, one of the world's classic appetizer combinations. If you like *vodka*, try some of the variations including *starka*, an aged type; or possibly the lemon-flavored *vodka*, but promise us (scout's honor?) that you won't drink the garlic-laden vodka so popular in the rural areas.

Russian beer is mediocre; much more interesting is *kvass*, a beerlike beverage (but slightly sparkling) made from fermented apples, bread or whatever is available. If you like yogurt or buttermilk, order some *kefir*; not too bad if you enjoy "dairy" drinks.

Here are a few pointers about eating Russian meals.

It takes, on the average, about two hours to get seated, attract a waiter's attention, order a meal, be told that there isn't any more something or other, get served and finally pay for the repast. Multiplying two meals (lunch and dinner) by two hours each means an average of four hours daily spent at the table. If you're impatient, bring along something to read to help pass the time If you like to eat meals in your room, learn the telephone number for room service and order your meal over the phone or have a waitress come to your room; then you can be comfortable while waiting for the meal to show up.

The principal tourist areas are Moscow, Leningrad and the Black Sea region.

Capital City

Moscow, unlike Paris or London, is a comparatively new city, with a history going back a mere eight centuries. At no stage of its development was it a beautiful, romantic place in the tradition of Paris; it lacks great parks and miles of trees because the climate is too rude during the bitter winter months. Russia never had a great architectural drive or famous designers; even during its most creative years, Italians and Germans came to design its principal buildings. Much of the principal part of Moscow was burned out when Napoleon set a giant fire before his hasty departure, and with it went many of the city's historic buildings.

At the turn of the century—the country's nearest approach to a merchant class with middle-class prosperity —whole series of apartment houses were built in the unimaginative, heavily ornamented style of the period. The classic apartment had seven or eight rooms for the typical family of that day, plus a couple of rooms for servants—and one bathroom. Today, with the city's acute housing shortage, several families are assigned to one apartment, all sharing in common the kitchen and bath facilities. Valiant efforts are being made to relieve the housing shortage, as can be seen by the rows of jerry-built apartment houses, but from all reports the authorities are lucky to construct new dwellings at a rate sufficient to account for the natural increase in population, compounded by the natural deterioration of existing structures.

Those who come expecting to find a handsome, gracious city will be disappointed; those who look for intellectual stimulation and consideration of an alien way of life will not be. But Moscow does have many sights worth seeing, if the mental preparation and adjustment is made.

The natural heart and center of Moscow is Red Square, an enormous open area about six city blocks long and two blocks in width. *Krasnaya Ploshchad*, as the square is called in Russian, involves an ambiguity, for *krasnaya* means both "beautiful" and "red," and therefore the designation of Red Square has no communist significance. It is here that the famous May Day parade passes; frequently throughout the year, other pageants and celebrations may be seen. Red Square has, at one side, famed Lenin Mausoleum, a severe marble structure; here are the embalmed remains of Lenin and Stalin. Usually there's a long line in front of the mausoleum waiting to enter; if you're inclined to go inside, the guard will occasionally allow the foreign visitor to enter without waiting in line.

Opposite the mausoleum is Moscow's leading department store, the *Gospodarstveni Universalni Magazin* (that is, the Universal State Store), which has been shortened to GUM, as was only natural and inevitable. It's pronounced "Gooom," however. The interior is a hodgepodge of large and small alcoves encircling an open area, with a glass-topped roof. Be prepared to walk upstairs and be prepared to find high prices.

At the end of Red Square is *St. Basil's Cathedral*, a smallish cathedral, but decorated in the most fascinating, unbelievable fashion. Surely this is one of Moscow's outstanding sights, with its asymmetrical towers and bright, strident color scheme, which surprisingly result in a refreshing architectural achievement. The cathedral was erected between 1544 and 1560 by Ivan the Terrible to commemorate his great victory over the Tatars (more correct than Tartars) in the battles of Kazan.

Red Square is also adjacent to the red-brick walls of the *Kremlin*, which escaped damage when Napoleon ordered the city set afire before his forced departure for home territory. The word "Kremlin" means "fort," and interestingly enough, if you visit other cities in Russia, you'll find other kremlins. No one knows for sure the earliest history of the Kremlin, but it is believed that the first fort was a wooden one, erected during the middle of the twelfth century. Today, there are Italianate brick walls surrounding an area of about sixty-five acres, roughly triangular in shape. Inside is the center of government for Russia.

Permission to visit the Kremlin may be readily obtained through Intourist and is something that should not—in fact, could not—be omitted from any visit to Moscow. Once inside, the visitor sees a series of well-maintained structures, some wooden, others of stone. The grounds are carefully tended and the visitor politely directed, by sign language, onto a prearranged series of indicated footpaths, which lead him through most of the highlights of the Kremlin. Official government buildings, of course, may not be visited by tourists. One of the stops is at the fairly small *Aruzheznaya Palata*, the Palace of Arms. Here are attractive exhibits of gold, silver and jewels; medieval armor; historical objects of significance to Russian history. There are displays of gifts made by foreign countries to Russian nobility, but if memory serves, nothing is displayed from the United States (unless added recently).

Other high spots within the Kremlin walls include the Great Kremlin Palace, Teremni Palace, the Bell Tower of Ivan the Great and the renowned Czar Kolokol Bell, which fell to the ground and broke. There is a large open area surrounded by three imposing cathedrals; in the Archangelsky Cathedral are buried many czars and their czarinas.

Another day, you'll want to visit Moscow's famed *metro*, the subway system of the city, which combines art with transportation. During some misguided period of Soviet development, the authorities determined to build a subway system to end all subway systems; thus, all stations were elaborately decorated with inlaid mosaics, statues, colored marble and anything that could be classified as "artistic." The local folk are proud as peacocks of their subway system, and who are we to say that the net result is nil? From the entrance until you can actually board a train involves a walk of what seems to be miles but is probably only several city blocks; the "art" itself is horrendous, the marble color schemes in the poorest of taste, the mosaic work pure cornball. But service on the trains is quite good; the cars are old-fashioned, perhaps, but transportation is swift and inexpensive, and after all, that's what matters.

Moscow University is another object of pride of the Russians, and here they have something worthwhile. Within a thirty-two-story structure there are thousands of students studying fiercely in their burning desire to overtake the United States. Every American visitor will want to visit the university and see the difference between the serious approach of these college students to the "snap course" approach of many of our own.

For some reason, the Intourist people don't seem to be terribly anxious for visitors to see the *Ostankino Palace*, a remarkable wooden building erected by a Russian nobleman about 200 years ago. If you can, try to visit this masterpiece of the fine arts of marquetry, carpentry and woodwork. The décor is rich and lavish, giving a fascinating insight into the fashion in which eighteenth-century noblemen once lived.

At one time or another, try to visit a local *hospital*, an English-language *school*, a session of the *law courts* and a collective farm, a *kulchoz*. In the summertime, be sure to take the *boat ride* on the Moskva River, which runs alongside the Kremlin walls. Another day, start alongside the National Hotel and walk up Gorki Street, one of the city's main thoroughfares: Moussorgski, the great composer, lived at number 22; across the street at number 21 is the *Museum of the Revolution*, formerly Razumovski Palace. Along Gorki Street there are interesting shops and fascinating sights; continue on to Pushkin Square, where you'll find Strastnoy Abbey and the offices of *Izvestia* (a leading newspaper).

SHOPPING ¶ As previously mentioned, the shopping and souvenir situation is none too satisfactory, because of the high prices charged. Even at the tourist rate for the ruble prices are high.

After considerable investigation, we can report that only a few items are worth bringing home, based upon price and quality. *Phonograph records*, particularly those made by noted Russian instrumentalists, are fairly moderate in price and well recorded; records are available in the long-playing speed, 33⅓, but don't expect to find stereophonic recordings. If you have developed a taste for *vodka*, why not consider bringing back a few bottles; many of your friends would be excited at the idea of owning a bottle of *Russian* vodka.

GUM, the Moscow department store, has a *"gift shop"*

on the main floor, displaying atrocious woodcarvings, gilt tea-glass holders, ceramics of a poor quality and other gimcracks and touristy nonsense at prices guaranteed to chill Paul Getty and others not ordinarily repelled by high prices.

If you have a child to remember with a gift, be sure to pay a visit to the *children's toy shop* at 7 Teatralny Proezd, where there are some fascinating items; many of the toys are calculated to amuse adults even more than children.

A Russian *camera* is worth considering if you're a photographic bug. While many of the models are outright copies of the German originals, it has been noted that newer versions indicate some original thinking. Don't bother buying the very cheapest models, because the American and German mass-produced low-priced cameras are better. From what we've been told, the cameras in the higher price range stand up fairly well.

If your home isn't decorated in the modern or contemporary style, look at the period *rugs* displayed at the shop at 10 Gorki Street. We doubt if you'll buy something, but look.

Antique collectors aren't likely to find any bargains at the famous shop at 9 Arbat Street, but who knows and who is more optimistic than an inveterate antique hound?

Don't buy, repeat DON'T buy: fur coats (the skins are good, the workmanship terrible); wearing apparel (the materials are poor, the styles way off); watches or clocks (high prices, inferior workmanship); perfumes (not in the same class with French by a thousand light years); typewriters (not very good, and impossible to service).

ENTERTAINMENT ¶ Moscow is renowned for its emphasis upon the cultural life, and after a few sessions with the local ballet and concert halls, you'll probably be inclined to agree that the reputation is not undeserved.

Not far from the Metropole Hotel is the world-renowned Bolshoi Theater; we hate to disillusion you, but that fascinating word "Bolshoi" merely means "big" or "grand." So, if you're desolated at the idea of calling it the Big Theater, just remember that every language has words that lose in the translation. At the Bolshoi, performances feature the ballet and opera. As to the *ballet*, it is superb and in the classic tradition, although a few new ballets are being gradually introduced. Not only is the dancing superb, but the orchestra that plays for it is equally remarkable. Orchestra seats are best, but the first rows of the balcony are passable; from the gallery you can see nothing but heads (of people in front of you). Tickets are about $5 for orchestra seats; these can be ordered through the Intourist representative in your hotel, but look at the schedule and request them as far in advance as possible.

The *opera* is none too good, we must report in all sadness. The day of great voices seems to have passed, and in truth, Russia, while rich in instrumentalists, is weak in vocal soloists. The opera shows this: the sets are handsome, the stage effects and costumes first class and the Bolshoi orchestra superb as always—but when the soprano utters her first squeaky, off-key notes, the whole performance falls apart. Go, we urge you, to see the stage craftsmanship, lighting and direction, but remember not to expect thrilling vocal passages. Most Russian opera voices couldn't make an American road company of a Schubert operetta.

Concert-goers will surely pay several visits to hear whatever is on tap locally; again, request tickets from Intourist as soon as you note something on the schedule that appeals to you. Performances are usually held at Tschaikovsky Hall, or at the State Conservatory. A fascinating evening may be spent in watching the Russian public's reaction to an American artist's performances, should there be one playing while you're in Moscow.

If you can speak Russian (and there aren't too many Americans who can qualify) or if you've always harbored a nostalgia for *drama* in the Russian style, visit the Maly Theater, which specializes in legitimate plays. If we disillusioned you about the meaning of the Bolshoi Theater, will it upset you to learn the Maly means "little"?

The Russian *circus*, if it's in Moscow, must not be missed. Some of the performers are routine; others are offbeat. The clowns are extremely good, but for us, the animal acts are unsurpassable, notably that of the talented (Russian) bear.

The *puppet* theater is absolutely tops; surely the world's best and most talented, without much question. Even though the dialogue will be lost to you, the movements of the almost human puppets will definitely amuse and delight; performances are at the Obratzov Puppet Theater on Gorki Street.

Don't bother about the *motion pictures*; most Russian films aren't too good for tourists because of the language problem. If you're absolutely dying of homesickness, call the American Embassy and ask about a screening of American films, which usually takes place once a week— inevitably a Western.

Night clubs, with floor shows, are foreign to Moscow —at least until some Russian official visits one in Paris or New York and decides it should become a part of the Russian scene. Many of the hotel dining rooms have music with dinner, and often feature American dance music, badly played, however. There's usually a vocalist of middling talent, but after a few vodkas, you'll hardly notice.

SPORTS ¶ Don't look for tennis or golf courses here, although it is true there has been talk of doing something along this line for tourists; at the moment, golf is non-existent and tennis facilities are very limited.

Sports in Russia are in the large-scale, public arena style. Vast groups of gymnasts and boring columns of marchers endlessly repeated are the sort of chauvinistic displays commonly seen here. Track events on the Olympic scale are likely to be scheduled at almost any given time; if these are to your taste, by all means go. *Horse racing*—with betting!—is currently a big rage here; betting has gotten to such a stage that the newspapers inveigh periodically against the evils of gambling, much in the fashion of American newspapers of some sixty or seventy years ago (we've been told).

MOSCOW HOTELS ¶ As you know, all hotel accommodations are in the hands of Intourist, the official government tourist organization. In the deluxe category, requests for particular hotels are sometimes (but not always) honored. In the middle of the busy summer season, it may be assumed that your request for a designated hotel will *not* be granted in the normal course of events. However, the hotel room situation in Moscow is very tight, and the local officials can scarcely be blamed if they concentrate on honoring the reservations first, and place secondary importance upon granting the request for a particular hotel. Almost without exception, however, when rooms with private bath are requested, the request will be honored. At present, by paying an extra fee, you can select your hotel.

National: Somewhat old-fashioned, but all things considered, probably the best hotel in Moscow. Small, centrally located, quite good food and service.

Metropol: Enormous, barnlike, Victorian style hotel with antique plumbing, high ceilings, red velour drapes and a very temperamental elevator. Some rooms are hundreds of feet away from the elevator. Well located near the Bolshoi Theater.

Ukrayna: A tremendous skyscraper hotel, very modern and up-to-date but located about twenty minutes from the center of town. Plenty of restaurants, shops, etc., but the service is extraordinarily slow.

Berlin (formerly the *Savoy*): Something like the National Hotel, but not quite so well located, and the service is somewhat indifferent.

Sovietskaya: Constructed for honored guests of the Soviet; tourists are sometimes accommodated. Rather luxurious, but very cold, chilly marble surroundings and atmosphere.

Leningradskaya: A brand-new eighteen-story hotel, quite good facilities, but out of the center of town. Fairly good-size rooms, almost modern surroundings.

MOSCOW RESTAURANTS ¶ Intourist (or your travel agent) will furnish you with meal coupons; these are surrendered for meals as indicated upon the coupons. The coupons are, of course, valid at your hotel, either in your own room or in the hotel dining room. Recently, Intourist has permitted the use of regular meal coupons for lunches and dinners ordered in several other restaurants; better inquire in Moscow as to which restaurants are included in the authorized list. In any event, you may (in fact, surely will) tire of the standard hotel food, and if your budget permits, you might want to try a meal or two on your own.

Aragvi: Probably Moscow's best restaurant, but of course, that isn't saying too much. The surroundings and décor have all the charm of the men's room at Grand Central Station, but the food is fairly good, the Georgian style music entertaining and, need we say, the prices are high?

Pekin Hotel: Not bad Chinese food, although you could do better in New York City. Be sure that you eat in the correct dinning room (of several) at the hotel; only one serves Chinese food, but you can tell from the oriental motifs on the walls.

Praha: Czechoslovakian cookery, quite good, but very expensive. As a break in the routine, you'll enjoy this very much.

Uzbekistan: Southern-style food (southern Russia, that is). Good Uzbekian food and wines from the Crimea.

Kiev: A sort of showplace of Ukrainian cookery, featuring all the dough-covered delicacies of that area; quite good.

SPAIN

National Characteristics

Spain is only one-twentieth the size of all Europe, but in recent years tourists have been flocking to it as if there was no other place on the continent. Those who did not include Spain on an earlier visit to Europe are doing so now. Most of those who have been in Spain before invariably come back. The Spanish landscape is a stunning collection of mountains and rivers, of barren plains and long, sudsy coastlines. Except for the parts bordering on France and Portugal, Spain's frontiers are the blue waters of the Atlantic and the Mediterranean. There are almost 2,000 miles of coastline, not counting the hundreds of miles of shoreland of the Canary and Balearic islands.

Most efforts to describe the Spanish national personality inspire a barrage of colorful adjectives—temperamental, high-spirited, dignified, explosive, haughty—but regardless of how writers differ otherwise, all conclude with one definitive hackneyed word: Proud. The peasant digging in his field is proud—you cannot buy his respect with mere money. The impoverished (ex-) grandee will not lower his dignity for any amount.

For once, the writers are in complete agreement. But pride goeth before a fall, another writer has said. Handicraft, pride in working with one's hands for a living and not taking the bread (or salary) of another means that the country lacks the industrial production so desperately needed to raise the living standards of the nation as a whole. The peasant tills his soil, scratching from it the most meager living imaginable. Instead of tractors and irrigation opening vast areas for large-scale cultivation, there is the solitary farmer who waters his crops by means of a bucket laboriously filled from the local well, just as his grandfather did before him.

The average Spaniard would rather walk alone down

his own hard road than ride in comfort, dependent upon any other man. He is gracious and kindly, even courtly with visitors from abroad. Ask a direction and expect to be taken to your destination in person. But make an appointment with a Spaniard and consider yourself lucky if he appears even an hour after the appointed time. His pride does not encompass your loss of patience waiting for his arrival. He desperately wants you to love his homeland, which is not at all difficult, and to admire it extravagantly. Is not Madrid the most beautiful of cities? Is not Spain the loveliest of countries?

He is much more reticent about his family, particularly his wife, who lives in almost Moorish isolation, a carryover from centuries gone by. American women, he thinks, are different—they belong out in the world—but Spanish women must be sheltered and protected. Therefore, while the Spanish husband leads his own life on the double standard, dining out, visiting his "little friend," the wife remains at home at his request (and insistence), protected from the cruel buffets of the outside world (and all its interests and entertainments).

When to Go

Spain is a large country with a wide range of climatic conditions, and generalizations can have only limited value. The "tourist" season begins in March and ends during early November; but at certain times of the year trips should be directed toward a region where the climate is best. In Madrid and the surrounding area, April–June and September–October are ideal; however, and there is no use in pussyfooting, Madrid can be very hot in the summer. Fortunately, the climate is exceptionally dry (the city is situated on a 2,000-foot plateau), and usually there is a tempering breeze (blowing off the adjacent Sierra de Guadarrama). To sum up: even during summer months, no matter how hot Madrid gets during the day, nights there should be pleasant. Good summer weather may be expected along the Costa Brava, to the northeast of Barcelona; the northwestern part of the country, particularly along the Atlantic coast from the French border, is also a prime summer vacation area. Majorca and all of the Balearic Islands are pleasant enough in summer months, although quite warm during the day; spring and fall are really best.

Now we must tackle a problem that cannot be avoided. One of the most fascinating parts of Spain is Andalusia, the southern part of the country in the Córdoba-Granada-Málaga-Cádiz-Seville region. From late June through August, this is undoubtedly the hottest part of Europe, with (shade) temperature exceeding 105 degrees Fahrenheit as a regular, normal affair. Even at night, temperatures drop sluggishly down into the 90s. It is with regret that we suggest that only the youngest, hardiest, most resilient tourist tackle Andalusia during the summer months. This is a winter resort country, delightful from October until May; unpleasantly humid and hot at other times. (During the late fall, winter and very early spring, cold days do come, and small hotels often will not turn on any heat, which means you may have to shiver around a small fire or miniature electric heater.) There is only one way of coping with Andalusia's tropical climate during the summer months: do your traveling very early in the morning, beginning as soon as 6 A.M. At noon, retire to a cool place for a siesta, resuming sightseeing when the heat breaks in the very late afternoon. If you aren't prepared to conform to this method, it is our sad duty to state that Andalusia should be omitted from your itinerary during the summer.

To recapitulate: If you come during the summer months, head toward the northwest Atlantic coast, the Costa Brava and the Balearic Islands, or limit your trip to Madrid and its surrounding area.

WEATHER STRIP: MADRID

Temp.	JAN.	FEB.	MAR.	APR.	MAY	JUNE	JULY	AUG.	SEPT.	OCT.	NOV.	DEC.
Low	33°	35°	38°	42°	50°	56°	61°	62°	55°	47°	40°	35°
High	48°	52°	57°	63°	72°	79°	86°	87°	76°	65°	54°	48°
Average	41°	44°	48°	53°	61°	68°	74°	75°	66°	56°	47°	42°
Days of rain	9	10	10	10	10	6	3	3	7	9	10	10

If it is August when you come, be sure to have confirmed reservations. With millions and millions of Frenchmen pouring into Spain by the conventional route of Port-Bou (on the east) and Hendaye (by the Atlantic) —not to mention passes and bypasses in the Pyrenees—

August is an extremely hectic, busy time. Crossing-the-border traffic is heavy, slow and hot. Locating an empty room in the tourist regions of Spain is impossible during mid-August. Yes, the word is *impossible*.

TIME EVALUATION ¶ On a month's vacation, the absolute minimum for Spain should be a week, but this is insufficient unless you're just planning to visit Madrid. However, a week would be sufficient for Madrid, plus quick visits to nearby sights (El Pardo, Toledo and El Escorial). If time is really short, Madrid could be reduced to five days. If you're planning to visit Majorca or the Costa Brava, allow about a week extra for each region. Inasmuch as Spain is a rather large country, and there is much to see, a whole month's vacation could be profitably spent in driving about, but the minimum auto trip would be not less than ten days, preferably two weeks.

PASSPORT AND VISA ¶ No visa is required. All you have to have for a visit of up to three months is a passport. For stays longer than three months, apply to the Dirección General de Seguridad in Madrid or to the Gobernador Civil in the provinces.

CUSTOMS AND IMMIGRATION ¶ The customs inspection has been just about eliminated, and after a quick glance at your American passport, inspectors will probably do nothing but smile and wave you into their country. You are allowed to bring in duty-free all personal travel articles, as well as such usual things as a camera, transistor, and pair of binoculars. Cigarettes are limited to a carton, but they rarely look. Or, in place of cigarettes you can have 50 cigars or 250 grams of pipe tobacco (a little over a half-pound). But, as we said, the Spanish customs inspectors are reasonable—if *you* are reasonable. As for pesetas, you know—money—you are permitted to take into Spain 50,000 of them and can leave with 3,000. There probably is a tiny saving if you buy pesetas beforehand in Zurich or New York, but not like in those old days. It is really not worth the effort to buy any sizable amount of pesetas in advance. But, whether going into Spain, or any country, it is always good to have a few dollars' worth of the local currency with you for tips, taxis or a glass of mineral water (or something). There are currency exchange booths at the border entry points, but at the time you cross the place might be closed or there might be a long waiting line. So have a bit of the Spanish money with you on entering. And don't worry about not being able to turn it in on your departure. You can cash it in at the border with no trouble.

TIME ¶ All Spain is six hours ahead of (later than) Eastern Standard Time. When it's noon in New York, it's 6 P.M. in Spain. When Daylight Saving Time is in effect in the United States, the time difference is reduced to 5 hours.

HEALTH ¶ In Barcelona and Madrid, you will be assured that the drinking water is absolutely safe, and we are sure that it is. However, if you've a tendency to be disturbed by changes in water, by all means drink the bottled variety. Outside of Barcelona and Madrid, under NO circumstances drink the local water, for this would be courting disaster in the form of "Spanish tummy," a disabling condition indeed. Make sure that any milk you drink has been pasteurized or boiled.

CURRENCY ¶ The value of the *peseta*, Spain's monetary unit, in American dollars varies with variations in the international currency market. There are coins of 1, 2½, 5, 25, 50 and 100 pesetas and banknotes of 100, 500 and 1,000 pesetas. The word peseta, by the way, is abbreviated as "pta." and the plural abbreviation is "ptas." The peseta is theoretically made up of 100 *céntimos*; but nowadays the smallest fraction of a peseta is the 10-cétimo coin. There is also a 50-céntimo piece.

PRICE LEVELS ¶ Spain is in the most favorably priced group of countries, but unfortunately—maybe the word is *inevitably*—the wonderful, often unbelievable, old bargain days have apparently gone forever. A cup of coffee is still not much more than a dime, and in general, everyday things are low-priced. But in a luxury restaurant you can easily spend close to $10 (per person) and a single room in one of Madrid's palatial hotels can cost $12, more or less. But what is so fascinating about Spain's prices is that you can get good food and pretty satisfactory hotel rooms for much less. The low-priced zone is generally almost anywhere but Madrid, Barcelona and a couple of major tourist centers.

TIPPING ¶ You'll find 15 percent added to your hotel bill, which theoretically should—but does not actually—cover all tipping. Give the baggage porter 10 pesetas for each piece of luggage, and hand the waiter who serves your breakfast in your room about 10 pesetas. The chambermaid, if she has been attentive and helpful, should also receive 10 pesetas for each day of your stay. Taxi drivers get 10 percent of the meter, but a 5-peseta tip should be the minimum because rates are so low. In the restaurants, the general tip for waiters is 10 percent. At railroad stations the baggage porters (*mozos*) expect at least 10 pesetas for each bag. In bars and cafes leave a few pesetas as a tip. Cloakroom attendants and movie and theater ushers should get 5 pesetas.

TRANSPORTATION ¶ *Taxi* rates are still low. For the first tenth of a mile the rate is 10 pesetas, and this amount is registered as soon as the driver "drops the flag" on the meter. From then on it works out to about 1 peseta for a tenth of a mile, or 10 pesetas for a mile. There are little, extra charges for baggage and also for journeying to outlying parts of a city. When a taxi is empty (and available), it will display a *Libre* (free) sign in the windshield. At night, a small green light carries the same message.

Bus trips are all right for short distances and in some areas (unless you're flying) are the sole means of public transportation. But in general they are crowded and can become tiresome after a couple of hours. Rates are extremely low. Sightseeing and tour buses are topnotch, very comfortable vehicles. Many of these services are run by ATESA (a state-owned organization, similar to CIT in Italy). In Madrid, ATESA is at 59 Avenida de José Antonio. The equipment used by this company is excellent, and there is a wide choice of tours—almost unlimited combinations are possible, the company itself says. There are seven-day Andalusian tours from Madrid and back; a three-day castle tour in the Madrid region; a five-day tour from Torremolinos through Andalusia and back to the starting point; and so on. Some tours are less expensive in the off-season. During the summer months, we hesitate (as previously mentioned) to recommend a southern trip through Andalusia by bus. Tours originate in Madrid, Barcelona and several other major cities.

expensive in the off-season. During the summer months, we hesitate (as previously mentioned) to recommend a southern trip through Andalusia by bus. Tours originate in Madrid, Barcelona and several other major cities.

Trains in Spain have been improving each season. This doesn't mean that the Spanish railroad (RENFE) is anything like the American ones (which aren't too great either!), much less the Swiss. But it is getting better all the time. The most interesting train rides in Spain are the famous *Talgo* trips between Madrid and Irún (on the French border) and between Madrid and Barcelona. These high-speed *Talgo* trains, invented by a Spanish engineer are diesel-powered. Something similar to the *Talgo* is the TAF, which is also a diesel but is not quite so fleety (if you know what we mean). The TAF series of trains was designed by Italy's Fiat. Whereas the *Talgo* features First and Second Class, the TAF trains carry only Second Class passengers (but in air-conditioned comfort). Both the *Talgo* and the TAF trains have dining cars, and both operate only in the daytime. They are extrafare trains, too. There are quite a number of TAF trains, so when planning to cover a big distance check beforehand to see if one of them serves the route you plan to travel. Something new has just been added to the Spanish railroads. As companions to the *Talgo* and TAF trains, TER trains travel between Galicia (in the northwest corner) to both Madrid and Hendaye (at the French border), from Cerbere on the French border via Barcelona to Alicante on the Costa Blanca, from Barcelona to Bilbao, and on a few other lines. A journey that once took as long as twenty-four hours has been cut to half that. Remember that on all extrafare trains and long-distance expresses you *must* have a seat reservation and your ticket in advance. If you do not have a reservation, you will not be allowed aboard. So get your place on a train reserved as soon as you can. There is a RENFE office in *every* Spanish city and in every town of any size, and you can buy your train tickets there with no difficulty. Or, have your hotel concierge get them for you. Railroad stations sell tickets on major trains only about an hour in advance of train time. Spain has three classes of train travel (First, Second, Third—with Third the lowest priced). Since rail fares are so low it is well worth the while to travel First Class always. Rail tariffs diminish slightly with the distance to be traveled. There is a special 25 percent reduction for a journey, or series of journeys, of 2,000 miles and of 7,500 miles. But that is an awful lot of mileage, and unless you're going to be in Spain for a while—and riding the trains—this type of ticket is not for you.

Iberia and *Aviaco airlines* link up all of Spain and its sunny islands at low rates.

Ships, if you have time, are a pleasant way of getting from one Spanish port to another. A popular journey is from Barcelona to Palma. Another favorite is from Algeciras to Tangier.

Local buses in Madrid operate from 6:30 A.M. to 2 A.M. The fare is very low.

Subway service is available both in Madrid and in Barcelona. It is called the *metropolitano*, or Metro. The Madrid subway operates between 6:30 A.M. and 1:30 A.M. The subway fare is even lower than the very-low bus fare.

COMMUNICATIONS ¶ On long-distance and overseas calls, telephone from your room or from an official telephone bureau (usually at or near the main post office in a city). A *letter* weighing no more than five grams costs something under a quarter by *airmail* to the U.S.A. *Telegram* service is so inexpensive—and good—that it often pays to telegraph, rather than write, for hotel reservations in Spain or from Spain to other parts of Europe.

INFORMATION POINTS ¶ The national government operates first-rate tourist information offices in the main cities, so don't hesitate to call upon them for ideas, help and directions in your travel and sightseeing plans. In Madrid there are three information offices. At the Torre de Madrid, right in the Plaza de España; at 2 Calle Medinaceli, right near the Palace Hotel and at the airport. The information offices are open daily from 9 to 9, except Sunday. In Barcelona, the office is at 658 Avenida de José Antonio. Hours are 9 A.M. to 1:30 P.M. and 4 to 7:30 P.M., closed on Sunday. Smaller cities have tourist offices as well. They usually are designated as Oficina da Información, and you will be able to get a handful of pamphlets and local maps at them.

EXCURSIONS ¶ From major cities there are half-day and one-day excursion trips to the major points of interest in the area. Rates, schedules and centers covered can vary slightly from one company to another. Generally, lunch as well as all admission fees and charges are included in the basic excursion price. In Madrid, the most specialized enterprise for local sightseeing tours is *Melia*, with seven offices scattered about the city. The most centrally located of these are at Princesa 27 (Hotel Melia Madrid), at Hotel Plaza and at Plaza del Callao 3. In Barcelona, we recommend taking your excursions with *Barcelonatours* which leaves from 5 Ronda Universidad and from Av. Generalísimo Franco 415; or *Terminaltur*, at 18 Balmes. Both are within a block or so of each other. Terminaltur, by the way, has an interesting office because the downstairs section is equipped with a pleasant snack bar.

GUIDES ¶ One of the many wonderful blessings in Spanish travel is the crackerjack guide service. It is topnotch and relatively inexpensive. Official guides can be obtained by applying at the government information offices (we gave you those addresses above, remember?). The rate is standard throughout Spain. If you engage a guide for a full day, you are also responsible for the guide's lunch and the transportation costs (if any) involved in your excursion. Guided trips at major monuments and points of interest are usually available on the spot, and it is advisable to join up—provided the attendant leading the group speaks English.

BASIC SPANISH

English-Spanish

Waiter: *Camarero*
Bill of fare, menu: *Lista de platos*
Napkin: *Servilleta*
Bread and butter: *Pan y mantequilla*
A glass of orange juice: *Un vaso de zumo de naranja natural*
Boiled egg: *Huevos cocidos*
1. soft: 1. *moles*
2. medium: 2. *meio duro*
3. hard-boiled: 3. *duro*
Fried eggs: *Huevos fritos*
Bacon and eggs: *Huevos con tocino*
Coffee, black: *Café negro*
Coffee with cream and sugar: *Café con natra (crema) y azucar*
Coffee with hot milk: *Café con leche*
Tea: *Té*
Water: *Agua*
Ice water: *Agua con hielo*

Mineral water: *Agua mineral*
Breakfast: *Desayuno*
Lunch: *Almuerzo*
Dinner: *Cena*
Shampoo: *Lavado de la cabeza*
Haircut: *Cortar el pelo*
Manicure: *Manicura*
I want . . . liters of petrol: *Deme . . . litros de gasolina*
Change the oil: *Cambiele el aceite*
Grease the car: *Engrase el coche*
How are you?: *Como esta usted?*
Fine, thank you: *Muy bien, gracias*
Please: *Tenga la bondad*
Thank you very much: *Muchas gracias*
Good morning: *Buenos dias*
Good afternoon: *Buenas tardes*
Good night: *Buenas noches*
Yes: *Sí*
No: *No*
Morning: *La mañana*
Noon: *Mediodía*
Afternoon, P.M.: *La tarde,* P.M.
Evening: *La noche*
Night: *La noche*
Sunday: *Domingo*
Monday: *Lunes*
Tuesday: *Martes*
Wednesday: *Miércoles*
Thursday: *Jueves*
Friday: *Viernes*
Saturday: *Sábado*
One: *Uno (una)*
Two: *Dos*
Three: *Tres*
Four: *Cuatro*
Five: *Cinco*
Six: *Seis*
Seven: *Siete*
Eight: *Ocho*
Nine: *Neuve*
Ten: *Diez*
Twenty: *Veinte*
Thirty: *Treinta*
Forty: *Cuarenta*
Fifty: *Cincuenta*
One hundred: *Cien (ciento)*
One thousand: *Mil*

ELECTRICITY ¶ As a rule you'll find 110 A.C. current throughout Spain, which permits the use of your appliances, although a special adapter plug is required. In some districts there are occasional installations of 120 A.C., so make local inquiry when outside of the largest cities.

Food Specialties and Liquor ¶ The complaint is frequently made by visiting Americans that Spanish food is heavy and oily, and to be factual, this is often the case. Spain is basically a hot country, although if you were in Madrid during January you might be inclined to doubt the accuracy of this statement. Perishable fats like butter are comparatively rare because of the heat, so olive oil is the more normal basis of Spanish cookery, and has been for countless centuries. In the best restaurants, fine delicate olive oil produces dishes of great flavor, but unhappily the poorer qualities of oil frequently used in smaller places are heavy and turn rancid quickly, and tourists often find the strong flavor objectionable.

Many first-time visitors expect to find Spanish food spicy and sharp in the Mexican sense, which it most certainly is not. With comparatively few exceptions, most provincial cooking is definitely on the bland side, completely suited to American palates except for the previously discussed problem of excessive olive oil. The only solution is to request that your dishes be prepared with butter, but it is not always available in the rural areas.

Meal hours are extremely troublesome for most Americans, particularly Midwesterners. In the morning, breakfast is brought to your room on a tray—it's almost always the same—the usual rolls, butter and jam, coffee or sometimes chocolate. But if you're a person whose appetite suddenly becomes awakened around the noon hour, Spain presents a problem, for lunch is generally unobtainable (except in a few tourist hotels) until at least 1:30 and sometimes 2 and . . . we hate to say this, occasionally 2:30. What does a starving American do? Well, of course there are loads of cafes around where you can get *something* to tide you over until the midday (?) meal. If you like an apéritif before meals, the cafes serve *tapas*, tiny hors d'ouvres, which should help you wait for lunch. Now that we've carried you along this far, we might confess that in some remote inns lunch is not infrequently served at 3 p.m.

When and if you finally do get lunch, you'll find it elaborate, with many courses and enormous portions. You'll find most restaurant waiters of a willing disposition, only too anxious to be of assistance, although scarcely as skilled as their French equivalents. But the generally gracious atmosphere of Spanish restaurants makes up for the lack of sophisticated service.

About tea time, 6 P.M. in Spain, you'd best look for a *pasteleria*, a pastry shop, at which to fortify yourself against a far-off evening meal—there is no point in further holding back the fact that dinner (or whatever you care to call it) won't be served until 9:30 P.M. Well, 10 is more like it. Of course, city sophisticates wouldn't want to have dinner until 10:30, although, if the peasants care to dine at the ridiculously early hour of 9:30, they can! Would you be interested in learning when smart cocktail parties begin in Madrid and Barcelona? Nine-thirty! The best hostesses in those cosmopolitan cities have their guest sit down to dinner at midnight, the chic starting time, so why should you complain about 10 P.M. dinner? How do you eat such a late dinner and then go to bed? The only apparent solution is to have the larger meal during the day and eat more lightly at night.

Fish dishes here are really superb, particularly if you're slightly courageous. The shellfish—shrimp, crab, oysters—are just about perfect, and of course, the fresh fish is almost unique. *Bacalau*, dried codfish, is something else; it may be very popular with the Spaniards, but not too many Americans can take to its exasperatingly fishy flavor. *Angulas* are the smallest eels you ever saw, but unless you're the sort of person who takes instantaneously to snails and octopus, we're afraid that the mental adjustment is too much for most people. This is not true, however, of a *zarzuela de mariscos*, a mixed seafood soup or chowder, which isn't exotic—just delicious. *Paella* is a marvelous rice dish with assorted shellfish and is easy to like; chicken and sausage are sometimes added, and the resulting local argument is reminiscent of discussions back home as to whether or not tomatoes belong in a clam chowder—nobody agrees, and *paella* tastes good either way.

If one dish had to be selected as typical of the national cuisine, probably the majority of votes would go for a *cocido*, a sort of soup-stew made in a dozen different fashions. First you eat the rich soup, then the vegetables and potatoes and last, the meats and sausage. Usually the basic ingredients include chicken or ham, plus chickpeas and potatoes, but from then on the cook plays by ear, adding anything in the kitchen not firmly affixed to the realty. Sometimes this is called *pote*, sometimes *olla podrida*, occasionally *puchero* or *caldo*—

but surely you get the idea—it's a New England boiled dinner not made by a Cabot or Lodge but by one Pedro Mendez Fernandez.

A soup that shouldn't be missed is *gazpacho*, a cold vegetable concoction served with croutons and diced vegetables. You'll probably never be served the same style twice. Sometimes *gazpacho* is prepared with a broth base, other times tomato. But it's always deliciously piquant, and just the thing for a hot day. Other high points of the Spanish cuisine are olives (in a million sizes, colors and shapes); raw, air-dried ham, *jamón serrano*, served as an appetizer; and of course the marvelous fruits of the country, most particularly the muscat grapes and golden melons.

Spain is famous for a wine that defies duplication— sherry. No amount of effort by California wine growers has imitated this Spanish product successfully. It is made by the complicated *solera* method, a series of connected barrels. There are three principal types of sherry: *fino*, a quite dry type, leaving the palate with the same taste as a dry martini; *amontillado*, somewhat sweeter and more to American taste; *oloroso*, the sweetest of all, as rich as a dessert. Many Americans drink Harvey's Bristol Cream, an extremely sweet *oloroso* sherry, before meals, which is of course regarded as sacrilegious by the Spaniards. A local wine called *manzanilla* closely resembles, but isn't, a sherry and is a fairly good before-dinner drink.

The local beer is extremely variable in quality, a far cry from the standard excellence of Danish or German brews, although better than the French efforts (the French don't even seem to try to make a good beer). Among table wines, you shouldn't have much trouble being satisfied easily and inexpensively. The two leading wine types you'll encounter are Valdepeñas and Rioja, with a slight edge being given to the Valdepeñas as to quality. Montilla is a typical dry white wine, more or less ideal with all shellfish, seafood or chicken. An inexperienced tourist can generally rely upon the bottler, and the most reliable names, to our way of thinking, are Marqués de Riscal, Marqués de Murrieta and Paternina. All of these bottle red and white wines and no concern need be felt for vintage years. If you are but little interested in wine, order *vino de la casa*, the unbottled house wine, which is sold at unbelievably low prices and is almost always quite satisfactory.

(Note: The advice on wine-drinking is doubly important because, except for Madrid and Barcelona, you should *not* drink the local water.)

Liking Spanish brandy is a matter of opinion; you'll have to make the decision. Don't expect anything like French cognac, for the Spanish product is milder and sweeter than most French types. Of them all, we suppose Fundador is about the best, or in any event the best known. Cider from the Austurias district is delicious, if only you can get it iced for you (you'll notice we didn't say to put ice into the drink). If the weather is warm and you yearn for a soft drink, try *horchata*, a milky beverage made from *chufa* nuts, something like almonds.

In hunting for a restaurant don't ask the nearest traffic cop or someone passing by in the street. The chances are that they eat all their meals at home and have not the vaguest idea of what type of restaurant would suit your taste.

Here is one thing to keep in mind, and it will make your traveling more pleasant: Spain is a very old country. But the tourism industry is new and growing all the time. All the top hotels and restaurants have a nucleus of highly trained, much-experienced personnel. But many of the employes are brand-new to the job of serving the international public. They mean very well, but at times they might fumble or misunderstand your order. So just be patient with them, please; all will work out well if you do.

The principal tourist areas of Spain are Madrid and the surrounding region, including Toledo. Ávila and Segovia; Barcelona and the Costa Brava; Majorca and the Balearic Islands; the north coast, with San Sebastián as its headquarters; Andalusia, Spain's deep south, chiefly centered in the area of Seville, Granada, Cádiz, Málaga, Torremolinos and Córdoba.

Capital City

Madrid is a remarkable city of about 2 million inhabitants in almost the geographical center of the country. The visitor arriving in the early-morning hours, by road, rail or air, will be intrigued by the mist that shrouds Madrid like a protective cocoon. (Notice we didn't call it *smog*?) This silklike mantle is *usually* swept away by the early-morning sun, and Madrid remains for the visitor's enjoyment on a golden platform. Unlike all other important Spanish cities, Madrid is isolated almost completely from the rest of the country on a 2,000-foot plateau. A visit to Madrid alone does not give a full picture of Spain's vast life and culture because the remainder of the nation has many different facets. Madrid is only *one* enchanting facet of Spain.

Madrid is a strikingly handsome capital, with broad, impressive boulevards, possibly second only to Paris in all of Europe for sheer beauty. The loveliness of the Castellana, an extremely wide thoroughfare, is accentuated at night when the trees are magnificently lit; on a mild summer's evening the whole effect is inexpressibly romantic. This is a city that eludes quick categorization or facile description. Madrid is old, dark and secretive; it is new, brash and modern. The answer lies in the Spanish Civil War, bitterly contested here from 1936 to 1939, in which large sections of the city were destroyed; the damaged portions were extensively rebuilt in the modern style—including skyscrapers, neon signs and motion picture palaces. A principal shopping street is frequently indistinguishable from a similar avenue in Seattle, but with a sudden turn into a dimly lit alley, paved with cobblestones, the pedestrian is carried back two and a half centuries in a matter of seconds.

It's not usual to head a city's list of sightseeing attractions with a museum, but only Madrid has the incomparable Prado. Paris has its Louvre, generally regarded as the world's greatest, but the Louvre is enormous, overpowering, impossible to cover with any degree of satisfaction (and, if truth be told, is slightly cold and difficult to love, like an imperious but wealthy dowager). Now, the Prado—well, one could fall in love on first sight with its charm. Small, almost intimate, this distinguished museum may, item for item, have the greatest collection in the world. Represented here you'll find El Greco, Ribera, Murillo, Rubens, Goya, Zurbaran and, of course Velázguez. "Las Meninas" ("the Maids of Honor"), generally considered Velázquez's greatest, has its own room for showing it at best advantage. Even nonart lovers are impressed by this wonderful collection, and if you'll take a tip from us, the best pictures are on the second and third floors (although we'd be happy even with the ground floor). If you're an El Greco enthusiast, you should know that some of the very best of his works are in Toledo, which must be visited by anyone who comes to Madrid.

Goya is represented by his famed "Disasters of War," a series of etchings executed in 1808 (yes, they had wars then). Ordinarily it's a good idea to wait for a rainy or cloudy day to visit a museum. Unfortunately, this system won't work too well for the Prado, because some rooms of the museum, particularly those featuring the Tintorettos are lit only by skylights, unbelievable as that may seem.

The Prado opens daily at 10 A.M. and closes at 6 P.M. from June through September. In other seasons of the year its closing time is a half-hour or an hour earlier. The Sunday and holiday hours are 10 A.M. to 2 P.M. When your legs weary (as they must get or you're not human), you'll find Retiro Park just behind the Prado. It's a charming green area and an ideal place to recuperate from whatever it is that you have to recuperate from—the weather, the emotional experience of the Prado or just tired feet. The Spanish have a talent for landscaping, as you'll soon notice, and Retiro Park is charming, restful to the eyes and in your present condition (after the Prado Museum) far too large to wander through. There is a zoo, there are little cafes and there is even a lake, where small rowboats may be rented, but did you come to Spain to row about on a lake? Even a Spanish lake? During the summer season, there are outdoor ballet performances in the park's theater, which begin at 11 P.M. (Yes, that's right.) To see the ballet, you'll have to take a very early dinner, say at 9:30 P.M., or else have an after-theater snack at 2 A.M. What are we saying?

The great painter Goya is buried in the Goya Pantheon, located in the Paseo de la Florida; here you'll see some of his frescoes depicting the royal and the not-so-royal. Now, as a rule, most tourists probably would be inclined to read this hastily and assume that, having once seen the Prado Museum, this building could be passed up—but don't, because you'll like the Goya Pantheon.

On the other hand, another sightseeing must—the Royal Palace—while richly furnished, offers little except lavish decoration on a large scale. We wouldn't say avoid it, but if time is short, you might do better to walk about Madrid on your own, wandering up and down old streets as your mood dictates. The Puerta del Sol is a central beginning point for a stroll in Madrid. Branch off in almost any direction and you'll find yourself with plenty to view and do, without any prearranged sight-seeing plan. The shopping is so attractive here that if we know Americans (and particularly American women), some reasonable amount of time will have to be devoted to this project. The most important shopping streets are José Antonio, Peligros, Serrano and Seville.

Madrid is well supplied with specialty shops and even with a few good department stores, but the most fascinating spot for miscellaneous objects and antiques is in the colorful "Rastro," Madrid's equivalent to the Flea Market of Paris. Here are fine shops, open carts and stalls; in fact, there is a little of everything in this old market, which is in operation from about 9:30 A.M. until 2 P.M. Sunday is the most lively day for a visit. In one shop you'll find a priceless set of antiques, in another some completely useless bits of junk. Do you want an old French clock? Twelve perfectly matched chairs? A painting believed (but not guaranteed) to be painted by Goya? They're here, and lots more, too. If you're planning to buy something for 2,000 pesetas that will be worth $5,000 when you get home, well, we don't know. A number of years ago, someone turned up a genuine Goya, so it *is* possible. On the other hand, a friend of ours at the Rastro had examined some Majolica ware and was discussing the price with her husband (who was vaguely opposed to the entire proposition). The shopkeeper broke into their conversation in broken, but perfectly intelligible English with "But, Madam, on Madison Avenue you would have to pay at least $50 more!" So you may assume that the shopkeepers know the value of almost everything they offer.

৪৯ Short Trips from Madrid

El Pardo

About ten miles from Madrid is El Pardo, the sumptuous (to say the least) residence of General Franco; there are some fine paintings and beautiful furnishings in a luxurious setting. Aranjuez makes for another interesting excursion; there is an unbelievable royal palace, but if you've gone to El Pardo, perhaps one palace per customer is enough. Make a choice, because two might be one too many.

El Escorial

There are two important sightseeing trips from Madrid that border on the compulsory: Toledo and El Escorial. Each involves an all-day excursion, and both are worth seeing, without any doubt. The question frequently arises as to which of the two should be visited when only one day is available for sightseeing out of Madrid. To this, it would seem, only one answer is possible, although, of course, this is a matter of personal taste and judgment. El Escorial is a magnificent monastery-palace, but it is only one building. Toledo, on the contrary, is a city filled with a wealth of worthwhile sights and has been declared a national monument, so the choice must inescapably fall to this historic, living museum of Spain's glorious past.

A THREE-DAY TRIP FROM MADRID

If you can manage several days for a trip around Madrid, you'll be able to combine Toledo, El Escorial, Segovia and several other points of interest in an ideal tour, which shouldn't be missed if you can spare the time. (You are, in fact, urged to make the time.) The trip may be made by bus (in large-scale tours) or by rented private car, or you can drive about in your own car. If you go on your own, leave Madrid by Avenida de José Antonio via route N-VI; later pick up route C-505 to El Escorial. (Description of El Escorial follows at the conclusion of this section.) From El Escorial, take an unnumbered road northward, bypassing Guadarrama and later joining route N-601 (left turn), then going through Navacerrada and San Ildefonso, which has the Palace of Philip V, often compared with Versailles. Actually, the gardens are its most attractive feature. Continue on to Segovia, where you could stay overnight at the Hotel Las Sirenas. Sightseeing in delightful Segovia is highlighted by the Alcázar, a fine building dating back to the eleventh century; the Monastery of Santa María del Parral; the sixteenth-century cathedral; the unbelievable Roman aqueduct, seemingly in almost perfect condition. The next day, drive from Segovia via route N-110 through Villacastin to the medieval walled city of Ávila, which, to many people, is even more fascinating than the equivalent

French town of Carcassonne. The mile and a half of thousand-year-old walls and almost 100 towers are enchanting (no, we're not going overboard in our enthusiasm). From Ávila, leave by the Puente Nuevo on route N-110, later changing to C-502, through Salobral, Villarejo del Valle and into Membeltran (see the Parish Church and the Castle of the Dukes of Albuqerque). Then through La Parra and into Arenas de San Pedro, a very old town. Proceed on to Talavera de la Reina, picking up route N-V to Maqueda, then N-403 to Toledo from where you can return to Madrid via route N-401.

Toledo

Three major excursion companies with sightseeing buses (Melia, Cook's, American Express) make daily trips to Toledo, leaving around 9 A.M. and returning about 7:30 P.M. The route by automobile is over route 401 for forty-four miles. If you wish, take the train from Atocha station (there is a good early-morning one). There are also interurban buses that will take you right to the Alcázar in Toledo (and depart for Madrid from the same point). The public buses (not the tour ones) are recommended only as a final alternative. However, if you get a seat on a bus, the ride is comfortable enough. Don't forget that Madrid has several railroad stations, and if you do much sight-seeing in various directions, the chances are you'll be leaving from a different station almost every day.

At one glorious period in Spain's history, Toledo was where the flamboyant royal court sat, and since church and state were closely intertwined, it became and remains today the religious center of Spain. Getting about in Toledo is slightly confusing, because the streets wander about at random in the Old World fashion; but Toledo is fairly compact and even if you get lost, it's just a matter of minutes to find your way again. Good solid footwear is essential on the cobblestones. The cathedral is probably the outstanding single sight (where you should surely see the Mozarabic Chapel, and the El Greco and Goya paintings located in the Sacristy). Then visit the Church of Santo Tomé, which houses one of El Greco's masterpieces, "The Burial of Count Orgaz," a haunting painting with ascetic faces and fanatical eyes that will follow you in your mind for days. Surely you'll want to see the home and museum of El Greco, which contains several of his greatest paintings, displayed, without fanfare, in simple frames. It's comforting to know that the master lived in comparatively good fashion during his lifetime. The Toledo Alcázar, once a magnificent building, unfortunately was almost entirely destroyed during the civil war. See also the remarkable interior, executed in the Moorish fashion, of the Del Transito synagogue, a remarkable medieval structure.

A good place to start your sightseeing is the Plaza de Zocodover, which is right in the center of town. On the plaza is the government tourist office, where you can obtain helpful literature on Toledo, as well as some maps. The name "Zocodover" is a tongue-twister, and it comes right out of Toledo's long and dramatic past. First, you must practice pronouncing it for a few times. Ready? Tho-ko-dough-vair. Easy, isn't it? It literally means "main marketplace" and comes from the old Moorish word "souk." If you would like to have a guide for your tour of Toledo, you can engage one at the municipal tourist office.

Some pointers about Toledo: Like most tourists, you'll probably be looking for the El Greco painting in the Church of San Tomé; you will find it in the chapel on the right-hand side, in the rear, nicely lighted. Tickets of admission (5 ptas.) are sold in a novelty shop across the way from the church entrance. In the fourteenth-century Del Transito synagogue you will marvel at the famous Cedars of Lebanon ceiling of sculpted wood and the intricately done marble panels of the windows; on the walls, there are ancient writings in Hebrew. When visiting El Greco's house, be sure to go up to the second floor (that is, one flight up) and see his studio. In the bedroom is a Moorish-style divan, where the artist apparently reclined while his dutiful wife spun away at the spinning wheel. It is all very domestic and artistic. The sacristy of the cathedral, by the way, is like a tremendous art gallery. It also has a fine collection of Belgian lace. From the Alcázar you can get a splendid view of the valley stretching out from Toledo and of the San Servando castle across the river. The Alcázar has been battered many times—the last time being in the two-and-a-half-month siege during the civil war. The restoration work has just about been completed.

It may be that you want to remain overnight in Toledo, and I would certainly second that wish. The very best place to stay is the brand new Parador Nacional Conde de Orgaz, located on a hilltop, with a wonderful view of the city. It's an extremely attractive hotel, but during the season, it might be well to phone ahead (through the hotel at which you're staying) and make a reservation. Off-season, there shouldn't be too much trouble in obtaining a room. If you can't manage a reservation at the Parador, try the Cigarral Monterey, which is located just outside of Toledo; it has a swimming pool and the food is rather good. If you really want to eat well, by all means head for a restaurant called Venta de Aire, which serves excellent meals, but is fairly expensive (for Spain). Also very delightful is the Meson Cardenal, located close to the walls of Toledo.

If you make the trip to Toledo—and I urge you to do so—and it's during the warm season (May through September), leave as early in the morning as you can, before 8 A.M. if possible; return in the evening when the heat has broken. The most comfortable way to make the trip is by hiring a private car or taxi for the day, but it's also the most expensive. It ordinarily takes about an hour and a half, and the countryside en route isn't especially interesting. But you won't regret visiting Toledo.

El Escorial

You can reach this sight by either train or bus in about an hour; the distance is approximately thirty miles. To get to El Escorial, there is fairly frequent train service from Madrid. Get the train at the North Station on the *lower level*. At El Escorial railroad station, taxis meet the trains and will take you to the palace (can't you hear yourself saying, "Take me to the palace, please"?) for a fixed, posted tariff. It is only a half-mile drive. The walk to the palace is easy, however, and on a mild day quite agreeable.

To get the solid facts over with quickly, El Escorial is an enormous monastery erected by King Philip II to celebrate a victory over France at St.-Quentin in 1557. It has been hailed as one of the world's greatest architectural masterpieces (although there are many carping critics); if it isn't the greatest, it certainly qualifies as one of the world's largest structures, a monstrous rectangle of a building several city blocks long and almost as wide, with courts and fountains galore, hundreds of rooms and thousands of windows. The corridors within stretch on for miles and miles and (more) miles until the tourist's feet cry out for relief. You'll see the imposing tombs of Spanish royalty and then visit the tiny Spartan apartment where Philip II lived in the monastic poverty required of the strictest order of monks. Just in passing, Philip II wasn't in absolutely the best of mental health just immediately preceding his death, seemingly driven by some inner compulsion to create this enormous monument as a symbol of his thanks for defeating the French. About two miles from the monastery is the *Silla de Felipe*, Philip's Chair, where the pixillated king was able to watch the construction proceeding. We must confess, at this point, that El Escorial is somewhat monotonous, chilly and very gloomy, although you may disagree. However, everyone owes it to himself to see this famous structure.

El Escorial is easy to get to—if you're driving, take route 6 to Guadarrama, then head south on route 600. You can't miss it—really! It's that big. It stands immense and dramatic in the middle of open country.

There are whole series of tariffs, depending on what you want to see and, also, how long you wish to take. A general visit, for example, lasts about three hours and costs about a dollar. The palace is open from 10 A.M. to 1 P.M. and from 3 to 7 P.M. Tickets go on sale before opening time in the morning, and sales cease a half-hour before closing. If you arrive an hour before closing time, you can make a quick tour at a bargain price. In the general palace visit, if you do not wish to see the new museums, the tariff is reduced. The same applies if you want to look at the museums *only*. Oh, yes—to take a peek at the private apartments of the kings will require a relatively sizeable expenditure. There are a number of other tariffs and combinations. We mention them to show you how huge El Escorial is and how smoothly organized everything is. English-speaking attendants accompany the visiting groups; you are not permitted to go it alone.

Valley of the Dead

This is one of the postwar architectural wonders of Spain—another massive monument on the order of El Escorial. Its basilica, which was tunneled through a mountain, is several hundred yards long, and the cross at the top of the hill is a couple of hundred feet high. The Valley of the Dead is ten miles from El Escorial and somewhat closer to Madrid. It is a national monument to those who died in the Spanish Civil War of a generation ago. The valley is dedicated, literally, to "the fallen" (*los caidos*), so it is often referred to as the Valley of the Fallen, rather than Valley of the Dead. The only entrance fee to the valley is a charge of about a dollar for each automobile coming into the park area. If you leave your car outside the park and walk, there is no fee (but we warn you—it's a long, uphill walk). There is a restaurant in the square at the approach to the cross, where you can get a fine meal. Excursion buses include El Escorial and the Valley of the Dead on daily all-day tours that cost about $5.

Ávila

This city is seventy miles from Madrid and can be reached by drive-yourself autos via route 6 to Villacastin, then routes 110 and 501. All the excursion bus companies make trips to Ávila, but they usually include it as part of some other tour. The tremendous wall, the main square (named after St. Teresa, who was born in Ávila) and the Plaza de la Victoria (also called Constitution Square) can be included on a pleasant walking tour of the town. A church has been built on the site of the house where (St.) Teresa was born. The railroad station of Ávila is about a mile from the center of town; there is fairly good service to and from Madrid. Of Ávila's few restaurants, we like Pepillo's (but eat upstairs—it is quieter). If visiting Ávila in the fall or winter, don't fail to bring something warm to wear. The town is at about 3,650 feet altitude, so it gets plenty of cool (ice-cold) breezes. Don't say we didn't tell you.

Segovia

Segovia is on the road to those castles in Spain that you always hear (and dream) about. Having seen Segovia, you might be content to remain there and forget about the other castles of Spain. Segovia is fifty-five miles from Madrid, and the road is not bad, but give yourself an hour and a half—maybe two hours—because the landscape is filled with hills, and the going is not fast. One or the other of the excursion bus companies has journeys scheduled to Segovia almost every day. Monday might be an exception, with no tours scheduled. The royal palace and gardens of La Granja are often scheduled with Segovia as a combination tour. There is a train from the *lower level* of the North Station, but we warn you that it is a long, sl-o-o-o-w ride. As in a number of Spanish cities, the railroad station is somewhat removed from the center of town, but a bus meets all trains, and a taxi ride costs only about a half-dollar. Lots of people (before us) have remarked that the Segovia cathedral seems to be floating through the air on a magic carpet—so we don't claim that as being original. In any event, it is called the "lady" of Spanish cathedrals because of its graceful, feminine lines. There are some guides inside the cathedral, but their knowledge of English seemed pretty shaky to us. Maybe it has improved by now. We doubt it, but we hope so. In the Treasure Room, in any event, you will recognize the huge carriage that is borne through the streets by four hidden men during processions. The carriage is topped off by a silver piece that reaches more than six feet above the vehicle. The carriage, too, is painted a dazzling baroque gold. There is an alcázar, which can be visited; this is recommended because there are some splendid views from the turrets. The stairway to the top, naturally, is one of those spiral affairs with plenty of steps, and they are slippery —so watch *your* step. A highlight of your visit to Segovia will be lunching at the Mesón de Candido restaurant, which is just a few yards from the old Roman aqueduct. Get a table on the upper floor so that you can gaze out upon the aqueduct while you eat. It is quite a magnificent setting, and incidentally, the food at the Mesón de Candido is excellent. The restaurant's specialties are roast suckling pig and lamb, so be certain to order one of them.

Cuenca

This is the Spanish town with the view. You can include this town as a trip from Valencia if you prefer, because it is just about halfway between there and Madrid. The distance from Madrid is just a bit over a hundred miles. If you have a car, all the better, because it is an agreeable (if slow) ride through the countryside east of the Spanish capital. There are farms, spinning windmills and lots of empty wide land en route, and the entire landscape provides an up-close picture of Spanish life. Follow route 3 from Madrid to Tarancón, then continue by route 400. Tarancón is a convenient midpoint where you can rest for a few minutes and sample a cup of coffee in the busy, crossroads cafe that is often crowded and always colorful. As we mentioned, Cuenca is the town with the view, so when you arrive go at once to the government tourist office (28 Calle Calderon de la Barca) and get a free map identifying the most popular observation points in town. Cuenca's cathedral is the only Anglo-Norman-Gothic one in Spain. The cathedral is in the Plaza Mayor. From there, if you have the time and energy, climb up to the chateau-prison on top of the nearby hill. It offers an excellent view. Otherwise, go down the street at the right of the cathedral. On your left, as you descend, watch for the famed hanging houses of Cuenca (the *casas colgadas*). They really are glued to the side of the high cliff—at least, it looks that way. One of them, Mesón Casas Colgadas, is a restaurant with an interesting view. Continuing on down the hill, you will come to the big crossroads, known as Four Corners. A few steps from here is the Togár restaurant, a fine place for lunch. Incidentally, the local archaeological museum has some interesting sculpture, but most fascinating of all (naturally) is the money collection—old Roman coins.

ACCOMMODATIONS ¶ Regardless of the degree of luxury offered or the price, hotels are almost without exception clean and inviting, although naturally there is a considerable variation in furnishings, modernity and bath facilities offered. In the southern cities the rooms may be practically opened to the outdoors by removing shutters; the floors are immaculate with cool tiles and the atmosphere pleasantly soft and pleasing. In the older hotels you'll often find no closet facilities, but the *armoire*, a sort of clothes cabinet, will work as well.

Spanish hotels are graded into five classes, but it has been our experience that the grading system has not developed as yet into a thoroughly scientific system. What we mean is that the classifications are often erratic, and in a First Class hotel in Madrid you might have to double-check to make sure that it really *is* First Class and not something further down the scale. By all means, in large cities choose only First Class or luxury hotels and stick to those that have been recommended to you. In smaller places the classification system works out pretty well, and can be a sound barometer. As an attempt to produce a more realistic classification, a new grading system was introduced in 1970. According to the new system only the following five (instead of the previous 50 and more) hotels have been classified as luxurious: Ritz in Madrid; Don Pepe in Marbella; Hostal de los Reyes Católicos in Santiago de Compostela; Hostal de San Marcos in León; and Hostal de la Gavina in S'Agaró on Costa Brava. The Son y Vida at Palma on Majorca is also in the luxurious class.

During certain festivals, rates may be increased and occupancy required for a fixed period of time. For example, during the fair in Seville, rates are (at least) doubled and all reservations must be made for a week. Inasmuch as only the hardiest and most durable traveler can last a full week in Seville during the fair, not only will the rate be double the normal charge, but you'll be paying for the days after your departure—or roughly triple the regular cost. The same goes for the big spring festival in Valencia. And as for Madrid, even in the socalled autumn off-season, it is often hard to get a room in the hotel of your first choice. Let's not talk about the hotel situation in Barcelona; that is almost always a difficult place. So line up your reservations early, and do not wait until the last minute. If you do arrive in one of the major cities at the time when hotel space is in short supply, check with a local travel agency. Spanish travel agencies specialize in booking hotel accommodations for newly arrived visitors, and the service charge is very small.

Throughout Spain, at various strategic points, the government has developed a system of *paradores* and *albergues*. The *paradores* are former palaces, convents or monasteries now converted into small hotels, usually of considerable atmosphere and luxury. There are also a series of *albergues*, small inns like American motels, which offer perfectly satisfactory accommodation to the motorist.

One of the finest of these converted old-time structures is the Hostal de los Reyes Católicos in Santiago de Compostela in the northwest corner of Spain, in Galicia. A truly twentieth-century hotel has evolved from a massive fifteenth-century *hospiz*, and it has everything from a bowling alley to a special seafood snack bar (and what delicious sea food!). A similar imaginative undertaking has been the Hostal de San Marcos at León, also in northern Spain. This sparkling establishment at one time was a monastery.

MADRID HOTELS

The city's five leading hotels (Ritz, Hilton, Melia, Plaza and Palace) are all luxury establishments, but have completely different personalities. All are excellent, all are more than pleasing.

Ritz: This is a marvelous place to stay, with lovely grounds and garden, good food; very convenient location. Rooms are often outsize, graciously furnished; and although this is not a new hotel, it is extremely well maintained.

Melia Madrid: Very modern, large (250 rooms) in a 25-story building with a beautiful view of the city from the upper 10th to 15th floors. Elegant interiors and good location near Plaza de España.

Castellana Hilton: A fairly new hotel with very attractively furnished rooms and suites (many with terraces). Very modern, very American; food is just fair. Located on a lovely tree-lined street about ten minutes from the center of activities.

Melia Castilla: Near Plaza de Castilla. The largest (1,100 rooms) and newest with very extensive convention facilities. Luxurious accommodations, several restaurants, swimming pool, tennis courts and what not.

Plaza: A practically new hotel, modern as today, with modern, handsome rooms. The Plaza is part of Madrid's first skyscraper and has its own swimming pool. This is perfect for those who like to be in the heart of things.

Luz Palacio: A very modern hotel on Paseo de la Castellana near Hilton; Madrid social events as well as conventions frequently take place here; so find out in advance if there is room.

Palace: This large, popular establishment (across the street from the Ritz) is also in the top group. Most of the rooms, although originally old-fashioned have been remodeled and now are quite attractive.

Wellington: A recently built hotel catering to a conservative clientele. 220 rooms, all with bath.

Eurobuilding: The newest, very modern addition to Madrid hotels. Accommodations consist of luxurious apartments, all with terraces. Large parking space and swimming pool. Located in a quiet suburban section near Plaza de Cuzco.

Colon: In a residential area near the Retiro Park, actually two very modern buildings, one called Colon and the other one Residencia Colon, connected by a nicely decorated gallery. Rooms have individual terraces. Two restaurants and rooftop swimming pool.

El Washington: A recent addition to the roster of Madrid

hotels and likely to become quite successful. Rooms are fair size and the atmosphere is generally pleasing.

Sanvy: Very pleasant rooms in this moderately expensive new hotel; swimming pool, outdoor terrace.

Suecia: Modern, fairly small hotel, very conveniently located, furnished in modern style. Has the Bellman Restaurant on its premises. Moderately high.

Waldorf: An ideal place for a stay of five days or longer; small, attractive apartments completely furnished. Moderately priced.

Fenix: A newish hotel on the beautiful Paseo Castellana with moderate-size rooms furnished in the contemporary style. Quiet, attractive location.

Menfis: A modern, efficient (rather than Old World) type of hotel, conveniently located near the Plaza de España.

Emperador: Quite a large, luxuriant establishment on the busy Avenida de José Antonio, and thus situated conveniently.

Barajas: Near the airport and one of the newest Madrid hotels and quite large (230 rooms); heated swimming pool, open-air restaurant; free transportation to and from the airport and the city.

MADRID RESTAURANTS

Jockey Club: The outstanding luxury restaurant in Madrid, specializing in French food, but with continental undertones. Smart, attractive and the best food in Madrid. Not cheap, but not so expensive as equivalent food in Paris, for example.

Horcher's: Homey, pleasant and housed in a rambling private house, this place specializes in German-style food, but there are also many local dishes. Quite good.

Las Lanzas: A modern and elegant restaurant near Prado. The quality of food is high and so are the prices. A favorite with local society.

La Trainera: An informal Basque restaurant serving excellent seafood, including lobsters, shrimp, oysters (in season) and crab.

Alkalde: A cellar restaurant, heavy on atmosphere, and really rather good; it features steaks and a fine crab soup.

La Gran Tasca: Be sure to go to the branch on Garcia Morata Street. Everyone who comes to Madrid wants to try the suckling pig; it's better here than at *Botín* and *Cuevas de Luis Candelas.*

Bellman: A comparatively recent arrival, this spot has made its mark among Madrid gourmets. Fine, fairly expensive food.

Club 31: A new, attractive spot, good food, somewhat limited menu; particularly good for lunch.

Botín: This atmospheric restaurant, a tourist favorite, features roast suckling pig. The food is generally mediocre.

Hogar Gallego: Among the better places specializing in regional Spanish cooking; emphasis on seafood.

Cuevas de Luis Candelas: Pretty touristy, fair food, but very atmospheric.

La Barraca: An authentic Valencian restaurant featuring paella Valenciana, rice with shellfish, chicken, red peppers.
Other places specializing in regional Spanish cookery: Gayango; Mesón de San Javier; El Bodegon; El Fogon; La Sevillana.

SHOPPING ¶ Although Spain isn't nearly so low-priced as it once was, it nevertheless offers a wide assortment of tempting merchandise and worthwhile souvenirs. But be sure to buy items that you'll *use* when you get home; the greatest bargain in the world isn't worth much if it winds up in the back of your closet because it doesn't fit or seems inappropriate in Portland, Oregon.

Women's clothing: Madrid is definitely moving along, making considerable strides, in fact, in the world of fashion. Among the outstanding couturiers (to designate someone who sets the style, as opposed to a dressmaker who copies the styles), we suppose Pedro Rodríguez and Balenciaga are Spain's leaders. However, we might as well mention that their creations involve a serious expenditure, say $200 or more for a beautifully made suit or dress. Better allow a minimum of five days or preferably a full week to permit several fittings. There are any number of less expensive, competent, skilled dressmakers who will whip up anything you like; prices run well under half (or even much lower) than at Rodríguez.

Suede coats and dresses are excellent, especially at Mitzou. *Gloves* are excellent values, with good styling, but in the very cheapest type, the stitching tends to open. *Knitwear* is a big local specialty, particularly sweaters —both daytime and evening types. *Lingerie,* particularly lace-encrusted petticoats and slips, is an excellent value, but the designs and cut are different from ours, so everything should be tried on for size or regret may follow. *Handbags,* usually in antelope or suede, are absolutely tops in style and value; we have seen Paris styles copied within a week and sold at one-fifth the French price; even under $10 you'll have a marvelous choice. Now about *shoes:* these are reputed to be the big, big bargain specialty of Spain. It is our thought that the ready-made local shoes are not suited to the American foot, in particular if yours is long and narrow (because the Spanish foot is short and wide). Custom-made shoes are relatively inexpensive, but require several fittings, so bear the loss of time in mind and allow at least a week. We suggest buying the open-toed straw-soled affairs, *alpargatas*, or beach and play shoes, where a precise fit is much less important.

Perfumes and *soap* shouldn't be overlooked. Maja (Chirurgia) soaps, perfumes and toilet water are authentically Spanish and not bad at all. If you aren't going to France, several French concerns bottle their products in Spain, and these are offered at moderate prices; the results, however, are not necessarily identical with the original French product.

Men's clothing: Spanish tailors will make up a tailor-made *suit* in a matter of several days, using British woolens; unfortunately, as a general rule, the result is not quite right. The best bet is to give the tailor one of your own to copy, rather than relying upon his measurements. We have no hesitation or doubts about vetoing the purchase of ready-made suits for men, because most Spaniards are not terribly well dressed. Men's *shoes* are another case in point: the ready-made are shoddily made and the tailor-made excellent, but time must be lost in a series of fittings: don't just assume they'll fit after the first try-on. Much safer values are sport shoes and bathing slippers. As to men's hats, ties, shirts and underwear: no, Spanish lisle socks are cheaper than French, but their wearing power is not high. Men's *gloves*, on the other hand, are extremely attractive and, best of all, low in price.

Another good men's buy are vests and *jackets* of suede and antelope. These come in various qualities (and prices) so be sure to buy the best one available. No matter what you pay for them, they will be lots cheaper than the same articles anywhere else.

Antiques are often marvelous values, particularly if you know something about them; shopping at the "Rastro" (previously described) is loads of fun, even if you don't buy anything. For serious shopping, don't go Sunday, when the area really is crowded, because that's the least satisfactory time to get the dealer's attention. Spanish *tiles* are wonderful for decorating a kitchen, fireplace or bathroom. Prices are low, but shipments frequently arrive broken; the travel time is often six months, so if you're prepared to wait, OK. Be sure to order more tiles than you need, because of breakage—and get insurance!

Wines, liquor and *food specialties* are among the most inviting bargains in Spain. If you like the brandy, you can take five bottles per person with you; of course, that goes for Spanish wines, too. It would hardly pay to bother taking the table wines, but the sherries are outstanding values, particularly the more expensive types. (Incidentally, Chicote's Bar in Madrid has a tremendous selection, plus a museum of liquor from all over the world that is a tourist attraction in itself.) Another possibility is the locally made nougat candy (Jijona is possibly the best); Spanish truffles are very cheap but can hardly match the French or Italian varieties; saffron, for cookery enthusiasts, is definitely a bargain, selling for a mere fraction of the American price.

Miscellaneous: Pottery and ceramics figures and dishes are undoubtedly attractive and cheap (but they break in transit occasionally—we're so cheerful!); Mariquita Pérez *dolls* stand eighteen inches tall, and any little girl will love you for bringing her one; *Toledo ware*, beautifully worked metal, is absolutely gorgeous but hardly inexpensive.

Imitations of Toledo ware are numerous, but the real thing is protected by the government. All you have to do is ask the dealer if what you are looking at is the genuine article. If the dealer says yes, you can be sure. Penalties for misrepresentation are stiff.

Here's a shopping tip for you, as far as transportation is concerned: Don't try driving your car on a shopping expedition through Madrid, and don't bother with the usual crowded buses. Instead, be on the lookout for the *microbus*, a comparatively new addition to the Madrid street scene (they were introduced in the latter part of 1966). These mircobuses are a compromise between taxis and regular buses. The fare is a few cents higher than the standard tariff on a bus—it is 5 pesetas on a microbus. But the advantage of microbus travel is that you can get on and off anywhere along the route—you don't have to wait for a regular bus stop—and you are always assured of a seat. Another advantage (or disadvantage) is that smoking is permitted. The bus stop for the microbus has a big M in front of the number of the standard bus line that it serves. Along the Avenida de José Antonio, for instance, you'll see "M-2."

ENTERTAINMENT ¶ An evening out on the town presents a somewhat different problem in Spain from elsewhere in Europe. For one thing, most people are only *beginning* to have their dinner at 10 P.M. (or even later); they're seldom finished before the witching hour of midnight, and most of the Madrid night clubs lock up at 1 A.M. except on Saturday nights, when the closing hour is extended until 2 A.M. (the suburban night clubs usually open just before midnight and close much later, when they're in the mood). Of course, one can always have dinner at a night club, but this is only for the very brave, say, jet-plane test pilots and others to whom life and safety have little meaning.

Night clubs are subdivided into two categories, like girls in Spain—good or bad; there are no gray places. In other words, the double-standard Spaniards recognize respectable places where a man can bring his wife and places where he can't, and never the twain shall meet. That is, his wife isn't supposed to meet the party girls he dances with on his nights off. Until quite recently, unescorted women could not visit a night club, but this rule has been relaxed at least to the extent that female American tourists are welcomed, although the local Spanish women would not be.

Caution to unescorted women: don't go slumming or wandering into real dives just for atmosphere; even the Spanish "hostesses" object and won't mind letting you know—but definitely!

Flamenco dance recitals are all the rage in Madrid and Barcelona, although they are authentically and originally a part of the Seville scene. Flamenco, in case you haven't previously seen it, is lively (often very!) Spanish gypsy dancing with sexy overtones, and not for the very timid or shy. No nudity, however. Many of the night clubs in Madrid have flamenco shows, but these are quite self-conscious and touristy—which may be the proper initiation, at that, to these uninhibited dances. Spanish people much prefer a *colmado*, which is not precisely a night club but a place where a party can rent a room, order a bottle of sherry and some ham and watch a group of authentic performers (whom you pay yourself); the *colmado* charges only for the food and wine. A simplification of the whole problem is to go (but not before 11 P.M.) to the ultrarespectable establishment called La Zambra (near the Ritz Hotel), where you'll be able to see some toned-down flamenco dancing and singing. For dinner and flamenco, you'll enjoy the Corral de la Moreria (located on the Calle Moreria); recommended.

Theatrical performances of straight plays are out of the question for most tourists, because (1) of the language barrier and (2) most of the productions are so ridiculously old-fashioned. If you like the tired-business-man's type of musical with lots of gay music, dancing, girls, ruffles and more ruffles, attend a *zarzuela* (which is lisped as thar-thu-ella), where a knowledge of Spanish is completely unimportant. Most times, you'll have a choice of the matinee (7:00 P.M.!) or the later show, at 11:00 P.M. You can have dinner after the matinee or before the evening show. If you should happen to be in Barcelona while the *opera* season is underway, don't miss seeing leisurely opera in the Spanish style at the Gran Teatro del Liceo; it's an experience, and just as a tip, may we suggest that you wander about the lobby during the intermission and glimpse social Barcelona at its most intriguing. You won't run into much concert music during the summer months, because the important orchestras are active, as a rule, only during the winter season.

Motion pictures are a problem, because almost all are dubbed in Spanish (and not very well at that), and you are offered the spectacle of Michael Caine being his bemused self in Castillian. If you see a western picture, you might get a laugh out of the Spanish-speaking cowboys, but this is not guaranteed. There are some English-language films shown in major cities. It is best to check with the local government tourist office.

Madrid has a very good *circus*, for which no knowledge of Spanish is necessary; there's a good-size *aquarium* at 8 Maestro Victoria; and Madrid's *zoo*, in the Retiro, is quite famous.

Probably the most inexpensive, and pleasant, way of seeing Madrid after dark—and having the possibility of seeing and meeting the people—is to drop into one or more of the nice little bars along the Calle de Barbieri. This is a tiny, narrow street just off the Avenida de José Antonio, and about a five-minute walk from the Palace Hotel. There are bars on both sides of the street for a hundred yards or so. One bar on Calle de Barbieri is even —should we say, inevitably?—called BARbieri. For about 10 pesetas you can get a nice glass of wine at the counter of one of these bars—or you can sit down at a table. A delicious *tapas* of some kind (olives, shrimps, etc.) is served with the drink, and the ambiance is friendly and convivial. These are not roughneck bars in any sense. As a matter of fact, you'll be goggle-eyed at the stylish, handsome couples who drop in for a pre-dinner, or after-dinner drink. Visit several of these bars and you will undoubtedly find one that suits your tastes. Los Corsarios is one of the most popular. If you get a bit hungry, go into the Mesón das Meigas (a combination bar-snack bar (in Spanish style) and order a bowl of *taza caldo gallega,* vegetable soup with ham in it. It costs 10 pesetas and is very good after (or before) a few glasses of wine.

SPORTS ¶ Everyone automatically assumes that bullfighting is the leading sport in Spain, but don't overlook the great importance of *soccer football,* which is followed by almost all of the country. The crowds attending a big match in Madrid are absolutely fantastic in size, enthusiasm and ferocity.

Bullfighting—is it or isn't it a sport? The Spanish proclaim it as the world's greatest, but Anglo-Saxons call it a spectacle or a pageant, refusing to classify it as a sport because the bull *never* wins. It has been called the manliest by some and denounced by others who say it should be prohibited by the SPCA. Well, in all truth, the bull doesn't enjoy the afternoon, but thousands of (Spanish) spectators apparently do.

If you want to go, you'll need tickets. (That's a brilliant thought!) For all practical purposes, your hotel porter or concierge is best qualified to get them, although at an advance in prices; be sure to ask for the shady, *sombra* side. Reserve a taxi or arrange transportation in advance, because taxis disappear about an hour or more before bullfight time; incidentally, if you're planning to see the whole show, better have the taxi wait for you (it's almost impossible to find transportation when the bullfight is over); arrange in advance a fixed price for the day.

Bullfights (*corridas*) commence precisely on time, which is more than can be said of almost anything else in Spain, including the trains. Actually, an Anglo-Saxon must have mistakenly translated the word "corrida," for it is not a "fight" but a "running" of the bull; in a given afternoon there are six corridas, and allowing fifteen minutes each, the whole spectacle will take about two hours. You must understand the proceedings, or it will all be wasted on you, for a corrida is as highly stylized as ballet, which in many ways it strongly resembles. The spectacle involves a prologue, three acts and an epilogue. Each corrida begins with the spectacular parade (the prologue), the wonderful sprightly music of the bullrings and the growing excitement of the spectators. The first act sets the scene for the drama to follow—the heart of this act consists in having the *picador* prick the bull three times, primarily to tire and weaken him. The second act features the *banderillos*, who thrust darts into the bull's shoulders. The third act is the tragedy itself, the death of the bull; the *matador* discards his large cape for a *muleta*, a small cape, and kills the bull with his sword. If he accomplishes this with only one stroke, quickly and facilely, he has done his work well and the crowd will roar its approval or, if the contrary, its disgust. The *torero*, the bullfighter, is rewarded by being given a part of the bull by the "president" of the fight according to the skill displayed—one ear means a good performance, two ears are exceptional; occasionally the tail is given, which signifies just about the ultimate in skill. (Incidentally, a bullfighter is a *torero*, never a *toreador*, and Bizet got the word wrong when he wrote *Carmen*.) The sad epilogue to the spectacle is the dragging of the dead bull from the ring.

The bullfight season runs from mid-March to mid-October. It gets underway in Valencia at the lively Festa de Fallas on St. Joseph's Day (March 19). The festa is much like the Nice Carnival, with the big papier-mâché figures parading through the streets. Zaragoza is the final wind-up point for the bullfight season. After that, if you still want to see more bullfights, you will have to leave Europe and go to Mexico or Caracas. The price of bullfight seats depends on the matadors, for the top ones mean higher prices.

During Spain's bullfight season every self-respecting town has a bullring in operation, so there will be plenty of opportunity for you to see a corrida (Barcelona has two big rings). The best cards, naturally, are in Madrid and Barcelona. Travel agencies schedule excursions to a bullfight, topped off by a stopover at a flamenco place.

Most Americans want to see a bullfight when they come to Spain. And they should—it's all part of the local scene. Not many go a second time.

There are many other sports in Spain besides bull-fighting, however. *Horse racing, ice skating* and *bicycle races* are popular. Madrid's *golf* course, Club Puerta de Hierro, is among the best on the continent. There is *dog racing* in Madrid, too, but whether that is sport or entertainment is up to you.

ᕱᕝ A Tour of Spain

Madrid to Valladolid—118 miles

Leave Madrid by driving out on Avenida de José Antonio onto route N-VI through El Plantio (bypassing Las Rozas), Torrelodones, Guadarrama, Tablada, San Rafael, and Villacastín. Then to Labajos and Sanchidrián; after about three miles watch for the right turn onto route 403 (sometimes marked on maps as 430) through San Martin Muñoz de las Posadas, Montuenga, San Cristóbal de la Vega and Olmedo; here you'll find the ruined castle of San Silvestre, the old town walls with seven gateways and the Romanesque Church of San Miguel. From Olmedo to Mojados and Boecillo and into Valladolid, a famous university town where Columbus died in 1506. Here you'll have a choice of hotels—the new Olid (built in 1969), the also first class Conde Ansúrez, the dignified Inglaterra and the more modest Flórida. Sight-seeing: the sixteenth-century cathedral; the university buildings and student life; the Museo de Escultura, the Sculpture Museum.

Valladolid to León—86 miles

Leave Valladolid by route N-601 heading for Medina de Ríoseco; later proceed through Berrueces (the road beginning a gradual descent), Mayorga and Alvires, climbing again as you drive through Grajalejo and Santas Martas (where the road levels off). Continue on through Mansilla de las Mulas and Arcahueja into historic old León. There is the luxurious Hotel de San Marcos, in a converted palatial medieval monastery, with 258 rooms, restaurant and flamenco programs in its nightclub; one of the top hotels in Spain. Also very good is the first class

Conde Luna with swimming pool. León is famous for its cathedral, possibly (a personal opinion) the most charming in all of Spain; the stained-glass windows constitute almost a complete wall. You'll want to see the former monastery of San Marcos (now hotel, described above), even if you don't stay there, and the Church of San Isidoro, but the entire town of León is atmospheric and picturesque.

León to Oviedo—74 miles

Leave León via route N-630 through La Robla, La Pola de Gordon, La Vid and Villamanin, climbing steadily uphill as you pass through Busdongo and at Puerto de Pajares reach the highest point (about 4,100 feet); here is the border between the provinces of León and Asturias. Then, a sharp descent through Puente de los Fierros, Pola de Lena, Mieres, Olloniego and into Oviedo, another ancient city. Here you'll find the quite modern Hotel Principado, the Second Class Pasaje and the Third Class España. Sightseeing: the fifteenth-century cathedral, the eighth-century Cloister of San Vicente; the grandiose Concistorial building.

Oviedo to Santander—155 miles

Leave Oviedo by route 634 through Colló, Pola de Siero, Lieres, Infiesto, Soto de Dueñas, Arriondas, Margolles and then into Ribadesella, a fishing port with a good bathing beach. Through Belmonte, Nueva, Villahormes (known for its ponds filled with crayfish and trout) and Posada. (From Posada an interesting side trip may be made to nearby Lledias to see the Cave of Avin, with interesting examples of prehistoric cave paintings.) Continue on from Posada to Llanes, an important port along this coast; here you could visit Santa María Church. Then follow the south shore of the Bay of Biscay (or the Golfo de Vizcaya, as the Spanish say) through San Roque, Buelma, La Franca, Lamadrid, Casar and Puente de San Miguel, where you make a left turn toward Santillana and the world-famed Altamira Caves. Don't fail to devote as much time as possible to the medieval village of Santillana, a true example of community right out of the Middle Ages. The wonderful paleolithic caves of Altamira were first discovered in 1868 and extend over four city blocks in length. The drawings are believed to date back some 15,000 or 20,-

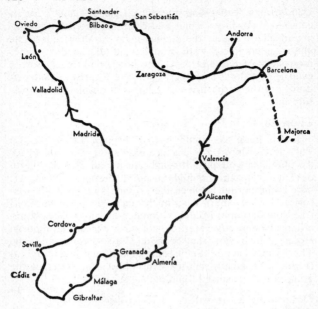

000 years, at which time some of our ancestors, in an artistic mood, decorated the caves' walls. The sketches are mostly representations of animals, in a roughly impressionistic style, chiefly drawn on the ceiling. Should you wish to remain overnight, there is the government Parador de Gil Blas, a pleasing small hotel—but be sure to phone ahead for reservations.

From Santillana, go back to the main road at Puente de San Miguel, make a left turn and drive to Torrelavega; then via route 611 to Barreda, Requepada, Arce and Igollo and into Santander, a very pleasant resort town, known for its fine bathing beaches. Here the choice of hotels would suit the most exacting: the recently completed luxury Hotel Bahia; the traditionally famous Old World Real; the slightly less expensive First Class Rex.

Santander to Bilbao—69 miles

Leave Santander, heading back again via route N-634 through Boo (sorry, didn't mean to frighten you), Astillero, San Salvador, Heras, Solares, Anero, Praves, Treto, Colindres, the small beach resort of Laredo, Islares (known for its lobsters), Mioño, Onton and San Salvador del Valle to Bilbao, an extremely important town of about 250,000 inhabitants. Here you'll find the luxurious Hotel Carlton and the First Class Almirante. This is a great town for hungry tourists. Don't eat at the hotels; Luciano is a remarkable fish restaurant, and Torróntegui is superbly set atop a roof and the food is excellent. Both places, however, are far from inexpensive. Sightseeing; the Museo de Pintura, with a fair collection of Spanish art; fourteenth-century Santiago Church; just outside of town a funicular trip may be made to Nuestra Señora de Begona, the Basilica of Begona.

Bilbao to San Sebastián—72 miles

The road goes through Amorebieta, Durango (which still retains some gates from the old town fortifications), Zaldua, Eibar (famous for its damask shops), Deva and Zumaya; this pleasing summer resort has a fascinating old port located at the mouth of the Urola River. You'll want to see San Pedro Church and the museum and the studio of Ignacio Zuloaga (a well-known Spanish painter) and a collection of his works, as well as others by famous artists. Then go through the fishing port of Guetaria, Zarauz (a resort town with a good beach and many sport facilities) and into San Sebastián, an internationally famous resort.

To this elegant community, the government, social leaders and everyone of any pretensions whatever move during the summer season, which reaches its height during the *Semana Grande*, the week of August 15. Here you'll be able to stay at the extremely luxurious Hotel Continental amid an atmosphere of high fashion and fancy tea parties; you may see more uniformed nursemaids than you ever thought existed in this servantless twentieth century.

The Hotel Londres e Inglaterra is a luxury establishment and has terraces facing the sea. Other good places to stay are the María Cristina and the Arana. Don't eat at the hotels; instead, have something much more interesting at the Casa Nicolasa, although this restaurant is moderately high in price. Basque food is served at Azaldegui and the view is most attractive; the prices are slightly lower, too. If there is a criticism to be made of San Sebastián, it must be laid to nature, for the town's location alongside the water backed by mountains causes moisture to condense—and you know that must mean drizzle, fog or, most likely of all, cloudy afternoons. Before you leave, drive to the top of Monte Igueldo for a view of the lovely coastline. An interesting trip of only six miles may be made to the toy village of Hernani; there are old houses, a heavily decorated church and several gilded palaces, none of which seems quite real.

San Sebastián to Zaragoza—162 miles

Leave San Sebastián heading south via route N-1 through Andoain and Tolosa, where you make a left turn onto route N-240. The road begins a gentle climb through Lizarza, Betelu and Lecumberri and goes on into Pamplona; here a stay may be made at the La Perla Hotel. This is the town where the bulls are permitted to run through the street in a wild local celebration around July 7 (San Fermin's Day) and don't expect to find hotel rooms at that time of the year without a definite, *confirmed* reservation. From Pamplona, take route N-121 (although N-240 continues for a short distance out of town), driving through Noain (known for its aqueduct), Tiebas, Barasoain, Tafalla, Caparroso, Valtierra, Arguedas (after passing this village, the ruins of an old Roman city may be seen on the left), Murillo de las Limas (known for the fiercest bulls in all Spain, or so it has been claimed) and Tudela. Here you take route N-232 southward along a very straight road to Mallén, Alagón, and Zaragoza, where the Gran Hotel, a luxury place, would be ideal. There are also the Oriente and Goya, and they are quite satisfactory. Zaragoza (also known as Saragossa, the other way of spelling it) was the birthplace of Goya, as you may have guessed from the hotel's name. This is an appealing university town of almost 250,000 people, filled with everything a big city should have—restaurants, shops, cafes, sights to see. Visit: the Museo de Pintura (open 9 to 1) for its collection of Goya paintings, also a notable one by El Greco; the cathedral, notable for the treasures within the walls; the Archbishop's Palace. But the high spot for most people is the Basilica of the Virgin of Pilar, an almost Oriental structure of considerable interest.

Zaragoza to Barcelona—185 miles

Leave Zaragoza by route N-II, going through La Puebla de Alfinden, Alfajarin, Osera, Bujaraloz, Candasnos and Fraga into Lérida. Here, if you're in the mood, explore the old quarter of the town, the cathedral and Santa María Castle.

SIDE TRIP TO ANDORRA ¶ From Lérida, a run of about ninety miles will bring you via route C-1313 to Andorra, a tiny independent republic whose mere existence is an anachronism in this world of twentieth-century power politics. Andorra is under the combined jurisdiction of two people of somewhat different personalities—the Spanish Bishop of Urgel and the President of the French Republic. The road travels through Artesa de Segre, Pons and then the small town of Seo de Urgel, formerly an important medieval stronghold. The route is rugged, the road mediocre, but Andorra has a certain Ruritania atmosphere that makes it somewhat unbelievable and therefore quite delightful. There are eight villages, including Andorra la Vella, the capital. A good place for an overnight stay is in tiny Encamp, a village of considerable charm, where you'll find the Hotel Rosaleda. You'll soon learn that Andorra's chief occupation is smuggling, for articles are offered for sale at considerably lower prices than in their country of origin, and this even applies to American cigarettes. You may return to Spain by the same route, or if you are hardy and don't mind poor roads, you could continue on into France, picking up route N-20, making a right turn back toward the Spanish border and then following route 152 south into Barcelona and rejoining the tour.

Leave Lérida by route N-II through Bell Lloch (which may sound Scottish but isn't), Mollerusa, Bellpuig (the road now climbing gradually), the ancient university town of Cervera, Jorba (and its old castle), Ingualada, and Bruch de Medio, after which the road begins a sharp descent. Continue on through Esparraguera, known for its Patraco Caves, filled with stalactites and stalagmites (do you remember which is which?), Mártorell, Palleja, Molins del Rey and Esplugas into the Mediterranean city of Barcelona, Spain's famous seaport. Luxury accommodations may be found at the world-renowned Hotel Ritz, at the new Presidente, Arycasa and Diplomatic or at the traditional and pleasant Colon; good rooms may also be had at the Condado, Continental, Florida, Manila, Las Masia and Roma hotels. La Rotunda Hotel is on the road to Mount Tibidabo, in a quiet residential suburb; many suites and almost all rooms have balconies. Should you wish to visit Montserrat monastery (see Side Trip below), there is the Hotel Abat Cisneros for those who enjoy an unusual setting and atmosphere.

Barcelona differs from other Spanish cities in the same fashion that Marseilles contrasts with the rest of France. Both are bustling seaports, filled to overflowing with individually distinctive personalities, worldly-wise and with customs of their own. If much of Spain sleeps away part of the day, this can hardly be said of lively Barcelona. Wander about its streets and see the life of the *ramblas*, the famous city walks, filled with bird and flower markets and strolling people enjoying life. See the cathedral, a treasure of a building in the comparatively unusual Catalan-Gothic style; then contrast its stylized proportions with the almost weird, unrestrained lines of the unfinished Church of the Sagrada Familia (Holy Family), whose architect, Antoni Gaudí i Cornet, felt himself unhindered by any previous architectural forms. You have a chance to see typical Spanish homes from various provinces of the country in an ideal setting, the outdoor Spanish Village. There are churches galore, museums for everyone, even a replica of Columbus's ship, in which he reached the New World, on exhibit in the harbor. If time permits, visit Montserrat, the famous monastery, to hear the choir singing at 6 P.M. At night, wander through Barcelona's Chinese district, see flamenco or have dinner at one of Barcelona's typical restaurants.

Casa Bofarull–Los Caracoles, close to the waterfront and just off the *ramblas*, is a fascinating and colorful place to dine. From early spring to late fall you can eat on the sidewalk. Set out (not before about 10 P.M.) and have dinner there. The food is strictly local—marvelous snails, *zarzuela* (mixed seafood stew), grilled chicken; in fact anything will be good and not too expensive. There's lots of room inside, too. That heavy-set balding man sitting at the table and looking as if he is doodling on the tablecloth is the proprietor of Los Caracoles. Actually he's autographing picture postcards of the restaurant for guests—and he'll do one for you if you ask the waiter. Assuming it's now about 11:30 or so (and the later the better), walk a few doors down on the narrow alley called Nueva San Francisco to a hole-in-the-wall bar–night club called Macarena; here you'll see some remarkably good flamenco dancing and hear some fairly good Spanish singing. Stay about an hour or so, have a drink or so, but *don't* buy any drinks for the performers and *don't* tip them.

Barcelona is a good city for a short layover if you're in the mood to explore an interesting city. There is quite a lot to see and do and eat, and the shopping is good, having that ultimate virtue of being low-priced. This might be a good place to park the car and use taxis, which are easily obtained at all hours and are extremely cheap. Style-conscious women might want to head for the dressmaking establishment of Pedro Rodríquez. You'll want to try some additional restaurants: Guria, with atmospheric and comfortable wooden and leather furnishings, very fine food, mostly Basque, expensive; Puerto-Joanet, in the port area, for seafood and especially fish soup; Amaya, a simple place with Basque and other dishes. If you prefer French-style food, there are two very good restaurants, both fairly expensive by Spanish standards: Parellada and Circulo Ecuestre.

SIDE TRIP TO THE COSTA BRAVA ¶ From here, proceed northeastward toward Spain's Costa Brava, the Rugged Coast; better phone ahead for reservations during the summertime, for this is indeed a popular region. Leave Barcelona by route 101 to Badalona, Mataró and Blanes, fronting onto a lovely bay. Then on to Lloret de Mar, more or less the beginning of the resort region; it is filled with hotels—all crowded during the season. Next comes colorful Tossa de Mar, the central point of interest for tourists—this is what you really expected Spain to look like! Here are wonderful old ruins, a fishing village atmosphere, a superb beach—and then suddenly the town will become overloaded with hundreds of tourists brought in wholesale by bus. In Tossa, try for hotel rooms at Reymar or Mar Menuda at the Menuda beach, at Rovira on the town beach, or at Florida, in town. Tossa, very recently, has been the destination point of plane loads of British all-inclusive tour groups, which on occasion (during July and August) flood the region to such an extent that no Spanish can be heard, only Lancashire and Cockney English. Incidentally, from here on, the road becomes increasingly difficult, with sharp curves, mediocre surface and, in fact, if it weren't because this place is so beautiful one might feel inclined to turn back —but no one will, we feel sure.

Seven miles north of Tossa is a sharp cutoff up the mountainside to the San Grau development (a little over three miles over the cliffs). There is a fine hotel there, but even if you don't stay you will like the big wide-screen view. Return to the main road and continue on to San Felíu de Guixols. The best places here are Hotel Reina Elisenda, Hotel Murlá Park, Montjoi at San Elmo and Alábriga at the San Pol beach (and we certainly hope you get a room). There is also a combination motel-hotel that is extremely nice, La Piscina; this might be a good all-around bet if you don't want anything too fancy or too expensive. The municipal museum at San Felíu is a good place to browse as a change of pace. It has an intriguing collection of guns, plus some vases and coins dug out of the local landscape. In the Palacio Municipal, Spanish artists present their works, with the exhibit changing every couple of weeks. For a good look at the sea, go to the Calasans promontory at the north edge of town. Boats, benches and a cosy garden give this lookout point a restful atmosphere. The Casa Buxo restaurant, by the way, specializes in a fish plate that is supreme and inexpensive. If you have no desire to explore the Costa Brava any further, head inland on route 250 in the direction of Santa Cristina. On leaving Llagostera you will meet a fork in the road. Take the southern, or left, part of this fork, route 253, to Vidreras, seven and a half miles away. A half-mile after Vidreras the road joins up with route 2, the main highway south to Barcelona. If you have time, however, do some further exploring of the Costa Brava, and pick out a beach for a bit of swimming. San Felíu is lovely, but lovely or no, we must (hesitatingly) admit that it has no beach and you'll have to drive elsewhere for a swim. Most likely, you'll head for S'Agaró, the outstanding resort spot of the coast, featuring its most luxurious hotel, the Hostal de la Gavina: the public rooms and halls are furnished in lovely antiques, the service is quite good and the food served on an attractive outdoor terrace is fair, although not extraordinary. But some rooms face an outdoor bowling alley, where the click of the balls may be clearly heard at 2 A.M., and other rooms face an outdoor night club, where microphoned expressions of love may be heard at 3 A.M. so be *sure* your room doesn't face in those directions if, like soft Americans, you expect to sleep at night. Adjacent to it is the Hotel de la Playa, not nearly so attractive, but what can you do if nothing else is available? Then there's Playa de Aro, a resort growing in popularity, with numerous hotels, some of the best among them, and all new, being Columbus, Aromar and Mar Condal. Next comes Palamós where the best hotels are Trias and Alba. Further up the Costa Brava, at Aiguafreda near Bagur, is the wondrous Cap Sa Sal Hotel (that's the name in Catalan, the language of the area).

Note: Hotels are being added to the Costa Brava all the time because the number of tourists increases each season; so inquire locally about new places to stay.

Excursion possibilities by bus from Barcelona are good. The only trouble is that they do not venture too far, stopping generally at Tossa. The departure time is 9 A.M., and the buses get back around 7 P.M. The tour is relatively inexpensive. If you want to, you can go swimming at Tossa. Dressing cabins are available for about a quarter. Some of the sightseeing companies give an extra dimension to their Costa Brava bus tour by making one leg of it in a boat. That gives a stupendous view of the coastline.

SIDE TRIP TO MONTSERRAT ¶ By car drive out the Avenida Generalísimo in the direction of Madrid. Montserrat, the "Holy Mountain" as it is known by the Catalan people, is only thirty-eight miles from Barcelona. It will take close to an hour and a half, whether you go by car, train or bus. En route you will see the former royal summer palace (now used by Franco) and the new university buildings that flank both sides of the road. It is best to approach the mountain from the eastern side. The scenery is less spellbinding, but it is easier going and you save yourself a half-dozen miles of mountain driving. Leave your car at the cable car station called AEREO. There is cable car service every twenty minutes from sunrise to sunset between the aerial railway station and the sanctuary at the top of the mountain. In case you come to Montserrat by train, the AEREO will also be your stopping point. Trains leave from Plaza de España in Barcelona a couple of times each morning, and there are several trains back in the afternoon. The train station in Barcelona for Montserrat is also a subway stop, so you should not have any difficulty in finding it. (As a matter of fact it is only a few subway stops from the university area.) Sightseeing excursion buses are probably the easiest means of getting to Montserrat; there are daily excursions by all the major companies, and the tariff is about $5. English-speaking guides at the sanctuary conduct one-hour tours every half-hour for a fee of about a half-dollar. Keep in mind that the boys' choir sings in the church at about 6:00 P.M. and plan your schedule accordingly. You don't need a guide for the church or the museum. In the museum, by the way, is a crown with 2,400 diamonds, more than 100 emeralds and several dozen pearls. In case you visit the mountain late in the day, remember that the boys' choir also sings in the evening after the seven o'clock vespers. The monastery has a pretty good restaurant if you want to have lunch or tea. A specialty, naturally, is paella Montserratina. If you would like to do some more cable car riding, take one to nearby St. John's peak. Two miles from the monastery is another cable car to St. Jerome's peak.

On your way back from Montserrat by drive-yourself car, take the route leading to Igualada and then follow route 244 to Villafranca. If you have been looking at the label on your wine bottles, you will recognize the name "Villafranca," and the sweep of vineyards will confirm for you that this is wine country. From Villafranca, you can really make a day of it by going along route 340 to Tarragona. If time does not permit this, you can save Tarragona for another, separate trip and return to Barcelona by route 340.

SIDE TRIP TO MAJORCA AND THE BALEARIC ISLANDS ¶ Barcelona is the customary starting point for a trip to the Balearic Islands, which usually means just one—Majorca —to most Americans. These fortunate islands are becoming increasingly popular with tourists, who find therein the fondest dreams of a vacation spot, or—absolutely nothing. It would seem reasonable to state that the majority of Americans do enjoy Majorca greatly, for the scenery is superb, the bathing superb and for once, the prices superbly low. Majorca is pleasant for a visit almost any time of the year except December through February, when the climate is damp and raw (as George Sand and Chopin found out one miserably unhappy winter); the remainder of the year there is excellent weather. During the busy season, July and August can be very hot, but the chance of steady rain is not too great. If you've never been to Majorca, go once and judge for yourself. Unlike another famous island (Capri), Majorca has more room to spread out and diversify its personality.

By air, travel time from Madrid to Majorca is about two hours; from Barcelona, under one hour; in season, there are several flights daily in each direction. The Compania Transmediterranea maintains boat service from Barcelona, usually departing at about 10 P.M. and arriving the following morning. The boats are quite comfortable, the staterooms somewhat small and the food pretty dull, but the trip is reasonably pleasant, except that the runs are made overnight and you don't really see anything except the insides of the ship until you arrive in the harbor of Palma in the morning. There are numerous interisland services by plane and boat, all increasing in frequency during the season as the islands become even more popular.

The Balearics consist of more than a dozen islands —some large and some tiny islets—but the biggest is Majorca (also spelled Mallorca); there are three other sizable ones—Ibiza, Minorca and Formentera. Majorca's offbeat capital is Palma, an attractive city with comparatively few sights other than the magnificent cathedral, but filled with wonderful old houses, slender streets and a charm-laden atmosphere. The harbor of Palma is one of the world's most entrancing sights (yes, almost like out of a travel folder!), best seen from a boat on entering the port, but pretty good any way you view it. Getting settled here is a choice of riches, for there are any number of excellent hotels. If you wish to stay in town you will find the best accommodations at the Jaime I at the corner of Paseo Mallorca and Avenida Jaime III, completely renovated in 1969, with rooftop swimming pool. But the main row of Mallorca hotels lines the western shore of the harbor. At the edge of the town

WEATHER STRIP: MAJORCA

Temp.	JAN.	FEB.	MAR.	APR.	MAY	JUNE	JULY	AUG.	SEPT.	OCT.	NOV.	DEC.
Low	36°	36°	42°	46°	54°	59°	61°	65°	62°	54°	48°	47°
High	56°	66°	62°	68°	78°	81°	85°	89°	84°	75°	68°	64°
Average	46°	51°	52°	57°	66°	70°	73°	77°	73°	65°	58°	55°
Days of rain	11	7	10	7	2	9	6	3	8	13	8	10

proper is the very modern Melia Mallorca (formerly Bahia Palace), with two buildings (one larger and newer and one smaller and not so new) and two swimming pools. Further down the shore are other leading hotels: Victoria (marvelous view, good food); Fenix (modern but somewhat functional); Mediterraneo (period-style furnishings and beautiful terraces); Alcina (good-size rooms overlooking the bay). The sightseeing boats stop in front of Hotel Ancina; their usual point of departure is the old port facing the old town.

If possible, stay at your hotel demi-pension, which will give you the chance to have a few meals out and do a little island sightseeing. In Palma you will find several good restaurants: El Patio, quite fashionable in the suburb of Terreno on the west shore; Mesón Carlos I and the intime La Broche, both in the old town; Lonja de Pescado, on the upper floor of the fish market hall in the old port, is more simple but has the best seafood.

Outside and inland (about 4 miles from Palma) is the luxurious hotel San Vida, which is quite excellent on all counts. It's usually filled with British tourists, with whom it's very popular. On the western shore of Palma Bay, at Calamayor, is the Nixe Palace Hotel, built against a cliff, right on the beach. At Bendinat, further down the coast on this side, is the small, picturesque Bendinat Hotel, perched on the rocks, directly overlooking the foaming green sea. The best in Palma Nova, a hotel settlement on a quiet, small bay, are Hotel Hawai above the beach and with terraces reaching down to the water, and Delfin Playa on the beach. There are several more new hotels at the nearby Magaluf beach but this place is so crowded and unpleasant, with rather unsavory vacationists crawling all over, that you may as well go to the Coney Island instead. Somewhat of an exception are the recently opened first-class hotel twins Antillas and Barbados. The best hotels on the eastern shore of the Palma Bay, in the Arenal section, are Garonda Palace, Playa de Palma and Cristina Palma.

Thirty-five miles from Palma—to the north—is the tiny fishing town of Puerto de Pollensa, which has about a dozen small hotels, medium-priced and lower; among the best are Daina, right on the waterfront, and Uyal at the beach on the coastal road to Alcudia.

If you hire a car (and incidentally drive-yourself cars have no mileage limitation), there are a few worthwhile excursions. Drive one day to the port of Sóller; the countryside is pleasant and, although the road is winding, the trip is worthwhile and you can, if you wish, have lunch at Sóller. But if time permits only one excursion, make your destination Formentor, at the northeast end of the island. Your road goes through Alcudia and then into Pollensa. From here, there is an absolutely spectacular drive to the island's tip of Formentor. Here you'll find one of the world's loveliest coves, much like a South Pacific island; it's almost unbearably beautiful. The only place to stay is the somewhat vaguely run-down Hotel Formentor, where the rooms are old-fashioned and none too large; alas, the food is poor—in fact, quite bad. But if you can put up with the seedy rooms and mediocre food, you'll be staying at one of the most attractive places you've ever seen.

One remaining possibility for a pleasant day's trip is to the Drach "Dragon" Caves; buses leave every day for this touristy proceeding. This is an interesting outing, but see one cave and you've seen them all, we always say; music in the caves is an unusual variation, however. The outlying islands of Minorca and Ibiza are much less built up and are therefore particularly attractive to the traveler who enjoys quiet, low-pressure surroundings, lots of nearly vacant beaches where days pass by in a gentle procession of lazy pleasure. Minorca, in particular, is noted for its archaeological sites, should an unexpected desire to see and do things overtake you. Roads on both islands are pretty bad, and the best sightseeing is from a coastal boat or on one of the native burros.

Barcelona to Valencia—209 miles

Leave Barcelona by route C-246 via Avenida de José Antonio, going through Esplugas, Cornella and Sitges, a resort town of ever-greater popularity. The English tourists have also discovered this town, and in the British press you see big "Come-to-Sitges" ads. When you arrive on the beautiful Sitges beach, you will realize that the advertising has paid off. Next, we go to Villanueva y Geltrú, another resort with an excellent bathing beach. Visit the Romanesque castle; then continue on to Vendrell, where route 340 joins, and from there into Tarragona. The best hotel in Tarragona is Imperial Tarraco, overlooking the beautiful belvedere called the "Mediterranean Balcony," and you have the same magnificent view from your hotel balcony. Hotel Lauria on the Rambla is less expensive and has a good restaurant and a swimming pool.

Tarragona offers fascinating opportunities for those interested in Roman ruins, for this ancient town was once the capital of all of Roman Spain. The sights on the outskirts of Tarragona probably should be seen first—or, at least, don't miss them. One we have in mind is the Arch of Bara, right alongside of the highway twelve miles from the Tarragona boundary line. A little closer in (about four miles from town) is a Roman monument to the dead that is known as Scipio's Tower. Three miles from Tarragona on route 240 (the road to Lérida) is a double-decker Roman aqueduct that is definitely worth a side trip. In town itself walk along the Archaeological Passage, a fascinating thoroughfare a bit over a mile long. It is a mile that will remain in your memory, especially if you do your strolling at sunset. This unique passageway is open from 9 A.M. to 8 P.M. The admission fee is 10 ptas. Allow yourself about an hour for this delightful walk. There is the Archaeological Museum, with a good display. One of the most wondrous items on display is an ivory doll—which moves (yes, indeed!). The museum's hours are 10 A.M. to 1:30 P.M. and 4 to 7 P.M.; admission is 5 ptas. Don't pass up the cathedral's treasury—the hanging tapestries are outstanding and you can see them between 10 A.M. and 1 P.M. and from 4 to 7 P.M. Here the entrance fee is a bit (not too much) higher: 15 pesetas. Allow yourself several hours to thoroughly view the Archaeological Passage, the museum and the cathedral's treasury. As a matter of fact, you would enjoy lingering at Tarragona for a day or two—maybe, even longer. Local food specialties are fish soup and a special way of doing the familiar paella. There is a fine *rosado* wine from the area. The seafood is excellent at the restaurant La Puda, located in the fishing port area.

Leave Tarragona by route N-340 through Villaseca de Salsina, Cambrils, Hospitalet del Infante (which gets its name from the Pilgrims' Hospice, a structure in the Gothic style), Perelló and Aldea; then to Tortosa (a quaint old village with many fine buildings). From Tortosa, continue to Vinaroz and Benicarló. About four and one-half miles after Benicarló, there is a left turn then it's four miles to Peñiscola, a medieval town perched on a rock; extremely colorful and definitely worth the short side trip; Peñiscola has had a fabulous, unlikely history, considering its small size. The Knights Templar built the interesting castle you'll see here; in its ramparts once lived Don Pedro de Luna (Benedict XIII) an ardent antipapist. Please don't miss seeing Peñiscola—after all, when will you be here again? Once back on the main road, continue on to Alcalá de Chisvert (with many fine old Roman ruins), Torreblanca, Oropesa, Benicaism and Castellón de la Plana, a small, quiet town with excellent climate, which makes it an ideal orange-producing area. Probably the single most important sight is the Capuchin convent, which has some fine Spanish paintings. For bathers, there are good beaches in the vicinity of town.

From Castellón, continue to Villarreal de la Plana, another town in the midst of orange groves; then come Nules, Almenara (with its eighteenth-century castle), Sagunto (old Roman ruins and castle) and finally the sunny seaport city of Valencia.

The luxurious Astoria Palace, right on Plaza Rodrigo Boté, is our first choice for a place to stay in Valencia. The Royal, Excelsior and Inglés should be tried if you cannot get a room at the Astoria Palace. For good food head for the restaurant Viveros, a glassed-in pavilion in the Royal Gardens, elegant and expensive. Marisquero, not far from the railroad station, has excellent seafood.

Valencia is a very modern city, lively, bustling and yet somehow light-hearted. Sightseeing of the compulsory sort: the museum, with some fairly good paintings; the Church of Corpus Christi; the cathedral; the Lonja de la Seda (the Silk Exchange), for its magnificent interior. This is rice-growing country, and a visit to see the fields is worthwhile; along the way you'll find restaurants specializing in the classic dish paella or arroz a la Valenciana, elaborate rice and seafood preparations.

Pointer: A note to summer travelers: From June through late August, the region to the south and west (particularly Andalusia) is sunbaked and extremely torrid. If you wish, trips may be made during the summer to these places, and many do go. However, if you are susceptible to heat and accustomed to air conditioning, Andalusia may be just too hot for comfort or enjoyment. If you do decide to go, plan to arise early (say, 6 A.M.), do your sightseeing and

quit before noon, with a possible resumption in the late afternoon. Those who have listened to this sermon and decided to return to Madrid from Valencia should take route 111, which goes directly back, a run of 218 miles easily made in one day.

Valencia to Alicante—112 miles

Leave Valencia by route N-340 going through Masanasa and Catarroja; at Silla, make a left turn onto route N-332. In driving along, note the peasant houses known as *barracas*, with their distinctive thatched roofs, typical of the local architecture. On the left you'll see Lake Albufera, twenty miles long, a freshwater lake protected from the sea by a long, steady growth of pine trees. Next come Sollana, Sueca, Cullera, Favareta and then Gandía, which deserves a little sightseeing. Originally an Arabic settlement, later a duchy belonging to the all-powerful Borgia family; see the Palace of the Dukes, notably the interior decorations of the Borgias' apartment; also the Collegiate Church. Then to Oliva (an old Roman community), Vergel and Ondara; here a left turn should be made to visit Denia (five and one-half miles), once a Phoenician town, with some marvelous remnants of the old fortifications. Go from Ondara to Gata de Gorgos, then drive through an unusual gorge toward Benisa, later passing through Mascarat Tunnel into Altea (orignally a Greek settlement) and then Benidorm, which in the past years has developed into one of the most fashionable beach resort towns in Spain. On each side of the former fishing village, which still remains the most colorful section of the town, there are two mile-long beaches lined with tall apartment buildings and hotels. Among the hotels are Corregidor Real with old Spanish interiors; Glasor and Dunes, each on opposite ends of the beach; and Planesia, on top of the promontory above the old town. There are several restaurants at the Poniente Beach (one of the two beaches; the other is Levante) right under the old town, serving very good seafood. Hogar del Pescador, is one. The road goes on through Villajoyosa and Campello; near San Juan, there are some very interesting old Roman ruins; then into Alicante, famous as a winter resort and for its extremely dry climate. This old Roman city rises steeply and picturesquely along the sides of a hill away from the harbor, almost every vantage point offering spectacular views of the Mediterranean. Sightseeing: the fortress of Santa

Barbara (elevator and motor road); the fortress of San Fernando with its large park and sports grounds; the old Santa Cruz quarter. In getting settled overnight or for a stay, you'll find the Carlton is the luxury hotel of Alicante; the Grand Hote is next best. On the San Juan Beach (about five miles away) are the Bonanza and the Playa. During July and August, this area is mobbed, so be sure to have hotel reservations. On the beach south of Alicante, near the airport, is Hotel Los Arenales with its terraced rooms turned towards the sun and a fine swimming pool (in addition to the beach).

Alicante to Almería—185 miles

Leave Alicante via route 340 toward Elche, a most unusual Spanish town with an intriguing Oriental aspect; the town is famous for its palm tree forest. Particularly renowned is the Palmera del Cura, a tremendous tree of imposing dimensions, the largest we've ever seen. Continue on to Crevillente (where you can buy some of the locally made hemp sandals), Albatera, Granja, Callosa del Segura and Orihuela, which, although originally founded by the Romans, has a curiously Moorish appearance and character. Then to Santomera, Monteagudo (with some ruins of Arab and Roman construction) and Murcia, capital of the province of the same name. If you should be fortunate enough to be here during Easter, you'll witness one of the most remarkable of Spain's religious processions. An interesting summer custom is that of protecting the streets from the excessive brilliance and heat of the sun by means of canvas lengths, called *toldos*. Sightseeing: the Provincial Archaeological Museum; the Cathedral of Santa María; the Salzillo Museum, featuring works by the noted sculptor.

Leave Murcia, departing on the Calle de Floridablanca, then through Librilla (with some old fortifications), Alhama de Murcia, Totana and later Lorca, a metropolis of considerable importance when it was a seventeenth-century art center; now it is a sleepy town, but very harmonious and pleasing to the eye. Sightseeing: the Church of St. Patricius; the Casa del Guevara; the Espolon Tower. Next, after a stretch of routine driving, Puerto Lambreras, Huércal-Overa, Vera, Sorbas (be sure to notice the town's site on a rock) and into Almería ("The Mirror"), originally a Phoenician settlement and later under the control of the Arabs. You are now in the heart of Andalusia, the real Andalusia, not the tourist version. If you come here during the late summer when the white grapes are being harvested, you'll be able to eat some of the finest in the world, vine ripened and luscious.

Almería is hardly a tourist town, so don't go searching for luxury hotels. However some good new hotels are available now in the city itself: Gran Hotel Almeria, facing the port, and Costasol on the main street (Generalisimo). About 6 miles west of the city, in a nice, private location on the sea is the very modern, new and luxurious Hotel Aguadulce.

Almería to Granada—113 miles

Leave Almería via route 340, following along the coast through Aguadulce (actually Sweet Water, just like a small western town in the United States), Adra (several interesting Phoenician and Roman ruins) and El Pozuelo, located in a fascinating scenic area; this whole region abounds with soft, evanescent charm—the somnolent countryside on the right hand, the blue Mediterranean on the left. On the horizon an occasional sail appears; there is the delight of watching the local people, filled with dignity, wandering along the road, leading or being led by their cattle. Next are La Rabita, Melicera, La Mamola, Castell de Ferro, Calahonda, Torrenueva and then Motril. Here you leave the coast, making a right turn onto route N-323 toward Velez-Benaudalla; the road climbs steeply through Durcal, Padul and into lovely Granada, situated in a unique setting of great beauty on three hills backed up by the Sierra Nevada mountain range.

At Granada you'll find the world-famous Hotel Alhambra Palace, one of Spain's leading hotels, encircled by a series of gardens. The other deluxe hotel is the Melia Granada. The newest (opened in Spring, 1969) is the first class, 175-bed Luz-Granada. The Hotel Washington Irving is very pleasant and less expensive. The Gran Hotel Brasilia, Residencia Kenia and Victoria are also quite good. However, for those who seek the unusual, there is a remodeled monastery, now a hotel, with beautiful gardens, and absolutely charming. It's the Parador Nacional San Francisco. But don't expect to get a room there without writing in advance. It's almost always fully booked.

Granada is a city that, being unique, takes a little knowing to understand. Many of Granada's charms are hidden, but most people become extremely fond of its stately homes, interestingly arranged on the sloping streets; the air is flower-laden and heavily perfumed, particularly in the early morning. There are many sight-seeing attractions, including the cathedral (where Ferdinand and Isabella are entombed), Charles V's palace, the Carthusian monastery, Generalife (the summer home of the Moorish Kings) and of course the fascinating gypsy district, the Sacro Monte. But to almost everyone, the heavily praised Alhambra is the outstanding sight. Among world-famous buildings, those probably most renowned are the Taj Mahal of India, Nôtre-Dame and Chartres cathedrals in France, the Parthenon in Athens and this remarkable edifice, the Moorish palace called the Alhambra. Granada and its proudest possession—the Alhambra, originally constructed by the Moorish rulers —were turned over to Ferdinand and Isabella of Spain in 1492, which must have been quite a year from all evidence. The Alhambra can be enjoyed only with peace and quiet, and that's hard to come by, for it is inevitably filled with guided tours, each following closely on the previous one's heels. Try to visit the Alhambra bright and early in the morning and really see it; otherwise, be prepared to be part of a horde of visitors. The original structure was damaged over the centuries, and the exterior restored by workmen who were apparently far from qualified. To see the Alhambra at its very best, go as early in the morning as possible before the crowds and tours spoil its inherent charm.

A word about the gypsy district, the Sacro Monte: some gypsies still live in caves in a colorful part of Granada known as the Albaicin. Don't feel too badly about the poor gypsies; you'll be surprised to learn that the cave interiors are lit by electricity, are frequently quite well furnished, seemingly lacking nothing but television sets, if you consider those a necessity. About the gypsies: as you approach the area, guides or local children will offer to take you to see the dancing—at fancy prices according to your degree of gullibility, but don't be taken in by nonsensical rates; about $5 is absolutely tops for a complete *zambra* display of songs and dances. Don't take too much money, or wear elaborate jewelry, because gypsies are basically thieves, and there's no point in being excessively polite and calling them light-fingered. The whole gypsy dance business has become practically a racket, we regret to say.

Granada to Málaga—84 miles

Leave Granada via route N-342, on the Avenida de Calvo Sotelo, heading toward Santafé (which is reminiscent, in name at least, of our own city in New Mexico), then through the River Genil valley, eventually coming into Lachar; follow the River Genil (and its Infiernos Altos, the Hell of Loja) into Loja, a medium-size town where typical Spanish pottery is made. Here, make a left turn onto route N-321 dropping down toward Málaga, an extremely attractive city of Andalusia.

Hotel Málaga Palácio with swimming pool and situated at the palm promenade near the port, and Hotel Lux Malaga, in a beautiful private park on the seaside and also with swimming pool, are now the best. There are a couple of national *paradores* here, and if you have developed into a *parador* fan, you probably will head for one of them: de Gibrálfaro and del Golf. In spring or fall or winter (in fact, anytime but summer) Málaga's climate is usually a delight and constitutes the chief attraction of the city, which is not otherwise too important for tourists. Sightseeing: the cathedral; the Sagrario, a Gothic structure with an interestingly decorated façade; the Alcázaba, a Moslem fortress constructed by Yusuf I of Granada. Drive up to Gibrálfaro (behind the Alcázaba), where the view is superb; there is a restaurant in the fortress. Don't leave Málaga without having *sopa Malagueña* (soup, in Málaga style), some boiled lobster, the broiled red mullet (usually with a teeny weeny bit—a quart—of garlic) and some of the rich Málaga dessert wine of this region.

Málaga to Algeciras—87 miles

Leave Málaga via route 340 heading for Torremolinos, a Mediterranean resort whose existence I do not understand. It has been publicized and glamorized, and I still don't know why. It has a fairly good beach and a fairly interesting shopping section, but it is overcrowded and completely lacking in atmosphere. It is so British that signs should be placed in the shop windows reading

"Spanish spoken here." For those remaining overnight the Pez Espada Hotel is a dead ringer for a Miami Beach hotel, with a similar atmosphere. However, hotels are being built by the dozens here, and you could make your own selection merely by looking around. Marbella, some twenty-eight miles farther along, has the Marbella Club, a hotel with very pleasant surroundings, much more suited to this region than Torremolinos' chrome-and-glass hotels. Also very good are the Melia Don Pepe, the Marbella Hilton (which has lovely grounds) and the Los Monteros. All of these are really quite nice for a visit. At Soto Grande, in the hills behind Marbella, there is a luxurious but small golf hotel, Nueva Andulucia, which has two 18-hole golf courses, two swimming pools, and a beach club. After Marbella, you'll come near the tiny fishing village of San Pedro Alcántara, where you have the chance of making a thirty-five-mile side trip to Ronda, driving on a poor road through some of the least restrained scenery in all of Andalusia. (If the coastal summer heat is too much for you, head for Ronda, high in the mountains, and cool off; the Hotel Reina Victoria at Ronda is quite modest, but the setting is superb. This atmospheric mountain retreat is another offbeat town, comparatively primitive and remote, for those who prefer the unusual to the beaten path.)

Continue on from San Pedro Alcántara through Estepona and Guadiaro. Near San Roque (a captivating little town), you'll see a sign indicating a left turn toward Gibraltar. At the moment you can't enter Gibraltar by this land route, because Spain is claiming the territory and has instituted a blockade of The Rock from Spain. You can't even enter Gibraltar by means of a boat from Algeciras or any other nearby shore point. There's no way of saying when the blockade will be lifted, and at the moment the only way to reach it is by air from Great Britain or Portugal; occasional cruise ships also stop there, but that's about it. You'll probably want to see The Rock, if only from a distance. If so, look for signs directing you to the town of La Linea; from here you can view rocky Gibraltar at fairly close range. However, there's an even better view of Gibraltar from Algeciras (coming up soon), although it's across the bay and much further away. If you do go to La Linea for a view, return to route N-340 (a left turn), and continue on to Algeciras.

Algeciras to Cádiz—80 miles

Leave Gibraltar returning through La Línea and picking up route N-340 (left turn) toward Algeciras, which has the Hotel Reina Cristina, an extremely luxurious establishment. (There is boat service, taking two and one-half hours, from Algeciras to colorful Tangier, North Africa, should you be interested in seeing something of this mysterious, intriguing bit of North Africa.) The road goes on to Tarifa, a fishing port, the most southerly spot of land in Spain. The route from here on to Chiclana is beautiful, passing through some extraordinarily attractive sketches, and the local traffic is fascinating to watch. After Chiclana, there is a left turn toward San Fernando (route N-IV) and Cádiz, a white town surrounded by the Atlantic (yes, at last the ocean) on three sides. Cádiz lacks important tourist attractions, but is a reasonably pleasant town to walk through.

At Cádiz, you could stay at the Atlántico in a magnificent park location and overlooking the sea, or at Playa Victoria, at the beach of the same name, on the way from the "mainland" to the old town.

Cádiz to Seville—93 miles

Leave Cádiz via route N-IV back to San Fernando, continuing on to Puerto Real, El Puerto de Santa María and Jerez (it must be pronounced Her-eth or no one will know what you're talking about), where the world-famous sherry wine is produced. Visitors are welcomed and are offered generous samples of the various types of wines, of which there are far more than you might have imagined. The hotels in Jerez are the new and first class Jerez with swimming pool, and the smaller but more atmospheric Los Cisnes with a beautiful green patio and the excellent restaurant La Parilla. While here be sure to visit the Carthusian monastery, three miles distant, in the village of Cartuja. Continue from Jerez on a fairly good road through routine countryside, stretching along drained marshland, finally coming through Los Palacios and Dos Hermanas and then into Seville. If you have an idea of visiting Seville during its traditional *feira*, held during April, *be sure* to have hotel reservations doubly confirmed, because rooms are otherwise unavailable.

Seville (Sevilla in Spanish) is without a doubt one of those rare places in the world that has something delightful for everyone; few leave it without a feeling of regret. (Of course, an exception might be made for someone who comes in torrid July and feels pleasure only when departing northward to a cool spot.) The hotel situation is excellent: the luxurious Alfonso XIII is elegant and lush, with atmosphere you can almost touch; Luz Sevilla, modern and luxurious, and the new Inglaterra, which belongs to the first class category, are both centrally located.

There are certain sightseeing requirements: to begin with, there's the Alcázar (a fourteenth-century castle); the lovely Giralda towers; the cathedral, which is basically Gothic but tinged with Arabic influence. But at the risk of imposing a personal preference, I would recommend the charming Old World district called Santa Cruz (it can be entered by a street near the Alcázar and the cathedral). For sheer delight, wander about the Santa Cruz district, peer into a courtyard or two and try to absorb some of the local color. Santa Cruz is at its best in the very late afternoon, when sunset adds its colors. Another pleasant pastime is wandering along the narrow, winding street called Calle de las Sierpes, Seville's most interesting street. Gourmets will be unhappy here; the food situation is extremely poor, and a good meal is hard to come by in Seville. About the best food in town is at the Hotel Alfonso XIII.

Portugal-bound motorists will leave Seville via route 630, later picking up route 433 to Aracena, then crossing the Spanish-Portuguese border, and on to Serpa and Beja in Portugal. If you're driving back to Lisbon, plan to stay overnight at the very pleasant Pousada de São Gens in Serpa; it's ideal for an overnight stop.

Seville to Córdoba—85 miles

Leave Seville by route N-IV to the east; about twenty miles along, you'll notice on the right hand the famous Necropolis, carved out of the rock by the Romans during the period of their occupation, with almost a thousand underground tombs that date back to the second century, B.C. One mile farther, you come to Carmona (which has many signs of its former rule by the Moors), then La Luisana (with salt lagoons), and Ecija, which may well be the hottest spot in Andalusia; if you're here during the cool season, visit the fortifications and towers. (During the summer months, we wouldn't blame you for continuing on without delay.) Then through La Carlota, after which care should be exercised in driving a comparatively difficult, steep road, and into Córdoba (or Cordova, as it is often spelled in English).

The top hotels in Córdoba are Melia Córdoba and Gran Capitán, both modern, comfortable and completely air-conditioned. A few miles outside of town, there is a new, rather elaborate hotel, the Parador Nacional de la Arruzafa, an extremely pleasant place to stay. As far as we're concerned, the place to go in the evening (say 9:30 or so) for dinner and entertainment is a simple *tasca*, or tavern. A most interesting one is called *Los Califas* (the Caliphs). It's a trifle difficult to find, being located on a narrow street in the colorful district of the old town called the Barrio de la Juderia. Here you'll find good food, impromptu music and singing and the peculiarly pleasing atmosphere of Córdoba. The Barrio de la Juderia, incidentally, is a sightseeing highlight of Córdoba; you can wander about its charming streets for hours without actually seeing any important sights, but merely absorbing local color. The Barrio is equally interesting by day or night.

Córdoba is a city of tremendous interest, possibly one of Spain's most fascinating old communities. Here is a place with two facets to offer: the sightseeing "musts" and also the unusual Moorish quality of the city, which, like a mysterious woman, seems to promise much if only her secret can be discovered. Many discerning tourists have spent days and weeks wandering about the narrow streets, peering into courtyards, looking blankly into space past flowered terraces, trying to understand what Córdoba is trying to tell them. Farfetched? Well, perhaps; walk on your own about the city in the late afternoon or early evening and see if you, too, do not feel an inexplicable something in the air.

For serious sightseers, there can be no question but that the eighth-century mosque, now a cathedral, is number one on everyone's list, and justly so. Originally, the mosque was dedicated, in the year 785, by the Moors to the pagan god Janus; a Christian altar was later built in the center of the building, despite the surprisingly bitter opposition of the local people. It is sad to relate that the altar seems out of place and overwhelmed by the mosque's fundamental magnificence. The interior is sheer wonder, the 900 columns seemingly endless, with a truly majestic overall effect; your eye is first taken aback, later delighted, by the diminishing symmetry of the mathematically arranged columns. It has been said that the mosque is best visited early in the morning or at sunset, and, undoubtedly, this is true, because shadows and reflections are softened, and the angular lighting effect produces an extraordinarily beautiful effect. See also: the Tower of the Malmuerta (near the Plaza de Colón); the bridge crossing the River Guadalquivir, built by the Romans; the Provincial Fine Arts and Archaeological Museum; the old Jewish district, with its *Sinagoga*, or synagogue, declared a national monument by the Spanish government. At night, visit the lantern-lit Plaza de la Dolores, picturesque and typical of Córdoba. Just fifteen minutes from town (six miles) are the excavations of an old fortress and its walls, built about the year 936; above is the Alcázar, with its famous columns.

Córdoba to Madrid—243 miles

This is a comparatively long run, but there is little to delay you on this portion of the trip, and the hotel situation en route in none too good; therefore an early morning start from Córdoba is recommended.

Leave Córdoba via route N-IV, going alongside River Guadalquivir, then crossing it on occasion as you proceed northward. Through fields of cultivation you pass Alcolea, Pedro Abad, Villa del Río; then comes a sharp climb toward Andújar, a town noted for its pottery production. Continue on to Bailén, an unimportant town in itself, but a crossroads for various automobile routes.

Leave Bailén via N-IV toward Guarromán, Carboneros, La Carolina, Santa Elena and Las Correderas; here is a narrow pass, the Despeñaperros, where the road is fairly difficult because of the many sharp turns and bends. Then to Almuradiel, Valdepeñas and Manzares, an ideal spot for a break in the day's run. The government's Albergue is a delightful place for lunch. If you plan to stay overnight in this area you could try the motel El Hidalgo in Valdepeñas, in a nice garden with a swimming pool; also the restaurant is good.

Continue on through Puerto-Lápiche, Madridejos, Tembleque and Ocaña into Aranjuez. If time permits, visit the Royal Palace and drive (or even walk) through the pleasing streets. Then on to Valdemoro, and finally into Madrid.

ॐ *Motoring in Spain*

A lot has been said about Spanish roads—and not all of it has been complimentary. But it can be now asserted that the highway situation is quite good, all things considered. Directional signs leave a lot to be desired, but you will not have too much trouble finding your way if you keep to *main* roads. Traffic keeps to the right and passes on the left. The usual international road signs are used.

You do not need any special papers for bringing your car into Spain. The registration for the automobile and your home-state driver's license—plus, of course, the Green Card (for the insurance proof)—are all that is needed. If you need any help about car matters, drop in at the Royal Automovil Club de España at 10 Paseo del General Sanjurjo in Madrid. Super gasoline is 12 ptas. a liter, or about 60 cents a gallon. Regular is 10 percent cheaper.

Although new gasoline stations are under construction, it's a very good idea to fill your tank whenever it's down by anywhere from one-third to one-half. This is particularly true on weekends, or in remote areas. You may locate a gas station, but find it closed for one reason or another—siesta, local celebration, or perhaps the owner's mother-in-law has a toothache.

When passing on the highway, it's part of Spanish law to signal in advance that you're about to pass. During the day, this is done by sounding your horn; at night, by flashing your lights. It is also part of the law that you signal your *return* to the right lane. Better remember this. By law, you must complete overtaking a vehicle within 15 seconds.

Of course, within city limits, such as Madrid, it's against the law to sound your horn, except in the event of an emergency.

If you find yourself behind a truck, see if any lights are flashing at the truck's rear end. If there are green flashes, the driver thinks you can pass him with safety; when it flashes red, it means there's another car approaching, or it's otherwise dangerous.

SWEDEN

National Characteristics

In banks, as well as in Stockholm's world-famous department store, N.K., it is customary for men to remove their hats. That will give you a clue to one striking aspect of the Swedish personality. The Swedes seem burdened with a code of formal behavior, much of it largely outmoded by changing standards of today's world. Yet, being social traditionalists, they cling to their habits all the more strongly as a means of protest. If a man offers another a light for his cigarette, etiquette requires him to take the match and hold it until the other's cigarette is lighted. Otherwise, he would be considered boorish. This formalism in social matters is difficult to reconcile with the nation's socialistic concept of government, induced by an otherwise extremely liberal-minded public.

Most Swedish people are hardly light-hearted or gay; the solid citizen is respected for his honest virtues, for his earning capacity, for his devotion to his family and for keeping his house in good order. The pleasures of carefree social life are minimized—entertaining friends or relatives is on a formal basis, and neighbors don't just drop in uninvited. Artistic leanings and tendencies are not encouraged—and to spare a thought on the subject, just how many Swedish painters and composers can be named? The average person doesn't lean in that direction, or if he does, is soon discouraged by his family. To generalize, the Swede is slow-spoken, deliberate and comparatively solemn. He is full of serious virtues—but a little spontaneity might be appreciated.

Swedes have a different approach to sex education and practice than Anglo-Saxons. While in their teens, Sweden's boys and girls receive explicit and clinical instructions (not vague generalizations) about sex and its relation to life. As might be expected, knowledge is frequently put to use. Even after marriage, for many Swedish people, sex has a somewhat different meaning than to most of us. Americans are puritanical, they say. Maybe we are. But Sweden, too, has a high divorce rate, so who knows?

Things move smoothly in Sweden, as if everything were rolling along on Swedish ball bearings. The Swedes strive hard to make life easier, and everyday gadgets are fashioned to be more functional and/or nicer to look at. The Swedes' expertise at designing has grappled with everything from the telephone to a champagne glass. They have been quite successful, too.

When to Go

The large majority of tourists come during the late spring and summer months and invariably head for Stockholm. This makes the city very crowded and at the same time increases the problem of getting hotel space. So, if you are planning to visit Stockholm in the period from mid-June to early September, be sure to have hotel reservations confirmed beforehand. The winter months are delightful for skiing, as well as for sightseeing. But you must come prepared for cold weather and be properly dressed for it. Even summer days can often be cool, and there are spells of rain or showers from time to time. The forewarned summer traveler will bring a lightweight raincoat, but he'll find that the weather will seldom break up a complete day or interfere with his planned excursion. The big festive occasion ushering in the arrival of spring is on April 30. It is called Walpurgis Night, and there are celebrations from lakeside to mountaintop. From then on the weather ought to be generally mild and pleasant.

WEATHER STRIP: STOCKHOLM

Temp.	JAN.	FEB.	MAR.	APR.	MAY	JUNE	JULY	AUG.	SEPT.	OCT.	NOV.	DEC.
Low	22°	21°	24°	31°	40°	49°	54°	52°	46°	38°	31°	24°
High	31°	32°	36°	46°	57°	67°	71°	67°	59°	48°	39°	33°
Average	27°	27°	30°	39°	49°	58°	63°	60°	53°	43°	35°	29°
Days of rain	15	13	14	11	12	12	15	16	14	16	15	17

TIME EVALUATION ¶ Stockholm itself requires about two to three days for sightseeing. The trip by auto to Uppsala can easily be done in one additional day. If you're planning to relax at Visby, which can be reached by boat or plane, add an extra week. The Göta Canal trip takes about three days; one way is enough—drive, take the train or fly back. Of course, an automobile tour of the countryside could be as leisurely as you wish, say, an extra week or ten days.

PASSPORT AND VISA ¶ Only your passport will be needed for a visit that does not last longer than three months. If you remain over three months, then you'll have to obtain a visa.

CUSTOMS AND IMMIGRATION ¶ You are allowed to bring in duty-free two cartons of cigarettes or 500 grams (a little over a pound) of tobacco; two bottles of liquor; and the usual travel articles, including camera, film, transistor and the like. Don't bring a dog with you, because there is a long quarantine period similar to the one in other Scandinavian countries and in England. There is no limit on the amount of non-Swedish currency you can take in with you, but if you have more than 5,000 Swedish crowns, you have to declare it at the border. Swedish customs have streamlined their operation at the Arlanda airport, just outside Stockholm. As you get off the plane and enter the customs inspection hall, signs direct you to either of two lanes: ARTICLES TO BE DECLARED and NOTHING TO DECLARE. If you (like most passengers) choose the nothing-to-declare lane, the odds are very much against your being involved any further in the customs routine. Baggage is brought into the hall on a conveyor belt, and the customs inspector only puts a to-be-opened tag on one or two pieces of luggage in the entire line of bags. If your bag is not tagged, you just ask a porter (they're dressed very nattily in burgundy-red jackets and blue overseas caps) to pick your luggage off the conveyor belt and take it to a cab or the air terminal bus.

HEALTH ¶ Water and milk are excellent any place in the country. There need be no special precautions taken for a trip in Sweden except to have sunburn lotion and sunglasses. They will be handy either for the snow in the winter or for the brilliant sun in the Lapp area during the summer.

TIME ¶ Six hours ahead of (later than) Eastern Standard Time. Thus, when it is noon in New York it is 6 P.M. in Stockholm. When Daylight Saving Time is in effect in the United States, the time difference is reduced to 5 hours.

CURRENCY ¶ The unit of currency is the *krona* (crown in English). The value of the krona in relation to the dollar depends on the current international monetary situation. The plural of krona is *kronor*, and the abbreviation is *kr*. The krona, or crown, is divided into 100 *öre* (pronounced or-uh).

PRICE LEVELS ¶ Price levels, as many other matters in Sweden, are middle of the road. A double room and bath in Stockholm can run to $20 or more, but you can also get satisfactory accommodations cheaper than that. Hotel prices in other cities are lower than the Stockholm level, as well. In Stockholm, Malmö and major resort centers a First Class meal at one of the best restaurants will generally be at least $5, but $3 to $5 is the average price that you will pay in most other places. At resort hotels, the inclusive price, which covers room and meals, is quite moderate; and if you plan to stay for three or four days or more, it is definitely worth your while to inquire about this special everything-included pension tariff.

TIPPING ¶ Hotels charge a 15 percent service charge, which is supposed to cover all necessary tips except to the porter who handles your luggage on arrival and departure. He should get about 1 krona for one bag; however 3 kronor is enough for four suitcases. The service charge in restaurants ranges from 12.5 to 15 percent and is usually included in the total bill. The waiter should be given a little extra—but not more than 5 percent of the bill—if he has been very attentive. Taxi drivers expect 10 percent of the meter, but not less than 1 krona. In theaters, at the opera and in some restaurants the hatcheck room will post a sign advising a minimum charge (usually 50 öre). It is the general rule to give a krona, whether or not a fixed charge is announced.

TRANSPORTATION ¶ The taxi situation is very good, and cab stands are near major hotels, the opera house, the royal castle and other major spots where tourists gather. Rates are relatively high, but the average fare will not run more than 4 to 5 kronor. If you see *ledig* on a cab, that means it's free, but you'll still have to pay, of course. You know what we mean. If you are at someone's home for the evening and are not near a cab stand, they can call one for you by phone.

Public transportation is excellent in Stockholm, with buses, trams and the subwaylike *tunnelban* prepared to take you just about anywhere. The basic ticket cost for riding on any or all of these various means of transportation is 80 öre, and within one hour from the time of the purchase of the ticket you can transfer from one line to another, or from bus to trolley or vice versa —or any other combination. The subway fare outside Stockholm—that is, to a point beyond the far-flung city limits—is 1.10 kronor. The subway, by the way, is already quite comprehensive but is being expanded. You can spot the subway entrances by a large sign with the letter T on it. During the summer, special tickets are on sale for tourists that at a flat price permit unlimited bus-tram-subway travel for specific periods.

Ferries are a popular means of transport in Stockholm, since the city is made up of fourteen islands and is connected by fifty-four bridges. The fares are low, and this can be a nice, very inexpensive excursion and a way of seeing the city. Highly recommended for sightseeing. For instance, from Slussen (which is between the Old City and the southern island in Stockholm) a ferry crosses the inland end of the Baltic, which is called the Salt Lake, and travels to the island of Djurgarden. The trip takes ten minutes, and a ferry leaves every twenty minutes. The fare is the same as on a bus.

The Swedish *railroad* is one of Europe's best. Many of its branch lines, as well as the main lines, are electrified. Fares are lower if you buy a round-trip ticket. Also, keep in mind that rail rates are reduced in accordance with the distance. Thus, the rate (per mile) for a 50-mile trip is higher than one for a 500-mile one. Many fine tours, especially in the summer, are scheduled by the railroad people, and this is the most economical way of making long voyages (assuming that your purpose is sightseeing). During the summer, for example, the Swedish State Railways operates a seven-day *Sunlit Nights Land Cruise* that whisks you up north to the land of the Lapps and of the midnight sun. It is not too cheap but you can have a wonderful, trouble-free trip, and you will live a life of luxury. It's a well-planned affair, with just about everything but tips and beverages included. There are folk dancers, country fiddlers, sightseeing tours and even impressive certificates that are suitable for framing or for showing to any doubting Thomas you encounter when you get home. The scenery is unbelievable—sometimes more so, sometimes less so—and astonishingly green because of the twenty-four hour brightness of the midnight sun. Well, what's wrong with this paradise? The fare per person is comparatively high, seven days is rather long to spend on a train, the Lapps are pretty scarce and the mosquitoes aren't. But loads of people have a marvelous time—so that's both sides of the picture. You'll have to make the decision as to whether you can bear those seven days—a *week*—on a train.

Bus tours are quite popular because of their variety and comparative inexpensiveness. They are also quite comfortable. One of the best bargains is the day-long visit to the glass factories—Kosta and Orrefors. The tour by bus starts from either Kalmar or Växjö. A number of times during the summer a coach-cruise is scheduled between Stockholm and Malmö (with departures originating in both cities). It's a five-day bus ride through the lake district, the area of the glass factories and Sweden's own chateau country. Or, you can take a three-day tour to Oslo, seeing much of Sweden's fascinating folkloristic area en route. The two-day coach tour between Stockholm and Göteborg is referred to as "the Blue Ribbon Tour" and is very popular. It leaves four times a week during the tourist season.

A variety of *boat* tours is also possible since Sweden is surrounded by all that water, and has so many islands. A really fine way to cruise on the water is to take a three-day tour of the canals by a steamer that covers the waterways between Stockholm and Göteborg. This tour originates in both cities.

By a combination of *bus and boat* you can really get to the top of Europe, touring the area of the North Cape, and seeing Norwegian fjords, the midnight sun and the mighty mountains of the Arctic. This tour leaves from Kiruna or Luleå and takes from seven to nine days. The rate is not too expensive, all things considered.

Finland is only an overnight boat trip away from Stockholm. You can leave the Swedish capital about 6:30 P.M. and arrive at Turku or Helsinki the next morning. In winter, the ship goes no farther than Turku (because of the ice in the Gulf of Finland), and you can proceed to Helsinki by a three-hour train ride. But in summer the ship goes all the way to the Finnish capital.

Air transportation is easy in Sweden, what with a network of twenty-three airports. There are two airports in Stockholm—international and jet flights use Arlanda; most domestic flights, Bromma.

COMMUNICATIONS ¶ Sweden is one of those European countries that keep the kind of postal hours tourists like. The Stockholm main post office is open every day in the week, for instance, and this is a big convenience for the postcard-writing American tourist. Monday to Friday the hours are 8 A.M. to 9 P.M.; Saturday, 8 A.M. to 6 P.M.; and Sunday, 1 P.M. to 3 P.M. *Airmailing* a letter to the United States costs around a quarter. Telephone service is excellent, although you might need some practice to handle the single-unit Swedish telephone instrument with the dial at the lower end. Long distance *telephone* calls should be made either from your hotel room or from the official telephone bureau at or near the main post office in cities and towns. Because of the language problem, it is always best to write out the text of *telegrams* and *cables* —preferably type or at least print—and hand them either to the concierge or to the telegram clerk at the post office for transmission. Service is excellent.

MIDNIGHT SUN ¶ Lapland is an excellent place for viewing the midnight sun. Its appearance varies with the latitude—and so does its duration. Here is an approximate timetable to enable you to track it down: Mount Kebnekaise, May 22 to July 22; Karesuando, May 26 to July 17; Riksgransen, May 31 to July 17; Kiruna, May 31 to July 16; and Abisko, June 12 to July 4. At Abisko and

Kiruna the midnight sun lasts a full twenty-four hours. In other cities, from Stockholm on north, it varies from three-fourths of the full twenty-four-hour day to nearly twenty-four hours.

QUEEN OF LIGHT ¶ The reverse of the midnight sun coin and celebrating is St. Lucia's Day, December 13, when the Queen of Light is honored all over the country. She is the traditional symbol of good winning out over evil and of light over darkness. The timing of the fete is quite appropriate, because December is the darkest month of the year. Each town and city has its "Lucia." The Stockholm Lucia is, in effect, the Queen of Light for the country as a whole. The celebration is particularly lovely in private homes. One of the girls of the family is chosen as Lucia, and early on the morning of the Queen of Light's day she arises before everyone else and prepares breakfast in bed for her parents. The breakfast tray features specially shaped currant buns.

HOLIDAYS ¶ New Year's, Epiphany, Good Friday, Easter Monday, Labor Day (May 1), Ascension Day, Whit Monday, Midsummer Day (June 24), All Saints' Day, Christmas, and Boxing Day (day after Christmas).

SWEDEN AT HOME ¶ Like her neighbors in Denmark and Norway, Sweden has been operating a program by which it is possible for foreign visitors to meet Swedish families with similar interests. More than a thousand families in Stockholm, Göteborg and several other cities participate in this getting-to-know-you program and serve as volunteer hosts to overseas visitors. The program is being expanded, with particular emphasis on cities throughout the country, so as to help draw tourists away from Stockholm, which is near or at the capacity point in midsummer. The official tourist office in Stockholm—or in any major city of Sweden—will give you details about how the program works and how you can get yourself invited into a Swedish home for the evening. This can be a highlight of your entire visit!

BASIC SWEDISH

English-Swedish

Waiter: *Uppassare*
Bill of fare, menu: *Matsedel*
Napkin: *Servett*

Bread and butter: *Bröd och smör*
A glass or orange juice: *Ett glas apelsinsaft*
Boiled egg: *Kokt ägg*
1. soft: 1. *lökokt*
2. medium: 2. *medium*
3. hard-boiled: 3. *hårdkokt*
4. egg cup: 4. *äggkopp*
Fried eggs: *Stekta ägg*
Bacon and eggs: *Bacon och ägg*
Coffee, black: *Kaffe utan grädde*
Coffee with cream and sugar: *Kaffe med grädde och socker*
Tea: *Te*
Water: *Vatten*
Ice Water: *Isvatten*
Mineral water: *Mineralvatten*
Breakfast: *Frukost*
Lunch: *Lunch*
Dinner: *Middag*
Shampoo: *Shamponering*
Haircut: *Hårklippning*
Manicure: *Manikyr*
I want . . . liters of petrol: *Jag vill ha . . . litter bensin*
Change the oil: *Byt olja*
Grease the car: *Rundsmörj vagnen*
How are you?: *Hur mår ni?*
Fine, thank you: *Tack, bra*
Please: *Var så god*
Thank you very much: *Tack så mycket*
Good morning: *God morgon*
Good afternoon: *God middag*
Good night: *God natt*
Yes: *Ja, Jo*
No: *Nej*
Morning: *Morgon*
Noon: *Middag*
Afternoon, P.M.: *Eftermiddag,* E.M.
Evening: *Afton*
Night: *Natt*
Sunday: *Söndag*
Monday: *Måndag*
Tuesday: *Tisdag*
Wednesday: *Onsdag*
Thursday: *Torsdag*
Friday: *Fredag*
Saturday: *Lördag*
One: *Ett*
Two: *Två*
Three: *Tre*
Four: *Fyra*
Five: *Fem*
Six: *Sex*
Seven: *Sju*
Eight: *Åtta*
Nine: *Nio*
Ten: *Tio*
Twenty: *Tjugo*

Thirty: *Trettio*
Forty: *Fyrtio*
Fifty: *Femtio*
One hundred: *Hundra*
One thousand: *Ett tusen*

ELECTRICITY ¶ In Stockholm and most of the country, 220 A.C. is the usual current, which means your appliances will not operate without a transformer; don't even experiment or you may burn out the appliance. Some of the larger hotels have transformers that you may borrow and use during your stay. When traveling in the outlying regions, make local inquiry, because 110 A.C. current is now being installed. However, because of the difference in cycles (the Swedes use 50 cycles whereas most American appliances are intended for 60 cycles), anything with a timer, such as an electric clock or phonograph, will still not operate properly. In addition, you'll need a special type of converter plug; however, if you bring the type of insert that is screwed into a lamp socket, you can use your regular appliance plug by inserting it into the lamp socket insert.

FOOD SPECIALTIES AND LIQUOR ¶ Let's begin with the meal hours. Breakfast (*frukost*) is often a large meal at resort hotels; in Stockholm, the custom is to have a continental breakfast of rolls, butter and jam and coffee with hot milk (although you can get eggs if you wish). The Swedish custom is to have a large glass of cold milk with breakfast, but no one will force you to drink it.

Breakfast is taken anytime from 8 A.M. to 11 A.M. in general, while lunch can start as early as 11 A.M. or as late as 4 P.M. But somewhere around 2 or 2:30 P.M. is usually the cutoff hour. Restaurants traditionally start serving lunch at noon on weekdays and at 1 P.M. on Sunday. Unlike other countries, there really are no fixed meal hours in Swedish restaurants. You can get a meal anytime—and it is up to you to decide what to call it.

Many people just have the traditional open sandwiches for lunch and the usual number is three. Select something with fish first, then meat and, finally, if you can manage it, cheese. As an alternative, you might have a selection from the hors d'oeuvre table (if there is one), which, as you know, is called *smörgåsbord* in Sweden. Unfortunately, the custom of serving dozens of appetizer items from which you make your selection is (and has been) disappearing from the local scene; this is a great mistake and should be immediately rectified by the Swedish tourist office, because it is one of the most interesting Swedish food customs. If you are fortunate enough to dine at a restaurant featuring smorgasbord, the proper etiquette to observe involves three trips to the table; your first plateful, by tradition, is fish and certainly one of the various herring dishes with some new potatoes if you're here in early summer; second, meat items like sliced ham or pork; and (gasp!) on your third visit, try the hot food in the chafing dish, plus one or two (or three!) of the cheeses. Many people go on to eat a large main course, the *varmrätt*, but the faint-hearted can stop before this point.

As a compromise, it has become the custom for a restaurant to serve a simple assortment of items from the smorgasbord, so that you don't have to get up to make your own selection; this service is called the *assietter* and consists of, say, a half dozen items, such as herring, sardines, cheese and a pickled salad. The more elaborate variety served in the better (meaning more expensive) restaurants is known as *delikatessassietter* (a mouthful in more ways than one); this should have a more varied selection and include shrimp, smoked salmon and several cheeses.

The official hours for dinner are from 5 to 8 P.M., but it can start as early as 4 P.M. You, of course, can eat after 8 P.M.—until midnight, as a general rule. But after 8 P.M. the dinner becomes "supper," and this quite frequently means a hike in prices. We're talking about Stockholm and the major cities. If you are off in Lapland or elsewhere in the countryside it will be a good idea to check about the local eating hours, especially in small resort hotels. You might have to go to bed hungry, otherwise, because the dining room might be closed when you turn up.

If you're invited to someone's home for dinner, arrive almost on the minute and expect to have dinner served shortly thereafter. Cocktails are not the general custom in Sweden, and there is, of course, usually no cocktail hour, but *snaps* will be provided, you may be assured. At a dinner, there is the problem of the *skål* (pronounced skawl). Don't take a drink until the host raises his glass and pronounces the magic word; thereafter, if you wish to drink, look someone in the eye (preferably of the opposite sex), say, "*Skål,*" and then you may drink. After the dinner, be sure to shake the hands of the host and hostess and say, "*Tack för maten,*" which means "Thanks for the food"; although it may sound archaic, it's good manners and should not be overlooked.

Now, how about *liquor*?: The national beverage is a clear, whitish liquor called *snaps,* also called *brännvin,* also called *aquavit.* In any event, it's a powerful drink somewhat like a vodka or dry gin—which means, in plain language, powerful. The alcoholic content varies from 40 percent to 46 percent; that should make it clear that one does not trifle with *snaps* or *brännvin* or *aquavit.* The various manufacturers put up their product with an assortment of spices and herbs: O.P. and Skåne (caraway taste), Överste (somewhat sweet), Angostura (made with Angostura bitters), Ödåkra (lightly spiced) and Taffel (without spices). *Snaps,* by law, may be served only with food, and something (at least a sandwich) must be ordered or liquor cannot be served.

Beer is quite good here, which is only natural because the salty smorgasbord cries out for beer. The most common types are pilsner, lager and pale ale, all with 3 percent alcohol; there is also a stronger beer with 4.5 percent content called "Export."

One of the happy surprises in the alcoholic beverage situation in Sweden is the presence of fine French wines at low prices—or, at least, a lot lower than you would expect to spend in this country that is such a long way from France's Rhone valley. There is a good reason for this. Sweden has a government-sponsored program to discourage the drinking of hard liquor. It therefore buys a very large amount of wine from French growers. Because Sweden is a major buyer of French wine, it gets both good wines and good prices. A bottle of a reasonably good Bordeaux wine, for example, will sell in Sweden for $1.50 or $1.75, whereas a bottle of locally made aquavit will cost about $5.50 and a bottle of Scotch close to $9. Sweden once had its share of crazy liquor laws, but restrictions on the sale of bottled liquor have been modified in recent years. The state-controlled liquor stores, called Nya Systemaktiebolaget (imagine saying that when you've had a couple of drinks!), are open daily except Sundays. Restaurants licensed to serve liquor can make it available starting at noon during the week and at 1 P.M. on Sundays.

Note: If you ask someone to direct you to the nearest bar, you are likely to wind up in a light-lunch place, cafeteria or establishment that specializes in milk and dairy products. Coffee is usually the strongest beverage available in a bar, but some of them do serve a light beer. For an establishment that has alcoholic drinks you should seek out a cocktail bar. Just to confuse this confusing situation a little more, we might point out that a *Konditori* is a pastry shop where you can have a cup of tea or coffee and a piece of cake. But in some of them, port and sherry are also on the bill of fare.

One of the great dining experiences of a European journey can be had from a waterfront position at the Opera House in Stockholm. In the opera building is the Operakällaren, a series of restaurants that Tore Wretman, the royal caterer, has made into what is probably Sweden's top place with a view to dine. Just across the Norrström, a section of the Baltic, is the royal castle. The masterpiece at the Verandah Restaurant of the Operakällaren is the noontime smorgasbord. It is as sumptuous, as immense and as varied as any in the civilized world. Wretman has what is said to be the second largest collection of menus in the world, and some of the items in his possession are in suitable frames on walls of passageways and corridors on the premises. He also has what is believed to be the second largest collection of cookbooks. (At least, there seem to be an awful lot of them in his office library.)

WHAT TO EAT IN SWEDEN

Sillssallad: Herring salad made with potatoes, apples and beets
Inkokt strömming: Pickled fresh sardines or smelts
Ärter med fläsk: Split-pea soup served with slices of pork
Kokt lax: Poached salmon prepared with dill
Gravad lax: Marinated salmon
Fiskbullar: Boiled fish balls, usually served with a sauce
Kräftor: Crayfish, a great specialty during August
Grytstek: A type of Swedish pot roast
Plommonspäckad fläskkarré: Roast loin of pork stuffed with prunes
Köttbullar: Meatballs, usually served with a cream sauce
Kokt rödkål: Red cabbage, usually served in a sweet-sour sauce
Sjömansbiff: Beef stew, often prepared with beer
Frikadeller: Meatballs, usually made with ground pork and veal
Kroppkakor: Potato dumplings stuffed with pork

Applekaka med vaniljsås: Swedish applecake with vanilla sauce
Pannkakor med sylt: Pancakes with jam; a Thursday favorite
Plättar: Small Swedish pancakes
Fattiga Riddare: Like French toast, served with jam
Frasvåfflor: Small waffles usually sprinkled with powdered sugar
Filbunke: Cold sour milk, often eaten with sugar
Kaffekaka: Coffee cake made with nuts and raisins; a local specialty

The principal touring areas are Stockholm, the lake district beginning with Göteborg and the far north country, including Lapland.

Capital City

Stockholm, a city of about 800,000, is undoubtedly one of the world's handsomest cities in its own quiet, unassuming fashion. With none of the flamboyance of Rome, the grace of Madrid, the almost theatrical magnificence of Paris, Stockholm has dignity (almost solemnity) and great physical beauty.

Originally founded as a fortress area to control the narrowing waterways, which it heads, the city has grown up somewhat haphazardly over the centuries on a series of islands—fourteen, to be exact. Stockholm has a remarkable feeling of breadth and freshness, due in part to its physical setting and the groupings of small islands that are joined by a series of interlocking bridges. This city has been called "the Venice of the North" (which it isn't in the slightest). The other travel folder name of "the City on the Water" at least has the merit of partial justification.

There are none of the broad boulevards of some continental cities here in Stockholm, unless you include—and correctly—the expansive, dramatic waterways. Views from the waterfront are excellent, such as the one from the opera building. The great point for viewing is from the southern island of Stockholm (Söder), which is across from the old town. An eight-story elevator, the Katarina, is at the edge of the Söder waterfront. The elevator is enclosed in a shaft that is independent from neighboring buildings, but once you get to the top floor, an open bridge seventy-five or so feet long connects to the office building of the Co-Operative Society headquarters. The Co-Op building has an inside elevator that is free—there is a small fee for the outer one—but taking it robs you of the chance of walking across the open ramp at the top and of getting a top-flight view of the city—looking out across Lake Mälaren at the City Hall, the Pantheon and all the church towers and steeples. It is a great panorama! From this distance, the City Hall looks more than ever like the Doges Palace at Venice. Atop the City Hall is a resplendent symbol, three gold-leafed crowns, which have inspired a local joke: There is a restaurant in the City Hall, and Stockholm people (when talking about eating prices to visitors) will say: "That's the only place in town where you can eat under three crowns." Speaking about eating, there is an interesting restaurant underneath the ramp connecting the Katarina elevator with the Co-Op building. The restaurant is suspended underneath the walkway like a gondola, and of course the viewing is fantastic. It possibly follows, too, that the food at the restaurant is only so-so. In case you are in the mood for a bit of walking when you finish your viewing from the Katarina elevator ramp, you can walk up the mountain street on the island of Söder (the largest of Stockholm's fourteen islands) and see some picturesque cottages and small houses in which artists live. It is a lovely section of town, and you would not realize that you are just a few miles from the center of Stockholm. There is also an excellent view of the Salt Lake from the roadway at the top of the hill. Unfortunately, the antique lampposts along the streets here are now fitted with electricity, and there is no evening lamplighter. Just the same, the whole setting is rather agreeable and soothing.

There is no single place or street in the city that is the hub of activity or a natural landmark that everyone knows instinctively and without question. The closest approach to this is Gustav Adolf Square, not far from the Grand Hotel and adjacent to the Royal Opera House. From this square, the nearest thing to a central starting point, cross the bridge onto Helgelandsholmen Island; on your right hand is the Riksdagshuset, the Parliament Building—large, imposing and extraordinarily dull. Just forget it and keep walking straight ahead onto the next island to reach the Royal Palace, whose style may be described as a reasonably homogeneous blend of French-Italian-Baroque-Swedish architecture, which is not said condescendingly, but as a fact. No one knows for sure how many rooms the place contains, although a reasonable guess of the number is just slightly under or over 600; this doubt is understandable, for after all, is a dining alcove entitled to be considered as a half-room or complete room? If the court is not in residence, visitors are permitted to wander through portions of the palace; from May through September usually from 10 to 3 weekdays, 1 to 3 Sundays.

After browsing through the Royal Palace, you'll probably agree that it is the biggest palace in existence still inhabited by a royal family. Incidentally, even if the king is not in residence at the time of your visit, please do not ask to see his living quarters. That part of the palace is out of bounds to visitors. The great spectacle at the Royal Palace is the changing of the guard. The ceremony is at 12:15 P.M. on Wednesday and Saturday and 1:15 P.M. on Sunday.

Behind the palace, you'll see the spires of the thirteenth-century *Storkyrkan* ("The Great Church"). King Gustav VI Adolf attends Sunday services there at 11 A.M. and sits in an ordinary pew, although there are special gilded chairs that are used on royal occasions. The church is open daily from 10 A.M. to 6 P.M. Among the interesting objects of art is the famous "St. George and the Dragon" wood carving of 1489. Right across the street from "The Great Church" is an inexpensive coffee shop that dates back to the fourteenth century. It is a fine place for a cup of coffee and a piece of cake to tide you over (until lunch or dinner). You first pick out the pastry you want, then serve yourself from a coffee pot on a big table in the middle of the room. Downstairs is a very interesting cave that is worth exploring.

Just a minute's walk down a narrow alley brings you to the Stortorget, the original main square of old Stockholm; here some bloody deeds have taken place, chiefly the murder of the Swedish nobility by Christian II of Denmark in 1520. On the opposite side of this gracious old square is the German Church; immediately behind the church is the heart of the old town, undoubtedly the most fascinating part of Stockholm for the tourist who dotes on the quaint and antique. Wander about at random, poking your head into courtyards, walking into alleys, visiting antique shops and drifting just as your mood dictates. Buy a little something here, have a cup of coffee at a *konditori*, a pastry shop; be sure to look for the narrowest street in old town, the Måren Trotzigs Gränd, measuring a bare forty inches at its widest point.

Stockholm's City Hall, the Stadshuset, is something that every tourist should see; leave Gustav Adolf Square (your previous point of departure) and walk to the right along the waterfront until you see the towers of the City Hall (built 1923–1932). Modern architects and designers have lavished praise on it, but some find fault with its barren surfaces.

In any event, the City Hall is generally regarded as a superb example of contemporary architecture, and its Golden Hall, or Salon, is extraordinarily colorful. The Nobel (Peace Prize) dinner is held in the Golden Hall. The doorway to it from the Three Crowns Room, by the way, consists of sliding doors, each weighing a ton. The reason they slide so smoothly back and forth is because (naturally) of the (Swedish) ball bearings. The Blue Room at the entrance to the City Hall is very striking: it looks like a huge Oriental courtyard. Because of Sweden's weather the upper part is covered with a roof, yet this is so high that you are not particularly aware of it. There is a guided tour of the City Hall daily at 10 A.M. and on Sunday at 10 A.M. and at noon. But at any travel bureau you can hire a licensed guide and visit the City Hall at any time. The general admission fee is small.

Another interesting spot is the National Museum, on the promontory near the Grand Hotel, which has a rather good collection of Swedish artists, both classical and contemporary.

A reasonably short taxi ride from the center of town brings you to Skansen, Stockholm's unique open-air museum, which in a vivid, interesting way provides an idea of Swedish customs and the way of life in bygone days. Complete buildings, including a manor house, have been lifted bodily from various parts of the country and brought to Skansen Village. One farmhouse was built in 1786 in the village of Bollnässtugan, in the county of Hälsingland. Skansen celebrated its seventy-fifth anniversary in 1966, so it itself is quite an old-timer. The village is spread out on seventy-five acres. There are many attractions—a museum, a zoo, a theater, outdoor concerts, dancing and several restaurants and outdoor cafeterias. The Yellow Room is particularly wonderful for evening dining because of the splendid view of the harbor and the central part of Stockholm. Dinner in the

Yellow Room (with dancing) is only about $5. In other restaurants at Skansen Village you can eat for $2 or so. The entrance fee to Skansen Village is lower in the winter than it is in the summer. To our way of thinking, Skansen is the ideal place to spend a few aimless, unplanned hours.

Stockholm has one outstanding tourist attraction, the salvaged seventeenth-century vessel *Wasa*. It is at the water's edge, a few hundred yards from Skansen, in a museum that has been built around it. The *Wasa*, a 1,400-ton vessel, was built during 1626–1628 in shipyards where the Grand and Strand hotels are now located, but it didn't have a very proud career. It capsized in the harbor on its maiden voyage, in 1628, when a sudden squall came up while it was en route to a naval base in the archipelago. The ship was found at the bottom of the harbor in 1956 and raised in 1961. It was put on exhibit almost immediately. To prevent the wooden hull from splintering and powdering away if it dried out prematurely, the vessel is sprayed continuously while a conservation process is being carried out. There is the sound of dripping water—and the sight—as if in an underground labyrinth of mineral springs, and the general dampness is worthy of a subtropical hothouse. But all this helps to make everything more realistic. A total of 14,000 catalogued items have already been recovered from the ship, and others are still being searched for. The recovered items range from a gold ring to a wooden lion that weighs a ton and a half. A study is being made of a new location for the *Wasa* and its museum, because the vessel, now that its bow and stern have been restored, is a bit too long for its quarters. In the summer it can be visited between 10 A.M. and 8 P.M. (in winter, till 5 P.M.). Every hour a film is presented, and a guided tour is conducted every half-hour. The admission fee is 3 kronor, and this includes the film showing and the guided tour. If you would like to have a special guide who will take you through the exhibit hall, the fee is 5 kronor. There is a nice *konditori* at the museum, which serves sandwiches, beer, milk and coffee, as well as several warm dishes.

Not far from Skansen is Rosendal Palace in Djurgården, a former royal summer palace built about 1820; the handsome interior is open weekdays from 11 to 4 and Sundays from 1 to 4. Even more interesting is the Pavilion of Gustav III in Haga Park, dating back to around 1790; open weekdays 12–4, Sundays 1–4.

The classic excursion from Stockholm involves a visit to Drottningholm, the summer home of the king of Sweden, beautifully located on a tiny island in Lake Mälaren; the easiest way to get there is by car or taxi, (about twenty minutes), or if you're romantic, take the little boat in front of the City Hall, a most pleasing forty-five minute ride. Just as Stockholm is erroneously called "The Venice of the North," so is Drottningholm called "The Versailles of Stockholm," and wouldn't you know it, Drottningholm isn't that either. There are lovely gardens, a theater museum, a Chinese pavilion, statues and lots of interesting and not so interesting things; open to the public when the royal family is not in residence, from 11 to 5 weekdays, 1 to 5 Sundays. Make inquiry about performances given in the old court theater: most of the shows are modernizations of the original works performed when this theater was at its height of fashion. This is something theater-lovers surely will not want to miss, and your hotel porter or concierge can make the necessary inquiries and arrange for tickets and transportation.

ஃ Excursion by Boat

One of the delights of Stockholm is in taking boat trips to places of comparatively small sightseeing importance, merely for the pleasure of the ride. Such a destination is Vaxholm, a miniature resort town in what is called the "Stockholm Archipelago," or if you wish to practice up on your Swedish, the Skärgården. Take the tiny steamer from the pier in front of the Grand Hotel (there are usually several sailings daily during the summer months) for an extremely enjoyable trip through the small charming islands of the archipelago, reaching Vaxholm in about an hour or so. The same trip can be made by car or rail-bus from Östra Station, but what would be gained when the pleasure lies in the journey more than the destination? At Vaxholm, there's the Hotel Vaxholms, with a quite good restaurant; the tiny town consists of a beach, a few shops and a miniature fortress, but it's the boat ride that makes all worthwhile.

Another possibility is Sandhamn, a summer resort with

a nice hotel; however the boat (also leaving from the pier near the Grand Hotel) takes three hours each way.

Of course, while on the subject of boat rides, everyone should take a trip called "Under Stockholm's Bridges," through the various canals, by way of and through the locks; departures every hour on the hour between 10 A.M. and 7 P.M. (May 19—September 15) from Karl XII Square, not far from the Grand Hotel and taking about two and one-half hours. Another boat trip leaving from this pier is the Royal Canal Tour, which goes through Stockholm's Baltic Sea entrance, cruises around Djurgården and the various piers and embankments; trips leave every hour from noon until dusk (May 1 to September 30) and take about an hour or so.

Beginning July 1, there is an all-day boat trip to Gripsholm, the renowned royal castle, with its rich collections and many fine historical portraits; boats leave from the Tourist Pavilion (near City Hall) on Sundays, Tuesdays, Thursdays, Fridays and Saturdays at 10 A.M., returning in the evening.

Short Trips

A day's trip to the university town of Uppsala is ideal for the visitor who doesn't plan to make an extended automobile tour through the country. Uppsala may be reached in slightly over an hour by train from the Central Station; in about one hour by automobile (forty-five miles via route 13); or by boat from Klara Strand, the pier in front of the City Hall, in about three to four hours. The last would involve an overnight stay in Uppsala. The wonderful old university town consists of two parts, the old and the new, both extremely interesting. The high spots include the famous fifteenth-century cathedral with tremendous spires, the Uppsala University buildings, campus and student body (who stage a marvelous festival on April 30, Walpurgis Eve), the combination Bishop's Palace and Museum of Archaeology called the Gustavianum, the University Library and sixteenth-century Uppsala Castle. Everyone will want to visit Gamla Uppsala, old Uppsala, about two miles north of the present city, where there are three royal burial mounds of the kings of the Yngve (yes, that's right) going back to the sixth century or earlier. There is also a ruined pagan temple dedicated to the god Wotan. Visit the inn at nearby

Odinsborg, where visitors drink that classic beverage of heroes, mead.

Visby is on Gotland Island, south of Stockholm; for those who like medieval towns, this easily may be the high spot of a trip to Sweden. Visby was just about the most important trade center of northern Europe during the twelfth and thirteenth centuries; at its height of power, the townsfolk erected a wall around the city some two miles in circumference. The old town is a maze of narrow alleys, fine old homes, towers, ruined churches—all reminiscent of Carcassonne in France and (is this heresy?) possibly even more interesting. Not only Visby but the entire island of Gotland is worth exploring for the fascinating old ruins of the ancient civilization that once existed here. From Stockholm, Visby may be reached by frequent daily plane service taking about an hour. Alternative railroad-ferry route: trains leave Stockholm each evening for Nynäshamn, where connections are made for an overnight steamer trip, an extremely pleasant interlude in your rigorous sightseeing. During the last week in July and the first week in August, performances of a medieval pageant are given in the ruins of Visby. (Those who are touring Sweden by automobile may take the four-hour ferry trip from Oskarshamn, about 260 miles south of Stockholm.) In Visby itself the best hotel is the Stadshotellet, consisting partly of a new section and partly of a remodeled, centuries-old inn. Just three miles north of Visby is the delightful resort hotel Snackgardsbaden; very pleasant, comparatively few rooms with private bath; ask for one of the cottages facing the water.

The famous Sunlit Nights Land Cruise throughout Sweden, run by the Swedish State Railways, as well as some of the "coach cruises" available, are discussed in the section on Transportation.

ACCOMMODATIONS ¶ The hotel situation in Sweden is somewhat disappointing. To be brief, other than at resorts, there are only three really deluxe hotels in the entire country: the Grand and Sheraton in Stockholm and the Park Avenue Hotel in Göteborg. What's more, it often is extremely difficult to get reservations at these hotels—particularly the Grand. This is so not only in the summer but even in the middle of winter. But wherever you go in

Sweden, there need be no hesitation about making an overnight stay at any hotel, regardless of its external appearance. Private baths are frequently hard to get during the tourist season, but immaculate rooms, spotless linens and a general air of hospitality may always be anticipated. Many of the resort hotels are extremely comfortable and luxurious, and every possible service and convenience may be expected.

If you arrive in Stockholm without a reservation, be sure to phone the Hotellcentralen, telephone number 24-08-80, and they'll help you get located. Incidentally, they almost always have an English-speaking person answering the phone. Even better advice: Never come to Stockholm without a reservation.

STOCKHOLM HOTELS

Sheraton-Stockholm: The newest and best hotel in Stockholm, with 500 rooms, pleasantly decorated, with views of the river and Town Hall. Central location. Restaurants and shopping arcade; parking facilities underground.

Grand: Formerly the leading hotel in Stockholm; marvelous location facing the waterfront. Most rooms are of good size, attractively furnished; front rooms have an excellent view. Reservations are difficult to obtain during the tourist season.

Continental: A new hotel, very modern with attractive rooms, good restaurant. Centrally located near railroad station.

Foresta: An excellent new hotel, located slightly out of central Stockholm. Very good rooms, attractively furnished; rates are quite moderate for this type of hotel. Numerous restaurants, quite good food.

Apollonia: A new, very fine hotel in the center of town, convenient to everything. Extremely pleasant, nice size rooms, well furnished.

Strand: An older, traditional hotel with a very good reputation; front rooms face the water. Many rooms are pleasantly redecorated; others not quite so attractive.

Palace: A comparatively new hotel, located atop an office building and almost totally lacking in atmosphere. Rooms are fair sized, and this place is OK in an emergency.

Anglais: Very new and quite nice, situated on an important shopping street. Rooms are quite attractive, and the atmosphere tends to be quiet and sedate.

KAK Hotel: A small, pleasant hotel belonging to the Swedish Automobile Club; to obtain reservations, one must belong to an affiliated automobile club, such as the AAA. Nice rooms, good location.

Bromma: A new hotel, quite large. Caters to those seeking modern, low-priced accommodations. Rooms are average in size.

Carlton: An older hotel, recently modernized; slightly out of the center of town. More expensive rooms are quite attractive and of good size; others are more modest.

Gillet: A small hotel on a busy square; fairly good location for shopping and sightseeing. Rooms are slightly above average in size, traditionally furnished; not too many rooms have private baths.

Stockholm City: A hotel located on the top two floors of an office building. Rooms are fairly small; there is no dining room. Good for business people.

Amaranten: The largest hotel in Scandinavia—it has 380 beds. Opened in 1970.

STOCKHOLM RESTAURANTS

I feel it necessary to warn you that dining out, at least in the luxury class, in Stockholm is a very expensive proposition. It's difficult to generalize, but a good dinner is rarely less than $10 a person, and can easily run to $25 each if you're not cautious. Don't forget to phone for a reservation. Remember, too, that although a service charge is included, a small additional tip (say the equivalent of 50¢ or so) is expected.

Operakällären: This delightful place is located in the Opera House. It serves an outstanding smorgasbord at noon and on Sunday evening. Of course, you may also dine on weekday evenings, and it's excellent and expensive. Phone 11-11-25 for a reservation.

Riche and Teatergrillen: Two restaurants under the same ownership. Riche is First Class, deluxe and expensive; Teatergrillen features grilled meats, simpler atmosphere, lower prices.

Källaren Aurora: Located in a wine cellar in the old town; lots of atmosphere, candle light, rather good food with emphasis on Swedish specialties.

La Ronde: Excellent cuisine served in an extremely pleasant, sophisticated atmosphere; emphasis on fine food and good service. Closed June and July.

Trianon: Beautifully situated on a small island, features very good French dishes. Not expensive.

Strand Hotel Terrace: Glass-enclosed terrace overlooking the harbor; seafood is the specialty here, although Swedish and French items appear on the menu. Ask for a table near the windows.

Rotisserie Brunkeberg: A simple rotisserie room in front but a fine, large restaurant in the back; specialty is roast ribs of Angus beef imported from England.

Gyldene Freden: Loads of authentic (and also spurious) atmosphere in this cellar restaurant; fairly high prices.

Piperska Muren: A rather small, pleasant place featuring both French and Swedish dishes. Terrace dining during the summer; not inexpensive.

Sturehof: A simple restaurant with complete emphasis upon

good fish preparations, particularly fish soups and stews. Comparatively inexpensive; offers a very good value.

Frati's Källare: In the old town in the cellars dating from the 16th century; good food, mainly Italian-type, medium priced but the wines are very expensive.

Fem Små Hus: Nine small rooms in five small very old houses joined together into one restaurant; cosy enough for old and young; good food.

SUBURBAN DINING NEAR STOCKHOLM

Stallmästaregården: A charming country inn featuring smorgasbord, and very good indeed. Available at lunch only, plus all of Sunday afternoon. Moderately high.

Nackanäs Wärdshus: Good Swedish dishes in this attractive country restaurant facing the lake at Nacka; a recommended short excursion from Stockholm, particularly suitable for lunch. Very reasonable prices.

Djurgårdsbrunns Wärdshus: A charming dining spot located in the Deer Park alongside a canal. Deluxe, superior cuisine; high prices.

Balloptikon: A glassed-in restaurant with marvelous views located on the Stockholms-Tornet, the new TV-radio tower.

SHOPPING ¶ Stockholm makes shopping a pleasure in many ways. For instance, in the old town, the Västerlånggatan, a narrow street crammed with shops and boutiques, has been off-limits to automobiles for the last few years, and shoppers can stroll and window shop with great ease and with no distractions caused by auto traffic. The street is about a half-mile long, too. What is greatly appealing to all visitors is the fabulous Downtown Shopping Center, which has been established near the Haymarket area. The shopping zone is several blocks square, and although there are several garages for parking cars (one above ground, two below), cars are not allowed on the main shopping thoroughfare itself. The street itself slopes slightly, and the sides of it are not parallel. Also, from underneath, the surface of the street is heated in the wintertime. Thus, between the heating and the sloping, no ice or snow accumulates, and rain water runs off at once.

While you're in Sweden you'll have to visit one of the fabulous shopping centers. An ideal one, if you're in Stockholm, is Farsta, which was opened in 1960 and at the time was the biggest one in northern Europe. Farsta is only a twenty-minute subway ride from the center of Stockholm. The shopping center is ten miles from the Swedish capital and serves an area of 150,000 to 200,-

000 inhabitants. Around the shopping center a town of 35,000 inhabitants has been built, and they live in splendid modern apartment houses and villas. The Farsta shopping center sells *everything*. Stockholm's three big department stores, including N.K., are represented at the center. Altogether there are about thirty-five shops, and their wares range from toothbrushes to boats and automobiles. One of the many fascinating features of this $30 million center is that no surface traffic is permitted. All merchandise for the shops is delivered through underground passages. Just walking around the center, in the open air, is a pleasure. Speaking of pleasures, too, is the center's restaurant near the N.K. shop. There are a couple of luncheon specialties that we recommend. One of them is *tunna fläskpannkakor*, which are very thin pancakes with little pieces of meat. Make sure they are well done, however. Another specialty is the *ärtsoppa med fläsk*. This is pea soup with pieces of meat in it; it is traditional to serve this on Thursday. The Farsta shops are open daily except Sunday from 9 A.M. to 6 P.M. and on Saturday from 9 A.M. to 3 P.M. On Friday, they stay open till 8 P.M. This is definitely something to keep in mind. The late night for stores in Stockholm is Monday, while the suburban shopping centers are open on Friday evenings. During the latter part of 1968 the biggest of these "satellite shopping towns" was to be completed at Skärholmen, which is a little farther out. No subway serves that area as yet, but it is being extended so that there will be public transportation for Stockholm people —and visitors. Parking is no problem at Farsta, incidentally. There are parking places for 2,000 cars.

Prices for Swedish articles are frequently (but not always) somewhat higher than for similar things in Denmark, although tempting values are still offered to the canny shopper.

Swedish *glassware* is world famous. The Orrefors crystalware is so superb that it takes no courage to recommend unquestionably just about any item bearing this label. The bowls and vases, particularly those with modern cut designs, are prize winners at exhibitions all over the world; the tableware is not precisely cheap even here, but considerably lower than at home. Kosta crystal is so good that it suffers only by comparison with the craftsmanship of Orrefors.

Modern furniture and Swedish Modern are almost a

byword in interior decoration; there should be no doubts about shipping anything home, providing it's insured. However, be sure to inquire whether the pieces will be sent "knocked down" and require assembling; if so, reassembly may be troublesome unless the man of the house is extremely handy.

Stainless steel flatware is exceptionally well designed and because it is informal, makes ideal everyday tableware—and best of all, requires no polishing to keep its bright luster.

Silver is beautifully treated here, although in all fairness Denmark's workmanship and prices are very *slightly* better; if you're not visiting Denmark, the Swedish silver is highly recommended. If silver articles are purchased, request the customs form that entitles you to a 20 percent luxury tax saving, providing the items are sent out of Sweden; don't fail to remember this point.

Household furnishings of all sorts are smartly executed here, notably textiles, printed linens, modern carpeting, ceramics, hand-carved wooden articles, lamps, brass and copper chandeliers and similar articles.

Gift items, that thorn in the side of otherwise carefree tourists, are easily managed here. Suggestions: *costume jewelry*, particularly types with the classic design of three Swedish crowns on a blue background; decorative, hard ebony *coasters*; heat-proof *tiles*; anything in the *cutlery* and *gadget* department; oven-proof *casseroles*; ceramic and metal *cigarette boxes* and *ashtrays*; stainless steel *pitchers* and *drinking glasses*; small *leather* articles; reindeer *gloves* for men and women; ice and sugar *tongs*; the famous "Bohus" *sweaters* and *scarves*; Swedish *dolls* for little girls on your list. Had enough?

Pointer: Swedish store hours are from 9 A.M. to 6 P.M. five days a week. Most stores are beginning to close somewhat earlier in the day on Saturdays, starting at about 2 P.M. or possibly 3 P.M.

ENTERTAINMENT ¶ If you come during early June, it's hardly necessary to discuss entertainment, for the city is filled with shows, spectacles and worthwhile attractions. Otherwise Stockholm at night has all the unfettered excitement of Wichita, Kansas, during Lent. Until quite recently, by edict of the stern municipal authorities, Stockholm had no *night clubs*; in the interest of tourism, this ban has been relaxed to a degree and the city has begun to exhibit signs of coming awake (or at least not going to sleep) in the evening. In midtown Stockholm there is the China Variety Theater, with a fair group of variety acts in the old vaudeville tradition, something on the order of the Palladium in London, although not nearly so star-studded. Needless to say, *motion pictures* are very popular in this land that produced Greta Garbo and Ingrid Bergman. English-language films are often shown in their original version.

The Royal Dramatic Theater is extremely active and produces many fine *plays*, but if you don't speak Swedish, what then? No, we couldn't really recommend a visit to the regular legitimate theater under those circumstances. Exception: musical plays are quite bearable if one should happen to come across them. But if performances are being given at the restored Drottningholm Court Theater (the 200-year-old playhouse), don't fail to attend, because the shows are based upon the original plays and operas given during the period of the theater's original existence; as previously mentioned, your concierge or hall porter can arrange tickets and transportation.

Have you ever heard Shakespeare performed in Swedish? You haven't? Then visit the theater at Skansen and you'll be able to tell everyone about it when you come home. In this regard, Skansen is a sort of central area for amusements; just go and wander about at random, eating here, visiting there, seeing a show or hearing a concert as the mood strikes you. If the weather is pleasant, this is one of the nicest ways to have an evening of impromptu fun.

The Royal Opera begins performances near the end of August; if you do go, try to see something with Scandinavian atmosphere, such as *Peer Gynt*; the Royal Opera Ballet offers first-rate performances if you're lucky enough to be in town during the season.

SPORTS ¶ *Fishing* permits are required; most tourist hotels are authorized to issue them at a cost of approximately $1; salmon and sea trout are the best game fish. The vicinity of the River Mörrum is the best area for the big salmon. *Deep-sea* tuna fishing in the Göteborg district has become increasingly popular. *Hunters* out for moose usually do best in Jämtland, some 360 miles north of Stockholm; the license for elk is expensive. While *golfing* is a comparatively foreign sport here, Stockholm has four courses—Kevinge, Lindingö, Saltsjöbaden and Djursholm. Elsewhere throughout the country, there are links at Mölle, Båstad, Göteborg and Tylösand. You'll seldom have to look far for *tennis* courts, because almost all the larger resort hotels have them.

Winter sports are very popular here and it often seems as if everyone (over the age of three) in Sweden skis. In the northern portion of the country, practically every locality has some facilities, but nothing should be anticipated resembling the ski resorts of Norway, which apparently have a partial monopoly of winter sports in this region. The Swedish places offering the best accommodations and facilities are Åre, Vålådalen, Östersund and Storlien. There is *skiing* in Lapland during the late spring, if you're looking for an off-season novelty; the famous place here is Riksgränsen. A marvelous "sport" is *skijoring*, in which skiers, who carry (or should carry) accident insurance, are pulled by horses; don't try this unless you have no dependents and lots of hospitalization. *Ice-skating* rinks are plentiful and are located in parks and other easily accessible places. Skates also can be rented without any difficulty.

ᎨᏍ *A Tour of Sweden*

Stockholm to Linköping—131 miles

Leave Stockholm from the Tegelbacken, going over the bridge onto Stora Nygatan, reaching Karl Johans Square; keep right and head onto Hornsgatan, which will lead into route 1. The first town is the industrial center of Södertälje. Next comes Vagnhärad and then Nyköping; should you want to stay overnight, the Hotel Standard is a pleasant, cozy place. The most interesting local sightseeing spot is Nyköpingshus (Nyköping Castle), now in ruins, but still extremely beautiful.

Continue on through Åby to Norrköping, a textile and paper manufacturing town; here too the Hotel Standard is the best. Eight miles along the route, you'll see eighteenth-century Lövstad Castle, which has a fine collection of books and art treasures. Next comes Linköping (you'll have trouble keeping all your "köpings" straight); here the two important attractions are the cathedral (constructed during the thirteenth and fourteenth centuries)

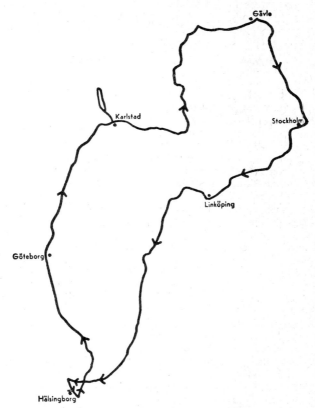

and the great castle with the Kungsträdgården, the King's Gardens. The largest hotel with the best accommodations is the Frimurarehotellet, close to the center of town.

Linköping to Hälsingborg—297 miles

Leave Linköping via route 210, passing, en route, Vreta Cloister, with its famous church and noted interior; then through Borensberg, which is on the Göta Canal; next comes Motala, which has a pleasant place to stay, the Stadshotellet. Here, you pick up route 8 heading southward near the east bank of serene (when it isn't rough) Lake Vättern to Vadstena, a small town that had an important history during the Middle Ages; this place, too, has a Stadshotellet for motorists who wish to remain overnight. Visit the Abbey Church and Vadstena Castle and walk through the picturesque streets of this quiet spot. The next town is Vaversunda, where bird lovers may hire a boat at the railway station for a trip to Lake Tåkern, a noted bird sanctuary; the best months for bird watching are May, September and October. Then to Alvastra, a resort town with a fine old Cistercian monastery; next comes Ödeshög, where a side trip of a few miles may be made to Rök Church, site of the Rök-stenen, the finest Runic stone (about ninth century) in Sweden and containing the longest Runic (which means old Scandinavian) inscription in the world.

From Ödeshög south on route 1, soon passing the ruins of Brahehus Castle, then to Gränna, famous for its pear trees, including a 300-year-old one; here you'll find the Gyllene Uttern, the absolutely charming Golden Otter Inn. Those who are spending time here might enjoy a boat excursion to Visingo Island, with noted ruins of a church and castle. Proceed on to Huskvarna, whose most interesting attraction is the Smedsbyn, the old part of town, very colorful and eye catching. Six miles farther along the south shore of the lake is Jönköping, famous for its match factories; places to stay at are the Store Hotellet and the Hotel Portalen. Sightseeing here should include the interesting Town Hall, the Gamla Värdshuset (the Old Inn) and the seventeenth-century Christine church. From here, there is a run of some forty-five miles through Vaggeryd, Skillingaryd and Värnamo, with a small folklore museum, the Apladen. Continue on alongside Lake Vidöstern into Lagan and Ljungby, which has the small and pleasing Stadshotellet, should you wish to stay overnight. Then through Traryd, Markaryd and Örkelljunga, where you make a right turn onto route 63 to Munka-Ljungby (now how do you pronounce that?); then to Ängelholm, a resort town with a fine public square, the Tinghusplatsen, the Palace of Justice Place. Continue on route 52 to beautifully located Mölle, where the sea meets Kullen Ridge; this whole region is absolutely magnificent, with irregular sea-worn grottoes and eroded caves; the Grand Hotel would be very nice indeed for a stay of a day or two. Leave Mölle via route 45 to Krapperup, site of a fine old estate with a sixteenth-century castle, moat and all the fairy-book trimmings; it's open for visits. On to Höganäs, a dull coal-mining town, through Viken, Kulla Gunnarstorp (another castle with moat to match may be seen nearby), then Sofiero, which is another of the King's summer homes; if possible try to be here from 1 to 2 P.M., when the beautifully landscaped grounds are open to the public. Next comes Hälsingborg, where the most interesting place to stay is the modernized Hotel Mollberg, whose history dates back some 300 years. The local sightseeing: St. Mary's Church (thirteenth century), the Kärnan (the remaining portion of what was once a fine castle); a drive out to Palajö, a nearby bathing resort. (Motorists leaving Sweden for a tour of Denmark will take the ferry here into Elsinore and pick up the appropriate portion of the Danish tour.)

Hälsingborg to Göteborg—149 miles

Leave Hälsingborg via route 1, which joins route 2 to Ängelholm. Fifteen miles along the way is the intersection with route 64. From here a left turn can be made to Båstad, a fine resort in a lovely setting and boasting of the truly charming Skånegården Hotel. Route 2 continues on to Laholm, whose leading sights are Lagaholm Castle and the quaint old part of town called Gamleby. Then to Halmstad, a seaport town. (An interesting side trip may be made by driving five miles to the west towards Tylosand Havsbad, a lovely beach and forested area; from here boats may be rented for a trip to the Tylö Islands, a sort of bird sanctuary with many medieval relics and Viking tombs.)

The road goes from Halmstad through Getinge, Slöinge and Falkenberg, a town with fascinating old streets, a ruined castle and a bridge across the River Ätran; here you'll find the Hotel Strandbaden. Then on to Varberg, guarded (very slightly) by fourteenth-century Varberg Fortress. In the fortress, there is a museum that contains the only completely preserved medieval costume, found on the so-called "Bocksten Man," a fully clothed body found in a peat bog. Continue along the coast through Åsa, Kungsbacka and Mölndal into Göteborg; here the outstanding hotel is the luxurious Park Avenue, undoubtedly Sweden's best and most elaborate establishment.

Göteborg, or Gothenburg, is an important city of almost 400,000, although because of its size, industry and comparative youth (only 300 years old), it can scarcely match Stockholm in tourist interest. But don't leave without doing some sightseeing: the Götaplatsen, the large centrally located square; the old town, with its fine old buildings, teetering on the edges of canals; the many museums of the city; Maritime Art, Arts and Crafts, Göteborg Oceanographic Institute. Don't miss a trip to Liseberg Amusement Park, with its restaurants, rides, attractions and concerts. There is a very pleasing tour on the old waterways through the canals and moats; boats leave hourly from 9 to 3 from Kungsportsbron. Another boat trip leaves hourly from 10 to 3 from Lilla Bommen, touring the archipelago and taking about one and one-quarter hours. During July and August, there are evening cruises on a large liner through the magnificent Bohuslän Archipelago off Sweden's west coast; departures on Tuesdays and Thursdays at 5:15 P.M., returning at 11 P.M. A new tourist attraction was added in 1971 when the seventeenth-century fortress on Nya Aelvsborg Island outside Gothenburg harbor was opened to the public. Special excursion boats take you there; the package deal includes the boat fare, a self-service lunch, and an eighteenth-century-style dinner in the evening.

Göteborg to Karlstad—161 miles

Leave Göteborg via route 7; the road passes through many large industrial installations, and some thirty-five miles later you reach Lilla Edet, where it is interesting to take a look at the old and new locks on the Göta Canal. Then Trollhättan, which has the pleasant Stadshotellet for those seeking an overnight stop; the leading attraction here is the enormous hydroelectric power station, which is open to visitors interested in hydroelectric power. Then to Vänersborg, famous (for reasons best known to itself) for the tremendous collection of African birds in its museum. The road proceeds on the west side of gracious Lake Vänern, although its beauty is soon lost to view, passing through Mellerud and then Köpmannebro, where the Dalsland Canal runs into Lake Vänern. Then Åmål, Säffle (the burial spot for the ancient hero, Olof Träjälja) and, shortly afterward, the village of Grums, the juncture with route 9; take a right turn to Karlstad, where the Stadshotellet is an extremely pleasant, almost luxurious hotel.

Karlstad is the point where motorists from Norway join the trip through Sweden, coming from Norway via Kongsvinger and Arvika, and Swedish route 232. This pleasant town has an open-air museum with an exhibition of folk and peasant arts.

Karlstad is also the starting point for an optional excursion to the Fryken Lakes; drive north via 232, then pick up route 234 to Sunne, returning by an unnumbered road along the eastern shore of Lake Fryken. Possibly even more pleasant is the steamer trip; drive north from Karlstad via route 232 to Kil and then proceed a few miles farther along to Frykstra, where the boats leave for Sunne (two and a half hours) or Torsby (five hours). If you should voyage to Sunne and want to stay overnight, there is the modest but pleasing Hotel Nilson.

Karlstad to Gävle—251 miles

Leave Karlstad via route 9 to Kristinehamn, facing onto the lake; then to Karlskoga, a manufacturing town of only routine interest, specializing in steelwork. A run of twenty-nine miles brings you into Örebro; here the Stora Hotellet is recommended. Sightseeing: Nikolai Church; the Kungsstugen, a sixteenth-century wooden building; the historic castle, with its moat, ramparts and museum.

Leave Örebro via route 10 toward Ervalla and Lindesberg, handsomely situated on Lake Lindessjön. Continue on through Guldsmedshyttan, Kopparberg, Grängesberg and Ludvika, which has a pleasant hotel, the Stadshotellet. (A beautiful side trip could be made from Ludvika by circling lovely Lakes Vasman and Bysjön, via Brunnsvik.) Leave Ludvika for Gräsberg and Borlänge, where you'll find the somewhat modest Hotel Saga. Next comes the important town of Falun, where a stay could be made at either the Stadshotellet or the larger Grand. The most interesting sights include the 700-year-old copper mine of the Bergslag Company (the oldest in the world, with a charter going back to 1437, given by none other than King Magnus Erikson), plus the mining museum.

Leave Falun via route 10 through Korsnäs, Hofors, Storvik, Ovansjö (which has an interesting medieval church) and Sandviken, a progressive steel community. Then through Forsbacka to Gävle, situated on both sides of the River Gävlean. The northern portion of the city is quite modern; the south bank has quaint old buildings. The most interesting sights are the Town Hall, the Church of the Holy Trinity and the sixteenth-century castle, known for its collection of portraits; should you wish to stay overnight, the Grand-Central-Hotellet seems to be the best.

Gävle to Stockholm—111 miles

The road goes on via route 13 to Furuvik, a seaside spot, then through Skutskär and Marma into Uppsala, the famous university town. To get settled, because you'll probably want to stay overnight, nothing could be more pleasant than the Hotel Rullan. Although the accommodations are simple, the Hotel Gillet is fairly good, too. Sightseeing: the university buildings and student body; fifteenth-century cathedral; the bishop's palace-museum called the Gustavianum; sixteenth-century Uppsala Castle. Be sure to visit Gamla Uppsala, the site of old Uppsala, with its famous burial mounds dating back to the sixteenth century.

Leave Uppsala via route 13 toward Alsike, soon thereafter reaching the junction with route 263, where a right turn may be made for a four-mile side trip to Sigtuna, a fascinating ancient village, which was once very important in the medieval world. Wander about the Stora Gatan, the narrow main street, and see the renowned old church and its murals; the ruins of various churches; the old Town Hall.

Continuing on route 13, you go through Märsta and into Stockholm.

Pointer: If you want to drive in Finland, there is a fine ferry service leaving from Norrtälje (forty-three miles northeast of Stockholm). The boats are very modern, the trip is extremely pleasant, the food is good and there are motion pictures and other distractions to amuse one. The trip takes about eight hours and lets you and your car off at Turku (Åbo), 109 miles from Helsinki.

ह Motoring in Sweden

Back in the late sixties highway traffic in Sweden shifted from the left-hand side of the road to the right. Nowadays, only Ireland and England remain with the driving-on-the-left custom—in Europe, that is.

To bring your car (or a rented one) into Sweden, all you need is its registration papers, a Green Card certifying that there is insurance coverage and your home-state or an international driver's license.

Gasoline is relatively expensive.

In general, there is no speed limit. However, in built-up areas you are not allowed to drive faster than 50 kms. (31 m.p.h.). Also, on some really busy summer weekends, highway traffic might be limited to 90 kms. or 100 kms.—about 55 to 62 m.p.h.

The most important main roads are well paved, fast and first rate. Many of the side or country roads are somewhat less satisfactory, with considerable mileage having only gravel or stone surface. Incidentally, when entering onto a major road from a minor road, it is essential for the motorist to come to a dead stop and wait until it is safe before turning.

That bane of motorists has hit Sweden—parking meters, although only in a few of the larger towns. Elsewhere, parking places are indicated by blue signs with the letter "P"; if a line is drawn through the "P," that means no parking. In Stockholm, there is parking on alternate sides of the street, depending upon whether the date of the month is odd or even; watch the other cars and be guided by them.

A round red metal disc with a horizontal yellow bar indicates "no entry," that is, a one-way street in the opposite direction (against you). Other one-way markers are usually indicated with directional arrows, which shouldn't be too confusing.

Swedish motorists are conservative and courteous as a rule; none of the dash of the Gallic driver, nor the wildness of the Portuguese. There is very little horn-blowing except in cases of emergencies; in cities, you might get a ticket for unnecessary noise.

The driving of a motor vehicle after drinking alcohol is seriously regarded here. If you are involved in an automobile accident, *regardless of whose fault it is*, you must submit to an examination and if your blood stream carries more than a very slight permissive amount, you will automatically receive a jail sentence if found guilty. Swedish motorists who plan to have more than *one* drink hire a driver or take a taxi in preference to the risk involved. This is extremely important, so do not disregard this point.

Between Göteborg and Stockholm is the 350-mile Göta Canal, a favorite with tourists; much of the trip is not through the canal but across lakes and down rivers, even venturing into the Baltic. The trip lasts two nights and three days, is usually booked well in advance and the meals served are fairly good. (Those who cannot spare the time or lack the patience for a complete three-day trip might enjoy going from Göteborg to Trollhättan by boat and returning by rail.)

The canal trip is an ideal way for all except motorists to get from Göteborg to Stockholm; if you want to make the trip, nevertheless, the steamship line has a combination fare including one-way steamer passage and return by air or train. Incidentally, the trip is just as easily managed in reverse from Stockholm to Göteborg.

About the voyage itself: cabins are tiny, very tiny, and there are no private baths. It's a slow trip and restless people might find three days of ambling along at a snail's pace just too much for them; others will be enchanted. There are sixty-five locks to pass through, and after you've seen a dozen—or two dozen—well, the novelty does wear off. On the other hand, it's a wonderful opportunity to see the lovely countryside, talk to some Swedish people and fellow tourists, relax and have a perfect rest. At many points, it's possible to go ashore for a half-hour or so while the boat is passing through the locks.

Here are some figures to keep in mind: from Stockholm to Göteborg it is 300 miles; to Hälsingborg, 349; to Malmö, 386.

SWITZERLAND

National Characteristics

This is a very old example of the kind of democracy where the votes of individuals settle all sorts of questions from a new sewer to an increase in the federal defense budget. The voting procedure is solemn and decisive, and in certain areas (such as Appenzell), it is spectacularly ceremonial, with the voters assembling in the main square and raising their hands publicly to cast their ballots. In short, it is all very democratic. What raises eyebrows among some visitors, however, is the news that women do not as yet have much of a voice in all this voting. In some parts of the country only men have the vote in certain elections. Women—according to the men—do not want to bother about voting. They have enough to do as it is, many men (and not a few women!) firmly believe. It is one of the many aspects of the Swiss and their country that will intrigue you and give rise to much conversation and private thoughts.

Switzerland's founding was on August 1, 1291—a very long time ago. The Swiss national day is only a half-holiday, but on the third Sunday of September there is a federal Thanksgiving, Repentance and Prayer Day, which was determined by the federal council in the nineteenth century. It is like an old-fashioned English Sunday. Everything is closed. The day is set aside for giving thanks to God for having spared the Swiss from wars.

The nation and her people have much to be thankful for. You'll run out of superlatives, or at least chatter along in clichés when you expound upon the scenery of Switzerland, the cleanliness and brightness of everything from a hotel room to the passageway in a railroad train and the ingenious, resourceful way the Swiss have for providing solutions to everyday problems even before they arise. For years, to furnish an example, traffic policemen in Zurich have been experimenting with the use of a closed-circuit television system to counsel them on shepherding trams and cars around "blind" corners. Railroad stations provide change dispensers so that the traveler using a baggage locker will not have to go hunting for the correct number of coins to put into the slot. This resourcefulness, however, requires the Swiss (and the visitor) to be on his toes, too. The traveler using a baggage locker in Zurich, for instance, who prepares for a visit to Basel by having the appropriate number of coins for the lockers there will be disappointed. The Basel lockers are priced differently than those in Zurich. This, of course, points up how independent, and different, one canton and one zone of the nation can be from another. Many things are standardized. But the people certainly are not!

The Swiss, fortunately, located in their own private mountaintop Shangri-La, feel themselves apart from the recurrent contestants of the European theaters of warfare. But just in case, the country maintains a citizens' army, in which no excuses are accepted—serve or go to jail. By remaining aloof and being constantly on the alert, the Swiss have built their small country and strong currency onto a rockbed of security. This, they inwardly think, entitles them to be smug. And they are slightly smug, in a pleasant way, undeniably and overtly content with their static way of life. Technically and scientifically, the Swiss move ahead by leaps and bounds; in the home, family relationships have not changed greatly over the past century.

Daily life is devoted to seeing that everything works efficiently and that everyone puts in a full day's work. The Swiss waste no time in being charming in the Gallic fashion, nor in the love of life exhibited by their Italian neighbors to the south. Humor and lightness and romance are foolish things, to be discarded early in life, before settling down to serious matters.

Persistence and personal integrity have made this country the most trusted of Europe; without question, the peoples of the world hand over their fortunes to the Swiss for safekeeping. Although Wall Street may deny it, the headquarters of international banking is Switzerland, the home of all the nervous, "hot" money of the world. In furtherance of this theme, the Swiss have made it a crime for anyone to disclose any information about the source or transfer of any funds in the country. In other banks of the world, the depositor receives interest; on special accounts left with Swiss banks, there is a charge made for leaving your money with them!

Switzerland has everything for the tourist; nothing goes wrong with his reservations, with his meals, with his train ticket. It must appeal strongly to American tourists—after France and Italy, Switzerland is the most visited country.

When to Go

Possibly the only month when you might not completely enjoy a visit in Switzerland is November. At that time—and often for the early part of December—the skies cloud over and rain falls, and the general atmosphere (and mood) is drizzly. But any other time of the year you will be welcomed with sun, snow and blue skies (the snow being confined, of course, to the winter months), with the bright, clear days showing up at any period of the year. December gets the skiing season started and Christmas and New Year's are extremely busy, social places at the great resorts (St.-Moritz, for instance). But there are lots of slopes filled with snow, and you'll be able to find good skiing from one end of the Alps to the other. Spring comes early to Zurich, and this is extremely pleasant, because at the city's front door is a long stretch of beautiful water (river and lake) and along the upper fringes of the skyline is glistening white snow caps. In general, American tourists have gotten into the habit of coming earlier than they used to and of staying longer. The best months are generally June through August.

WEATHER STRIP: GENEVA

Temp.	JAN.	FEB.	MAR.	APR.	MAY	JUNE	JULY	AUG.	SEPT.	OCT.	NOV.	DEC.
Low	28°	28°	31°	41°	50°	57°	60°	59°	51°	42°	35°	29°
High	30°	37°	44°	52°	61°	66°	70°	69°	63°	53°	42°	35°
Average	29°	33°	38°	47°	56°	62°	65°	64°	57°	48°	39°	32°
Days of rain	12	13	13	15	15	15	14	13	12	12	12	13

TIME EVALUATION ¶ Each of the more interesting cities of Switzerland (Bern, Lucerne, Zurich, etc.) is entitled to at least two days of sightseeing. A reasonable amount of time for driving about the country would be about ten days—a week, if time is short—but as much as two weeks, should you be fortunate enough to have the time.

PASSPORT AND VISA ¶ You only need to have a passport for a stay of up to three months. No visa is required. But for a longer stay, you will have to apply for a visa. Because of the many foreign nationals searching for work in Switzerland, the government has been tightening up immigration and residence regulations in recent years. So settling down in Switzerland for an indefinite sojourn is not quite so matter-of-fact as it used to be.

CUSTOMS AND IMMIGRATION ¶ Swiss customs can be comparatively routine, without so much as a question being asked of you. Once the inspector sees the American passport in your hand, he usually waves you onward. But this is not something to be taken for granted. In any case, if the inspector asks you whether you have anything to declare, reply to him courteously and frankly. If you have only the usual travel articles with you, say so. If there is something special in your baggage, tell him that at once. You are allowed to bring into the country, duty-free, two cartons of cigarettes *or* 100 cigars *or* 500 grams (a bit over a pound) of tobacco. As for alcoholic products, you can have in your baggage two bottles of wine, or one of wine and one of hard liquor. If you have a dog (or cat) with you, you must have a vaccination certificate certifying that the animal has been inoculated against rabies within the past thirty days. The certificate must be written in English, German, French or Italian.

HEALTH ¶ The water, the milk and anything and everything are safe to eat or drink. Switzerland is just about the most sanitary country in Europe. If you're disturbed by a change in drinking water, regardless of how safe it may be (and many people apparently are), you have a choice of numerous bottled waters. Don't forget to bring your sunglasses into the mountains with you, winter or summer. Spread a little lotion or cream on your face to prevent sunburn. Switzerland is laced with miles of cable cars, ski lifts and funiculars, which rise to great heights *literally*. If you have ever experienced any heart disturbances, it might be best to stay off this means of transportation when the altitudes are higher than normal.

TIME ¶ Switzerland is six hours ahead of (later than) Eastern Standard Time. When it's noon in New York, it's 6 P.M. in Zurich. When Daylight Saving Time is in effect in the United States, the time difference is 5 hours.

CURRENCY ¶ The Swiss *franc* has long been recognized as a strong, stable currency. But its value changes, too, in accordance with changes in the value of the dollar and other currencies on the world money market. The franc is divided into 100 *centimes* (the French word) or into 100 *rappen* (the German equivalent to centimes). There are absolutely no restrictions on the amount of money you can take into Switzerland or carry with you on leaving. Changing money is easier here than anywhere else. Exchange offices operate in all major railroad stations daily, and late into the evening. You can cash just about any kind of money in return for just about any kind. In other words, Swiss money does not have to be included in the transaction in any way. You can therefore, if you wish, change United States dollars for Italian lire. Swiss coins will take some getting accustomed to. The various coins are in silver, nickel or copper, according to their valuation. Here's how it works:

Silver: 5-franc, 2-franc, 1-franc and 50-centime (or rappen) pieces
Nickel: 20-centime, 10-centime, and 5-centime pieces
Copper: 2-centime and 1-centime pieces

If you like to study the color of the money, this will help you do it:

1,000 francs: rust
  500 francs: light red
  100 francs: dark blue
   50 francs: green
   20 francs: mauve
   10 francs: reddish brown
    5 francs: brown

PRICE LEVEL ¶ Switzerland has a reputation for being more expensive than it really is. Of course, if you travel deluxe all the time—luxury hotels, luxury restaurants, etc.—prices will be high. But in general they can be considered on a medium high level, or at least average with those in other parts of Europe. But, as we said, if you "go luxury" you will spend perhaps $20 (or more) for a single room in Zurich and a bit more than that in a major resort center such as St.-Moritz. Of course, this will be a very good room with a bath, whereas one without a bath might be a third less or even half the price. The hotel prices in Switzerland also include breakfast (the continental *petit déjeuner*). Dining out will cost anywhere from a couple of dollars (at nice modern American-style combination snack bar-restaurants) to $6 or even more. One wonderful thing about budget trips to Switzerland—the country is so immaculate and appetizing, and so accustomed to dealing with tourists, that any restaurant or hotel, no matter how low priced, will be satisfactory.

TIPPING ¶ The government has decreed the amount of tips for hotel guests—that is, the level of the service charge. If you are there less than three days, the hotel will add 15 percent to your bill as the charge for service. Over three days, it is 12 percent. Thus, you are not required to do any additional tipping except for the baggage porter, who should receive approximately 1 franc for each piece of luggage. However, 3 francs are enough for four pieces of luggage. If the maid or waiter serves you breakfast in your room, you should give her (or him) 1 franc per person a day. The concierge is also entitled to be remembered if he has done something to make your stay easier, more pleasant or worthwhile. The valet for shining your shoes each night—provided you have left them outside your door on retiring—should be given 1 franc a day. The service charge is normally added to restaurant bills, but if the waiter or waitress has been especially good, leave some extra change (never more than 5 percent of the bill). Taxi drivers should receive 10 to 15 percent of the meter (never less than 1 franc) —and that's enough, because taxis are expensive. Give washroom and coat-room attendants at least a half-franc.

TRANSPORTATION ¶ *Taxi* fares are not only sky high but just short of stratospheric; by all means, avoid taking cabs whenever possible. In some cities, they're merely expensive, but in others their rates are absolutely outrageous; this is one of the few black marks that can be given to the Swiss tourist authorities, who are otherwise so competent and diligent about protecting the rights of visitors. In the interests of saving money, take the small (*klein* or *petit*) taxi, which is about one-fourth cheaper than the large taxis; however, after 11 P.M. this differential is removed and all taxis charge the same prices.

The Swiss Federal *railroad* system is not just a means of transportation from one point in this lovely country to another. It is a delightful experience, whether you are in First Class or in Second Class on the train between Zurich and Basel, or whether you are moving across the top of the Alps on the section of highest rail trackage in Europe. The Swiss operate their trains on perfect schedules and with excellent equipment, and everything about them also satisfies the visitor. To make rail travel as inexpensive as possible the railroad has a special holiday ticket, which cuts the normal rate 50 percent. So work out your itinerary—the places you want to visit and the order in which you will visit them—and get a holiday ticket. If you are going to do an extensive amount of sightseeing by train in a particular region of Switzerland, you will probably save yourself a good amount of rail fares if you get a "regional seasonal" ticket that is sold in the summer. They are available for such areas as the Bernese Oberland, Lake Lucerne, Locarno, Montreux-Vevey, Lugano, Appenzell and the Grisons. Distances are so short in Switzerland—the country is only 200 miles long and 100 miles wide—that the usual train ride is only an hour or two, and you don't have to concern yourself with sleeping-car berths or couchettes. However, if you travel by train between Switzerland and capitals of other European countries, a complete line of overnight train accommodations is available. Incidentally, a little more than half of the railroad lines in Switzerland (1,500 miles) are operated by the Swiss Federal Railway system; 1,200 miles of remaining trackage is served by private companies. But the whole system is integrated, and it is something that may be interesting, although not noticeable, to the average traveler. From many major tourist centers or cities, such as Interlaken, there are low-priced comprehensive train tours to other parts of the country. At Interlaken, for example, there is a day-long round-trip excursion to Zermatt. This type of excursion is scheduled in the summertime—early June to early September—and is repeated several times a week.

Traveling by means of *buses* of the Swiss Postal Motor Service is one of the most rewarding and inexpensive ways of seeing the glaciers, alpine meadows and snow-capped peaks of Switzerland—not to mention the lakes and the flower-bedecked dales. The buses travel *everywhere*—this is no exaggeration—and they keep to a time-table as precise and as sure as any train. Usually you can include the bus section of your journey in a holiday railroad ticket. The buses also make a long list of excursions from major centers throughout the country during the summertime, but even in the winter maintain regular service between many towns and cities.

Streamer travel on Lake Constance and Lake Zurich is a marvelous sea-level way of seeing the country's sights. The lakeside towns, either because of their location or for some deeper intrinsic reason, are invariably beautiful and will evoke all manner of comments and compliments from you. On Lake Constance you can do some international sightseeing by cutting across the water to Austrian and/or German ports of call.

Airline service is not usually practical for the visitor in Switzerland because of the short distances between points. *Swissair*, the national airline, is one of the world's great international air companies and not only serves cities within Switzerland but operates to far-off corners of the world.

Note: Baggage porters at railroad, bus and air terminals expect at least 80 centimes for each package or piece of luggage. This is a minimum fee, and it is usually the custom to give them a flat 1 franc for each article.

COMMUNICATIONS ¶ *Telephone* service is probably as good as any place in the world, and there is an excellent dial system throughout the country. You can direct-dial from one point in Switzerland to another without any difficulty. In fact, if Switzerland was not the very first European nation to have direct-dialing (before World War II), it was one of the first. Local telephone calls in Zurich are inexpensive. Post offices have booths for local and interurban calls, and usually someone is on duty to assist you. In the main railroad station at Zurich a telephone bureau, staffed by multilingual clerks, will help put you in communication with anyone anywhere. Similar service is provided at railroad stations and/or post offices throughout the country. A three-minute telephone call to the United States costs from $12 up. You can reverse the charges, too, if you wish.

There is a marvelous service that provides information (on the telephone) about hotel accommodations, the weather, road conditions and other matters of tourist concern. All you do is dial 11 and phrase your question. Other numbers helpful for you to keep handy are 10, telegrams; 14, international calls; 161, correct time; 162, weather forecast; 163, highway conditions; 164, sports results; 168, newscasts. These numbers, by the way, remain the same from city to city.

You can send a *telegram*, or cable, from the nearest post office. But of course, the easiest way is to hand it to your hotel concierge. Telegrams within Switzerland are not expensive. The cable service to the U.S.A. is excellent.

An *airmail* letter to the United States is around a quarter, and often service from Zurich to New York is only overnight. Post offices generally are open from 7:30 A.M. to 6:30 P.M. during the week and until 3 P.M. on Saturday. Often they close for an hour or an hour and a half at lunchtime. The main post office in Zurich has an Urgent Window (*Dringlich Schalter*), which is open evenings and for short periods on Sunday. There is a surcharge of a half-franc for this service, but if it is merely a matter of a letter or two that you are mailing no extra charge is made.

BASIC SWISS ¶ Language will be no problem at all in Switzerland. This is one country where it can be truly said that practically everyone speaks English. (Don't try out this generalization at the top of a mountain or deep in some valley.) Also, the French-speaking area of the country is not quite so linguistically flexible as the German-speaking section around Zurich. Otherwise, we repeat that English is spoken everywhere and multilingualism is one of the many fascinating characteristics of the Swiss. Switzerland has three official languages: German, French and Italian. The largest number of people speak German; the next largest-spoken language is French (around Geneva, Lausanne, Montreux). Italian is spoken in the Ticino district, near the Italian border, and particularly in Locarno and Lugano. Many of the German-speaking people (especially those from Zurich) also speak French. But not too many of the French-speaking people are fluent in German (or even Italian for that matter). The German-speaking Swiss have a special dialect, which they use among themselves, that is pronounced as "Schwee-zer Dootch." This Swiss-German dialect is completely unintelligible to anyone else, so don't get depressed if it is too much for your high school German. There is also another language called Romansch, an ancient tongue spoken in the area near St.-Moritz as well as in a few other linguistic pockets in northern Italy. It has a Latin base but from then on goes off on its own. In any event Romansch is not one of the languages you will normally encounter on your usual itinerary.

ELECTRICITY ¶ Some places in Switzerland continue to provide 145 A.C. current, but an increasing amount of 220 A.C. facilities have been installed. If you haven't been to Switzerland in a couple of years, you will probably notice the progress made in obtaining a standard service of 220 A.C. Of course this is not going to help you with your 110 A.C. American-oriented appliances. A transformer will be needed. You will also have to have international (round prongs) plugs. Swiss hotels are very good about posting little signs in the bathroom to let you know the type of electricity in use. So look for one of these signs near a wall outlet in the bathroom.

SPAS ¶ About 250 mineral springs are among Switzerland's natural resources, and a tenth of them have been developed for the use of health-seekers. Bad Ragaz is one of the favorites. It has been a popular spa for centuries. Back in the very long ago, monks used baskets to haul visitors up and down between the mountaintop and the bottom of the gorge, through which water flows at a rapid, frothy rate. All this has changed, of course, but Bad Ragaz remains as wonderful as ever. It is one of the continent's finest resorts, even if you never go near the water.

WORKING HOURS ¶ Banks generally are open from 8 A.M. to noon and from 2 to 4 P.M., Monday through Friday. Stores follow an 8:30 A.M. to 12:15 P.M. and 2 to 6:30 P.M. schedule, which is shortened on Saturdays to 5 P.M. Some stores continue the habit of closing for a half day during the week—usually Monday. In large cities and in major resort centers, shops often forgo the noontime closing and keep open straight through the day.

FOOD SPECIALTIES AND LIQUOR ¶ Since breakfast is usually included in the hotel room price, you will probably have it at the place where you're staying. This is more convenient for those people who like to dress leisurely and eat in their room. But it is not helpful for those who enjoy the possibility of eating the way the local people in a country do. Your hotel room meal—or the one in the breakfast dining room, if you choose to eat there—will be the so-called continental type. That means rolls, bread, marmalade, jellies and butter. But it can be different, if you wish. Most hotels are prepared to serve you bacon and eggs, breakfast foods or whatever—including *fresh* orange juice. But the price will be similar to what you'd spend for the same thing in a hotel room in the United States. A number of hotels, to facilitate the early-morning breakfast trade, have breakfast rooms, separate from the large dining room. To experiment on breakfast, pass up the hotel one (even though paid for) some morning and drop in at a local lunch counter or even a cafe. You can still get rolls and bread and butter and jellies, but the chances are they will be different from the ones at the hotel. Also, you will have the chance to do some picking and choosing—and that can be pleasant. In any event, you'll have the opportunity to see exactly what the Swiss themselves eat.

Lunch is usually about noon or 12:30 P.M. In hotels, and at resorts, this is a multicoursed affair. But if you dine in a city restaurant, you can eat anything from a sandwich to a steak with French fried potatoes. The Swiss have been very alert to pick up many of America's food-serving habits and techniques. Illustrated menus and overhead display panels translate food specialties and dishes smoothly, so that there is no language problem when ordering. There is seldom any afternoon tea at a city hotel, but resort hotels will serve it (because they have been badgered for years by English tourists, and in Switzerland the tourist is always right). The ideal way of having an afternoon tea is to visit a special tea room. These abound—that is exactly the word—in large cities, such as Zurich. They are the type of tea room you would envision also—generally rooms with a couple of dozen very small tables (mostly occupied by women). The guest orders tea or coffee from the waitress, and while this order is being attended to another waitress passes by with a tray of pastries. From this tray you select what you wish—and how many pieces. You don't have to take any of the pastry if you do not wish to, naturally. The beverage and pastry transactions, by the way, are handled separately. These tea rooms are very reasonably priced, and for a half dollar or so you can have a fine snack for yourself during a lull in your sightseeing or shopping. No one will rush you along, either. Most tea rooms do not serve alcoholic drinks. Those that do are generally called cafes, rather than tea rooms. The thing to watch for is a sign at the door which says *Alkoholfrei* (No Alcohol). If you do not wish tea or coffee in one of the tea rooms, you can have a glass of mineral water, a Schweppes or some other soft drink.

One of the most delightful tea rooms in Switzerland (or anywhere) is the Kranzler on the Bahnhofstrasse in Zurich, right near the Union Bank of Switzerland. The walls are decorated with wallpaper, and mirrors hang resplendently. The Kranzler is on two floors, and a winding stairway (like one in a castle or palace that is on your itinerary) connects them. What will catch your eye on entering is not so much the furnishings, but the big glass showcase of pastries and cakes. You can pick what you wish, and the waitress will serve you at your table.

Because Swiss stores and offices close relatively early, and also because every place closes up at midnight, the people have a tendency to avoid wasting time. That means they start their dinner hour early (around 6:30 P.M. or so) and then have the full evening before them. Couples usually drop into cafes for a predinner drink or precede a restaurant meal with a cocktail. In hotels the evening meal (which is either dinner or supper, depending on the management) is an elaborate affair in the international hotel routine.

You will be able to get something to eat at any time of the day in a Swiss city. Restaurants open somewhere between 8 and 9 A.M., and those serving breakfast get started at 6 A.M. The railroad station cafeterias and restaurants keep early-morning hours, starting somewhere around 4 A.M. or 5 A.M. and remaining open till 11 P.M. or midnight. Usually you can get cold dishes in railroad restaurants at any time of the day and in many places hot dishes are served throughout the day also. The railroad station restaurants are comfortable places to eat, and the food is not expensive at all. Sad to relate, the Swiss style of mediocre cooking has been wished innocently upon the world and is now the general cookery style of deluxe hotels all over the world, including Zanzibar. Originally, the nationalistic hotel style was French; then along came British tourists who complained that the sauces were too rich; so the hotelkeepers modified the sauces. Along came the Italians, who objected to the lack of noodles, spaghetti and flour dishes; so these were added. Then came the Americans, who wanted roast beef and steak on the menu. The Swiss, ever obliging, have evolved a style of international cookery designed to please everyone, which, as might have been foreseen, pleases no one. The Swiss are marvelous chocolate and cheese makers, but as cooks, well, . . . "routine" is probably the word we're seeking. Everything is appetizing-looking and fresh, but this dish lacks something and that dish misses something else. It's a repetition of the old adage—you can't modify an Italian dish to satisfy an Englishman and still please an Italian who knows what the dish should taste like. But don't blame the Swiss for this; put the fault where it should be—upon the visitor who wants to eat the same food he does at home. All of this has been carping criticism, however; in point of fact, you'll eat well, if unspectacularly, anywhere in Switzerland, with the full knowledge that everything is fresh and wholesome.

Swiss cookery as a nationalistic style does not exist; although there are quite a few regional specialties, most of the dishes have been borrowed from the country's neighbors—France, Italy and Germany. As you travel from canton to canton (roughly like our own states), you'll notice variations depending upon the background and closeness to these three neighbors. If you dine only at deluxe hotels and restaurants, you'll always be served the various "international dishes," such as chicken in cream sauce, sautéed veal and tournedos of beef. To eat local specialties, it's usually necessary to try small, local restaurants.

This is cheese country, although, naturally, you won't get "Swiss cheese," which, of course, is an Americanization of the classic Switzerland cheeses—Emmental and Gruyère. Cheese is the basis for little *ramequins*, miniature pies made with these varieties; you'll frequently encounter cheese soup, which is rather good, providing the weather is brisk. Another favorite is *raclette*: a large chunk of cheese (usually Bagnes) is melted (often before an open fire) and scraped onto your plate to be eaten with boiled potatoes, pickles and little onions. An inexperienced American usually can manage only a half-dozen scrapings, but local people can consume two dozen (and often more!) portions at a sitting.

Of course, the favorite cheese dish, without doubt, is the *fondue*, a mixture of grated cheeses, white wine and a touch of potato flour and garlic (if there is such a thing as a touch of garlic). The fondue bubbles over an alcohol lamp and everyone spears pieces of bread on the tines of a long fork, dunks in the bubbling mixture and nervously conveys the mixture to his mouth, meanwhile hoping for the best. This is a rich dish and at its best from September until June; the Swiss don't normally eat fondue during the summer months, although tourists will assuredly want to try it. By the way, don't drink water or beer with fondue, or the cheese *reputedly* will become indigestible; the custom is to drink white wine or *Kirsch* (clear cherry liquor). *Fondue Bourguignonne* is a meat dish you cook yourself. Small pieces of steak are cooked quickly in oil and then dipped in a variety of sauces. A delicious novelty, so try it if it appears on the menu.

There are a few other important aspects of Swiss cookery: the love for noodle and flour dishes is particularly in evidence near the Italian border; the national mania for sausages of all types, shapes, colors, weights and ingredients is surpassed only by the Germans; then, last, there is the national predilection for gooey (and that is the only word) desserts of unbelievable calorie count.

Among the strong drinks, the Swiss are fond of *marc*, which, like the French version, is a potent, somewhat crude type of brandy. *Kirsch* or *Kirschwasser* is a clear, white cherry brandy and pretty good, too. Among the soft drinks, *moscht* is a type of cider that isn't bad; but we can't find it in us to say kind words about Swiss beer, which is definitely poor (sometimes downright bad). There is also a weird liqueur, reportedly made from alpine roots, herbs and flowers, called *Appenzeller Bitter*, which tastes exactly as though it were made from alpine roots, herbs and flowers.

Swiss wines are delightful and completely unimportant

in the world of wines (with one or two exceptions). Of lower than customary alcoholic content, they ship badly, so if you find a wine you enjoy tremendously here, don't make the mistake of sending it home. As wine experts say (with a pompous air befitting a wine expert), "They do not travel well." Among the red wines, *Dôle* has a characteristic masculine quality reminiscent of a middle-class Burgundy; most of the others are pretty thin. On the other hand, almost any white wine is sure to please: if you want a selection or two, look for the Neuchâtel types. *Dézalay* (which the experts think is the best) and the highly regarded *Fendant* white wines.

Zurich has some 2,000 restaurants and among the most popular of them are the "Mövenpick" establishments. One reason is that they are thoroughly modern and yet seek to present their food in a classic, traditionally pleasing setting. The other reason, we guess, is because the food is quite good and not at all expensive. The word "Mövenpick" is meant to bring to mind a seagull picking up a snack. There are a number of the Mövenpicks throughout Zurich, as well as Switzerland. You'll find them in Bern, Lucerne, Lausanne and Geneva, for instance. Each has its own personality, and some are much more stylish than others. Their founder is an enterprising gentleman named Ueli (pronounced *Willy*) Prager. Perhaps the most popular of the Mövenpicks is the one on the Dreikönigstrasse in the middle of Zurich. The Black Bull Room (one of four rooms) serves Angus beef, prime ribs and other choice cuts of meat with background music all evening and a setting of black-leather chairs, red tablecloths and silverplate. At the entrance is a large hors d'oeuvre table with platters of fish, salmon, shrimps and other tempting appetizers. The general menu features the Angus beef with baked potato, horseradish sauce and salad for less than $4.

A big hit with American businessmen who live and work in Zurich is the chain of Silberkugel snack bars, which have counter service. They are patterned after American food-serving places, but have been given a very fine Swiss touch and are bright and pleasant. The word "*Silberkugel*" means "silver ball," and you enter one of these establishments through a doorway that looks like a huge silver ball. The Silberkugel in the Löwenstrasse in Zurich is very popular. One of the features of these places is that everything possible is automatic—

and the food is not touched by human hands as it comes to you. If you order a sandwich it is served all wrapped up, and that is the way you get it on a plate. A drawback (maybe, maybe not) is that the menu is limited. There will be a salad every day—but only one type of salad. The next day it will be a different one. They do nicely with hamburgers, too.

WHAT TO EAT IN SWITZERLAND

Bernerplatte: Steamed ham, pork, boiled beef and sausage served with a boiled potato and hot sauerkraut

Geschnetzeltes: Small pieces of broiled veal served with a white wine sauce and *Roesti*, fried potatoes

Leberspiessli: Skewers of bacon and calves' liver

Klopfer: A type of mild sausage

Bundnerfleisch: Thin slices of air-dried meat; an interesting appetizer

Roesti: A favorite fried potato dish

Raclette: Melted cheese served with boiled potatoes

Fondue: The classic dish of Switzerland; a melted cheese and white wine preparation served in a casserole

Croute aux morilles: Wild mushrooms served on toast

Saucisse au foie: Very much like liverwurst

Piccata Luganese: Veal, sausages and chicken livers

Zupfe: A twisted, braided bread

Kirschtorte: A pastry dessert sprinkled with sugar and flavored with *kirsch* (cherry brandy)

Lebkuchken: A type of cinnamon cake with a symbolic bear made with white icing

Emmental: What we know as Swiss cheese

Gruyère: Another cheese similar to what we call Swiss cheese but without holes

Vacherin du Jura: Like our own cream cheese, but slightly astringent

The principal tourist areas are really the entire country of Switzerland, which constitutes one tremendous vacation, sightseeing and resort region.

Capital City

Bern is rather picturesque, located chiefly within a loop of the River Aare, although recent growth and development have been outside the old portion of town. The most distinctive features of the ancient city are the overly decorated water fountains, the arcaded shops, the floral areas, the cobbled streets and the towers and ramparts. Bern has retained its medieval aspect, more so than almost any other important city in Switzerland. Although there are many touristic sights, what Bern has to offer is quiet charm, the pleasure of wandering about and discovering delightful nooks and corners on your own; a cup of coffee at a tiny cafe; a delightful flower-be-decked square in an obscure medieval part of town that almost seems to become your own personal property. While here, a stay could be made at the centrally located Hotel City; luxury accommodations at the Bellevue-Palace and Schweizerhof hotels.

Bears have been a feature of the city of Bern for many hundreds of years and are still a part of the heraldic device of the municipality; therefore the Bear Pit, maintained by the city, is considered as obligatory sight-seeing. The clock tower, the Zeitglockenturm, which puts on a marvelous show of mechanical figures each hour, is an attraction that has amused the local citizenry (and nonlocal tourists) for more than 400 years. See the cathedral (*Münster*), whose construction was begun in 1421 and, if possible, try to visit this lovely building when an organ recital is given. But the best of Bern's sights are (as previously mentioned) the quaint old cobbled streets, particularly the Junkerngasse, and in fact almost any part of the Nydegg, the old quarter. In the Bundesplatz is an imposing Florentine building called the Bundespalast (where the legislative groups sit), but Bern being the kind of city it is, there are several outdoor fruit and vegetable markets held in front of it each Saturday. (Can you imagine that happening in front of the Capitol in our own Washington, D.C.?)

The Bern market is a colorful sight. From miles around farmers bring their flowers and fruits and vegetables. The main market days are Tuesday and Saturday, and a different square or street is the site. One of the oldest markets is the one for butter, cheese and meat, held on a street near the cathedral. The right to hold the market goes back almost 200 years.

Just south of Bern is the funicular railroad that goes to the top of Gurten mountain; this runs from Wabern, where the ascent is made. From the top, there's a marvelous view of the region, but don't worry about views, because if there's anything Switzerland has (besides wristwatches), it's views. Another possibility is a short trip to the northwest, where you'll find the Bremgarten-wald, or Bremgarten Forest, which is delightful for wandering about on a warm day. Nearby is the Wohlensee,

Lake Wohlen, an artificial lake, where boats may be hired.

Out in the countryside around Bern some people still wear the national costume. At the time of a festival the gay costumes are especially in evidence, and people come into town with them. A big festival you will enjoy is the Onion Market on the fourth Monday in November. Onions naturally feature the fare served on this occasion (along with cheese cakes), and there is dancing and singing hour after hour.

FLOWERS ¶ Flowers are sprinkled everywhere in Switzerland, from the edges of the snow-packed peaks to the great wide valleys. From May to July the alpine meadows bloom with lively flora. By the end of April, the slopes lower than 2,500 feet are already brimming with color. First to arrive are the crocuses; then, the little gentians. From then on it is a cascade of beauty and color tumbling down the slopes.

SHOPPING ¶ When shopping, naturally, Swiss watches are the number-one bargain, as every tourist knows. It should be borne in mind that no bargaining is possible, for the prices are fixed all over the country, the problem being simply one of selection; reliability and quality are always assured. That is not to say that a $20 watch is in the same class as a $400 one, for inherent differences must exist before there could be such a price differential.

Let's clear up the nomenclature: a *watch* is a timepiece usually worn on a wrist, although it may be the pocket type or even made into novelty rings or pins. A *clock* is the larger type, not made to be worn but intended to be used in the home or office. A *chronometer* is a watch that has undergone tests by the official Swiss government agency that tests timepieces, but many very fine watches are never certified as chronometers. The term "chronometer" is not necessarily a guarantee of a greater degree of excellence, for all watches are factory tested and many manufacturers do not submit their products to the government agency. A *chronograph* is a watch with added features: for example, stop watches, moon phases and the like. The important factor to remember is that these watches are *extremely* complicated to design, manufacture and assemble and no bargains are possible; unless you are prepared to invest a substantial amount of money, don't buy a chronograph. Repairs on these complicated mechanisms are often prohibitively expensive; even their maintenance is high, for it usually costs about $35 merely to clean and oil an average chronograph!

Now for a few general pointers about watches: *jewels* are used by watchmakers at points of stress in the instrument; except in the more elaborate chronographs, 17 jewels are considered sufficient for all purposes. Thus, a 21-jewel watch is not necessarily better than a 17-jewel one, and since the "jewels" are frequently synthetic rubies costing only a few pennies each, the manufacturer gains practically nothing by leaving them out.

Self-winding watches aren't entirely a luxury, because the idea is to keep the mainspring fully wound, thus assuring a constant tension, which results in a more accurate watch. The winding occurs through the action of a weight inside, which swings about with the movement of the wearer's wrist; one type of self-winder operates by means of a weight that is able to make a complete circle, the other through a weight operating in a restricted area. Since both work satisfactorily, no distinction need be made. Incidentally, these watches do not always work well for very sedentary or elderly people, whose movements are apt to be limited.

Waterproof watches are not intended for swimmers, although probably the watch will keep on running should you accidentally be wearing one while taking a swim; but don't keep this practice up regularly, for it can't possibly do the watch any good. On the other hand, water-resistant watches offer only a degree of protection against moisture. It should also be borne in mind that the main advantage of a waterproof watch (which can only be opened by a watchmaker) is that it is sealed against air, dust and moisture, all detrimental to operation and efficiency.

The *escapement* is the device by which the driving power of the watch is released so as to operate the regulator; that is, the familiar sight we have all seen in which one tooth of the wheel escapes with each swing of the pendulum. (If you can't remember, look inside your watch at the next opportunity.) In any event, if this mechanism is not jeweled, don't buy the watch; the so-called "Roskopf" or "pin-lever" escapements are so poor that their repair is not only difficult but often impossible.

There are highly styled and nonjeweled models available, however, at low cost. These are usually guaranteed for a year; if the watch doesn't work, it is replaced by a new one.

Now about quality categories: there can be no question but that the finest watches are made by three firms: Patek Philippe, Vacheron et Constantin, and Audemars Piguet, to list them in their accustomed order of merit. Any watch in this category is bound to be a superb timepiece. The cheapest timepiece in this class would be about $150 for a stainless steel case, and Patek starts at about $250; gold watches begin at $300 and can cost considerably more; many unusual novelty watches sell for $1,000 or even higher. Watches of this caliber should last a lifetime. But remember that the stainless steel case and the gold case usually have the identical movement, even though there may be a tremendous price differential.

The second category (in alphabetical order) includes the following: Girard Perregaux, Gübelin, International, Jaeger-Le Coultre, Longines, Movado, Omega, Piaget, Rolex, Ulysse Nardin, Universal, Vulvain and Zenith. These are all fine watches and generally range from $70 to $200, with some few exceptions.

The third category (alphabetically) includes: Borel, Consul, Cyma, Doxa, Eterna, Invicta, Juvenia, Marvin, Mido, Nivada, Recta, Roamer, Solvil, Tissot and Zodiac. Some of these watches begin at about $30.

As a generalization it may be assumed that you'll save anywhere from 40 percent to 60 percent on your watch by making your purchase in Switzerland. The 40 percent figure applies to the most famous name-brands; the 60 percent saving is only possible on the lesser-known watches. The luxury tax has been removed at the present time, and it is no longer necessary to ask for an export certificate. Each tourist is permitted to export (duty free) up to five watches, so, if you're planning to bring home presents for a dozen or more friends, better give this rule a little thought.

A good place to do your shopping in Switzerland is along the Bahnhofstrasse in Zurich. It is an elegant street of top-quality stores and boutiques. Gübelin, which also has a place in Lucerne, is one of the continent's finest jewelry stores. Butcherer, a few doors away, is the largest watch dealer in Switzerland and has superb display rooms, where you can look at—or buy—Piaget watches that range from $450 to $10,000 (this is diamond-studded, of course). You can also buy "boys' watches" for $8 and up, but they are not guaranteed.

Grieder, which is also in the Bahnhofstrasse, has a fine selection of clothes and fashion-wear. It also has a special Club 17 for young people. In Jelmoli you will find a very stylish boutique, along with all the wide range of merchandise found in a big store. For shoes, go to Löw on the Limmatquai. Across the river, too, is Globus, which sells all sorts of things and is very modern-minded and therefore quite popular with the young (and young-minded) folks. If you are looking for some of Switzerland's fine tablecloths, blouses and embroidered goods, go to Sturzenegger on the Bahnhofstrasse. Incidentally, we should mention that Grieder started out as a silk house three generations ago and since then has added haute couture, Dior shoes (and all his clothes) and a wide range of beauty products. The quality of everything at Grieder is very high; prices are also high. If you are looking for the one-of-a-kind Swiss souvenir—actually originals—then you will be interested in the *Heimatwerk* on the Uraniastrasse, near the Rudolf Brun Bridge.

The famous *chocolates* of the country are excellent, but bulky to carry about; shipment recommended with some hesitation. Nothing wrong with sending some chunks of Swiss cheese for those who would appreciate such a gift. If you aren't going to Germany, there is a good selection of cameras and optical goods with prices just about identical with (or slightly higher than) those in the country of origin. *Embroidery and laces* are attractive, if you like embroidery and laces—although available all over Switzerland; if you're visiting St.-Gallen, do your shopping there, for the prices and selection are better. *Toys* are marvelous, but not necessarily inexpensive; *dolls* for the little girls on your gift list are bound to please. *Sportswear*, particularly ski clothes, are absolutely superb.

The Swiss *portable typewriter* is the Hermes, and it's a fairly good machine, very light and reasonably sturdy. Whether this make is better or worse than the Italian Olivetti is an argument we have to avoid. One thing is certain: the Hermes is price-fixed in Switzerland and has been the subject of several price cuts in the United States, so the cost differential isn't very great. *Motion picture cameras* (Bolex) and *binoculars* are of unexcelled quality, should you wish anything in this line. The famous

Skira art books (Swiss-printed) sell for considerably less than at home and can be shipped without difficulty.

Don't buy touristy junk like replicas of mountains, "souvenirs of ———" and other nonsense. Ready-made clothing is very unstylish and expensive and should be avoided. Don't buy any watches except in legitimate, obviously respectable shops.

MOUNTAINS ¶ All those Alps may look alike to you, but they really aren't. Almost all the central and western Alps are entirely of limestone (or nearly so). In the Valais, Tessin and the Grisons, they are granite.

ENTERTAINMENT ¶ All over Switzerland, at varying times during the tourist season, there are local festivals and these should not be missed if at all possible. Lucerne has a fine music festival and also a night lake carnival; at Interlaken, there's the William Tell celebration, which now takes place every year; Geneva has a high old time during the *Fetes de Genève*; Zurich has a sort of all-purpose festival in June with ballet, art shows, concerts, opera. Pick up a folder at your hotel when you first arrive in Switzerland, and check the dates of the various festivals and try to match your schedule to them.

Geneva is proud of its famous *orchestra*, the Suisse Romande, which *is* very good although not in the first rank of great orchestras of the world. Local music, including yodeling, is often encountered at various resort hotels; it should be remembered that the average Swiss knows as little about yodeling as the average American does about hillbilly music and square dancing.

Night clubs in Switzerland are mostly intended for tourists; the local folk seldom attend except to take visiting Americans. Just in passing: Swiss night clubs are not for budget-minded travelers, because drinks run about $3, champagne averages $20 or so, and everything else is proportionately expensive.

The *Kursaal*, casino, is the center of resort hotel activities and don't forget that almost every resort hotel bill has a small item called "kurtax," which you pay to cover your use of the casino. The *Kursaal* is a sort of all-in-one amusement area, with small-scale gambling, dancing, refreshments, shows, and other pastimes. The gambling is limited in scope (say, a dollar or so per bet) to prevent any undue losses and (possibly) to prevent undue breaking of the bank. In some of the more elaborate *Kursaals,* there are likely to be important concerts by world-renowned soloists, dance recitals or ballet performances or, in small communities, some displays of local folk music and dancing. In any event, on quiet evenings after dinner, almost everyone heads for the *Kursaal,* as you should, unless, after a few visits, you find the proceedings dull.

There is a gambling casino at Arosa, Bad Ragaz, Baden, Bern, Brunnen, Davos, Lausanne, Locarno, Lucerne, Lugano, Mobtreux, and St. Moritz.

In Zurich drop in at the Queen Anne, a finely furnished discothèque, where you can slouch on a comfortable divan, have a drink, and listen to some comforting music. For something on the livelier side, go to La Ferme; as the name implies, it is a barnlike discothèque with authentic farm implements and fixtures and a few divertissements and attractions that were never dreamed of back on the farm, such as silent movies being flashed on a screen during the evening. This is a place where you can eat a fine dinner or just have a drink. It is not on the expensive side at all. An evening's entertainment that is tailored to tourists—and is popular with them—is provided by the Kindli restaurant. There the Schmid Family sing, dance and carry on in an uninhibited, agreeable way, giving you a panoramic picture of Swiss folklore. The place is done up in the style of a peasant farm-house, and you will enjoy the special dinner that is served, including fondue Bourguignonne, which is not inexpensive and is well worth every centime. For jazz music, try the Africana or the Atelier; they serve nonalcoholoc drinks. The Hazyland is a happy-go-lucky night club and there are top international stars here from time to time. The Petit Palais, in the Baur au Lac Hotel, is a famous night spot with Zurich people and their guests, and has an outdoor garden during the summer. The Terrasse is also a fine night club. There is also a Petite Terrasse, which specializes in strip-tease, so don't confuse them. The Plaza Hotel has several entertainment rooms, where the time passes happily and merrily.

SPORTS ¶ Some *horse racing* in the larger cities with pari-mutuel betting permitted. Lots of *football* (soccer) wherever you go, and if you've never seen a game, one visit might be in order.

In the winter months, *skiing* is the most important active sport; there are hundreds of places to ski all through the country and almost as many schools devoted to the fine art of skiing. All winter sport facilities are unexcelled, probably the finest and most elaborate in the world. When the snow is gone, the mountains are still there, so the Swiss (and assorted tourists) devote themselves to the harrowing sport of *mountain climbing*; since practically all of Switzerland seems to be either hilly or mountainous, wherever you are is mountain-climbing territory. Of course, the most popular region is Zermatt, with you climbing the Matterhorn (you, not us).

Somehow, somewhere, the Swiss have discovered a few places where the terrain is level enough for playing *golf*; but in the whole country there are only about thirty courses, and at that, most of them are quite hilly. Championship matches are always held at the Crans-sur-Sierre course in the Valais district; the altitude here is 5,000 feet. Other important courses are at Lausanne, Lucerne, Zurich and Geneva. *Tennis* can be played at almost every fair-size hotel or resort area; a few places feature night tennis, particularly at Lugano. Lots of *trout fishing* in Switzerland; the local tourist offices will be of great assistance if you want to wet a fly. But don't expect to do any *hunting*, because all the good land is privately owned.

Bicycling is also a popular sport. Bring along your own bike, if you wish, or rent one at any railroad station of the Swiss Federal Railways.

❧ A Tour of Switzerland

Bern to Interlaken—36 miles

(Note: See the section on France for a tour from Konstanz through Zurich, Lucerne, Interlaken, Montreux and Chamonix.)

Leave Bern by the Kirchenfeld Bridge, which crosses the River Aare at a height of 115 feet; then onto the Thunstrasse (road), picking up route 6 through Muri, Rubigen, Münsingen, Nieder-Wichtrach and Thun, an ancient town featuring and proud of its town hall, near which you'll find the twelfth-century castle of Duke

Berthold. Follow the south shore of the Thunersee (Lake Thun) through Gwatt and the pretty resort town of Spiez, where you'll find the Hotel Bahnhof-Terminus. Then through Faulensee and Leissigen into Interlaken. Very large and luxurious in an old-fashioned way is the gracious Victoria-Jungfrau, a well-managed, pleasant place; the food is quite good, too.

Interlaken, a quiet town full of visitors during the season, is actually pretty much without attractions of its own, but has come into popularity as a base for excursions into the surrounding area. Wander about the Höneweg, the main street, lined with shops selling all sorts of things you really need—such as foot-high beer mugs and toilet paper rolls that play Swiss tunes. This town, always crowded with busloads of tourists, has a mania for mountain railways; if you'll take our advice, don't waste too much time on the lesser railroads, but save your energies for the Jungfraujoch trip, the mountain excursion to end them all.

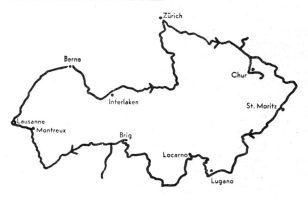

SIDE TRIP TO JUNGFRAUJOCH ¶ Drive south on route 70 to Wilderswil and Zweilütschinen and on route 71 to Lauterbrunnen; here you should visit the nearby Trummelbach Falls, quite impressive. Lauterbrunnen is the starting point for the railroad trip to the Jungfraujoch; the trip takes about two and one-half hours, and if you get an early start, you'll be able to return to home base at Interlaken that night, even though you'll probably be tired. If you want to take our advice, stay at Interlaken in preference to the mountain hotels—the thin air will often disturb your sleep and digestion. (If you wish, you can leave by train from Interlaken—the station is Interlaken-Ost—at greater cost.)

The train (Wengernalp Railway) goes from Lauterbrunnen to Wengen (a town that can be reached only by railroad) and then to Kleine Scheidegg, at 6,777 feet; and don't be surprised to find this little town bursting at the seams with visitors. (CAUTION: those with heart trouble or high blood pressure should not venture higher, except on competent medical advice.) At Kleine Scheidegg, you change for the Jungfrau Railway, constructed at the turn of the century and still a truly remarkable engineering feat. The train goes through Eigerwand and Eismeer (via tunnels hewn out of solid rock of the mountains) and finally arrives at the Jungfraujoch, the very highest railroad station in Europe (11,340 feet). The hotel here is the Berghaus (without private baths), and you could stay overnight for the magnificent views at sunset and sunrise, providing the altitude doesn't bother you. Take it gently here, avoid too much exertion and eat and drink with great moderation, because mountain sickness can be very uncomfortable. Sightseeing: besides gaping at the wonderful panorama, take the elevator to the Meteorological Observatory, from which you can go through the Sphinx Gallery to the Jungfrau Glacier. Another interesting sight is the Ice Palace, an ice-enclosed skating rink (but we're even shivering writing about it!). You'll return to Klein Scheidegg to change trains back to Lauterbrunnen. If you've driven by car to Lauterbrunnen, you'll want to return there to pick up your auto; if you've come from Interlaken by train, it's possible to return by another route from Kleine Scheidegg, via Grindelwald, a perfectly delightful little resort town.

If you're in the mood for a few days of luxurious rest, there is a new hotel located on the north shore of Lake Thun (the Thunersee) at the village of Merligen, about eight miles west of Interlaken. The Hotel Beatus is marvelously situated on the shores of the lake, the rooms are attractive and it's ideal for a few days' break in driving.

A mile and a half downtown Interlaken is a new eighteen-hole golf course. It is located near Neuhaus on Lake Thun. The course is something like four miles long, and par is a neat 72. Yes—a golf pro is on hand, too.

Interlaken to Zurich—113 miles

(The choice of route depends upon the time of the year: the route described herewith goes through the Susten Pass, which is open only from the middle of June until almost the end of October. If you're traveling through the area during that period, follow this section of the tour. If you're making the tour at any other time of the year, the Susten Pass will be closed, and after Brienz, you should pick up route 4 heading north through Sarnen, Lucerne and Zug, rejoining the tour at that point.)

From Interlaken via routes 6 and 20 (parallel routes), continue alongside the north shore of Brienzersee (Lake Brienz), passing through Ringgenberg, Brienz, Meiringen and Innertkirchen, where you make a left turn following route 20 toward Nessenthal and Gadmen. Soon afterward you come to Wendenwasser Bridge, and a few miles along is the Hotel Steingletscher; here you might enjoy a short walk to see Stein Glacier. Next comes famous Susten Pass, where there is a tunnel cutting through the mountain at an altitude of about 7,300 feet. The road continues to Meien and Wassen, where you make a left turn onto route 2. Continue through Wiler, Gurtnellen, Amsteg, Ersfeld, Altdorf and Flüelen. Here, you begin to follow along the eastern shore of a part of Vierwald-stättersee, that is, Lake Lucerne, heading through Sisikon, Brunnen, Schwyz Arth (also called Arth am See); then alongside the eastern shore of the Zugersee (Lake Zug) and into the town of Zug, a famous walled town noted primarily for its medieval atmosphere and aspect and secondarily because it is where *Kirsch*, the cherry brandy, is made—and you can reasonably expect everything (edible) possible to be liberally sprinkled with it. In Zug, see the Town Hall, the Convent of the Capuchin, St. Oswald's church and the Zytturm, the Clock Tower, with a remarkable astronomical clock. (Lucerne is only a short side trip from here; details in the section on France.)

From Zug, continue on route 4 through Baar, Sihl-brugg, and Adliswil into Zurich, Switzerland's largest city, charmingly located at the northwest end of Lake Zurich. The city's main shopping street, the Bahnhof-strasse, lined with lovely trees, is just about as interesting as any in Europe and a wonderful place to dispose of your surplus money (what surplus?). Sightseeing: the Fraumünster, (thirteenth-century cathedral); Grossmünster (Great Cathedral); Rathaus (Town Hall); National Museum, devoted largely to Swiss art. Take a trip to Zürichberg and ride the funicular to lofty Dolder, a famous beauty spot. Just a half-hour's drive from Zurich is the thirteenth-century village of Regensberg, an absolutely delightful retrogression into time and space. Take the little train from Selnau railroad station to Utliberg, from which there is a marvelous view and where there is also an adequate restaurant. The famous old and grand hotel here is the Baur au Lac; the Bellerive is similar but a touch less grand. However, you'll find much more modern accommodations at the Zurich Airport Hilton, which has a swimming pool (if it ever gets that hot in Zurich!). The Hotel Continental is another possibility, being comparatively new and quite pleasant.

If you stay in Zurich for several days, it might be pleasant to dine in some of the town's restaurants. Da Bernasconi features French-Italian-Swiss food; it's very good but quite expensive. Very good, also quite expensive is Giangrossi, with Italian specialties. After dinner, head for Zurich's most interesting street for night life, the Münstergrass, which begins its winding course near the Grossmünster. You'll find a large number of theaters, cafes, night clubs and so forth. Or, if you're a serious lover of music, get tickets for the state-supported opera company, which specializes in modern, often experimental, operas; it features a Richard Strauss festival every June.

Zurich is the starting point of several lake trips at the shore end of the Bahnhofstrasse; the most popular ride is to Rapperswil on the north side of Lake Zurich.

Sightseeing tours of the city are scheduled daily at 9, 10, 10:30, 2, 3:30 and 5 during the summer; and at 10:30 and 2 in the winter. The charge is not very much. In summer, the Zurich-by-Night tour begins at 8.30 P.M. Starting point for the tours—and the place to get tickets— is the tourist office in the main railroad station.

Zurich to Chur—79 miles

Leave Zurich via route 3, driving along the southwest shore of the lake, passing through Thalwil, Horgen,

Wädenswil and Richterswil. (*Side Trip*: just ten miles to the southeast via route 155 is the town of Einsiedeln, famous for its Benedictine abbey.) Continue on through Pfäffikon, Lachen and into Näfels. From Näfels to Mollis, Filzbach and Obstalden, after which you begin to approach the Walensee, Lake Walenstadt. Riding along its south shore, you pass near Mühlehorn, with an incomparable location, then Murg, Mols and Walenstadt. Then comes Berschis, where you might like to investigate St. George's chapel: next Ragnatsch, Heiligkreuz and Sargans (noted for a thirteenth-century castle).

SIDE TRIP ¶ Sargans is the point for a trip into that anachronism of the twentieth century the Principality of Liechtenstein, with a population of 14,000 living contentedly in sixty-one square miles. Leave Sargans via route 13 to Trübbach and Weite and, at Sevelan, take a right turn toward Vaduz, the capital (if a village can be called a capital). Liechtenstein is governed by a prince, and although affiliated with Switzerland politically and economically, it prints its own stamps (and tourists keep buying, thus more than balancing the tiny national budget). A visit here is a step backward into time except on an overcrowded Sunday; for lovers of the unusual, the timeless and quiet romantic charm, Liechtenstein is heartily recommended; the best place to stay in Vaduz is the Waldhotel.

From Sargans, drive to Bad Ragaz, a favorite Swiss spa; you'll want to see Tamina Gorge. (From Bad Ragaz, there is a pleasant ride south to visit another thermal spa, Bad Pfäfers.) Then on to the industrial centers of Landquart, Zizers and Chur (also known as Coire). Chur is a medieval town, seemingly unchanged over the centuries, and the finest entertainment is walking about through the quaint streets; the town has an ancient history, with Roman records going back some 2,000 years. The only important hotel is the somewhat modest Steinbock, but since Chur is such an excellent base for sightseeing trips through this region, the Grisons, a stay should be made here. Sightseeing: the Bishop's Court and Palace; the Rhaetian Museum; St. Martin's church; twelfth-century Cathedral of St. Lucius. From Chur, a delightful short excursion of nineteen miles may be made via route 65 to Arosa, following the winding mountain road. Here you find the highest health resort in the country, and possibly the most chic vacation spot in Switzerland, a headquarters for the international set.

(Again, a choice of routes. The main tour proceeds to Davos and then goes through the Flüela Pass, a road normally open only from June through October. If you are traveling through this region before June or after October, it would be advisable to head south from Chur via route 3 and rejoin the tour at St.-Moritz, a distance of forty-five miles.)

Chur to St.-Moritz—75 miles

Leave Chur via route 3 northward through Zizers, and near Landquart, take a right turn onto route 28. The road goes through Grüsch, Schiers, Küblis, Saas, Klosters (a tremendously popular ski resort); there is an aerial tramway ride leaving from the railroad station to ascend Gotschnagrat mountain. A pleasing hotel here is the Pardenn-Sporthotel, and a smaller hotel is the Chesa Grichuna. From Klosters, proceed (via a mediocre road) to Laret, Wolfgang and Davos-Dorf and Davos-Platz, both of which constitute one renowned health resort, although recently more emphasis has been placed upon the unique location as a winter resort. Many hotels are closed during the summer months, but the Schweizerhof, Flüela Sport, and Victoria remain open. From Davos-Platz, you backtrack to Davos-Dorf, then turn right back onto route 28 for the ride through the Flüela Pass, ordinarily closed except during the summer months beginning in June. This is an exciting drive of only sixteen miles, but filled with some of the finest scenery of the country, particularly when you pass the Weisshorn, over 10,000 feet high. The Flüela Pass road ends at Susch, where you make a right turn onto route 27, heading for Zernez, whose location could scarcely be excelled. Continue on through Brail, Cinuos-chel, then Zuoz (with its fine old sixteenth-century houses), La Punt (a tiny village), Bever, the resort community of Samedan, Celerina and finally St.-Moritz, one of the most popular gathering places of international society.

We think you'll like the Hotel Monopol, although it is not the most luxurious place in this luxury-loving town. The famous deluxe hotels are the Suvretta House and the Kulm and Palace hotels; expensive but excellent. Now, at the risk of being considered an iconoclast, we must confess that large-scale, super-duper resort operations do not precisely thrill us; on the other hand, since St.-Moritz goes on forever and ever, there are undoubtedly thousands of people who *do* like large-scale fashionable resort operations. Although the town itself is completely devoid of interest, there are a million and one distractions and entertainments for the visitor, including every sport facility you ever dreamed of, plus a few extra. Before you leave St.-Moritz, make a short excursion to nearby Pontresina, which is also an attractively situated resort, with some of the oddest architecture you're likely to encounter on the entire trip. Just before Pontresina is the funicular for the top of the Muottas Muragl, from which there is a spectacular view of a spectacular countryside.

St.-Moritz to Lugano—77 miles

Leave St.-Moritz on route 27 toward Champfer, passing Silvaplana, then the Lake of Silvaplana, followed by the Silsersee (Lake Sils) and Maloja, a small resort town. The Pass of Maloja begins a descent in a series of sharp hairpin turns, which aren't dangerous, although careful driving is required. The gradual down-mountain run continues through Casaccia, Vicosoprano, Promontogno and Castasegna (notice the Italian names?), after which you cross the Swiss-Italian border. Continue on via route 37 toward Santa Croce and Chiavenna. Here, you pick up route 36 for a drive of thirteen miles (passing Lake Mezzola), until you reach a right turn in the direction of Gravedona; be sure to watch for this turnoff, and, incidentally, this route was and may still be unnumbered. The road travels along the northwest shore of magnificent Lake Como, one of the most beautiful of the Italian lakes, passing Gera, Gravedona, Dongo (Mussolini was captured here on April 27, 1945, while trying to escape from Italy) and Rezzonico into Menággio. At Menággic, take a right turn through Porlezza, and after crossing the border, pass through Gandria and into Lugano, situated on Lake Lugano.

Lugano has been extremely fortunate in its location and enjoys much better weather than any Swiss city is normally entitled to; flowers bloom earlier and later than elsewhere, birds sing (even in the early morning, when you'd rather they'd shut up), the air is usually balmy and gentle and life can be very relaxing and luxurious, particularly at the best hotels along the lake, such as the Grand Hotel Palace, the Splendide and the Park Hotel au Lac. There is even a motel, the Vezia, located just two miles north of Lugano on route 2. For those who like the unusual, La Romantica is a tiny, extremely luxurious and elegant hotel just three miles south of town in the direction of Melide, with excellent food served by candlelight.

Sightseeing in Lugano should include the various churches, but especially Santa Maria degli Angioli (for its frescoes) and San Lorenzo; there are also funicular rides from Cassarate to the top of Monte Bre. But no one should fail, weather permitting, to take a boat ride on Lake Lugano; there is frequent service through the northeastern part of the lake, touching at Gandria and Porlezza. Another boat runs south to Melide, but whatever the route, the lake is absolutely delightful.

Lugano to Locarno—26 miles

Leave Lugano by route 2 to Taverne, Bironico, passing Mount Ceneri on the right hand, and into Cadenazzo, where you make a left turn onto route 22 to Quartino; later there is a turn onto route 21 to Gordola, Minusio and Locarno, a small town, peaceful and unassuming, nestled on a bay that is a part of Lake Maggiore. A pleasing lakefront hotel here is the La Palma; not too far away is the neighboring lazy resort of Ascona, also extremely attractive. Sightseeing: the Madonna del Sasso, a famous sanctuary, may be reached on foot, but most people prefer the funicular; Rusca Castle, partly in ruins, but very attractive. Boat trips to lovely Stresa and to the Borromean Islands, but allow a complete day; however, there is quicker service to the islands from Verbania, which will be reached shortly along on the tour.

If you like splendid markets, this area is the place for you. Market day at Locarno is the first and third Thursday of the month. It is every Wednesday at Luino, Sunday at Cannobio and Saturday at Intra and Domodossola.

In case you wish to have more activity than browsing through a public market, we'd like to point out that right near the public gardens of Locarno are five fine tennis courts. The court fee is about a dollar an hour.

Locarno has many interesting attractions. First of all,

why not wander about the center of town, the Piazza Grande, with its pleasant arcades? Behind Locarno, facing south, are several interesting villages to explore: drive up to Orselina, Brione and Monti della Trinita. Only a few minutes from Locarno is Ascona, an attractive art colony. If you stay for a few days in Locarno, it might be interesting to eat at either (or both) of the town's two very good restaurants, Los Gatos and Da Emilio; both are expensive, however. For those who enjoy bathing, it would be pleasant to stay at the Bellavista Motel, eight miles from Locarno at the village of Vira-Magadino, for the motel has its private beach.

Locarno to Brig—87 miles

Leave Locarno via route 21 through Ascona, soon viewing Lake Maggiore from steep heights on the left-hand side; then through Brissago (famous for its irregularly shaped slim cigars), and shortly afterward, the Swiss-Italian border. Once in Italy, we drive through beautiful scenery, passing Cannobio and Cannero and into Verbania, which is divided into two parts—Intra and Pallanza. From here, motorboat trips may be made to the Borromean Islands, which are definitely worth a visit; be sure to see the unspoiled Isola dei Pescatori, Fisherman's Island.

From Verbania, continue on to Gravellona (passing Lake Mergozzo en route), then to Domodossola, whose chief attraction is the marketplace, the Piazza del Mercato. (You are now going through the Simplon Pass, open from late April until the middle of November; at any other time of the year, cars may be shipped on railroad flatcars through the pass.)

From Domodossola, drive through Preglia, Crevola d'Ossola and Iselle, and then cross back into Swiss territory. After the border, you come upon Gondo (also called Ruden); about three miles farther along is Gondo Gorge, a rugged and startling bit of scenery. Then a climb into Gstein (Gabi), the village of Simplon, the Simplon Pass *itself*, Berisal, Schluct and Brig (or Brigue, as it is often spelled). An excellent place for a stay here is the extraordinary, bright and cheerful Hotel La Couronne.

SIDE TRIP TO ZERMATT ¶ Undoubtedly high among the outstanding touristic attractions of Switzerland is Zermatt, adjacent to the Matterhorn, 14,701 feet high. The

Matterhorn came into particular renown in 1865 when only an Englishman (Edward Whymper) and his two guides survived, three other Englishmen being killed, in the first successful ascent of the mountain. Controversy raged as to whether the ropes had been cut or were broken during the descent, and poor Whymper came in for considerable criticism, although no guilt was proven.

Drive from Brig on route 9 to Visp and leave your car there, taking the Visp-Zermatt Railroad (completed in 1891). It's true that you can drive farther along to St.-Niklaus, but since the purpose of this trip is to see, why drive and lose all benefit? The railroad trip operates partially by rack and pinion (if that conveys anything to you) and reaches Zermatt in one and one-half hours of absolutely superspectacular scenery, passing cataracts, gushing waters with every view worthy of a picture postcard, except that your view will be in 3-D. If you wish to make your trip to Zermatt even faster, you can fly there by helicopter. Zermatt itself is most attractive should you wish to remain overnight. The town is the starting point for mountain-climbing excursions in this area, including an ascent of the Matterhorn, which can be accomplished, since Whymper showed how, by anybody in good physical condition (at least that's what they keep telling us!). But most tourists content themselves with the less arduous enjoyment of a cogwheel railroad trip from Zermatt to Gornergrat; it's a ride that is the final touch to your emotions; now you may say (with a reasonable degree of truth) that you've seen everything—in the way of mountains, that is. In the Zermatt area there are altogether some 80 hotels and boarding houses providing about 10,000 beds. The best hotels are Zermatter Hof and Mont Cervin.

Brig to Montreux—85 miles

Leave Brig by route 9 westward to Visp, Turtmann, Susten, Pfyn and Sierre, an important tourist town famous for the dryness of its climate. There is some interesting sightseeing: the four-turreted castle of the Vice Dominies; Goubing Tower; the monastery of Geronde. Then through the tiny wine village of St.-Leonard and into Sion, where the Hotel Treize Etoiles is the best in town. Sion is worth strolling about to see Nôtre-Dame Cathedral; the Sorcerer's Tower; Tourbillion Castle; the

Town Hall and its renowned astronomical clock. Continue on to Vétroz, Ardon, St.-Pierre-de-Clages, Riddes, and Martigny, where you could stay overnight at the comfortable Hotel Central.

From Martigny, continue on route 9 through Vernayaz, Evionnaz, then into Bex, famous for its brine baths and thus often called Bex-les-Bains, or even colloquially as X-'n-Pains. From Bex to Aigle (an extremely attractive little town at the beginning of a wine district), then through Roche, Rennaz and Villeneuve on Lake Geneva. About a mile or so after Villeneuve, you come to the famed Castle of Chillon, believed to date back to the thirteenth century; it was this famous castle that Byron dealt with in his poem "Prisoner of Chillon." In the dungeon, visitors are shown where the patriot François Bonivard was incarcerated for his valiant efforts to liberate Geneva. Incidentally, in case you're worried about Bonivard, he was freed by rebels in 1536—some four years later. Then into Territet and shortly thereafter the world-renowned resort of Montreux, one of the most beautifully situated towns in Europe (no, we're not just carried away with emotion—it's a fact). There's always something doing in Montreux: there is water for swimming and mountains to climb or to ascend by mountain railroad, and if the quietude settles down to mere bedlam and excitement, the municipal authorities will surely put on some festival or another—that is, if there are any free days. Two standard sightseeing trips here are to Glion (a pleasant, subdued resort community reached by rack railway), then on to Caux and another rack railway to Rochers de Naye, with a further magnificent (ho-hum) view of the surrounding area.

Montreux to Bern—79 miles

Leave Montreux by route 9 toward Clarens (actually almost a suburb of Montreux) and into Vevey, famous for its Swiss chocolates. Then come St.-Saphorin and Chexbres; now you are in the wine-producing region of Cully, an extremely pretty village. Next through Lutry (famous for its Lavaux white wines) and into Lausanne; here the Beau Rivage is the standard, old-fashioned luxury hotel fronting the lake; the Victoria Hotel is quite good, but only breakfast is served. If you want to stay at a pretty good motel, there's the Motor Inn Parking

Hotel (now there's a mouthful!), located on the Avenue Rond-Point. The rooms are fair enough, there's plenty of parking space, and they even have a passable restaurant. The city seems to be equally divided between the ultra-modern (there is even a seventeen-story skyscraper) and the ancient, which is inevitably much more interesting to tourists. Sightseeing: the Town Hall (an interesting architectural specimen of what has been called, with some justification, the Ugly Gargoyle School of Architecture); the twelfth-century Gothic cathedral, extremely pleasing in appearance; the Bel-Air Tower; the streets of the Old Town, *La Cité,* and the open-air markets; the Château-St.- Maire, formerly the bishop's castle. If you can still manage to ride in a funicular, there's one here, the oldest in the country, running to Ouchy (yes, that's its name). Lausanne is a wonderful starting point for lake excursions to Montreux or Geneva. Directly across the lake on the south shore are lovely Evian and Thonon, which surely warrant a visit, if only for the boat ride.

Leave Lausanne heading north by route 1, passing through Epalinges, Chalet-à-Gobet, Bressonnaz, Moudon, the tobacco-producing town of Lucens, Henniez, then through a wooded area into Payerne, which is famous for its eleventh-century Abbey Church, often considered the finest Romanesque church in the country. Next come the hamlet of Corcelles, Dompierre, Domdider and Avenches, an important town in Roman days. There are some interesting Roman ruins to the east of the town; there is also the fifteenth-century Town Hall. From Avenches we descend, proceeding to Murten (also called Morat), located on the Murtensee, or Lake Murten. This charming little town is like something removed intact from the fourteenth century—towers, decorative fountains, arches, ramparts, bastions, gateways, narrow streets. Next to Löwenberg, dropping down to Gümmenen, Mühleberg, Frauenkappelen and then back into Bern, the starting point.

ᔰ *Motoring in Switzerland*

Gasoline and oil are not very expensive, comparatively. Prices on these items might be a little higher in the mountains. Logical, no?

To bring a car into Switzerland you'll need only its registration papers and a Green Card certifying insurance coverage. To drive, your home-state driver's license is perfectly satisfactory.

Traffic keeps to the right, with passing on the left, as usual. In built-up areas, 31 miles per hour (50 kilometers) is the limit, but on the open road there is no speed limit, although a motorist is supposed to have his car under control at all times. Occasionally, lower speeds may be called for in industrial or city areas. Special notice with regard to *built-up areas*; it is essential to remember that a car or even a bicycle on the right-hand side (even when entering from a minor road onto a main street), has the *absolute* right of way. On *highways* those on major roads have priority over those entering from minor roads. Don't blow your horn except in emergencies when driving through cities.

The road communications are headed by autobahns, many of which have been completed. The cities of Zürich, Basel and Bern are now connected by autobahns. The main roads are good and well surfaced, but occasionally disturbingly narrow, although there are a number of wide roads with several lanes in each direction. Mountain (alpine) roads are frequently unpaved and dusty; remember that postal buses (easily identified by yellow markings and a three-toned musical horn) have the right of way over all traffic. When the road narrows, you must stop and let the bus have precedence, even if you must back up or pull over to let it through. Besides postal buses, traffic going up a mountain road has precedence over any vehicle going downhill, as you might expect. You'll often see telephone booths, along the mountain roads; there is no charge for service calls for autos with foreign license plates. On mountain roads, no matter how attractive the scenery, it is essential for the driver to give his complete attention to the traffic (of which there is more than enough during the summer months) and to negotiate the hairpin bends with extreme care. A particular warning about the passenger buses: the drivers of these enormous vehicles know the roads but they frequently approach blind corners at excessive speeds, so be extra cautious.

There can be no question that June through September are the ideal months for traveling in Switzerland; at other times of the year, *always* check road conditions, particularly those through mountain passes, which are frequently snowed in for varying periods of time.

You can identify the origin of most Swiss autos by the first two letters on the plate—BE designates Bern, LU means Lucerne, etc.

ACCOMMODATIONS ¶ If not everyone agrees about other matters in Switzerland, they all concur in the fact that here are the best hotels in the world. Over one hundred years ago it was quite fashionable to "do the continent," and Switzerland became a major tourist center. Thus, for more than a century the Swiss have been a nation of hotelkeepers, specializing in catering to a wide variety of tastes and trying to satisfy them all. Naturally, some hotels are more attractive and more elaborate than others, but even the smallest, more economical Swiss hotel will be absolutely immaculate and with good service, although some of the fancy trimmings and gold braid will be lacking. Most Swiss resort hotels were built in the old tradition of large, open areas, lots of elaborate old world décor and rooms comparable in size to Grand Central Station; even the bathrooms are the size of small living rooms. But elaborate or plain, brass buttons on the uniform or no, the Swiss know everything there is to know about hotel keeping. If you order something, room service will bring it quickly and the food will be hot and there will be ice if you ask for it and everything is very efficient. Many American hotel owners insist on Swiss-trained personnel for their executive staff, and a few years in a Swiss hotel is considered an essential ingredient in the background of every would-be hotel man.

There are something like 7,500 hotels and pensions in Switzerland, with about 180,000 beds. By quick calculation on your household IBM computer you can see that the relation between beds and hotels means that most hotels are relatively small. As a matter of fact, only a few dozen have more than 200 beds. Even the biggest hotels almost invariably are family operations that one generation after another has been managing with skill and graciousness.

Americans will notice that when a meal is ordered in a room, the waiter brings it course by course. This is a nice change from the American system, which calls for everything to arrive at the same time, so that you nibble at the salad while watching the ice cream melt away swiftly, much like the snow on an alpine peak in the late spring.

You will have no trouble finding a place to eat in Switzerland, either. The country has more than 20,000 restaurants, inns and cafes that serve meals.

BASEL HOTELS AND RESTAURANTS

Trois Rois au Rhin: The "Three Kings Hotel" is exceptional; each room individually decorated. Pleasant dining terrace; good food.

Alban-Ambassador: The newest and the largest in Basel, with 100 luxurious rooms and 20 suites; grill room, bars and an underground garage for 100 cars.

Wirtshaus zu St.-Jakob: At town's edge, attractive restaurant with dining terrace; very charming. Fairly good food, quite high.

BERN HOTELS AND RESTAURANTS

Bellevue Palace: A "grand-palace" style hotel; quite large, with attractive rooms. Panoramic view of Alps.

Schweizerhof: Old, but modernized hotel. Entrance is simple, but rooms are pleasant. In center of town.

Kornhauskeller: The best place to absorb local color while having a typical meal of the region; not too expensive.

GENEVA HOTELS AND RESTAURANTS

President: A palatial, impressive structure with attractive rooms, many with exceptional views; luxurious and expensive.

Intercontinental: Opened in the fall of 1963, this hotel seems destined to be one of Geneva's very best. Several different restaurants; attractive rooms.

Richemond: Excellent west shore location; fine hotel near gardens. New wing is very luxurious but more expensive than traditional portion of the hotel.

Suisse: Modern hotel in center of town; pleasing, fair-size rooms are not too expensive. No meals are served.

Le Gentilhomme (in the Hotel Richemond); *Le Béarn*; and *Plat d'Argent:* these restaurants are all famous for excellent French food; quite expensive.

Brasserie Bavaria: Homier, friendlier and more atmosphere than the above restaurants; local food, not too expensive.

LAUSANNE HOTELS AND RESTAURANTS

Lausanne-Palace: The big, "grand" hotel of Lausanne. Large rooms overlooking the lake; fairly expensive.

Château d'Ouchy: A remodeled castle with lots of atmosphere; rooms in the tower are large, others are moderate size. High prices.

Aux trois Tonneaux: Pleasantly decorated, Swiss-French food; moderate to expensive.

Du Monde: Four miles east of Lausanne; charming restaurant with view of vineyards; meals are very good; not inexpensive.

LUCERNE HOTELS AND RESTAURANTS

Grand Hôtel National: Exceptionally good, very large deluxe "palace" style hotel; beautiful situation on the lake; fairly high priced.

Palace: More modern than the Grand, with inviting, good-size rooms; somewhat less expensive.

Luzernerhof: Rather new, quite small, all rooms with bath; good location; moderate prices.

Wilden Mann: Celebrated restaurant with centuries-old tradition; food is fair; expensive. Rooms are available.

Stadtkeller: If you want some entertainment, this atmospheric restaurant has good food, music, yodeling. Not too expensive.

LUGANO HOTELS AND RESTAURANTS

La Romantica: A very small, interesting hotel in its own park. Good rooms, attractively furnished; fairly expensive. Good meals, too.

La Perla Motel: Motorists would like this hotel and motel situated on the road between Lugano and Ponte Tresa. Swimming pool, restaurant; quite inexpensive.

Orologio: Very good restaurant, often featuring local Italianate specialties. Fruits and vegetables are exceptional; moderately high.

MONTREUX HOTELS AND RESTAURANTS

Montreux-Palace: The name describes this hotel; large, good reputation. Very expensive.

Lorius: A small, unassuming hotel near the lake; medium-size rooms, not all with bath. Moderate prices.

Traverne du Château de Chillon: Attractively situated on the lake near the chateau. Good food; rather expensive.

ZURICH HOTELS AND RESTAURANTS

Baur au Lac: Zurich's outstanding hotel; good reputation. Good rooms, dining terrace, view of lake. Expensive.

Continental: A new, modern, good-sized hotel in the center of town; all rooms with bath; first class.

Atlantis: The newest hotel, scheduled to open during 1970 in a quiet spot at the foot of the Uetliberg hill in the suburbs.

Motel Sihlbrugg: Fifteen miles from Zurich on Lucerne-Zurich road; rooms are pleasant, and there is a restaurant close by; inexpensive.

Vetlinerkeller: Atmospheric old restaurant in old part of town; food is slightly above average, but quite expensive.

YUGOSLAVIA

National Characteristics

Yugoslavia has been a pacesetter in a couple of interesting ways. It was the first of the behind-the-iron-curtain countries to enthusiastically open its doors to Westerners. In fact, the doorway is now so far ajar that there is not even the semblance of a curtain hanging in the Adriatic breeze. During recent years, Yugoslavia has saluted tourism in spectacular ways. It completely abolished the need for a visa for everyone. The visa has now been reintroduced for citizens of those countries which do not let Yugoslav citizens enter without a visa. However, obtaining one is a formality which takes only a few minutes. You can get it at the border.

The republic of Yugoslavia is on the upper end of the Balkan peninsula, surrounded on the north by Austria and Hungary; on the south by Greece and Albania; on the east by Romania and Bulgaria; and on the northwest by Italy. There is also the shining Adriatic separating Yugoslavia from Italy on the west.

The Balkans have always been the scene of intrigue, nationalistic struggles and power politics. Rulers and wars come and go, but the basic personality of the Balkan area in which Yugoslavia is snugly fitted goes on forever, despite these many changes.

To the philosophical people of this beautiful country, life must be lived from day to day; the historic centuries brought both wonderful and terrible moments, and who knows what the future may bring? How much easier it is to act as if the colorful old cities and majestic mountains had not been witnesses to such marvelous or horrible events.

The Yugoslav man in the street (and that's precisely where he spends a good part of his life) chauvinistically admires his country's land, mountains, plains and seacoast. The people are poor, you say? It will all be better tomorrow, or, surely the day after. His country has enemies? Maybe they'll have a change of heart and leave little Yugoslavia alone. In fact, he declares with vehemence, why doesn't everyone leave Yugoslavia alone, that is, everyone except tourists? But tourists haven't been leaving Yugoslavia alone; they've come here steadily and in increasing numbers until today there is almost a tidal wave of them. The friendly Yugoslavs welcome all, enjoying seeing them come and, wonder of wonders, hating to see them go. For the people are extremely hospitable and still unspoiled by the excesses that tourism can bring on.

Life, even in the cities, is on the low-pressure side. This is no place for Madison Avenue ulcers, for sleepless nights, for supersalesmanship or big business. Everyone works for the state, no one is unemployed or likely to become so; there can be no accumulation of wealth except within specific limitations, so why work too hard?

When to Go

Along the Dalmatian coast, in the Split-Dubrovnik area, the weather is pleasant from late March through most of October, but you should remember that July and August frequently have torrid days, with temperatures in the 90s. The remainder of Yugoslavia may be toured, with a reasonable assurance of good weather, from May through September, if you keep in mind that an inland town like Sarajevo can have real heat waves for several days at a time during the summer months. Naturally, if you can't come at any other time, July and August are all right, although you'll draw an additional dividend in better weather and more easily obtained reservations during the spring and early fall. The advantages of summer travel is that many festivals and celebrations occur during those months.

WEATHER STRIP BELGRADE

Temp.	JAN.	FEB.	MAR.	APR.	MAY	JUNE	JULY	AUG.	SEPT.	OCT.	NOV.	DEC.
High	39°	42°	55°	63°	74°	78°	84°	84°	78°	63°	50°	40°
Low	27°	28°	37°	44°	52°	58°	60°	59°	54°	45°	35°	30°
Days of rain	12	13	15	14	15	16	12	10	12	12	12	13

TIME EVALUATION ¶ On a month's trip to Europe give Yugoslavia about a week on your schedule. Of course, if you're planning to drive along the coast from Venice down to Dubrovnik, two weeks would be ideal for a leisurely paced trip. Belgrade and Zagreb could easily be covered in one day of sightseeing each. Needless to say, you could easily spend a month at one of the resorts, if you wanted a good rest.

PASSPORT AND VISA ¶ The visa for U.S. citizens was re-introduced in 1969 but you can get one at the border in a matter of minutes. Before planning your trip, check on current visa requirements at the nearest Consulate General of Yugoslavia in the United States. Their ad-dresses are: 816 Fifth Avenue, New York; 38 East Bellevue Place, Chicago; 3030 Pacific Avenue, San Fran-cisco; 301 Fifth Avenue, Pittsburgh; and (the Embassy) 2410 California Street, N.W., Washington.

CUSTOMS AND IMMIGRATION ¶ The customs requirements are rather precise and in general are more restrictive than other western European nations. There are oral and written declarations, for instance, and if you have items falling into the written-declaration category, you must keep a copy of this list until you leave the country. It probably is obvious to you, too, that on leaving the country you should have with you all the items listed on the declaration that you made out when you arrived. If you have one camera, one phonograph with a "reason-able" number of records, one transistor, one tape re-corder, one portable radio, one pair of binoculars and one of several different kinds of sports gear (fishing tackle, for instance), you are permitted to make an oral declara-tion. But typewriters, bicycles, sports boats, portable TV sets, a complete camping unit and objects of a relatively expensive nature have to be declared in writing. As for cigarettes and tobacco, the customs people will generally permit each traveler to have with him a carton of ciga-rettes, or a couple of dozen cigars, or about a quarter of a pound of tobacco. One bottle of liquid refreshment (especially if it is no stronger than wine) will usually be passed by without any fuss. But we should also state that as in many other countries of Europe, tourism is more important than bothering about the individual tour-ists and their usual paraphernalia. Ninety-nine times out of a hundred, no one will bother you at the border unless you have a half-dozen cameras and scores of rolls of film. Don't try to mail your undeveloped film out of the country—that can really lead to headaches.

There is no limit on the amount of foreign currency you can bring into Yugoslavia, but you are limited to only a few dollars' worth of Yugoslavian money (100 dinars, to be exact). On leaving you can take with you only 50 dinars. The Yugoslavs are worried about the excessive importation and exportation of Yugoslavia's currency because the country is making an all-out effort to stabilize the money and stamp out black marketing. At every customs point there is a money exchange where you can easily cash your foreign currencies into Yugoslav dinars at the special tourist rate. Don't attempt to smuggle any dinars.

HEALTH ¶ The water in large cities is potable; however, if you tend to be troubled by change of water, there are bottled mineral waters obtainable at very reasonable prices wherever you go. As a matter of precaution, tap water is best avoided in rural areas, although the residents drink it with impunity. With all the good wine and beer available, drinking water should not present too much of a problem. Much of the milk is unpasteurized, so exercise care.

TIME ¶ Yugoslavia is six hours ahead of (later than) Eastern Standard Time. Daylight saving time is not observed. When it's noon in New York, it's 6 P.M. in Yugoslavia. When Daylight Saving Time is in effect in the United States, the time difference is reduced to 5 hours.

CURRENCY ¶ The unit of currency is the *dinar* (pronounced deen-er). Those of you who may have been in Yugoslavia a couple of years ago will remember the large numbers of dinars involved in changing a few dollars. The value of the dinar has remained more or less the same, but as a means of convenience instead of there being 1,500 dinars to a dollar there are now 15. This has been accomplished by chopping off the last two numerals in the case of 100 dinars and making it 1 dinar. It will be a bit confusing for a while because new notes and coins are circulating at the same time as the old ones. Shops, also, are quoting prices the old and the new way.

Fluctuations in the international money market affect the actual value of the dinar in relation to the American dollar.

PRICE LEVEL ¶ Yugoslavia on the basis of most price indexes, including rule of thumb, is probably the least costly nation in Europe for the traveler. Certainly, its transportation is the least expensive, and hotels and meals are also not high. At the Metropol Hotel in Belgrade, for example, you will pay about $13 for a double room. Deluxe hotels in a major resort such as Dubrovnik will be a few dollars higher. Full board rates in the leading hotels average about $11 to $12 a day per person— which is very reasonable, indeed. If you dine at public restaurants, you'll rarely pay more than $3, with beer or wine included.

Pointer: Avoid the occasional black-market operator who may sidle up to you on the street, in the hotel lobby or at a newsstand. The Yugoslavs issue receipts for transactions involving the exchange of dollars into dinars. No one ever asks to see them again, but they *could*. Exchange your money only at officially authorized places.

TIPPING ¶ Here is one country where tipping hasn't become a nuisance. Most hotels and restaurants make a service charge and that takes care of everyone, unless you feel personally inclined to offer an extra coin for special service; sometimes it will be gratefully accepted, sometimes politely declined because, theoretically, everyone is working for the state, and the practice of tipping is frowned upon. If your largesse is refused, don't insist. You'll find that almost without exception, everyone who renders service (including maids, waiters, hotel employees) are more than willing to be helpful, without expectation of a tip. However, in my opinion tipping helps a *great* deal in Yugoslavia. If you tip, about 10 percent is standard.

TRANSPORTATION ¶ Connections to major Yugoslav cities by *air* are made by Yugoslav Airlines, JAT, which has been building up a fine record both in domestic as well as in international flights. Some domestic services are maintained only during the summer season, but others are scheduled all year around. So you will have no difficulty getting to the country's lakes, mountains or seashore in a hurry. There is service throughout the year to Belgrade, Zagreb, Titograd, Ljubljana, Dubrovnik, Mostar, Sarajevo, Ivangrad, Skopje, Pristina and Tivat. Seasonal flights are made to Hercegnovi, Zabljak, Split, Ohrid and Vrnjacka Banja. A number of foreign airlines, of course, also fly into Yugoslavia.

Trains in Yugoslavia have those wondrous storybook names like Orient Express, Balkan Express and Simplon. But although the names of these celebrated international trains evoke romance, mystery and things exciting, they do not necessarily guarantee a smooth, fast trip. As a matter of fact, rail service in Yugoslavia, although improving, is still shaky. The most interesting part of the country, the Dalmatian coast, facing the Adriatic, has no railroad running along the shore, although there is service from the coast running inland. (The government, in apparently a we-can't-do-everything-at-once gesture, has built a fine auto highway along the coast, however.) Rail rates are low. On international trains traveling overnight you can get excellent sleeping-berth accommodations in First Class as well as *couchettes* in Second Class.

Bus service is reliable and goes everyplace, even where the daring motorist would hesitate to venture. Unfortunately, many local buses are overcrowded during the summer season. The tourist (except those hardy souls in search of local color) will do well to avoid these but instead to ride the "luxury" buses where seats can often be reserved; these are comparatively fast (at least faster than the train) and cost less than First Class train travel.

Automobiles are usually hired with chauffeur only. Drive-yourself cars have just become available and may be rented in many large cities or resort areas. Inquire at your hotel. Be absolutely sure to inquire about insurance coverage. Should you wish a car and driver, contact the local *Putnik* (a semiofficial tourist office) in any of the larger towns. Rates are fairly reasonable and since roads are not too well marked, use of a driver is advisable if you plan to visit remote regions.

Taxis are available, although not in great number; if you must catch a train or plane, you should order a taxi in advance to ensure prompt transportation.

This is a country by the sea, and a beautiful sea, at that, so there are many opportunities for traveling by *boat*. Coastal steamers cover the ports along the beautiful shoreline. Other boats operate to and from the mainland and some of the many offshore islands. From Venice, Bari and Ancona in Italy there is frequent service by ship to Yugoslavian ports. It is also possible to take lengthy cruises (up to two weeks) that originate in Venice, cover Yugoslavian ports and voyage as far as Greece and the Middle East. Tariffs are relatively low, and accommodations and the food are generally satisfactory.

COMMUNICATIONS ¶ An *airmail* letter to the United States costs about a quarter. Surface mail is much cheaper, but is extraordinarily slow. It would take almost a month for a letter to reach the United States by ship, so be sure you have enough stamps on your mail to dispatch it by air. Local *telephone* calls are cheap, and the service has been improving. For overseas telephone calls, book them through your hotel operator.

ELECTRICITY ¶ Most of the country uses 220 volts A.C., but there exist some few places where you'll encounter 110 A.C. Better inquire locally before using your appliances; transformers are rarely available.

FOOD SPECIALTIES AND LIQUOR ¶ The meal hours aren't too troublesome here. Breakfast is served in your hotel room, as a rule, and consists of the inevitable rolls, butter, jam and a choice of tea or coffee (neither of which are too good). Lunch and dinner are similar, usually beginning with enormous portions of soup followed by equally enormous portions of meat, salad and vegetables, a course that the Yugoslavs don't feel is worthwhile unless it is stuffed with rice and meat. The Yugoslavs have what may only be described as a mania for hot peppers, pickles, chopped onions and relishes. Go gently, at least at first. If you'll accept a suggestion, avoid the steaks; the local butchers simply do not know how to cut a steak to suit American tastes. You'll do better to follow the national cuisine, for it's better prepared than their version of continental food; of course, this involves acclimating yourself to rich, oily dishes flavored with onions and/or garlic and lots of paprika (don't forget that Yugoslavia borders on Hungary). For dessert, there's always ice cream, which is extremely popular throughout the country. The cakes and tarts are fairly similar to what you're accustomed to and should present no problem except for the fabulous calorie count. We recommend the Yugoslavian version of Hungarian strudel, here called *strudla* and prepared with apples, poppy seeds or whatever else happens to be available or in season. Don't order the ordinary coffee, because to be downright crude, it's horrible. You'll fare better with your own instant coffee, or, if you want an authentic coffee drink, try the *turska kava*, thick Turkish coffee, which the Yugoslavs have adopted as their own; the cups are minute, the servings not inexpensive, but for the true blue coffee lover this is the only solution.

Bottled beer is drinkable, but whether it's more than that we're not willing to say; the draft beer is quite good. Yugoslavian wines are not only good but very good, and they're so cheap that it hardly pays to drink water. Wines come in white (*belo*), pink (*ruzica*) and red (*crno*). Wines are served by the pitcher or jug except in the best places; order a small quantity, say three-tenths of a liter by telling the waiter "*tri-deci*." The most famous white wine, suitable with fish or chicken is *Zilavka*, very smooth and delicious, and available only by the bottle. Among the reds, the *Cabernet* and *Dingač* are excellent with any meat dishes. Actually, you'll hardly go wrong in ordering any of the regional wines and deciding which suit your individual taste.

All of Yugoslavia seems to be engaged in the raising of plums, which inevitably become either prunes or brandy, known as *slivovitz*; it is also called *slivovica* or *rakija*, and name it what you may, it is strong and potent and you'll hate it. At first, that is. The local people don't believe in drinking slivovitz until quite late in the day, say, 10 A.M. or so. With this, you order a cup of black coffee, and it's difficult to say which is stronger. Later on, it seems to be a fixed rule to have a plate of appetizers, *meze*, with slivovitz; which item is the excuse for which, we never did find out. Incidentally, if you're driving along a country road and get hungry, look (or ask) for a *gistiona*, a country inn, where you can buy meat, sausage, bread, fruit and cheese, plus wine, for about 50 cents or so. It is also worthwhile when you're trying to reach a certain destination and don't want to make a typical Yugoslavian stop to eat a two-hour Yugoslavian lunch.

What to Eat in Yugoslavia

Ajvar: Cold, chopped eggplant relish
Čorba od pašulja: Thick bean soup with pieces of ham
Dalmatinski pršut: Smoked ham, served as an appetizer
Alaska čorba: Thick soup-stew, sometimes quite spicy
Ribji gulaš: Fish prepared with a considerable amount of paprika
Musaka: A ground meat dish, prepared with eggplant and potatoes
Čevapčići: Small lengths of grilled ground meats shaped into sausages
Raznjiči: Small pieces of roast pork, usually served with bits of bread
Lonatz: Peppers, vegetables and meat in a thick stew
Djuveć: Rice, vegetables and meat in a stew-like mixture
Sarma: Vine leaves or sauerkraut with rice-meat mixture
Pečeno prase: Roast young suckling pig
Kachkavalj: A cheese made from sheep's milk
Potica: Rich butter coffee cake prepared with nuts
Lokum: The sweet gelatin candy we know as Turkish Delight

REPUBLICS ¶ Yugoslavia is a socialist federal republic and is formed by six socialist republics, many of whose names are familiar to you already, we are sure, whether you have visited the country or not. The republics are Bosnia and Herzegovina, whose capital is Sarajevo; Montenegro, with Titograd the capital; Croatia, with Zagreb the capital; Macedonia, with Skopje the capital; Slovenia, with Ljubljana the capital; and Serbia, with Belgrade the capital. Belgrade serves also as the capital of Yugoslavia itself. The republics were set up on the basis of nationality; Slovenian is the language of Slovenia, Croatian of Croatia, Serbian of Serbia, Macedonian of Macedonia. Serbian—here the complications begin—is also the language of Montenegro, and both Serbian and Croatian are spoken in Bosnia-Herzegovina, which is populated by Serbs, Croats, and Moslems (how the Moslems got there is too long to explain). Slovenian and Croatian are written in the Latin alphabet, while Serbian and Macedonian are written in the Cyrillic.

The principal tourist areas are the capital city of Belgrade, the northern resort area centering around Bled and the Dalmatian coast, particularly between Split and Dubrovnik.

Capital City

Belgrade is everything to Yugoslavia—its largest metropolis, the capital of Serbia and the headquarters for all the government offices. The city has recovered since the Germans dropped explosives one lovely Palm Sunday morning, killing about 25,000 people in one tragic hour. Belgrade is located in the midst of rolling green hills. The leading tourist sight is the fortress in Kalemegdan Park and its various gates and tower. Other important attractions include the university buildings; the Orthodox cathedral; Barjakli mosque, a reminder of Turkish occupation days; the Ethnographical Museum, with exhibits of local costumes; the National Museum, although most of the frescoes are copies, not originals. Just a short ride from midtown Belgrade is Topcider, a suburb, where you'll find a pretty park with a summer theater and restaurant. Belgrade, being on the Danube (although most people think Austria has a monopoly on that river), can offer several boat excursions; the most interesting trip involves two days through the Djerdap Ravine. If you can allow only one day for a boat trip, visit Golubac to see the fortress. An interesting one-day journey by car may be made to Fruska Gora, a mountain range; drive about forty miles northwest from Belgrade to Sremski Karlovci, around which there are many old monasteries worth visiting. Or, if you wish, go eastward along the north shore of the Danube to Vinca and Smederevo, site of a remarkable fortress built during the troubled days of fighting with the Ottoman Turk forces. Only twelve miles from Belgrade is the town of Avala, which has not only a monument to the nation's unknown hero, but a tall TV tower with an observation restaurant; it makes a pleasant destination for a Saturday or Sunday lunch.

HOLIDAYS ¶ The national holidays are January 1 and 2, May 1 and 2, July 4, November 29 and 30. The six republics also have their holidays. They are: Serbia, July 7; Montenegro, July 13; Slovenia, July 22, Bosnia and Herzegovina, July 27; Croatia, August 2; Macedonia, October 11.

SHOPPING ¶ Yugoslavia is far from being a shopper's paradise, for most fine articles are imported and sell for high prices. The most attractive items, should you find any use for *peasant clothes*, are native blouses and skirts; they make excellent gifts for children. *Gold* and *silver filigree* jewelry is worthwhile, particularly in Peć, where it's much cheaper than elsewhere.

Small *carpets* and *rugs* are interesting and cheap, but quite bulky; if you're returning home by sea, no problem; if by air, better ship it *yourself*. *Hand-carved wooden objects* are better made in Austria, but if you must have a Yugoslavian souvenir, what can we say? . . . *Ladies' blouses* are overembroidered and overelaborate, but perhaps you'll find one to suit. A little girl on your list would surely like a *Yugslavian doll* in national costume. The locally made pottery you'll see displayed along the roadside is primitive and amusing, but need we say (in a deep voice of doom) that pottery breaks easily? How about a Turkish-style *coffee-grinder* with an oversized hand crank? Don't overlook the possibility of bringing back some of your favorite *Yugoslavian wine*, because it's not readily obtainable, to say the least, in the United States. Or some *slivovitz*—what are we saying? Be sure you sample the famous cherry brandy of the country —*maraskino*—everyone seems to like this; if you do, it's good value.

HOURS ¶ The day, in general, starts early and ends late. In between there is a big pause, however. Most places are open from 7 A.M. to 2 P.M., but banks close at 11 A.M. That does not leave you much time for dawdling over your breakfast-in-bed coffee if you have been slow in rising. Shops and the travel agencies (which will be a major point of contact for you while in Yugoslavia) also have afternoon hours, during the summer, from 5 to 8 P.M. In the winter, they normally are open from 8 A.M. to noon, and from 5 to 7 P.M. Some of these schedules vary slightly from one republic to another or from the coastal to the mountain areas. Restaurants have a very long day, opening somewhere around 6 A.M. and operating until midnight. The night clubs get started around 9:30 or 10 P.M. and call it a night at 2 A.M. Shops, banks and travel agencies are not open on Sundays.

ENTERTAINMENT ¶ During the tourist season, you'll often see announcements (sometimes in English) of *folk danc-*

ing in national costumes; watch for these and inquire locally, for you never know when you'll run across a colorful show. Of course, in Dubrovnik and Bled there are frequently festivals where you're almost certain to see at least one performance; the best group is the Kolo ensemble of singers and dancers—absolutely exciting! Speaking of Dubrovnik, there is a *drama festival*, which runs from about June 15 to July 15—and you have the chance of hearing Hamlet as you have never (repeat, never) heard it before. Also in Dubrovnik during July and August there is an almost continuous series of dance, music and opera performances.

Zagreb and Belgrade have quite a lot of *opera*, fairly well performed, too; seats are very reasonably priced, and you should attend at least once. The opera houses often present *ballet* performances, marked more by enthusiasm than by professional skill, but go anyhow. There is quite an active legitimate theater, but oh, that language barrier! There are very few night clubs, except in Belgrade, although Dubrovnik has one modest spot, and others are scheduled to open. Loads of motion picture theaters, but try to attend one in the open where you can sit at a table and enjoy the lovely night air as much (or more) than the movie.

SPORTS ¶ Although scarcely in a class with Austria or Switzerland for *winter sports*, Yugoslavia is becoming more important all the time—good facilities at Bled and Planica, and there is even a ski lift at Kranjska Gora. The most popular sport for most tourists is *swimming*, along the Dalmatian coast in the blue waters of the Adriatic; here too, *skin diving* has developed rapidly in popularity. *Hunting* for deer and game is particularly good, but licenses are surprisingly expensive. From June through August, there are *deep sea fishing* excursions leaving from Rijeka (not too far from the Italian border). Marvelous *fishing* for brook and rainbrow trout, which come in good sizes; inquire locally or watch for other fishing enthusiasts. There are *tennis courts* at many of the leading resort hotels. Yugoslavia has always welcomed a great influx of mountain climbers in search of new worlds (mountains) to conquer.

Note: All that Adriatic coastline will look mighty inviting to the underwater swimmer and photographer. But before you snap on your underwater breathing apparatus and get your camera in focus, check to be sure whether this type of activity is permitted in the area where you happen to be. There are restrictions at some places and a permit is required. So, check and be sure.

Pointer: The trip below largely follows the shore road along the Adriatic and is extremely interesting. However, should you wish to drive through the center of the country, there are newly opened and rather good roads running all the way through Yugoslavia. The entire stretch fom north to south is well paved and fast, extending 740 miles. Yugoslavia may be entered from southern Austria or, more commonly, from Trieste. The road runs through Ljubljana, Zagreb, Belgrade, Paraćin and Niš Grdelica to the Greek border at Djevdjelija; it is then just a short run to Salonika.

৪৺ A Tour of Yugoslavia

A recent development in Yugoslavia is the availability of drive-yourself cars. However, the car probably has to be returned to the same point from which originally rented. For local sightseeing, it is possible to fly to some places, such as Zagreb or Dubrovnik, and rent a drive-yourself car. However, for a tour of the country, you should rent your car outside of Yugoslavia. Coast roads have been improved to the point of being excellent, all the way from Trieste, Italy, to south of Dubrovnik.

Trieste to Senj—93 miles

Leave Trieste via route 14 toward the Yugoslavian border, which lies just beyond the village of Basovizza. Then via route 12 through Hrpelje, Obrov, Rupa and Matulje; shortly thereafter there is a right turn (route 9) for Opatija, possibly the most luxurious resort town of Yugoslavia; the best hotel here is the Kvarner. Then on to Rijeka (once called Fiume), through Sušak, Bakar, Kraljevica into Crikvenica, which has the Hotel Mira-mare. The road goes on through Selce and Novi into Senj, which has a few remaining old houses, although the town took a battering during the war years. From Senj, boat trips can be made to the various islands off the coast —Cres, Rab and Krk. (Now how do you pronounce Krk? We're glad you asked—it's pronounced Krk, with the emphasis on all three letters.) Should you want to see one of the islands, perhaps the best bet is a visit to

Rab and its delightful capital town, called, you guessed it, Rab. Make reservations at the pleasant Imperial Hotel; there are no motor vehicles, and the small town has a medieval appearance.

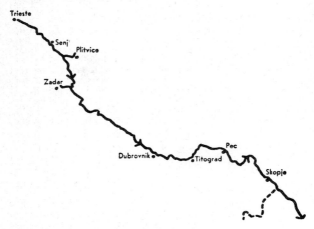

Senj to Plitvice—51 miles

The road from Senj to Plitvice is only partly paved, and the unpaved portion (about half) is miserably bad.

At Senj, if you wish, you may follow route 12 along the coast to Zadar; but it is more interesting to turn left at Senj toward Melnice, Zuta Lokva and Otočac. After you leave this town there is a left turn (don't worry about the number of the route anywhere in Yugoslavia) to Vrhovine. Then come Babin Potok, Priboj, where there is a left turn to Plitvice and its chain of lakes; this is undoubtedly one of the most beautiful parts of the country and should not be missed. There are sixteen lakes connected by a series of terraces and waterfalls, and the entire area is delightful; at Plitvice, you'll find the very good Hotel Plitvice.

Plitvice to Zadar—171 miles

Return by the same route to Senj; what looks like a shorter road to the coast on most maps is impossibly slow. At Senj, turn left and follow the lovely coast road south and into Zadar; here you have the choice of Beograd and Zagreb hotels (why do they select such confusing place names?). Zadar offers the chance for interesting boat trips to the Kornati Islands; this whole region is famous for fishing.

Zadar to Dubrovnik—233 miles

From Zadar take the main road back through Zemunik following route 12; then come Benkovac, Zazvić, Skradin, Gulin, Šibenik, an old town and the tourist center of this area. A little over 16 miles beyond Šibenik, on the same route, is the lovely old fishing town of Primošten and across the bay from the town there is the new Adriatic hotel group where you'll find low prices, modern facilities and good food. Continue to lovely Trogir (a marvelous medieval town that warrants a little exploration). Then into the wonderful resort town of Split, made famous by the Emperor Diocletian, a man who knew a good thing when he saw it, and he saw it in Split. All in all, the new Marjan Hotel is easily the best. You'll want, of course, to visit the palace, the Town Hall and the wonderous old streets of the city.

Continue on from Split to Omiš, Dubci and Makarska, which is a beach resort; the Hotel Beograd here is delightfully located. Makarska (sometimes spelled Markarska) is just about the most (all right, one of the most) beautiful spot, scenically speaking, in the country. It has an attractive little harbor with very good bathing beaches, the whole surrounded by forests of pine trees. Makarska is the best of all possible combinations. Then on through Podgora, Drvenik, Gradac, Pioče Metković and Trsteno (and there are no vowels missing from that place), an attractive area. Then on to the best of all, old Dubrovnik, worth several days' stay on even a hurried trip. You'll find the Hotel Argentina the most luxurious, although the Excelsior is excellent; the newish Villa Dubrovnik is modern, small and pleasant. The hotel food is pretty good, although not great. However, for variety, try some of the places specializing in grilled meat and sausages, such as the Mimoza Restaurant.

This unique medieval town seems misplaced in the twentieth century, but it is wonderfully lost, a place overbrimming with charm. Wander about Dubrovnik's old city, walk through the ancient fortifications, visit the cathedral, the museum, the various monasteries. Be sure to take a boat ride to Lokrum, where there is a very good beach. A regular excursion begins at 6 A.M.(!) and involves a bus ride from Dubrovnik to the Moslem-Oriental town of Cetinje, passing around beautiful Kortor Bay. Another favorite excursion, but beginning at a more reasonable hour, is the run from Dubrovnik via route 7 through Ljubova and Tvrdoši and into Trebinje, a Moslem town with many mosques and colorful markets.

Dubrovnik to Titograd—131 miles

Continue on from Dubrovnik through Cavtat, then into beautiful Hercegnovi, famed for its marvelous climate, circling Kotor Bay into Cetinje; here you can make a lovely side trip along the coast to Budva, Bar and the unbelievable beauty of Sveti Stefan (St. Stephan), a miniature village built out into the sea. If you like the unusual, don't fail to stay at St. Stephan, for the entire village is really a hotel. Believe it or not, the individual stone houses are actually hotel rooms (usually with sitting rooms), and the streets of the town serve as the equivalent of corridors for the hotel; meals are taken at a main building. It's all completely charming, offbeat and delightful (particularly if it doesn't rain). Five minutes' walk away, at Milocer, there is another interesting place to stay: the remodeled summer home of Queen Marie, very pleasant but not nearly as unusual as St. Stephan. On the other hand, should it rain, it's very comforting to have the dining room inside. From Bar, there is a direct road back to Titograd, the capital city of Montenegro; here the leading hotel is the Crna Gora. From Cetinje, it's a direct route to Titograd. (From Titograd on, the roads are quite bad; be sure your car is in excellent condition.) Or else return to Italy.

Titograd to Peć—111 miles

Leave Titograd via route 6-A heading toward Andrijevica, with the passable Komovi Hotel; then on to Peć, one of the most colorful old towns of Yugoslavia, its many fascinating streets apparently lifted intact from an Oriental setting. Be sure to wander about the Okolj district, filled with tiny shops and almost like a stage setting for *Kismet*; the Hotel Korzo is Quite pleasant for an overnight Stay. (Don't try to drive from Peć to Kosovska Mitrovica; the road is extremely bad, although scheduled to be improved.)

Peć to Kačanik—95 miles

Head south from Peć to Dečani, only a matter of ten miles, to visit the remarkable monastery of Dečani. This noteworthy group of buildings in Romanesque style was originally constructed in 1335; the interior and its frescoes are extraordinary. Unfortunately, there is no place to remain overnight.

On through Djakovica and into Prizren, the fascinating fourteenth-century capital of Serbia. Visit the monastery and Sinan Pasha's mosque and see the renowned frescoes in the Bogoridca Ljeviska church. From Prizren, head northeast, passing through Suva Reka, Dulje, Crnojevo; at Stimlje, turn right toward Uroševac and Kačanik.

SIDE TRIP ¶ Those who don't mind mediocre(!) roads should certainly journey to Ohrid, an old town filled with medieval monasteries, churches and artistic treasures. Follow the main route south to Titov Veles, then make a right turn onto route 16 for a run of thirty-six miles to Prilep, then twenty-four miles to Bitola, a town with many fine old monasteries and mosques. From here, passing through Resen, it is a matter of forty-five miles to reach Ohrid; by far the best hotel here is the Palace. Motorists driving on to Greece can continue around beautiful Lake Ohrid, crossing the Yugoslav-Greek border, then heading eastward to Salonika to rejoin the Greek tour.

To the Greek Border—132 miles

Head south via route 4 to Titov Veles, a road that follows the River Vardar; you'll want to see the St. Dimitri church and St. Pantelemon monastery. Then on to Gradsko and Negotino, cutting through graceful Demir Kapija Pass, continuing on to Gjevgjelija and across the border into Greece.

૭➤ *Motoring in Yugoslavia*

Formalities for bringing a car into Yugoslavia are the same as they are in other European countries—which means that there is not much to it. All you need are the registration papers for the automobile and the Green Card certifying insurance coverage. If you don't have one of these, its equivalent can be obtained on entrance for a small amount.

The pleasure of driving in Yugoslavia has been increased considerably in recent years by the organization of a mobile service that provides emergency repairs and gives first aid. It also keeps the road clear of such obstacles as stones from rock slides. Here's one wrinkle that will add zest to your driving: In Macedonia, Bosnia, Serbia and Herzegovina place-names are usually written in Cyrillic characters. K in Cyrillic and K in the Latin alphabet are written more or less the same way. But the other letters are dramatically different, except for J, M, O and T, which do bear some resemblance to their Latin colleagues.

Almost every town has at least one gasoline station, and these should not be overlooked if your tank is less than half full, and particularly if night driving is contemplated. There is a 10 percent discount with special gas coupons. Gasoline (super) is inexpensive, relatively.

Driving is on the right, passing on the left. There is a speed limit of 50 miles per hour on the open roads and 30 in built-up areas. Outdoor, overnight parking is allowed except in the largest cities.

Yugoslav roads have a fairly poor reputation, but the situation is improving swiftly. Almost all of the northwestern part of the country, near the Italian and Austrian borders (Republic of Slovenia), has paved roads in excellent condition. Road crews have completed paving the road from Rijeka down the Dalmatian coast all the way south to the Albanian border. The Ljubljana-Zagreb-Belgrade highway varies in quality. The Ljubljana-Zagreb section was completed most recently and still is in excellent condition, while the Zagreb-Belgrade section is only fair and is deteriorating. The Zagreb-Belgrade section does not have over- and under-passes and one has to be very careful about cars (to say nothing of peasant carts) suddenly turning into the highway. Except for the areas and roads mentioned, the roads are generally in fair to poor shape.

This latter fact should not deter any but the most timid motorist; while most of the unpaved roads are surfaced with gravel or dirt and are of variable quality, all may be used without undue difficulty. The careful driver will be sure to have a spare tire and see that his car is in good condition before undertaking trips on side roads; but we are not overemphasizing the difficulties, although the Yugoslav government is engaged in a large-scale effort to improve conditions for auto travelers. Tremendous strides have been made already, and tourist roads should soon be in generally excellent condition. Before leaving the main roads, inquiry may be made at any office of *Kompas*, *Generalturist*, *Putnik* or any other governmental travel agency or at local tourist offices for last-minute information.

MISCELLANEOUS ODDITIES ¶ During the summer months, most city people work from 7 A.M. to 2 P.M. So if you see large numbers of people promenading about in the afternoons with apparently nothing to do, it's because they begin their work at such an unearthly hour.

If a Yugoslav makes an appointment with you, don't be surprised if he shows up late; many people are punctual, many are not.

Lots of handshaking here; on meeting, on leaving and occasionally, in between times.

Don't ever expect to eat a meal in a hurry in Yugoslavia; relax and enjoy a leisurely (two-hour) dinner.

ACCOMMODATIONS ¶ Hotels are rarely elaborate except for a few in Belgrade, Zagreb, Ljubljana and some of the resort cities. Most of the others are usually (but not always) clean and comfortable.

You'll be welcomed and made to feel at home, but patience must be exercised with regard to room and meal service, because large-scale tourism is something new here. Don't be disturbed if it takes a half-hour (or longer) to get a cup of coffee in the morning, because lunch will often necessitate two hours and you might as well get in practice. Hotels are classified as A, B, C, D, but there are only about ten A hotels in the country. As a rule, while motoring off the beaten path, you'll have to be satisfied with B accommodations, which really aren't bad although not very luxurious; the C and D hotels are something else indeed. Bring your own soap to all hotels.

Remember that staffs are actually working for the government, because there is no private hotel ownership in Yugoslavia. In theory there would seem little incentive to be of more than routine service; nevertheless you'll find everyone helpful and anxious to please.

The leading hotel in Belgrade is unquestionably the

Hotel Metropol. All rooms have private baths. Other class A hotels include the Majestic, Palace and Moskva, but none of these really rates with the Metropol.

BELGRADE HOTELS AND RESTAURANT

Yugoslavia: A new and absolutely enormous hotel, located on the right bank of the Danube River. This hotel is the country's pride and joy, and has several dining rooms and bars, a swimming pool, Finnish sauna, and so forth. For Yugoslavia, fairly expensive.

Metropol: Quite modern, very good hotel with large rooms. Prices are moderate.

Dva Ribara: Generally regarded as Belgrade's best restaurant. Food is good, but service is somewhat slow.

ZAGREB HOTEL AND RESTAURANT

Esplanade Intercontinental: The old traditional Esplanade was taken over by the Intercontinental chain and successfully refurbished and polished up. Several restaurants, among them Taverna Rustica, with local-type food and folk accent. Very nice on all counts.

Split: A very fine restaurant located in Ilica specializing in fish brought in fresh from Dalmatia.

LJUBLJANA HOTEL AND RESTAURANT

Slon (*"Elephant"*): Not the largest in the city, but it has the best service and the most individualistic facilities. Folk-type restaurant in the basement featuring local specialties. Recently renovated.

Sestica: An old restaurant which was a stage coach post house some 150 years ago; good Slovenian-style food, which closely resembles Austrian.

INDEX